Wavell

Also by Victoria Schofield

Kashmir in Conflict
Afghan Frontier: Feuding and Fighting in Central Asia
The House That Fell Down
Old Roads, New Highways: Fifty Years of Pakistan (ed)
Kashmir in the Crossfire
Every Rock, Every Hill: The North-West Frontier and Afghanistan
Bhutto: Trial and Execution
The United Nations

Wavell

Soldier & Statesman

VICTORIA SCHOFIELD

JOHN MURRAY

© Victoria Schofield 2006

First published in Great Britain in 2006 by John Murray (Publishers)
A division of Hodder Headline

The right of Victoria Schofield to be identified as the Author of the Work has been asserted by
her in accordance with the Copyright, Designs and Patents Act 1988.

1

A CIP catalogue record for this title is available from the British Library

ISBN 0 7195 6320 8

Typeset in Monotype Bembo 10.75/13pt
by Servis Filmsetting Ltd, Manchester

Printed and bound by
Clays Ltd, St Ives plc

Hodder Headline policy is to use papers that are natural, renewable and recyclable products and
made from wood grown in sustainable forests. The logging and manufacturing processes are
expected to conform to the environmental regulations of the country of origin.

John Murray (Publishers)
338 Euston Road
London NW1 3BH

To my family

Contents

Illustrations   ix

Maps   xi

In Memoriam   1

I   THE SOLDIER'S SON

1. A Late Victorian   7
2. Life in the Army, 1901–8   17
3. Staff College, Russia and the War Office   30

II   WAVELL'S ASCENT

4. War in 1914   49
5. Palestine with Allenby, 1917   65
6. Peacetime   81
7. Manoeuvres   95
8. Prelude to War   113

III   COMMANDER-IN-CHIEF

9. Middle East Command, 1939   127
10. Holding Africa, 1940   145
11. All Fronts, 1941   165
12. Churchill's Axe, 1941   194
13. Conflict of the Hemispheres, 1941   212
14. Supreme Commander, 1942   230

15. Adversity's General, 1942   254
16. Field Marshal, 1943   276

IV   FROM SOLDIER TO STATESMAN

17. Designated Viceroy, 1943   291
18. Wartime Viceroy, 1944–5   308
19. Viceroy at Peace, 1945   333
20. Unity or Partition, 1946   348
21. Dismissal, 1947   368
22. The End   379
23. Wavell's Legacy   397

Abbreviations   405
Notes   407
Acknowledgements   476
Sources and Bibliography   479
Index   489

Illustrations

1. Archibald Goodall Wavell
2. Archibald Graham Wavell
3. Archibald Percival Wavell, aged 7, in India
4. Scholars at Summer Fields, 1896
5. A.P. Wavell, aged 15, at Winchester College
6. Lieutenant A.P. Wavell, The Black Watch, aged 27
7. Cranborne Lodge
8. Eugénie Marie Quirk in 1914
9. Colonel and Mrs Wavell, 1931
10. Wavell zaps the Italians (cartoon)
11. Wavell studying maps
12. Generals Auchinleck and Wavell
13. Felicity Wavell
14. Joan Wavell
15. Wavell, Queenie and Archie John Wavell
16. Leonie Lemartine otherwise Gladys Redwood Robinson
17. Joan Bright, June 1943
18. Wavell's personal staff
19. Winston Churchill on board HMS Prince of Wales
20. The Prime Minister and his 'top brass'
21. Alanbrooke and Wavell, Teheran, 1942
22. Commander-in-Chief's house, New Delhi
23. Field Marshal Wavell on reconnaissance in Burma
24. Wavell in Burma with Generals Alexander and Slim
25. A.P. Wavell at his lectern
26. The Hon. Simon and Mrs Astley on their wedding day
27. Daisy Ribbands
28. Wavell and Ivor Jehu
29. The Viceroy Lord Wavell at Imphal in 1944
30. Wavell awarding a posthumous VC, 1944
31. 'Can they make up the Jigsaw?' (cartoon). The Cabinet Mission, 1946

32. The Cabinet Mission: Sir Stafford Cripps, Lord Pethick-Lawrence and Rt. Hon. A.V. Alexander with the Viceroy, Lord Wavell
33. Wavell on his morning ride from Viceregal Lodge
34. Lord Wavell greets his successor as Viceroy, Lord Mountbatten, March 1947
35. Wavell, Colonel of the Regiment, with Lt-Col Bernard Fergusson
36. Re-dedication of War Cloister, Winchester College, 14 November 1948
37. Wavell's grave, War Cloister, Winchester College

Photographic credits: 1, 2, 3, 5, 6 and 7, Wavell Estate and Executors of Ann Grantham; 4, Hill & Saunders, Oxford and Executors of Ann Grantham; 8, 13, 14, 15, 18, 20, 21 and 24, Wavell Estate and John Connell Estate; 9, Charles Burrell; 10 and 16, Patricia Box; 11, 28, 29 and 30, Maybe Jehu; 12, 22 and 23, T.A. Bird; 17, 25 and 26, Joan Bright Astley; 19, author's collection; 27 and 35, Lt-Col F.J. Burnaby-Atkins; 31, Pethick-Lawrence Collection, British Library; 32, 33 and 34, The Wavell Estate; 36, The Warden and Fellows of Winchester College; 37, Araminta, Lady Aldington.

Maps

1. The Middle East in the Second World War   xii
2. South & South-East Asia in the Second World War   xiv

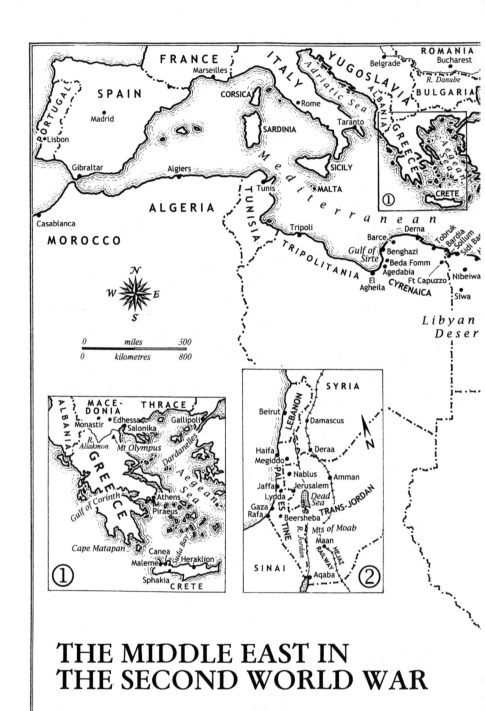

THE MIDDLE EAST IN
THE SECOND WORLD WAR

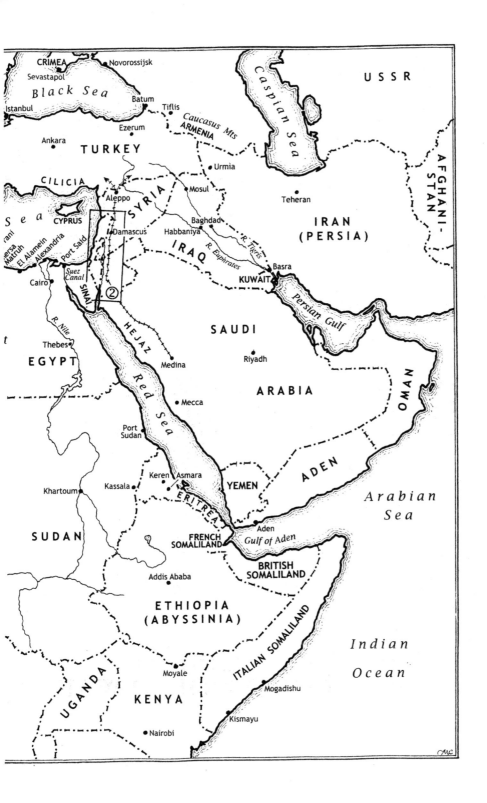

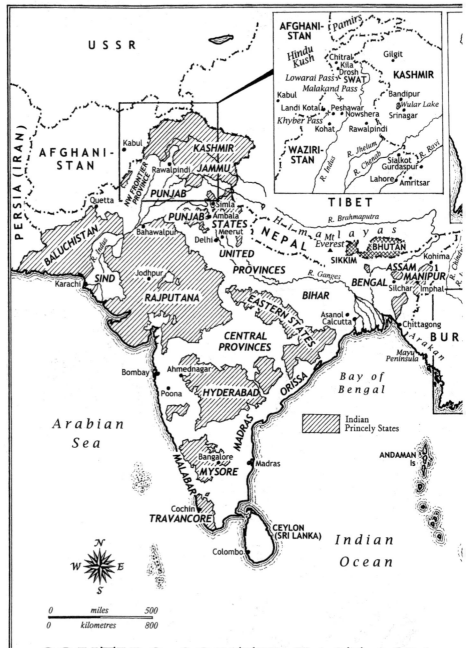

SOUTH & SOUTH–EAST ASIA
IN THE SECOND WORLD WAR

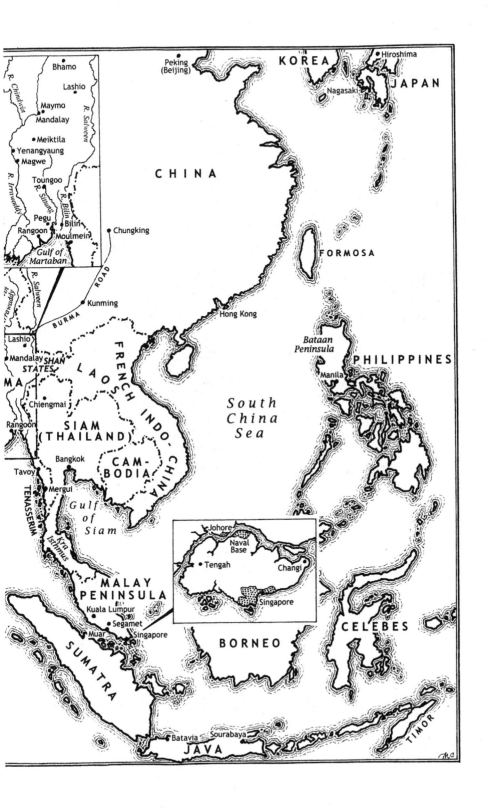

In Memoriam
Winchester, 14 November 1948

Write on the stones no words of sadness –
Only the gladness due,
That we, who asked the most of living,
Knew how to give it too.[1]

Frank Thompson, Polliciti Meliora

G REY STILLNESS HUNG in the air. War Cloister, set in the heart of Winchester College and surrounding a garden of remembrance, was unseasonably filled with visitors, patiently waiting. In London, at Buckingham Palace, Princess Elizabeth, elder daughter of George VI, was soon to give birth to her first child. But the minds of the visitors assembled on the north, south and east sides of the Cloister at Winchester were focused not on the new but on the old, in a service of dedication and remembrance. Almost as soon as the boys of the school had passed through the east porch and taken their places on the west side, the Chapel clock struck twelve.

A fanfare of trumpets sounded. The Warden and Fellows and the Headmaster of the school, Walter Oakeshott, passed through the east gate. With them came a thick-set man, blind in one eye, deaf in one ear: Earl Wavell of Cyrenaica and Winchester, PC, GCB, GCSI, GCIE, CMG, MC, scholar of the college from 1896 to 1900, Field Marshal and former Viceroy of India. The most distinguished living Wykehamist had returned to his old school on this solemn November day to take part in a service of re-dedication in memory of former students. To the names of the five hundred Wykehamists inscribed on the walls around the Cloister after the First World War had been added 270 more, of those who had fought and fallen in the Second World War. These new inscriptions were placed on the inner sides of the main buttresses of the stone columns, facing the names of their predecessors. When a second fanfare of trumpets sounded the choir, dressed in red and white, moved towards the west side, followed by the bishop, his chaplain and the chaplains of the college. In 1924, when War

Cloister was dedicated by the Duke of Connaught, a different congregation had sung 'Finita iam sunt proelia' ('Now the battle is over').[2] Twenty-four years later the same hymn was sung again. Earl Wavell then spoke:

> Today we dedicate again this Cloister to the memory of the 770 Wykehamists whose names are inscribed in it . . . I need say little to you of their services in this last war. They fought, they endured, they died, in advance or retreat, in victory or disaster; on the Atlantic, on the Pacific, in the Mediterraenean; in the steaming jungles of Burma, on the hills of Italy; on the beaches of Normandy; in the fighter aircraft in the Battle of Britain, in bombers over Berlin; in other places all over the world by sea and land and air.

With the bishop and chaplains behind, a microphone in front, Wavell stood erect, hands by his side, in full military uniform. He spoke without notes. He knew only too well the theatres of war in which the men had fought. As Commander-in-Chief in both the Middle East and India, for four years Wavell had been directly involved with overseeing their movements. The high proportion of casualties among Wykehamists, he said, demonstrated that the school's alumni had always served their country 'with an unhesitating spirit of service and self-sacrifice'. 'In thankfulness of their example,' he concluded, 'and in determination to be worthy of it, we dedicate their names here, to live for evermore.' The service continued with prayers and sentences uttered by representatives from the four sides of the Cloister. The bishop then dedicated War Cloister 'to the honour and glory of Almighty God and to the sacred and perpetual memory of our brothers, who in two World Wars have given their lives in the same faith'. From a lone bugle the 'Last Post' sounded; after a minute's silence came the 'Reveille'. The service ended with a final hymn, 'City of God how broad and far', and the first verse of the National Anthem.

Wavell died eighteen months later. His coffin was brought from London and he was buried in the heart of the Chantry Cloister, close to where he had stood the last time he was there. The stone plaque embedded in the grass is simply inscribed:

5 May 1883

W A V E L L

24 May 1950

He rose to join the famous, yet unmoved
Was he by all the outward signs of fame.
Staunch was his spirit, honoured and beloved.
As player or as captain in the game
That we call life, how clean his record proved.
Wide was his vision, ample was his aim;
Much did he witness through a poet's eyes,
While with a soldier-statesman's active mind
He spurned the counsel of the over wise.
With that robustness which he had defined
In lesser marshals, when the vital hour
Of tense decision came he took command,
For other mighty victories to flower
From the initial purpose of his stand.

J. Osborne Harley[3]

I
THE SOLDIER'S SON

I

A Late Victorian
Colchester . . . Summer Fields . . .Winchester

Without courage there cannot be truth: and without truth there can
be no other virtue.   Sir Walter Scott[1]

FAMED AS THE name of Wavell became in twentieth-century Britain, its
origins dated back to the time when a group of marauding Norsemen
settled in the north-west of the Cherbourg Peninsula in northern France
around AD 600 and called themselves Seigneurs of Vauville.[2] In 1066 the de
Vauvilles crossed the Channel with their kinsman, William 'the
Conqueror'. As England became their home, their name altered to de
Wauvil, Wayvil, Weyvill and, eventually, Wavell. By the nineteenth century
this family history was part of the oral tradition handed down to young
Archibald Wavell. His grandfather, General Arthur Goodall Wavell, was a
soldier who had served not only in India but in the revolutionary armies
of Mexico and Chile. 'I have always had a liking for unorthodox soldiers
and a leaning towards the unorthodox in war,' the future Field Marshal
wrote. 'Perhaps it is inherited; my grandfather was a soldier of fortune.'[3]

In the mid nineteenth century Arthur Goodall settled at Somborne
House, Little Somborne, in the beautiful and still unspoilt countryside of
the Test valley, between Stourbridge and Romsey in Hampshire. His fourth
son, Archibald Graham, was Wavell's father. He too joined the Army and
was commissioned into The Norfolk Regiment. In August 1880 he married Eliza Bull Percival, known as Lillie, whose family came from Cheshire.
Their first child, Florence Anne Paxton, was known as Nancy. The
Norfolk Regiment was at that time based in Colchester in Essex and the
Archibald Wavells were still living there, in a tall redbrick three-storey
semi-detached house at 10, The Avenue when on 5 May 1883 Lillie gave
birth to their second child, a son. He was called Archibald after his father
and Percival, his mother's maiden name. Soon afterwards Lillie was preg-
nant again. Her last child – christened Lillian Mary and known as Molly –
was born in 1884. Lillie suffered from crippling arthritis and 'whether

owing to her naturally retiring disposition, to ill health or the fact that her husband himself ruled the family in true Victorian fashion,' writes Wavell's early biographer and contemporary, Jack Collins, 'Mrs Wavell does not seem to have played any dominating part in the shaping of the character and mind of her only son.'[4] Archibald's relationship with his sisters was always close. In later life he confessed that he might perhaps have 'come the man' over them too often; but their mutual correspondence suggests a strong bond between them which broke only with his death. Of his uncles, he hardly knew his father's eldest brother Arthur, who died in 1891, but believed that there was probably 'a strong family likeness' in character between him and his other uncles, William and Llewellyn, his godfather. Wavell described Llewellyn from recollection as 'a small, wiry energetic little man, deeply religious, very charitable and with a real love of the British soldier and devoted to his welfare at a time when very few bothered about the soldier once he was off parade.'[5] Two of Wavell's six aunts had died before he was born.

The first five years of young Archibald's life were spent in Britain. A typical child, one of his earliest recollections was of attempting to turn a somersault while paddling in the sea at Dornoch, a holiday resort with beautiful golden sands on the north-east coast of Scotland. Soaked clothes were the inevitable result, and years later he still remembered the 'ignominy' of walking back home through Dornoch, wet and in disgrace.[6] In the autumn of 1888 Major Wavell rejoined his regiment in Gibraltar after a period in a staff appointment. Lillie and her three small children went with him, and another recollection was of nearly creating an 'international incident' when he inadvertently 'tumbled' across the Spanish frontier and had to be retrieved.[7] The Gibraltar posting lasted only a few months, and the regiment then moved to India; yet again, the family followed. The Norfolks were at Wellington, a station in the Nilgiri Hills, south-west of Bangalore in southern India. Here the small boy learnt to ride, and one of the first photographs of him shows a relaxed child sitting on a fat white pony. For the rest of his life Wavell remembered India as a place 'where the sun and air of a fine climate gave my body a good start in life'.[8]

When the Norfolks were ordered to Burma in 1891 Major Wavell decided to exchange regiments. To live in India with one's family was considered acceptable; to do so in Burma, with its unhealthy climate, was not. A fellow officer recently promoted to command the 2nd Battalion, The Royal Highland Regiment (The Black Watch) wished for financial reasons to serve abroad. Since Wavell was in line for a command, the two men agreed to an exchange. Promoted to lieutenant-colonel, Archibald Graham Wavell took over his new battalion in Limerick; the following year, 1893, The Black Watch – as the regiment was familiarly known, from the 'watch' they had kept on the Highlands and the dark tartan they wore – was transferred to Maryhill Barracks on the north-west side of Glasgow.[9] The family had no Scottish blood, but by this exchange Wavell's father started a connection with the regiment that was to be continued in future generations.

Colonel Wavell's return to Britain meant he could educate his son in England without having to consign him to the care of spinster aunts during the holidays, the fate of so many boys sent to boarding schools 'at home' while their parents remained abroad. Until now, Wavell had shared his sisters' governess. Already he had developed a love of reading; family folklore has it that when visitors arrived he would disappear under the table with his book to avoid interruption. He had also acquired a love of poetry that was to endure his whole life, and exhibited an exceptional memory. 'Horatius', 'with its arresting stanza about Lars Porsena and his Nine Gods', was the first poem he learnt by heart: 'Admiring aunts used to give me threepence for reciting it from beginning to end; a wiser uncle gave me sixpence for a promise to do nothing of the kind.'[10] Like any Victorian child, much of his life was spent with his sisters in the nursery. He was shy and sometimes tongue-tied in adult company.[11] Archibald Wavell's contemporary Kenneth Buchanan, who lived in Lanarkshire, not far from the Wavells' home on the outskirts of Glasgow, recalled that one afternoon Archibald and his father rode over from Maryhill Barracks to Cambuslang, five miles from Glasgow, to return his father's call on the regiment. It was a ride of some fifteen miles, through the city of Glasgow, which Buchanan considered 'no mean achievement'. His first observation of Archibald Wavell was that 'he was shorter than myself, but stocky and probably half a stone heavier'. Buchanan, already at the school Wavell was shortly to join, remembered telling his family that he'd found him to be 'a funny, quiet sort of chap!'[12] Wavell celebrated his tenth birthday in May 1893, and the next decade of his life fashioned the man he became.

In the autumn of 1893 Archibald Wavell left his family to attend Summer Fields, a prep school in Summertown, north Oxford, established in 1864 by Gertrude Isabella Maclaren, the second wife of Archibald Maclaren, pioneer of gymnastics and founder of the Oxford University Gymnasium. The idea was that Gertrude, or 'Mrs' as she was known by the boys, would teach them, and her husband would look after their physical well-being. Initially 'Mrs' had relied on the local vicar to teach the boys divinity, and the organist to teach them music. But in 1870 a Welshman and graduate of

Brasenose College, the Reverend Charles Eccles Williams, had arrived, followed soon afterwards by the Reverend Hugh Alington; known as 'Doctor' and 'Bear', they married the Maclaren daughters. Mrs Maclaren's husband had died in 1884, but the *mens sana in corpore sano* motto of the school continued to be upheld. In 1891, as Summertown grew into a suburb 'and Summerfields, Summerhills and Sommervilles arose in such numbers that letters were constantly going astray', Mrs Maclaren had changed the school's original name of Summerfield to Summer Fields.[13]

By the time Archibald Wavell started at Summer Fields in 1893, it was a flourishing school of ninety boys and ten masters. Mrs Maclaren had virtually handed over its running to her son-in-law Dr Williams and her own son, Wallace. Three forms were taught, seated on benches, in the large, wood-panelled 'New Room', overlooking the playing fields. On the walls were hung wooden boards listing in red script the names of those who had won scholarships, whose achievements it was hoped the boys might emulate.[14] The academic timetable was mainly classical. In the top form the boys were expected to be able to compose prose and verse in Latin and Greek and to understand works such as St Mark's Gospel and part of the Acts in the Greek Testament; the *Ajax* of Sophocles; and selected passages from the works of Herodotus, Livy, Xenophon, Virgil's *Aeneid*, *The Odyssey*, Ovid and Horace. In later years, contemporaries marvelled at the breadth of Archibald Wavell's classical mind: undoubtedly the origins lay in his early education.[15] There was no chapel in the school grounds and so every Sunday, their threepenny pieces in their pockets, the boys went in a crocodile to the local church of St John the Baptist, across the Banbury Road.[16]

In addition to football and cricket in their season, once a week the boys walked to the gym. There were 'Fives' courts in the playground, and the boys also played golf with hockey sticks and fives balls on a primitive golf course. A 'unique' amusement, called 'Torpids' after the Oxford boat races, consisted of hurdle-races on the bumping principle, each competitor taking the name of a college boat club at either Oxford or Cambridge. They also had a 'dribbling' game which involved dribbling a football around the hurdles until a boy could shoot it through the goal at the end. In summer the boys went swimming in the Cherwell River which skirted the grounds of the school, and where they had a specially reserved bathing place.

However, life was very different from the comfort, even luxury of prep schools today. During term time the boys saw little of their parents. As noted by old boy Nicholas Aldridge: 'Schoolmasters were remote and often unpredictable giants. Big boys seldom deigned to notice little boys, except to cuff them, and were in turn feared or worshipped by the little boys, who behaved in the same way themselves when their turn came to be cocks of the roost.' There was also a ritual about clothing. Like every other boy, young Archibald Wavell would have been instructed that he must always wear a vest, change his shoes when going outside, and wear a felt hat if the sun was shining. Surprisingly, however, for sport 'one simply flung off one's jacket and sometimes one's waistcoat and then weighed in, braces, boots, trousers and all.'[17] Caning was a regular occurrence, and the 'Black Book' recorded misdemeanours. Apprehensive new boys received Mrs Maclaren's good-night kisses.[18] Already nearly 60 when Wavell arrived at the school, she had become very short-sighted and sometimes wore two pairs of glasses 'when she meant business!'[19] Wavell appears to have settled into Summer Fields without any difficulty, and never showed any signs of being homesick; an often-repeated story describes how 'as soon as he arrived at the school, he was introduced to a group of boys, began to play with them, and after a few minutes strolled over to his parents, remarking, "You can go now. I shall be quite all right." '[20]

Throughout Wavell's time at Summer Fields, Dr Williams was impressed by his all-round mental and physical capacity. 'Words like "capital", "grand", "most promising" sparkled through his reports from Archibald's first day in the school to the last.'[21] In December 1894 Williams wrote to Colonel Wavell: 'The Villain has again won his Form Prize, you see. He has been first in most subjects, as usual. We think him a child of great capacity and what pleases us most is that he goes up gradually accumulating knowledge and experience without the slightest effort, having his foundations very firm and sound.'[22] Contemporaries remembered him as a sturdy, quiet-mannered boy, a little small for his age, 'handsome and with a quick, shrewd gleam of humour in his eyes'. They also recognized his exceptional ability to learn. 'Lessons appeared to come easy to him, in fact he seemed to do less work than the average,' recalled Kenneth Buchanan. He was already demonstrating the quiet reserve and detachment which became the hallmark of his character for the rest of his life. Buchanan described him as inclining to be 'shy and uncommunicative', rather untidy in appearance, 'yet meticulously tidy in his work'.[23] 'About his intelligence there was never any doubt,' wrote another contemporary. 'His mind flowered quickly; he absorbed knowledge with an almost daunting ease, and remembered everything he learned.'[24] With another boy, Norman Grundy, Wavell started a school paper – 'written in long hand and passed around the Vth form (scholarship form) and to others who wanted it. It was rather primitive.'[25]

Like any schoolboy, Wavell enjoyed things that made him squeal. Nearly fifty years later he wrote to a contemporary, Robert Lightfoot: 'I can remember our finding an earwig and someone, and I think it was you, telling a gruesome story about earwigs which got into one's ear while one was sleeping and ate their way through the brain and came out quite white at the other ear!'[26] According to Buchanan, Wavell did not shine particularly at games 'but used to go very straight for his man at football'.[27] By his own admission he was not a good cricketer, but in his last year he captained the Second XI, and played several times for the First XI. And for at least one boy Wavell was a 'schoolboy hero'. Robert Dundas was a year younger and thought the older boy 'terrific', recalling 'a very solid little boy, with resolution and a low centre of gravity, and very hard to knock over at soccer'.[28]

Within eighteen months of Archibald's arrival, Dr Williams had written to Colonel Wavell suggesting that his son had a good chance of a scholarship to Eton or Winchester, 'if you would like that'.[29] The following year Williams wrote describing Wavell as 'a capital boy . . . he has pleased me especially in his Latin work, but he has no weak points and has a rare good head and memory.'[30] By this time Wavell had been joined at Summer Fields by his cousin Jack Longfield, two years his junior.[31] In the summer of 1896 Wavell was one of twelve boys at Summer Fields who won scholarships, three of them to Winchester. Dr Williams was obviously pleased with Wavell's success. 'I fully trust that, please God, he is going to make a good – perhaps a great – man.'[32]

Winchester was in some ways an obvious choice. Several Wavell ancestors had passed through the college, and his first cousin, Arthur, son of his deceased eldest uncle, was already there. As he had at Summer Fields, Wavell settled in to Winchester easily. 'He was a square, silent, self-contained youth,' noted one of the older boys, A.L. Irvine, who acted as 'pater' to Wavell during his first few weeks.[33] Academically Wavell's early promise continued, and he later recalled that examinations never worried him and that he had probably therefore 'gained places above my real merit'.[34] He was able to expand his general reading, and indulge his growing love of literature. All the boys learned poetry during 'Morning Lines', and for Wavell this 'laid a foundation on which my memory ever since has been building and furnishing'. The *Winchester College Song Book* contained many verses that he remembered for the rest of his life, one of his favourites being Robert Browning's 'Muckle-Mouth Meg'. The verses of Tennyson and Wordsworth, on the other hand, 'never registered' on him. 'I think he [Wordsworth] got a bad start with me, in that the first of his poems I was made to read as a child was "We are Seven", and its utter bathos repelled me even at that age.' As far as Wavell was concerned, Tennyson's poetry was like 'eating an egg without salt, whereas Wordsworth's was eating one with sugar.'[35] With Browning, Wavell's other favourite poet was Rudyard Kipling; the works of both had 'courage and humanity'.[36] Shakespeare, written in blank verse, he found hard to memorize, but seeing it acted was different, and prompted a lifelong interest in going to the theatre.[37]

During Wavell's time the Headmaster of Winchester, Dr W.A. Fearon, took the somewhat radical decision to abandon the compulsory study of Ancient Greek, one of the few subjects in which Wavell did not excel. He read the account of Xenophon and his ten thousand 'with intense boredom', perhaps because his teacher never troubled to explain the story – of how Xenophon, a Greek general in the service of the Persians, led a retreat of ten thousand men from the Tigris to the Black Sea. 'They were interested only in irregular verbs, and syntax . . . it was many years later, after I had seen most of the ground, that I realized how interesting it might have been and how the young imagination might have been stirred to adventure.'[38] He also found it difficult to compose Greek prose, because he never understood the system of accenting in Greek 'and was reduced to haphazard sprinkling': one of his teachers called it 'the pepperbox method'.[39] The only Greek author who inspired him was Homer, and he always regretted not being able to read The Odyssey in the original.

Wavell and the other boys studied in cubicles known as 'toys' in one big room, probably the explanation for the renowned Wykehamist characteristic of being able to concentrate in the middle of chaos.[40] He also experienced 'fagging', or the 'sweating' phase, as it was called, which meant being answerable to the demands of the prefects. For half a term he was the 'junior' or 'fag' to Raymond Asquith, eldest of three brothers at the school whose father, H.H. Asquith, was Home Secretary in William Gladstone's government.[41] Although Archibald's shyness was much commented on in his later life, a contemporary at Winchester recalled that he and Wavell were part of the same 'pitch-up' or clique of boys, which the Senior Boys called the 'Pandemonium Pitch-up'.[42]

Following boarding-school custom, Wavell wrote regularly to his parents and sisters. The earliest surviving letter, dated 'Winchester, 1896', describes to his elder sister Nancy the game of football, demonstrating the sense of humour characteristic of his letters throughout his life: 'If you have never seen a game of footer, as played at present, you have missed something. However if you want a fairly good idea of it, take a bit of ground and water it well and thoroughly till it is a cake of mud and there are little pools here and there and a big one in the middle.'[43] With other Wykehamists from Summer Fields, Wavell returned to his prep school to play in the annual Old Boys' match. As the 1897 *Summer Fields Magazine* recorded, all their XI played 'pluckily but . . . were greatly outclassed . . . the Old Boys really played an excellent game; Wavell being most conspicuous in the forward division.'[44] In later years, Wavell downplayed his ability: 'I mistrusted my personal courage and toughness. Though I passed as plucky enough a football player, I knew how often I was tempted to funk.'[45]

During the holidays Wavell enjoyed shooting with his father. Once, when they were out after duck, he stumbled on a patch of boggy ground and the gun's muzzle plunged into soft wet earth; he later had the chance of a shot and raised the gun, but did not fire. When the keeper came to clean the gun, both barrels were found to be plugged tight with mud, from the muzzle downwards. What would have happened if he had attempted to fire the gun is all too obvious.[46] The Wavell children often visited their Longfield cousins – Jack and his sister Katherine – whose family had a house at Mallow, County Cork, in southern Ireland. Jack had gone on to Harrow, but the two boys remained close. On a swimming expedition, Jack encouraged his cousin to dive into the Blackwater River, which was in flood. As Wavell later recalled, he took a 'header' off the highest part of the bank, hit a rock, 'nearly scalped' himself, and emerged with a bleeding head. A local doctor stitched him up, and he was 'all right in a few days'. The scar remained with him for the rest of his life.[47]

In July 1898 Colonel Wavell finished a tour of duty at Perth commanding the regimental depot and was moved to a staff appointment at the War Office in London. The family therefore left Scotland and found a house at Englefield Green, not far from Windsor Castle. Archibald Wavell's last academic year at Winchester coincided with the Boer War in South Africa, a war which marked, as Wavell wrote many years later, 'a turning point in our history. It was the climax of British Imperialism, of the time – the last time – when we were aggressively sure of ourselves and of our destiny.'[48] The 2nd Battalion, The Black Watch was one of the first British units to be sent to South Africa, as part of the 3rd (Highland) Brigade, commanded by Major-General Andrew Wauchope, Colonel Wavell's successor and former second-in-command in Perth.[49] In early December 1899, as part of a three-pronged offensive, the British attacked the Boers on the hill of Magersfontein; but the Boers, with their superior marksmanship, were well prepared to meet their attackers and British losses were high. Wauchope was one of the first of fifteen officers to be killed; his cousin, Lieutenant Arthur Wauchope, was severely wounded, his bright new gaiters drawing the Boer fire.[50] News of the battle – one of many reverses for the British in what was known as 'Black Week' – arrived at Winchester at tea time. After looking solemnly at the list of war dead and wounded – his father's friends and contemporaries – sixteen-year-old Archibald Wavell abruptly left the room. In January 1900 – four weeks after the defeat at Magersfontein – his father, promoted major-general, was sent to South Africa to command the 15th Brigade, part of a corps of cavalry and infantry with which the new Commander-in-Chief, Field Marshal Lord Roberts of Kandahar – 'Bobs' Roberts – was proposing to take the offensive. Two months later, on 15 March, Roberts entered Bloemfontein, capital of the Orange Free State. General Wavell, who had been hospitalized with enteric fever, later became Military Commander of Johannesburg.

In different circumstances, Wavell's obvious academic ability would have secured him a place at Oxford or Cambridge, or in the Civil Service. But while it is not clear exactly when his father decided on his son's future, it seems to have been a foregone conclusion that Wavell would follow his father into the Army. As he later admitted, though he did not have any special inclination for a military career, to go against his father's wishes would have required far more 'independence of character' than he possessed. The decision met with a strong protest from Dr Fearon, who (in a letter much quoted by later commentators) wrote to the general in dismay: 'I regret to see you are sending your son to the Army Class, and I hasten to assure you this desperate step is not necessary, as I believe your son has sufficient ability to make his way in other walks of life.'[51] Wavell later suggested that this was not a very tactful comment to make to a soldier.

The first uniform he ever wore, while still at Winchester, was that of the school's 'Hampshire Regiment', forerunner of its Officer Training Corps and 'a rather forlorn little band', as he later recalled. Membership was voluntary, but one of the prefects, having discovered that Wavell's father was a soldier and that he was going into the Army, took him off to the Armoury and very firmly enrolled him as a 'voluntary recruit'. 'So, in a not very well-fitting red tunic, with a rather weighty Martini [rifle], I toiled my short legs – I was small then – on marches where everyone else always seemed out of step; or skirmished pantingly over Teg Down and wondered whether I was really going to like soldiering.'[52] Throughout his time in the 'Hampshires' Wavell appears to have been indifferent to rank, and never became a lance-corporal. His excuse was that he would have quite enough drilling later on, so he would do the minimum now.[53] On one occasion, however, the schoolboys received praise beyond their expectations. It was a big Public

Schools field day, and a regular Army battery was taking part in their exercise. During the manoeuvre, the boys were supposed to retire in a hurry, 'so hurriedly that I and a few other of the smaller or lazier ones were left behind and lay down to rest in a sheltering ditch.' Up came the Army battery and stopped not far from Wavell and his colleagues. The opportunity was too good to miss, and the delighted schoolboys poured their blanks into the battery which an umpire then declared out of action. The following day Wavell and his friends found themselves mentioned in the local paper, whose columnist noted that 'our reverses in South Africa were hardly surprising when a handful of Winchester schoolboys lining a ditch could put a regular battery out of action.'[54]

Wavell left Winchester in the summer of 1900, just seventeen years old, after what he remembered as a 'good half'. He had passed fourth of his entry into Sandhurst, and 'the Winchester correspondent' of the *Summer Fields Magazine* congratulated him 'for his excellent performance'.[55] Spending only four years at Winchester rather than the customary six meant he missed the chance of being a prefect, or Captain of the School. Montague Rendall, second master in Wavell's last year, recalled 'a sturdy independent figure, moving with complete composure among all and sundry'.[56] Rendall also recognized that Wavell had a great deal of 'latent power', and that it would help if he became more communicative as he grew older. 'He is a boy of much ability,' he wrote to General Wavell, 'literary and other. I hope he will develop a little socially. He is at present needlessly shy and reticent in manner, but it is a fault on the right side.'[57] Although the education he received made a lasting impression, Wavell's assessment of himself during his schooldays was sadly negative. 'I must have been an unattractive boy – very self-centred and rather bumptious but clever enough to keep out of trouble and on the right side of people . . . I was not popular with my contemporaries and rather lonely, for the same reason as at Summer Fields: there was too much ego in my cosmos.'[58] Over the next fifty years he returned time and again to his old school, which he referred to as his 'spiritual home'.

2

Life in the Army, 1901–8

My father, while professing to give me complete liberty of choice, was
determined that I should be a soldier.   A.P. Wavell[1]

THE ROYAL MILITARY College, Sandhurst, an impressive building with
tall portico columns and guns from the Battle of Waterloo, marked a
significant change from the cloisters of Winchester College.[2] Throughout
Wavell's time there he lived in a residential block near the stables. Once
more he was treading in the footsteps of his first cousin Arthur, who had
passed out of Sandhurst the previous year.

Some of Sandhurst's more archaic practices, such as flogging, had been
abolished a generation earlier, but much remained the same. As part of their
training the young cadets had to make sketches and scale diagrams of fortifications of a kind probably unchanged since the Crimean War. As he had
with his schooldays, Wavell later downplayed his abilities, modestly describing his experience at Sandhurst: 'The bookwork gave me no trouble, but I
was not good at the drill nor at field sketching, which was at that time considered a necessary qualification for an officer. I had short legs and no sense
of music or rhythm so found great difficulty in keeping step, and I was not
naturally smart, which was the great military virtue at that time, though I
was always well enough turned out to keep out of trouble.'[3] Of his immediate circle of friends there is scant record, but there was one with whom
he developed a lifelong friendship: John Greer Dill.[4] Dill did not share
Wavell's intellectual ability, but there was mutual admiration and understanding. Soon after Wavell started at Sandhurst his father returned from
South Africa to England and an appointment as Chief Staff Officer, 3rd
Army Corps, to the Duke of Connaught, Queen Victoria's third son and
Commander-in-Chief in Ireland. The family continued to live at Englefield
Green, and at weekends Wavell cycled from Sandhurst to visit them. On
two occasions he was caught without lights on his bicycle. The fine was five
shillings, but when the young cadet appeared before the Farnborough Petty

Sessions court the Chairman, who happened to be his uncle and godfather, Colonel Llewellyn Wavell, doubled the fine to ten shillings.[5]

So great was the demand for junior officers to fight in South Africa that Wavell's training at Sandhurst lasted only two terms instead of the usual eighteen months. Together with 139 other cadets he took only one set of exams, at Christmas, gaining 'a very high aggregate'. His papers in Tactics, Engineering and French were 'exceedingly good'.[6] He may have had mis-givings about his performance, but with less than nine months' training, he passed out 4th in the Order of Merit. His conduct was described as 'exemplary'.

It was a new century, and a new era was dawning. On 22 January 1901 Queen Victoria died, and was succeeded by her eldest son. Wavell joined the Army on 8 May 1901, three days after his eighteenth birthday. His Commission, signed by the new king, Edward VII, addressed him as His Majesty's 'trusty and well beloved'. He was gazetted to The Black Watch and posted to the 2nd Battalion, which his father had commanded for four years in the early 1890s. The loyalty he felt to the regiment lasted a life-time. Although an Englishman, Wavell came to recognize and admire the characteristics of the Highland Regiment: 'the clan feeling, the toughness, the fierceness in assault, the independence of character, the boundless self-confidence in his own powers in all circumstances and conditions.'[7] The 2nd Battalion was in South Africa and the 1st in India, so after a few weeks' leave, which he spent in Ireland with his father, in early June Second Lieutenant Wavell joined the 'Details' of The Black Watch – effectively a recruits' drill course – at Edinburgh Castle. After Winchester and Sandhurst, for two months a bleak room at the top of Edinburgh Castle was his home. As he recollected, all the winds of Scotland whistled through it, according to their season, and it was appropriately known as 'the Rookery'. Here, Wavell later recalled, the new subalterns rocked if the wind was blowing and cawed like rooks. 'And as young rooks cast debris from their nests to the occasional annoyance of those on the ground level, so we used sometimes to amuse ourselves by driving old golf balls from the roof in the general direction of Edinburgh city.'[8]

After his two months 'on the square' in Edinburgh, Wavell went off to spend six weeks in Kent at the School of Musketry at Hythe. Another friend from those early months of soldiering was Charles Henderson, with whom he shared a love of poetry. Charles was known as 'Long Man Henderson', because of his height and to distinguish him from Neville Henderson, also in the regiment, known as 'Piccanin'.[9] Wavell's sturdy build earned him the nickname 'Podgy', which stuck to him for at least a decade.[10] After Hythe Wavell enjoyed a month's leave and then returned to Edinburgh, from where on 29 September 1901 he set off for South Africa with a draft of 115 Non-Commissioned Officers and men. It was a grey evening and the streets between the Castle walls and the entrance to Waverley station were lined with people who cheered as the band of young men in their kilts and khaki tunics passed by. Relatives were allowed onto the station platform, and the train left to a mixture of tears and cheers.

The young subalterns travelled aboard 'a most excellent seaboat', the SS *Custodian* of the Harrison Line. During his time at sea Wavell wrote as many as seven letters a week to his family, but since nothing very exciting happened, there was little to record: 'We have not been shipwrecked, on fire or seen the sea serpent,' he wrote to his sister Nancy. He was, however, learning a new skill – photography – and he shared every step with his sisters. Among them was having to withstand gratuitous comments from his cabinmate, who was 'a great expert in the art'. Every time he started to take a photo, his companion would caution him: 'You silly ass that'll never come out, your subject's in the shade, the sun is shining right on your lens, and you've got the thing all focused wrong and that's not the right stop to use.' His letters were full of his characteristic humour, more playful than dry at this time. 'I am awfully sorry for the horses on board,' he wrote after three weeks at sea. 'Fancy standing on your legs for over three weeks if you had been a horse accustomed to lie down at night.'[11] When the ship stopped at Las Palmas in the Canaries, off the west coast of Africa, he posted a bundle of letters and sought out interesting stamps for his own and his sisters' collections.

The SS *Custodian* reached Durban on 29 October. By early November Wavell was in camp near Standerton in the Transvaal, south-east of Johannesburg and west of the Drakensberg mountains. Fortunately he had a good batman – 'McA' – who on arrival took 'complete charge' of his personal comfort. 'Within an hour he had gone through my equipment with an experienced eye and named several articles of which I was deficient – a mug for shaving water was one.' By the evening 'McA' had procured everything necessary. Since there was no shop in sight, Wavell wanted to know their provenance. 'He merely said: "There they are, sir, that's all you need to know, and you needn't be afraid to find your friends missing them." '[12]

Wavell's battalion was part of a mobile column commanded by Colonel Mike Rimington, who had previously raised and commanded an irregular corps of Guides; wearing wild-cat skins around their felt hats, they had achieved notoriety as 'Rimington's Tigers'.[13] The four companies of the 2nd Battalion that formed Rimington's column were attempting to round up the Boers in the south-eastern Transvaal. Although there was plenty of excitement for the cavalry, riding hard to search out the enemy, for the infantry – the 'foot sloggers' – there was a considerable amount of 'trekking' but little fighting. It was, as Wavell recorded, 'not very exciting work'.[14] In contrast to the bleak room at the top of Edinburgh Castle, on the South African veldt most of Wavell's nights were spent in a bivouac shelter, into which he crawled each night 'like a tired puppy'. This kind of soldiering was unpredictable and exhausting. 'Last night, I thought I was going to get some sleep at last as no orders to move had come,' he wrote to Nancy early in January 1902, 'but at 3.15 a.m. this morning a sergeant put his head into my bivouac and told me reveille was at 3.45 and parade at 4.50 a.m. We started about 5 a.m. and got here at 12 noon about. It is very nearly 20 miles so it was pretty good marching.'[15]

In early 1902 Rimington's column was undertaking two drives north-west from Harrismith towards the Bloemfontein–Johannesburg railway line. The objective was to trap the Boers against some blockhouses built as part of Lord Kitchener's 'scorched earth' policy of containing Boers and their families within enclosed areas or 'concentration camps'. At the end of one drive, on 28 February, Wavell noted in his diary: '1,100 Boers snaffled'.[16] The following day the 2nd were relieved by the 1st Battalion, The Black Watch, just arrived in South Africa from India; Wavell then returned to Harrismith for three months' garrison duty. As part of his training he was required to attend the court martial of a reservist whose fortitude had given way under the strain of war and who had committed a deliberate act of insubordination. Wavell was only nineteen but, wiser perhaps than his superiors, who showed a singular lack of understanding of the circumstances which had caused the offender to court his own dismissal, and he absorbed a lesson he never forgot. 'Obviously,' he wrote many years later, 'one cannot discharge men simply because they get bored with war – almost everyone does – but it is a commander's job to prevent men reaching a breaking-point of discipline.'[17]

Wavell's letters home brought vital supplies in return: pipes, tobacco, cigarettes, chocolate, butterscotch, cake and plums, which he described as 'very acceptable'.[18] He was still collecting stamps and taking photographs, sending films home for Molly to develop and also photographs 'of more or less interest'.[19] He showed a thrifty turn of mind, keeping an eye on what things cost: for example, a film for his camera was five shillings rather than the three it cost at home, though he was not surprised since the main customers at the stores (which stocked anything 'from a helmet or pair of breeches to a box of matches or a toothbrush') were officers off columns halted for only a short while, 'so the stores charge what they like'.[20] Despite the war, his letters to his sisters continued to be light-hearted. He teased Nancy about coming-out parties, and how 'awfully well' she looked in a photograph he had seen of her as a debutante.[21] 'I suppose the Dublin season is about over now,' he wrote at the end of March, 'and you have taken off the war paint and hung up the scalps.'[22] On another occasion, he told Nancy he wished he could send her the cold he had got, so that it would reach her in time 'to make it a reasonable excuse for not going to Church on Sunday'.[23] He also asked her to send him *Clara in Blunderland*, a political parody of Lewis Caroll's *Alice in Wonderland*.[24]

Negotiations for peace between the Boers and the British had begun on 23 March; at the end of May, the Boer leaders signed the Treaty of Vereeniging. Wavell had been sent to join his battalion on a blockhouse line near Retief's Neck, scene of a battle the previous year involving both The Black Watch and The Seaforth Highlanders. 'Heard peace was declared,' he recorded in his diary on 1 June.[25] The Black Watch was not among those chosen to garrison the country, and for a while Wavell and his companions did not know whether they were going immediately to India or to a posting in the Mediterranean. 'Not much to do,' he recorded. 'A few partridges to shoot and rode into Bethlehem for polo occasionally.'[26] 'I sometimes hit the ball now,' he told Nancy, 'which I never used to before.'[27] At the end of June the 2nd Battalion returned to Harrismith where it was joined by the 1st, and for a brief exceptional period the two were stationed together.[28] During a football match between officers and sergeants in early July Wavell tackled a larger opponent, fell and broke his left shoulder blade, collar bone and the tip of another bone. He went immediately to hospital, his shoulder was set the next day, and it was nearly three weeks before he was able to get out of bed for the first time, his shoulder in splints. He was advised that he would be unable to use his arm for a month, so he applied to be invalided home: 'It is most infernally dull down here, especially with only one arm available.'[29] Sick leave was granted, but it took time for the arrangements to be made, and he chafed with annoyance and boredom. At the beginning of September he complained to Nancy that he was still 'immured in hospital', waiting 'for a mythical hospital ship', but his sense of humour remained intact. He had made a study of hospital cooking, and amused himself by sending his sister two recipes: soup entailed washing dirty plates with warm water, pouring the result into a saucepan, rescuing a bone from the kitchen terrier for flavour and adding the contents of the pepper pot and a handful of sand; fish sauce required two handfuls of dried grass, chopped small and mixed with two ounces of flour and a pint of water, served cold.[30]

In mid September Wavell finally was transferred to Natal, on the coast; on 1 October – a year after he first set sail for South Africa – he began the journey back to England; two days later, his battalion left for India. Wavell spent a cold and wintry leave at home. His shoulder was still recovering and of little use for most active sport, but he continued to ride, and later recalled an amusing episode from this time. His horse Kitty had an 'excitable' temperament and 'no paces between neutral and top gear'. When she bolted one day while he was out hunting, he was unable to control her with only one arm. Horse and rider cantered past the hunt at breakneck speed, knocking riders to the right and left. Having left the field well behind him, Wavell tried 'to sneak off' home, but to his dismay encountered them again around the corner, whereupon he was roundly ordered by the Master to take his 'circus-horse' home before he got himself 'or something much more valuable' killed.[31] Wavell spent nearly four months on sick leave. Though his shoulder healed, he was left unable to raise his left arm straight up over his head. Wavell's father, now 59, had retired in November with the honorary rank of major-general, renting a house in Ascot for his family while he sought a permanent home. After Wavell left for India the general eventually settled on Cranborne Lodge in Dorset on the Cranborne Estate owned by the Cecil family. A large house on three floors set in beautiful grounds surrounded by a high wall, and conveniently located in the village of Cranborne, it was to be the Wavell family's home for twenty years.

When Archibald Wavell sailed for India at the end of February 1903, Britain controlled an empire upon which, proverbially, the sun never set. The King's representative in India, the Viceroy, personified its potency. Under his administration in the west, east and south of the subcontinent lay the vast provinces of the Punjab, Bengal and Madras, collectively larger than Europe, stretching from the Khyber Pass bordering Afghanistan in the west to Assam, which shared a rugged frontier with the ancient kingdom of Myanmar (or Burma, as the British called it). Interspersed with the provinces were numerous semi-autonomous 'princely states' ruled by maharajas, nawabs, nizams and princes. On no account could a state enter into a relationship with Tsarist Russia, lately perceived to be Britain's main competitor in the region. The first Viceroy of the twentieth century was George Nathaniel Curzon, who had not yet celebrated his fortieth birthday when he assumed office. Tall and resplendent in his imperial robes, he would have been no more than a shadowy figure to a young subaltern embarking on his second posting overseas.

Wavell's new home was the military cantonment at Ambala in the heart of the Punjab, and he could look forward in peacetime to a comparatively easy existence with the opportunity to indulge in a good deal of sport, as regimental duties permitted. Another subaltern in The Black Watch, the Hon. Malise Hore-Ruthven, later recalled his 'silence, modesty, sense of humour and inimitable likeableness',[32] but it seems he was not always silent: fifty years later a private soldier who had served with him for some years remembered that 'He joked and talked a lot, and his memory was very good on soldiers' families.'[33]

Lord Kitchener was also in India at this time, having left South Africa at the end of the Boer War to be appointed Commander-in-Chief of the British forces in India in 1902. He brought with him a reputation as a ruthless and capable leader, and immediately instituted a series of reforms relating to the training and disposition of both Indian and British Service formations. The Commanding Officer of the 2nd Battalion, The Black Watch for most of Wavell's time in India did not fit the new Kitchener mould. Wavell recalled the Hon. Henry Edward Maxwell, DSO (for his services in South Africa), known as 'Chumpy' and then in his late forties, as 'a fat, heavy man, barely mobile'. Shrewd, pleasant and witty, he was 'no bad judge of men, an able and impartial dispenser of justice, clever with his tongue or pen'.[34] Wavell did not however rate him highly as a tactical leader, or as a trainer of a battalion for war. As far as he could recall, the men hardly did any battalion or brigade training, and no manoeuvres on a large scale.

During the summer the battalion moved from Ambala to the cooler climate of Solon, half-way to the hill station and viceregal summer capital, Simla. The only flat open space in sight was the gravel parade ground. Little training was done, and with Thursday a holiday, and work finishing at lunchtime on most other days, time hung heavily. One hot afternoon Wavell sought out Piccanin Henderson, and made him put on boxing-gloves for a fight. They were well-matched in height, but Henderson was quicker on his feet, while Wavell was heavier. A heavy swing Henderson landed on the side of Wavell's nose left it slightly crooked ever after. On another occasion, Wavell succeeded in breaking a couple of Henderson's ribs. The two men also took up fencing; Wavell managed to cut Henderson's hand. 'He did every damned thing – every possible sport,' Henderson later recalled.[35] When the battalion returned to Ambala at the beginning of the cold weather in October 1903 Wavell bought ponies and played polo, even though he did not class himself as a good horseman. 'I certainly have not the figure of a horseman. I have short, stout legs. But I had a fairly strong seat and fairly good nerves in those days and passed for a reasonably good rider for an infantryman.'[36] At Solon Wavell had also acquired a dog, 'Smiler': 'a terrier of sorts with a dash of bull terrier or bull-dog in him.' He was 'hard as nails', would have faced a tiger in defence of what he considered 'his rights and prerequisites', and had been known to make 'improper advances to a tigress'. When Wavell left India he gave Smiler to Long Man Henderson; Henderson took Smiler with him back to Solon, where he disappeared.[37]

Nearly fifty years after the Indian Mutiny, the internal security of the Empire in India was of less concern to the British Government than the threat posed by Russia on India's northern frontier; in addition, peace had to be kept in the frontier regions bordering Afghanistan, inhabited by war-like tribesmen who had mounted a serious rebellion against British author-ity at the end of the nineteenth century. To cope with these twin threats Kitchener reduced the garrisons in the 'safe' parts of India. The Black Watch therefore moved up from Ambala in the Punjab to the military can-tonment at Peshawar, the 'first town' of the North-West Frontier Province of British India, in 1901 demarcated by Lord Curzon as a separate admin-istrative unit from the Punjab. To the west of Peshawar lay the Khyber Pass, traditional invasion route from Central Asia into the subcontinent.

In the absence of any particular current threat, Wavell settled into a life of sport and soldiering. His first period of leave was spent shooting in Kashmir. As the most northerly state in India, ruled by Maharaja Pratap Singh under the firm guidance of a British Resident, Jammu and Kashmir constituted British India's northern frontier, bordering both China and Russia. In peacetime this land of lush valleys and stupendous mountains was an ideal place for rest and relaxation for the British officer. After shooting ibex in Baltistan he moved on to Bandipur on the vast Wular lake in the valley of Kashmir, west of Srinagar. Here he looked for black bear, leopard, and the Kashmir stag known as the 'bara singh'. When it began to snow, he returned to Peshawar. Wavell played golf, polo and regimental cricket, was in the football team, and won several point-to-point races with the Peshawar Vale Hunt. He also found time to captain the regimental hockey team. He shot snipe and duck, often in the company of Long Man Henderson, and his letters to his family are full of failures and successes met with in trying for 'a good head', or to shoot a leopard 'who of course did not appear'.[38] Bears he described as being 'most inconsiderate animals', since they usually fell over a precipice when killed.[39] He continued to collect stamps for his sisters and also for himself, announcing rather cheekily that he was open to being bought out on 'moderate terms'.[40] He responded enthusiastically to news of his sisters' diverse activities. He might be going on 'ripping' hunts, but he thought of Nancy going to plenty of balls – to the extent that she hardly ever seemed to honour their parents' 'humble home'.[41]

Wavell was also making more lasting friendships. Arthur Wauchope, cousin of General Andrew Wauchope, who was killed at Magersfontein in South Africa and had himself been badly wounded there, had rejoined the regiment at Ambala. Wauchope was interested in the arts, books, architecture, developments in science, history and politics, and Wavell was immediately drawn to him intellectually. 'He was very kind to me and became one of my greatest friends . . . I have owed a great deal to him, in those years, and ever since,' Wavell later acknowledged.[42] Another Black Watch officer, Amyas Borton, known as Biffy, joined them in Peshawar. Wavell enjoyed his company because he was 'witty, light-hearted, full of enterprise and ready for any form of sport but not specially good at any.'[43] Wavell's ability to concentrate was a continual source of surprise to his companions. 'When he was reading, nothing disturbed him; to attract his attention you had to shake him,' noted Archie Bulloch, another officer who had also been wounded at Magersfontein. Yet he could put aside this concentration of effort and with equal zest have a quotation-swapping contest with Long Man Henderson.[44] Discovered reading a French book while supposedly studying to pass his examinations in Urdu, and questioned on the apparent waste of his teacher's time and his own money, Wavell explained that reading a French book was the only way he could keep awake to understand what his teacher was saying.[45] Despite his unorthodox methods, he succeeded in passing both the Lower and Higher Standard exams; he also learnt Pashtu, the language spoken by most of the tribes of the North-West Frontier.

Needless to say, such pleasures as shooting in Kashmir, travelling when not on duty, civilian clothes and books had to be paid for. As a second lieutenant, Wavell's pay was 5s. 3d. a day; officers were generally assumed to enjoy private means. In later life, he was candid about the state of his finances. While his father made him an annual allowance of £200, he also encouraged him to patronize his own expensive tailor and to play polo, racquets and other sports. Wavell did not therefore think his father could be justified in making any complaints if he ran short: 'I knew there was plenty of money in the family to rescue me if I got into trouble.' Perhaps, he remarked, he would have done better if his father had given him a larger allowance and required him to live within it.[46] When he passed his Pashtu

Higher Standard examination, he put his reward money – which amounted to about £45 and, as he admitted, provided the main incentive for studying for the exam in the first place – towards stabling for one of the three or four ponies that were probably his greatest extravagance. Occasionally he tried to retrieve his financial situation by betting on a steeplechase or a regimental point-to-point, and promotion to full lieutenant in August 1904 brought an increase in pay to 6s. 6d. per day.

In the winter of 1904–5 each unit had to undertake the Kitchener Test, to determine its level of efficiency. Whereas The Gordon Highlanders, also in the North-West Frontier Province, embarked on serious training, The Black Watch, under Chumpy, treated the idea of a competitive test with disdain. When the results were made known, The Black Watch was at the bottom of the list. 'It was not so much that we were badly trained, as not trained at all – a grand lot of chaps, scrambling along mostly in blissful ignorance of how ignorant we were,' remarked Malise Hore-Ruthven. Even so, Wavell's studious behaviour set him apart. 'I for one', continued Hore-Ruthven, 'was lazy about dull routine jobs and only interested in polo and racing, but Wavell was industrious – we all took off our hats to him for that, and the results showed its value and his character.'[47]

In April 1905 Wavell went to England on seven months' leave, arriving home in early May. For about £10 he had secured a 'third class' berth. The sanitary arrangements he described as 'awful', but neither he nor his companions had any qualms about using the first class facilities instead, and Wavell judged that they had 'quite a good voyage' to Marseilles and onwards to London.[48] It was his first visit to Cranborne, and there General Wavell entertained his son's friends generously. One who came to stay was his Wykehamist contemporary Stephen Phillimore, who was studying at the theological college at Cuddesdon, near Oxford. He was also a keen shot, but the shoot arranged during his visit was 'disappointing': 'I don't know where all the birds got to, there's a lot of heath all round and I think they must run out into it,' Wavell wrote apologetically afterwards, at the same time describing how on another occasion they had succeeded in getting 'rather a nice mixed bag for four guns' consisting of '10 brace partridges, 31 hares, 5 pheasants, 9 rabbits, 1 snipe and 1 golden plover'.[49] While he was on leave Wavell also stayed at the Junior United Services Club in London. The hundred pounds he had saved while on active service in South Africa was soon spent, and to restore his finances he placed a bet on the races. His horses – whose names, Hammerkop and Merry Andrew, he remembered for over thirty years – finished first and second; thinking he had made £40, he had 'a final bust' in London on the strength of it. Unfortunately, the bookie refused to pay 'on some pre-text', and so he was worse off than before. Whether or not General Wavell knew of his son's financial situation, when the time came he paid for him to return to India by P&O first class. The young subaltern was travelling in the same ship as the new Viceroy, Lord Minto, shortly to take over from Lord Curzon.

Wavell was 23 in May 1906, and his sisters wanted to know what useful present he would like. He opted for a large knife with lots of implements and blades, since every one he possessed, down to a small pocket-knife, had been blunted by skinning and cleaning the bear skin, 'so that I can't even sharpen a pencil except with the dinner knife'.[50] Having become proficient in Urdu and Pashtu, he began to learn Persian. But still his teacher struggled to hold his attention and, as he confessed, he generally went to sleep because he got ' bored to tears' with translating 'the books of my brother's son are good'.[51] Editing a newspaper with Long Man Henderson was far more fun. The *Cherat Times*, named after the hill station between Kohat and Peshawar to which the companies went in turn to escape the summer heat, had a 'crude' humour that appealed to the soldiers; its appearance was eagerly awaited, and Wavell even sent his sisters copies for their amusement.

An integral part of a regiment's Frontier duties each year was relieving the battalion stationed in Chitral, scene of the famous siege of 1895, in the foothills of mountain ranges twice the height of those in Europe border-ing Afghanistan and Russia. Feeling that this was 'a part of the world one's unlikely to have a second chance of going to', Wavell went on a transport course and then managed to get himself attached to the column as the transport officer.[52] The march from Nowshera, south of Peshawar, and back generally took five to six weeks. Setting out in the autumn of 1906, from Nowshera they marched over the Malakand pass and through the beautiful Swat valley to Chakdara, from where they crossed the Lowarai pass to Kila Drosh, the headquarters of the battalion. Here there was a week's rest while the relief took place. Kila Drosh was only about twenty-five miles from Chitral – a morning's ride – so Wavell decided to hire a couple of ponies and see it for himself. His enthusiasm at the prospect was only dimmed by regret that he had forgotten to get film for his camera.[53] As he later recalled, the path was narrow with a rock wall on one side and a sheer drop into the river on the other. Much to his alarm, the ponies insisted on trotting on the edge of the precipice rather than in the middle of the path: 'I realized later that their normal employment was as pack-ponies and that, with a bulky pack on each side, they had learned the necessity to keep well away from the rock wall.'[54]

At the beginning of 1907 Wavell's battalion was required to take part in organized manoeuvres for the first time. He was working on the exams for promotion to captain at the time, and claimed that the papers 'absolutely defeated' him. His powers of self-assessment were as usual inaccurate, and instead of failing, as he had predicted, he passed the written part of the examination with distinction. Promotion, however, was still a long way off, and after over four years in India he was beginning to think more seriously about the direction his career might take. 'What old people we are getting to be sure,' he wrote to Nancy on her twenty-fifth birthday in March.[55] Wavell was not yet 24 and if he continued as he was he faced the prospect of at least another four or five years of regimental duties. However, one of his friends had served in Somaliland in the King's African Rifles, and Wavell, hearing that his battalion was to move from Peshawar back to the Punjab, to the less exciting military cantonment of Sialkot, thought of requesting a tour of duty with the KAR. His father, however, anxious for his son to spend some time at home, suggested a tour of duty at the Regimental Depot in Perth instead, during which time he could work for the entrance examination to the Staff College. Eventually they reached a compromise: Wavell would return home to try for the Staff College examination; if he did not get in, he could apply to go to Somaliland.

In November 1907 The Black Watch made its move from Peshawar to Sialkot. Betting losses compelled Wavell to sell some of his ponies, and while he was sorting out his finances he was sent on a month's staff attachment to Rawalpindi, as part of his qualification for Staff College. In early 1908, while he was there, there was trouble with the Zakka Khel, a subtribe of the Afridis living in the Bazar valley, south of the Khyber Pass, and from Kitchener's headquarters in Simla came the order for a punitive expedition to set out under the command of General Sir James Willcocks. There was a pile of telegrams, and one Wavell was asked to decipher contained a request for a British subaltern who had passed the Urdu Higher Standard examination, to command an ammunition column: Wavell immediately composed a letter putting his own name forward. There were 'some rather awkward inquiries' as to who had recommended Lieutenant Wavell, but since he had shown initiative and was sufficiently qualified, he was allowed to form the column and to proceed to Fort Jamrud, at the southern end of the Khyber Pass.

In the heat of the preparations for this expedition Wavell passed his financial problems on to his father in rather careless haste, earning himself a stern letter of reprimand from the general – who regretted his anger when he learned that Lieutenant A.P. Wavell was commanding the ammunition column against the Zakka Khel in the Bazar Valley. An engagement was fought at the north-eastern end of the valley with the loss of some men, but Wavell and his column were spared any hazardous encounters. What was described by *Punch* magazine as 'Willcocks' Week-end War' was over in a matter of days.[56] It was Wavell's first independent command on active service, and he never forgot it.[57] To the medal with four clasps he had received in South Africa was added another medal with one.

After finishing his attachment at Rawalpindi, Wavell returned to Sialkot to pack up his belongings and set sail for England. In later years he described the time he had spent in India as 'certainly some of the best years of my life . . . in those years I came closest to knowledge of the common Indian people. I learnt enough of the language to speak with the villagers where I camped and shot, with my *shikaris* in the hills of Kashmir where I was several times alone with them for many weeks and with the soldiers of India with whom I served.'[58] It was more than thirty years before he returned.

3

Staff College, Russia and the War Office

Of all the officers who came under my notice, I should consider
Wavell by far the ablest.   Field Marshal Sir William Robertson[1]

$\mathbf{A}$RCHIBALD WAVELL WAS back in England in the spring of 1908. He spent
the summer at Cranborne studying for the Staff College examination
while his father diligently watched over him – sending him inside to study,
as Wavell later recalled, when he would have preferred to be outside playing tennis. For a few weeks before the exams he also went to a crammer
in London, but he later derided this method of instruction: 'After a very
short time at the crammers I decided that I could learn the military subjects better by myself, and concentrated mainly on mathematics and French
. . . they taught very little real useful military knowledge and I did not waste
time on their military history.'[2] With about five applicants jostling for each
of the 35 places offered that year, the competition was stiff. For once, however, Wavell did not appear to be at all concerned about his prospects. He
spent all July on holiday, playing golf in Scotland with Arthur Wauchope,
a member of the Royal and Ancient Golf Club overlooking St Andrew's
Bay.

Wavell may have felt confident about his future, but the Staff College
exams were the most challenging he had faced since Winchester. One-
third of the applicants had been 'nominated' – put forward by their senior
officers as having 'marked ability' in the field or 'special aptitude' in General
Staff studies – and they needed to pass only in the obligatory subjects,
which included mathematics, military engineering, military law, military
topography, military geography, tactics and a foreign language. But since
Wavell was 'too young and too undistinguished' to receive a nomination,
to secure a place he also had to qualify in certain voluntary subjects: more
mathematics, military history, and a second language. Wavell chose French
as his obligatory language, and Hindustani. In all, he sat eighteen three-
hour papers. 'Curiously enough, the only paper I really thought I had done

very well, Military Geography, was the one in which I got the worst marks.'[3] When the results were announced in September, Wavell's name came first, with 85 per cent.

In January 1909 Wavell entered the Staff College at Camberley. The Boer War had prompted an overhaul of the military system. The brief given the Secretary of State for War, Richard Haldane, was to inject new energy into the War Office and to re-fashion the Army as an 'Expeditionary Force' to be kept in readiness for service abroad, supplemented by the formation of a Territorial Army made up of the former militia, yeomanry and volunteers. Haldane's next objective was to modernize and expand the General Staff, and for this the Staff College was the obvious recruiting ground; it was the main and (until the foundation of the Imperial Defence College) the final gateway to extra-regimental promotion.

Wavell was considerably younger than his contemporaries at Staff College, and still a subaltern. The reserve of earlier years was still in evidence. Ivo Vesey of The Queen's Regiment, who was seven years older, observed that when Wavell arrived at Camberley, he was very shy. But 'within a fortnight he was completely absorbed into the spirit of the college . . . he was first rate on paper and very enthusiastic on the sporting side.' But it seems his love of poetry 'never showed up at Staff College'.[4] Wavell's close friends, as he recalled them in later life, were limited to a handful: of these, Everard Calthrop was 'the most attractive'. His father was an artist and he himself 'artistic to the fingertips'. On one occasion Calthrop arrived to stay at Cranborne on a bicycle with one shirt and his washing kit, which he thought was 'ample equipment' – but, said Wavell, it shook his very conventional mother to the core.[5] Vesey too stayed with the Wavells at Cranborne, recalling 'a very happy quiet house', the General as 'charming, kind and gentle' and a good host. Archibald and his sisters, Nancy and Molly, were devoted to their father, Archie, as he was called by his family, was the 'apple' of his eye.[6]

The Commandant of the Staff College was Major-General Sir Henry Wilson, who was quite happy, as Wavell recalled, to refer to himself as the 'ugliest man in the Army'.[7] Wavell also remembered his geniality and humour: 'He had a very quick and agile brain, a ready wit.' Wilson was atypical of his time and place, for rather than staff or tactical work, he was much more interested in 'higher strategy, in the relations between statesmen and soldiers'. His lectures explored such themes as impending war with Germany, where military reorganization was taking place at an alarming rate, the size of the British Army, and the need for conscription. Wavell enjoyed them, but believed that it might perhaps have been better if there had been more emphasis on practice, less on theory: 'It was never rubbed into us that all operations were entirely dependent on transportation, and it was not till much later in my career that I really realized this truth.' He also thought that not enough attention was paid to morale, 'how to induce it and maintain it'.[8] The aspiring staff officers studied military law, martial law and international law, as well as what constituted the 'occupation of a foreign territory', provost duties, discipline, and the treatment of prisoners-of-war. Wavell sat through lectures, wrote essays, drafted plans, wrote out orders. The syllabus included a detailed study of the American Civil War and Wavell discovered the campaigns of Lieutenant-General Stonewall Jackson and his use of ruses and feints. The introductory lecture asserted that the 'cause' of the war was not 'slavery', and that it was 'an international more than a civil war'; on his copy, in neat handwriting, Wavell noted: 'both sides believed they had a just cause.'[9] Reconnaissance work was also part of the syllabus, and at a time when both motor cars and the 'mechanization' of the Army were still in their infancy, the students went about sometimes on horseback but mainly by bicycle.

Wavell took full advantage of the sporting side of life at Camberley; riding with the Staff College Drag Hunt was in any case compulsory, causing considerable 'pain and grief' to many non-equestrians. At Cranborne – two hours away by train – he shot in season, and in January 1910 he took Nancy skiing at Gstaad in the Bernese Oberland with a party of Staff College friends. These were the early years of skiing as a sport, and they had the slopes almost to themselves. No one was very proficient, and they had no instruction. His gunner friend Watty – Herman de Watteville – was 'a keen but indifferent skier' and the rest of the party went up and down hill 'by the light of nature', with very frequent falls.[10]

As part of the second-year Staff College course, large-scale exercises took place at centres within reach of Camberley. In Wavell's opinion they were on far too grand a scale, and should have been broken down into exercises for divisions and brigades. The students did short tours with various arms of the service, and Wavell went on manoeuvres on the Berkshire Downs with the cavalry brigade; the new Inspector-General of Cavalry was Major-General Sir Edmund Allenby, a man with a reputation for brusqueness.[11] Wavell noted the 'explosions' which might follow a misdemeanour, but also saw that Allenby – known as 'The Bull' – had a sense of humour. 'Only the few who knew him well recognized his mental powers,' he wrote later.[12] Wavell is said to have observed prophetically, 'That's the man I should like to go to war under.'[13]

During Wavell's second year at the Staff College Wilson was replaced as

Commandant by Major-General Sir William Robertson.[14] Wully, as he was known, had been born in Lincolnshire, the son of a Scottish tailor, and had worked his way up through the ranks of the army; he was 50 when he became Commandant. Wavell considered him a 'blunt, commonsense practical soldier'. Unlike Wilson, Robertson did not believe political matters to be any concern of the Army. Second-year Staff College students were required to submit a military history paper demonstrating knowledge of previous campaigns. In Wavell's year, he and his contemporaries had to respond to the question 'How far are the strategical and tactical lessons drawn from the campaigns of 1815, 1862, 1866 and 1870 confirmed or modified by the experience of the recent wars in South Africa and Manchuria?' Under the inspiration of Wilson's teaching, Wavell wrote an essay which took into account both the political and strategic aspects of the campaigns. But it was not to Robertson's liking. He praised Wavell's work as 'excellent', but added a cautionary warning: 'I am sorry that your efforts have not been more constantly directed towards military matters . . . The discussion of questions of policy and political matters generally leads to no practical result nor benefit of any kind to the soldier, nor is it his business.'[15]

Despite Robertson's rebuke, Wavell passed out of Staff College with one of the two 'A' grades awarded; the other went to Vesey, to whom Wavell gave his own accolade: 'he was the star turn of our term, the perfect staff officer, hard-working, accurate, sensible.'[16] Vesey for his part noticed how the shy young officer who arrived at Camberley in 1909 had increased in confidence, and that his character 'was very much developed'.[17] Wavell had his own views about the training he had received: 'A good staff officer must be able to produce clear orders or instructions at very short notice. We did not do enough of this.'[18] Among his contemporaries, Wavell's talents were evident. 'There was no question,' recalled Bob Wallace, who had been with him in India, 'that if any of his class were going to the top, [he] would be one of them.'[19] Lieutenant A.P. Wavell was now entitled to have the important initials 'p.s.c.' – 'passed Staff College' – recorded after his name in the Army List. He was 28 and still unmarried and he might have spent another decade with his regiment. But Robertson presented him with an alternative: the War Office wanted an officer from Wavell's intake at Camberley to go to Russia and learn Russian; in the Commandant's opinion, Wavell was that officer.

Wavell arrived in Russia as the Tsarist empire was entering its twilight. His home for the next year was a third-floor flat in a street to the west of the Kremlin. His 'landlady' was a widow, Madame Ertel, and with her lived an assortment of women, among them her 20-year-old daughter Natalya, who delighted in talking to him in English rather than Russian when her mother was out of earshot.[20] There was also another paying guest, Reuben Ivanovitch, a student from Armenia. Madame Ertel initially called Wavell 'Archibald Archibaldovitch', until he made it clear he preferred 'Mr Wavell'. She had not previously had a British officer to stay and Wavell was something of a novelty: the Ertel household was also a new experience for Wavell. The late Mr Ertel had been a friend of Chekhov and had known Tolstoy,[21] and over the next few months Wavell grew accustomed to a constant stream of visitors – writers, artists, students, professors, actors and actresses – who would come in the evenings after dinner and sit until late, drinking tea. 'I am in a thoroughly intellectual circle,' he wrote to his mother soon after his arrival.[22] On the other hand, as far as he could make out, no one took any exercise and they ate excessive quantities of food. Reuben Ivanovitch could eat fifteen or sixteen pancakes at a time, served with melted butter, sour cream, egg, salt fish or caviare, while at best Wavell could manage 'about six if I get plenty of exercise afterwards'.[23]

Madame Ertel was not just Wavell's landlady: 'She was a very good teacher, liked teaching and worked me very hard,' he recalled, adding that she thought him very lazy. 'Russians when they do work, work incessantly, and by their standards I was idle. But I worked pretty hard by mine.'[24] By the end of his first lesson he could say 'Tell me please the way to the Kremlin' correctly. But the difference in temperament between teacher and student became evident even at this early stage: Wavell refused to say his sentence to at least a 'dozen people' on the street, as Madame Ertel asked him to. His reasons were threefold: he did not want to go to the Kremlin; he already knew where the Kremlin was; and he would not understand the answers he was given.[25] He worked as diligently as he could, but was often lonely. In the morning he had his lessons, followed by lunch; he then went to his room and worked. Afterwards he went for a walk, had tea at Muir and Merrilies, which he described to his family as 'the Moscow equivalent of Harrods', then returned home to work until supper. Madame Ertel tried hard to please her English guest by asking him for English recipes, but the only ones he could think of were for plum pudding and mince pies. He did, however, write to ask his mother whether she had one for haggis.[26]

Wavell had arrived in Moscow at the start of Lent, so all the theatres were closed and he had to make do with the Opera, concerts and the ballet. He told his mother that the Bolshoi's performance of Arend's ballet *Salambo* was magnificently staged, the dancing wonderful; in April he confessed to Nancy that he had been rather jovial, going to the Opera twice and the ballet once in a week; *La Traviata* was 'good', *Romeo and Juliet* 'terrible' – Romeo had a fine voice, but his appearance was so 'horrible' that it was difficult to appreciate his singing, and he took an 'unconscionable' time to die.[27] With the arrival of spring Wavell joined a football team of students and schoolboys formed by a Russian doctor, a keen fan of the game. The team's ideas about time were not what he was used to. The game was supposed to begin at 3 p.m., but nothing happened until 3.30; then, when finally it appeared that play was about to start, 'a representative of the Moscow sporting paper usually appears with a camera and delays the start for 10 to 15 minutes while the teams are solemnly photographed.'[28] Half-time was long enough for the players to drink tea and smoke cigarettes.

Another diversion was the arrival in April of Wavell's Staff College contemporary Cuthbert Fuller of the Royal Engineers; Fuller had fallen for his former teacher, the Princess Sophia Shahovsky (whom he later married) and had returned to Moscow to requalify in Russian.[29] When Fuller proposed a holiday Wavell accepted, and on 8 May they set out with another language student, Captain George Churchill, an Indian Army officer in the Medical Corps,[30] for the Volga, the Caucasus and the Crimea. They took a train from Moscow to Nijni-Novgorod, famous for its fairs; it was a welcome change, despite such mishaps as losing their luggage and missing a connection. From Nijni-Novgorod they proceeded south by boat along the Volga to Tsaritsin (later Stalingrad, now Volgograd). The ship's timetable was erratic and meals – consisting almost entirely of borscht and caviare (the best Wavell had ever eaten) – might be served at any hour. Fuller's leave ran out and he had to leave them at Tsaritsin; Wavell and Churchill (whom Wavell described as 'not very intellectual but a pleasant companion') journeyed onwards by train to Vladikavkaz and thence by road across the Caucasus mountains to Tiflis (Tbilisi) and by train to Batum (Batumi) on the eastern coast of the Black Sea. A leisurely four-day trip by steamer took them to Novorossijsk and eventually to Yalta in the Crimea, where they disembarked. From Yalta they went by road to Sevastapol by way of the battlefield of Balaclava, setting for the ill-fated charge of the Light Brigade.[31]

Wavell was back in Moscow by the end of May. The heat was not yet oppressive, but he complained to his mother that his few friends were out of Moscow so he had no one to go about with in his spare time, and that he was getting 'steadily worse' at Russian.[32] In June the Ertel family moved out of Moscow to stay on a small estate owned by Madame Ertel's brother-in-law at Yegorovka in the central Russian province of Tambov, forty miles from the nearest railway station. In the heat of the Russian summer,

Madame Ertel and Wavell came to literary blows. Wavell produced a bundle of papers set for the military interpretership exam and, not surprisingly, Madame Ertel had difficulty understanding all the technical terms. One morning she was correcting a translation of Wavell's from English into Russian: 'She scored out one sentence and rewrote it. I said I had no doubt my translation was bad Russian and hers was good, but that what she had written was not what the English meant.' Madame Ertel insisted that it was and Wavell maintained that he ought to know the meaning of his own language, whereupon Madame Ertel 'flung out of the room in a temper.'[33] She asked her daughter to back her up, but Natalya had to tell her mother that she was wrong, and Wavell's translation was correct.[34] Apologies were exchanged, but the atmosphere remained strained. International events could also be a source of friction. When in July Germany sent a gunboat to Agadir ostensibly to protect some 'Hamburg merchants' allegedly threatened by French interests in Morocco, Wavell insisted that Europe was being driven to the brink by Germany, and that the Russians would unite to defend their country. The Ertel family disagreed; Russia, they said, could not fight, and if the Government declared war, there would be a revolution.

In September Wavell secured another break from his rather claustrophobic life with the Ertels when he received permission to attend the manoeuvres of the Grenadier Corps, second in rank to the Guard Corps of the Tsarist Army, and he spent a week attached to the Fifth Kiev Regiment of the Corps near Moscow. With the exception of the Military Attaché's formal attendance at the manoeuvres held at St Petersburg, British officers had not previously been allowed to see Russian army training, 'So I was quite a novelty.' When he put on his kilt for a formal parade, he created 'a veritable sensation'. Wavell was impressed by the hardy physique of the soldiers, but he thought their officers' lack of education a noticeable defect, as was their reluctance to take responsibility. They were also very ignorant about the British Army, believing, for example, that British soldiers lived on a diet of chocolate creams. Wavell could only account for this misconception by supposing it to be based on reports of Queen Victoria sending chocolate to the soldiers in South Africa.[35]

After the all-male environment of his regiment and the somewhat staid atmosphere of family life in Dorset, Wavell's year in Russia was exposing him to a more 'social' life than he had previously experienced. According to Cuthbert Fuller, Wavell was 'fond' of a young Russian girl, Lydia Arbatskaya, with whom he used to go ice-hilling. This unusual sport involved tobogganing down a steep run onto an ice-rink, and the trick and excitement was to manoeuvre the toboggan around the semi-circular wall of the rink to return to the bottom of the run. As Fuller recalled, it was proposed that Lydia should go with them on their trip to the Volga, he and Churchill acting as chaperons, but her father forbade it.[36] In October 1911 Wavell met a young woman who introduced herself as Leonie Lemartine, in Russia on a three-month contract as an opera singer. In fact she was 'working in intelligence' under Sir Mansfield Cumming[37] and the name she gave Wavell – and by which he always called her – was her 'stage name'. She was really Gladys Redwood, aged 26 and recently widowed; she had left her two small children in England to undertake a special assignment which involved tracing a man who was believed to be 'a double agent'. Wavell probably knew nothing of this at the time, but for the rest of his stay the reticent army officer and the theatrical young lady had 'good fun' together in Moscow.[38] Wavell left Russia on Christmas Day, 1911. He may have felt somewhat uneasy in the Ertel family, but on the whole his memories were positive: 'I have always since liked the Russians better than any other foreigners I have met.'[39] In early January 1912, after a little extra coaching, Wavell sat his interpreter's exam, and his 'first class' result earned him the letter 'L' after his name in the Army List, as well as a monetary reward. Soon afterwards he and Nancy went off again to Switzerland to ski.

To date Wavell had notched up one year's experience in South Africa, five years in India, two years at Staff College, and nearly a year in Russia; in March 1912, still comparatively young for the job, he was appointed to the War Office as a GSO3 (grade three staff officer) with the rank of Acting Captain. In the huge complex of buildings close to the nerve centre of government in Whitehall his first assignment was to the Russian Section, to write a handbook on the Russian Army. For a short period he was then transferred to the Military Training Branch and the section in charge of the Officers' Training Corps. The summer of 1912 was enjoyable for his job was to visit school OTC contingents across the country. His open-top car and a careful choice of route meant he could visit schools and friends at the same time, and work became a series of house parties. Afterwards he was rather disappointed to be posted back to the Russian Section. Here he was under the Director of Military Operations and Intelligence, his former Commandant at the Staff College, Henry Wilson. Staff Officers who worked in 'I' were known as 'the newspaper snippers', from the popular belief that they spent an inordinate amount of time cutting up foreign newspapers for articles that might reveal some military secret. 'I seemed irrevocably committed to the career of a staff officer,' he later recollected.

'I never really cared for Intelligence work, though I think it may have helped me later on to have a knowledge of it.'

In later life, Wavell was inclined to be critical of his younger self. 'I wish I had spent my spare time (not that I had a very great deal) more profitably, in writing or some other hobby. I read a certain amount, especially of military history, but on no particular plan. In fact I think I rather wasted my time.' Yet by his own admission he hated to see a job of work badly done, and was always prepared to put in extra time in order to improve it. There is a slightly forlorn note in his assessment that 'I had found that I could hold my own and get along in any company I was put in, with both officers and men in my regiment. But I had few close friends, and I was diffident of my powers of leadership.'[40]

Wavell's home while he was at the War Office was a furnished flat at 53a Pall Mall, above Wilkinson's Sword and Razor shop, and his rent was £120 a year. Of his former Staff College friends, he lunched frequently with Everard Calthrop, who was also at the War Office. He, ever unconventional, introduced Wavell to a Chinese restaurant in Soho, one of the few to be found outside Limehouse. The French engineer and pioneer aviator, Louis Blériot, had crossed the Channel in his monoplane in July 1909, inspiring many civilians and soldiers to take up flying, and Wavell and Calthrop both enrolled for lessons. But when Calthrop told his family they objected and he withdrew. Wavell had no intention of telling *his* parents, but when he found he could not interest any of his other friends at the War Office to join him, he too gave them up. 'I wonder what my fate would have been if I had taken up flying then . . . I might have become a pioneer of the Royal Air Force, but should quite likely have killed myself, as I am not much of a mechanic and a bit careless.'[41]

Compared with regimental life, Wavell's current existence was a sedentary one, though he played hockey and cricket for the War Office. Weekend breaks might be spent visiting his parents at Cranborne, and he shot during the season and golfed on courses near London whenever possible. Longer breaks from London took the form of two return visits to Russia. In 1912, he spent three weeks attending manoeuvres north of the Caucasus mountains, attached to the Caucasian Corps, and in the summer of 1913 he was in Russia again, to attend the army's manoeuvres near Kiev. He saw nothing to alter the impressions of his first visit: the Russian soldier was a first-class fighter, but higher command was weak and equipment was inadequate. The Russians had few aircraft; Wavell received permission to visit the Army's main aviation centre outside Kiev. He was taken up in a plane that then crashed on landing – fortunately 'with no damage done, except bruises'. On his way home, Wavell was unexpectedly detained on the Polish frontier by Russian police; for the first and last time he found himself under arrest, locked in a cell. Before leaving England, he had been given the document customarily issued to officers bound to observe foreign manoeuvres, detailing information the War Office would like, if possible, to obtain; Wavell had tucked it away and forgotten about it. On his return from Kiev, his Moscow hotel room was searched by the secret police. Whatever they thought they had found, it was enough for Wavell's arrest at the frontier to be ordered. During the interrogation that followed Wavell remembered the questionnaire and managed to remove it from among his papers before he could be asked about it. The Russians, baffled, had to release him. Recalling the episode in later life, Wavell commented: 'It was lucky that I managed to get hold of it [the questionnaire] and prevent their finding it, or I might have had a lot of trouble.'[42]

Wavell's knowledge of Russian had led to him being asked to do some translations for the Historical Section of the War Cabinet, currently at work on a history of the 1905 Russo-Japanese War, and this had brought him into contact with Major Ernest Swinton; like Wavell a man of considerable literary talents, Swinton approved his speed and accuracy and commended his style.[43] Another of Wavell's assignments was the translation of a laudatory book on Tsar Nicholas II by Major-General Andrei Georgievich Elchaninov. Since it entailed a significant amount of work – the translation of 149 printed pages – Wavell asked for and was granted a fee of £15, and his authorship of the translation was recognized by the addition of his initials 'A.P.W.' under Elchaninov's name.[44] Subsequently, much to Wavell's surprise, additional thanks came in the form of a gold watch, engraved with the Tsar's monogram; perhaps it was also a veiled apology for his arrest.[45]

It was an age of visionaries and clairvoyants and some time in 1913 a young woman with the initials M.M. wrote an assessment of Wavell's character based on his handwriting; thirty years later Wavell still had the paper, but had forgotten the lady's name. If her analysis was indeed founded on his handwriting alone, it demonstrates extraordinary insight:

A.P. Wavell. Your handwriting shows a very well regulated mind and a sequence of ideas – you are intelligent and cultivated and have a command of language. You have excellent judgement and reasoning power. There is a desire to be liberal, but not extravagant; you like to do things well, if possible – you are fairly economical from necessity, rather than from choice. There are signs of literary taste and poetry. Artistic taste – without however the power of execution, is shown. There is also some imagination. You are logical and critical – you are energetic and a man of physical activity. Your writing shows neither sympathy nor affection, and you are not demonstrative. Your will is fairly strong, but you are not very firm or frank, and there is some indecision. Poetic feeling is strongly marked. This may mean you are fond of poetry. Versatility of mind, quickness, independence, lucidity of mind are all indicated. You are inclined to be selfish and impatient and have a fairly quick temper. Your handwriting shows a love of travel. You should have good health. You are truthful, but cautious and reserved – orderly. Jealousy is not indicated. Some of your letters show pride, ambition and a desire to win. Some again show a want of calmness and self-restraint.[46]

Wavell was now thirty years old, and on 20 March had finally been promoted to the rank of captain. As he later admitted, he had no settled plan for his life, but took things as they came. Everything he had done to date had been mainly at the instigation of his father, who had also more than once indicated that it was time for him to marry. On occasion the General had gone so far as to introduce him to young women whom he considered eligible. But as Wavell subsequently wrote, whereas he might have deferred to his father in matters regarding his career, he had no intention of marrying to please him, or even of consulting him.[47] As it happened, in the spring of 1913 Wavell was reportedly 'in love', and had even made a proposal of marriage to a 'sweetly pretty' girl. But she was much younger than he, and had turned him down.[48] Later in the year he expressed a 'fondness' for Caroline, the youngest of three daughters of Canon Bernard, a neighbour at Wimborne. 'She's such a nice dainty little person and clever, but – I wonder if she ever lets herself go,' he mused in a letter to Nancy, relaying the information that their mother had also tried to 'pump' him to find out whether or not Nancy had 'any man in tow': 'So like Mother,' he commented, 'and she wasn't even really interested or anxious about it, merely curious I think. No wonder we're secretive and reserved, you and I.'[49] Wavell was also still in touch with 'Leonie', who referred to him affectionately as 'old sobersides' because he was so quiet. The opera singer–spy introduced him to a side of London he had not previously experienced. 'On one occasion, they went to a nightclub,' recalled Leonie's daughter, Peggy. 'My mother described how he was sitting there staring into space. When she asked him if he was enjoying himself, he replied: "Oh, yes, it is fascinating. I have never seen anything like this before." ' Their friendship continued, but in December 1913 Leonie married her second husband, Esmond Robinson, an unsuccessful businessman and 'compulsive gambler'.[50]

Then Wavell's cousin Veronica (known as Vere) Bellairs – Arthur and Raymond's sister – took 'a very attractive' girl to the polo and asked him to accompany them.[51] Eugénie Quirk, known as Queenie,[52] was the daughter of Colonel John Owen Quirk, CB, DSO, who had commanded the 41st (the Welch) Regiment, in which Vere's father and brother Arthur, had served. Queenie's mother, also Eugénie, was the daughter of Octavius O'Brien of the Protestant Unionist branch of the family, and claimed descent from Brian Boru, King of Ireland in the eleventh century. As Queenie described her parents: 'My mother was beautiful and clever. She loved music and parties and old furniture. My father was an unselfish darling, a fine fighting soldier.'[53] Miss Quirk had already shown herself to be an intrepid traveller, visiting Australia in 1911, when she stayed with the Governor-General, Lord Denman, whose wife was related by marriage to Queenie's godmother Augusta, Lady Edward Spencer Churchill.[54] Recalling their first meeting, Wavell described his future wife as 'slim and attractive in a large hat', and also remembered that she kept them waiting for a quarter to half an hour – 'not unusual with her', as he afterwards discovered.[55] After this initial meeting, they continued to see each other regularly.

In the War Office, Wavell was well placed to follow events as they unfolded, not just in Europe but in Ireland too, at the time when Home Rule was being hotly debated in Parliament. In early March Asquith as Prime Minister had moved the second reading of the Home Rule Bill in the House of Commons. The Ulster Unionists were vociferously opposed to Home Rule, demanding that six counties remain part of the United Kingdom; under the terms of the bill the six Ulster counties were excluded from its provisions for six years; the Unionists wanted their exclusion to be permanent. The Secretary of State for War, Colonel J.E.B. Seely, and the First Lord of the Admiralty, Winston Churchill, took a particularly stern view of Ulster resistance, and intimated that force would be used if necessary. On 18 March General Sir Arthur Paget, the General Officer Commanding in Ireland, arrived in London for talks with Seely and the Chief of the Imperial General Staff (CIGS), General Sir John French.[56] In his absence, orders were given at the Curragh, the main British military cantonment in Ireland, that ammunition be distributed to every man in the barracks. Returning to Dublin, Paget signalled to Seely that administrative arrangements for the movement of troops to Ulster were in progress; he then called the generals and brigade commanders of the troops in Ireland together to inform them that he had been given orders to move into Ulster. Many officers in the regular Army were Ulstermen by birth or affiliation, and the difficulty of their position was recognized: officers who were domiciled in Ulster would not be required to take part in operations; any commanding officer who gave similar indulgence to those not domiciled in Ulster would be court-martialled, and any officer who refused to take part would be dismissed from the Army without pension rights. Brigadier Hubert Gough, who commanded the 3rd Cavalry Brigade, immediately handed in his resignation; when he indicated to the officers the choice they had to make, they resigned en masse.[57]

Mindful of his father's military career and his service in Ireland, Wavell took pains to describe to him in detail – and in the strictest confidence – the situation as it evolved. It appeared likely to affect him personally, as Henry Wilson, his superior at the War Office, was an Ulsterman, and made no secret of his objections to the use of the Army against his countrymen. 'It seems that if the Government will not give a pledge that the Army is not to be used against Ulster, Wilson himself and probably a good many others will resign. He certainly will if the Government take any steps to punish Gough and the others. In fact he called us in to ask us, if any of us were thinking of resigning in support of Gough.' As Wavell told his father, discipline was being shaken and the Army was being dragged into politics. 'The idea of the officers of the Army going on strike, which I think is what it really amounts to, over this business, is to my mind absolutely disastrous.'[58] When Wavell arrived at the War Office on Monday 23 March, he heard that a number of people already had their resignations in their pockets. Confronted with the possibility of a mass resignation by senior officers unless Gough and the officers of the 3rd Cavalry Brigade were reinstated, the Government gave way. However, Wavell did not approve, confiding to his father his feeling that the 'victory' of the Army over the politicians would have disastrous consequences: 'How are you to use your Army to keep law and order against strikers when once the officers have successfully resisted an attempt to use them to enforce a law which they do not approve?' In Wavell's opinion, the mistake lay in the Government's attempt to 'hold a pistol' to the officers' heads in attempting to coerce them by threatening dismissal and loss of livelihood. 'It is inconceivable to me how an English Government could have done such a thing.'[59]

In the end, despite the tremendous furore in Parliament and in the press, the implications of the 'Curragh mutiny' were not as disastrous for the reputation of the Army as Wavell had feared. Recent events had however played a significant part in forming his opinions about the proper relationship between soldiers and politicians. He was especially critical of Seely – who resigned, along with the CIGS, Sir John French – and of Winston Churchill, who he felt had been instrumental in pushing the Government to adopt such an aggressive stance.[60] Asquith's defence of his Government, by refusing to admit that there was ever any intention of using troops against Ulster and insisting that their presence was merely required to keep law and order, did not impress: in Wavell's opinion, the Government was 'lying hard to try and hush the matter up and save themselves'. There was, as he wrote in another letter to his father, no doubt that the Government had intended to crush Ulster: a war staff was being mobilized in Dublin, troops were being moved from Aldershot, and the Navy was also on alert. 'Can you conceive a Government doing such a thing before the Home Rule Bill was even law?'

Wavell understood the motivation behind Gough's resignation, but at the same time believed that the Army should have obeyed orders – not because he wanted them to fight their countrymen but in the hope that when people realized they were on the verge of civil war, 'there would have been such an outcry to insist that the matter should be settled at once without bloodshed, that the Government would not have dared to carry out their scheme and would have been compelled to compromise the Ulster question at once.' As far as Wavell's position on the General Staff was concerned, the Government's climb-down had at least spared him a difficult decision. The whole of the General Staff of the War Office was threatening to resign if the Government persisted in its action against Ulster: 'Holding the views I do, I should have thought it wrong to resign, but I should have been in a very small minority, I think, and it would have been a question whether it would have been right to resign against my convictions for the sake of maintaining a show of unanimity among the General Staff. It would have been a pretty hard alternative to face.'[61]

During the summer of 1914, as the problem of Ireland preoccupied many in Britain, a situation more alarming still for Wavell and his contemporaries was developing in Europe. Over several decades a series of treaties of mutual assistance had in theory 'balanced' power on the Continent. As far back as 1882, Germany, Austria-Hungary and Italy – resentful of France's seizure of Tunis on the coast of North Africa – had joined in a 'Triple Alliance', renewed every five years. As the nineteenth century drew to a close, Marshal Alfred von Schlieffen, Chief of the German General Staff since 1891, was formulating a strategy based on the presumption that in any future conflict Germany's enemy would not be Russia, as earlier planners had believed, but France, where the loss of Alsace-Lorraine to Germany in the 1870–1 Franco-Prussian war remained a contentious issue.[62] France having fortified her frontier, von Schlieffen's plan was to disregard Belgian neutrality – guaranteed by France, Britain and Prussia since 1839 – and first move into Belgium.[63] In 1904 the Anglo-French Entente

Cordiale was ratified as a cross-Channel counterweight to the combined
power of the Triple Alliance; three years later Britain and France entered
into the Triple Entente with Russia. The plan to send a British
Expeditionary Force into Europe if and when Britain's allies were threatened dated from Haldane's reforms of 1906; five years later, a firm commitment was made that, if Germany were to turn belligerent, Britain
would sanction the despatch of a force of 160,000 men to take its place
beside her French allies in the projected line of battle.[64] In view of Britain's
naval supremacy, so jealously guarded, the Government's objective was to
defeat Germany by creating an economic blockade. But before this 'economic warfare' could be effective, the BEF was regarded as necessary to
bolster French resistance against Germany on land.

The catalyst for the outbreak of hostilities occurred on Sunday 28 June
1914. Archduke Franz Ferdinand, nephew and heir to Franz Josef,
Emperor of Austria, and Inspector General of the Army, was in Bosnia,
where the Habsburg army's summer manoeuvres were taking place. In the
opinion of Serbian nationalists, Bosnia – a former province of the Ottoman
Empire, occupied by Austria in 1878 and annexed in 1908 – was still sub-
jugated by 'foreign oppressors'. Ignoring warnings that his presence – on
the anniversary of Serbia's defeat by the Turks at the Battle of Kosovo in
1389 – was ill-advised and might provide the nationalists with a target, the
Archduke and his wife Sophie, Duchess of Hohenberg, processed through
Sarajevo. There was indeed a plan to assassinate the Archduke: the first
attack failed, wounding an officer in the next carriage, but later, as the
Archduke and his wife were on their way to visit the wounded officer in
hospital, another assassin – Gavrilo Princip – succeeded in drawing his
revolver. The Duchess took the first bullet; a second hit the Archduke. The
Austrian Government might have exacted a swift, domestic retribution but
hesitated to move against the Serbs – and risk antagonizing Russia – without an assurance of German support.

Diplomatic exchanges took place over the next few weeks, as emissar-
ies from the two countries assessed the potential repercussions of widen-
ing the conflict. Russia announced that she would defend the Serbs – her
Slavic brothers – and vacillated between partial and general mobilization.
On 28 July – a month after the assassination – Austria declared war on
Serbia; when the Austro-Hungarian Army mobilized, Germany followed
suit. On 1 August, after all attempts to resolve the matter had failed, Russia
and Germany declared war on each other. France then came out in support of Russia. When German troops swept across the Belgian frontier, in
accordance with von Schlieffen's plan, the British Government had no

alternative but to abide by its commitment to send troops to the Continent. The formal declaration of war on Germany came on 4 August. Italy remained neutral, but almost by default the Central Powers recruited a new ally, Turkey, whose overtures to the Entente Powers had been rejected. Turkey did not become openly belligerent until the end of October, but the presence in the Dardanelles of the German battleships *Goeben* and *Breslau* in early August gave the Entente powers an indication of her new-found allegiance.

When war was declared, King George V, first cousin of both Kaiser Wilhelm of Germany and Tsar Nicholas II of Russia, spoke of a 'terrible catastrophe', but few in Britain were of the same opinion. A sense of jubilation prevailed among the crowds who gathered outside Buckingham Palace, singing and dancing before going home after midnight on 4/5 August. Only Kitchener, immediately appointed Secretary of State for War, appeared to realize that those who rejoiced would not in sober truth be 'home by Christmas': his appeals were for a hundred thousand men to enlist for three years, or however long the war lasted. Throughout August men flocked enthusiastically to the recruiting offices. Wavell had been enjoying a period of leave in Dublin, but as soon as the Army began to mobilize he was summoned back to the War Office. Like so many others, his youth had been spent in the evening glow of a golden age; for them, life as they had known it would never again be the same.

II
WAVELL'S ASCENT

4

War in 1914

I shut my eyes and turned them on my heart.
As a man calls for wine before he fights,
I asked one draught of earlier, happier sights,
Ere fitly I could hope to play my part.

Robert Browning[1]

When one looks back, the bitter disappointment of those left behind
at the outset of war appears ridiculous.   R.J. Collins[2]

MUCH TO WAVELL'S disappointment, he was not chosen as a member
of the British Expeditionary Force. Although his distress may now
seem 'ridiculous', his feelings mirrored those of many who were left
behind. Wavell was a regular soldier and, like his fellow officers in The
Black Watch who were literally sharpening their swords in preparation for
their departure, he wanted to be where the action was from the start.[3]
None of those who set off to fight with such naïve bravado had any idea
that the war would drag on for four years, that so many would not return,
that Britain's eventual victory would be but the portent of future conflict.
Wavell was feeling 'too utterly depressed', for it seemed to him it would
never be possible to make up for having missed the beginning.[4]

Confusion was the lot of those who remained behind at the War Office.
Wilson and nearly half his officers had joined the BEF. Wavell had no 'immediate master', and although he was still only a GSO3 officer, there were occasions when he had to 'act as if I was a GSO1 or even higher up'.[5] Soon after
the outbreak of war a rumour spread that large numbers of Russian troops,
recognizable by the snow on their boots, had landed in the north of Scotland
and been sent straight to France. Since Wavell's friends and relations knew
he was back working in the Russian Section, he found himself overwhelmed
with praise for the 'skill and secrecy' with which the operation had been
arranged. His disclaimers were met with a knowing look, as if to say, 'Of

course you have to pretend to know nothing, but you don't have to keep it a secret from us.' For the rest of his life Wavell considered this to be one of those instances which demonstrate 'the capacity of the human race to deceive itself, and of the unreliability of human evidence.'[6]

Meanwhile, following Britain's declaration of war, the BEF had begun to mobilize under the command of the former Chief of the Imperial General Staff, now Field Marshal Sir John French. On 9 August they began a steady embarkation, their destination the French ports of Boulogne, Le Havre and Rouen.[7] The four infantry divisions and one cavalry division, with thousands of horses, were divided into Corps I and II; the Field Marshal was not under the executive command of the French Commander-in-Chief, General Joseph Joffre, but it was agreed that the British would operate according to the French 'Plan 17'. Less precise than von Schlieffen's plan, this envisaged an offensive against the Germans either in Lorraine or into the Ardennes; Belgian neutrality precluded any attack on Germany in the north. In hindsight Wavell was critical of the French plan, which he believed was based on 'faulty intelligence and a faulty conception of war'; it was, he said, remarkable that the French recovered so well from its consequences.[8] As was soon all too clear, the French had miscalculated the extent to which the German forces would extend to the west; as a result, the left flank of the BEF was immediately threatened by the Germans who, marching brazenly through Belgium, had forced the Belgians to withdraw from Liège and Namur into the fortress of Antwerp. On 23 August the Germans engaged the BEF at Mons, a small Belgian town near the French border south-west of Brussels. The superiority of German numbers prompted Sir John French, rather than risk total annihilation of his men, to order British forces to retreat. In command of II Corps, General Sir Horace Smith-Dorrien attempted to make a stand at Le Cateau, but after severe casualties he too was obliged to retreat.[9]

Despite these setbacks, it did not occur to Wavell that the Allies might be in danger of losing the war. And in early September the French and British struck back. In what became known as the first Battle of the Marne they halted the German advance, forcing them to withdraw beyond the River Aisne. The arrows on the map at the War Office, which Wavell looked at daily, began to creep forwards – eastwards – instead of backwards. All this time he was 'importuning' his friends to see what they could do to get him across the Channel. As he told Nancy, they now had to wear uniform at the War Office, which gave him the opportunity to break in his new boots, 'but I hate dressing like a soldier when I'm doing the work of a clerk'. In anticipation of his departure at some stage his family had sent him various items which might be useful in the field, as well as some 'first rate' slippers, for which he expressed his thanks; he now, he said, had everything he needed 'except orders to go'.[10] Finally, even as Wavell was writing despondently to Nancy, declaring that he wished he'd never gone near the Staff College or Russia, which he felt had hindered his selection as a member of the BEF, the order came for him to go to France.[11]

Wavell was still seeing Queenie regularly, and on the night of 18 September, after working late at the War Office, he proposed. 'I had made up my mind some time before that she was the person I should like to marry,' he later recalled. 'But my courtship was peculiar and should have warned her of my egoism, since it consisted mainly of grumbling at having been left out of the Expeditionary Force, and pessimistic forecasts that the war would be over before I got a chance to take part in it. She was very sympathetic, although she probably wanted to slap me.' Queenie accepted, warning her future husband that she was lazy and unpunctual. 'I knew the latter already. I don't think I warned her of any of my failings; I wanted to marry the girl.'[12] But Queenie was not the only woman he was thinking about. Earlier in the day he had gone to say goodbye to Leonie. 'He asked me if I would have married him, if I hadn't married Esmond – I said of course I would – he then told me that he thought he ought to get married and was going to propose to Queenie Quirk.' Leonie, who was still fond of Wavell, recalled that he wrote to her a few days later to tell her Queenie had accepted him, and listing her good qualities: 'rides well to hounds', et cetera. 'I believe I wrote and asked him if he was buying a wife or a horse – thank goodness he had a sense of humour.'[13] Ten days later, Wavell was in France. He left in a hurry, for which he apologized to Nancy, thanking her and Molly for packing up his rooms: 'It must have been a very grubby job.' At the same time he was anxious to share his excitement over his engagement. 'Isn't she a perfect darling?' he asked his elder sister. 'I think I am very lucky.'[14]

Wavell's destination was the General Headquarters of the British Army in the wooded green valley of Aisne, where the BEF had taken up its position after the Allied victory at the Marne. With the rank of acting major and graded as a GSO2, he was put in command of the Intelligence Corps, a group of about forty men recruited on the basis of their knowledge of languages or because they could 'ride a horse or a motorcycle'. Remembering that he had kept his files from his Staff College days, one of his first requests to Nancy was to send his notes on reconnaissance, which he felt might be of some use. To demonstrate his new – albeit temporary – rank, he also asked her to see if she could find a pair of their father's old major's metal crowns for the epaulettes of his coat, remarking ruefully that he could well be demoted before he had time to wear them.[15]

Having finally got himself to France, Wavell was dismayed by how little he had to do. By the end of September, fighting in the Aisne had 'trenched itself into immobility'.[16] In an attempt to gain the advantage both German and Allied forces began to race northwards to the sea, trying to outflank each other, and thereby created a 'Western Front' that ran from the North Sea to the mountains of neutral Switzerland. To establish a position to the left of the French near the coast and reduce their lines of communication (as well as filling the gap between the French and the retreating Belgians, who had been unable to withstand the German attack on Antwerp), the BEF made its way northwards by train or road from Aisne to Flanders. By the time they had taken up their respective positions, the gap in the line of trenches through which a decisive move could be made had narrowed to this dreary stretch of land in Belgium. In the distance lay the city of Ypres. As Wavell recollected: 'Then began the long, desperate struggle of the Germans to break the British line at Ypres and to gain the Channel ports.'[17] At GHQ Wavell continued to chafe at his inactivity, for which he tried to compensate by making his own reconnaissances, on occasion by air. His friend Amyas Borton was with the Royal Flying Corps, and Wavell sometimes accompanied him, armed with a revolver in case they met a 'Boche': 'We did on one flight, and Amyas shouted to me to be ready with my revolver and went in pursuit of the enemy. The observer's seat in the back of the plane was wretchedly cold and my fingers were frozen out of all feeling.' Wavell was heartily relieved when they failed to catch the German plane. 'I was very doubtful whether I could shoot off my revolver when I wanted to; also I had a suspicion that the Boche would probably be armed with a more effective weapon.'[18]

While Wavell was fretting over his own inactivity, the first offensive at Ypres began; it lasted nearly a month and, by Wavell's account, although 'the Regular forces of Great Britain [were] almost annihilated . . . they had saved Europe from German domination'.[19] Towards the end of the battle, in mid November, Wavell was at last given an appointment in the front line as a Brigade-Major in the 9th Infantry Brigade, 3rd Division, headquartered near Hooge on the Menin road in the Ypres salient. The Brigade Commander, Brigadier-General Douglas Smith, was also a newcomer to the scene, his predecessor having recently been wounded; Wavell was therefore able to demonstrate his usefulness. As the brigade commander's chief of staff he relieved him of routine staff work in preparing orders, and also acted as an important link with the battalion commanders. Normally the brigade would have numbered approximately 5,000 men but the 9th – comprising men from the 1st Northumberland Fusiliers, the 4th Royal Fusiliers, 1st Lincolnshire Regiment and 1st Royal Scots Fusiliers – had already suffered heavy casualties, which included most of the senior officers.

Archibald Wavell's first taste of combat on the Western Front – literally on the day of his arrival with the 9th Brigade – involved regaining some stables which German soldiers had occupied in part of the line held by the Northumberland Fusiliers. 'It was decided to muffle the wheels of an 18-pounder, to manhandle it up the road in the dark to within 100 yards or so of the stables, rapidly put a dozen rounds into the stables, and then rush them with 30 or 40 men, the only reserve battalion we could muster.' As Wavell proudly reported, the stables were recaptured without loss – on the British side: the artillery fire at close range proved deadly for the Germans.[20] The 9th Brigade were soon due to be relieved by a French contingent, for a much-needed period of rest behind the lines. They looked forward to hot food, washing their lice-infested clothes, playing football, and generally enjoying some free time. But they 'were critical days in November,' recalled Kenneth Buchanan, Wavell's prep school contemporary, who had also recently joined the 9th Brigade as Staff Captain. 'We had many anxious incidents, but Wavell was always calm and imperturbable; nothing would ever rattle him, and he inspired confidence. He was exceptionally tough and never spared himself. He set himself to know every part of his front and daily or nightly tramped many miles.'[21] As Buchanan also observed, Wavell felt it important to visit the trenches. What he saw was depressing: 'The trenches were a single line of very poor construction, badly sited, undrained with very little wire to protect them. In the rain they became knee-deep in mud and I found the whole garrison of a trench sitting on the parapet; preferring the risk of enemy bullets to the mud in the trench.' In an effort to improve the conditions, Wavell initiated a 'factory' to make duck-boards and mud scoops. 'We were the first brigade to do this.'[22]

The offensive in which Wavell and his 9th Brigade played their part lasted until 22 November; thereafter the approach of winter with its snow and sleet, as well as mutual exhaustion, led to something of a lull in the fighting. Throughout the winter of 1914 the 9th Brigade was constantly on the move, holding different sectors in the Ypres Salient. Wavell's experience in the front line made him critical of the strategy of his superiors, which was to hold on to every yard of ground and every trench, 'however worthless' and full of water, in preference to taking note of and obtaining valuable ground – high ground, or ground concealed from the enemy – which might prove more useful. An example of the High Command's 'utter folly' was the first of the trench-warfare attacks, ordered in mid December. 'Not the way to win battles; but battles in which no one believes should not be fought.' The 9th Brigade's role, prior to the main attack, was to capture 'The Petit Bois' – the strongest point in the German line, which was well entrenched and heavily wired. When Wavell ordered the 1st Lincolnshire Regiment, the battalion closest to it, to attack the Petit Bois he felt 'rather like a murderer . . . they took it very well and said they would have a try, but had no hope of success.' Towards midnight, half frozen, they emerged from their trenches and plodded towards the German line; not surprisingly, they were met with a volley of fire. Unable to cut through the wire, they sustained 40 casualties out of fewer than 120 men. A German soldier, as was later related to Wavell, rather than kill them all, stood up, threw a clod of earth at them, and shouted in English: 'Go home, you damned fools.'[23]

As 1914 drew to a close most of the soldiers in the front line, despite the demands made on them and the conditions in which they were living, accepted their circumstances, supremely confident in ultimate victory. Wavell was among those officers fortunate enough to be able to take a week's leave at Christmas, and he arrived in England on Christmas morning. As he was to discover, the Christmas holidays were being celebrated as usual, 'for the sake of the children'. Shopkeepers had put up signs advertising 'Business As Usual During Alterations To the Map of Europe'. Christmas trees were on sale and the theatres of London were packed. Barrel organs ground out variations of 'It's a long way to Tipperary', and a discordant version of 'La Marseillaise'. But the weather was dreadful. For days southern England was enveloped in pea-soup fog. Gales and blizzards swept away church steeples, billboards and trees. Wavell went immediately to Windsor to spend Christmas day with Queenie, who was staying with her godmother, Lady Edward Spencer Churchill. Three days were spent at Cranborne. Nancy had set up a hospital for the war wounded and he took time to visit it, later commenting that she was doing 'splendid' work.[24] His last three days were spent with Queenie again, at her parents' flat in Knightsbridge. They decided that they would get married on his next leave.

Back in Flanders in the New Year Wavell found himself 'desperately busy', with less time for all his customary letters, often written in pencil on scraps of paper. 'We've been out of the trenches for 3 days and only go back again tomorrow,' he told Nancy on 7 January. 'We do 4 days in and 4 days out now. We used to do 3 in and 6 out.'[25] Wavell's thoughts were with his future bride, whom he 'hated' leaving, and he was also brooding over the objections his father 'for some reason' had raised to his marrying before the end of the war.[26] Having reviewed his son's financial position, General Wavell had decided not to increase his annual allowance of £200 if he went ahead with his plans. The acrimonious correspondence about money continued over several weeks. Clearly it was a typical father–son relationship. Writing to Nancy, Wavell conceded that he was probably to blame because he was liable to say what he thought – 'an expensive luxury and tactless'. On the other hand, at times he found the attitude of his father 'maddening'.[27]

Whenever it was possible Wavell continued to reconnoitre the various sectors under his command. When visiting the 4th Royal Fusiliers, who were holding the sector of trenches opposite Petit Bois, he was privy to an episode that culminated in mayhem at Brigade HQ. Robert Pipon, a contemporary from Summer Fields and Winchester serving with the 4th, had returned from his leave with a supply of 'fire' balloons.[28] As Wavell recalled, 'in the raw winter night Pipon amused himself by sending them up to draw fire from the German trenches' and the 'Boches' seemed to enjoy it too. Then one balloon, after soaring over the German lines, either rose into an upper current of air or was caught by a change of wind direction and 'sailed back over the British lines, high up and going fast'. Wavell returned to his Brigade HQ to be kept awake for the rest of the night 'by frantic telegrams reporting a Zeppelin over our part of the line'. Since reports to do with Zeppelins were always given priority, he had to take serious note of them. 'It was only next morning, when I examined them, that I realized that the Zeppelin was undoubtedly Pipon's fire balloon.'[29]

Such distractions as this apart, for the Brigade most of the days of early 1915 were either dull, spent sitting in their rest station behind the front line, or dangerous and uncomfortable, in the trenches. 'We go back into trenches again tonight for ten or twelve days, I suppose,' he wrote to Nancy at the end of March. 'Not much rest these days, and it's a fairly great strain. Two of the brigade staff have collapsed and departed sick.' After five months of it Wavell was himself feeling weary, but remained 'fit'. 'We've hardly got a company officer in this brigade who has been through the whole winter with us, they get hit or go sick sooner or later.' As well as various friends, his cousin Jack Longfield, who had joined the Norfolks, was in the front line. In March the two cousins met. 'I hope he gets some other job soon. He's done long enough in the trenches and is lucky to have lasted so long,' Wavell commented.[30]

After Christmas Wavell spent more than three months in Europe without leave; on 19 April, with the situation 'very quiet at present', he was able to return home.[31] He had been writing daily to Queenie and the date for their wedding had been fixed. General Wavell still obstinately refused to increase the allowance his son had been receiving for fourteen years. 'I don't know why my father was so sticky,' Wavell later said. 'He was a generous man as a rule.'[32] This disagreement notwithstanding, on Thursday 22 April Archibald Percival Wavell and Eugénie Marie Quirk were married at Holy Trinity Church, Sloane Street in Knightsbridge. The reverential atmosphere of this red-brick church designed in 'Gothic spirit' was far removed from the death and deprivation with which Wavell was becoming so familiar. Queenie had no sisters to act as bridesmaids, but her godmother Lady Edward was present as one of the witnesses. Even as the bride and groom emerged into the sunlight, they saw the news displayed on the billboards: 'Ypres. Big Battle. Huns Use Gas.'[33]

The Germans had used gas on the Eastern Front against the Russians in early January, but it was not lethal. By April they had discovered that chlorine could prove fatal when released from pressurized cylinders in favourable wind conditions. As Wavell and Queenie were preparing for their wedding, across the Channel the Germans, having subjected the Allied positions to a heavy bombardment, released 6,000 cylinders containing 160 tons of gas over the Western Front. On a light east–west breeze the gas floated in a greyish-green cloud towards the Allied trenches. The effect was instantaneous: thousands of men, clutching their throats, coughing and turning blue in the face, ran from their positions, leaving a gap 8,000 yards wide in the Ypres defences. Yet the Germans did not have sufficient reserve infantry to push forward into the breach, and the Allies succeeded in holding the line. The gas attack marked the start of the second offensive at Ypres, and when Wavell first saw the news he thought he would have to cut short his honeymoon and return to the front. But the 9th Brigade was just outside the immediate area of the attack, and he was not ordered back. After a reception at Lady Edward's town house, 28 Grosvenor Street, off Park Lane, Wavell and his bride spent three days at her house in Windsor and four days at Cranborne; their last three days together were spent at Jules's Hotel in Jermyn Street, near Piccadilly Circus.

There is no doubt that Wavell loved Queenie as deeply as his reserved character permitted him to love anyone. He was not by nature a demonstrative man, and had grown up in a Victorian environment where emotions were not shown. By his own admission, he was also not only 'self-centred', but inclined to be secretive, and throughout his life he maintained friendships with other women. The day after his marriage he wrote to assure his Moscow friend Leonie Lemartine that although he was now a married man there would always be 'a very warm corner in his heart' for her. He also took Queenie to meet her. After he had returned to Flanders Queenie shrewdly wrote to Leonie – or Gladys, as she called her – mentioning that she knew from Archie 'of his great affection' for her, and that she did not expect him to give up his old friendships.[34] Queenie's forbearance served her well: she and Wavell remained happily married for 35 years.

By early May 1915 Wavell was back in the trenches. The second Battle of Ypres was still raging. 'There's been desperate fighting to the north of us all day,' he wrote home. Fortunately the 9th Brigade was positioned to the south of Ypres, so though the bombardment continued, all was relatively quiet with only the 'ordinary casual shelling'. Wavell had just celebrated his thirty-second birthday, and as usual Nancy had wanted to know what he would like as a present; he suggested a case for bank-notes: 'They make them for 5 franc notes and I always have a bundle of them on me I don't know what to do with. I'd love one if you gave it me and it would be most useful.'[35] The 9th Brigade escaped further gas attacks but continued to move from one sector of the salient to another to relieve those brigades which had been affected.[36] 'Although', as he later recollected, 'the smell of chlorine came to Brigade HQ, it was never sufficiently strong to compel us to use our very primitive gas-masks – flannel helmets with a talc eyepiece – soaked in some chemical.'[37]

Ever since Wavell's arrival at the front he had been shuttling backwards and forwards in and out of what was regarded as 'the fire zone'. He put on as brave a face as possible when writing to his family. It was 'an unpleasant part of the world', but what he had to do was 'all in a day's work'; 'with luck' they would get into 'these Huns and kill some of them'. With their superior infantry the British could, he said, walk over the German infantry any day, if only they had enough guns and ammunition and 'could stick out the gas'.[38] Light relief was a rarity. On one occasion the 9th were sent a basket of two carrier pigeons, to be tried out for sending messages from the trenches when communications were cut, as frequently happened. Brigade HQ duly passed them on to one of the battalions with instructions to send a message back, to see how long it might take. The first bird reached its destination bearing the signal 'This pigeon is sent off at 12.00 hours. Unless we receive acknowledgement of this message before 12.30 we propose to have the other one for lunch as they can't be any good.' As Wavell recalled, HQ received the message in time, and the second pigeon was saved.[39]

On 16 June 1915 the 9th Brigade took part in an operation in the Bellewarde area of the salient. 'It was one of those minor attacks on a narrow front that were so often ordered at this period in the war in order to "support" attacks many miles away. They were supposed to attract enemy reserves, I imagine. They never had the slightest effect on the main attack; and being on a narrow front nearly always failed with heavy loss.' According to Wavell, this particular attack was made in about 'the worst possible place', the extreme tip of the Ypres Salient, which was exposed to observation and artillery fire not just from the front and both flanks but from the rear as well, 'so pronounced was the salient'.[40] The objective was to capture three lines of enemy trenches near Bellewarde Lake, close to Hooge. Despite the poor location, Wavell believed that the plan – which involved leap-frogging from trench to trench – was good.[41] In the early afternoon, when there appeared to be a lull, he left the dugout for some fresh air and to try to see what was happening. Suddenly the Germans started a heavy barrage. Wavell was hit on the left side of his head. It was not clear whether he had been hit by a bullet from a rifle or a machine gun, or a piece of shrapnel from a high-explosive artillery or mortar shell, but his injury could well have been fatal. 'It went through my left eye but just missed everything vital. I was bandaged up and sat in the dugout for a bit; but as my right eye also began to close and I could be of no further use, I accepted the brigadier's suggestion that one of the orderlies should take me back to the dressing station near Ypres.'[42] With both eyes nearly closed Wavell was 'practically blind'. The only way he could see anything was to prop open his right eye, painfully, with one or both hands. The shelling continued, and at one time as they were walking across the fields he and the orderly were blown into a ditch and covered with earth. At the dressing station they found an ambulance on the point of leaving for the casualty clearing station the other side of Ypres. Instead of waiting to have his eye dressed, Wavell climbed into the ambulance.

At the casualty station Wavell was given a tetanus injection and then morphine.[43] He woke up in the Rawalpindi General Hospital near Boulogne. What remained of his left eye was immediately removed. Queenie was informed of his injury by telegram; initially the doctors thought he was more seriously wounded than proved to be the case – the telegram intimated that his sight in both eyes might be permanently damaged – so she was given special permission to travel to France to be with her husband. 'Q came over at once, bless her, and held my hand.'[44] Fortunately only the left eye was affected, and at the end of June they went home together for Wavell's convalescence.

This was a 'wonderful' and unexpected interlude in the war Wavell had been so desperate not to miss. Professionally, however, it was unquestionably a setback: he lost his appointment as Brigade-Major and the pay that went with it; but he was awarded the Military Cross for gallantry and good service with the 9th Infantry Brigade at Ypres, and at the end of July received it personally from King George V at Windsor Castle. Pride in his MC was initially tinged with disappointment, since he knew he had been recommended 'very strongly' for the DSO.[45] Yet at least, as he must have kept reminding himself, he had survived and retained the sight of one eye. On 30 September, while Wavell and Queenie were in Dornoch, his cousin Jack – the boy in whose company he had spent so much of his youth – was killed by a sniper during 'enemy action'. He was just 28.

In October a medical board passed Wavell fit to return to active service; from that time onwards a little leather box containing everything he needed for the care of his eye accompanied him everywhere. His next appointment was as a GSO2 to the 64th Highland Division at Perth. Realizing that the division was unlikely to go overseas, he wrote to his friends in France asking them to find him a job. In November 1915 he was ordered back to GHQ, and bade Queenie, now expecting their first child, another fond farewell. GHQ was about to shift from St Omer to Montreuil and Wavell was assigned to work in the 'operations' branch of the General Staff, responsible for organizing the training of new recruits. His disappointment at not being back in the front line was tempered by the knowledge that at least he was working under an exceptional officer. Brigadier John Burnett-Stuart had 'probably the best and quickest brain in the Army of his rank' and became Wavell's 'guide and friend' at once.[46] A re-shuffle had taken place in the High Command: Sir John French had been recalled to Britain and replaced by General Sir Douglas Haig, I Corps Commander. In the weeks and months that followed the names of yet more of Wavell's friends were added to the 'roll of honour' printed daily in *The Times*. Shortly before Christmas Everard Calthrop, still in Wavell's opinion a man with the most 'charming character and manners', was killed.[47] In January 1916 came the death of another cousin – Arthur, in whose footsteps Wavell had followed at Winchester and Sandhurst. He was killed not in the trenches of Belgium or France but in a little-known skirmish in East Africa.[48]

By the spring of 1916 the British Army held a continuous line from the east of Ypres to the River Somme. The weather remained 'vile', which Wavell hoped would be bad for the latest 'Boche' offensive at Verdun on the River Meuse.[49] Wavell had been able to augment his periods of home leave by giving lectures at training schools in Britain. Whenever possible he returned across the Channel by air with Amyas Borton, who had himself been seriously injured but was now flying again. Wavell's father travelled out to see him, and the two went as close to the front as visitors were permitted. During this time, Wavell's thoughts were also with his wife. Their first child – a boy – was born on 11 May; he was named Archibald John – after his father and his maternal grandfather – and always known as Archie John. A month after the birth Queenie engaged a nanny, Daisy Ribbands from East Anglia, straightforward and gentle. From this point on, wherever the Wavells went, Nanny went too, loyally sharing their lives.

Wavell was able to go home soon after Archie John's birth. 'I can remember well my first sight of him with his proud mother and the thrill it gave me,' he later wrote.[50] But while he delighted in his infant son, the death toll for 1916 on the Western Front and elsewhere was growing out of all proportion to any military gains. The 'attrition battles' of Verdun and the Somme were supreme evidence of the futile stalemate in which both sides remained locked. At GHQ Wavell was no longer a witness to the carnage, and perhaps for this reason his comments seem strangely detached from the human tragedy around him. He later described his work at the time as 'dull', and the period as 'uneventful'. In October, as the Battle of the Somme was drawing to its muddy and ruinous close, Wavell was ordered to report to the Chief of the Imperial General Staff at the War Office. Six years previously, as Commandant of the Staff College, Wully Robertson had suggested Wavell learn Russian; as CIGS, he now had another surprise appointment in mind.

Arriving in London, Wavell – now a major – went directly to see Robertson. His new job was to carry out 'liaison duty' with the Russian Army of the Caucasus while the current liaison officer returned to Britain. Wavell was not pleased, and told Nancy that the 'blighters' had ordered him to Russia.[51] He had wanted to return to France, and the Russian appointment – expected to last for three or four months – seemed an unnecessary diversion; it did, however, carry the rank of acting lieutenant-colonel. On 4 November 1916 he set out for Tiflis, taking passage from Hull to Bergen in a Norwegian ship, the *Jupiter*. Four months previously the HMS *Hampshire* on a similar route, taking Lord Kitchener to Russia for talks with the Tsar, had been hit by a German mine off the Orkneys and sunk with no survivors.

Norway was neutral, and *Jupiter* steamed towards its destination fully lit, apparently unconcerned that she might be seen by German U-boats. The Germans knew that British officers and military and diplomatic despatches frequently travelled by this route to Russia, and Wavell had been warned that the ship might be stopped by a U-boat or a German destroyer. He had no intention of spending the rest of the war in a German prison, so he took with him some old dungarees; if the ship were stopped, he planned to put them on and pretend to be one of the crew.

From Bergen Wavell went on by train to Oslo, where he met his predecessor on his way home. The outgoing liaison officer had his wife with him, so Wavell immediately wired Queenie to make arrangements to join him. He journeyed onward through Finland, at that time still part of the Russian Empire, and on 12 November reached Petrograd, as St Petersburg had been known since 1914 in rejection of a Germanic-sounding name. After four days he set out again, and arrived at Tiflis – which he had last visited six years earlier – on 21 November; he later recalled that the train never arrived so punctually again during the next six months.[52]

Wavell's immediate enemies were now the Turks, and his job was to keep the General Staff at the War Office informed of events on the Caucasus front, especially with regard to any changes in the state of the Turkish troops opposing the Russians. In early 1915 the Russians had defeated the Turks and captured Erzerum in Turkish Armenia; the following summer, they then advanced into Asia Minor on a broad front and captured Erzinjan. When Wavell arrived the Russian front had moved well beyond these two towns and the Turkish Army had suffered considerably in their attempts to mount a counter-offensive. What the Turks might do next was important to the British because any withdrawal of Turkish forces from the Russian front was likely to mean a corresponding increase of strength in the Turkish Army facing the British in either Palestine or Mesopotamia. The British Government also hoped that the Russian Army in the Caucasus might be used to assist them in Mesopotamia and the Persian Gulf. But when Wavell visited the front he found that the high morale of 1914 was gone: 'The Russian soldier was tired of being launched at strong positions with little artillery support and uncut barbed wire. He had lost confidence in his officers.'[53]

The man with whom Wavell was to 'liaise' was the Governor of the Caucasus, the Grand Duke Nicholas Nicholaivitch, uncle of the Tsar. As Commander-in-Chief of all the Russian armies, he had successfully led the campaign against the Turks in Erzinjan and Erzerum, and thereby incurred the Tsarina's jealousy. Her suspicion of his popularity was such that when the previous Governor of the Caucasus died she had persuaded the Tsar to appoint his uncle governor, and himself assume the position of Supreme Commander. Wavell thought the Grand Duke, an immense 6 feet 7 inches tall, the most impressive-looking man he had ever met. He spoke fluent French but no English, 'though I think he understood it. He gave me the choice of talking Russian or French with him, and I decided that my

Russian was better.'[54] Official access to the Grand Duke was through his Chief of Staff, General Bolkhovitinov.

In December Queenie made the first of what were to be many journeys to join her husband in an overseas posting – having first overcome the objections of the Foreign Office who referred her to the War Office, who referred her back again to the Foreign Office. Leaving Archie John with his nanny at Cranborne, Queenie and her maid, a young Norfolk girl called Grant, set out for the Caucasus. Wavell was delighted by her arrival, and later recounted proudly how she had succeeded in persuading her travelling companions to open the window in their railway carriage, without knowing a word of Russian. They stayed at the Hôtel l'Orient in Tiflis; according to Queenie it had only its food to recommend it, but Wavell described it as 'fairly comfortable'. As batman Wavell had a young boy from Siberia named Stepan; he also had the services of a cipher officer, George Scott, who played the violin and enjoyed writing poetry.[55]

On Christmas Day 1916 the Wavells were the guests of the Grand Duke. In addition to other Russian delicacies, they feasted on 'recognizable' plum pudding, with small hard currant buns rather like rock cakes. Apart from Wavell's official duties in Tiflis there was little or no social activity, so Wavell and Queenie found themselves going for long walks in the mountains. On one occasion they got lost. As Wavell recalled, Queenie helpfully suggested that if he could tell her where London was she knew that Piccadilly runs east and west. When finally they returned, Scott's relief was palpable. During their absence he had been worrying about what he would have done with Wavell's body in the event of an accident – whether it should go back to London, and how he would make the arrangements.[56]

In early 1917 Wavell was informed that General Frederick Maude, who had recently taken command in Mesopotamia, was expected to capture Baghdad imminently.[57] To assist the advance, Wavell was requested to propose to the Grand Duke that his forces should attack Mosul in Turkish-occupied Syria. Colonel Chardigny, the French liaison officer, had similar instructions; but Chardigny also wanted to make it clear that, in line with the agreement reached between the Foreign Office envoy Sir Mark Sykes and France's Georges Picot in 1916 allotting Mosul, post-war, to the French sphere of influence, as soon as the city was captured the French flag would be raised above it.[58] Together they went to see General Bolkhovitinov. Wavell made the request on behalf of the Allies, then Chardigny made known his position regarding the French flag and Mosul. Well aware that such a demand would not endear the proposed offensive to the Russians, Wavell feigned ignorance of the terms of the Sykes–Picot agreement. When Bolkhovitinov asked for a translation of the Frenchman's oration, Wavell adapted Chardigny's sentiments: 'He is only saying,' he told the Russian, 'how glorious it will be to see the flags of the Allies floating over Mosul.'[59] The request for assistance was communicated to the Grand Duke and he gave his assent but, as Wavell realized, the Russians were in no position to advance on Mosul. With five and a half million casualties in two and a half years of war, the Imperial Russian Army was already disintegrating. The troops had no ammunition, and the civilians no food. In early March revolutionary protest erupted on the streets of Petrograd, and to the Tsar's distress the troops sided with the rioters. A few days later Tsar Nicholas abdicated and for a short period the Grand Duke resumed supreme command of the Russian Army; but his appointment was cancelled by Russia's new leader, Alexander Kerensky, who became War Minister in May and Prime Minister in July.

Wavell had already spent more than the anticipated three months in Tiflis and was anxious to return to Britain, but in early April he was instructed to go to Asia Minor to visit Erzerum and Erzinjan. Leaving Queenie behind in Tiflis, he set out on 11 April. Soon after his arrival he received three telegrams from the War Office, assigning him a permanent post with the Russian Army on the Urmia front in Persia. Yet again he was displeased, feeling he was being 'unfairly' treated. As he said in a letter to his father, if he went to Persia, he would not be able to take Queenie: she had not been well, and was not fit enough to 'rough' it. But he also realized that it would be very dull for her to remain in Tiflis on her own and difficult – in the prevailing circumstances – for her to go home alone. 'They might at least have given me some warning,' he continued grumpily. Moreover he had been promised (twice) by the War Office that once the previous liaison officer returned to Tiflis, he would be able to return to England. To compound his annoyance, he had been in Russia since November: if he had to go directly to Persia, he would have no summer clothes.[60]

In the end, the War Office took Wavell's protestations to heart and the posting to Persia was cancelled; he and Queenie were able to return home in the early summer of 1917. The revolution was paralysing many aspects of Russian life, and travel was even more chaotic than Wavell's previous experience. Their journey from Tiflis to Petrograd took ten days but they finally reached England, travelling by way of Finland, Sweden and Norway.[61] Despite Wavell's reservations about going to Russia, he subsequently admitted that it had given him a break from the tedium of routine military work, which he had discovered could be 'as dull in war as in peace'.[62] He had also been on his own, without the support of regiment, brigade or HQ, which was good for his self-reliance. His experience as a liaison officer in the Caucasus and as brigade-major with the 9th Infantry Brigade led to his advancement to brevet lieutenant-colonel at the age of 34, dated 3 June 1917.[63] He was not required to make an official report, but told the General Staff at the War Office informally of his conviction that the Russian Army was likely to 'run out', and therefore should not be relied upon. Initially, his superiors may not have believed his appraisal, but events soon proved him correct. In October 1917, under the leadership of Lenin and Trotsky, the Bolshevik faction of the revolutionaries seized power. Soon afterwards discussions for an armistice with the Central Powers were begun.

After his Russian interlude Wavell wanted to go back to the Western Front, where he was sure of being assigned a GSO1 post in command of an infantry division, but yet again his hopes were dashed. Instead, he was sent as liaison officer between the Chief of Imperial General Staff at the War Office and the Commander-in-Chief in Egypt, General Sir Edmund Allenby. 'I had hoped for something more active, nearer the front line. However, I couldn't refuse. I had to make the best of it.'[64]

5

Palestine with Allenby, 1917

And he gathered them together into a place called in the Hebrew
tongue Armageddon.   Revelation xvi, 16[1]

WAVELL'S APPOINTMENT AS liaison officer to the Commander-in-Chief of the Egyptian Expeditionary Force took him to an area which cartographers had long chosen to define by reference to their own understanding of where the world began. Thus for people living in Europe, the 'Near East' – now known as the Middle East – started in Egypt and ended at Persia. Since the sixteenth century it had embodied much of the land under the rule of the Ottoman Turks, a multi-lingual, multi-racial empire comparable to that of the Habsburgs in Europe. One of the ancient highways of this empire was the region which ran along the eastern rim of the Mediterranean: Palestine. As Wavell noted, all the great conquering nations had passed that way: Assyrians, Egyptians, Persians, Macedonians, Romans and Arabs.[2] With the prospect of winning the war on the Western Front still bleak, the War Cabinet under Lloyd George as Prime Minister had become increasingly divided between those 'Westerners' who believed that all possible means should be used to defeat Germany in the West, and the 'Easterners' – of whom Lloyd George was the most ardent advocate – who thought that continuing to strike at Germany's weaker allies would reap greater dividends. Despite the failure of the Allied offensive against the Turks at Gallipoli, the War Cabinet believed an offensive into Palestine would not only distract the Turks from any possible counter-attack against Baghdad but also safeguard British control over Egypt and the Suez Canal – and, consequently, access to Britain's empire in India. In the wake of the carnage of the Somme, it would also serve to boost the Allies' confidence in their eventual ability to win the war. In early 1918, the then Commander-in-Chief of the Egyptian Expeditionary Force, General Sir Archibald Murray had laid the groundwork for such an offensive by securing Sinai east of Suez as far as Rafa on the coast, but two attempts – in

March and April – to force the Turks out of Gaza in southern Palestine had failed, resulting in heavy casualties and loss of morale.[3]

Lloyd George decided to introduce more 'resolute leadership' by replacing Murray. The Prime Minister turned to Allenby, Commander of the Third Army in France, who had been unable to capitalize on his April victory at Arras and whose uncommunicative relationship with Haig was impeding cohesion at the top. When Lloyd George and Allenby met in London, the Prime Minister outlined his objective: Allenby should aim for Jerusalem, in the heart of Palestine. Its capture, he suggested encouragingly, would make a fine Christmas present for the British nation.[4] At midnight on 28/29 June Allenby assumed command of the Egyptian Expeditionary Force;[5] three weeks later Wavell arrived at GHQ in Cairo. The challenge facing him as liaison officer was to maintain a relationship of trust with both Robertson as CIGS at the War Office and Allenby, the C-in-C in the field – the man 22 years his senior whose skills of leadership had so impressed him during his Staff College training in 1910. Wavell immediately recognized his good fortune in working for someone who took his junior officer into his confidence: 'A smaller man might have regarded an emissary from the War Office as some sort of a spy and have treated him with suspicion.'[6]

As Wavell immediately discovered, Allenby had firm ideas about his proximity to the projected area of battle: to be closer to the field of action, he planned to move GHQ from the relative comfort of Cairo to a camp near Rafa, the most forward point secured by Murray in Sinai, just south of the Turkish front at Gaza. Allenby also distributed copies of the Bible so that his men could study the military campaigns of Joshua, who in the Old Testament was Moses's successor in leading the Israelites in their conquest of Canaan, the ancient coastland of Palestine. On one occasion Wavell was able to persuade his friend Biffy Borton, who had also been posted to Palestine, to fly him along the front from Gaza to Beersheba for an aerial view of their forthcoming battleground. Wavell's reconnaissance showed him that the town of Gaza was protected by tall thick cactus hedges, which made the city 'more impenetrable than a barbed wire entanglement of the same size'. Running north-east to south-west was the Ali Muntar Ridge, 'the real key to the defences of the town' and, as Wavell commented, by tradition the spot to which Samson had carried the pillars of Gaza as described in the Old Testament.[7]

For the third Allied offensive against Gaza, where the Turks were well entrenched and flushed with pride at having twice resisted an attack, Allenby needed to adopt fresh tactics. 'The plan itself was simple, as are almost all good plans in war,' recalled Wavell, '– to concentrate a superior force against the enemy's left flank, while inducing him to believe that his right would again be attacked.' It was, as Wavell realized, a tried and tested formula that had been used by Lord Roberts in South Africa against the Boers – and Allenby, as a squadron commander, had seen it in action. A high priority was to ensure that Beersheba was captured before the Turks had time to destroy the wells, without which the offensive could not continue.[8] Wavell returned to London in August to put his other 'boss', Wully Robertson, in the picture and outline Allenby's requirements in terms of men, machines, aeroplanes and equipment, including medical units. Robertson sat through his exposition of the plan of action in apparent boredom, frequently getting up out of his chair to look at maps of other regions; but when Wavell had finished he proved that he had heard every word, acceding to all Allenby's demands, except that he was unable to provide all the requested artillery. As Wavell later appreciated, the proposed campaign 'made Palestine the most important theatre outside Europe for the rest of the war', while British actions in relation to Palestine at that time involved the British Empire in 'fresh commitments and perplexities when the war was over'.[9] Throughout the summer of 1917 the Foreign Secretary, Arthur Balfour, had been engaged in talks with the Zionists working to secure a Jewish homeland – to gain their support, while cutting the ground from under any German efforts in that direction. In any future disposition of the oil-rich Middle East, the British Government also wished for strategic and political reasons to stake its claim to a British sphere of influence against competing demands from the French, Russians and Italians. On 3 September Balfour presented the War Cabinet with a public statement which endorsed his private commitment to the Jewish community. Not everyone in the War Cabinet supported the idea of a Jewish homeland, but two months later the wording was finally agreed.

By the time Wavell was back in Palestine, GHQ had been shifted to its new headquarters north of Rafa, where 'there was no shade and the temperature often rose to 110 degrees . . . there was constant dust; all cuts, even scratches, turned septic . . . only a regular sea-breeze kept the heat down and made the nights reasonably cool.' There was also the danger of 'sand-fly fever', which left those it attacked limp and exhausted for many days. England was so far away that there was little chance of respite, and many of the men had not been home for over two years.[10] Yet again Wavell found himself working with a Staff College contemporary, Guy Dawnay, Brigadier-General on the General Staff.[11] Since motorized vehicles were still comparatively scarce and there were very few roads, the force Allenby was assembling was dependent on horses; thousands of camels were used for supply and transportation from the railhead north of Rafa. As authorized by Allenby, the plan was for the Desert Mounted Corps, which included Australian and New Zealand brigades as well as the Yeomanry Mounted Division and the Imperial Camel Corps, with the bulk of General Sir Philip Chetwode's XX Corps, to be used for the main attack against Beersheba. Once Beersheba and the wells were secure, a secondary 'feint' attack on Gaza was to be made by XXI Corps, prior to the main attack. As there was no question of hiding the tremendous moving caravan of men and animals which comprised XX Corps and the Desert Mounted Corps, a key element of Allenby's strategy lay in making the Turks think the move to Beersheba was merely a distraction from their main attack on Gaza; Wavell was present when the 'haversack' ruse designed to effect this was sanctioned. Allenby's intelligence officer, Major Richard Meinertzhagen, 'contrived to be chased by the Turkish outposts, pretended to be wounded, and dropped, with other articles, a haversack stained with fresh blood containing papers, letters, money.' The information the papers contained persuaded the Turks that they were genuine, and that the British were indeed preparing for an attack on Gaza.[12] As a result the Turks were prompted to publish an official warning against officers carrying written orders, and the officer who had picked up the haversack was rewarded.[13]

The attack on Beersheba was fixed for the night of 30/31 October, 'so timed that the light of the full moon favoured this night approach. The weather, however, was sultry and airless, and a dense pall of dust lay heavy on the marching columns.'[14] Already the Royal Navy had begun a heavy bombardment of Gaza, giving substance to the idea that the town was again the real target. The Turks at Beersheba were completely taken by surprise, 'not at the fact of an attack taking place, but at the unexpected weight and direction of that attack.'[15] It was, as Wavell later commented, like pitting a county cricket eleven against a village team.[16] Only once the men and animals had watered at Beersheba could the main attack on Gaza begin. Since an estimated 48 hours would be required before the 'delivery of the main blow', the 'second act' of the plan – the diversionary feint against Gaza – was ordered for the night of 1/2 November. It too was successful.

On that same 2 November, as Allenby and his troops battled once more to take Gaza, far away from Palestine, Balfour made his Declaration, writing to Lord Rothschild, former Member of Parliament and influential financier. Once hostilities were over, he said, 'His Majesty's Government view with favour the establishment in Palestine of a national home for the

Jewish people, and will use their best endeavours to facilitate the achievement of this object, it being clearly understood that nothing shall be done which may prejudice the civil and religious rights of existing non-Jewish communities in Palestine, or the rights and political status enjoyed by Jews in any other country.'[17] While the wording was diplomatically vague, the meaning behind 'the establishment . . . of a national home' was clear: Jews should be allowed to go to Palestine and settle in such numbers as the land could accommodate. As Wavell later wrote, few at the time realized the 'significance or danger' of the declaration.[18]

In Palestine there was now 'an awkward and unrehearsed pause before the curtain could rise on the third act'.[19] Unforeseen circumstances, including heavy fighting in the hills north of Beersheba, prompted General Chetwode of the XX Corps to seek a postponement of the main attack on Gaza from 4 to 6 November. Wavell watched how Allenby weighed up the consequences of the delay, then took his decision. He first wanted to determine whether or not the delay was essential, and immediately went to Beersheba by car to talk to Chetwode. 'One [that is, Wavell] who drove with him that day can testify to the force and energy that he radiated.'[20] In terms of Wavell's own military schooling, it was an invaluable lesson in dealing with a setback: 'To listen patiently to all the administrative arguments, to weigh them up quickly, to change his preconceived purpose at once, and having decided to do so, to do it with confidence and cheerful encouragement to his subordinate in spite of the risks he knew it involved, showed him a great man and was a lesson in the art of leadership.'[21] When the attack took place, the Turks were unable to withstand the force of the three divisions against them. On the morning of 7 November XXI Corps entered the deserted fortress of Gaza, as thousands of Turks streamed 'north along the coastal plain in hasty retreat'.[22] Yet again the politicians attempted to take advantage of their respective military conquests. This time their pledge was to the Arabs: a joint Anglo-French declaration was issued in Palestine and Syria, stating as their goal 'the complete and final liberation of the peoples who have for so long been oppressed by the Turks and the setting up of national governments and administrations that shall derive their authority from the free exercise of the initiative and choice of the indigenous populations.'[23]

Although Wavell took no physical part in this third – and final – battle for Gaza, with two other officers he was able to see part of the Turkish retreat from the top of Ali Muntar Hill on the outskirts of the city. For a while they stood watching the Turks make a last attempt to shell the British Brigade headquarters. Suddenly noticing the spectators on top of the hill, the Turks swiftly altered the direction of their guns and turned the battery on Wavell and his companions. A speedy escape through a gap in the maze of cacti surrounding the south of the city ensured their survival. Overall the operation had been an unqualified success, and the two-day delay had not significantly affected the outcome. But water was short, which meant that the Desert Mounted Corps were unable to carry out the 'sequel' to the breaking of Gaza envisaged by Allenby, which entailed an immediate combined strike at the retreating Turks, to prevent them escaping to the north; when they finally attempted to do so, they had lost the advantage. As Wavell noted, it was another military lesson: 'the ideal exploitation by mounted troops is not a pursuit, but an interception. It aims to strike, not the rear of the retreating enemy columns, where the sting is, but the less protected flanks or head.'[24]

Then, on 16 November, Jaffa fell. Far from being disappointed at no longer being on the Western Front, Wavell was in high spirits. 'Darling Nancy,' he wrote, 'we've had great doings out here and it's been a most wonderful success' – thanks, he said, due chiefly to General Allenby. And, true to form, as the infantry and cavalry continued to traverse the ancient highway towards Jerusalem, Wavell was finding his surroundings 'most interesting in every way', commenting to Nancy that he was re-learning a lot of biblical history forgotten since his boyhood.[25] The Turks were not yet defeated, however, and under the direction of their German commanders were able to withdraw in sufficient order to mount a counter-offensive as they continued their retreat northwards. The pursuit of the Turkish Army again provided Wavell with some lessons for the future. 'The pursued has a greater incentive to haste than the pursuer, and, unless he is demoralized, a stronger urge to fight. It is only natural that the soldier who has risked his life and spent his toil in winning a battle should desire relaxation in safety as his mead of victory, and that the general and staff should feel a reaction from the strain.' Allenby could have chosen to halt, to let his soldiers rest, or to press onwards so as not to lose the advantage. Wavell believed that the 'surest test' of Allenby's strength of will was the energy he put into continuing to pursue the Turks into the hills and there engaging in some of the fiercest fighting of the offensive, carried out in driving wind and freezing rain. But, despite formidable fortifications around Jerusalem, 'the Turks defended with less than their usual tenacity.'[26]

By dawn on 9 December the Turks had left Jerusalem after an occupation lasting four centuries. Soon after midday the mayor emerged to surrender the keys of this holiest of cities to Major-General John Shea, commander of the 60th Division.[27] Two days later – on 11 December –

Allenby formally entered Jerusalem on foot through the Jaffa Gate, the main entry to the old walled city, traditionally only opened to a conqueror. The Guard of Honour represented the nationalities of all those who had taken part in the campaign – English, Scottish, Irish, Welsh, Australian, New Zealand, French and Italian. A guard of Indian Muslim troops stood watch over the Haram-el-Sharif, sacred to Muslims throughout the world. Allenby's proclamation was then read to the citizens in English, French Arabic, Hebrew, Greek, Russian and Italian.

Wavell was one of twenty officers invited by Allenby to join the procession. Close by walked Colonel T.E. Lawrence, who had been active in leading the Arab rebellion against their Turkish masters and had recently escaped from imprisonment (and, according to his account, torture) by the Turks.[28] Although he had not contributed to this specific victory, Allenby 'was good enough' to include Lawrence in the procession as a staff officer. As Wavell recalled, he appeared happy that day, 'with jests at his borrowed uniform and at the official appointment that had been loaned him for the ceremony.'[29] In years to come, the two men, ostensibly so different, became friends, based on their shared literary tastes and love of poetry. Lawrence's presence may have personified the Arab contribution in the overall offensive, but also included in the party was Dr Chaim Weizmann, a renowned scientist whose manufacture of a synthetic form of cordite had helped the war effort. Following Balfour's Declaration, he had travelled with a small group of friends to meet Allenby at his headquarters. On reaching Jerusalem Weizmann laid the foundation stone of a new Hebrew University, signifying one small step towards the creation of a Jewish homeland in Palestine. Allenby however, already aware that the capture of Jerusalem posed political as well as military problems, had refused to let the Balfour Declaration be published in Palestine. As Wavell noted, the only flag permitted to be flown while Britain was in military occupation was the Union Jack.[30] In the newspapers at home, this victory and the ceremony provided a welcome distraction from the continuing losses on the Western Front. As far as the British people were concerned, Jerusalem had indeed been handed to them for Christmas.

Wavell returned to England almost immediately to report to Robertson on the success of the campaign. Before he left he showed Allenby his report, in which he had noted the failure of the Desert Mounted Corps to cut off the Turks after the fighting at Beersheba. Although Allenby had criticized the slow pace at which the cavalry progressed, he was not pleased that Wavell should have mentioned it in his report. 'Have you ever commanded mounted troops in pursuit?' he demanded of the startled junior officer. But Wavell had 'the temerity' to stick to his guns: 'I maintained my view that the mounted troops should have done better.' Nevertheless, he offered to delete the offending remarks if Allenby so wished. 'He was an alarming person when angry, and though I was not afraid of him and argued the point, I found myself at the end of it pouring with perspiration though it was not a warm evening.' When Allenby's legendary temper subsided he offered Wavell a drink, the incident apparently forgotten. Allenby never again said 'a harsh word' to Wavell, and used Wavell's report – without the criticism of the cavalry – as the basis for his own despatch on the operations.[31]

Wavell was able to spend Christmas with Queenie and their son, whom he had not seen since the summer, and his own family at Cranborne. He was expecting to return to Palestine, but yet again Robertson had something different in mind: Wavell was to attend the recently formed Supreme War Council at Versailles, where the future of Palestine was being discussed. The decision to form a War Council had been taken the previous November in Rapallo at a meeting of the Chiefs of the Allied Governments of France, Britain and Italy. The objective being to try to coordinate their respective thinking on the direction of the war, each country was to send a military representative. Henry Wilson was Britain's, and Wavell was to be on his staff. The appointment was another of Robertson's surprises accepted by Wavell with reluctance: if he were not to return to Palestine, he wanted either a command or a staff job in the field. But Robertson insisted that he must go, on the grounds that 'the most awful nonsense' was being talked about Palestine in Versailles, and it was important to have someone present who knew about the region. It was also no secret that Robertson disliked the mechanics of the Supreme War Council, and was not pleased, as CIGS, at having to assume the role of 'the errand boy' of Wilson and 'a pack of foreigners'.[32]

Wavell arrived at Versailles in January 1918. Following Russia's military collapse and the new government's continuing discussions regarding an armistice with Germany – eventually signed at Brest-Litovsk on 3 March – there was general anxiety among the Allied representatives lest freedom on the Eastern Front should enable the Germans to transfer more divisions to the Western Front and mount a crushing attack on the Allied, French and British armies in the spring. The United States had entered the war in April 1917, and American soldiers were playing an increasingly important role, but their army was not expected to arrive in strength until September 1918. Both Haig and Robertson therefore believed it was necessary to muster all possible forces for a defensive stand on the Western Front.

Lloyd George arrived with an impressive contingent of advisers and based himself at the Hôtel Crillon. He and Henry Wilson disagreed with Haig and Robertson, still maintaining that the war could be won by defeating Germany's ally Turkey, and that a further offensive in Palestine, extending to Damascus (and possibly Aleppo), would produce the desired result as far as Turkey was concerned. Wavell found himself in the difficult position of presenting views which, although acceptable to Robertson and Haig, were in direct conflict with those of the Prime Minister and Henry Wilson. In his paper he made the case for forcefully resisting the Germans in the West. Unless sufficient reinforcements were provided and the number of railways doubled, an advance to Damascus and Aleppo would have no real effect and would entail maintaining long lines of communication across difficult terrain, against an enemy whose fighting spirit was by no means extinguished. Wilson was not receptive to the opinions expressed by Wavell; when the Supreme War Council met at the end of January, he ignored Wavell's paper and presented his own plan: a defensive stand should be taken in France; at the same time, the Allies should undertake 'a decisive offensive against Turkey with a view to the annihilation of the Turkish armies and the collapse of Turkish resistance.'[33]

After lengthy meetings, a compromise was eventually reached – the offensive against Turkey would be mounted on condition that, as the French insisted, no 'white' – that is, European – troops were diverted away from the Western Front. Robertson, who believed that such a course of action would hinder Britain's attempts to win the war, was not to be won over: Wavell recorded him leaving the meeting with a face 'like a thundercloud'. As was later revealed, an undercurrent of mistrust ran through the proceedings from the start. Lloyd George believed Robertson to have deliberately instructed Allenby to exaggerate the strength of the Turkish enemy opposing him and to apply for an extravagant reinforcement of troops before continuing his advance on Aleppo, enabling Robertson to rule out the project as impracticable, and thus retain these troops for the Western Front.[34]

Wavell was never comfortable in Versailles. He considered the sumptuous surroundings inappropriate to the task at hand, and felt the British section was overstaffed. Once the discussions relating to the Palestine operations were over, he found he had little to do. To pass the time he put up three papers on manpower to Brigadier-General Frederick Sykes, who was on the General Staff of the Supreme War Council.[35] Sykes, however, seemed to absent himself frequently, travelling back to London with half a dozen large boxes full of documents, and never reviewed Wavell's papers or addressed the problems he had raised. In early February Wavell himself took a week's leave in London, indicating that he would do no more work until he got some answers. When this produced no effect, he requested permission to resign his appointment: Wilson was surprised that he should wish to relinquish a position 'so much at the heart of things'. But even though no job awaited him, Wavell stuck by his decision. After spending nearly two weeks in England, he returned to Palestine as a 'pool' officer without an appointment, 'trusting to my friends at GHQ in Palestine to find me one'. Versailles he later recollected as 'an unprofitable interlude, which gave me a poor opinion on the higher direction of international war'.[36] On 8 February the War Cabinet decided that Robertson and Wilson should exchange positions. Robertson refused; ten days later he read in the newspapers that he had 'resigned', and that Wilson was the new Chief of the Imperial General Staff.

Wavell arrived back in the Middle East in late March, and it seemed he had landed on his feet when he was appointed to the General Staff of a new Corps – the XXII – which was to be raised. For the first time he was entitled to wear the insignia of a brigadier-general – the crossed sword and baton – on his shoulders. When he reached Palestine, however, he heard that the divisions which would have constituted the Corps had been sent to the hard-pressed Western Front where the Germans, as predicted, after finally signing an armistice with Russia in March 1918 had mounted a murderous offensive across the Somme. Replacing his crossed swords and batons with a colonel's stars, Wavell was then briefly appointed GSO1 in charge of training at the main HQ in Cairo. But within a very short time he was once more changing the insignia on his shoulders: on 18 April Allenby appointed him Brigadier-General, General Staff, XX Corps, under General Chetwode's command. Although his predecessor had described Chetwode as a 'rum 'un', Wavell admired him for having 'the best and quickest military brain' he had ever known, as well as 'an extremely good tactical eye for ground and a great gift for expressing a situation clearly and concisely'.[37] Early on in their relationship Wavell asked how much of the work which passed through his office Chetwode wanted to see: 'Just what you think necessary to show me,' was the reply. 'I shall find out soon enough whether you are doing your job or not.'[38] And even though Chetwode did not have Allenby's qualities of 'drive and determination', Wavell found him easy to work for. After the fall of Jerusalem British headquarters had moved to a hostel on the Mount of Olives which had been erected by Kaiser Wilhelm II for German tourists who wished to visit the Holy Land. By the time Wavell arrived, the German nuns who had run the hostel had been dismissed for security reasons, with a detrimental effect on the standard of the cooking.

During Wavell's absence much had happened in the planning of Allenby's future course of action. In the wake of the Supreme War Council's decision to continue the offensive beyond Jerusalem, the South African leader General Jan Christian Smuts, who had joined Lloyd George's War Cabinet, arrived for discussions with Allenby.[39] Although the arrival of a politician reportedly 'bored' Allenby, Smuts was impressed with the soldiers' fitness and by their confidence in Allenby. It was decided that British and Imperial forces would remain on the defensive in Mesopotamia while Allenby took all the troops that could be spared and advanced through Palestine and Syria, with Damascus and Aleppo as his eventual destination. By the middle of April British troops, after securing the Jordan valley, had moved their line to the north and east of Jerusalem. But the next stage – advancing across the River Jordan into the mountains of Moab to capture Amman – presented greater difficulties: heavy rainfall hampered two attempts. In addition, the German offensive on the Western Front was proving more deadly than could have been anticipated. Instead of ordinary infantry the Germans were using groups of the first 'storm troopers', armed with light machine guns and flame-throwers, the dreaded *Flammenwerfer*, which Wavell called an experiment in 'frightfulness'.[40] With German troops advancing to within 35 miles of Paris, the priority yet again was to send as many reinforcements to Europe as possible, and Allenby was obliged to part with two European divisions. He could only bide his time and prepare for a decisive attack in the autumn. He therefore dug in for the summer – 2,000 feet below sea-level in southern Jordan; men and animals were obliged to remain in an area where according to the official military handbook, as Wavell noted, 'nothing is known of the climate in summer-time, since no civilized human being has yet been found to spend summer there.'[41]

Throughout the long hot summer Wavell was able to utilize his previous training experience behind the lines to build a new Corps under Chetwode's command. Experienced brigades were broken up so that men who had not seen action could be incorporated. The Indian battalions which had come from Palestine needed to be absorbed and trained. Wavell's experience of a decade before with his regiment in India was useful, with his knowledge of Urdu and his understanding of Indians. He was able to appreciate Chetwode's 'good eye for the ground' when it came to working out an offensive strategy for XX Corps's front, and also to take pride in his own successes: 'I take a little credit for an appreciation I drew up at this time, that if the Turks did attack they would do so in a certain way and on a certain part of our front. When we advanced in the autumn, amongst captured Turkish documents was found a plan for an attack on our front which almost exactly reproduced that attributed to the enemy in my appreciation.' In addition to the scorching heat – the temperature rarely dropped below 130 degrees Fahrenheit in the shade – there were natural hazards, among which Wavell never forgot the predominance of fleas in the villagers' houses in the hills, from which the inhabitants had already fled. The British forces had hoped to occupy them as strong points, but 'owing to the number, size and ferocity of the fleas, so long deprived of their natural fodder', this proved impossible. The only thing the men preparing the defences could do was 'to work entirely naked and brush the fleas off one another'.[42]

Allenby's strategy for the next stage, the occupation of the rest of Palestine, was based on the instrument of war he knew best: the horse. Throughout the summer the Cavalry Corps too endured the heat in the Jordan valley; the horses tolerated the conditions better than the men, but they too had become listless and tired, short of exercise and nutritious forage.[43] The original plan would have allowed most of the Turkish forces to retreat and escape, but Allenby now determined on an extension to it that aimed at the destruction of the Turkish armies in Palestine. As Wavell observed, the plan which had gradually been formulating in Allenby's mind was based 'partly on thought and study – of the history of previous campaigns, of the topography of the land, of Intelligence reports on the state of the Turks – and partly on personal observation and experience during the fighting in the first half of the year.' It involved a ride of more than 50 miles, across hills held by the Turks to enter the plain of Esdraelon, at least 30 miles behind Turkish lines, behind the railway that served the Turkish troops, cutting off their lines of retreat. 'There is no parallel in military history to so deep an adventure by such a mass of cavalry against a yet unbroken enemy. . . . The long Turkish domination of Syria and Palestine, and the military power on which it was founded, were to be given the death-blow in the grand manner.'[44]

Yet again Allenby adopted various ruses designed to mislead his enemy. This time he wanted the Turks to think his attack would be directed inland, rather than along the coast, so he set up a 'dummy' GHQ in Jerusalem and rumours of a troop concentration were spread. And to create the appearance of a large force, the horse lines were crowded with fifteen thousand dummy horses made of canvas stuffed with straw on a framework of bamboo and wooden poles. Many sported real horse rugs across their backs, real nosebags on their dummy heads. Mules drawing sleighs created clouds of dust that made it look as though the horses had gone to water. West Indian 'labour' battalions marched noisily down to the Jordan valley by day, only to return quietly at night by lorry. New camps of old, unserviceable tents were pitched, occupied by a few men to provide the necessary signs of life and movement.[45] On the real flank of attack, troops and horses were moved by night to north of Jaffa and hidden in the orange groves, where the irrigation channels provided the necessary water. No one was allowed to light a fire, and no one moved until night time. Wavell, present as Chetwode's BGGS at the main conferences, saw how Allenby's optimism and enthusiasm for this great enterprise infected the other commanders. He never forgot the dummy horses; when it was his turn to plan an operation involving ruse and guile in the Western Desert in 1940, he used the modern equivalent: dummy tanks.

Part of Wavell's administrative duties at headquarters involved building up dumps of ammunition and stores near the front line, never forgetting that transport was limited and would be non-existent once the offensive began because it would be in use elsewhere. Wavell's assessment was that, although 'it would be a close run thing', they could just about manage to bring the ammunition up in time. Chetwode, however, was doubtful, and repeatedly expressed his fears. Although Wavell reassured him, Chetwode's doubts permeated his subconscious: 'For three nights running I woke up – or thought I woke, I must have still been half asleep – to hear quite clearly the roar of the opening artillery barrage that preceded our attack, and realised that there was only enough ammunition up for a few minutes' bombardment owing to my failure to get up the ammunition: I then woke up completely and realised that it was a dream.' After making additional calculations, Wavell decided to go to Egypt for a few days' leave, in order to 'rid myself of any dreams'.[46]

Before the main offensive, scheduled for 19 September, there were, as Wavell later wrote, 'two curtain-raisers to the great drama on the coastal plain'. The first was carried out by Lawrence, who had returned to lead the Arabs; under his command, and with much-publicized slaughter, the Arabs finally succeeded in cutting vital communications on the Hejaz railway at the Deraa junction. The second 'curtain-raiser' was the offensive involving XX Corps's attack on Nablus. Apart from indicating – erroneously – to the Turks where the main attack was to take place, the raid was intended to give experience to some of the new Indian units. More careful planning went into this operation, such as lighting up a deserted village with dummy gun flashes to draw fire from the Turks, issuing the men with felt-soled boots, and laying bundles of dried grass on the rockiest parts of the gully to muffle the horses' hooves. Wavell's job during the battle was to run the HQ at Ramallah, a few miles north of Jerusalem. Assessing his performance in later life, his sense was that 'on the whole the staff work went all right'. The reports by others on his conduct at this time were less dismissive, and helped build him a reputation as 'tireless, thorough, accurate, reliable and self-reliant'.[47]

The main thrust of Allenby's offensive began at 4.30 a.m. In Wavell's opinion it was not a 'soldiers' battle' but the manoeuvre of 'a great master of war'. The dramatic cavalry ride through the plain of Esdraelon north of the ancient fortress of Megiddo epitomized all the drive and physical energy Wavell had so admired in Allenby since his arrival in Palestine. 'The action of the XXI Corps was exactly that of men pushing open a wide and heavy door of which the hinges were in the foothills and the handle by the coast. Rightly, the greatest leverage was exerted at the handle end; there was the thickest concentration of troops and guns, and here were the leading cavalry divisions, ready to pass through the moment the door was even ajar.'[48] Wavell was alive to the fact that they were passing over a battlefield where an English commander had won 'a notable victory' more than seven hundred years previously, when on 7 September 1191 Richard the Lionheart had 'outmanoeuvred and outfought a worthy opponent in Saladin'. Since Saladin's army had included Turkish bowmen and Richard's 'international force' contained an English contingent of horse and foot, 'it was not the first time that the ground over which the cavalry now rode had felt the victorious rush of English chivalry in pursuit of Turks.'[49] On the sidelines, the diversionary raids of the Arabs drew away scanty Turkish reserves and contributed to Allenby's success by protecting his eastern flank.

Trapped in the ravines and hills, the descendants of those medieval Turks were no longer in a position to put up a fight. With the capture of Beisan ('where Saul's dead body had hung')[50] and Jenin, Allenby's forces immediately pushed onwards to Damascus. Throughout the battle, Allenby himself was never far from the front line: 'Long distances over indifferent tracks in heat and dust had no effect on his determination to see for himself how things were going.'[51] On 1 October his forward troops, a brigade of Australian Light Horse, passed through the Syrian capital – 'famous for trade rather than for war' – in pursuit of a Turkish column. Soon afterwards Lawrence and his Arabs reached the city. By the end of the month, Allenby's forces were in Aleppo. Wavell was the first to recognize the scale of the achievement. 'In less than six weeks Allenby's army had captured

75,000 prisoners and 360 guns, and had moved its front forward 350 miles. Its own casualty list had been little over 5,000 . . . The greatest exploit in the history of horsed cavalry, and possibly their last success on a large scale had ended within a short distance of the battlefield of Issus where in 33 BC Alexander the Great first showed how battles could be won by bold and well-handled horsemen.'[52] During the later stages of the battle Wavell remained in Nablus 'with very little to do', and was therefore quick to take advantage of an opportunity to fly to Damascus with Borton. 'It was quite an exciting trip,' he later recalled. The landing-ground near Damascus was too small for the plane, and 'Amyas only avoided what might have been a disastrous plunge into a deep, broad ditch by using the wing of a smaller machine as a brake to ours; the smaller machine was badly damaged but we pulled up practically unhurt on the edge of the ditch.'[53]

By the time the armistice with Turkey was signed on 31 October, Wavell had applied for some home leave: Queenie was expecting their second child and he was anxious to return to England. Meanwhile, on the Western Front the Germans had finally succumbed to the pressures of the Allied counter-offensive, which now included reinforcements from the United States. Food shortages and low morale had led to strikes and protests throughout Germany. Bulgaria and Austria had already sued for peace. Just before the Turkish armistice, German sailors mutinied at Kiel. In early November General Erich von Ludendorff, who had for so long kept alive the prospect of a German victory, was dismissed by Kaiser Wilhelm II; wearing false whiskers and coloured spectacles, he fled to Sweden. Days later the German government was overthrown, and the Kaiser and his family left for Holland. On 8 November armistice negotiations began near Soissons in the Aisne valley. In the early hours of the morning of 11 November 1918, the agreement was signed by military and civilian representatives of the armistice delegation in a parked railway car; then, at the eleventh hour on the eleventh day of the eleventh month, after four years, the guns of war fell silent. Incredulously, men raised their heads above the trenches. Wavell had just reached Paris. The following day he arrived to find a carnival atmosphere pervading London. Previously darkened streets were alight. Flags adorned shops and houses. The crowds gathered outside shouted: 'Have we won the war?' and the response came: 'Yes, we've won the war!'[54]

Of all Wavell's experiences to date, it was the time he spent with Allenby in Palestine that made the most lasting impression. Not only did he learn from his active involvement in day-to-day events; he also stored up for the future the strategic and tactical manoeuvres he had witnessed.

While commentators praised the power of the cavalry, Wavell saw it in the context of the general value of mobility, 'however achieved'. Of the greatest importance, he stressed, was training: 'In France we never had, after the first year of war, any troops that were really well trained – judged by the pre-war standard. In Palestine, with the lower percentage of losses and the less continuous fighting, there was time available for training, and sufficient pre-war personnel capable of imparting instruction. Herein lies the explanation of how the infantry was able on many occasions to assault and capture strongly fortified positions with no great weight of artillery behind it and without the aid of tanks.'[55] (They were introduced on the Western Front at the end of the war). It was Wavell's good fortune to have been young enough at the time of the Palestine Campaigns to profit from and perfect their lessons: on the practice ground in the nearer future and in the as yet unforeseen war that lay ahead. Of all his experiences, Wavell wrote and thought more about Palestine than about any of the other campaigns in which he was involved. For the rest of his life, Edmund Allenby was to him the personification of 'greatness'.

6

Peacetime

War creates as many fresh problems as it solves old ones.   A.P. Wavell[1]

Few soldiers' families can have been so much together and so happy
as we have.   A.J. Wavell[2]

PEACETIME BRITAIN PRESENTED no hope of a return to pre-war
frivolity. Of a total estimated death toll of nearly eight and a half million, over 900,000 were from Britain and the Empire.[3] A high proportion
were junior officers and they were the 'lost generation', mirrored by a
generation of deserted women. Those who returned from the war could
not forget those who did not. Thousands of the injured, gassed, shell-
shocked, blinded remained traumatized by their experiences. The 'war'
poets, especially those who lost their lives, captured the sentiment of sadness mingled with pride. The words of 'In Flanders Fields', written by
John McCrae, a military physician who died in 1918, became the epitaph
for the departed:

> In Flanders fields the poppies blow
> Between the crosses, row on row
> That mark our place; and in the sky
> The larks, still bravely singing, fly
> Scarce heard amid the guns below.
>
> We are the Dead. Short days ago
> We lived, felt dawn, saw sunset glow,
> Loved and were loved, and now we lie
> In Flanders fields.[4]

Rudyard Kipling, one of Wavell's favourite authors, had lost his only son
John, and put his grief to verse in 'My Boy Jack': 'Have you news of my
boy Jack? / *Not this tide.* / When d'you think that he'll come back? / *Not
with the wind blowing and this tide.*'[5]

In Europe the established order of the Austro-Hungarian and Ottoman empires had broken down but there were as yet no stable 'nation states' to take their place. As Wavell commented, it took longer 'to conclude peace than war' with Turkey. The Treaty of Lausanne, though not signed until 1923, left open the question of the status of the oil-rich region of Mosul, which was in turn handed to the newly founded League of Nations to resolve in 1925. The border between Turkey and the new kingdom of Iraq – the former Ottoman provinces of Basra, Baghdad and Mosul – was not delimited until 1927. In Britain the semblance of peace was fractured by fighting in Ireland between the Irish republican party, Sinn Fein, and British troops. The 1918 election had returned Lloyd George as Prime Minister in a coalition government; the Labour Party had gained more seats than the Liberals, and for the first time sat in Opposition. Demobilization of the largely conscript army resulted in an overwhelming number of unemployed ex-servicemen. Women who had played an essential role in factories and in public transport in the absence of their menfolk found the struggle for their political rights not yet won. Britain had not, like France and Belgium, been ravaged by warfare across its landscape, but German air-ships had given London its first taste of aerial bombardment.

Except for losing his left eye Wavell had had an 'easy' war, but he had lost numerous friends as well as three first cousins – Arthur Wavell, Jack Longfield, and Reginald Norton Knatchbull, Aunt Betsy's son, ten years his senior, who had died on active service in 1917.[6] Another cousin, Arthur's brother Raymond, had been posted missing at the end of November 1914, shortly after Wavell's arrival in Flanders; interned in Holland in February 1918, he was not repatriated until January 1919. Among the five hundred Wykehamists who fell in the war, Raymond Asquith, Geoffrey Smith and Geoffrey Clark were 'the three most brilliant and attractive men' Wavell could remember from Winchester. Then there were his contemporaries from Summer Fields: Clement Peto, who had gone on to Harrow and was commissioned into the 10th Hussars, had been killed at the first Battle of Ypres in 1914; George Cholmley was missing, presumed killed, when his submarine was sunk in the North Sea in October 1914; Richard Powell, a King's Scholar at Eton and then at Cambridge, was killed in action in 1915; Reginald Vaughan-Thompson, also a contemporary at Winchester, who had become a solicitor, was killed in action in 1916; the Hon. George Herman-Hodge, another Summerfieldian and Wykehamist, died of wounds received in action in 1916; John de Luze Simonds, who had won a scholarship to Winchester from Summer Fields a year after Wavell and had joined the Royal Artillery, was killed in action in 1917 – all people in whose company Wavell had grown to manhood. 'No wonder we lacked leadership in those post-war years,' he observed many years later.[7] Everard Calthrop was perhaps the most sorely missed from among his Staff College friends. Like Amyas Borton and Bob Wallace, others had been severely wounded: 'Long Man' Henderson was wounded three times within the space of ten months, and retired from the army in 1919; Neville Henderson was wounded at Loos in 1915 and retired in 1921.

Professionally, at 35 Wavell was well placed for future advancement. Despite the time he had spent on sick leave following the loss of his eye, and the fact that he had not held a command, he was a brevet lieutenant-colonel with experience as an acting brigadier-general. He had shown himself both competent and thorough in his work as a staff officer. From a personal standpoint, returning to London as a married man with a child represented a marked change in his way of life. Apart from periods of leave he and Queenie had not spent much time together since the Caucasus, nearly two years previously. Their new temporary home was a small house at 10 Cliveden Place, near Sloane Square, close to the church in which they had married and near the Quirks' home in Knightsbridge. Wavell's parents were still living at Cranborne, and on 18 November his father celebrated his seventy-fifth birthday. His sisters, both near him in age, were still unmarried. In 1917 Nancy had been decorated for her hospital work; just as she applauded his achievements, Wavell took pride in hers, writing from Egypt that she deserved the award for 'all her hard work'.[8] Archie John was now a toddler of two and a half, and on 3 December Queenie gave birth to their second child – a girl, named Eugénie after her mother and grandmother but known always by her second name, Pamela.

Britain might no longer be at war, but there was no time for the Wavells to establish what might be thought an ordered family life. Soon after Pamela's birth Wavell was informed that he was to return to Egypt, to XX Corps. He arrived in Cairo in mid January 1919; within a short time he was appointed Brigadier-General, General Staff in place of the same Brigadier-General Bartholomew from whom he had taken over his position under Chetwode, and who was returning home. Many years later J.R. Macdonald, a young staff officer at the time, recalled an early encounter with his new Brigadier-General: 'It was my duty on the staff of XX Corps to provide him with two chargers on his appointment to us as BGGS. I knew nothing about horses but had them paraded at our HQ on the Mount of Olives in Palestine. He inspected them and then turned to me and said in the kindest way, "Yes, Macdonald, but I would like a horse with two eyes." Believe it or not, I had got I suppose the only one-eyed horse that Remounts had in hand!'[9] Wavell's superior was Major-General Sir Louis Bols, Chief of Staff at GHQ. When Bols became ill and returned to England on leave, Wavell took on his work in addition to his own. War restrictions on travel were still in force, so Queenie and their two children could not immediately join him.

Allenby still had his headquarters in Palestine. As Commander-in-Chief he was responsible for the administration of an expanse of territory that included Egypt, the Sinai, Palestine, Transjordan and Syria, as well as Cilicia as far as the foothills of the Taurus mountains in southern Turkey. Wavell's task was to assist him. Throughout this vast terrain they faced difficulties both 'diverse and troublesome'. Allenby was also finding that the thoroughness of his victory had stimulated the growth of a strong feeling of Arab nationalism. For purposes of simplicity the area – known as Occupied Enemy Territory Administration or OETA – had been divided into four districts: Palestine (south); Syria and Transjordan (west); the Lebanon and other parts of Syria (east); and finally Cilicia (north). As all four districts came under Allenby, 'complex problems of currency, finance, public works, police, justice, refugees, poor relief, and so forth were referred, in three languages, to his headquarters for decision.'[10]

One of the first problems confronting Allenby was the refusal of the Turkish generals to disband their armies as stipulated by the Armistice. Allenby had no brief to enter militarily into Turkey and so in early February he went directly to Constantinople, which was under Allied occupation, on board HMS *Téméraire*, with Wavell by his side. 'We were only about thirty-six hours in Constantinople. Allenby held a meeting at which the Turkish Ministers of Foreign Affairs and of War represented Turkey.' According to Wavell, the meeting showed the C-in-C at his most dominant. 'The Minister came prepared to discuss and argue; Allenby merely read out his demands, which included the removal of Ali Ihsan [leader of the Turkish generals], handed them a copy, and insisted on immediate acceptance without discussion or argument.'[11] The Turks were so impressed by Allenby that they 'accepted meekly and it was all over in five minutes or little more'.[12] In early 1919, as the European allies debated the future of Germany and Turkey at the Versailles Peace Conference, Allenby was summoned to France. An additional delegate at Versailles was Feisal Ibn Hussein, the Hejaz leader of the Arab revolt. For a while T.E. Lawrence was also present as Feisal's adviser and translator, but when it became clear that the European powers were not going to adhere to their wartime promises, he left the conference. Feisal was later made King of Iraq and his brother Abdullah King of Transjordan. As Wavell realized, the problems of the Middle East were only just beginning. The proposal to create a Jewish homeland had already set Jewish and Arab nationalists on a collision course.

Allenby, accompanied by Bols, remained in Europe in early 1919. During his absence Wavell assumed the role of Chief of Staff, and General Bulfin, commander of XXI Corps, became acting Commander-in-Chief. When riots broke out in Egypt, where nationalist sentiment was reacting against the suggestion that Egypt should continue as a British protectorate, Allenby returned at once. He assumed the office of High Commissioner, while remaining Commander-in-Chief. In Syria the French too were having to deal with rising Arab nationalism – supported, they believed, by the British. Soon after Allenby's return from Versailles, he showed Wavell a Foreign Office telegram about French concerns that Lawrence, who had not resurfaced since leaving Versailles, might be on his way to Damascus to help Feisal in a rebellion against France. Allenby made Wavell answerable 'with his head' for ensuring that Lawrence did not pass through Egypt on his way to Syria: Wavell duly gave instructions that he should be notified if and when Lawrence arrived. A few weeks later, on a report that Lawrence was at Shepheard's Hotel in Cairo, Wavell immediately sent a staff officer to fetch him. Lawrence arrived looking 'rather ruffled', without belt or cap, and when Wavell intimated that he was suspected of being in Egypt on his way to raise a revolt in Syria, he was 'distinctly aggrieved'. Wavell explained that 'the apprehensions were those of the French and Foreign Office only'.[13] Lawrence duly returned to England.

In May 1919 Queenie was able to join her husband in Egypt; in October, Nancy and Nanny Ribbands arrived with the two children, leaving Molly at home with Wavell's ageing parents. The Wavells and Bols shared the Villa Heller, a large house in Gezira, along the right bank of the Nile, owned by an Austrian. The loss of his eye meant that Wavell was no longer able to play polo, and he settled instead for tennis and golf at the Gezira Sporting Club. He and Queenie also developed the habit of enjoying an early-morning ride around the race track. Wavell's horse, Napoleon, 'a roughish ride' but with 'the heart of a lion', would jump anything 'or have a try'; Queenie usually rode a chestnut 'with good paces' but 'no courage'. This particular horse had fallen out of favour by carrying Wavell into a very muddy canal one morning when he was wearing a new pair of jodhpurs. Sunday afternoons were spent on long rides in the desert, and during the shooting season Wavell took a day off now and then to try for duck or snipe in the Delta. Archie John had his first mount while they were in Cairo, a donkey lent by an Egyptian neighbour. The family also acquired a dog, a mongrel female terrier called Susan. Wavell later recalled her contracting a misalliance – 'or probably several' – and producing 'a litter of variously coloured and shaped puppies.'[14]

Towards the end of 1919 Allenby handed over his position as Commander-in-Chief to General Sir Walter Congreve, VC, who as General Officer Commanding-in-Chief, Egypt and Palestine became Wavell's new superior. Allenby stayed on as High Commissioner, but there was no longer the daily contact he had become accustomed to enjoying. Mindful that concerns elsewhere meant the Middle East was losing its strategic importance, in an attempt to assist his career Allenby had suggested to the Army Council that Wavell should be further promoted. But the response came back that, at 36, Wavell was too young. Allenby then tried to secure Wavell's appointment to command a brigade; yet again he was deemed 'much too junior'. In early 1920 Bols was appointed Military Governor of Palestine, leaving Wavell as the most senior general staff officer in Cairo. Inevitably, the demand for employment among more senior officers on half-pay meant it was only a matter of time before Wavell was informed that his position as Chief of Staff was required by someone more senior. The children, nearly four and one, went back to England at once to stay with their grandparents at Cranborne; Wavell and Queenie returned to England in early April, and Wavell was given four months' leave. Recognizing that time was passing, he attempted to re-establish contact with some of his pre-war friends: 'I wonder where you are now and what you are doing,' he wrote to his Wykehamist friend, Stephen Phillimore, now Vicar of Seaforth in Liverpool. 'Somehow during the war I never found time to write to my friends and keep in touch with them. I know you were with the Grenadier Guards in France most of the war and got a MC and bar and I always meant to write and congratulate you and hear your news . . . If you find time, write and tell me what you are doing.'[15]

At his age, Wavell's military career could either move forward or stagnate. He was still anxious to command a battalion, but the only position available was a second-grade post as a junior instructor at the Staff College, which had reopened in May 1919. It was too much of a step down the military ladder; and so, after more than a decade's absence, having last served as a junior subaltern in India in 1908, Wavell returned to his regiment. At the end of August 1920 he sailed from Southampton in command of a mixed draft of troops bound for Antwerp on their way to join the British Army of Occupation in Germany. The 2nd Battalion, The Black Watch was stationed in some former German army barracks in the Marienburg quarter of Cologne. Wavell's friend Arthur Wauchope, who had served in the trenches and in Mesopotamia and been wounded twice, was in command. Rather than give Wavell a company, Wauchope used him to run tactical training courses and to look after the Regimental Institute; as Wavell later commented, this was the same as doing the second-in-command's work, although he was not the senior major. Despite his long absence he readapted easily to regimental life, and helped to produce *The Red Hackle*, the regimental magazine. It was during this time that he 'joined the ranks of the "Doodlers": when listening to 'Commanding Officer's orders', he amused himself by drawing ladies' hats. According to his adjutant, these 'tended to grow more ornate as the case before him grew more complex or serious.'[16]

Once more Queenie and the children followed in his wake, and Wavell moved out of barracks and into a billet: the mansion of a wealthy German cigar merchant, 'decorated after the fashion of a liner's saloon'.[17] In late January 1921 a fortnight's leave for skiing in Gstaad ended disastrously when Wavell ran into a small ravine and hurt his right knee badly. Back in Cologne, rather than make him use his knee and prescribing massage, the regimental doctor bandaged it and confined his patient to a sofa. Wavell felt his knee never fully recovered from this cosseting. Shortly afterwards the 2nd Battalion was moved to Lublintz in Silesia. Under the terms of the Treaty of Versailles, a plebiscite was to be held to determine whether Silesia should belong to the newly established republic of Poland; when fighting broke out between Germans and Poles, an Allied force was despatched to restore order. With his wounded knee, Wavell was not fit for active service, and so remained in Cologne to look after the families and the administrative details. The only other officer left behind was a young subaltern. Looking back on this time, Wavell felt that the subaltern must have hated his job, for he recognized that he was a bad invalid, and probably very 'impatient and peevish'.[18]

After six weeks Wavell was fit enough to rejoin the battalion in Lublintz and was temporarily in charge while Wauchope took command of an improvised brigade. By the middle of April the situation in Silesia had improved and The Black Watch were able to return to Cologne. Wavell was then sent back to England for a course – required to qualify for command of a unit – at the Senior Officers' school. Yet again the family packed their bags and followed. Nanny took the children to Cranborne, Wavell reported to Inkerman Barracks at Woking, and Queenie, expecting their third child, went to her parents' home in London; in July she gave birth to another girl, Felicity Ann. Wavell was not impressed by either the instructors or his fellow students at Woking; the Commandant described him in his confidential report as 'self-reliant and showing distinct character – well above the standard of officers attending this school.'[19]

In the autumn Wavell returned to Lublintz, where hostilities had once more broken out between the Germans and Poles. His old friend from the North-West Frontier, Archie Bulloch, had taken over command of the battalion in May 1921; in November he was recalled to take over the Depot at Perth, and Wavell stood in until a new commander could be appointed. The situation in which the battalion found itself was akin to active service, since the German *Freikorps* and Polish guerrillas were engaged in constant skirmishes. To make the situation more deadly, the countryside was flat and featureless but full of forests, and therefore suitable terrain for surprise attacks and ambushes – and, as Wavell recalled, the Allied forces were regarded as 'fair game' by both sides. He took charge of training, adapting the old Frontier system of using picquets, and even managed to give a lesson in guerrilla tactics: six of the regimental band were disguised as German farm labourers and put in a potato-picker's lorry from a neighbouring farm; as the lorry went past a marching column, these men 'zestfully' hurled potato 'grenades' at the 'enemy' and beat kettledrums to simulate machine-gun fire.[20]

Wavell's return to his regiment proved short-lived. At the end of December 1921 he was appointed Assistant Adjutant-General at the War Office in London. The Adjutant-General was Lieutenant-General Sir George Macdonogh, who had been Director of Military Intelligence during the war.[21] As Wavell was to learn, the Adjutant-General was responsible not only for finding the number of men estimated by the General Staff as necessary for the Army, but also for obtaining from the Treasury the money to pay them. Professionally, Wavell was at a crossroads. After four years as a brevet lieutenant-colonel his promotion to full colonel in June 1921 was automatic, but took him off the regimental list and onto the general list; he therefore had to give up his long-cherished ambition of commanding a battalion. If no job were immediately available, he would go on half-pay. As things stood, Wavell felt he was better off accepting the staff grade appointment, which while it lasted would increase his pay and give him some domestic stability. Out of the twenty years since he had joined The Black Watch and set sail for South Africa, he had spent only eight with the regiment: 'Not a very good regimental record,' he later commented. 'But I think I can safely say that my heart has always been with the Regiment, and that I have ever since done all that I could to further its interests.'[22]

When Wavell took up his new appointment, the Army's main concern was still demobilization. By the end of 1920, the three and a half million men in uniform at the time of the Armistice had been reduced to 370,000. In 1922 the 'Geddes Axe' – wielded by the Rt Hon. Sir Eric Geddes – reduced the number still further. Geddes was appointed by the Chancellor of the Exchequer to chair a committee to advise on questions of national expenditure, and his suggestions fell hardest on the Army. The Royal Navy always retained its prestige as the 'senior service', and the Royal Air Force still had a novelty value, but the Army was increasingly hailed as the 'Cinderella service', short of men, money and equipment.[23] In peacetime, the Army Annual Act passed by Parliament guaranteed the army's pay for another year. If more officers were registered than had been authorized, they could not be paid unless further authorization was granted by Parliament. There was also the question of the Army's reorganization for the future, if and when another conflict arose. As the General Staff pushed for more men and more money in the name of modernization, the Treasury was pulling in the opposite direction, trying to cut costs now that the war was over.

Wavell's immediate superior, the director of Recruiting and Organization, was Ivo Vesey, the Staff College friend he had so admired. According to Vesey, Wavell always thought very carefully at conferences before he gave his views, which were 'very sound ones after everyone else had uttered'.[24] While admitting its necessity, Wavell found deskwork uninspiring compared with his previously active life, but his contemporaries acknowledged his industry: 'Hard working, thorough and painstaking, he showed himself to be an outstanding "A" staff officer in what must often have seemed to him dull routine work.' His reports and memoranda were 'clear, concise and to the point'.[25] In later life Wavell was able to recognize the benefits of a full understanding of the financial control exercised by the Treasury over the Army.

Despite rising unemployment, spreading pacifist sentiment and a period of economic retrenchment, the early 1920s were 'roaring'. No one then talked about 'the First World War', of course: it was 'the Great War', the like of which they hoped never to experience again. The Wavells once more settled into a new home in England at 5 Hobart Place near Victoria Station. Living in central London meant that Wavell had to rely for exercise on a weekly game of golf at the Sandy Lodge Golf Club in Middlesex. On occasion he went to Cranborne to visit his parents, especially during the shooting season, and he and Queenie enjoyed the races. Of those friends who had survived the war, he remained in touch with Amyas Borton, now also a colonel. Borton was shortly to be married and, in mid January 1923 Wavell went to stay with him at his parents' home at Cheveney in Kent. He left a parody of the poem 'The Perfect Guest' 'rather pointedly' inserted in the Visitors' Book. Wavell's poem was called 'The Imperfect Guest':

> He left his work – without a sigh,
> He left his ailing babes to cry,
> He left his wife to mind the lot
> (Though she'd been asked, and he had not),
> Arrived at half-past ten at night,
> Demanding food and drinks and light,
> Came down to breakfast late, at ten,
> And ate enough for seven men.
> Then sallied forth with gun and cartridges
> To hunt his host's most treasured partridges,
> And as they passed him in full sail
> Discharged his piece without avail,
> (Tickling them only in the tail).
> Spent Sunday like the worst agnostic
> Yet failed to solve the week's Acrostic.
> The way he gorged at every meal
> Made even stolid Banshee squeal.
> The bathroom weigh-machine by bounds
> Recorded his increasing pounds.
> He went back, unashamed, to Town.
> Will they again invite him down?

A postscript noted that: 'He shot with fierce but fruitless vim, / Yet took two brace away with him.' Banshee was the Bortons' dog.[26]

Queenie was expecting their fourth child, and the day after their eighth wedding anniversary, on 23 April 1923, a third daughter, Joan Patricia Quirk, was born. She shared her birthday with Allenby, now aged 62, who was still in Cairo. In May Wavell celebrated his fortieth birthday and Archie John his seventh. He was in his last year of primary school at Gibbs in Kensington; the following year he would follow in his father's footsteps to Summer Fields. But in the wake of all the birthday celebrations came mourning. On 17 May Wavell's last surviving aunt, Betsy, died. She had outlived her husband by two years, both saddened in their old age by the loss of their son Reginald in the war. Elizabeth Florence's death meant that of the ten children fathered by Arthur Goodall Wavell, only one remained: Wavell's father, Archibald Graham.

After eighteen months in the Adjutant-General's department, in July 1923 Wavell was transferred back to the General Staff as a GSO1 at the War Office. Yet again he was working under Jock Burnett-Stuart, who had been appointed Director of Military Operations and Intelligence (MOI). 'Jock was as brilliant as ever, and as caustic, very easy to serve, difficult for his superiors to control.'[27] When Burnett-Stuart returned from the Lausanne Conference which finally settled the terms of peace with Turkey, he found one of Wavell's poetic offerings on his desk, entitled 'From Nathaniel in Wonderland':

> I sent a message to the Turk,
> I said 'To sign you cannot shirk'.
> The Turk replied, 'Go easy, Nat,
> You mustn't hurry us like that.'
> I said, 'We cannot leave it so,
> The answer must be "Yes or No"' . . .
> I tried until my head went fut
> To make them sign the Treaty, BUT ——.[28]

After reading the poem, Burnett-Stuart observed that there could not have been a better description of what had happened at the conference.[29] Turkey had finally agreed to surrender its claims to all non-Turkish territories of the former Ottoman Empire, leaving the question of Mosul to be resolved by further negotiations. Wavell found his work more interesting than previously, but he was at the War Office during a 'depressing period' of the Army's life and so the fruits of his labours were 'disheartening'. The prevailing mood in Government was that there was no need to prepare for another war for at least the next ten years, and anti-war feeling was reinforced by the growing influence of the Labour Party which briefly held office in 1924 with the pacifist Scottish politician Ramsay MacDonald as Prime Minister of a minority Labour Government. As well as plans for operations for which there were no forces available, Wavell found himself working on schemes for the redistribution of the Army, when – with a complement which was less that at the outbreak of the war in 1914 – there was 'hardly any' Army to redistribute.[30] Even when a Conservative Government under Stanley Baldwin replaced Labour at the end of 1924, no determined action to re-arm was taken. Winston Churchill became Chancellor of the Exchequer but he too subscribed to the belief that defence planning should proceed on the assumption that there would be no major war for ten years. Since funds were short, the three services scrambled indecorously for what money there was.

The man entrusted with pushing forward the interests of the Army was General the Earl of Cavan, currently Chief of the Imperial General Staff and former Commander-in-Chief at Aldershot: despite four years' experience in the European war he was far less assertive than either Lord Beatty at the Admiralty or Lord Trenchard at the Air Ministry.[31] Trenchard argued that the RAF could be more effective than the Army in the defence of Britain's imperial interests in Iraq and Palestine, the North-West Frontier of India and Singapore, and since one of Wavell's tasks was responsibility for Coastal Defence, the debate about the defence of Singapore was particularly relevant. 'There was a hot controversy between the RAF, which claimed to be able to defend Singapore with torpedo-bombers alone, and the Navy and the Army, who challenged them to prove their case.'[32] In this instance, Cavan and Beatty's views prevailed.[33] Big guns were installed and provisions to improve the naval base were agreed. Twenty years later Wavell himself was in supreme command, and the respective claims of the three services were put to the test.

Wavell's appointment at the War Office officially ended in December 1925 but he did not leave until after his successor had arrived in early 1926. He then spent nearly nine months on half-pay, which in reality meant a reduction of his salary by nearly two-thirds, to less than a retirement pension. Despite the loss of income, Wavell saw the advantages of this break. 'The ordinary peacetime routine is killing. I should like to see promising officers given a year or so of some civil employment, or travel, at some period in their career.'[34] And, even before he left the War Office, Wavell himself was developing another string to his bow: he had accepted an offer to write an article on the Palestine operations in the Great War for the new edition of the *Encylopaedia Britannica*. The military adviser was Captain Basil Liddell Hart, wounded in the war and invalided out of the Army in 1924, who was already enjoying a reputation as an expert military historian.[35] Liddell Hart was delighted with Wavell's contribution: 'I cannot refrain from a note of congratulation – it combines literary style with clearness and simplicity, perfectly easy to follow and yet of value to military as well as general readers.'[36] The article was, he went on, exactly what he would like all contributions to be. Wavell, obviously pleased, responded immediately: 'Praise from a military writer of your calibre is indeed worth having and gratifying to a novice like myself.' He then touched on his ideas of generalship, a subject that continued to exercise his mind for the rest of his life: 'As you know, victories are often, one might almost say usually, won by the general who has the instinct and courage to realize when the *correct* military solution is the wrong one and the risk should be taken.'[37] As a useful supplement to his income, Wavell then undertook other writing projects: book reviews in *The Times* and the *Times Literary Supplement* and for the *Army Quarterly*. He also corrected Army examination papers.

Between his work and his writing, Wavell was spending a considerable amount of time thinking about the way the Army was going to have to develop. He was personally not in favour of disarmament, and though he was still too junior to influence decision-making, he gave an early warning against complacency when he indicated that new ideas in military science might come from Germany. 'Defeat is a more fertile mother of reforms than victory,' he noted, pointing out that even a strong nation could be speedily struck down if not prepared.[38] In 'War and the Prophets', which came to be regarded as one of the most visionary articles he produced during this period, he set out his thoughts, endorsing the views of Liddell Hart and of Colonel 'Boney' Fuller, another revolutionary thinker and keen advocate of tanks.[39] Like the prolific military writer, the German General Hans von Seeckt, these men were suggesting that future warfare would be decided by superiority in mobile mechanized forces and machine production. As Wavell was himself coming to realize: 'Armies must, in the nature of things, change and develop very slowly during peace, since they have always to be ready for action, and can never discard a weapon, an organization or a tactical doctrine till a new one has been proved by long and careful experiment.' At the same time, it was of little use 'to build a tank that is too heavy or large to pass over the normal bridge or along the normal road or street'. Looking to the future, he predicted that 'the mobility of practically the whole nation and its resources' would begin at once. Therefore soldiers as well as statesmen would have to study carefully the civil organization of their countries, the morale of the average citizen and the needs of home defence. In retrospect, Wavell thought his essay was 'not at all a bad forecast of the War', considering the date – 1926 – it was written. He submitted it in an essay competition, but it was rejected as being 'too futuristic'[40] or, as Liddell Hart recalled, 'too advanced and visionary for practical purposes'.[41] It was later published in the November 1930 edition of journal of the Royal United Services Institute, of which his old Staff College friend Herman de Watteville, another survivor of the European war, had become assistant military editor. The Royal United Service Institution[42] subsequently provided another outlet for Wavell's talents. He had also embarked on another, bigger project, a contribution to a series of studies, *Campaigns and their Lessons*, edited by Major-General Sir Charles Callwell for the publisher Constable. Once again he had been requested to write on the Palestine Campaigns.

Throughout the 1920s Wavell's parents continued to live at Cranborne Lodge in Dorset, although the old General – now over eighty – had become both rather lame and very deaf. While he was on half-pay it suited

Wavell to stay with his parents, so he sold the lease of Hobart Place, stored their furniture and left London. For a brief time the Wavell children, aged nine, seven, four and two, led a country existence. Mary Eden, then also aged nine, remembered frequent picnics with them and the Salisbury children at Mudeford, near Christchurch; all the children, shepherded by their nannies, were smartly dressed in smocks, with hats to protect them from the sun. Mary and Archie John also rode their ponies together. At Cranborne, the top floor was reserved for the children. Mary recalled that even though they were so young, they used to play bridge, with Joan, the youngest, as 'dummy'.[43] It was a peaceful if unexciting time for the family, remote from the prevailing 'class war' which came to a head with the nine-day General Strike in May 1926.

Among the friends Wavell saw in Dorset was T.E. Lawrence. Feeling self-conscious about his fame as 'Lawrence of Arabia', in 1922 he had joined the Royal Air Force as John Hume Ross; he later took the name of Shaw and spent more than two years with the Tank Corps at Bovington, from where he would arrive at Cranborne, unheralded, on his outsize motor cycle. Wavell was impressed by Lawrence's intellect; as he later wrote, 'one felt always when he departed that one had wasted one's opportunities: with so keen and intelligent a mind one should have discussed weighty and serious problems. And one had spent the hours of his visits in talk of casual every day matters, amused and charmed by his fresh outlook and shrewd comments on people and things.'[44]

Lillie Wavell had for long been little better than an invalid, crippled with arthritis, and for some time not really 'sensible'. In later life Wavell described her as a woman of 'no character and little understanding' and confessed that he never really had 'much affection' for her. In view of her suffering he considered his mother's death on 24 June 1926 a 'happy release' for her as well as his father and sisters. On the night before the funeral the old General asked if someone would watch over her coffin in the village church of St Mary and St Bartholomew in Cranborne; Queenie, who had been fond of her mother-in-law, volunteered. She remained by the coffin all night, lit by a single gas-jet; at daybreak, Wavell took her place.[45] Eliza Bull Wavell was buried in the graveyard of the church. After her death the General moved from Cranborne to Hightown, near Ringwood on the edge of the New Forest. The house was called Little Somborne after Little Somborne House, near Stockbridge, where he had lived as a child. Nancy and Molly, now in their forties, continued to live with their father. Over the next decade, the General watched as his son rose in the ranks, rivalling both his own achievements and those of his father, that soldier of fortune, Arthur Goodall.

7

Manoeuvres

*L'homme est l'instrument premier du Combat: étudions donc l'homme dans
le combat, car c'est lui qui fait le réel.*   Ardant du Picq[1]

AFTER A SOMEWHAT 'lean' period on half-pay throughout most of
1926, Wavell's next appointment was as a GSO1 to the 3rd Infantry
Division at Bulford Camp on Salisbury Plain. For the third time in his military career he found himself serving under Jock Burnett-Stuart, a chief
who could not have been 'more to my liking'.[2] Soon after Christmas
Wavell and his family moved to the village of Brigmerston near
Durrington, overlooking the rolling hills and green fields of the Avon
valley. He later described Brigmerston Farm House as 'the first, the small-
est and the happiest of our official residences'. It had 'no pretension to distinction or beauty' but was 'pleasant and comfortable like a buxom country
lass'. There were stables for the horses and ponies, a paddock, and a tennis
court. They added a saddle-room and accommodation for a groom,
Peacock. Ever alive to the fascination of words, Wavell noted happily that
Peacock married their cook and their daughter was named Gloria: 'I have
been looking ever since for Hollywood to advertise Gloria Peacock as a
film star – the name seems to demand it.'[3]

The three and a half years Wavell spent on Salisbury Plain were among
his happiest in the Army. Every morning he cantered to his office across the
fields, accompanied by his hound puppies. These he once confined to a
small room where back files (or 'p.p.' – previous papers) were kept: when
he went to release them, he found that 'hardly a file was intact'. From his
own point of view 'no great harm was done, for a hound puppy can digest
practically anything' – but the head clerk was almost in tears. Luckily
Burnett-Stuart was amused, and delighted in telling his superiors that he
could not reply to certain correspondence because it had been 'eaten by the
GSO1's hound puppies'.[4] The Wavells had also acquired a spaniel called
Peter, a good 'golf dog' who never got in the way but was capable of

finding any lost ball. His only embarrassing habit was to retrieve any ball he saw in a bunker, having 'the correct instinct' that his master must not have meant it to be there.[5]

Wavell's work was more challenging than it appeared. Earlier in the year the ageing Earl of Cavan had been replaced as Chief of the Imperial General Staff by General Sir George Milne; he, having become interested in restoring mobility to land warfare, authorized the formation of the first-ever experimental 'mechanized' force, under Burnett-Stuart's command. This mechanized force was to consist of armoured cars, light and medium tanks and mechanized artillery, engineer and supply units, as well as one fighter and one reconnaissance squadron of the Royal Air Force (formed in 1919 from the Royal Flying Corps and the Royal Naval Air Division). The man appointed to command the experimental force was R.J. Collins, Colonel Commandant of the 7th Infantry Brigade and former Director of Military Training in India.[6] While Collins struggled to make sense of the administrative problems relating to a force utilizing such a wide variety of vehicles, Wavell worked with Burnett-Stuart on devising tactical exercises, as well as undertaking the normal duties of a chief of staff. In hindsight, Burnett-Stuart recollected an occasional and surprising lack of focus: Wavell 'wouldn't work if he could get someone else to do it for him – particularly me. Idle is not exactly the word for him – because he was always absorbing something – but he would always put off setting exercises for divisional manoeuvres.'[7]

Wavell was certainly developing his career as a military historian. Although he claimed not to have any expert knowledge 'of any particular branch of the military art',[8] he continued to write articles for the *Encylopaedia Britannica* under Liddell Hart as Military Editor. His contributions included articles on the Army and the campaigns in Russia during 1914–18, and, as always, his attention to detail was meticulous. He once had occasion to complain to Liddell Hart that a bibliography had been added at the end of his contribution, over his initials, which included works he had either never heard of or knew to be misleading, and omitted the 'best and authoritative' accounts; he suggested quite stiffly 'that the writer of the article might be given a chance to compose his own bibliography'.[9] Wavell's other major literary enterprise was his book about the 1916–17 Palestine Campaigns, which he dedicated to his father. In the final chapter, 'Lessons of the Campaigns', he examined themes to which he was to return time and again: the value of mobility, training, and the power of surprise, all of which he believed would restore to the infantry the offensive power lost during so much of the Great War. The book was published to immediate praise from Liddell Hart: 'This is one of the best military histories of a campaign that has been written in English. It is admirably clear, lightened by frequent "literary" touches, and contrives to give an extraordinary amount of details and facts for study without tiring the reader.'[10] As a 'young author', Wavell was however dissatisfied with the financial rewards. By the terms of his contract with the publishers, John Constable & Co., he had agreed to make over all the rights to them for a flat fee of £70. By the time he had paid for typewriting and given away copies to all relatives 'who expected them', his profit was less than £50. In later life he considered that he had been a 'fool' to sign the contract, but also that it was 'sharp practice' for a reputable firm like Constable to present him with a contract, assuring him that it was their 'usual' one. 'Q[ueenie],' he said, was 'more practical', and would undoubtedly have made a better deal.[11]

On 27 November 1928, after two years' experimentation, the Secretary of State for War, Sir Laming Worthington-Evans, announced that the 'armoured force' was to be disbanded so that the experiment 'might' be extended in an alternative way – that is, by reinforcing the infantry divisions with armoured machine-gun carriers, thereby creating a 'mixed' brigade. Liddell Hart, invited by Wavell to see the opening exercise, later noted that 'the armoured force had succeeded too well in inducing depression among the troops of the older arms, and the General Staff felt that something must be done to restore their confidence and interest.'[12] At the annual Staff Conference at Camberley in the New Year of 1929, Wavell presented a report in which he highlighted the disparity between an infantry division able to move at two and a half miles an hour when challenged by an armoured force travelling at four times that speed.[13] He also urged the need for improved communications, to enable a new armoured force to operate on as wide a front as possible. Above all, as Wavell later recalled, 'the armoured force had made people think and it was certainly valuable experience to have been so closely connected with it'.[14]

At home in Brigmerston, as Jack Collins observed, Wavell enjoyed his life as a family man. Here he lost his normal tongue-tied manner and became the 'life and soul of the party'.[15] Collins's daughter Ann remembered Wavell as always being kind to young people 'and not intimidating'.[16] Queenie's father had died in 1928 but the General lived on with Wavell's sisters in Ringwood, still able to play bridge and attend meetings. T.E. Lawrence continued to visit, as ever 'witty and enlightening on any subject that was raised' and always 'at his ease, simple, sympathetic, and unaffected'.[17] Archie John was now in his last year at Summer Fields, and in the summer Wavell accompanied him to Winchester to sit for a scholarship.

'He was not very bookish in those days, and in fact hardly ever read,' Wavell later recalled. As they were waiting for his interview with the Headmaster, they noticed schoolmasters coaching other boys on books they planned to say they had read. 'Archie John asked me what he was to say if asked about his reading. I told him to tell the truth and not pretend that he had read books which he had not.' Wavell later learned that when asked what he read, Archie John had replied that he did not read much. When questioned further he admitted to reading the cricket scores, and the 'occasional' Edgar Wallace; whereupon the Headmaster laughed, remarking that 'it was probably the first really honest answer he had had that morning'.[18] Archie John failed to win a scholarship, but was awarded a Headmaster's Nomination and started at Winchester in the autumn of 1929.

Then early in 1930 the Wavell family's mildly bucolic existence centred on ponies and hound puppies was disrupted when, after nearly four years on the Plain, Wavell was told that he had been nominated to command a brigade. Aged 47, he was promoted to the rank of brigadier. The transition from a staff appointment to command turned him into 'a new man': 'There was to be no more talk of lack of interest, of aloofness, even of lethargy at times.'[19]

At the end of June 1930 Wavell left Brigmerston Farm House to take command of the 6th Infantry Brigade in the 2nd Infantry Division in the Aldershot Command, quartered at Blackdown, a barrack town built on a ridge to the east of Aldershot. The family's next home was a pseudo-Tudor villa, Blackdown House, on the outskirts of Aldershot at Deepcut Camp. Although they could still 'slip onto horses and ponies every morning through the garden into open country', for Wavell it was a 'derurulization' and 'suburbanization'. His office was within walking distance – gone were those enjoyable five- or six-mile rides with his hound puppies. Yet in this new environment there was an opportunity for Wavell to make his mark: 'At Aldershot I should have very critical eyes on me, and I knew that the ability to command of one who had been on the staff for so long would be under close test.' Looking back on his performance later, however, he believed that the responsibility 'turned' him in on himself: 'It is certain anyway that I have never been so carefree or able to enjoy life as much since leaving Brigmerston.'[20]

For the first time Wavell found himself in a position of comparative independence, answerable only to his divisional commander, Major-General Henry Jackson, recently home from India where he had served as Director of Military Training at the Army Headquarters.[21] Years later,

Wavell told Jackson that he believed the best job a soldier could have was the command of a brigade. The 6th Infantry Brigade was part of I Corps, one of the original corps of the BEF, and therefore enjoyed special prestige. Captain Eric Dorman-Smith of The Northumberland Fusiliers, called 'Chink' because with a narrow head and pointed ears he was said to resemble the regimental emblem, the Chinkara antelope, joined Wavell as brigade-major in early 1931; their paths had crossed in the Great War, when Dorman-Smith was a subaltern.[22] Wavell was always interested in the broader aspects of training, and found Chink 'invaluable . . . I could control his ideas and sort out the good from the bad and keep him on practical lines.'[23] At Aldershot the two men worked on a number of imaginative schemes. 'The devising was primarily that of Dorman-Smith,' noted Liddell Hart, 'and Wavell showed his responsiveness not only in adopting them but in carrying them out.'[24] Much to Wavell's surprise, he discovered that he was good at both the practical and the theoretical sides of his new job. 'I started without much confidence in my capacity for command, and was not sure that I should make a success of it. I soon found to my relief that I could make up my mind and act quickly in handling my brigade, and could give orders without hesitation, not only in the field but in the various administrative problems.'[25] His manner also made him popular. 'At Blackdown, Archie for all his remoteness of speech was everybody's friend,' recollected Dorman-Smith. 'He especially liked to play golf with his subalterns in the several battalions; he seemed to know everybody . . . he never fussed and preferred to let things ride where he could and yet was always there when needed. He'd turn up quietly, stand by without interfering and then perhaps go off, having said only "Very well".'[26]

Wavell's interest in the mechanization of the Army stood him in good stead when the 6th Infantry Brigade was chosen to take part in a number of experiments, becoming a 'mechanized' infantry brigade by the addition of a light tank battalion.[27] Wavell did not personally handle tanks, but he watched how they were used, advising on concentration and deployment. He also suggested, through demonstration, that the existing Army divisions were too large, and should be replaced by smaller, more mobile formations. To make the point, he weighed down his division with all the equipment and transport prescribed by army regulations, with the result that it extended for fifteen miles and blocked traffic.

When possible, Wavell also took it upon himself to broaden the horizons of the ordinary – less ambitious – officer who might not aspire to Staff College and whose military experience would therefore be limited to the regiment. With this in mind, at the end of October 1931 he took about forty men on a tour of the Mons, Marne and Aisne battlefields so that they could see for themselves the terrain which had cost so many lives. Another novel experience for the 'barrack-bound majors', as they were known, was the visits he organized to the newly opened Metropolitan Police College, the Port of London Authority, and the headquarters of the rudimentary Air Defence of Great Britain. By the second year of his command, Wavell's performance was becoming more widely recognized. Kenneth Buchanan, commander of the 2nd Brigade, remembered him as 'one of the outstanding trainers of troops, [who] introduced a humour and liveliness which were greatly appreciated. I used to meet many of Wavell's officers, and they were all of one voice, that they were learning something all the time from him.'[28]

As at Salisbury, Wavell also used his time at Aldershot to read and to write. In Liddell Hart he had found a ready sounding-board, and the two continued their discursive correspondence. Asked to prepare reading lists for Staff College candidates, Wavell enlisted Liddell Hart's help; his aim, he said, was to include books which were personal and human, not 'horrid little cram books'.[29] Wavell also shared aspects of his life at Aldershot with Liddell Hart. 'It's a difficult job this modernization of infantry,' he confided in May 1932, 'especially in our army – I think infantry are beginning to recover a bit from the shell-shock and machine-gun paralysis of the war.'[30] From his vantage point Liddell Hart watched the progress of Wavell's career. He had already noted Wavell's growing reputation as 'an original thinker'; the exercises he carried out formed part of his appeal. Dorman-Smith believed that Wavell came into his own because he was working with other original thinkers, and that his role was that of 'the catalytic agent'. 'Nothing short of a tactical revolution and a military renaissance developed from the Blackdown experiments of 1932,' he later noted.[31] But Wavell's background was still not widely known beyond his inner circle and when he was appointed an aide-de-camp to King George V in 1932, a columnist described him as 'a good-looking Scot of sturdy build and charming manners' with a fine war record, adding that 'few men know the Near East as well as he does.'[32] The appointment was largely honorific but entitled Wavell to wear the Royal Cipher on each epaulette and, on ceremonial occasions, aiguillettes on the right shoulder.

Of all the exercises Wavell and Dorman-Smith devised for the 6th Infantry Brigade at Aldershot, the *pièce de résistance* was carried out in August 1932. The objective was to accustom soldiers to think and act quickly during a succession of unexpected and surprising circumstances, no matter whether or not they were tired and confused or what they did or did not know. Presented by 'The Blackdown and Deepcut Strollers', the exercise was billed as 'a stirring Drama of Love and War in Four Acts, entitled *Araminta of Antelopia* or *The Non-Stop Princess*'. A fictitious synopsis set out the relations between the four 'small, independent and quite undemocratic' states of Equestria, Deepdown, Antelopia and Subsilvania, together with the dynastic matrimonial arrangements of Princess Araminta, the beautiful daughter of the reigning Archduke of Antelopia, 'a proud but peppery father'. Araminta, 'a slender slip of a gazelle', was represented by a life-size doll. Wearing a long coat and two-piece suit, complete with hat, gloves and handbag (acquired by Queenie and Dorman-Smith's wife Estelle from the newly opened shop Marks and Spencer), the Princess reviewed the troops in a baby Austin motor-car, accompanied by an ADC.[33] The last day's fighting involved the combined forces of Antelopia, Deepdown and Subsilvania – the 6th Infantry Brigade – in an attempt to drive out the Equestrian forces. The whole exercise, said Wavell, interested the troops and 'kept them well on their toes' for four days.[34] As recollected by Dorman-Smith, it was 'a tremendous romp'. Courtesy of the pilots of No. 4 Squadron, RAF, 'Archie and I took to the air and dive-bombed parts of the Brigade in bivouac with flour-bags. Typical of Archie . . .'[35]

In hindsight, Wavell attributed his successes in the training exercises to the fact that he was using more 'cunning'. 'My opponents, and indeed every other commander, kept a large proportion of their available force as a reserve, in attack or defence. I normally deployed the whole of my force in attack, on a wide front. My argument was that a battalion a mile or two away to the flank was just as handy as a reserve as if it was a mile or two behind, and usually much better placed to come in on the enemy's flank. And the enemy was kept guessing where I should concentrate and was likely to become dispersed.'[36] As Dorman-Smith observed, Wavell usually 'beat' his fellow brigadiers before they had committed all their forces.[37] During the exercises, rather than remain in headquarters, Wavell invariably visited his commanders to gain an appreciation of the situation at first hand. He also made use of a team of specially trained liaison officers and, he believed, paid greater attention to intelligence-gathering than the other commanders, 'both in the matter of obtaining information and in getting across false information to the enemy'.[38]

Wavell was also emerging as a lecturer respected by officers in the Aldershot Command who were applying to Staff College. If he was lacking in charisma before an audience, Wavell managed to hold his hearers' attention because of what he was saying, whether it was urging the value of a proper study of military history, or discussing methods for training, the theme of a lecture delivered to students at the Staff College at Camberley in December 1932. In February 1933 he delivered the same address – in shortened form – to a wider audience at the RUSI in Whitehall. As always, his aim was to get away 'from the pedantry and dullness of the barrack-square and to train for war almost as a sport.' He started by what, to the casual listener, might almost appear to be hair-splitting: 'I will begin by emphasizing the words "for war", not "for *a* war" . . . in training I hold that it is a positive advantage to have to train simply "for war" and that training for "*a* war" is a positive danger. Because the war you train for never happens; it certainly did not either for the French or ourselves in 1914.' In contrast to an earlier definition of a good soldier as being an 'athlete, stalker, marksman', Wavell introduced a lowlier note: 'the qualities of a successful poacher, cat burglar and gunman would content me.' Expressing sentiments which possibly shocked the more conservative of his listeners, he proceeded to explain the importance of training for the unexpected: 'However wrong things may go on exercises and manoeuvres, and however hopeless a muddle they may seem to be, remember that war is always a far worse muddle than anything that can be produced in peace. So that straightening out muddles is really the best possible practice in training for war; also, if you keep your head and temper, the most hopeless-looking muddle has a marvellous way of sorting itself out – both in war and in peace.'[39] Liddell Hart, who was in the audience, was delighted to find 'how closely our views coincided'. But he was disappointed when the 'arch-conservative' General Harry Knox, former Director of Military Training at the War Office, expressed his 'strong disagreement' with the views expressed and Wavell back-pedalled: he might be thinking along original lines, but he still felt it important publicly to defer to his senior officer's greater experience and knowledge.[40]

On 16 October 1933, at the age of 50, Wavell was promoted to the rank of major-general. He could stay on as a brigade commander until the New Year, then would have to go on half-pay again until he was given an appointment appropriate to his new rank. Of his time at Aldershot he recalled that 'I had certainly worked harder than on the Plain, had much less leisure and a great deal more responsibility. I became in fact a much more serious soldier than ever before.'[41] Promotion also meant giving up their quarters, Blackdown House. The usual inventory was taken before they 'marched out', and one bolster, one fish-kettle, and nine black coal scuttles were found to be missing. Wavell knew very well that Queenie had appropriated the bolster, covered it in brocade and given it away as a wedding present 'at short notice' two years previously; and he surmised that the fish-kettle had probably been used to boil bran-mashes for the stable; but he was not prepared to admit that they had made away with *nine* coal scuttles – at a cost of 27*s*. 3*d*. each. His correspondence about them with the War Office continued throughout 1934, during the course of which he went off to the Middle East and the relevant letters got lost, leading him to recall some early advice: 'If you can keep correspondence circulating long enough you can get away with almost anything.'[42]

Wavell spent more than a year on half-pay. For a while he and his family settled into a house in Camberley, shared with Ivo Vesey, his wife Geraldine and their two sons. Vesey was also on half-pay, having just finished his four-year appointment as Director of Staff Duties at the War Office, and he and Wavell played 'a good deal' of golf. Hunting was too expensive and had to be abandoned, but the girls kept their ponies. To Wavell's delight Archie John – now a tall, lanky, red-haired boy – having entered Winchester as an avowed non-reader, had returned home one holiday with books on history, sociology, and other 'hard matters': civics, politics, economics. The transformation was due to the Assistant Master, Walter Oakeshott, who had come to Winchester in 1931. Henceforward father and son shared their literary interests. Wavell had already put Archie John's name down for a college at Cambridge, with a view to giving him a broader education than if he went to Sandhurst. But the old General was insistent that his grandson should join the army and, as Ivo Vesey – a witness to the discussions – recollected, 'grandpa's word was law'.[43] During this period Wavell supplemented his finances by agreeing to rewrite Volume II of the *Field Service Regulations* – the main text book of the British Army, on which it trains for war. 'A very interesting job,' he wrote to Liddell Hart, 'but I expect that you will be disappointed with the results.'[44] In response, Liddell Hart sympathized with the constraints suffered by 'official' authors. Jack Collins, who saw the first draft, noted that 'it was attractive to read, alive, picturesque and would have been far less stodgy and more interesting reading than the bowdlerized version which was all that a staid General Staff were in the end prepared to father.'[45]

In April 1934 Wavell was chosen to take charge of a Middle East reconnaissance tour. Burnett-Stuart had been appointed GOC, British Troops in Egypt, and among his concerns was the safety of the airfields on the Indian air route, particularly at Habbaniya in Iraq. Experience had shown that the best way of reinforcing the small number of troops that might be available to protect the airfield was with a mobile column from Egypt, which would travel across the desert from Palestine. With Wavell in charge, a small party was sent to reconnoitre the most likely route from Haifa to Baghdad. Arthur Wauchope, knighted and promoted to general, was currently serving as High Commissioner for Palestine and Transjordan. After a week with Wauchope at Government House on the Mount of Olives, Wavell set out on the recce, leaving Queenie and Archie John to enjoy Wauchope's hospitality, the girls having stayed at home in the care of Nanny and Queenie's mother. The route Wavell and his companions took for the most part followed the oil pipeline then under construction from Palestine to Iraq. Lawrence Pendred, as Staff Officer, Intelligence, Transjordan and Palestine, was detailed to assist them, and later described Wavell's visit as the 'highlight' of his five-year tour. As they flew from Jerusalem to Haifa, Pendred drew Wavell's attention to the battleground over which Allenby had fought. Wavell made no comment, but Pendred nevertheless considered 'it was a great moment!' From Haifa, the recce started at the Yarmuk valley. 'Wavell had to concentrate hard on his driving, especially on the old route which was cut up by camel tracks and strewn with lava. His endurance was extraordinary. At the day's end, we others were flaked out, but would find him in his tent working away at his notes or reading poetry.'[46] The ten-day recce led Wavell and his companions to realize, as had Allenby before them, that the main obstacle was the rift of the Jordan valley, lying a thousand feet below sea level, and the danger of being delayed by rainstorms which could turn the desert into a swamp.[47]

Another break came at the beginning of December, when Wavell attended a three-week staff course in France at the École des Maréchaux (so-called on the assumption that all those who attended it were of sufficient calibre to become 'Marshals'). He took with him Liddell Hart's latest book, *The Ghost of Napoleon*, which he wanted to read 'in the appropriate atmosphere'.[48] Usually one British officer was invited each year to attend the course, cumbersomely titled 'Cycle d'Information des Généraux et des Colonels', but in 1934 the Director of Military Intelligence John Dill – Wavell's Sandhurst contemporary – had got permission for three major-generals to attend – Wavell, James Marshall-Cornwall and Bernard Freyberg. Both Wavell's companions had a certain distinction: Marshall-Cornwall had been Military Attaché in four European countries in four years and spoke fluent French, while Bernard Freyberg had won the VC in the Great War.[49] Dill wanted to verify reports from the British Military Attaché in Paris regarding the high standard of training and efficiency of the French Army. With their wives and 16-year-old Pamela Wavell the British contingent stayed at the Hôtel Majestic in the Avenue Kléber. 'Each morning we drove out to Versailles', recorded Marshall-Cornwall, 'to attend the lectures and take part in the exercises in the open country.' In the evenings the three visitors discussed their impressions. They were generally unanimous that the much-vaunted efficiency of the French General Staff did not live up to expectations, and that their attitude smacked of 1916 static warfare. No manoeuvres were envisaged in a future war, and it was expected that the division would attack on a narrow front supported by a mass of artillery. 'It was not only a reversion to the methods of 1914–18, it was Napoleon's tactical folly at Waterloo all over again.'[50]

By the end of the course the British had concluded that, far from being 'leaders in military doctrine', the French had made no progress since the end of the Great War. 'They had, for instance, no conception of exploiting the ability of armoured divisions in tactical manoeuvre,' Marshall-Cornwall later noted.[51] To their surprise, nor were the three asked anything about the British Army, its methods or equipment: 'If they had asked our opinion at times it would have been of value from their point of view, especially upon all questions affecting the employment of tanks.'[52] The climax of their stay was a luncheon at Les Invalides hosted by the Military Governor of Paris, General Gouraud, a distinguished veteran of the Great War, who amused them with his description of the various arms of the military: 'The general gives an order to the infantryman. The infantryman, being rather stupid, does not well understand what the general wants, but goes out and engages the enemy. The general gives an order to the artilleryman. The artilleryman understands it perfectly, but being much cleverer than the general goes and does something quite different. The general gives an order to the cavalryman. The cavalryman smiles politely and goes off to water and feed his horses.' As Wavell later recollected, they all assured Gouraud that 'things were arranged differently in the British Army!'[53]

After this visit, Wavell further discussed the theory of war with Liddell Hart. 'Now for some argument and criticism,' he wrote on 5 January, 'which I know you will welcome. First of all, is there any true "theory" of war, and isn't a study of theory really rather dangerous than otherwise for the soldier?' He then developed his theme, 'that those who study theory too much become obsessed with some particular theory which they try to apply to every situation'. Wavell was already thinking along lines which he continued to explore for the rest of his life: 'There is nothing fixed in war, except a few elementary rules of common sense, and study of history should be directed not to evolving any theory or formula, but to observing what strange situations arise in war, what varying problems face a commander, how all rules may sometimes be broken with successful results, and especially the influence of human nature and the moral factor.' He also expounded his views on alternative plans of battle; while acknowledging the value of alternatives, he came down on the side of having only one plan and putting all one's weight behind it; in support of his argument, he quoted Mark Twain: 'The fool says "Put not all your eggs in one basket"; the wise man says "Put all your eggs in one basket, and *watch that basket*".'[54] Liddell Hart was so stimulated by his correspondence with Wavell that 'willy-nilly' he set aside what he was doing to respond at once with a seven-page letter typed single space – agreeing, disagreeing, explaining his own thoughts on the 'fixed' and 'variable' nature of warfare and the relative importance of having alternatives in battle.[55]

Wavell's next appointment was to replace Jackson as commander of the 2nd Infantry Division, and brought him his first aide-de-camp. The Candidate he interviewed was Bernard Fergusson, who had joined The Black Watch in 1931, the son of General Sir Charles Fergusson, a Corps Commander in the Great War, and a cousin of Arthur Wauchope on his mother's side.[56] Like Wavell he was a writer of poetry. Wavell met him at Windsor station, 'bare-headed, in an old tweed coat and flannel trousers – and bore me off to luncheon in the bosom of his family', at Lady Edward Spencer Churchill's house. The interview included a spirited exchange with the teenage Archie John, when Fergusson confused T.S. Eliot with Ezra Pound. On their way back to the station, Wavell asked Fergusson whether he would be prepared 'to take them all on'. Fergusson said, 'I've never been an ADC before, and I may make an awful mess of it,' to which Wavell replied: 'Well, I've never had an ADC before; I may make an awful mess of you.'[57]

In late February 1935, the Wavells were staying with the old General in Ringwood when he had a heart attack after taking an almost cold bath 'as his custom was'. The following day he had improved and the family hoped he would rally, but he then collapsed and died peacefully in the early hours of 2 March, at the age of 91. He had become very deaf, but his brain had remained clear. 'It is merciful in a way,' Wavell wrote to a distant cousin, Edward, with whom he shared an interest in the family lineage, 'for his legs were beginning to fail him, and if he had got over this attack he might have been a complete invalid . . . I shall miss him a great deal . . . he is a great loss but he had a good life.'[58] Looking back, Wavell described his father as 'rather an autocrat in family life, as was the tradition of his age . . . he was a kind and indulgent father to me, and I wish I had been more attentive to him in his old age.'[59] General Archibald Graham Wavell was buried with Lillie, his 'beloved wife', in the graveyard at Cranborne. Pamela wanted to go to the funeral, but was considered too young. Demonstrating the will-power and determination inherited from both her parents, she borrowed one of her mother's black dresses and went anyway.[60] The General's death improved the Wavells' financial position: when the estate was finally settled, it was sworn at £94,000.[61]

On 11 March 1935, after fifteen months on half-pay, Wavell took over command of the 2nd Division at Aldershot. Chance had also brought together a group of officers 'with dazzling futures', noted his new ADC, Fergusson; in command of Wavell's former brigade, the 6th Infantry, was Brigadier Henry Maitland Wilson, identifiable by his girth, and known as 'Jumbo';[62] Brigadier Victor Fortune, another Winchester and Sandhurst contemporary and distinguished soldier, in command of the 5th Infantry Brigade;[63] and Colonel Arthur Smith, a Coldstream Guardsman permanently lamed from the Great War, in command of the 4th Guards' Brigade.[64] Wavell's official home was Churchill House, entirely 'urbanized' in Victorian stucco on the edge of Aldershot Barracks and Farnborough town. At last, as he was amused to note, 'the fecundity of his consort' tallied with the size of house to which his rank entitled him. A colonel was expected to have two children, a brigadier three; finally, as a major-general, he was entitled to a house large enough for a family of four children.[65]

Daily life fell into a comfortable routine. Fergusson remembered that he would call at Churchill House in the evening with a map and a sheet of paper from each brigade, indicating what companies would be practising which exercise and where the next day. Wavell would then choose two or three that were close to each other, and select a rendezvous for the grooms and horses. The following morning Fergusson reappeared and they drove to the rendezvous. After arranging where to pick up the car and the grooms, they would then spend a few hours on horseback watching the troop movements. Fergusson, who did not like riding, related how Wavell loved to gallop through the trees 'with his head close to his horse's shoulder', which he called 'wooding'. Once Fergusson's horse bolted, and covered a good half-mile before Fergusson succeeded in pulling up. Wavell soon appeared alongside. 'It's more usual', he said with amusement, 'for the ADC to ride *behind* his General.'[66]

Not long after his father's death Wavell lost another friend. In late May T.E. Lawrence, recently discharged from the RAF, was riding home on his motor-cycle from Bovington Camp to his cottage when he swerved to avoid two boys on bicycles; his motor-cycle crashed and Lawrence, fatally injured, died five days later. Wavell described it to Nancy as 'a tragic business . . . I can't help believing that he would have found some great work to do if he had lived. He was the most impressive and attractive man I ever met.'[67] Although, as he told Nancy, his friendship with Lawrence was neither 'deep nor intimate', it was one of his 'most valued privileges and boasts'.[68] Wavell also regretted that he had never talked to him on the subject of regular defence forces and the professional soldier: 'I always felt that his company and his comments on indifferent matters and life in general were too good to interrupt for serious discussion.'[69]

The provisions of the 1911 Manoeuvres Act permitted the Army to carry out training exercises in the countryside, and Wavell's time in command of the 2nd Division was marked by some of the most ambitious manoeuvres yet undertaken by the Army. The highlight, for which James Marshall-Cornwall stood as Chief Umpire, was an enactment of the mythical battle for the Golden Fleece which took place over several days in the Sussex countryside. The 4th and 5th Brigades, as the Argonauts, made an imaginary landing near Worthing and then had to secure the 'Fleece' – obtained from a local butcher and dyed yellow – from its custodians, the 6th Brigade, and escape with it. The troops worked through the usual stages of advance, attack, retreat and defence, but its theme so fired their imaginations that the exercise lived on in people's memories. Among the spectators was Brigadier Claude Auchinleck, formerly an instructor at the Staff College at Quetta, who had recently distinguished himself in action against the Mohmand tribesmen on the North-West Frontier of India.[70] Wavell continued to reflect on the nature of warfare and the effects of natural hazards: 'If I had time and anything like your ability and industry to study war,' he wrote to Liddell Hart, 'I think I should concentrate almost entirely on the "actualities" of war – the effects of tiredness . . . fear, lack of sleep, weather, inaccurate information, the time factor . . . The principles of strategy and tactics, and the logistics of war are really absurdly simple, it is the "actualities" that make war so complicated and so difficult, and are usually so neglected by historians.'[71]

To those close to Wavell, it was remarkable that he succeeded in writing anything serious, for as Fergusson pointed out, it was never done 'in seclusion': 'They were all works which, one would have thought, called for complete isolation and a Trappist silence. They were in fact brought forth in a welter of daughters borrowing three-ha'penny stamps, and puppies chewing at his boot-laces, and a series of bulletins about what was happening in the stables and who couldn't come to luncheon.'[72] Most of the Wavells' entertaining was 'necessarily duty stuff', but the house was also full of Pamela's 'debutante' friends, fellow cadets of Archie John's from Sandhurst, or young subalterns invited to help entertain the debutantes.

Vesey had noticed when they shared the house at Camberley that Wavell had 'a quiet humorous way' with Queenie but was decidedly vivacious with the girls, who were quick at repartee.[73] Many over the years recalled sitting next to Wavell in stony silence, but Arthur Smith's daughter Auriol remembered how much he made her feel at ease.[74] He even 'looked with favour' on a game Fergusson introduced into the household, 'which involved plunging up or down the front and back stairs, and diving through the service hatch'. Wavell usually umpired, but occasionally took part.[75] There were 'no limits' to his kindness. Fergusson got into debt and fell behind on payments for his car. When the bailiffs arrived to repossess it Wavell, hearing of Fergusson's distress, immediately proffered £100 'if that would help'.[76] He also strove to improve his ADC's military education: 'He made me read military history, prescribing and often giving me the books, and cross-examining me not so much on their contents as on what lessons I had deduced from them.'[77]

Towards the end of 1935 Wavell explained some of his current thinking to a wider audience when he lectured at the RUSI on 'The Higher Commander'. Jock Burnett-Stuart was in the chair. As usual, Wavell's clarity of thought led him to make distinctions which to him were self-evident. First, it was important to distinguish between the man fitted for independent command, confident in his knowledge and ability and delighting in responsibility, and the man who was a competent 'executive general', excellent at handling and administering troops. 'An army needs both types, the difficulty often is to recognize which is which and to prevent the wrong one being "pulled out of the hat".' Referring to the pious Greek who set up an additional altar 'to the unknown god', Wavell believed it was necessary, when remembering some of the great generals, to add one more memorial, 'to the unknown leader' – in other words, 'to the good company, platoon or section leader who carries forward his men or holds his post and often falls unknown. It is these who in the end do most to win wars.' Wavell also made certain proposals for the continuing education of soldiers and for promoting men according to merit, combined with better training. In the question-and-answer session that followed, his foresight was applauded, but it was also recognized that a shortage of time and money presented an obstacle.[78]

Those around Wavell during his time in command of the 2nd Division were aware of his emerging talent. 'Young as I was,' wrote Bernard Fergusson, 'it was obvious that [his] contemporaries were looking to him as something of a prophet. A stream of Major-Generals used to travel down to Aldershot to pour out their hearts to him. I would serve them with sherry, bang the door to pretend I had gone out of it, and settle down to eavesdrop.'[79] Among those who came were John Dill, still Director of Military Intelligence and Operations, and Jack Gort, Commandant of the Staff College.[80] Another was Alan Brooke, recently appointed Director of Military Training at the War Office, a job Wavell had turned down in May 1936, on the grounds that he had already had ten years of training.[81]

There were critics as well as admirers. Brian Horrocks, brigade-major to the 5th Infantry Brigade, readily admitted Wavell's keen intelligence, but considered that his lack of social graces put him at a disadvantage: 'This brilliant, imaginative brain lay behind the most expressionless, poker face I have ever come across . . . On arrival young officers were warned that if they met a man who looked like a gamekeeper and said nothing, he was certain to be the divisional commander.' He also found much to admire: 'He instructed staff officers to reduce reports to the shortest possible length. After much mental wrestling, he would receive one which had been pared to the bone. Wavell would then take a pencil and effortlessly reduce it by a quarter.'[82]

About this time Wavell embarked on another literary project, one that took him far longer than he might have expected. Allenby had died in May 1936, and soon afterwards his widow asked Wavell to write her husband's biography. He accepted; he was busy but, he thought, 'not so busy that I could not hope to complete the work in reasonable time'; he discovered, however, that it was 'not easy to write and command a division at the one time.'[83] And since Allenby had left no record of his life and no papers, it took 'many months' to collect the necessary material.

In the late summer of 1936, for the first time in more than twenty years Wavell returned again to Russia, leading a British delegation to observe manoeuvres at Minsk. Although he was obliged to admit that his Russian had 'a thick layer of cobwebs and rust', he was pleased to have the opportunity of comparing the new Soviet Army with the old Russian one.[84] Travelling by train via Aachen, Berlin and Warsaw – and furnished with several slabs of 'marching chocolate' to tide them over any long gaps between meals during manoeuvres – the delegation arrived in Minsk in early September.[85] Wavell observed nothing new or original about the tanks the Russians were using, which were copied from foreign designs, 'But their performance is well ahead of similar types in our service. Their reliability also appears remarkable.' Dress and equipment were similar to those of pre-war days: 'The load both on man and horse is, by our standards, heavy and clumsy . . . The officers generally seemed keen, confident and business like.' Wavell and his companions also saw 'grading' machines in action – the predecessors of bulldozers – which could excavate an anti-tank ditch. Of spectacular interest was an air drop of about 1,500 infantry – the 'paratroopers' of the Second World War; Wavell considered this development to be 'of doubtful tactical value'. In conclusion, he noted that the officers were 'younger, keener and probably better educated' than those of the old Tsarist Army.[86]

During their stay the British party enjoyed lavish hospitality, including visits to the theatre, luncheons and banquets. They were also, 'somewhat embarrassingly', presented with numerous bouquets of flowers and, when they left, with 'munificent' amounts of caviare.[87] The manoeuvres ended with a firework display and a grand parade during which 1,000 tanks 'thundered by the saluting base throwing up a blinding dust'.[88] Wavell met the Soviet Union's Defence Minister, Marshal Voroshilov, who spoke earnestly and presciently 'on the peaceful aims of the Soviet Union and the desire to co-operate with Great Britain in facing the German menace, which he considered very real and urgent.'[89]

By the end of 1936 Wavell was in no doubt that war clouds were once more looming. In 1934 Adolf Hitler, Chancellor and Supreme 'Fuehrer', had withdrawn Germany from the League of Nations; a year later military conscription was established. In the same year, the Fascist Italian government of Benito Mussolini invaded Abyssinia, deposing the Emperor Haile Selassie. Then came Germany's unchallenged occupation of the Ruhr, the vital mining and manufacturing region on the right bank of the Rhine occupied by French and Belgian troops in 1923 when Germany refused to pay her quota of wartime reparations. In the Far East, Japan's invasion of Chinese Manchuria and subsequent withdrawal from the League of Nations was a portent of belligerence to come. Finally, in the Middle East an uneasy situation had been developing between the Muslim Arabs and the Jews in Palestine. Initially it was hoped that the Royal Air Force would be able to deal with the violence that erupted, but when discontent flared into open rebellion in 1936 Dill, promoted to lieutenant-general, was sent as GOC Palestine and Transjordan with two divisions to restore order. The alarming nature of the situation was brought home to the troops under Wavell's command in the 2nd Division as they practised their manoeuvres in the English countryside when they had to relinquish equipment for use by the 1st Division in Palestine.

In December 1936 Edward VIII abdicated, and in May 1937 Stanley Baldwin resigned, to be succeeded as Prime Minister by his Chancellor of the Exchequer, Neville Chamberlain. A Cabinet reshuffle introduced new faces, including Leslie Hore-Belisha as Secretary of State for War. He admitted to knowing nothing about the Army, but his stated objective was to get rid of the old generals – anyone over sixty – and bring in fresh blood.[90] With this in mind, Liddell Hart was requested to prepare two memoranda on the reorganization of the Army; his list of 'noteworthy' generals described Wavell as 'outstanding'. He also suggested that Wavell had not only 'great ability but marked originality, if a bit inclined to the "professional" point of view. Does not impress at first sight.'[91] Wavell was soon afterwards informed by the Military Secretary at the War Office, Charles Deedes,[92] that there was likely to be a change of command in Palestine: the Chief of the Imperial General Staff wanted him to know that, 'in the interests of the Country, he hopes that you will be ready to take over the Command in Palestine if you are asked to do so.'[93] Wavell was not enthusiastic. 'I have said I will go,' he wrote to Nancy, 'but it is going to be a terrible upset moving out of this house at short notice, disposing of children, horses, ponies, dogs, cars, servants, furniture, etc. etc.'[94] However, after nearly twenty years in Britain, Wavell recognized the challenge. 'Palestine will be no sinecure, but it will be more interesting than training skeleton units at home,' he wrote to Liddell Hart. 'This would have been my *12th* successive training season with a regular division at home!'[95]

8

Prelude to War

In the British Army today, there is only one good general [Wavell], but he is incomparably good.   Field Marshal Wilhelm Keitel, 1939[1]

WAVELL'S APPOINTMENT TO Palestine was officially confirmed by the War Office on 16 July 1937. 'The work will be very interesting,' he wrote in reply to his cousin Edward's congratulations. 'I only hope I shall manage to do it.'[2] The appointment was officially a secret prior to its announcement, so Wavell found himself sorting out his hot-weather khaki uniform and doing some of his own packing 'lest the servants at Churchill House should grow suspicious!'[3] Queenie and the children were to remain in England until appropriate accommodation could be found.

Travelling overland to Marseilles, Wavell went by P&O to Cairo. Dressed in civilian clothes for the journey, he had automatically brought an umbrella with him. Only half-way across France did he realize that 'nothing could be more useless' than an umbrella in Palestine.[4] In Jerusalem Wavell stayed at the King David Hotel, where Dill had a suite of rooms, and formally took over command from him on 12 September.[5] Two decades previously he had accompanied Allenby on his victorious procession through the Jaffa gate; he now sat down – generally before breakfast – to write Allenby's biography, recreating the story of the life of the man whose most famous exploits he had witnessed.

There was no official residence, and Wavell had to find suitable accommodation for his family. He finally settled on two flats in the affluent Katoman quarter, a predominantly Christian/Arab neighbourhood on the south-west side of Jerusalem, and took pleasure in designing some of the furniture himself, to be made at the local prison. Special care was taken with the measurements of his own desk. The children subsequently described their new home as 'lovely', but Queenie found it 'horrible' and never quite forgave her husband 'this breach of accepted marital etiquette' in choosing their accommodation himself.[6] A member of his staff,

Brigadier George Brunskill, remembered that Joanie was especially sad to have left their dog behind in England; Wavell duly arranged for it to be sent to Palestine. On another occasion, he was hurriedly changing for 'a very important dinner' when Felicity entered his room in great distress: while shopping in the bazaar she had lost a string of pearls. Wavell, said Brunskill, 'could not have been more kind and patient in soothing her before deciding that I was to enlist the help of the police.'[7] Shortly after his family's arrival Archie John, who had joined the 2nd Battalion, The Black Watch in early 1936, was posted to Palestine – just in time to mount the first guard on his parents' new home.

As was always his way in any new appointment, while apparently making the least effort possible, Wavell succeeded in inspiring loyalty. Dudley Clarke, who later served on Wavell's staff in the Middle East, recalled a typical first encounter. His orders were to escort Wavell from Jerusalem to Haifa, and 'as if to put me at my ease' Wavell asked him when he had joined. 'In 1916, Sir,' Clarke replied. About an hour passed, and Wavell spoke again: 'I meant, when did you join this Headquarters?' Like others before and after him, Clarke soon learned to respect Wavell's silences, 'and even to understand them. From this strange relationship I gradually became imbued with an abiding affection for the man himself.'[8]

Wavell was aware that Palestine was simmering with revolt. Under the Turks, Arabs and Jews had lived in mutual poverty and comparative harmony. Balfour's 1917 Declaration confirming Britain's support for a national home for the Jews conflicted with promises made to the Arabs, however, and relations were further exacerbated after 1933 when Jewish migrations to Palestine increased following Adolf Hitler's rise to power in Germany. Wauchope's view as High Commissioner was that the immigrants could benefit Palestine's economy, but the Arabs reacted violently against both the Jewish settlers and the British administration, whose officials they regarded as responsible for the influx. As well as adopting a policy of military containment, the British Government had set up a Royal Commission under Lord Peel, former Secretary of State for India, to investigate the causes of the unrest and to resolve 'once and for all' the Jewish–Arab problem. It recommended the termination of Britain's 1920 mandate and the partition of Palestine into three sections: an Arab state, a Jewish state, and specific areas of religious or strategic importance which would remain under British mandate. The Arab and Jewish states should be given independence at once, with Britain retaining control over foreign policy and defence.

Initially Arab opinion regarded partition as a possible solution – but the extremists led by Haj Amin el Husseini, the Mufti of Jerusalem, aggressively rejected it. Before Wavell's arrival, anticipating arrest, he had claimed the right of sanctuary in the Haram-el-Sharif, the Muslims' holiest mosque in Jerusalem. From here he directed a subversive campaign against the Jews and their 'co-conspirators' – the British. The Zionist Congress meeting in Switzerland in August 1937 had accepted partition in principle, but considered the proposed boundaries unacceptable. As a soldier, Wavell was in Palestine to keep the peace; but he was also personally concerned by the deteriorating triangular relationship, his closeness to Allenby during the Great War and his friendship with Lawrence having made him particularly aware of the circumstances leading to the growth of Arab national consciousness. While sympathizing with both communities on humanitarian grounds, on the basis of tenure Wavell believed the Arabs had the greater claim to the country.[9] He also thought that, left to themselves, the Jews could make 'mincemeat' of the Palestinian Arabs.[10]

Wavell's brief in Palestine was to provide 'aid to the civil power'. The Palestine Command came under the War Office, so for the first time he was acting on his own, as an independent commander. Dill had had two divisions with which to quell the rebellion in 1936; now, in a period of supposed calm, Wavell had just two infantry brigades to keep the peace. Soon after his arrival he had to deal with the consequences of the murder on Sunday 26 September of the District Commissioner of Galilee Lewis Andrews and his police guard on their way to the Anglican church in Nazareth. Andrews, an Australian who spoke both Arabic and Hebrew, was perceived as a 'friend' of the Jews, and therefore a ready target for Arab extremists. In response, the civil administration declared 'military control', a reduced form of martial law. Warrants were issued for the arrest of several important Arab leaders: some were caught, others fled. Wavell suggested setting up military courts to try offences related to the carrying of weapons and sabotage, and these were finally authorized in mid November. One of the first men to be tried was a leading Arab extremist, Sheikh Farhan, who had gone to ground in a small village on Mount Gilboa; found guilty of several murders, he was hanged on 27 November. His execution was deemed to have had a 'salutary' effect, but a group called 'The Muslim Society of Sweden' published a resolution condemning Wavell as 'one of the most prominent bloodhounds sent to the Near East after the World War' – presumably a reference to the tracker dogs used to locate Sheikh Farhan – and announcing that his 'outrageous crimes' would never be forgotten.[11]

In the normal course of events Wavell would have expected to remain for about eighteen months in Palestine, but after little more than a month he learned of another reshuffle at the War Office. In October 1937 the question arose of finding a successor to Jock Burnett-Stuart, who was retiring the following spring as General Officer Commanding-in-Chief, Southern Command. Liddell Hart, who was still advising Hore-Belisha, recommended Wavell. 'There were objections to this, naturally,' he noted, 'since it meant picking him out from the major-generals' list and giving him preference to any of the lieutenant-generals who might be available.'[12] Liddell Hart was also discussing with Hore-Belisha the 'bigger' question of getting 'new blood' into the Army Council with the appointment of a new Chief of the Imperial General Staff. 'Is there anyone who isn't tame?' Liddell Hart was asked. 'I want a real gangster.' Liddell Hart suggested Dill or Wavell – the latter the better if the choice were to be carried as far down as Wavell's rank.[13] But when Wavell returned briefly from Palestine to be interviewed by the Cabinet, Hore-Belisha was not convinced: 'He made a disappointing impression by the way he talked,' recorded Liddell Hart.[14] Several days later, Hore-Belisha and Liddell Hart again discussed Wavell. 'When I said that Wavell did not impress at first sight, H.B. said that for CIGS it was necessary to have a man who did.'[15] For the new Chief of the Imperial General Staff Hore-Belisha therefore chose Jack Gort, former Commandant of the Staff College, who had just spent two months as Military Secretary. It was agreed that Wavell would be appointed General Officer Commanding-in-Chief, Southern Command.

Meanwhile, knowing that he would soon be packing his bags yet again, Wavell continued to deal with the volatile situation in Palestine. On the evening of 5 November two soldiers of the 2nd Battalion, The Black Watch were shot in the back while out walking in Jerusalem. Bernard Fergusson, back in the regiment after two years as Wavell's ADC, had recently been appointed Brigade Intelligence Officer and was on the spot at the Jaffa Gate Police Station. Wavell gave orders for the battalion to carry out the necessary retaliation, but the Commanding Officer advised against using men who, emotions stirred by the murder of their comrades, might themselves run amok. No other troops were available, however, and in Wavell's estimation this was their only chance to catch the assailants, who had been traced to a nearby village. He therefore told the CO that he would trust the discipline of his old battalion, and that they were to carry out the operation. Wavell spent 'an unhappy night', but in the morning heard that all had gone well.[16] Fergusson later recollected that even in the major crises that lay ahead of Wavell, he never saw him show anxiety 'as much as on that evening'.[17]

The Arab offensive continued throughout the winter. As part of his general strategy, instead of scattering his soldiers the length and breadth of the country Wavell decided to hold certain strategic points while keeping mobile columns ready to strike where necessary – effectively utilizing the tactics of a mobile mechanized infantry, as devised at Aldershot. When the roads essential for wheeled transportation ran out, donkeys were taken to the point in lorries, to continue the journey by available tracks. Wavell had full air support when necessary from Air Commodore Roderic Hill, the Air Officer Commanding the RAF,[18] and frequently travelled on reconnaissance missions with Hill in preference to making dusty road journeys that were all too likely to trouble his eye. He also enjoyed a temporary resumption of his flying lessons: 'Whenever I could manage it I flew a two-seater dual-control machine, took charge of it in the air and had a flying lesson from the pilot. Roderic Hill was very good about letting me fly, and actually allowed me to land and take off by myself once.'[19]

During this period Wavell came into contact with Orde Wingate, a man twenty years his junior. The name immediately attracted Wavell's attention because he had long known and admired General Sir Reginald Wingate, a cousin of Orde Wingate's father.[20] A fluent Arabic speaker, the younger man also spoke Hebrew and Yiddish. 'When I met him I realized that there was a remarkable personality behind those piercing eyes and rather abrupt manner,' Wavell later recalled. Wingate was an ardent Zionist with a reputation for being 'rather an oddity, clever but eccentric', and had created a Jewish police force ('the beginnings of the Army of Israel') to protect the settlers whose homes were under constant threat not only from Palestinian Arabs but also from those to the north who crossed the designated border between Palestine and Syria. Wingate's next proposal was to raise an irregular corps of Jewish men – 'stiffened' by British officers – who, operating almost always at night, would assume a more active role in defending the settlements. His immediate superiors saw its potential for exacerbating armed conflict between Arab and Jew; in the face of their criticism, Wingate decided to seek authorization at the top.

The circumstances of their meeting and Wavell's agreement to the scheme illustrate both Wingate's extraordinary tenacity and Wavell's ability to put aside established protocol if an enterprise appeared worthwhile. Instead of seeking an audience with Wavell by ordinary – and possibly obstructive – channels Wingate chose to intercept Wavell's car on his return from a military station: 'Wingate knew the road and the hour and was waiting for him. When the outriders of the escort had passed, and the general's car came in sight, Wingate stepped into the road and held up his hand.'

When the car stopped, Wingate climbed in and began to explain to Wavell 'with fervour and eloquence' his plan for raising what were to be known as Special Night Squads (SNS) under Wavell's command. Although Wavell did not share Wingate's Zionist beliefs, he appreciated the enthusiasm with which the younger man expressed his unorthodox scheme, and agreed to it. The SNS came into its own after Wavell had left Palestine and Wingate received the DSO for his part in its operations. Wavell retained in a corner of his mind 'an impression of a notable character who might be valuable as a leader of unorthodox enterprise in war, if I should ever have need of one.'[21]

In Palestine Wavell started to play polo again, and golfed on a course near Jerusalem. He also initiated the Ramleh ('sand') Vale Hunt – in the absence of any foxes, the hounds were obliged to pursue jackals. His horse was a one-eyed mare who rode through prickly pear hedges and fruit groves 'with oranges flying in all directions'.[22] In their season he went partridge shooting, and sea-bathing at Jaffa. At his desk, when not focusing on operations in Palestine he continued work on his biography of Allenby. 'This is a restless and disturbed country,' he noted. 'The very great majority are all for peace, but there is a minority determined that there shall not be peace. And sniping from the hills, and sabotage, and assassinations are not easy to deal with.'[23] The prospect of the appointment he was shortly to assume in Britain set him randomly to thinking of what would be the most essential military requirements in any future conflict. As expressed in a 'note', these included the need for close cooperation with the RAF, air defence of London, modernizing of drill, uniform and equipment and good propaganda.[24] He also wrote conscientious reports, in a style rather different from that of the average military bulletin. To his description of an action he had been obliged to mount against a band of Syrians who had been terrorizing villages in Galilee he added this postscript, lest the beauty of the place be overlooked: 'It is a shame to fight in Palestine in the Spring. The two villages where the battle took place are surrounded by orchards in full blossom and there is a mass of wild flowers of every kind on the hills.'[25]

Liddell Hart, meanwhile, anxious to benefit further from Wavell's literary skills, in February 1938 requested him to contribute to the volume on 'Infantry in the Next War' in a new series looking to the future. But Wavell, already behind with his biography of Allenby, thought it wrong to put it aside to work on something else and therefore declined. Liddell Hart was so keen for Wavell to do it that he proposed arranging to have publication put off until the autumn. 'No one is likely to combine ideas and the capacity to express them as well as you could, so I hope you may now feel able to give me a favourable answer.'[26] Wavell wrote back immediately: 'Sorry, but NO. It will take me all my time to finish Allenby by the end of the year, and I've got to get acquainted with my new Command and all sorts of problems.'[27]

Arthur Wauchope retired in February 1938; in his farewell radio broadcast he exhorted his listeners to 'pray for the peace of Jerusalem: they shall prosper that love her.'[28] Wavell was sad to see his friend go, but 'he has been living on his nerves and courage for years and working at high pressure.' Wauchope's successor as High Commissioner was Sir Harold MacMichael, former Governor of Tanganiyka Territory, a little older than Wavell, who described him as seeming good, 'but I doubt if he realizes quite yet what he is up against'.[29] Soon afterwards Wavell and his family were again packing their bags for home, and the furniture Wavell had designed was put up for sale. At the beginning of April the family – minus Archie John, who remained with his regiment in Jerusalem – embarked at Port Said on board the SS *Orontes* with their 71 pieces of luggage. Wavell had spent only eight months in Palestine, and was dissatisfied with his achievements: 'Dealing with the rebellion was a very unsatisfactory and intangible business, and I don't think I produced any better answers than anyone else. But I think I kept it within bounds and did as much as I could with the troops available.'[30]

Wavell – now a lieutenant-general – arrived in Salisbury in April 1938 thinking, as he had of Palestine, that his new posting would be 'most interesting'. Government House, at the southern end of Salisbury under a steep hill, was large and comfortable with a garden, lawns and paddock, but 'not in any way attractive'. And 'as usual' – Wavell later recalled – his wife wanted 'a good deal done' in the way of redecoration, so they had to spend two months in the White Hart Hotel, which annoyed him because he 'hated' hotels, and did not much mind 'exactly what shade my rooms are'.[31] The house was ready by July; hitherto it had been generally agreed that Wavell should have 'a really nice room' for his own use, a generosity so successfully executed 'that my wife and daughters and dogs and ADCs and their friends conducted most of their affairs, by interview or telephone, in the study.' This time Wavell deliberately selected a very small room on an upper floor: 'This was condemned by my family as definitely an anti-social act, but I did get more homework done.'[32]

As the Wavells soon discovered, the atmosphere in England had changed considerably during their absence. In February, Anthony Eden had resigned as Foreign Secretary in protest at Neville Chamberlain's appeasement of

Italy under Mussolini's dictatorship; in March, Hitler had announced the *Anschluss* with an unwilling Austria, and immediately looked menacingly towards Czechoslovakia; Fascist Italy had also joined hands with Nazi Germany. Nevertheless, Neville Chamberlain still earnestly hoped that through diplomacy he could achieve a satisfactory resolution of Britain and Germany's deteriorating relationship. In Wavell's view the situation looked 'a little quieter for the moment, but it is ignominious to have to wait on the words of these dictators, and to know that their word is valueless.'[33] Chamberlain already had his critics in Parliament, foremost among them a party of independent Conservatives led by Winston Churchill, now an ardent advocate of rearmament.

In Salisbury Wavell was in familiar surroundings but with far greater responsibilities, over an area extending from Portsmouth to Land's End and inland to include Gloucester, Oxford and Reading. He was also responsible for coastal defence, the ports of Southampton and Bristol, and the land defences of Portsmouth and Plymouth. 'I like the job and the West country but it's an enormous area,' he noted.[34] To command the brigade at Portsmouth Wavell had requested a promising colonel, Bernard Montgomery, just returned to Britain after spending three years at the Staff College at Quetta in India.[35] Montgomery, who had just lost his wife, threw himself into his work – but he also incurred the wrath of the War Office by leasing out War Department land near Portsmouth without permission. He considered his action fully justified, for his aim was to raise money to improve the welfare services for married families in his garrison, but he was warned that he faced the prospect of being promoted no further. Wavell took a different view: 'He was really rather amused that I had improved the Garrison amenities, at the expense of the War Office, all square and above board,' Montgomery recalled. 'He backed me and kept the file on the move between the War Office and Salisbury.' When Montgomery was later promoted to major-general and sent to Palestine, the issue was dropped.[36]

While Wavell was in Salisbury, Major-General Alan Brooke had command of a new 'Mobile Division', re-formed in 1937 after its dissolution in 1929. In the event of war and the requirement for a British Expeditionary Force to be sent to Europe, Wavell, as General Officer Commanding-in-Chief, Southern Command, was also 'Corps Commander designate' of II Corps. The acknowledged shortage of men and equipment led to a decision that any Expeditionary Force would consist only of I Corps and the Mobile Division; II Corps would mobilize six months later, by which time it was anticipated that there would be enough reserves.

★

At this juncture, Wavell's career might have taken a completely different direction. In early May he received a letter from his old friend General Sir Ernest Swinton. Now almost 70, he was Chichele Professor of Military History at All Souls College, Oxford, and nearing retirement: he wanted to know whether Wavell would be interested in having his name put forward for the professorship. Although Wavell believed that he should be making history rather than writing it, he responded positively: 'There is nothing I should like better than your job, and the neighbourhood of Oxford would suit me well to settle down in when I finish soldiering.' His appointment at Southern Command was due to end in April 1941, by which time he would be 58. Under present regulations generals were not employed after the age of 60 and Wavell realized he would be unlikely to get another military appointment. In an ideal world, Swinton's suggestion would have come a year or so later; but, he wrote, 'I should so much like the work at Oxford that, so far as my personal inclinations go, I should be prepared, if by any chance I was selected, to give up my appointment here at once.' He felt constrained, however, to add an important proviso: 'I must consider the interests of the Army, especially at a time like the present, when the danger to the country may become so pressing so soon that one has to regard oneself as almost on active service already.'[37]

Wavell was also again in regular communication with Liddell Hart, who was keen as always to tap into his strategic knowledge, though by the summer of 1938 his admiration of him as a military commander had waned: 'I went down to visit [Wavell] at Salisbury and was dismayed to find that he had become only a shadow of the man he had been, having developed a hesitancy and conservatism that he had never shown before.' Liddell Hart even went so far as to say that he believed his 'strong recommendation' of Wavell the previous November had been a mistake. From that time it was his belief that both Wavell and Dill had passed their peak 'by having to wait too long for opportunity'.[38] They remained friends for the rest of Wavell's life, but Liddell Hart no longer pushed Wavell's name forward when opportunity offered.

Wavell meanwhile, unaware (and had he not been, no doubt unconcerned) that Liddell Hart's opinion of him had changed, continued to fulfil his duties as best he could. When he was not reviewing formations and units, much time was spent in consultation with the Army Council at the War Office. The inner circle consisted of men Wavell knew and liked – Gort, the CIGS, as well as Generals Bartholomew and Dill, GOC-in-Cs, Northern and Home Command, respectively. But preparing for war was a slow and fitful business. Important developments like radar were kept secret. And as Wavell noted, since there were no large-scale manoeuvres, there was no possibility of practising the art of command in the field. The only major exercise with troops at brigade level was carried out in July at the instigation of Montgomery and with the assistance of Admiral of the Fleet 'Ginger' Boyle;[39] the objective was for the brigade to make a landing at Slapton Sands, near Dartmouth. Wavell was unimpressed: 'It was a pitiful exposition of our complete neglect of landing operations.'[40] As an unwelcome postscript to this exercise, on the way back to Salisbury, Wavell's driver ditched their car in a farm dung-heap.

Wavell was struck by the general fitness and keenness of the territorial divisions, but otherwise disappointed. 'They are magnificent material for the most part. But it is pathetic to see how much a uniform tends to cramp a man's natural commonsense and instincts. I suppose it is an almost inevitable characteristic, and that if we all put on wigs we should talk like Lawyers, or try to.'[41] A more personal worry was the news that Archie John had been blown up in a truck by a landmine in Palestine; fortunately the injury was only to his foot, but severe enough for him to be invalided home. In his leisure moments Wavell still managed to play golf and have 'good fun' in what was to prove his last season's hunting in England with his wife and daughters, riding over the Wiltshire Downs with the South and West Wilts packs. The biography of Allenby was going slowly.

The political crisis in the country was deepening, and as Wavell noted, the dictators seemed to have it 'pretty much their own way at present'.[42] In September the Prime Minister went to Germany to meet Hitler. By the terms of the 'Munich agreement', regarded by many as ignominious, German military occupation of the Sudetenland region of Czechoslovakia was accepted, Britain and Germany signed a pact, and Chamberlain returned to Britain boldly stating that he had achieved 'peace with honour'. The British public remained divided. There was no desire for a return to the dismal and tragic circumstances remembered by many from 1914–18; at the same time, the threat posed by German expansionism was too great to be ignored. Writing afer the Second World War, Wavell recalled having been among those who believed Britain should have declared war at the time of Munich. He realized Britain was unprepared but believed the Germans were even less ready; looking back, he thought they made better use of the year's respite achieved by Munich.[43] To his 'intimates' Wavell's immediate reaction was outrage: 'How can we hold our heads up again? We don't deserve to be great and we'll end up a second-rate power.'[44] Archie John had become interested in politics, and during his convalescence sat in the Public Gallery at the House of Commons to hear Winston Churchill, a leading opponent of appeasement, fulminate against the Government amid cheers from the Opposition benches. Gort was preoccupied with the consequences of the 'Munich crisis', so in the autumn it was Wavell who directed a big War Office exercise between the Aldershot and Southern Commands. The theme of his directives was to encourage those taking part to make do with what they had rather than bemoaning the insufficiency of equipment and reserves of men, which were painfully obvious.

Christmas 1938 was spent at Northwick Park with Lady Edward Spencer Churchill's son George. It was unseasonably cold, and the 80-mile journey from London took five hours. In the King's New Year honours, Wavell was appointed a Knight Commander of the Bath, and plain Mrs Wavell became henceforward 'Lady Wavell'. Not since Sir John Weyvill, MP, noted in 1358 as 'holding lands in Sussex and Somerset', had there been a title in the Wavell family. Wavell's promotion elicited the customary letter of congratulations from his cousin Edward, and Wavell's characteristically modest reply: 'I have got a good deal higher than I ever expected or deserved.'[45] In early 1939 Wavell took Felicity and Joan to Austria for two weeks to the mountains at Wengen, where they stayed in the Falken-Hotel. The girls, 16 and 14, took to skiing 'like ducks to water'; Wavell found, after his long absence from the slopes, that 'it was a much more fearsome sport' than he remembered it, and that he was 'too frightened and decrepit to ski' any more.[46] The knee he had injured in 1921 hurt him, and the pace had increased a great deal, with so many more people, 'all going hell for leather all the time'. Even while on holiday he kept up his usual correspondence, writing to Liddell Hart about the desirability of sending an army to the Continent in another European War, 'though the safety of London has stuck out as our first military (and air force) commitment for years'.[47]

In accepting an invitation to deliver the Lees Knowles lectures at Trinity College, Cambridge in February 1939 Wavell chose not to speak on a particular campaign or period of history, as his predecessors had, but to 'inflict' upon his audience some broad observations on 'generals and generalship': comparatively few of them, he said, would become generals, but many were likely to 'suffer, perhaps even to triumph, under generals'. The first lecture (expanded from Wavell's talk to the RUSI on the 'Higher Commander' in December 1935) was given after dinner on Friday 17 February. In it he referred again to the qualities of 'the good general', who must have physical and moral courage; his second lecture, a few days later, focused on the general in relation to his troops; his third dealt with the relations of higher commanders to their masters, 'the statesmen who direct them'. He ended by exhorting his audience to realize that 'war is not a matter of diagrams, principles, or rules'.[48] Perhaps no more than thirty undergraduates, all of whom were in the Officers' Training Corps, attended the lectures, and they attracted no attention outside this immediate circle.

The situation in Europe was deteriorating still further. Germany's invasion of Czechoslovakia in March directly contravened what Chamberlain believed had been agreed at Munich. The governments of Britain and France immediately pledged their support to Poland, should she be similarly attacked; guarantees were also given to Greece and Romania. At government level there were hurried attempts to make up for lost time; production of tanks and guns was speeded up. The Territorial Army was doubled in size and, for the first time during peacetime, conscription was introduced. Forty years after Wavell's own passing-out parade, he took the salute at Sandhurst. Loyalty and obedience were the themes of his address. His drive and determination throughout this period belied Wavell's customary affectation of laziness, revealing it as an illusion: 'He would like to have been [lazy], but he wouldn't allow himself to be,' noted his ADC, Michael Fox (who had replaced Fergusson). In more than two years he took only a fortnight's leave.[49]

For Wavell change was once more in the air. On 6 July George Giffard, his former GSO1 at Aldershot and now Gort's military secretary, wrote to ask whether he would like to be considered for appointment to the newly created post of 'General Officer Commanding-in-Chief, Middle East'. In the knowledge that war was imminent, Wavell accepted without hesitation. Officially appointed on 28 July, he set out immediately. At Marseilles he boarded the P&O liner *Comorin*, and crossed the Mediterranean to Egypt. For him, the 'inter-war' years were over. The man who loved family life, riding to hounds and reciting poetry, the man who was so evidently bored by mundane routine, was about to be challenged more than he had ever thought possible. 'So ended my last year of peace and the old, pleasant, comfortable life of soldiering and sport in England.'[50] He was 56 years old.

III
COMMANDER-IN-CHIEF

9

Middle East Command, 1939

North Africa has always been one of the great battle-grounds of history. Rome and Carthage there decided their long drawn-out contest for the Empire of the Mediterranean – the world of their day.

A.P. Wavell[1]

GENERAL SIR ARCHIBALD Wavell – as he was now styled – took up his new job as General Officer Commanding-in-Chief, Middle East on 2 August 1939. Apart from his brief posting to Palestine in 1937/8 and his reconnaissance mission in 1934, he had not served in the Middle East for over twenty years. 'It will be interesting here, I think, but a bit hectic if we have a war,' he noted soon after his arrival.[2] His brief was to command all British forces based in Egypt, the Sudan, Palestine and Transjordan, and also Cyprus, over an area extending approximately 1,700 miles from north to south and 2,000 miles from east to west. If war broke out, his command would be increased to include Kenya, British Somaliland, Aden, Iraq, and the shores of the Persian Gulf. But while war clouds hung over Europe, the only immediate threat came from Italy: her empire in Libya bordered Egypt to the east. Further south, Eritrea, Italian Somaliland and Italy's recent acquisition of Abyssinia (Ethiopia) – known collectively as Italian East Africa – bordered the Sudan, British Somaliland and Kenya. Throughout 1939 the prevailing hope in London was that as long as Mussolini was not 'provoked', the Italians would take no further aggressive action in North or East Africa.

Of Wavell's vast new command, the only terrain with which he was familiar was Palestine. Of the areas in which he was to travel over the coming years, undoubtedly the most challenging was the Western Desert, extending from El Alamein, 80 miles west of Alexandria, to El Agheila in Libya on the Gulf of Sirte, which marked the border between Cyrenaica and Tripolitania. Along the coastline a few habitable areas, linked by road and rail, had grown up. In ancient times, part of this coastal strip had been the granary of the Roman world; since then, lack of rain had turned it into desert, with little vegetation and virtually no water. The men involved in military operations under Wavell's command were to discover that they were as much at war with the all-pervasive sand as with their fellow human beings. In summer and in winter, it could be bitterly cold. Flies were a constant menace. When a sandstorm blew, everything stopped, 'making you feel that you will never see light and air and feel coolness again'.[3] Wavell's political responsibilities involved maintaining contact with the Government's representatives in the area, especially Sir Miles Lampson, Britain's Ambassador in Egypt and High Commissioner to the Sudan.[4] A conference known as the 'weekly waffle' became a regular feature of Wavell's relationship with Lampson. It took place in Lampson's Victorian study, 'cluttered with furniture, books, photographs and flowers' and dominated by a life-size portrait of Kitchener over the fireplace and a similar one of Allenby on another wall.[5] After a few meetings, Lampson wrote of Wavell: 'I am coming to the conclusion that when one gets to know him better, he is rather a good fellow.'[6] Additional less frequent contact was maintained with the High Commissioner for Palestine and Transjordan, Sir Harold MacMichael, whose acquaintance Wavell had already made in Jerusalem in 1938; and with Britain's officials in Cyprus, Aden and British Somaliland, including Lieutenant-Colonel Sir Stewart Symes, Governor-General in the Sudan since 1934.[7]

Together with the naval Commander-in-Chief Admiral Sir Andrew Cunningham[8] and the Air Officer Commanding-in-Chief, Middle East, Air Chief Marshal Sir William Mitchell,[9] Wavell was also responsible for co-ordinating Britain's strategy with her allies in the area, France, Turkey, Greece and Romania. In addition, since Indian troops provided some of the forces in Somaliland and Aden, Wavell had to consult with the Commander-in-Chief in India, General Sir Robert Cassels.[10] Finally, by the terms of the 1936 Anglo-Egyptian treaty – signed following Italy's invasion of Abyssinia – Egypt was also an ally: Wavell was responsible for training the Egyptian Army as well as for the defence of Egypt – Britain's priority being to safeguard the Suez Canal and thus access to Britain's empire in Asia.[11] His task was immense, and not only because of the distances involved but also in terms of the different languages spoken, the different military and political organizations and the varying outlook of the countries involved.

Even before Wavell reached Cairo he had begun to assess the requirements of his new command and the possible future actions of both Italy and Germany. The 'Notes' he wrote on his outward journey from Britain show an early awareness that Hitler, as the first step in his bid for world domination, was likely to attempt a 'grand coup' by advancing eastwards against Poland, Romania and Greece. Italy, Wavell believed, would be kept neutral at the outset; even so – whether or not Italy was 'openly hostile' or 'nominally neutral' – Britain's only possible counter to German aggression would be a swift domination of the Mediterranean. He therefore saw the need not only to plan for the defence of Egypt but also to take counter-offensive measures against Germany in eastern and south-eastern Europe.[12]

At the outset, administration of the troops in Wavell's field of operations remained the responsibility of the War Office. To assist with planning and coordination Wavell had a small staff, the 'founding members' numbering just seven. His Chief of Staff was Brigadier Arthur Smith, in Egypt since 1938 and with whom Wavell had worked in Aldershot. According to Wavell, Smith had 'a delightful sense of humour, was the very soul of honour and uprightness, organized a staff well and ran an extremely happy show.'[13] Smith considered Wavell 'a splendid man to serve. Not only a wonderful soldier, but so human and always, unobtrusively, doing kind acts for people.'[14] The team also included a naval liaison officer and four staff officers, one of whom, John Benson of The Black Watch, a GSO3, had written to his brother-officer Bernard Fergusson asking for guidance on how to deal with his new 'boss'. Fergusson immediately focused on the taciturn side of Wavell's character: 'If he doesn't want to talk, don't make conversation. He usually doesn't . . . he is a most loyal and affectionate person to work for, and will back you up through thick and thin. He is very accessible.' He also warned Benson that 'he can bite, and sometimes bites just on account of liver. But it is all over at once.'[15]

These men constituted the staff of the new General Officer Commanding-in-Chief, Middle East. They worked from four rooms in the same cheerless Edwardian hotel on the banks of the Nile that was Headquarters to the British troops in Egypt commanded by Wavell's old friend Major-General 'Jumbo' Wilson, in Cairo since late June. In Palestine the military governor and commander of the 7th Division was Major-General Richard O'Connor, who had arrived shortly after Wavell's departure in 1938.[16] An intelligence section was set up in July 1939 to coordinate all aspects of intelligence affecting North and East Africa, the Middle East and the Balkans, organized by an Australian, Colonel Walter Cawthorn – known as 'Bill'.[17] His task in Cairo was not only to provide strategic intelligence and coordinate political intelligence for the three Commanders-in-Chief; he also acted as Wavell's political adviser, and as joint services representative on the Middle East Joint Planning Staff. Throughout their association Cawthorn had the highest regard for Wavell, describing him as 'the greatest man I ever met'.[18] Later it was realized that administration from London was not practical, and Wavell's small organization grew to include over a thousand men, necessitating a move to a modern block of flats known as 'Grey Pillars' at the southern end of Garden City.[19]

Wavell immediately adopted his customary 'hands-on' approach, and this included reconnoitring his new terrain. The day after he assumed command he wrote to the CIGS, Jack Gort, asking him to urge the Air Ministry to provide him with a suitable plane 'with good speed and radius'.[20] A week later he set out for Aden by way of Port Sudan: 'D— hot, 10 hours in the air each day for four days starting 4 a.m. each day.'[21] Back in Cairo Wavell wrote again to Gort, describing the 44 hours' flying time the journey had taken, in an 'ancient' Vickers-Valentia plane so slow that its pilots joked that in a strong headwind, it would stand still in the air or fly backwards.[22] 'A more modern machine' would have saved two days, 'besides a great deal of discomfort'.[23]

Planning for a desert war was one challenge; having the resources to act offensively if need be was another, especially when, as Wavell already realized, his own forces were vastly inferior in numbers to those of the Italians, who had an estimated 215,000 men in Libya alone – nine divisions in Tripolitania, five in Cyrenaica. At Wavell's disposal was the equivalent of two divisions, which included the incomplete Mobile (Armoured) Division.[24] In mid August, the 11th Indian Infantry Brigade of the 4th Indian Division – later famous as the Red Eagle Division – arrived from India. But Wavell remained critically short of mechanized transport, which reduced his potential mobility. To counter his deficiencies, his standing order, as reported by war correspondent Alan Moorehead, was 'to make one man appear to be a dozen, make one tank look like a squadron, make a raid look like an advance'.[25] The Viceroy of Italian East Africa, the Duke of Aosta, was no more anxious for war than his British counterparts, but the size of his force – a quarter of a million men – was more than formidable when compared with the limited contingent of troops in British East Africa.[26] To the south, under the command of Major-General William Platt, approximately 9,000 British and Sudanese troops garrisoned Sudan's long frontier.[27] To protect Kenya, there were only about 8,500 British East African troops.[28] On the meagre plus side of Wavell's balance sheet was the fact that he had enough space and, provided it could be harnessed, sufficient labour to build the necessary military installations; and for transport there was the railway along which Wavell had travelled in 1917 between Suez and Palestine's deep-water port at Haifa.

On 18 August Wavell was off again, this time to Alexandria to meet his naval and air counterparts, Cunningham and Mitchell, for the first time, aboard HMS *Warspite* in Alexandria harbour. It was immediately clear that none of them had any detailed instructions as to what to do in the event of hostilities – and even as they were meeting, the magnitude of the threat they faced changed with intelligence of the Nazi–Soviet pact due to be signed on 23 August. As Wavell wrote to his former divisional commander at Aldershot, General Sir Henry Jackson, while news from home seemed to indicate people's conviction that there would not be a war, he believed what was called 'wishful' thinking should be described as 'woolly': 'News smells of mustard gas and antiseptics and other unpleasant things.'[29] Nor was he averse to pointing out to Gort how dissatisfied he was with the defensive mentality of the Government.[30] For the time being, since the Italians on his western frontier appeared quiet, Wavell's chief concern remained the Suez Canal. Italy was technically neutral, so the British could not close the canal but were obliged to permit unimpeded passage to friend and potential foe alike.

While Britain, by design, avoided provocative moves in North Africa, her increasing involvement in the European theatre was creating a network of obligations. On 25 August the Polish foreign minister Josef Beck negotiated an Anglo-Polish treaty of assistance whereby Chamberlain assured Poland that Britain would help Poland to protect her neutrality 'by force if necessary'.[31] The probability of war with Germany was such that even if Italy were to remain neutral, it was essential for all services to advance their state of readiness. On Friday 1 September, as Wavell had foreseen, Hitler moved rapidly into Poland; Mussolini announced Italy's 'non-belligerence', affirming her neutrality. Wavell had only been waiting for the inevitable, and the following day he wrote to Gort suggesting that Britain was making 'a rather pompous, long-winded, old-fashioned entry' into the war compared with the summary methods used by Hitler. He also questioned Gort over the extent to which Italy should be allowed 'to build up her stocks of aeroplane fuel and munitions in East Africa' and let her submarines 'roam the seas unchecked'.[32] But even as he wrote, Neville Chamberlain, at last bowing to the pressure of his Members of Parliament and the country, announced in the House of Commons on Sunday 3 September that war had formally been declared against Germany. Gort immediately relinquished his position as CIGS and became Commander-in-Chief of the British Expeditionary Force to France; General Sir Edmund Ironside, who had commanded the British Expeditionary Force to Archangel during the Great War, took his place.[33] Chamberlain formed a small War Cabinet and invited Winston Churchill to assume the position he had held in 1914: First Lord of the Admiralty.

Wavell's role immediately changed from a 'planning' one to an 'operational' one. 'Our strategy in the Middle East must be an Imperial strategy,' Ironside informed him.[34] O'Connor and his 7th Division were immediately ordered from Jerusalem to Cairo and then to take up a defensive position in the desert, west of Alexandria, between the white-walled town of Mersa Matruh – the terminus of the railway and the metalled road, two hundred miles from Alexandria – and Maaten Baggush. When it became clear that for the time being the Italians were holding to their declaration of neutrality, despite the declaration of war on Germany, O'Connor shifted his division to more comfortable quarters at Mersa Matruh, where the main base for desert operations was subsequently established. Throughout this period Wavell was invariably working a twelve-hour day, taking an hour off for lunch and dinner. It was a far cry from the 'idle self-indulgent old age' which he had once thought he was going to enjoy.[35] If he did no other work in the evening, he took up his manuscript of Allenby's life. He also enjoyed his early-morning ride, a habit he continued whenever he could, wherever he was and in whatever capacity.

Now that Britain was at war with Germany, it was even more imperative to develop a satisfactory relationship with Britain's allies in the region. French troops were stationed in North Africa, Syria, the Lebanon and French Somaliland, and it was understood that a combined Anglo-French strength would present a more formidable challenge to the Italians than British forces in isolation. The Commander-in-Chief of the French forces in Syria was General Maxime Weygand, Marshal Foch's right-hand man during the Great War. Soon after the declaration of war Wavell went to Beirut for discussions with Weygand, whom he had already met briefly in Cairo and assessed as a 'sagacious ally'.[36] With potential German moves into southern Europe at the forefront of their minds, their discussions focused on the strategic importance of Salonika, and of safeguarding this 'gateway' to the Aegean from Macedonia in Greece. On this visit Wavell – still without his own transport – travelled once more in an old Valentia, whose pilot immediately returned to Cairo. When the meeting was over, Wavell found himself with no way of getting back to Egypt. Weygand put a far more comfortable plane at his disposal, and instead of reprimanding his ADC for the nonsense he had made of arrangements, Wavell settled down agreeably, suggesting that they should send their plane away again 'next time we come'.[37]

Of Britain's other allies, the newly created Kingdom of Iraq needed careful handling. By the terms of the 1930 Anglo-Iraqi treaty, Britain had the right to maintain RAF bases at Habbaniya and Basra, and to move military forces through the country; in the event of war, the British retained the right to make use of all transport and communication facilities. Feisal, installed as monarch when the Kingdom of Iraq was created under a British Mandate in 1921, had died in 1933, shortly after the formal termination of the Mandate, and it had soon become apparent that his son Ghazi did not share his father's pro-British sympathies. Instead, as a 'pan-Arabist' he had demonstrated support for the Palestinian Arab uprising in the 1930s. King Ghazi's sudden death in a car crash in 1939 left Iraq in the hands of a minor – his son, Feisal II – and the Regent, Abdullah, the new King's uncle, who displayed a willingness to accommodate British interests. On the outbreak of war the British Government requested Iraq to sever all relations with Germany and to intern all German citizens. In mid September, Wavell flew to Baghdad to discuss the situation. Yet again the flying bogey for which he became famous was lying in wait: on the return journey, his plane crashed. With typical *sang-froid*, before he had been cut free from the wreckage Wavell was already giving orders for another plane to come and pick him up. The remainder of his journey was no more trouble-free, for the replacement plane had to make a forced landing near Jerusalem, which involved spending a 'most uncomfortable' night under the stars.[38]

The country for which Britain had the highest hopes as a potential counter to German aggression was Turkey. As Gort wrote to Wavell in September, 'The Turkish Army is a formidable body of troops. If Turkey comes in against the Germans there is no possibility of Turkey being overrun such as there is in a country like Romania whose army is not of high value.'[39] In late October Wavell flew to Ankara to sign an Anglo-French treaty of 'mutual assistance' to Turkey, yet again in a Vickers-Valentia. He left Cairo before dawn for the 700-mile journey, and once more his arrival at his destination was an achievement in itself. This time his pilot, refuelling in Cyprus, inadvertently landed on an airfield which was undergoing repairs, and punctured the plane's tyres. In the absence of any ground staff, the tyres had to go to a local garage for repair. When he finally arrived, Wavell was able to atone for his lateness and please his hosts by giving the correct Turkish greeting to the Guard of Honour. Accompanied by General Weygand he met Marshal Fevzi Cakmak, Chief of the Turkish General Staff. By the terms of the agreement, both France and Britain pledged to assist Turkey if the country were to be attacked by a European power or if it became involved in war through an act of aggression in the Mediterranean; most importantly from the Turkish Government's point of view, Turkey was not to be involved in war with Russia. Following the signing of the accord, French and British military missions were to be sent to Turkey, and steps would be undertaken to improve telephone communications between Ankara, Beirut and Cairo. As to Germany's future actions, Cakmak thought that 'the Germans must finish the war quickly and therefore must produce new surprises. Time is against Germany but in favour of France and Great Britain.' On the whole Wavell remained silent during these discussions, interrupting less frequently than Weygand, who argued energetically in favour of taking a more active stance. But though he endorsed Weygand's appreciation of the situation, Wavell considered his lack of resources left him with little to contribute, and so contented himself 'mainly with a watching brief'.[40] It was also evident that Turkey was unwilling to be drawn into greater belligerence, and the military missions never materialised.

It was in the course of this visit that Wavell, staying with the ambassador and debating whether or not he should wear his sword to meet the Turkish representatives, encountered an unusual woman. Freya Stark, unmarried and in her middle forties, was an acclaimed travel writer and had worked on the *Baghdad Times* during the 1930s. Her book *The Valley of the Assassins*, inspired by her travels in Persia, had won her the Triennial Burton Medal of the Royal Central Asian Society. Wavell made a lasting impression: 'I met . . . an officer with many ribbons, active, not tall, with grizzled hair and a steadfastness as of friendly granite all about him; and, in his general expression, a look of gaiety and youth. He carried with simplicity a rare atmosphere of greatness.'[41] This Turkish visit provoked Wavell to renewed complaints of the bad image created by having to travel in such an antiquated plane: 'I was questioned by many senior Turkish officers on the speed of the machine and how long the journey had taken.'[42]

Inevitably, the broader political and military problems of the day were not the only ones with which Wavell had to deal. Personal differences developed among his subordinates, and it did not take long for his commander of the Armoured Division, Major-General Percy Hobart, to fall foul of Jumbo Wilson, although the two had known each other since Staff College in 1919.[43] As Wavell later recalled, Wilson told him that 'he could not have Hobart as a Commander any longer' since he had disregarded 'definite instructions given him as regards the training and handling of his Force'. Wilson, a more conventional soldier, also criticized Hobart as one whose 'tactical ideas are based on the invincibility and invulnerability of the tank to the exclusion of the employment of other arms in correct proportion'.[44] On the grounds that 'Hobart was not trusted as a

Commander by either his superiors or many of his subordinates', Wavell acquiesced and in November 1939 Hobart was 'retired'.[45]

Wavell had been separated from his family for more than three months, and it was long enough: despite the dangers, in late November Queenie and his daughters travelled out from England in a troopship full of soldiers and sailors bound for the Middle East and India.[46] The Wavells shared the Residence used by Jumbo Wilson and his wife Hester, a large white house, the 'pleasantest' on the island of Gezira, with palms and bougainvillea. It was not big enough for the whole family however, so Felicity and Joan lived briefly in a *pension* with Nanny Ribbands before moving to an apartment close by. In front of the house were the riding track and the golf links and the sports club was only a few minutes' walk away across the polo grounds, but the house itself was quiet and secluded: 'Too comfortable a place from which to conduct a war, and too many distractions?' Wavell wondered in later life. 'Perhaps, yet I believe that heavy responsibilities can be better shouldered if there are opportunities to relax.'[47] That Wavell had his family with him caused some comment, but ever since Queenie travelled out to be with her husband in Russia in 1916, this was Wavell's – and more especially Queenie's – style. Auchinleck, who later exchanged commands with Wavell, saw the presence of his family as entirely characteristic: 'To try to run a war with a houseful of women intent on social activities keeping an ADC whose main job seems to have been to send bouquets of carnations to Cairo ladies, would have been impossible for me, but then I was not A.P.W.'[48]

The Wavell ladies did not intend to sit idle. Queenie took on responsibility for providing amenities in canteens for the troops in and around Cairo and was frequently to be seen behind the counter in the Services Club in Cairo. Pamela, known as 'Pam' and nearly twenty-one, had passed her first aid examination before the war and joined the Voluntary Auxiliary Division (VAD), working as a nurse in the Scottish hospital outside Cairo; Felicity or 'Fizzie', eighteen, found secretarial work in her father's headquarters; and Joanie – called 'the Trooper' – still only sixteen, went to the French school. Just as in pre-war days, their lives revolved around their animals. 'It was fifty times more important to find out the name of a new horse, or that the dog had just had six puppies and what we were going to call them,' recalled Araminta MacMichael, the High Commissioner's daughter, later a friend of Joanie's and who frequently stayed with the Wavells on holiday from Jerusalem. 'That's where General Wavell got his relaxation.'[49] But if life in Cairo seemed to carry on as if there were no possibility of war, at GHQ there was a distinctly different atmosphere. 'I found,' said Lieutenant-Colonel Dudley Clarke, who had travelled out on the same troopship as the Wavell family to reconnoitre a land route between Mombasa on the Kenya coast and Cairo, 'that no one had any illusions whatever that Italian neutrality would not continue past the point where it suited Hitler to whip in Mussolini.' Two walls of Wavell's office were covered with maps. 'Around the borders of Cyrenaica, Eritrea, Abyssinia and Somaliland coloured flags showed the stations of the armies, lined up like opposing teams at the start of a football game and waiting only the whistle before the fight was on.'[50]

No sooner had Queenie and the girls arrived in Cairo than Wavell had to return to England. But by the time he reached London in early December, the Chiefs of Staff – Admiral Sir Dudley Pound, First Sea Lord, Air Chief Marshal Sir Cyril Newall, Chief of Air Staff, and the CIGS, Ironside – had already concluded their discussions on Middle East military policy.[51] Britain's vulnerability in the Middle East in the event of Italy entering the war was recognized, but it had been decided that there was no point adding to British forces in the region before the necessary bases and communications to sustain their operations had been developed. Wavell maintained friendly relations with Ironside but did not have much confidence in his judgement, and was dissatisfied with the outcome of their meeting. 'I cannot remember that our discussion on the Middle East situation bore much fruit,' he later recollected. 'He talked to me a good deal about iron ore from Norway and the importance of denying it to Germany.'[52] Throughout Wavell's stay – 'spent practically entirely inside the War Office'[53] – the only Government minister he met was Hore-Belisha. In addition to spending five days in London, Wavell formed part of a delegation including the Chiefs of Staff and Hastings Ismay, the Secretary of the Committee of Imperial Defence,[54] that travelled to meet their French counterparts at the Château de Vincennes outside Paris. Wavell's continuing admiration for Weygand was bolstered by the discovery that they appeared to be the only ones advocating a forward policy in the Balkans to prevent Germany gaining the upper hand.[55]

On his way home from Paris to Cairo Wavell stopped at Algiers and flew on to Tunis to meet General August Noguès, Commander-in-Chief of the French forces in North Africa and inspect the impressive Mareth Line which divided French Tunisia from Italian Libya.[56] Unable to leave Algeria because of yet another air delay, Wavell signalled somewhat provocatively to the War Office that he proposed to use the Italian air service via Tripoli; as a result a plane was despatched at once to return him to Cairo. By the end of 1939,

Wavell was confident that war in North Africa was inevitable. Writing in later life, he maintained that Britain's policy of doing nothing that might provoke the Italians was 'quite misguided'. He knew Italian agents were operating in British territory, but was not given permission to send his own agents into Italian territory. 'Stores continued to pass through the Suez Canal to Italian East Africa, and we even continued under a pre-war agreement to inform the Italians of our reinforcements to the Middle East.'[57]

According to directions for future policy in the Middle East, outlined by Chamberlain's War Cabinet and issued on 15 January 1940, Wavell was to start building a base organization in Egypt and Palestine; preparations were also to be made to equip and maintain a force of nine divisions. In addition, plans were made to defend the Anglo-Persian oilfields. The land route from Haifa to Baghdad reconnoitred by Wavell in 1934 was to be maintained in the event of traffic through the Red Sea being interrupted. Additional forces were to be raised for the Sudan and Kenya. Wavell was also to assume command of British land forces in East Africa and British Somaliland as well as any future forces sent to Turkey and the Balkans, including Greece. From mid February, instead of 'General Officer Commanding-in-Chief' his title was to be 'Commander-in-Chief, Middle East'. He took the change in status with his usual modesty, observing to Nancy that it made little difference 'if any' but put him on a level with 'Gort in France and the C-in-C in India'.[58] Uppermost in his mind was how far they were from a state of preparedness. 'Troops are gathering here gradually . . . But there is a lot of training and equipping to do and time may be short.'[59]

Surveying his large command kept Wavell busy. 'No one seems to know which way Hitler will spring next Spring,' he noted at the end of January.[60] Assuming that Italy's entry into the war was imminent, he concluded that except in British Somaliland, as far as a ground attack was concerned the situation was 'remarkably satisfactory' – unlike the defences against air attack. But he lacked the resources for any counter-attack into Libya; in fact, without adequate reinforcements Britain was still not in a position to undertake any offensive operations against Italy by land or sea.[61] Wavell realized he would not get all the reinforcements he thought necessary, but took some comfort from the arrival of cavalry from Britain and a British infantry battalion from the Far East. It had also been agreed that Expeditionary Forces from Australia and New Zealand would be sent to the Middle East. In early February Chamberlain sent Anthony Eden, back in the Cabinet as Secretary of State for the Dominions, to Cairo to gain a better appreciation of the situation on the ground. Wavell in general mistrusted politicians but developed a liking for Eden, who had served with distinction in the Great War; Eden for his part was impressed 'by Wavell's quiet but firm analysis of his many responsibilities. He made no attempt either to gloss over the shortcomings of his command or to complain about them. He just told a straightforward story. I liked him from this first meeting and our friendship was to grow very close and last until his death.'[62] Together they went to Port Said to greet the new arrivals from New Zealand and Australia, successors of the 'Anzacs' who had played such a courageous role at Gallipoli.

Hailed as 'Anzacs' in the local press, their arrival brought two new generals under Wavell's command. Major-General Bernard Freyberg, whom Wavell had known since their joint visit to Versailles in 1934, commanded the New Zealand Division;[63] the Australians were commanded by General Thomas Blamey, mentioned in despatches seven times during the Great War.[64] Welcome as they were, these 'Dominion' forces presented Wavell with administrative problems. In the previous war the Anzacs had been treated as part of an 'imperial' force: they were not required by their governments to operate along 'national' lines as a separate, cohesive unit, and the British did not hesitate to use individual battalions to make up shortages in their own brigades. Now, the Australian and New Zealand Governments were adamant that their respective divisions should not be used 'piecemeal', and Wavell was irked by a situation which denied him units he desperately needed to make his forces operational. Blamey stood firm by his government's decision, but Freyberg's loyalties were divided: technically still a British army officer on secondment, he was yet committed to following the New Zealand Government's directives. Unfortunately for both Wavell and Freyberg, this conflict of interests resulted in heated arguments which strained both their friendship and their working relationship.[65]

While Wavell was focusing on preparations for war, his domestic arrangements were beginning to run more efficiently with the introduction into his household in early 1940 of a new ADC, Peter Coats.[66] He had enlisted with the Middlesex Yeomanry and soon found himself in the Middle East. The first member of the Wavell household he encountered when he went for his interview was Queenie: 'She was ample, motherly and Irish . . . she had a pretty face and dazzling smile, and her eyes were a very bright blue; just below one was a little black birthmark which made her look as if she had started to apply mascara and then thought better of it. In fact, she wore no make-up at all.' He also met Pamela, 'slightly severe, but beautiful', with, as he was to discover, 'a rollicking sense of humour'.

Wavell then appeared; after a brief talk, he asked Coats if he would like to be his ADC: 'I said I would, and that I only hoped that I would be up to it.' Wavell asked whether Captain Coats rode: 'I answered boldly that I did but was not much good at it. He smiled and said "I see . . . Bernard Fergusson was not much good at it either."' Like many others, Coats initially found Wavell's impenetrability disconcerting: 'It was a long time before I got over my shyness . . . his silences were alarming and sometimes he did not even seem to hear one's pathetic attempts to make conversation.'[67]

In mid March Wavell was on his way to South Africa, accompanied by Coats, to discuss what assistance the South African Union could offer and whether South African troops would be permitted to serve north of the Equator. Their first stop was Khartoum – 'oven hot' – where they stayed at Government House, built on the site of the old one: the steps where General Gordon had been killed were still visible. At Mozambique they became civilians, 'changing into crumpled flannel suits' before landing.[68] Finally they reached Cape Town, where they stayed at the Mount Nelson Hotel. Coats felt like 'a Cape Gooseberry', sometimes participating in the discussions, at others sitting apart, sorting out press cuttings. Wavell conferred daily with the South African Prime Minister, Field Marshal Smuts, whom he had never met, though Smuts had been in Palestine with Allenby in 1917. On the return journey, they were flying over Tanganyika, with jungle stretching endlessly on all sides, when the flying gremlin struck again and the plane had to land quickly. Their arrival at a small village aroused considerable interest among the local people. Wavell and his companions were taken to the local guest house, where the proprietress met them dressed in a grand ball gown and rubber boots. It so happened that it was the night of the yearly dance, and the hotel was full. As Peter Coats recalled, someone gave up a room to Wavell and he went to bed reading James Handley Chase's new thriller, *No Orchids for Miss Blandish*.[69]

When Wavell returned to Cairo he reported the outcome of his South African visit to Ironside. He had been impressed by what he saw, but 'how far Smuts and the Government can commit Union forces to the war I am naturally unable to say.' Everything possible, he said, should be done to encourage the South Africans in the effort they were making; it was his sanguine conclusion that it depended on Smuts – already in his seventieth year – remaining healthy and in power. Wavell lamented again the damaging effect of the policy of 'not provoking' Italy on his preparations. According to his assessments, even though they had been 'at war' since September 1939, it would be at least six months before they were in a position to undertake any offensive operations by land against Libya: 'Quite frankly, our policy seems undecided and hesitating, with the result that valuable time is being lost . . . So long as Italy's hostility is possible we must continue to take all reasonable precautions.'[70]

The situation in Europe was ominous and preparations were being made in the desert for battle, but entertaining in Cairo continued. When Wavell returned from South Africa in March he hosted a large party for Prince Mohammed Aly, heir to the Egyptian throne if King Farouk failed to produce a son.[71] 'Bishops, flood-lit Highlanders dancing reels under the palm-trees, Matrons, Maids, Saris, Sarongs, Black faces, White uniforms, and the hero of the party, Prince Mohammed Aly, in spongebag pants, red Tarboosh and carnation, and an emerald in his tie the size of a golf ball,' observed Coats. As a change from Wavell's other duties, he had also to deal with the problem of 'illicit wives'. Several women had managed to get out to Palestine to be with their husbands, but the divisional commander was now insisting that they leave. Ensconced in the bosom of his own family in Cairo as he was, Wavell felt he was not on very strong ground and claimed he did not have the authority to send them home: it was up to their respective husbands to tell them to go. 'So they remain,' recorded Coats, 'and Palestine is more like Ladies' Day at Ascot than ever.'[72]

On 9 April German forces entered Denmark and Norway. The Danish Government capitulated immediately, but Norway attempted to hold out, requesting assistance from the Allies. Wavell's immediate reaction to news of the German invasion was to assess the impact of Hitler's sudden successes on the minds of the Italians, and how his command might respond. 'From the military point of view, no offensive action against Libya would be possible without very extensive administrative preparations requiring many months,' he wrote to Ironside. 'Given adequate forces offensive naval and air action can be taken. It is therefore essential to know what naval and air forces will be available to meet Italian hostility.'[73] No clear instructions came. When General Sir John Dill was called back from his position as Commander of the 1st Army Corps in France to act as Vice-Chief of the Imperial General Staff, Wavell wrote him a note of welcome which voiced his own frustration: 'I am frankly alarmed at the slowness and heaviness with which our whole military machine still seems to move after nearly nine months of war. It apparently all comes from the strict financial control, which is still being imposed, but I do hope the machinery can be speeded up a bit.' Yet again he stressed the importance of bolstering the Royal Air Force.[74]

In the office, Wavell was deep in military problems; at home, he and Queenie celebrated their silver wedding anniversary on Monday 22 April.

Coats gave his 'new General' a paper-knife inscribed with the names and dates of their stops on the South Africa trip, which 'surprised and delighted' him.[75] He was beginning to understand Wavell: 'I have discovered he loves toys. He sulked for two days recently because he had lost a plastic pencil sharpener in the shape of a bulldog. And once he gets to them, he really enjoys parties, of which there are a spate at this moment.'[76] There was also another newcomer to Wavell's General Staff: Lieutenant-Colonel Eric (known as John) Shearer, Commandant of the Intelligence School in Britain, had been sent out to the Middle East to organize a Field Intelligence Section.[77] Accommodation was at a premium in Cairo, so he shared the apartment in which Felicity and Joan were living, supervised by Nanny Ribbands. Joan celebrated her seventeenth birthday on 23 April and started to work with Shearer, Pam continued to nurse, and Felicity was working on the cipher staff at GHQ.

At dawn on 10 May 1940 Germany invaded Belgium and Holland, deftly skirting the Maginot Line built to defend France; that evening Chamberlain resigned as Prime Minister, to be succeeded by Winston Churchill. He immediately set up a National Coalition government, selecting as Lord Privy Seal Clement Attlee, leader of the Labour Party and 'long versed in the House of Commons'. They 'worked together with perfect ease and confidence'. Churchill retained most of the previous Government's ministers: former Viceroy of India Lord Halifax remained as Secretary of State for Foreign Affairs,[78] Eden became Secretary of State for War. As Secretary of State for India and Burma Churchill brought in Leopold Amery, Conservative MP and a contemporary from his schooldays (who Churchill had once pushed into the swimming pool at Harrow)[79]. When the House of Commons was summoned to give the new Government a vote of confidence, its members thrilled to Churchill's rhetoric: 'I have nothing to offer but blood toil, tears and sweat . . . You ask, What is our policy? I will say: It is to wage war, by sea, land and air, with all our might and with all the strength that God can give us . . . You ask, What is our aim? I can answer in one word: Victory.'[80] For the next five years Churchill's dominant personality held the British war effort together. He also assumed the portfolio of Minister of Defence, giving him full control over the conduct of the war and the armed forces. Overnight the Military Wing of the War Cabinet Secretariat became the Office of the Minister of Defence, headed by Hastings Ismay, who as Secretary for the Committee of Imperial Defence since 1938 already had considerable experience of the Government's inner workings.[81]

Wavell absorbed the news of Churchill's accession with his customary reserve. Privately he was less enthusiastic about it than some of his colleagues. Benson recalled having been asked by Wavell the previous year what he thought of Chamberlain as Prime Minister: 'Naturally I was taken aback as a very junior officer to be asked a question like this but I believe he asked lots of young officers these sort of questions in order to sound out the general feelings of officers in his command.' Benson replied that he thought they might get 'better results' if someone like Churchill was Prime Minister. 'Wavell's reply to this was, "I see; perhaps, but Churchill was not very successful over Gallipoli in which he was one of the prime movers if not *the* prime mover." '[82] Meanwhile, discussion of war plans with the French continued. The question arose of the island of Crete, south of the Greek mainland. Both because the British did not wish to violate Greek neutrality before Italy had entered the war and because they did not have sufficient resources, the Chiefs of Staff in London were urging Wavell to encourage the Greeks to stiffen their defences on Crete. A meeting with Weygand in early May revealed that it was France's intention to defend Crete once hostilities with Italy appeared imminent, and Wavell was able temporarily to shelve his concern, having once more warned the Chiefs of Staff how weak they were in air power.[83] In Europe the situation was deteriorating rapidly. The Germans had already captured Brussels and were moving with speed and determination through France towards Arras and Amiens. As in the Great War, the British Expeditionary Force in the north under Gort's command was vulnerable to annihilation.

Wavell continued to observe Italy's reaction to Germany's successes: 'Musso looks to me rather like a man who has climbed up to the top diving board at a swimming pool, taken off his dressing-gown and thrown a chest to the people looking on. I think he must do something; if he cannot make a graceful dive, he will at least have to jump in somehow; he can hardly put on his dressing-gown and walk down the stairs again.'[84] In the circumstances, he considered it necessary to evaluate what might happen if the war continued to go badly for Britain. On Friday 24 May he sat down and wrote a short four-page document headed 'The Worst Possible Case'. As he envisaged it, 'The Worst Possible Case' was Britain in a state of siege, the Middle East cut off and attacked by Italy, possibly reinforced by German air and land troops, and Egypt and other Middle Eastern peoples 'frightened, unfriendly or hostile'. He proceeded to analyse the problems he would face, and how he would deal with them. The final page of his document, entitled 'Immediate Arrangements', stipulated the necessity of controlling Egypt and seizing all means of communication.[85]

Towards the end of May Ironside became Commander-in-Chief, Home Forces and John Dill succeeded him as CIGS. For Wavell, a friend in such direct contact with the Prime Minister would be an advantage. From Dill's point of view, if and when 'Musso tries to come the jackal', he said in a short note to Wavell, it would be a great relief to know that he was in charge in Egypt.[86] But even as the ink was drying on Wavell's 'Worst Possible Case', the situation in Europe was becoming unsustainable. German attacks continued along the French coast and the British Expeditionary Force had already withdrawn to the bridgehead around Dunkirk, from where it was evacuated over the next few days. Wavell again assessed the situation, this time taking into account the availability of oil. His analysis was positive: 'We are bound to win the war' because 'oil, shipping, air power, sea power are the keys to this war'. Germany was short of oil and its naval power was not equal to that of the Allies; unless Germany could obtain oil in sufficient quantity, Germany could not pursue the war. To win the war, therefore, Britain needed to focus on preventing Germany from obtaining oil, which meant keeping the seas open to Allied shipping and closed to that of Germany. Writing on 28 May to congratulate Dill on his appointment as CIGS, Wavell enclosed his appreciation, adding: 'We shall be all right, but we may have some difficult moments.'[87]

Bad feeling was already developing between Wavell and the new Prime Minister, however. Churchill, concerned that Hitler was about to attempt an invasion of Britain, instructed Wavell to despatch eight battalions from Palestine; Wavell, concerned about his own theatre of command, was reluctant to part with them. As Churchill saw it, the situation in Europe demanded their immediate return: 'It is quite natural that General Wavell should look at the situation only from his own viewpoint. Here we have to think of building up a good army in order to make up, as far as possible, for the lamentable failure to support the French by an adequate BEF during the first year of the war,' he wrote to Anthony Eden on 6 June.[88] The despatch of eight battalions from India somewhat relieved the situation, but Churchill did not forget Wavell's unwillingness to help.

Wavell watched and waited, and on 4 June he, Admiral Cunningham and the new Air Officer Commanding-in-Chief, Air Chief Marshal Sir Arthur Longmore (who had replaced Mitchell in mid May),[89] received identical messages: they were reminded that although forces in the Mediterranean had to be on the defensive, in view of the dire situation in Europe, local offensive action should be taken against the Italians where possible.[90] It was an indication of what was to come, and during the weekend, events reached a climax. Wavell's dispositions had been made, and on

8 June O'Connor was informed that he was to take over command of the Western Desert Force, which included not only his 7th Division – now known as the 6th because the number seven had been given to the Armoured Division, the former Mobile Division raised by Hobart, now commanded by Major-General Dicky O'Moore Creagh – and the 4th Indian Division, under the command of Major-General Noel Beresford-Peirse.[91] O'Connor's arrival left Wilson free to concentrate his attention on British troops in Egypt. Nevertheless, as Wavell stood poised at the brink of war he knew that, while he had some of the best soldiers the British Army could offer under his command, his forces remained numerically inferior to those of the Italians. Not one formation was either fully equipped or fully trained. There was still a shortage of ammunition, equipment and transport.[92]

Finally, on the night of 10/11 June, at one minute past midnight, Italy's long-awaited declaration of war was made. Looking back at this period later, Wavell did not hide his annoyance over Britain's policy. 'Right up to the end of May our Foreign Office would hardly admit that war with Italy was really likely. I do not know whether the Italians skilfully threw dust in the eyes of our Ambassador or whether it was just wishful thinking . . . But I am sure that a more robust attitude towards Italy during the period of waiting instead of our weak-kneed and apologetic attempts at appeasement would certainly not have increased the danger of war and might perhaps have lessened it. And our preparations would have been less hampered.'[93] The following day Wavell went to meet Sir Miles Lampson at the Embassy; of the Embassy staff among those present were Michael Wright, Terence Shone and Ernest Besly.[94] With the exception of Lampson, an Etonian, all were Wykehamists, and in solidarity they were wearing their Old Boy's ties.[95] War had finally come to the Middle East.

10

Holding Africa, 1940

Wavell's star rose high at an early stage of the war. The glow was the more brilliant because of the darkness of the sky.

Basil Liddell Hart[1]

WITH ITALY'S FORMAL entry into the war came the opportunity for which Wavell had been waiting: 'I had given instructions for offensive action on the Italian frontier with Egypt to be taken immediately on the declaration of war.'[2] In Europe, events were moving towards an ultimate confrontation between France and Germany. On 17 June Wavell was playing golf at Gezira; his game was interrupted by his Intelligence Officer John Shearer, who arrived with the dramatic and appalling news that France had capitulated. Like Sir Francis Drake with his game of bowls, Wavell finished his round. It was entirely characteristic: 'I thought for a moment if there was anything I could do about it. There wasn't. So I went on with the game and was rather pleased that I did the next two holes in three and four.'[3] When Wavell returned to his office, he wrote a brief 'Order of the Day'. The tone was sombre: 'Our gallant French Allies have been overwhelmed after a desperate struggle and have been compelled to ask for terms. The British Empire will, of course, continue the struggle until victory has been won . . . Dictators fade away – the British Empire never dies.'[4] Within the space of two months – from the moment of Germany's offensives in Europe to the entry of Italy into the war and the fall of France – Wavell had been transformed from the commander of a valuable outpost into a key figure. At his suggestion, approved by Churchill, a Cabinet Sub-Committee on Ministerial Policy in the Middle East ('the Middle East Committee') was set up. Its members were Eden, Amery and George Lloyd, the Secretaries of State for War, India and the Colonies, respectively.

Wavell had hoped that the French might fight on, but their surrender put an end to any plans for cooperation and shared defence either in the Middle East or in North Africa. On 22 June Marshal Henri Pétain, the octogenarian

Prime Minister of France, agreed to the Armistice signed at Compiègne, permitting a government to be set up at Vichy. Churchill, however, wanted to encourage individual French officers in the colonies to join the British and on 1 July he informed Wavell by cable that he was trying to gather together a force of five to ten thousand French officers and soldiers under Charles de Gaulle, who had been the French Under-Secretary for National Defence before the capitulation. 'Do not therefore on any account discourage the rallying of good men to our cause upon consideration local to your own command,' he instructed Wavell.[5] Wavell, as so often, had his own point of view, and disagreed with the policy as voiced from London. Because of his vulnerability on so many fronts, he wanted Syria to remain stable and neutral. 'To disrupt it by removing large numbers of the best French officers would be bad policy,' he later explained. 'It might result in disorder in Syria, which I did not want, and in Vichy sending out officers definitely hostile to the British. I did not think the gain of a certain number of French officers without units was worth the risk of this.' Eventually Wavell 'struck some sort of a bargain' with General Eugène Mittelhauser, who had replaced Weygand, now serving as Defence Minister in Pétain's government: he would not encourage French officers to desert to the Allied cause, if Mittelhauser would enable the Polish Brigade, stationed in Syria, to come over fully armed.[6] Wavell's cautious response earned him criticism in London and also from de Gaulle, because by observing the Armistice, France would inevitably be obliged to assist Germany.

As instructed by Wavell, immediately war was declared O'Connor's Western Desert Force began to attack the Italians. On 14 June the Italian forts at Capuzzo and Maddalena were captured. London voiced immediate approval. 'All these operations are of immense value at this time and publicity of our remarkable local successes has also importance,' Dill cabled Wavell on 26 June.[7] Yet already the novel conditions of desert warfare were beginning to take their toll on British machinery. At the end of July O'Connor was obliged to withdraw his tanks to conserve them for a larger battle. Henceforward their role was to be taken by the motorized infantry and guns of the 7th Armoured Division Support Group, commanded by Brigadier W.H.E. 'Strafer' Gott.[8] Even at this early stage Wavell was keen to exploit any chance of operating behind enemy lines. His long-standing interest in the use of unconventional methods received a boost with the unscheduled arrival of Ralph Bagnold in Cairo. A veteran of the Great War, in the 1920s Bagnold had undertaken expeditions to Sinai, Transjordan and the Libyan desert. He retired from the army due to ill health in 1935, but on the outbreak of war he was recalled and posted to a routine job in Kenya.[9] A collision in the Mediterranean sent his ship into Port Said for repairs, and Wavell arranged for him to be transferred to the Middle East Command. As early as November 1939 Bagnold had suggested the formation of a force to guard the 700–mile frontier with Libya; Jumbo Wilson, mindful of the British Government's insistence at the time that no moves should be taken to antagonize Italy, had rejected the idea. After Italy's declaration of war Bagnold revised his proposal and submitted it directly to Wavell, who lost no time in agreeing to the formation of a self-contained motorized force which would penetrate as far as possible into the Libyan desert. All branches and departments of the Army were ordered to cooperate and give Bagnold whatever he needed.[10]

The force Bagnold created, originally called the Long Range Patrol, became the Long Range Desert Group or LRDG. After just over a month's preparation, three patrols each consisting of two officers and twenty-eight men were ready to go. On 27 August Wavell visited their base to bid them 'god speed'. 'The old boy seemed as if he's dying to come with us,' remarked one of the departing men.[11] Operating in small independent columns, the group succeeded in penetrating nearly every part of the desert. As well as bringing back information, the patrols attacked Italian forts, captured personnel and transport and grounded aircraft as far as 800 miles inside 'enemy' territory. Wavell was quick to congratulate Bagnold. Their efforts, he said, had only been achieved 'by careful organization and a very high standard of enterprise, discipline, mechanical maintenance and desert navigation.'[12]

In conjunction with O'Connor's offensives in the Western Desert, Wavell regarded the destruction of Italy's East African Empire as the lynch-pin of his campaign. In his opinion, the best way to destroy the Italian hold on East Africa was to foment a rebellion among those still loyal to the deposed Ethiopian Emperor, Haile Selassie, aimed at restoring him to his throne.[13] Wavell's real tool of revolt, however, was a bald and bespectacled British colonel, Daniel Arthur Sandford.[14] A former gunner, and acting treasurer of Guildford Cathedral, Sandford had previously been an adviser to the Emperor and had an intimate knowledge of the Abyssinian tribal hierarchy. As soon as Italy declared war, Wavell instructed Sandford to come to Cairo, to raise a rebellion. Events moved even faster than anticipated with the unexpected arrival of Haile Selassie himself. Using a fictitious name – Mr Strong – he reached Egypt by flying-boat on 25 June. Since it was not deemed politic to permit him to land on Egyptian soil, he spent the night aboard his flying-boat before continuing his journey to Khartoum, this time using the name of Mr Smith. Once news of the

Emperor's arrival in the Sudan reached the ears of his former subjects, they flocked to see him. Soon afterwards, Sandford crossed over the border into Ethiopia with four colleagues and two wireless sets at the head of a special 'Mission 101'.[15] As in the Western Desert, Wavell's offensive strategy here involved directing 'small mobile forces' to occupy the main locations on the frontier. They could not withstand attacks for long, he knew, but they could at least fight a delaying action and inflict some losses on the Italians. To no one's surprise, when in mid July the Italians did succeed in capturing the small post of Moyale in Kenya, they made such dramatic propaganda of it that it appeared Wavell had lost a major engagement. 'The War Cabinet sent me some very critical telegrams and the authorities in S. Rhodesia and S. Africa showed signs of nerves!'[16]

In mid July Wavell travelled south again, to Kenya and Sudan, where he met Haile Selassie for the first time. 'The Emperor was an attractive personality, although not always easy to deal with.' During their discussions Wavell felt that he had to 'disabuse' him of the idea – instilled by some 'moron' in the Foreign Office – that a large force could be put at his disposal to help him regain his kingdom. On this as on subsequent occasions, he found that although Haile Selassie appeared to understand French and English, he would speak only Amharic – and since the Amharic interpreter spoke only Arabic, 'conversation had to filter through at least three languages – on one occasion four, when it was found that the interpreter of Arabic knew no English, only French.'[17] In London, at a meeting of the Middle East Committee in July, Leo Amery suggested that 'an ideal man' to lead the insurgent Ethiopians would be 'a certain Captain O.C. Wingate'. When the suggestion was communicated to Wavell, he plucked his memories of Wingate from the 'pigeon hole' of his mind and accepted his appointment to General Headquarters in Cairo – with an important pre-condition: on no account was Wingate to visit Palestine. In the years since he had worked under Wavell in Palestine in 1937/8, the creation of a Jewish Fighting Force had become his overriding passion. This ardent advocacy of Zionism had gained him a certain notoriety, and it was feared that he might upset the Palestinian Arab population. Disappointed and angry at the prohibition, Wingate arrived in Cairo in September.[18]

On Churchill's assumption of the premiership, Wavell had immediately found himself at the receiving end of a barrage of questions regarding deployment. In some respects it was no more than he might have expected. He was constantly putting forward the case for reinforcements: it was therefore only natural that the new Prime Minister should want an accurate record of where various troops were employed. The object of Churchill's

immediate interest was the South African Brigade, which Wavell had seen
disembarking at Mombasa during his recent visit to Kenya. Where was it,
Churchill demanded indignantly, and why was it not playing any part
in the Middle East? A soldier of Wavell's temperament found this sort of
'barracking', as he called it, tedious. Communicating through Dill, he gave
factual responses to Churchill's enquiries. The South African Brigade, he
said, was only partially trained; the men also needed to become acclimat-
ized, and to learn anti-malaria precautions. Above all, Wavell spelled out
the full scale of the logistical difficulties, among them geography, climate,
deserts, distances: 'It all looks so simple . . . on a small-scale map.'[19] His
own immediate requirement was for the 7th Armoured Division to be
brought up to its full strength and for a second armoured division to be sent
from Britain, together with an armoured regiment: 'We cannot continue
indefinitely to fight this war without proper equipment and I hope that
Middle East requirements will be delayed no longer.'[20]

But as Wavell's shopping list increased, so did Churchill's desire for
results. The increasingly argumentative tenor of their respective telegrams
led Eden to suggest to Churchill that Wavell should return to England at
the beginning of August, to 'talk over his difficulties with us'.[21] Wavell was
duly informed that a Sunderland flying-boat would pick him up at
Alexandria, but even as he was preparing to depart, the Italians chose to
advance into British Somaliland. Colonial conquest had left the region
divided between Britain, France and Italy, and the Italians saw British
Somaliland as a 'ripe plum', ready to fall. Strategically it was relatively
unimportant, and Wavell had decided that it would only be worth putting
up a fight if the small force already present could be augmented. Before
leaving for England on 4 August he issued the necessary instructions,
which included the despatch from Aden of his own regiment, the 2nd
Battalion, The Black Watch, to the capital, Berbera. Jumbo Wilson was
entrusted with the decision whether and when to evacuate.[22]

Wavell had not been to London since his brief visit at the end of 1939.
Much had changed. Since July, following Hitler's instructions to
Reichsmarschall Hermann Goering 'to begin the great battle of the
German Air Force against England', an atmosphere of extreme tension had
prevailed. If the German Luftwaffe triumphed against the Royal Air Force,
it would be only a matter of time before the land invasion began. Even
Wavell's journey from Egypt was fraught with danger. Shearer, who
accompanied him, described how 'coming over we were attacked, and had
to descend to sea-level . . . German aircraft also chased us far into the
Atlantic the night before we landed at Plymouth.' During the flight Wavell

spent time rehearsing until he was 'word perfect' what he was going to say to the War Cabinet, and 'spouting poetry by the yard'.[23]

On Thursday 8 August the Prime Minister and the General came face to face. Wavell had known of Churchill the politician for more than a quarter of a century, since the controversies over the Curragh mutiny in 1914 and Gallipoli in 1915 brought him to public attention. Rather than erasing the animosity of their recent telegrams, the meeting provided ample proof of their differences: Wavell, the taciturn general whose reputation had been built on integrity and hard work according to a military schedule; Churchill, the charismatic and bullying politician prepared to work all hours, who now – at this critical time in Britain's history – was the one man upon whose every word the populace hung. As Wavell reviewed the situation in front of the Chiefs of Staff and the Middle East Committee, the deficiencies being experienced in the Middle East were made manifest. 'The outcome of this meeting,' noted Eden, who praised Wavell's account as 'masterly', 'was a strong recommendation by our Committee and the Chiefs of Staff that the despatch of convoys taking reinforcements to the Middle East should be hastened.'[24] But Wavell's reticence irritated the Prime Minister, and led him to think his Commander-in-Chief lacked mental dexterity. 'It was soon apparent that they did not see eye to eye on every point,' recollected Ismay.[25] Churchill's 'interrogation', noted Shearer, 'seemed to me to become increasingly curt,' leaving relations 'between these two magnificent men . . . irretrievably damaged.'[26] Wavell was instantly aware of their differences: 'I do not think Winston quite knew what to make of me and whether I was fit to command or not.' But he was also critical of Churchill: 'He never realized the necessity for full equipment before committing troops to battle. I remember his arguing that because a comparatively small number of mounted Boers had held up a British division in 1899 or 1900, it was unnecessary for the South African Brigade to have much more equipment than rifles before taking the field in 1940.' Wavell recognised the greater theatre of war in which Churchill was operating, but believed his tactical ideas had 'crystallized' at the South African war.[27]

After the meeting Wavell walked through the streets of Westminster with Dill and Shearer to Dill's flat in Ashley Gardens, where he was staying. Their conversation, as related by Shearer, revealed Wavell's wounded pride. He told his companions of Churchill's invitation to Chequers the following day: 'I'll be damned if I'll risk further treatment of the kind to which I have just been subjected,' he said, to which Dill responded: 'Archie, no one would deny that you have had unbearable provocation. But he is our Prime Minister. He carries an almost incredible burden. It is true you can be replaced. He cannot be. You must go to Chequers.'[28] Realizing that Dill was right, Wavell acquiesced. In addition to Wavell, Churchill's guests included Eden, Dill, Pound, and Ismay. Once the Churchill ladies had withdrawn after dinner, discussions took place. The atmosphere between Churchill and Wavell remained cool, but a decision was taken to send half the strength of the tank force in Britain to the Middle East. As noted by Eden, who was just getting to know Wavell, 'the Commander-in-Chief was not a man who could be drawn out, or one to make a special effort to please, but there was agreement as to what should be done.'[29] Churchill's private secretary John Colville also observed the damaging effect of Wavell's reticence: 'Churchill tried his hardest to elicit the General's views and was met with the silence of shyness.'[30]

In London on Monday 12 August a third meeting with Churchill took place at the Prime Minister's preferred time, late at night. The main point at issue was the route by which the tanks and other equipment should be sent to the Middle East. Churchill wanted them to get there as soon as possible, and suggested they go by way of the Mediterranean; Dudley Pound maintained that this route was too dangerous, and that they should go via the Cape of Good Hope, a point Churchill eventually conceded. But he chose once more to question Wavell on the disposition of his troops. As related by Ismay, 'an unfortunate incident brought matters to a head. Churchill was trying to scrape the pot in order to get things moving against the Italians in East Africa and suggested that West African Frontier Force troops might be brought round to the Sudan to release British troops to be used to operate against the Italians. For some reason Wavell blurted out the foolish comment, that West African troops could not stand the climate of the Sudan!' Although Wavell later withdrew his statement, 'the damage was done. Churchill had got it into his head that here was another general who could think of nothing except making difficulties.' As Ismay recalled, he was so afraid Wavell was going to get himself sacked that he nearly 'plucked' up courage to ask for a personal interview, to explain that he was not handling Churchill in the correct way: 'But I felt that I did not know him well enough and was too junior; so I blurted it all out to John Shearer in the hope that he would pass it on.'[31]

The following day Wavell presented himself at Eden's office. 'He was clearly upset at last night's proceedings and said that he thought he should have made it plain that if the Prime Minister could not approve his dispositions and had not confidence in him he should appoint someone else.'[32] Although Eden and Dill tried to defend Wavell, Churchill's confidence had been shaken. 'I am favourably impressed with General Wavell in many ways,' he noted in a letter to Eden, 'but I do not feel in him that sense of mental vigour and resolve to overcome obstacles, which is indispensable to successful war.' Instead, Churchill said, he found a 'tame' acceptance of a variety of local circumstances which was 'leading to a lamentable lack of concentration upon the decisive point'. In the same letter he once more recommended a number of changes in the disposition of the forces in the Middle East in order to meet the 'impending' Italian attack: 'Pray do not forget that the loss of Alexandria means the end of British sea power in the Eastern Mediterranean, with all its consequences.'[33] Eden's opinion of Wavell, as expressed to Churchill, was unequivocal: neither he nor Dill knew of any general officer in the Army 'better qualified to fill this very difficult post at this critical time'.[34] Churchill backed off, but conceded only that Wavell was 'a good average colonel' and would make 'a good chairman of a Tory association.'[35] As Eden later surmised, 'the truth was that Churchill never understood Wavell and Wavell never seemed to encourage Churchill to do so.'[36] His first encounter with Wavell so disappointed Churchill that he even 'toyed with the idea' of replacing him with Bernard Freyberg, whom he had known since the Great War.[37] At the time of Wavell's visit Freyberg too was in England, overseeing the training of the second 'echelon' of New Zealand troops, diverted from Egypt during the invasion scare. On reflection, however, Churchill decided that the time was not yet right for Freyberg to take on such a complex command. He also discussed with Eden the possibility of Claude Auchinleck, currently GOC-in-C, Southern Command, as a replacement, but it was eventually decided that they did not have enough evidence 'to compel a change which at the moment might have very bad effect on morale throughout Middle East.'[38] In his history of the Second World War, Churchill toned down his reaction to Wavell: 'While not in full agreement with General Wavell's use of the resources at his disposal, I thought it best to leave him in command. I admired his fine qualities, and was impressed with the confidence so many people had in him.'[39]

During Wavell's absence in London, the fate of British Somaliland had been sealed: in the face of an Italian attack which lasted for three days, British troops could do little except pull back. On the day Wavell was preparing to leave London Major-General Godwin-Austen, who had taken command of the British force, signalled GHQ in Cairo: either he could evacuate immediately, or casualties would be extremely high. Jumbo Wilson, acting in Wavell's absence, decided in favour of evacuation and signalled his decision to Wavell in London. When Wavell told Churchill, the Prime Minister appeared to consider it of no great significance, except that it freed the troops involved for more important defence work. The evacuation went smoothly: with The Black Watch fighting a rearguard action, the majority of the troops were safely embarked on HMAS *Hobart*.

When he returned to Cairo Wavell broadcast on the Egyptian BBC, the second time he had spoken on the radio since the outbreak of war. He showed no hint of his difficulties with Churchill in London: 'I was in England during a week of continual heavy air attacks and I saw no sign of depression or even anxiety in any circles.' At the same time, he seemed to be raising the curtain on the next act: 'The Middle East will have a great part to play in final victory; we must be ready to play it.'[40] Before Wavell's departure from London on 15 August, Churchill had dictated an eighteen-point 'General directive for Commander-in-Chief Middle East', which was put before Eden and Dill on 16 August though it did not catch up with Wavell in Cairo, as a signal, until the 23rd. Once deciphered, it made more than three foolscap pages, closely typed, of detailed instructions which left Wavell feeling that the Prime Minister did not 'trust me to run my own show and was set on his ideas'. It was an exceptional document for a Prime Minister to send a Commander-in-Chief. Writing in later life, Wavell stated that he 'carried out such parts of the directive as were practicable and disregarded a good deal of it.' In particular he ignored the Prime Minister's directive to render all water supplies between Mersa Matruh and the Alexandria forces 'depotable'; nor did he follow instructions to render the tarmac road from Mersa Matruh to Alexandria impassable. As he put it, he had 'an inkling all the time that I might want it before the Italians'.[41]

Repercussions of the evacuation from Somaliland, however, raised the temperature again. Wavell believed the best aspect of Britain's enforced withdrawal was the comparatively small number of casualties – 260, of which 38 were killed, with 222 missing or wounded, compared with an estimated 2,000 Italians dead; when Churchill realized how few there had been on the British side, he took it to indicate that the British forces had not put up a good fight. He immediately telegraphed Wavell, ordering him to suspend Major-General Godwin-Austen and conduct a court of inquiry. Wavell had known Godwin-Austen since Aldershot, and judged the situation differently. He at once cabled Churchill that 'a big butcher's bill was not necessarily evidence of good tactics'. According to Dill, this remark 'roused Churchill to greater anger' than he had ever seen before.[42] In the larger interests of the war, Churchill chose not to persist either with the suspension of Godwin-Austen – now commanding a Division in Kenya – or with the court of inquiry. But the damage to the relationship between Prime Minister and General appeared almost irreparable.

Mussolini, meanwhile, was watching for an opportunity to strike at the British forces in North Africa. Wavell was anticipating just such a move and, with the exception of a few battalions held back for internal security, nearly all available trained forces were concentrated in the Western Desert, under O'Connor's command. Ideally they would fight a 'forward' battle, encouraging the Italians as far eastwards as Mersa Matruh, with the objective of isolating and destroying them. Even at this early stage, however, Wavell had asked his staff to study the possibility of an offensive into Italian-held Cyrenaica. In planning the operation, he suggested that they should 'avoid as far as we can the slow ponderosity which is apt to characterize British operations'. He also stressed the need for 'a proper air component with our force', and asked pertinent questions: whether they had 'all the topographical information about Cyrenaica that we can possibly get, have we suitable maps, do we know all about water supplies?'[43] On Friday 13 September the anticipated Italian offensive began. Italian forces with tanks and artillery crossed the border between Libya and Egypt and halted at Sidi Barrani, 60 miles into Egypt but still 80 miles from Mersa Matruh, where the Western Desert Force lay. Sidi Barrani was only a small village, but Italian radio announced its capture as a major achievement. After erecting a monument to celebrate their passage into Egypt, the Italians dug themselves in, creating a semi-circle of defensive camps.

While the Italians were busy in North Africa, the weight of the Axis alliance was growing. On 27 September Germany, Italy and Japan signed the 'Tripartite Pact' in Berlin, its aim to establish the 'New Order' in Europe and 'Greater East Asia'. Embodied in the pact was the commitment that each would declare war on any third party which joined the war against one of the three. On 4 October Hitler and Mussolini met at the Brenner Pass in South Tyrol, and Hitler formally offered to supply Italy with mechanized and specialist troops.[44] Mussolini grudgingly accepted, agreeing that he might need assistance when – on the assumption that Mersa Matruh would soon be taken – he advanced on Alexandria. Wavell, meanwhile, contemplating the possibility of a German air attack on Egypt, sent a request to Dill for immediate RAF, anti-aircraft and anti-tank reinforcements. Eden responded at once: 'In view of your telegram to the CIGS of 7 October and wide developments likely to take place affecting your Command have decided with concurrence of PM to pay you a flying visit and hope to arrive Alexandria 14th.'[45]

As Wavell evaluated the enemy he had also to deal with problems in his own command, in particular with Freyberg, who, while he was in England, had heard from his second-in-command that GHQ Middle East was proposing to disperse New Zealand forces; he had thereupon gone to Dill and reminded him that these forces were in the Middle East on the understanding that they should not be used 'piecemeal'. Returning to Cairo in late September, Freyberg found that although Dill had assured him the New Zealand Division would not be dispersed, Wavell had felt justified in making what dispositions he believed necessary for the greater good. When Freyberg raised the matter with Wilson and Wavell, he later said, he felt that he was being treated as a 'fifth columnist'.[46] The fact that Freyberg obviously enjoyed a good rapport with Churchill while Wavell's own relationship was so difficult only increased the tension.[47]

Eden arrived in Alexandria on 15 October, but it was no 'flying visit': he remained for over two weeks. Churchill, still fretting that there were too many troops in Kenya, was anxious to know Wavell's plans for the Western Desert. Wavell greeted Eden warmly but, mindful of Churchill's 'desire to have at least one finger in any military pie', had no intention of disclosing the plans which he had been formulating ('very roughly') to counter-attack the Italians simultaneously at Sidi Barrani and on the top of the escarpment at Sofafi.[48] His orders to Wilson and O'Connor were to carry out a 'five days raid' in a two-pronged attack. Instead of splitting the British forces, O'Connor thought it would be better to advance through the gap between the Italian camps at Sofafi and Nibeiwa, thereby cutting the Italian defences in two; he would then swing north to attack them from the rear. Wavell accepted the alterations, but the operation remained classified as a 'raid'. The British forces were afterwards to withdraw to Mersa Matruh.

While Wilson and O'Connor continued to work out the strategy of their proposed 'raid', Wavell and Eden travelled north and east, to Palestine and Transjordan. 'We talked of the country and politics and persons and also of Meredith and George Moore, so that the time passed very happily until we were beyond Jericho,' Eden recalled.[49] They also went west, to Mersa Matruh, visiting the various contingents encamped in the Western Desert, and at the end of October to Khartoum. Haile Selassie was a guest of the British Government in the Sudan but, annoyed that he was not being kept informed of the operations taking place within his kingdom, was demanding the status of an independent sovereign in alliance with Great Britain; a ministerial conference had been called to discuss his grievances. Landing at night, Wavell and Eden went immediately to the palace where Symes, the Governor, was waiting. 'Khartoum was still hot, even in the lofty rooms of the Palace which Kitchener had rebuilt. We were glad', Eden remembered, 'to sleep on the roof and to be wakened by the sun as it rose over the desert.'[50] Breakfasting every morning on iced coffee, Wavell spent three days embroiled in what proved to be 'stormy' meetings. Taking the view that the Emperor had the 'right to rebellion', and was fighting a war of liberation, Eden was 'determined that we must help him without stint' and that he should both be informed of events inside his kingdom and have a say in the distribution of weapons.[51] Haile Selassie's idea for a treaty of friendship was not pursued, but it was agreed that the Ethiopian rebels should be called, as the King was requesting, 'the Patriots'. In addition, two regular army officers were to be sent to Khartoum to liaise between the British military authorities, Mission 101 in the person of Colonel Sandford, and the Emperor. The two officers chosen were Orde Wingate, and Major Tuckey from the Deputy Quarter-Master General's department. 'I should like to have seen the meeting between Sandford and Wingate,' Wavell later wrote. 'Few people looked more like a fiery leader of partisans than Wingate, few looked less like one than Sandford – solid, bespectacled, benevolent – who was in his way as bold and as active as Wingate.'[52] But the rigours of travel were taking their toll on Wavell. The return flight from Nairobi, where they visited outlying garrisons, was disagreeable: seven hours in burning heat over a lunar landscape in a service plane.

While Wavell and Eden were in Khartoum, the Italians invaded Greece. Wavell was ordered to send reinforcements to Athens and an infantry brigade to Suda Bay, on the north shore of Crete. 'All this meant a considerable drain on my resources, and led to my disclosing to Eden my plans for an early attack on the Italians.' His initial reluctance to do so lay not only in a desire to avoid Churchill making detailed plans on his behalf – he knew his only hope of success lay in absolute secrecy, and the Italians 'had so many tentacles in Cairo'. But since Eden was proposing to 'sap his strength' in aircraft, guns and transport, Wavell was obliged to outline his offensive 'to prevent my being skinned to an extent that would make an offensive impossible'.[53] He subsequently recognised that the disclosure to Eden had had its benefits: it was largely Eden's support 'which enabled us to obtain the air reinforcements on which the success of the plan greatly depended.'[54]

Throughout October and November the Western Desert Force was strengthened with the arrival of additional regiments for the 7th Armoured Division and the 4th Indian Division. More importantly, the fifty-seven 'I' – infantry – or 'Matilda'[55] tanks of the 7th Royal Tank Regiment promised by Churchill arrived from Britain. Heavy and heavily armoured, 'nothing much apart from big holes in the ground or impossible terrain could stop them,' recalled Tom Straker, a member of the 4th New Zealand Brigade, which with the 6th Australian Division was being kept in reserve between Mersa Matruh and Alexandria. 'Not many army cannon could penetrate their armour. But because of their great weight, they developed mechanical problems and it was difficult to keep them serviced and in action.'[56] On 2 November Wavell gave Jumbo Wilson a formal written directive detailing his instructions to O'Connor for an offensive. He accepted responsibility for the enterprise, and the tone was upbeat: 'In everything but numbers we are superior to the enemy. We are more highly trained, we have better equipment. We know the ground and are better accustomed to desert conditions. Above all we have stouter hearts and greater traditions and are fighting in a worthier cause.'[57]

Eden was back in London on 8 November and went at once to see Churchill; Dill and Ismay were summoned, and Eden described Wavell's proposed offensive, code-named 'Compass'. Churchill was delighted, wished he had known about it earlier, and purred, as he said himself, 'like six cats'. 'That is putting it mildly,' recalled Ismay. 'He was rapturously happy, believing that Britain was finally going "to throw off the intolerable shackles of the defensive".'[58] It was at once decided that 'Compass' should take priority, and should be given all possible support. A curtain-raiser to the offensive was provided by the Royal Navy: an attack by the Fleet Air Arm on the Italian fleet in Taranto harbour effectively put half Mussolini's battle fleet out of action.[59]

On 14 November, while acting as a pall bearer at Neville Chamberlain's funeral in Westminster Abbey, Churchill was ruminating on Eden's information about the proposed offensive in the Western Desert. After the service, before sitting down to lunch, he wrote Wavell a cable of encouragement: 'The general political situation makes it very desirable to undertake operation of which you spoke to Secretary of State for War . . . It is unlikely that Germany will leave her flagging ally unsupported indefinitely. Consequently it seems that now is the time to take risks and strike the Italians by land, sea and air.'[60] Wavell, a man of measured responses, did not reply directly to Churchill, but to Eden. On 16 November he confirmed that the operation was in preparation but 'not possible to execute this month as originally hoped'. Once again, Wavell's constant reference to his deficiencies irritated Churchill – inevitably viewing the bigger picture. 'I fully understand your difficulty, but you must also see mine . . . If, as seems probable, Germany immediately attacks Greece through Bulgaria with or without Bulgarian aid, we shall certainly be bound to urge Turkey to the utmost to enter the war. Turkey will either refuse in which case Greece will soon be ruined; or Turkey will come in, in which case she will make most heavy demands for arms, troops, ships and air.'[61] As Churchill minuted to Dill and Eden, a victory in Libya would 'probably turn the scale' and leave them free to move troops to the new theatre. 'How long would it be before the Germans could strike at Greece through Bulgaria? There might just be time for Wavell to act in Libya before the pressure becomes decisive.'[62] But whatever the exhortations from London, Wavell was deliberately playing his cards close to his chest.

The success of Wavell's campaign in the Western Desert – the first great victory of the Second World War – has been told and re-told with an almost misty-eyed reverence. O'Connor's army – immortalized as 'Wavell's 30,000' – had approximately 120 guns, 275 tanks and sixty armoured cars. Because of the continuing shortages, part of the plan involved putting in position a brigade of rudimentary 'dummy' tanks. British air support was inferior to that of the Italians in a ratio of five to one. In the effort to maintain secrecy, 'as few people as possible were made aware of the plan . . . Practically nothing was put on paper. The fact that General Wilson and myself lived in the same house and met daily was of assistance. I attempted, through certain channels known to my Intelligence, to convey to the enemy the impression that my forces in the Western Desert had been seriously weakened by the sending of reinforcements to Greece and that further withdrawals were contemplated.'[63] O'Connor had also suggested that a rehearsal of the 'moonlight' portion of the approach march would be necessary. The date for the rehearsal, called Training Exercise No. 1, was 26 November; Training Exercise No. 2 – the actual operation – was to be held on 'a day in the second week of December'. The rehearsal – carried out on a plateau south of Matruh with replicas of the Italian camps at Nibeiwa and nearby Tummar based on aerial reconnaissance photographs – went off well. Most importantly, it was realized that there must be no delay between the tanks forcing the entrance and the first wave of infantry reaching the perimeter.

Even as the dress rehearsal was taking place, Churchill was peppering Wavell with more directives: 'If success is achieved, presume you have plans for exploiting it to the full. I am having a staff study made of possibilities open to us, if all goes well, for moving fighting troops and also reserves forward by sea in long hops along the coast . . . without wishing to be informed on details, I should like to be assured that all this has been weighed, explored, and as far as possible prepared.'[64] Dill was also warning Wavell of the consequences of inaction: 'You will appreciate that developments in Greek theatre are likely to lead to further persistent demands for our assistance which will be more difficult to resist so long as your forces are not actively engaged.'[65] Wavell, however, was following his own instinct. As he indicated in his last directive to Wilson before the offensive, though he hoped to capitalize on any success, he was thinking much less grandly than Churchill: 'I am not entertaining extravagant hopes of this operation, but I do wish to make certain that if a big opportunity occurs we are prepared morally, mentally and administratively to use it to the fullest.'[66]

Wavell also had to bear in mind his other theatres of operation. With the 'rebellion' in Ethiopia under way, he wanted – if the desert offensive worked out as he hoped – to start his offensive in East Africa by recapturing Kassala in the Sudan, taken by the Italians in July. For this he needed reinforcements, and on 2 December he met General Platt and General Alan Cunningham (Andrew's younger brother),[67] commanders of the forces in Sudan and Kenya respectively. Wavell informed Platt that in about the middle of December the 4th Indian Division – in an operation codenamed 'Emily' – would begin to move from the Western Desert to the Sudan; they would be replaced, he had decided, brigade by brigade, by the 6th Australian Division, currently held in reserve east of Matruh, under the command of General Iven Mackay.[68] Wilson knew of his intentions, but in general the strictest possible secrecy was observed. When O'Connor received his final orders from Wavell on 5 December, there was no mention of the proposed transfer.

Churchill was still being kept in the dark about operations in the desert, and his impatience was growing. As late as 6 December, Wavell sent Dill a cable in which he expressed his fear that too much hope was being placed on the operation 'which was designed as a raid only'.[69] On the grounds that he did not want to worry the Prime Minister and that Wavell was playing down the situation to avoid disappointment, Dill did not show the cable to Churchill. But the Prime Minister was insistent. 'If, with the situation as it is, General Wavell is only playing small, and is not hurling on his whole available force with furious energy, he will have failed to rise to the height of circumstances.'[70] As Wavell later explained, his reticence was due to his apprehension that Churchill 'might urge me to do too much, as limitations of supply and transport never made any great appeal to him.'[71] Then, on Saturday 7 December General Sir Archibald Wavell, his wife and daughters went to the races at Gezira. This was not in itself unusual, but they normally did so 'as quietly and unobtrusively as possible'. On this occasion, they arrived 'in a fleet of cars, with flags flying'.[72] Press photographers were accommodated. In the evening Wavell hosted a dinner party at the Cairo Turf Club at which all his senior commanders were present. But as the ostensibly frivolous social activities of Cairo were played out, deep in the desert the operation to encompass the enemy had begun.

To ensure maximum success, O'Connor had to get into position the night before the 'raid'. This required him to move his forces through open desert for some 75 miles. In subsequent operations, tank-transporters and tank-towing vehicles conserved the tank tracks and engines; O'Connor had none, but by the evening of 8 December he had reached his advanced HQ, near the main Mersa Matruh–Siwa road. Wilson set up his HQ at Maaten Baggush. To 'disconcert the enemy' and prevent them from carrying out reconnaissance flights while the formations were moving forward, British warplanes bombed Italian camps and British gunboats bombarded Sidi Barrani and Maktila, near the coast. By early morning the 4th Indian Division had succeeded in smashing through the Italian defences. With the capture of Nibeiwa camp, south of Sidi Barrani, the first objective had been achieved.

Wavell's very public appearances over the weekend were the culmination of his efforts to ensure secrecy while his commanders in the field moved forward. He had already made arrangements – described by war correspondent Alexander Clifford as unprecedented[73] – to hold a press conference in Cairo at 9 a.m. 'We have attacked in the Western Desert,' Wavell announced. Lest the correspondents become too excited, he continued: 'This is not an offensive and I do not think you ought to describe it as an offensive as yet. You might call it an important raid.' Further action would depend on what supplies and petrol they were able to find. Wavell also assured himself that the journalists had had no inkling of the impending attack.[74] As Bonner Fellers, the US Military Attaché in Cairo, later revealed, Wavell had told him that they were going to do manoeuvres. 'So up I went as an observer, and Goddamit – it was the works!'[75]

Wavell heard the details of the capture of Nibeiwa camp around 3 p.m. He had taken time off to play a round of golf and once more it fell to Shearer to walk across the fairway to bring him important news of Italian prisoners taken. Throughout the rest of the day, the 4th Indian Division under the command of Beresford-Peirse pushed on; the next objective was Sidi Barrani on the coast. That night Wavell sat and drafted a 'Special Order of the Day'. Describing the result of the fighting in the Western Desert as one of the decisive events of the war (and echoing his words to Wilson on 2 November), he pointed to the advantages which the British and their allies had over the Italians: 'In everything but numbers, we are superior to the enemy. We are more highly trained, we shoot straighter, we have better equipment. Above all, we have stouter hearts and greater traditions and are fighting a worthier cause.' With almost Churchillian rhetoric, he went on: 'The harder blows we strike against the servants of tyranny and self lust of power, the sooner we shall bring peace and freedom back to the world.'[76] On 10 December the Western Desert Force captured Sidi Barrani, bringing to a successful conclusion the first phase of 'Compass'.

When news of the victory reached Churchill, he was ecstatic. 'While it is too soon to measure the scale of these operations,' he stated in the House of Commons on 12 December, 'it is clear they constitute a victory which, in this African theatre of war, is of the first order, and reflects the highest credit upon Sir Archibald Wavell, Sir Henry Maitland Wilson, the Staff officers who planned this exceedingly complicated operation, and the troops who performed the remarkable feats of endurance and daring which accomplished it.' Churchill's cable to Wavell was rapturous: 'I send you my heartfelt congratulations on your splendid victory, which fulfils our highest hopes. The House of Commons was stirred when I explained the skilful Staff work required, and daring execution by the Army of its arduous task.'[77] Even at the summit of his success, Wavell was busily sharing this praise: 'I sent at least three telegrams home during the course of the ops to the CIGS or PM pointing out much of the credit was due to Dick [O'Connor] and asking that due publicity should be given to him and others, as I felt the limelight was coming much too much on myself who had only done the general direction.'[78] 'It was very lucky,' he wrote to Dill, 'to get four such outstanding commanders as Jumbo, O'Connor, Creagh and Beresford-Peirse in one show.'[79]

In the meantime, the Prime Minister had decided to find out more about his Commander-in-Chief. 'I believe there was a book written by Sir Archibald Wavell,' he wrote to Ismay in a personal minute on 11 December. 'Let me know what its name is and let me have a look at it.' Ismay immediately borrowed from the War Office library Wavell's two books (*The Palestine Campaigns* and his recently published *Allenby*, which he had been obliged to suspend at the victory at Damascus, pending publication of a second volume).[80] Not surprisingly, Wavell's frequent correspondent Basil Liddell Hart had also been reading *Allenby*, and subsequently gave him the same frankly critical treatment in print as he was accustomed to giving him privately: 'The value of his account of his old chief, Allenby, lies in the flashes of critical perspicacity which illuminate an otherwise rather too formal biography . . . his account of Allenby's operations shows signs here and there of the brakes of professional reticence having been put on his critical faculty.'[81]

While Churchill had been addressing the House of Commons on 12 December, Wavell was on his way to see Jumbo Wilson at his headquarters in the desert. As far as he was concerned, despite Churchill's stated desire to capitalize on their success in the Western Desert and his own instructions to Wilson to make every attempt to 'exploit' their victory, his decision to send the 4th Indian Division to the Sudan at their moment of triumph and replace them with the Australian 6th Division still held. O'Connor, informed of Wavell's decision only on 11 December, regarded it as 'a most unwelcome piece of news'. Certainly the transfer would create administrative difficulties – but it also meant that valuable transport was taken up with exchanging the divisions, rather than moving the captured Italians back to Mersa Matruh and, unfortunately but inevitably, this would delay the British advance along the coastline. Only when the transfer – which took three weeks – was complete were they able to move on their next military objective, the fortress of Bardia, into which the Italians had withdrawn under their garrison commander, whose splendid moustache had earned him the nickname of General 'Electric Whiskers' Bergonzoli.

In accepting the drawbacks of the exchange of forces, Wavell was mindful of the larger picture. Even before the Western Desert offensive, the campaign in East Africa had been a major component in his bid to drive the Italians out of Africa, and in this he was both supported and cajoled by Churchill, Smuts and Dill, all of whom favoured an East African offensive. Writing to O'Connor after the war, Wavell maintained that his decision to exchange the divisions was the right one. It was, he said, 'a matter of shipping':[82] a convoy had come into Suez and Wavell planned to use some of the returning ships to transport part of the 4th Indian to Port Sudan.[83] It was also evident that what Wavell had anticipated as merely a large-scale 'raid' to stun the Italians in the desert while he continued with his offensive against them in East Africa had developed its own momentum. Before the repercussions of the transfer had become evident, Churchill was envisaging supreme victory in even more hyperbolic terms than he had used in his earlier cable: 'The Army of the Nile has rendered glorious service to the Empire and to our cause . . . We are deeply indebted to you, Wilson and the other commanders,' he cabled on 16 December. 'Your first objective now must be to maul the Italian Army and rip them off the African shore to the utmost possible extent.'[84] Despite their earlier unpleasant exchanges, the relationship between Wavell and Churchill was in harmony. Responding to Wavell's requests for supplies, Churchill amused himself with a biblical reference: St Matthew vii, 7, ('Ask and it shall be given you; seek, and ye shall find; knock, and it shall be opened unto you'),[85] to which Wavell's riposte was 'St James, chapter i, verse 17, first part ["Every good gift and every perfect gift is from above, and cometh down from the Father of lights, with whom is no variableness, neither shadow of turning"]. More aircraft are our immediate need and these you are providing. Additional anti-aircraft also much required.'[86] Letters of congratulation flooded in. Wavell was especially delighted by a cable from the Kipling Society in London which referred to Mussolini's defeat as the jackal Tabaqui's discomfiture. He replied hoping that soon Shere Khan's hide would be on the council rock – Germany being the tiger Shere Khan whom Tabaqui reverently followed.

In Cairo, the news of British successes in the Western Desert was at the same time thrilling and curiously remote. 'Amazing that we live with no blackout,' marvelled Hermione Ranfurly, 'with good restaurants and shops and plenty, while the struggles, dangers and discomforts of the Desert continue nearby. Sadly, wounded or "on leave" soldiers bring us news of more and more friends who are missing or dead.'[87] As it happened, the Countess of Ranfurly's name was known to Wavell as that of a woman who had demonstrated the sort of courage and determination he admired. When her husband Dan, the 6th Earl, was posted to Palestine with the Nottingham Sherwood Rangers Yeomanry at the outbreak of war she had followed him to the Middle East, and had been doing voluntary work in a Soldiers' Rest Camp on the edge of Haifa and working as a part-time secretary to the District Commissioner's wife.[88] After the Italian offensives all Yeomanry wives were ordered to return to Britain. Hermione, determined not to do so, jumped ship at Cape Town – the ship was later torpedoed and sunk – and made her way to Cairo. GHQ in Cairo demanded that she should return to England, she persistently refused, and managed to get a job with the fledgling Special Operations Executive. When news of Hermione Ranfurly's predicament came to Wavell's attention in December, he wrote giving her permission to stay because of her 'certain valuable qualifications'. She was overjoyed: 'Astonishing that, with operations going on in the north, south, east and west of his big theatre of war, he should find time to sign a letter to a typist.'[89] Wavell was also earning the respect of the wounded. During one of his visits to the hospital outside Cairo, where Pamela was working, he met a young officer, Major Jock MacKinnon of the 2nd Cameron Highlanders, who was recovering from a bad injury to his leg. As MacKinnon related many years later, the Commander-in-Chief, in an old bush shirt and no medals, sat at the end of his bed for about twenty minutes. 'I thought what a man to be able to behave like this to a young chap like myself. Subsequently I had a letter from his ADC saying they would send the car for me to sit in the garden at the house when I was up to it.'[90]

Before the attack on Bardia, Wavell again visited the front. 'It would be impossible to say what great pleasure and assistance these visits gave to me,'

O'Connor recalled, 'and also to all other Commanders and units which he visited. He listened patiently to all our difficulties and made notes of everything; and I always received a wire from him on his return to Cairo, regarding which of my many demands he was able to supply. I felt the greatest confidence in him and knew that he would support me to the full in any bold action. Inaction was what he could not do with. All my instructions emanated from him.'[91] Administrative difficulties were beginning to emerge. Water was short, and every drop had to be transported some eighty miles up from the Siwa Road to the Sidi Barrani area. All the prisoners 'had to be fed, watered and guarded, and eventually brought back to Matruh'. And, as Wavell made clear in a cable to Dill, transport was as so often his 'chief anxiety . . . these desert operations at such distances are throwing very heavy strain on all vehicles'.[92]

Nor were the administrative difficulties all: beneath jubilation on the surface, vestiges of discord remained. The New Zealand Division was still not complete and had therefore not taken part in the offensive, though Freyberg believed his men had contributed to the victory by undertaking non-combative tasks, thus releasing British forces for the attack. Another meeting between Wavell and Freyberg on 27 December ended in a clash, 'when things were said that cannot be too quickly forgotten . . . It was not a pleasant situation to be treated as a "black sheep" by one's old friends in the British Army, with whom I had spent so many happy years. But the British generals greatly misunderstood my character if they thought that I and the New Zealanders would allow ourselves to be bulldozed.'[93] At the end of December the three Commanders-in-Chief – Wavell, Cunningham and Longmore – met in Cairo. They decided that their priority was to advance into Libya, at least as far as Tobruk. Unlike Sidi Barrani, Bardia was considerably better fortified than the camps they had already captured, protected by wire and anti-tank ditches, and concrete posts with machine guns and anti-tank guns in position along the seventeen-mile perimeter. The attack was to be supported by an artillery barrage. Wavell spent the next two days in the desert overseeing the final preparations. On 30 December General Mackay of the 6th Australians decided to postpone the attack, planned for 2 January, for twenty-four hours, to bring in additional ammunition. Wavell was back in Cairo to celebrate the New Year with his family. As he proudly felt, the first stage of 'Compass' had gone like 'clockwork'.[94]

11

All Fronts, 1941

If to die nobly is the chief part of excellence
To us of all men fortune gave this lot
For hastening to set a crown of freedom upon Hellas
We died possessed of praise that grows not old.
                    Simonides, Greek lyric poet[1]

A T THE BEGINNING of 1941 Wavell's reputation was glowing, but his New Year's Day broadcast from Cairo was nevertheless subdued. 'The first day of a new year is a time to look back to the year that is gone and forward to the year that is coming, to weigh one's gains and losses in the past and to take stock of one's hopes and fears for the future.' After reviewing the events of the year, pointing out the difficulties they still faced and paying tribute to Britain's friends and allies, he concluded: 'If we maintain the spirit and unity of these last six months of 1940, all will be well. Let us think further ahead still and make it our resolve to maintain this spirit and unity, not only through the war but after it. Have you ever thought what a world we could make if we put into our peace endeavours the same energy, the same self-sacrifice, the same cooperation as we use in the wastefulness of war?'[2]

On New Year's Eve Henry Channon III, MP – known always as 'Chips' – Parliamentary Private Secretary to R.A. Butler, Under Secretary of State for Foreign Affairs – had arrived in Cairo and was staying at the British Embassy with the Lampsons. As a friend and Oxford contemporary of the Yugoslav Regent Prince Paul, he was en route to Belgrade: the Foreign Office had sanctioned the visit, in the hope that Channon might be able to encourage the Regent to support Britain's war effort or, at the very least, to desist from siding with the Germans. Channon was undeniably excited at the prospect of 'making history', but the stop-over in Cairo suited him for personal reasons: he had recently met Peter Coats and they had begun an intimate relationship. Coats so admired his 'Chief' that he was anxious he and Channon should like each other. 'Chips was worldly and brilliant and had a quick, seemingly comical way of talking, which one had to get used to. He was the exact opposite of General Wavell.'[3] Channon took an instant liking to Wavell. 'We had a long conversation,' he noted, 'and I saw how lovable and gently distinguished he is . . . His charm completely engulfed me.'[4]

Far from Cairo, in preparation for continuing the offensive in the Western Desert, on the nights of 1 and 2 January the Royal Air Force bombed Bardia. The Royal Navy also shelled selected targets. At 6 a.m. on 3 January, in the Australians' first action in the war, the 6th Division began the land attack. After two days the Italian garrison surrendered, yielding yet more prisoners, tanks and guns, in their thousands. On the evening of the victory Wavell was hosting a 'mammoth cocktail party'. 'The Victor of Bardia hardly mentioned his latest victory: typical,' observed Channon: 'all goes according to plan; Wavell does his thinking alone, walking, or on the golf course.'[5] He had been successful in North Africa, but other aspects of Wavell's command required attention. Italian East Africa remained a priority, and on 6 January he flew to Khartoum to see General Platt. Initially Platt's attack on Eritrea had been planned for March, but the apparent weakening of Italian resolve prompted Wavell to bring it forward to 19 January. And all the while, he was being subjected to Churchill's searching scrutiny of the administrative aspects of his command. Soon after Bardia the Prime Minister sent what he obviously thought was a diplomatically worded cable: 'I am sorry to jar the hour of your splendid victory by awkward matters of housekeeping . . . You have well over 350,000 troops on your ration strength and the number of units which are fighting or capable of fighting appears to me disproportionately small . . . I beg you to convince me that you will continually comb, scrub and purge all rearward services.'[6] Wavell responded with corresponding tact that he would ensure they were not 'over-insured' or 'over-lavish' in any direction.[7]

An even greater concern for Churchill was the situation in the Balkans. From 'Ultra' intelligence reports he knew that German forces were gathering in southern Romania, in all probability to help the Italians in Greece and Albania.[8] In early January, as the storming of Bardia was being consolidated, additional intelligence indicated that a German attack on Greece, Yugoslavia and Bulgaria could be launched as early as mid January. Mindful of the guarantee of military support to Greece and Romania given by the British (and French) governments in 1939, following Italy's occupation of Albania, Churchill was looking closely at the Middle East Command to determine what forces might be available for the Balkans. Wavell, however, was anxious to continue the advance to Cyrenaica 'while we have Italians on the run'. He also believed that, indirectly, victory in the Western Desert would help the Greeks 'more than sending small additional amounts of transport that might be spared.'[9] But Anthony Eden, who had been appointed Foreign Secretary again, was suggesting that aid to Greece would help to influence Turkey to form the projected 'Balkan bloc'.

Churchill had therefore decided that support for Greece should take priority once Egypt's western flank had been made 'secure', and ordered both General Wavell and Air Chief Marshal Longmore to proceed at once to Athens, there to determine exactly what assistance the Greeks would require: 'Destruction of Greece will eclipse victories you have gained in Libya, and may affect decisively Turkish attitude, especially if we have shown ourselves callous of fate of allies. You must now therefore conform your plans to larger interests at stake. Nothing must hamper capture of Tobruk, but thereafter all operations in Libya are subordinated to aiding Greece, and all preparations must be made from the receipt of this telegram for the immediate succour of Greece up to the limits prescribed.' For good measure, Churchill also informed Wavell that Smuts had cabled 'almost identical views'.[10]

Regardless of his other commitments, Wavell still managed to make time for corresponding with his family, friends and colleagues, and on occasion their daughters too. Discovering that nineteen-year-old Araminta MacMichael, daughter of the High Commissioner in Palestine and Transjordan, was making a collection of military buttons, he made a point of sending her any he found. On 13 January she received an envelope enclosing a button with the note 'more coming';[11] when she wrote back thanking Wavell's ADC, the Commander-in-Chief let her know with playful indignation that he was collecting the buttons for her himself. But even as Araminta MacMichael was opening the envelope containing the military button, Wavell was on his way to Athens to meet King George II of the Hellenes and his Prime Minister, effectively the dictator of Greece, General John Metaxas.[12] Two days later Longmore arrived.

Wavell stayed at the British Embassy and hosted 'an enormous luncheon' in honour of Metaxas at the Hôtel Grande Bretagne. 'The table was decorated with hundreds of narcissus,' recalled Coats, who as Wavell's ADC had organized the lunch, 'but, as there seemed to be no vases, the flowers just lay on the tablecloth, wilting but scenting the whole room.'[13] The Greeks found the discussions unsatisfactory. Since Yugoslavia was neutral, the Germans were most likely to attack Greece through Macedonia; the Greek Commander-in-Chief, General Alexander Papagos, requested for its protection nine British divisions, plus air support. Wavell was obliged to inform him that he could spare only two or three divisions. On the grounds that it would merely provoke the Germans into attacking, Metaxas rejected this limited contingent. Wavell suggested that, on the contrary, the despatch of a small British force to Salonika might encourage both the Turkish and Yugoslav governments to enter the war on the British side. The Greeks remained unconvinced, and the offer was refused. Wavell and his party left Athens on Friday 17 January, returning to Cairo by way of Crete. Having felt constrained to carry out Churchill's instructions, Wavell was relieved by the Greek refusal. Had he been obliged to make good his offer, he would have had to halt his advance on Tobruk. Privately, he believed that to send inadequate troops would be a 'dangerous half-measure'. By the time the issue was discussed again, the Greeks had a new Prime Minister. On 29 January, in his seventieth year, Metaxas died of throat cancer. Much to his surprise, Peter Coats was accused by name on German radio of having poisoned the General at the Hôtel Grande Bretagne luncheon – the only time in his life, he said, that he was accused of murder.[14] Metaxas's successor Alexander Koryzis, a banker with little political experience, reaffirmed Greek determination to resist a German attack.

Wavell's moments of relaxation were rare. In mid January he and Queenie had a 'domestic evening' dining with Freya Stark, now transferred to the Ministry of Information in Cairo (to whom Wavell had sent a pot of honey acquired in Athens). 'General Wavell sat twinkling with his one eye and quoting poems about Samarkand and talked about the Caucasus.' No one would think, she said, that 'he had just brought off one of the biggest victories of the war.'[15] General Platt's attack into Italian East Africa was scheduled to begin on the revised date of 19 January, but the Italians withdrew unexpectedly from Kassala, and Wavell ordered Platt to pursue them into Eritrea as rapidly as possible. Meanwhile, the rebellion in Ethiopia gained its figurehead when Haile Selassie, accompanied by British representatives and his personal entourage, crossed the frontier.

On 21 January the attack on Tobruk began. The perimeter was twice as long as that at Bardia, the garrison not as large. By dusk one-third of the area was in British and Australian hands, and the following morning Australian forces entered the town. Yet again thousands more Italians became prisoners of war. In the wake of this victory Wavell immediately went to Tobruk and Bardia, and made an aerial reconnaissance of the stretch of coastline towards their next objective, Benghazi. 'Tobruk less damaged than expected and should be usable as port very shortly,' he cabled Dill on his return. 'Pace of Australian attack probably prevented more demolitions being carried out.'[16] When Churchill heard the news he sent Wavell another laudatory telegram with 'heartfelt congratulations' on the third of the 'brilliant' victories which had 'transformed' the situation in the Middle East. Yet with the Luftwaffe now operating in the Mediterranean from Sicily and British shipping under sustained attack, Wavell realized it was only a matter of time before his troops were pitted against the Germans. 'I wonder what Hitler will do next. I rather expect a busy and difficult six months in the Eastern Mediterranean.'[17]

Channon returned from Belgrade with the information that Prince Paul, while professing himself violently anti-German, hoped Britain would not do anything 'rash' like sending troops to Greece, which he believed would draw the Germans further into the Balkans. According to Channon the Regent wanted to be able to hand over a peaceful Yugoslavia when his nephew King Peter came of age; news of the Foreign Office proposal to declare a United Balkan Front and Wavell's January visit to Athens had caused him to shake visibly with rage.[18] Since Peter Coats was suffering from a bad chest, Wavell suggested that he take a few days' leave and accompany Channon to Palestine and Transjordan. Inevitably, Wavell's name came up as a topic of conversation between them: 'His silences, his one eye which saw so much more than other people's two. His susceptibility to people who were not shy with him – attractive, elegant women', among whom they included the Ambassador's wife, Jacqueline Lampson. They both marvelled at Wavell's remarkable memory for poetry, and Coats recalled that his hope of visiting Petra had prompted Wavell to recite some lines of John Burgon's poem: 'These the gay walls, through which in days of old / The tide of life so rapturously roll'd' – so much less 'hackneyed', in Coats's opinion, than the too-familiar 'rose-red city half as old as time'.[19]

On 28 January Wavell flew south once more to confer with his commanders in the Sudan and Kenya. With Coats away he was accompanied by his former ADC Bernard Fergusson, now serving as GSO2 to James Marshall-Cornwall, Britain's liaison officer between the C-in-C Middle East and Turkey. As Fergusson noted, 'we dropped back into our old relationship as though I had never left him.'[20] Their first stop was Khartoum, to meet Platt, whose next objective, following the Italian withdrawal from Kassala, was the town of Asmara. From Kenya, Cunningham proposed to undertake operation 'Canvas' – the capture of Kismayu – within the next two weeks. Following his discussions with Platt and Cunningham and a visit to the Headquarters of the 1st South Africa Division, Wavell was scheduled to leave Nairobi at six in the morning. But the aircraft was not serviceable, and while they waited, they breakfasted at the airport. 'As the sun rose,' recalled Fergusson, 'it became obvious that all the rank and fashion which had come to see us off had counted on the darkness to conceal the fact that they had postponed shaving until after we had gone.'[21] Back at his desk in Cairo Wavell cabled to inform Dill of his instructions for the execution of 'maximum effort' against Italian East Africa over the next two months. He also discovered that during his absence the Joint Planning Staff in London had been continuing their discussion of a possible British plan of action in the Balkans. As Churchill had minuted on 31 January: 'We must not overlook the decision we have conveyed to General Wavell that once Tobruk was taken, the Greek–Turkish situation must have priority. The advance to Benghazi is most desirable, and has been emphasized in later telegrams. Nevertheless, only Forces which do not conflict with European needs can be employed.'[22]

In the Western Desert, the strategy for O'Connor's attack on Benghazi was for the Australians to put pressure on the town of Derna along the coast road while the 7th Armoured Division attacked Mechili inland. But by the time they reached Mechili, the Italians had already withdrawn. Eric Dorman-Smith – who had on Wavell's orders been with O'Connor since Sidi Barrani, to report on the offensive – flew to Cairo seeking Wavell's permission for O'Connor to intercept the departing Italians. As he later recalled, Wavell appeared preoccupied, as was his habit, with marshalling the pencils on his desk in parade-ground drill, taking them up in handfuls, forming them into fours and threes. Every so often, when Dorman-Smith paused, Wavell observed: 'Yes, Eric, I see.' At the end he looked up. 'Tell Dick he can go on and wish him luck from me. He has done well.'[23] On 4 February Wavell flew up to Cyrenaica for further discussions with O'Connor. They decided to 'take a bold course' and cut off the Italians south of Benghazi. Wavell then returned to Cairo, and as the 'Battle of Beda Fomm' raged, the Australian and British forces succeeded in completely vanquishing the Italian 10th Army: at dawn on 7 February General Bergonzoli surrendered. Allied forward troops took up position in front of El Agheila, the most westerly town of Cyrenaica, close to the border with Tripolitania. O'Connor immediately told Dorman-Smith to draft a signal to Wavell. It began: 'Fox killed in the open . . .'[24] For Wavell, the victory brought more acclaim. With two divisions, one of them armoured, his commanders had since December destroyed ten Italian divisions.[25] After Beda Fomm, O'Connor was anxious to capitalize on their successes, but since his stated mission – the capture of Benghazi – had now been achieved, he needed fresh instructions. He therefore sent Dorman-Smith across the desert again to meet Wavell in Cairo.

Meanwhile, Channon and Coats were back in Cairo. Air Chief Marshal Longmore had organized a 'men's dinner' at which the Australian Prime Minister Robert Menzies was present; he was passing through Cairo on his way to London, flying on the same plane as Channon. Wavell, seated next to Channon, appeared 'silent and bored at first . . . he only thaws gradually. I noticed that he focuses badly with his one eye and that he sometimes upsets things.' During the dinner they listened to Churchill on the radio, praising his military commanders in the Middle East for their continuing victories in the Western Desert. 'Wavell, Commander-in-Chief of all the Armies of the Middle East, has proved himself a master of war, sage, painstaking, daring and tireless,' he declared. 'Operation Compass will long be studied as a model of the military art.'[26] According to Channon, Wavell hid behind the door during the Prime Minister's effusion, only resuming his place when the eulogy had finished. Channon remained slightly bemused by Wavell: 'I can't get over Wavell's modesty, his lack of surface brilliance, his intellectual detachment and seeming boredom with military matters. He is on a high scale and as great as he is charming.'[27]

As victory in Cyrenaica was being celebrated, the Balkans once more beckoned. On 8 February the new Greek Prime Minister, Koryzis, asked Churchill if they could discuss again the support Britain might be able to give should Germany enter Bulgaria. Having failed to persuade Turkey to form a Balkan front, Churchill was receptive, and on the evening of 10 February chaired a meeting of the Defence Committee at which the pros and cons of continuing the advance to Tripoli and/or assisting the Greeks were discussed.[28] As minuted, Churchill believed that 'it would be wrong' to abandon the Greeks, who were 'putting up a magnificent fight.'[29] On 11 February Wavell, who had tentatively suggested that 'Tripoli might yield to a small force if despatched without delay',[30] received a telegram authorized by the Defence Committee informing him that he should now give Greece and/or Turkey priority. 'This rules out any serious effort against Tripoli, although minor demonstrations thitherwards would be a useful feint. You should therefore make yourself secure at Benghazi and concentrate all available forces in the Delta in preparation for movement to Europe.'[31] The reaction expressed jointly by Wavell, Longmore and Cunningham pointed to the logistical difficulties, both in terms of the burden placed on the Royal Navy in safeguarding supply routes and in terms of shortages of anti-aircraft guns and aircraft. But Churchill at this stage did not want to consider such impediments. Nor did he take note of the odds which would be against them on land if the latest (inflated, as it happened) Ultra reports – indicating that 23 rather than 9 German divisions were in Romania – were to be believed.[32] On the morning of 12 February Dorman-Smith, having completed the arduous 570-mile drive across Cyrenaica, went into Wavell's office. Instead of the maps of the Western Desert that had previously adorned the walls, he found Wavell looking at maps of Greece and the Balkans. 'You find me busy with my spring campaign,' he said.[33] On the same day, German forces landed at Tripoli.

To give Wavell 'the very best chance of concerting all possible measures, both diplomatic and military, against the Germans in the Balkans', Churchill had notified him that he would be sending Dill and Eden to Cairo; after assessing the situation there, he expected them all to go on to Athens and possibly to Ankara.[34] Even if a feasible military initiative for Greece could not be agreed, Crete had to be kept 'at all costs', along with any Greek islands suitable for use as air bases – though these, together with a possible advance on Tripoli, would be but 'consolation prizes after the classic race has been lost'.[35] Rather than expressing the concern he had felt after his January visit to Athens about the wisdom of sending forces to Europe, the tone of Wavell's next communication to Churchill, on the evening of 12 February, was cooperative if cautionary. He intimated that while they would 'do their best' to frustrate German plans in the Balkans, Greek and Turkish 'hesitations' and Yugoslav 'timidity' were making his task difficult.[36] According to his written *aide-mémoire*, the first thing to determine was the minimum garrison necessary for Cyrenaica, and its composition.[37] Before Robert Menzies left for London, Wavell made a point of discussing with him what troops the Australians might offer as part of a proposed 'expeditionary force' to Greece.

In London, Dill expressed his concern that all the troops in the Middle East were fully employed and none would be available for Greece – whereupon, as he later related to Major-General John Kennedy, the Director of Military Operations,[38] Churchill lost his temper, 'the blood coming up his great neck and his eyes began to flash'. According to Dill, he said: 'What you need out there is a Court Martial and a firing squad. Wavell has 300,000 men.'[39] At this stage, both Dill and Kennedy believed that Churchill and the War Cabinet were trying 'to force an unsound policy down Wavell's throat, and down the throats of the Greeks and Turks', and that any forces sent there were 'certain to be annihilated or driven out again.'[40] Wavell, however, had changed his mind about Greece. In this, it is clear that his thinking had been influenced by Colonel William Donovan.[41] Known as 'Wild Bill' and a close friend of Frank Knox, the US Secretary of the Navy, Donovan had initially been deputed by President Roosevelt to go to England as his representative, to determine whether Britain could hold out against Germany following the fall of France. Returning to England in December, he spent a further three months in Europe. In the course of their discussions, he made Wavell understand the need to keep a foothold in the Balkans; he also impressed upon him the importance of favourably influencing American public opinion at a time when the Lend-Lease Bill – by which Britain was to receive virtually unlimited supplies from the United States – having been passed in the House of Representatives, was still to be heard in the Senate.[42]

The news from East Africa was encouraging. By 14 February, after severe fighting – but six days ahead of schedule – the Italians had been forced to evacuate Kismayu, leaving behind thousands of gallons of petrol and aviation fuel. Cunningham's next objective was Mogadishu, capital of Italian Somaliland, 'a bare, treeless town on the edge of the desert'.[43] Platt's forces were continuing their offensive in Eritrea, but the route to Asmara was proving harder than they had expected. Aerial photographs of the region around Keren showed 'a wild immensity of peaks, knife-edge ridges, precipices, gorges and narrow defiles'.[44] After nearly a week of attacks and counter-attacks, Platt's advance came to a halt while the 5th Indian Division was moved up to assist the 4th. In Ethiopia, Sandford – promoted brigadier – was acting as political and military adviser to the Emperor, as well as leading Mission 101. Deep inside the country Wingate was moving forward with his irregular army which, believing that he was 'wielding the sword of the Lord and of Gideon', he had renamed his 'Gideon' force. Writing in later life, Wavell admitted that he had known little of Wingate's exploits until afterwards. 'The enterprise once launched had to take care of itself while I directed the regular operations against the north and the south of the Italian East African Empire.'[45]

By the middle of February Wavell was at the summit of his military career. On 14 February he issued a Special Order of the day outlining the success of 'Compass' in the Western Desert: 'The Army of the Nile, as our Prime Minister has called us, has in two months advanced over 400 miles, has destroyed the large army that had gathered to invade Egypt, taking some 125,000 prisoners and well over 1,000 guns besides innumerable quantities of weapons and material of all kinds. These achievements will always be remembered.' As usual, he paid tribute to the ordinary soldier: 'The spirit of quiet resolution that during these operations has animated all ranks in all places – the combatant under fire in the fighting line, the driver making his way over bad tracks in a dust storm, the mechanic working long hours on repair and maintenance, the pioneer unloading stores, the signaller, the engineer, the medical personnel – will continue and carry us through all dangers and difficulties.'[46] In Britain, the newspaper head-lines were triumphant: 'Wavell's Wave Sweeps over Libya', 'Wavell: Warrior of the Desert', 'Wavell: Hero of North Africa'. The February edition of the *Illustrated London News* had Wavell's portrait on the cover, captioned 'A master at war'.[47] The three lectures on 'Generals and Generalship' Wavell had delivered to those few students in Cambridge in early 1939 were reprinted in *The Times*. As the leader article accompanying the first lecture stated: 'General Sir Archibald Wavell is a student of war and of military his-tory. His latest exploits prove him to be gifted in high degree with the imaginative daring which is the hallmark of the great commander who reached that higher and rarefied atmosphere wherein so many others cannot easily breathe.'[48] There were eulogistic Letters to the Editor. On 21 February W.R. Titterton of 30 Clare Court, WC1 wrote: 'I have never read anything on generalship as illuminating as the articles published in your columns this week from the pen of the victor of Libya.' Pointing out that 'many great military leaders have been inarticulate', Mr Titterton enthused still further: 'it is an incomparable portrait that every patriotic Briton will treasure. This is Wavell, who touches this touches a man.'[49] Wavell, Cunningham and Longmore were promoted up the knightly ladder, appointed GCB – Knights Grand Cross of the Most Honourable Order of the Bath; Jumbo Wilson was appointed GBE – Knight Grand Cross of the Most Excellent Order of the British Empire. O'Connor, Beresford-Peirse, Creagh and Mackay received knighthoods. But even as the laurels of victory were being awarded, Wavell was facing a still more formidable challenge.

The Middle East Command's main focus of attention was now the Balkans. Eden and Dill had left London on 12 February but bad weather meant it took them three days to reach Gibraltar, where Eden finally read his sealed instructions: his principal object was to send 'speedy succour' to Greece, and to this end he was to initiate any action he considered necessary with the Commander-in-Chief Middle East, the Egyptian Government, and the Governments of Greece, Yugoslavia and Turkey. Eden's instructions were in line with his personal views: 'Britain has never regarded her treaties as scraps of paper: her word remains her bond. If therefore Greece called on Britain for help, the latter was ethically bound to send all the help she could spare.'[50] While Wavell waited for his guests to arrive, he was already determining which troops would make up the 'Lustre' Expeditionary Force for Greece. On 17 February he informed Freyberg that the completed New Zealand Division was to be the advance guard of an 'Imperial Force' which would include the 6th and 7th

Australian Divisions, under the command of General Thomas Blamey, plus the independent Polish Brigade and the 1st Armoured Brigade.[51] On the same day Wavell wrote out a four-page appreciation, arguing the pros and cons of the venture. Although he was not under any illusions about the risks, he now believed the political reasons to be inseparable from the military ones, first in terms of keeping Greece 'in the field', secondly by encouraging Turkey to fulfil her treaty obligations, and lastly by encouraging Yugoslavia 'to resist German domination'.[52]

On Wednesday 19 February Wavell revised this appreciation, using as its title a favourite quotation from the eighteenth-century British General James Wolfe: 'War is an option of difficulties.' His conclusion came down on the side of action. 'I think we are more likely to be playing the enemy's game by remaining inactive than by taking action in the Balkans. Provided that conversations with the Greeks show that there is a good chance of establishing a front against the Germans with our assistance, I think we should take it.'[53] That afternoon he met General Marshall-Cornwall. 'Wavell then told me, obviously with a heavy heart, that he had decided to send the expeditionary force to Greece. I was horrified and said I was sure that it was a gamble which could only lead to military disaster. Archie replied slowly: "Possibly, but strategy is only the handmaid of policy, and here political considerations must come first. The policy of our Government is to build up a Balkan front."[54] Later Wavell dined alone with Donovan, whose advocacy of the importance of forming a Balkan front once more impressed him.[55] When Eden and Dill arrived, weary from their travels, Wavell greeted them with the words, 'You have been a long time coming.' Eden, feeling the reproach unjustified, attempted to explain their delay, but Wavell moved the subject forwards: 'As you were so long I felt I had to get started, and I have begun the concentration for a move of troops to Greece.' Both Dill and Eden, well aware of Wavell's earlier opposition to intervention in Greece, breathed a sigh of relief 'that Wavell's mind was apparently in tune' with their instructions.[56]

In a cable to London on 21 February Dill summarized the collective view of himself, Eden and the three Commanders-in-Chief: although the risks were considerable, 'inaction would be fatal'.[57] Eden's cable said that they were agreed they should do 'everything in our power to bring the fullest measure of help to Greeks at earliest possible moment'. He also informed Churchill of the forces which were to be left to garrison Cyrenaica.[58] But Churchill was now back-pedalling, and had already told Eden: 'Do not consider yourselves obligated to a Greek enterprise if in your hearts you feel it will only be another Norwegian fiasco . . . If no good plan can be made please say so. But of course you know how valuable success would be.'[59] When Eden received this telegram, he sent a detailed response reminding the Prime Minister that, discussing the matter in London, they had been 'prepared to run the risk of failure, thinking it is better to suffer with the Greeks than to make no attempt to help them.'[60]

Before a final decision was made another conference was arranged with the Greeks and on Saturday 22 February a delegation that included Wavell, Longmore, Eden and Dill went once more to Athens. Before meeting the King, Wavell discussed the situation with Sir Michael Palairet, the British Minister in Athens, who was also a keen advocate of intervention.[61] According to Harold Caccia, First Secretary at the British Legation, who was present, Palairet informed Wavell that following Metaxas's death, it would be the King – rather than Koryzis – who decided whether to accept British aid.[62] It was therefore up to Wavell to persuade the King. Palairet's briefing instigated a particular train of thought in Wavell's mind, and instead of confining himself to his usual limited interjections, he expressed himself more fully: 'Wavell held forth, and said, well, he'd have to remind us that the situation in Greece was not unlike that in North Africa; . . . the question was not really how many divisions could [the enemy] deploy, but if they could all be brought into action at once.' In other words, Wavell was thinking not simply in terms of how many divisions would be pitted against each other, but of the relative advantages of the terrain.[63]

Throughout the day further discussions took place at the Royal Palace at Tatoi outside Athens. Speaking in French, Koryzis said that Greece would fight to the last, with or without help from Great Britain: the Greeks' honour was unstained and their courage was boundless.[64] Wavell sat making notes in pencil on sheets of Palace writing paper emblazoned with the Greek crown. Much attention was focused on the line which they believed could be held against a German attack from Bulgaria. In such an event it would be impossible to continue offensive operations against the Italians in Albania, and it was therefore important to establish a line behind which the Greeks fighting in Albania could withdraw. In Wavell's opinion, if the Yugoslavs did not join in on the side of the Allies, the only possible line was that of the Aliakmon River, approximately seventy miles long and with natural protection from the mountains. Four gaps made it vulnerable: one on either side of Mount Olympus, a third the river valley itself, and the fourth at Edhessa, through which a road and railway leading from Yugoslavia passed to the port of Salonika in Macedonia.

Much also depended on the attitude of Turkey and Yugoslavia, but there

Archibald Goodall Wavell: 'I have always had a liking for unorthodox soldiers – my grandfather was a soldier of fortune'

Archibald Graham Wavell: 'He was a kind and indulgent father,' said Wavell when the General died in 1935

Archibald Wavell in India aged 7: India's 'fine climate gave my body a good start in life,' he later wrote

Scholars at Summer Fields, 1896. A.P. Wavell is standing, second from the right. On his left is Norman Grundy, with whom he started a 'rather primitive' school paper

Wavell, aged 15 at Winchester. He later regarded his school as his 'spiritual home'

Wavell, aged 27, a subaltern in The Black Watch. 'My heart has always been with the Regiment,' he said in later life

Cranborne Lodge, the Wavell family's home for more than twenty years

Eugénie Marie Quirk, known as Queenie, in 1914. Wavell described her as 'slim and attractive'. They were married in 1915

Colonel and Mrs Archibald Wavell at The Hon. Judith Denman's marriage to Walter Burrell, August 1931

اللى فيهم !!

الجنرال وايفل يطهر جو مصر من الهوام الموسولينية ...

Wavell zaps the Italians. The caption reads: 'Up and at them! General Wavell protects the air of Egypt from the Mussolini swarm.' Wavell's victories against the Italians in 1940 and 1941 boosted morale at a time of disaster in Europe

Wavell in his habitual position, studying the scene of battle

Generals Auchinleck and Wavell in the Middle East. In June 1941 the two men exchanged commands: Auchinleck became Commander-in-Chief, Middle East, and Wavell Commander-in-Chief, India

Felicity Wavell, Wavell's middle daughter, known as Ferocity by Wavell's ADCs because of her determination

Joan Wavell: she fell in love with Wavell's ADC, The Hon. Simon Astley

Wavell, Queenie and their only son, Archie John. 'Few soldiers' families can have been so much together and so happy as we have,' Archie John said

Leonie Lemartine otherwise Gladys Redwood Robinson. Wavell met the 'opera singer/spy' in Moscow in 1911; she called him 'old sobersides' because he was so quiet. They remained in touch for more than forty years

Joan Bright, who worked in the War Cabinet Secretariat. Wavell met her in 1941 and she became one of the many correspondents to whom he wrote long descriptive letters from India

Wavell's personal staff: Sandy Reid Scott, whom Wavell described as 'one in a million', The Hon. Simon Astley 'the quickest-witted and most efficient ADC I have ever had', and Peter Coats, who worked loyally for Wavell for six years

Winston Churchill in August 1941 on his way to Placentia Bay, Newfoundland, where he signed the Atlantic Charter with President Roosevelt. *HMS Prince of Wales* was sunk off Singapore four months later. Wavell's most testing relationship throughout the war was with the Prime Minister: 'I do not think Winston quite knew what to make of me'

was no time to wait for Greece's neighbours to declare themselves. Both Papagos and Wavell believed that if the Greeks withdrew three divisions from Western Thrace and Macedonia, with the additional support of another Greek division from Albania, and provided the British moved their forces at once from Egypt, they would be able to hold the Aliakmon Line against superior German numbers. Towards midnight on 22 February agreement was reached: with all possible speed they would assemble a joint force of seven and a half divisions – four Greek, three and a half British – and one armoured brigade. The British force was to come under Papagos's command; if there was a difference of opinion between the British commander and Papagos, it was to be referred to Wavell; if Wavell and Papagos disagreed, the matter would be referred to the British Government. Wavell noted that their greatest obstacle was German air superiority, but believed that, as long as they acted rapidly and in secrecy, there was a reasonable chance of success. While Eden and Dill journeyed onwards to Turkey, Wavell returned to Cairo to prepare for the movement of forces to Greece.

The scene was now set for the series of disasters which culminated in Wavell's replacement as Commander-in-Chief Middle East four months later. Before the Greek venture he had been in full control of his command; after the decision to intervene in Greece, events followed their own course. At the precise moment Wavell was signing away his forces for the Greek venture, confirmation was received that a German patrol had been sighted in Libya.[65] At a meeting of the War Cabinet in London, the Chiefs of Staff endorsed the decisions taken in Greece: 'It goes without saying that the expedition must be a gamble, but our representatives on the spot, after conference with the Greeks, and full examination of the Greek plan, evidently think there is a reasonable prospect of successfully holding up a German advance.' Not for the first time, political considerations seemed to override military: 'Even the complete failure of an honourable attempt to help Greece need not be disastrous to our future ability to defeat Germany . . . On balance we think that the enterprise should go forward.'[66] At no time was Allied inferiority in the air discussed, nor what the effect would be of denuding the Western Desert of what air support there was. Churchill, whose own enthusiasm for the venture had waned, also emphasized that Wavell favoured the operation, 'although he was inclined to understatement, and so far had always promised less than he had performed, and was a man who wished to do better than his word.'[67]

As Wavell was preparing his troops for departure to Greece, the news worsened. On 1 March German forces crossed the River Danube from

Romania into Bulgaria, and Bulgaria joined the Tripartite Pact. In Athens, Eden and Dill discovered to their dismay that Papagos had not withdrawn Greek forces from Thrace and Macedonia to the Aliakmon Line as promised, reportedly because he had believed the withdrawal was contingent upon Yugoslavia declaring her position. Moreover, with the Germans now in Bulgaria, Papagos was reluctant to begin withdrawing Greek forces lest they be attacked while doing so. Wavell returned to Athens for further discussions, and before he left sent a cable to the War Office detailing the forces left in Cyrenaica. Although the presence of German forces in Libya was unquestioned, Wavell did not believe an attack eastwards across the desert was yet imminent. In his opinion, shipping risks, difficulties of communications and the approaching hot weather suggested that an offensive was unlikely to take place before the end of the summer, and therefore skeletal forces in Cyrenaica should suffice.

In East Africa, the pincer movement of Platt and Cunningham was having its effect. On 1 March Wavell was able to report that the Italians were evacuating Italian Somaliland, giving Churchill the opportunity to respond with some humour: 'At present we seem to have swapped Somalilands with the enemy.'[68] Over the next three days, between 2 and 4 March, the British and Greeks haggled over the respective forces which would be positioned on the Aliakmon Line. Eventually a compromise was reached. But even before he knew of the Greek failure to withdraw, Churchill was recommending that Eden look for an escape clause. 'Loss of Greece and Balkans by no means a major catastrophe for us provided Turkey remains honest neutral,' was his opinion on 5 March.[69] Meanwhile, the increasingly lukewarm attitude perceptible in London caused the three Commanders-in-Chief, with Eden and Dill, to review the situation once more. While Longmore and Cunningham pointed to the changed circumstances which made their positions less favourable, Wavell continued to assert that provided the forces could be disembarked in Greece, there was a 'good prospect' of success, 'The results of [which] would be incalculable and might alter the whole aspect of the war.'[70] The decision to proceed was reluctantly endorsed. As Andrew Cunningham noted: 'At the final meeting in Cairo with Wavell, Eden and Dill, I gave it as my opinion that though politically we were correct, I had grave uncertainty of its military expedience. Dill himself had doubts, and said to me after the meeting: "Well, we've taken the decision. I'm not at all sure it's the right one."' No sooner had they decided to send an expeditionary force than they were thinking 'of how we should bring them out'.[71]

On 6 March Smuts arrived in Cairo for a meeting with Eden, Dill and

Wavell on Middle East strategy. He too saw the dilemma of undertaking a venture of which the success was so uncertain; at the same time, he endorsed it: 'I think it is still possible to transform this apparently promising situation for the Germans into disaster for them and from this front pave the way to victory.' If the Allies did not stand by the Greeks, he said, they would be 'held up to public ignominy'.[72] Finally, on 7 March, the War Cabinet approved the expedition to Greece. Yet again Wavell agreed: 'I am sure the decisions were the right ones though they will bring us new hazards and anxieties.'[73] Operation 'Lustre' began that same day with the departure of Bernard Freyberg and the first echelon of the New Zealand Division.

At this critical juncture, Wavell had to welcome the Prime Minister's 29-year-old son Randolph, who had been posted to the Middle East as a General Staff Officer (Intelligence) at GHQ.[74] 'I do not know whether he will be able to get leave to come to your Headquarters, or whether you will be there when he can. Assuming, however, that these difficulties do not make it impossible, it would be a pleasure to me to make him known to you personally, and I shall be grateful for any kindness you can show him agreeably with the Service,' Churchill wrote to Wavell in a letter of introduction.[75] Randolph eventually met Wavell at Gezira, and reported back to his father: 'He is not very talkative but he seemed very well.'[76] Later Wavell informed the Prime Minister that his son was 'looking remarkably well and in very good spirits.'[77] At this time Wavell was also entertaining celebrities from India as part of a scheme agreed with Auchinleck, who had taken over from Cassels as Commander-in-Chief in India in February, to educate Indian public opinion 'and make our task of pulling our weight in the war correspondingly easier'. Among those who had already visited the Middle East was the Nawab of Bhopal, Sir Hamidullah Khan, former Chancellor of the Chamber of Indian Princes. Auchinleck also had a request: could Wavell spare any captured Italian AA artillery, heavy or light, or both? 'I know that you must have many demands on you for these guns, but perhaps you might be able to spare us a few.'[78]

As Wavell was discussing Greece, he had at the same time to consider Cyrenaica, to where he and Dill flew soon after returning from Athens. O'Connor, exhausted and suffering from stomach complaints, was in hospital. XIII Corps was now commanded by Lieutenant-General Philip Neame, VC, former GOC in Palestine and Transjordan and briefly commander of the 4th Indian Division in 1940.[79] What remained of the 7th Armoured Division which had sustained so much of the fighting had returned to Cairo, to be replaced by the 2nd (minus its 1st Armoured Brigade Group, which was being sent to Greece); they were supported by the 9th Australian Division, commanded by Major-General Leslie Morshead.[80] But the combined force was ill-equipped and inadequate. Signals equipment and transport were lacking. As Wavell later wrote, it was not until his March visit that he discovered the deplorable state of the tanks: 'They were in fact completely worn out before they ever left England.'[81] He also understood the error he had committed in not reconnoitring the terrain. Preoccupied with Eden and Dill and discussions about the Balkans, 'I imagined that it was an escarpment similar to that running east from Sollum, with only a very few passages fit for vehicles . . . when I actually went out and saw the escarpment, I realized that it could be ascended almost anywhere and was no protection.' In addition, he had failed to recognize the strategic importance of the Salt Marshes near Agheila. 'If I had gone out there and seen for myself what a formidable barrier they could be made, I think I should certainly have insisted on our pushing our force down to those marshes, whatever the supply difficulties were. As it was, we stopped short of them, and allowed the Germans passage through them.'[82] As Coats, who accompanied Wavell, later recalled, this visit symbolized the end of 'the short halcyon few months of continual victories in the desert, a time which had effectively knocked Italy out of the war and made my Chief a figure of world-renown.' In a few weeks the dream was to be shattered 'with our troops reeling back, everywhere, before the Germans.'[83] It was now known that the 5th Light Panzer Division, equipped with light and medium tanks, was commanded by the audacious general Erwin Rommel, who had earned the Knight's Cross of the Iron Cross at the time of Allied surrender in Normandy in June 1940.[84] German intervention to help the Italians in North Africa was originally intended as a 'rescue' operation – code-named 'Sunflower' – but after reconnoitring, Rommel realized that the British presence in Libya was considerably smaller than the Germans had at first believed. On 19 March he returned to Berlin seeking permission to attack the British in the Western Desert at the earliest opportunity. But the generals at home were still thinking less aggressively than their commander in the field: pending further instructions, Rommel was only authorized to conduct a limited offensive around Agedabia.

In Cairo after his visit to the Western Desert, Wavell once more surveyed the situation in East Africa. On 20 March he reported to London the slow progress and bitter fighting taking place over Keren, amid the high peaks and passes. In the Balkans, as the 'Lustre' force was disembarking in Greece, diplomatic attempts to encourage the Yugoslavs and Turks to join the Allies continued; Prince Paul, however, was still reluctant to commit himself. After a particularly weary day in the midst of their deliberations

Wavell and Dill had already gone to bed when Eden decided he wanted the two men to listen to the cable he proposed to send Churchill; Coats had just time to rouse the two generals to receive Eden and Longmore. They sat side by side on the sofa in their dressing gowns but so exhausted were they that when Eden paused for some appreciative response to the cable he was dictating, he saw that the two were sound asleep. The following day Wavell gave Longmore a piece of paper headed 'Most Secret and Very Personal: The Jug (with apologies to Lewis Carroll)'. Especially relevant were the following verses:

> I sent a message to the Jug,
> I told him not to be a mug.
> I said he must be badly cracked
> To think of joining Hitler's pact.
> The Jug replied: 'But don't you see
> How difficult it is for me.' . . .

> I took a pencil large and new,
> I wrote a telegram or two.
> Then someone came to me and said
> The Generals have gone to bed.
> I said it loud, I said it plain,
> 'Then you must wake them up again.'

> And I was very firm with them,
> I kept them up till 2 a.m.
> ('Wasn't that rather unkind?' said Jacqueline.[85]
> 'Not at all,' said Anthony firmly. 'We want Generals,
> not dormice. But don't keep interrupting.')[86]

When Randolph Churchill saw the poem, he sent his father a copy.

Britain's entreaties to the Yugoslav Government – 'The Jug' – were to no avail: on 25 March, under pressure from Hitler, who wanted to use the Yugoslav railways to reach Greece, the Prime Minister signed a pact of allegiance.[87] Less than two days later, in a bloodless *coup d'état*, the armed forces overthrew the government. Prince Paul was deposed and a new Government was established under the young King Peter, as cheering crowds filled the streets. But the change of government only made Papagos more reluctant to move Greek forces to the Aliakmon Line, hopeful instead that the Greek divisions on the Bulgarian border would be able to join forces with the Yugoslavs. The Yugoslav *coup d'état* also infuriated Hitler, who vowed 'revenge', detailing 29 divisions and 2,000 aircraft for his Balkan campaign.[88]

There was never any question at this time of dealing with one issue in isolation, a fact to which Wavell was becoming accustomed. No sooner had the 'Lustre' force disembarked in Greece than Cyrenaica began to give him 'increasing cause for anxiety'.[89] Contrary to Wavell's forecast, Rommel had gone on the offensive as soon as he returned from Berlin. On 24 March a German reconnaissance unit seized El Agheila – the gateway between Tripolitania and Cyrenaica. Lacking sufficient reinforcements to counter-attack, as instructed by Wavell, Neame and Major-General Gambier-Parry, who had taken command of the newly arrived 2nd Armoured Division, intended to mount a delaying tactic by means of a gradual withdrawal as far as and beyond Benghazi, if necessary. Churchill, learning of the Germans' advance, expressed concern, observing that it was their 'habit to push on whenever they are not resisted. I presume you are only waiting for the tortoise to stick his head out far enough before chopping it off. It seems extremely important to give them an early taste of our quality.'[90] Wavell meanwhile had returned to East Africa to work out how Platt might break the deadlock at Keren. Personal observation of the ground yet again proved invaluable: 'As soon as I had a good look at the position, I said to Platt that it looked to me as if the way through was straight up the main road, neglecting the high peaks to north and south.'[91] This new approach was adopted, Keren was finally taken, and the way was open for a move on Asmara.

Returning to Cairo after overseeing the Battle of Keren, Wavell contemplated the implications of Churchill's instructions to chop off the tortoise's head. He pointed out tactfully that he had taken a 'considerable' risk in Cyrenaica after the capture of Benghazi 'in order to provide maximum support to Greece . . . Result is I am weak in Cyrenaica at present and no reinforcements of armoured troops, which are chief requirement, are at present available . . . Steps to reinforce Cyrenaica are in hand . . . My own chief difficulty is transport.'[92] At sea, Admiral Cunningham's victory in late March against the Italians at the Battle of Cape Matapan off the coast of Greece had boosted morale, but the situation in the Western Desert remained critical. On 30 March Wavell informed Neame that a large contingent of German troops was arriving in Tripoli. Countering his previous instructions regarding a gradual withdrawal, Wavell was now encouraging Neame to make a stand to prevent the Germans from crossing the stretch of land from El Agheila to Benghazi.

It was unfortunate that at this decisive moment Wavell felt the need to make a change of command. Neame had seemed confident of his ability to cope with the shifted emphasis of his orders, but in the event Wavell was dissatisfied with his style of command; on the afternoon of 2 April he flew to the Cyrenaica headquarters at Barce for consultations. The Brigadier, General Staff, John Harding, was also far from happy at the way Neame was handling things, and begged Wavell to send O'Connor back to replace Neame.[93] The following day – with Rommel menacingly positioned north of Agedabia – O'Connor was recalled. As he later admitted, he was not happy 'at the thought of taking over command in the middle of a battle which was already lost'.[94] Arriving at Barce he suggested to Wavell that, since he did not know the divisions now making up XIII Corps, he should remain to help Neame instead of taking command. He later regretted his decision, maintaining that it was the 'worst proposal' he had ever made.[95] He also pointed out to Wavell that 'it was no good having two of us up at the same time. So if you wanted me up, it would have been better for Neame to go.'[96] In the meantime Rommel's forces succeeded in taking Agedabia and he pressed home his advantage towards Benghazi. Under heavy air attack and unable to hold their forward positions, all the beleaguered XIII Corps could do was to withdraw. As noted by Harding, Wavell characteristically managed to inspire 'complete confidence that all would work out well, really without doing much about it and that again was typical of the man.'[97]

To add to Wavell's concerns, the Middle East was becoming volatile. Anti-British sentiment was running high in Iraq, and the Foreign Office had acted upon its concern by appointing Sir Kinahan Cornwallis as ambassador.[98] A friend of King Feisal I, he had been adviser to the Iraqi Ministry of the Interior throughout the 1920s and early 1930s and had considerable knowledge of Arab politics. Before taking up his appointment, Cornwallis flew to meet Wavell. Their discussions at GHQ in Cairo left Cornwallis in no doubt that Wavell would find it difficult to spare any troops for Iraq and that military support, if needed, was most likely to have to come from India. Then on 1 April the former Prime Minister, Arab 'nationalist' Rashid Ali el Kailani, staged a *coup d'état*, declaring himself head of a National Defence Government. Abdullah was deposed and a new Regent was installed. Prince Abdullah fled, making his way to Basra and then Transjordan. Rashid Ali protested his allegiance to Britain, but the British were worried about radical influences on his government; of particular concern were the former leader of the Palestine rebellion, Haj Amin el Husseini, who had taken refuge in Iraq, and a group of army officers known as the 'Golden Square' who were opposed to Britain's 'imperialist' presence in Iraq. In Wavell's view, Rashid Ali's questionable allegiances left his eastern flank vulnerable to infiltration by the Germans, who were already operating in Vichy-held Syria. If Iraq turned belligerent, Britain's oil supplies to Haifa would be endangered, as would Basra, where the British had plans for a base to accommodate American Lend-Lease supplies.

Hard-pressed as Wavell already was, his immediate reaction to the changed situation was to suggest that Iraq should be placed under the India Command. In early March he had agreed with Auchinleck that if any military operations were necessary in Iraq, they would first be organized from India, a decision with which the Chiefs of Staff had concurred. Yet when the Iraqi coup took place, the Chiefs of Staff immediately cabled Wavell to enquire what forces he would have available. His response was unenthusiastic: all he could send was a battalion from Palestine. When the same request was put to Auchinleck, he agreed to divert an infantry brigade of the 10th Indian Division to secure Basra, together with a field regiment of artillery. Unfortunately, Churchill did not forget this negative response from Wavell at a time of crisis. To add to Wavell's concerns, in early April General Charles de Gaulle had arrived in Cairo. He planned to extend the authority of his Free French Army over Vichy-held Syria, and for this he wanted Wavell's help.

With the exception of East Africa, by the first week of April the situation on all fronts was critical. With Rommel advancing in the Western Desert and Iraq potentially hostile, Wavell faced the alarming prospect of being caught in a pincer movement at the Nile. On Saturday 5 April came Germany's long-anticipated declaration of war on Greece and Yugoslavia. On 6 April German bombers hit Belgrade, killing thousands of civilians, and destroyed the Greek port of Piraeus. In a simultaneous invasion the German *blitzkrieg* began crossing into Yugoslavia and northern Greece from Romania, Hungary and Bulgaria. Against the onslaught, as the Germans were well aware, British forces were a 'mere drop in the ocean by the standards of continental warfare'.[99] Jumbo Wilson, officially in command of the 'Lustre' force (renamed 'W' Force), realized it was a 'flimsy' one, the more so because to protect Tobruk Wavell had been obliged to withdraw the Australian 7th Division and the Polish Brigade. The 6th Australian Division was still in transit. Wireless contact in the Greek mountains was problematical, and it was difficult to determine where Wilson's HQ should best be sited. Heavy snowstorms impeded movement.

Palm Sunday, 6 April, was Wavell's blackest day. As he sat in conference in Cairo with Eden, Dill and his Chief of Staff, worse news was on its way. That evening O'Connor, Neame and Dan Ranfurly, their ADC, having delayed too long before leaving Barce and got lost, were captured by a German motor-cycle patrol; later, Gambier-Parry was obliged to surrender. The Germans also took possession of a large number of British vehicles, and of documents detailing British operations and the personalities involved. As Churchill noted, Rommel had torn 'the new-won laurels from Wavell's brow and thrown them in the sand.'[100] News of the British generals' capture did not reach Wavell until the evening of 7 April, delivered by a GSO1, Francis (Freddie) de Guingand, who said he had never seen the Commander-in-Chief so moved.[101] Wavell immediately asked the War Office to put up 'any five [captured] Italian generals' in exchange for O'Connor, but the idea of a barter was 'rather primly' rejected as unprecedented.[102] The following day, accompanied by Major-General John Lavarack, commander of the 7th Australian Division, who was to be appointed Neame's successor in the Cyrenaica Command, Wavell flew to Tobruk. Strong winds and driving sand made visibility difficult, but his appearance had a 'tonic' effect on the 'unshaven, weary group of officers' who had come to meet him.[103] His message was insistent: as the only supply port east of Benghazi, Tobruk must be held.[104]

By the time Wavell was ready to return to Cairo, it was late afternoon and the weather had further deteriorated. As the pilot was attempting to take off, a wheel seized up. While this was remedied Wavell retired to a nearby hut, where he was offered warm beer by a group of pilots. Major the Earl Amherst, a member of GHQ staff who had begged a lift from Tobruk to Cairo, recalled how for a short while Wavell thrilled his audience with an account of the battle against Rommel. When the plane was ready, he took his leave. Fifteen minutes into the journey, the oil pressure on one engine went to zero: the pilot landed, cleared the oil filter and took off again: after another twenty minutes the oil-pressure gauge was down again. According to Amherst, Wavell was imperturbable, greeting any fresh information with his habitual 'I . . . see.' Eventually the pilot had to make another forced landing, in an unknown part of the desert near Sollum. As he did so, the aircraft swung violently and the left wing and tailplane were torn off. A desert patrol was seen in the distance, and on the chance that it might be unfriendly it was decided that Amherst should remain with the crew while Wavell walked northwards alone on foot. If the patrol was indeed hostile, it was hoped that Wavell could somehow escape; if friendly, they could go after him. Briefly it seemed that their worst fears would be fulfilled: when the approaching vehicle stopped, its occupant got out and challenged Amherst and the crew in an unknown language. Then, slowly, out of the half-light there emerged a friendly Sudanese soldier. After going 'missing' for six hours, the Commander-in-Chief spent the night in Sollum, returning to Cairo the following day.[105]

Remembering the hospitality he had received from the pilots in the hut, he sent their squadron some champagne.

The strategic potential of Tobruk made its capture an obsession with Rommel, and he was anxious to attack before the British could prepare its defence.[106] In the early hours of 14 April the offensive began. Thinking it had been immediately successful, Rommel went forward at dawn, only to realize that anti-tank fire had prevented his tanks from advancing. The repulse of the German attack on Tobruk by the Australians was important because, as Churchill noted, it was the first time they had 'tasted defeat'.[107] Tobruk might have held, to Wavell's relief, but Greece was proving a disaster. The Yugoslavs having put up little resistance, the Germans had already succeeded in pushing through the Monastir Gap, the gateway to Greece from Yugoslavia. Elsewhere in Wavell's vast command, however, East Africa was paying dividends: after the capture of Asmara on 1 April, Platt's forces had taken the port of Massawa, and on the 6th General Cunningham had entered Addis Ababa. Nevertheless, the Ethiopian countryside was still occupied by large numbers of Italian forces, and with Rommel continuing to proclaim the Suez Canal as his objective, it was still feared that the Germans might reach Cairo by the summer and move onwards to the Sudan and Ethiopia.

Despite the near-disaster of Wavell's return from Tobruk he was in the air again on 11 April, flying to Mersa Matruh before going on to Jumbo Wilson's headquarters in Greece. Without additional support, it was obvious that 'W' force could not withstand the Germans for much longer: when once they established themselves beyond the Aliakmon Line, it was no longer a tenable line of defence. As Wilson observed, at the end of a long day Wavell was extremely tired, and slept in his tent where he sat, not making it to his bed.[108] Throughout the Balkans the German advance continued; on 13 April they occupied Belgrade. Returning to Cairo, on 15 April Wavell held yet more discussions with Air Chief Marshal Longmore and Admiral Cunningham. They concluded that a complete withdrawal from Greece was their only course of action. On 17 April the Yugoslav Government capitulated. The German High Command was delighted by these Allied reverses. 'In London they are being forced to watch one illusion after another crumble to nothing,' noted Hitler's propagandist, Josef Goebbels. 'All they can do is to stutter lame excuses. We hit home relentlessly.'[109]

On Saturday 19 April Wavell made his last visit to Greece, to discuss evacuation plans. As he did so, Churchill was contemplating the appointment of a deputy to assist him in the Middle East. Dill, who took this as an implied criticism of his friend, opposed the suggestion: it might, he said, appear that Wavell was about to be removed, which in turn would diminish his confidence and hence his performance. Moreover, while he recognised that Wavell had 'many balls on which to keep his one eye', Dill suggested to Churchill that he also had a 'first class' Chief of Staff – General Arthur Smith – who could act in his name.[110] Among Wavell's colleagues on the spot, however, there was a belief that the Commander-in-Chief was shouldering his burdens single-handedly. As the Deputy Air Officer Commanding-in-Chief, Middle East, Arthur Tedder, noted: 'The team at GHQ really gives me the shudders. Wavell I think is a fine man, but the rest?!!! They swing daily from easy optimism to desperate defeatism and vice versa.'[111] Coats, who accompanied Wavell to Greece, believed that it was 'madness' to risk this perilous journey, for the Germans were closing in; even as their plane landed, the sirens wailed and bombs began to fall. But 'the countryside looked beautiful, with fig trees and flowers. Brown-faced peasants waved as we sped by.' The situation which greeted Wavell was even more chaotic than on his previous visit. The day before his arrival, Koryzis had risen from a meeting of his ministers, locked himself in his bedroom and shot himself. He had been less than three months in office. At meetings with the King and Papagos plans for evacuation were discussed, but the decision itself was postponed until a new Prime Minister could form a government. Wavell was having giddy spells, doubtless caused by the pressure under which he was working, and he appeared 'tired, depressed and down'.[112] Late that night he drove to see General Blamey at his headquarters near Thebes and narrowly missed being fired upon by an Australian ambush. In the back of Wavell's car he and Blamey discussed evacuation plans, studying a map by torchlight. 'Heavy rain thudded on the roof of the car, like a depressing obbligato to the words of the two men.'[113] The following day Wavell had one last meeting with the King, and afterwards instructed Wilson to prepare for withdrawal. The pilot of the plane taking Wavell back to Cairo, fearful that the German Luftwaffe would score a hit, 'hedge-hopped towards the sea, and, like a wounded mallard, skimmed over the water towards Crete'. Wavell picked up *Antony and Cleopatra* to read, but fell asleep. His cable to Churchill from Cairo was without elaboration: 'Consider time has come to prepare public in official communiqué for impending Greek collapse.'[114] St George's Day – 23 April, which was also Joan's eighteenth birthday – passed grimly. Unable to resist the German advance, the Greeks capitulated. That night King George and his government were evacuated to Crete; the following day the evacuation of British and Dominion troops began.

★

On his return from Greece Wavell had to focus immediately on the Western Desert. Although Tobruk was holding out, Rommel's forces remained outside the perimeter and the Germans' capture of Sollum, Capuzzo and the Halfaya Pass had brought them literally to the doorstep of Egypt. To make matters worse, Ultra intelligence indicated that another Panzer division with nearly 400 tanks had just reached North Africa. While presiding over the withdrawal from Greece, Wavell had informed Churchill of the Allied weakness in armour. In greater detail he told Dill how out-numbered they were compared with the Germans. On 21 April Churchill had urged the Chiefs of Staff to agree to send a further contingent of tanks with all speed, regardless of cost. The operation was code-named 'Tiger', and more than 300 tanks, known as 'tiger cubs', guns, vehicles and planes were despatched. In this instance Churchill was prepared for the convoy to run the gauntlet across the Mediterranean, instead of taking the longer and safer route around the Cape. At the same time, he wanted a report on the recent 'severe' defeat in the Western Desert. Wavell chronicled the reasons with clarity, noting mainly that the offensive had occurred at least two weeks before it was expected. He admitted he had been wrong in telling Neame to withdraw, and that it would have been better if British tanks had counter-attacked immediately. He set a pattern by taking full responsibil-ity for the defeat.[115] Without censure, and hiding his frustration, Churchill replied: 'We seem to have had rather bad luck. I expect we shall get this back later. Every good wish.'[116]

Churchill was also hiding the fact that, once again, he was annoyed with Wavell. In the current situation Wavell had decided to look again at the 'Worst Possible Case' plan for a withdrawal from Egypt that he had drafted the previous year. Dorman-Smith was involved in its reconsideration, and one proposal was the implementation of a scorched-earth policy in the event of a withdrawal; as he recalled, 'when I took the idea to APW he said that he was damned if he'd create a famine in Egypt and struck out most of our precious details. I admired his humanity then enormously because by making it easier for the Egyptians he also made it easier for the enemy – he was prepared to chance that.'[117] Finally on 24 April the revised plan was despatched to the War Office. Three days later, dining with Brooke, the Director of Military Operations Major-General Kennedy, Ismay and others at Chequers, Churchill questioned Kennedy on the security situation in Egypt. Kennedy warned that if German supply routes remained uninterrupted, they might be able to come at Egypt from both east and west, and retreat might be necessary. Churchill's response was heated: 'His eyes flashed and he shouted: "Wavell has 400,000 men. If they lose Egypt, blood will flow. I will have firing parties to shoot the generals."' Kennedy tried unavailingly to convince the Prime Minister that Wavell was no defeatist, and when he mentioned that Wavell had prepared a plan of withdrawal from Egypt, Churchill 'fairly exploded'. The following day he demanded to see the plan, then ordered that there should be 'no whisper' of any plans for the evacuation of Egypt or for closing or destroying the Suez Canal. That the plan was Wavell's – against whom he was already prejudiced – perhaps exacerbated his reaction; but Wavell was not alone in thinking it important to be prepared for the 'Worst Possible Case'. The Chiefs of Staff made it clear that, however confident they might be of victory, they believed 'it would be tempting providence to disregard the possibility of the reverse.'[118] The 'Worst Possible Case' plan and Churchill's reaction to it demonstrated yet again how different was the attitude of the two men: Churchill the politician, bearing the supreme burden, could not contemplate defeat; Wavell the general was prepared to stare defeat in the face so that he could prepare to meet it, if and when it came. Although it hardly helped Wavell's position, Rommel too was facing difficulties with his superiors. General Halder, the chief of the army general staff, believing Rommel to have overstepped his orders in the Western Desert, had sent his deputy, General Friedrich von Paulus, from Berlin to North Africa to report on his activities.

By 29 April Operation 'Demon' – the Allied evacuation from Greece – was complete. Of approximately 58,000 men, the Royal Navy succeeded in evacuating the majority. In the circumstances, casualties were relatively light. Of those evacuated over half were taken to Crete, where about 16,000 Italian prisoners were also being held; the rest were transported to Egypt. Their losses were exacerbated by Germany's heavy bombardment of the port at Piraeus which meant that all heavy equipment – tanks, field guns, anti-tank guns, machine-guns and transport vehicles – was lost.

On 30 April Wavell flew to Crete. He had already foreseen its strategic importance following the Italian attack on Greece in October 1940, at which time the Greeks had invited the British to maintain their forces on Crete and a temporary naval base for refuelling had been established; Wavell had also despatched two battalions, and these were periodically strengthened. But such was the pressure of events elsewhere that resources had remained inadequate and the naval base at Suda Bay had never become the Mediterranean 'Scapa Flow' Churchill had envisaged. No consideration had been given to the advantage of using Crete as a base from which to bomb the Ploesti oilfields in Romania, and Germany's rapid advance through the Balkans made the island's vulnerability painfully obvious. Ultra intelligence was already suggesting that the Germans would attack by airborne assault, and even as Greece was being evacuated Wavell was receiving emphatic cables from Churchill suggesting that this would present 'a fine opportunity for killing the parachute troops', and insisting that the island must be stubbornly defended.[119]

Wavell, looking 'drawn and haggard', presided over a meeting held at a small villa between Maleme and Canea to assess Crete's defence. Freyberg, who together with Wilson had been safely evacuated from Crete, recalled that after preliminary discussions with Wilson, he was informed by Wavell that he had been nominated by Whitehall to take over command of Crete.[120] He was reluctant to do so, feeling that his responsibility was to the New Zealand forces, but when Wavell impressed on him that it was his 'duty to remain', he accepted. When the formal part of the meeting was over Wavell spoke privately with Freyberg, informing him for the first time of the Ultra intelligence that was continuing to provide the British Government with exceptionally accurate information about German war plans.[121] He then returned to Alexandria and Cairo, where yet again the fate of the Western Desert hung in the balance.

In the first four months of 1941 Wavell had plummeted from glorious success to near disaster. Cyrenaica, so ably won, had been lost, and Egypt was in danger. 'Succour to Greece' had been a failure and the proposed Balkan front had never materialized. Crete was now under threat. Iraq had turned from friend to foe, and Syria was hostile. No commander in military history had faced such severe challenges in such unfamiliar circumstances. Neither Wavell's analyses during the inter-war years nor his attempts to train for 'war' rather than 'a war' had prepared him for the most difficult assignment of his life. That he weathered the strain and – despite failures – continued to retain the respect of his men is testimony to the confidence he inspired as a leader.

In the luxury of post-war hindsight, his decision to commit troops to Greece, which was militarily perilous and left the Western Desert exposed, was one of the most controversial aspects of Wavell's generalship. Many of his admirers, including men in the field, have gone to their graves believing that Wavell was only the instrument of Churchill's desires, and that only because of Churchill's insistence was the expedition not called off when the chances of success receded. But the facts speak otherwise. As Wavell both expressed publicly and wrote privately, he considered that 'from a military point of view the expedition to Greece was by no means the hopeless and quixotic affair that it has appeared in the light of what happened.

Actually, the plan on which it was originally conceived had a very good chance of success. But certain actions taken, or rather not taken, by the Greeks, after the plan had been agreed, the events in Yugoslavia and our weakness in the air, led to our being turned out so speedily.'[122] It was Papagos's refusal to withdraw from Macedonia and Thrace, resulting in fewer Greek divisions being available to support the British and Dominion forces, which led Wavell to describe the operation in his report as 'ill-starred' from the first.[123] He was aware of the political advantages, however: 'By supporting our ally Greece, we encouraged others to resist, for instance, Turkey and Yugoslavia.' He also believed that Britain's assistance to Greece would convince the United States and other countries 'that we meant to fight it out to the end.'[124] As Longmore later noted, all those who were present at the meeting on 22 February at Tatoi, including Eden, had been 'impressed by the Greek assurance that they were determined to resist a German invasion, if necessary alone . . . The decision, taken at the time it was, to support Greece was the correct one however unfortunate the result. It was too late to call it off when Rommel began to make his presence felt in Libya.'[125] But it was the assessment of Wavell's staff officer John Benson that Wavell 'thought himself' into the position, 'with great success and afterwards, when the expedition was a failure − and this is where I always thought him to be such a great and selfless man − he never tried to blame anyone else.'[126]

From the information available, and warnings to the contrary notwithstanding, Wavell did not believe Rommel would be in a position to advance across the Western Desert as soon as he did. Had he fully appreciated Rommel's character and drive, he perhaps would have taken care not to leave his western flank so exposed, an error he later admitted. 'I had certainly not budgeted for Rommel after my experience of the Italians.'[127] On the ground, the decision to provide succour to Greece was disastrous for North Africa. As O'Connor noted in the memoirs he wrote as a prisoner-of-war: 'The fact that we did not go on to Tripoli will always be a matter of controversy, but how we could take the risk of leaving Cyrenaica with a completely inadequate protection and send an equally inadequate force to Greece, I cannot understand. If we had neither gone to Greece nor Tripoli the situation would have been far better, as we then should have been able probably to hold Cyrenaica, and certainly Crete, without the very serious losses on land, in the air, and on the sea which we have suffered.'[128] At the time, the DMO at the War Office, John Kennedy, also believed that 'a small force rushed on to Tripoli might well have eliminated the enemy threat from the North African shore for the rest of the war . . . Wavell did suggest sending on such a force, but rather tentatively. He was told from London to hold hard until the Balkan situation had been cleared up. This direction from London was a bad mistake, which I pointed out at the time . . . But the biggest mistake was committed by Wavell when he did not insist on sending at least a small force in a bold attempt to seize this great prize.' However, Kennedy also acknowledged that the pressures brought to bear on the Commanders-in-Chief in the Middle East were 'far too great. There had been a constant flow of directives and suggestions regarding both major and minor policy. The Directives can be justified partially, and only partially, upon the ground that political considerations and other considerations of Government policy were involved. They might also be justified on the ground that they were not couched in the terms of definite orders. But they have been pressed far too hard.'[129]

Eric Dorman-Smith, who had shuttled back and forth across the desert, was adamant that an attempt should have been made to take Tripoli. 'Had we gone to Tripoli we could have forced Italy out of the war, just when Hitler was attacking Russia. Our whole world status would have altered, and when the USA entered the war we would have been in a strong position to remain at least an equal partner. Besides which, the North African campaign would have been unnecessary.'[130] More than twenty years afterwards, O'Connor remained steadfast in his view: 'What I really complain about was that the War Office planning staff never really got down to an appreciation of the possibility of the capture of Tripoli and what its capture would mean to our strategy.'[131] Even at the time, Leo Amery in a letter to Dill advocated a move on Tripoli as the 'open sesame' of the war: 'The advance to Tripoli should not be considered merely as the exploitation of Wavell's success in North Africa, but as the key to any future operations on a serious scale against Sicily, Sardinia, or in the Balkans.'[132] Rommel's view was that 'if Wavell had now continued his advance into Tripolitania, no resistance worthy of the name could have been mounted against him – so well had his superbly planned offensive succeeded . . . in comparison with Tobruk and Bardia, the defence works round Tripoli were totally inadequate.'[133] In the whole North African débâcle, Neame's reputation suffered the most. But his task had not been easy. Wavell's 'vacillation, contradictory instructions and obvious lack of rapport and trust' must have placed an intolerable burden on his subordinate. As his son later wrote: 'Where my father was at fault was in failing to win his superior's support and trust – but then he was neither the first nor last who found Wavell difficult to communicate with.'[134]

Before his death, Wavell once more reassessed the decisions taken in the spring of 1941. While he stood by his decision that the Greek offensive had been worthwhile, he no longer held to the view he had expressed in February 1941 that Tripoli 'might' have yielded to a small force despatched at once. Instead he wrote: 'As for the advance to Tripoli, Italian opposition could be discounted as small and likely to be easily overcome . . . but even so our own resources were not equal to the task. Our armoured vehicles were worn out by an advance of 500 miles; we had not enough mechanized transport to maintain even a small force for an advance of another 500 miles to Tripoli.' In the air and on sea the British and Dominion forces were 'still numerically inferior to the Italians, without any German reinforcement.'[135] A decade and a half later, Longmore concurred: 'Any serious advance after the capture of Benghazi, 6 February, would have meant a bad mauling by the German Air Force then assembling in Sicily . . . there was [also] the human factor of the general exhaustion of our troops, not to mention their commanders. Hindsight is apt to deny such considerations.'[136]

On 1 May 1941, in recognition of the supreme effort made by British, Australian and New Zealand troops in Greece, Churchill cabled Wavell: 'We have paid our debt of honour with far less loss than I feared.'[137] The Prime Minister's sentiments were echoed by Field Marshal Smuts: 'Honour was saved and a given pledge was kept. These are not small things in world affairs.'[138]

I 2

Churchill's Axe, 1941

There went out of Cairo and the Middle East, one of the great men
of the war.

Alan Moorehead[1]

THE BEGINNING OF MAY in North Africa is always unbearably hot.
Despite the exigencies of the past four months, life in the Wavell
household continued much as usual with the addition of a new house
guest: Hermione Ranfurly, on whose behalf Wavell had interceded at the
end of 1940. Her husband Dan had been captured with O'Connor, Neame
and Gambier-Parry, and she was recuperating from a severe bout of 'gyppy
tummy' and chicken pox. When they met, Wavell recalled how his own
wife had followed him across Russia in 1916: 'For sheer obstinacy there is
not much to choose between you.' He also told Hermione not to worry if
she did not get immediate news of her captured husband. 'He spoke so
kindly, I had a struggle not to cry.'[2] She was able to observe Wavell at one
of the most stressful periods of his life. 'Unhurried and quite slow in movement and speech, he exudes serenity – as if he knew trouble well and had
often stared it in the face . . . he talks very little, but listens to everyone
carefully and when his daughters came home and talked of their jobs you
might have thought they were as important as his.'[3]

Wavell's 'serene' exterior notwithstanding, he was facing new and yet
more daunting challenges. During the inevitable post-mortem, the Greek
tragedy weighed heavily on everyone – and, as Wavell realized, the
Germans' next target was likely to be Crete. Furthermore, the eastern flank
of his command was still volatile, both in Iraq and in Syria, where German
intelligence activity had intensified. In the Western Desert, Rommel had
made another attempt at Tobruk on 30 April; but once more Tobruk held
and he had to withdraw. Unfortunately, Ultra intelligence was giving both
Churchill and Wavell a misleading appreciation of future German moves.
According to the decrypts, General von Paulus had instructed Rommel not

to endanger what he had already gained by continuing the offensive at Tobruk, and not to advance beyond Bardia and Sollum until the arrival of the 15th Panzer Division and its substantial reinforcement of tanks; his order also described the exhaustion of the German troops. In light of this information, Churchill fired off another insistent cable goading Wavell into further immediate action, lest leaving the Germans 'quiet' enable them to gather supplies and strength for a forward move.[4] Wavell, as measured in his tone as ever, reassured Churchill that he had already issued orders for an offensive, code-named Operation 'Brevity', to be commanded by Strafer Gott, whose objective was to recapture the forward positions near Sollum and the Halfaya Pass. If 'Brevity' was successful, the Germans would be driven back from the perimeter of Tobruk.

Emboldened by the reverse in Allied fortunes, Rashid Ali had signed a secret treaty with Italian and German representatives in Baghdad. When Sir Kinahan Cornwallis, the British Ambassador to Iraq, informed him that the second brigade of the 10th Indian Division was due to arrive in Basra to protect the town and the oilfields, Rashid Ali refused permission for any more troops to land; he also demanded a cessation of flying activities. On the same day, two Iraqi infantry brigades appeared on the plateau overlooking the Royal Air Force training station at Habbaniya, fifty miles west of Baghdad; when the Iraqis were requested to withdraw, they refused. Without issuing an ultimatum, lest 'any warning of our intentions would be used by the investing forces as an opportunity to forestall our attack', on 2 May British aircraft bombed the Iraqi troops. They in turn began to shell the British garrison at Habbaniya, which had also become a refuge for British women and children awaiting evacuation to India.[5] Cornwallis found himself besieged in his Embassy in Baghdad. Churchill in London was watching the situation with concern. It was vital, he believed, to preserve the security of the oil pipeline, as well as communications with Turkey through Iraq; he therefore insisted that all attempts should be made to relieve Habbaniya and Basra.

Initially events in Iraq, which came under the India Command, were not top of Wavell's list of priorities. But on the day the Iraqi bombardment began, Churchill cabled that, since relief could most easily come from Palestine, Iraq should become part of the Middle East Command. As always, Wavell's reluctance to assume further responsibility was related to his limited resources. He indicated to Churchill that he would make a show of force from Palestine, but warned that the single brigade he was able to send would be 'too little and too late'; he therefore urged Churchill to pursue a political settlement with the Iraqi government rather than become more involved militarily. Dismayed by the number of fronts on which he was having to fight, after defeating Hermione Ranfurly at a game of back-gammon after dinner, he remarked, 'You seem to be the only enemy I can be sure of defeating these days.'[6]

Wavell's current leisure reading – Francis Bacon's essay 'Great Place' – struck a particular chord: 'Men in great place . . . have no freedom, nei-ther in their persons, nor in their actions, nor in their times. It is a strange desire to seek power and to lose liberty: or to seek power over others and to lose power over a man's self.' As he commented, 'I don't believe I did seek it, consciously. I was just too vain and too stupid to avoid it.'[7] On 5 May – Wavell's birthday – he officially assumed control of northern Iraq. 'Nice baby you have handed me on my fifty-eighth birthday,' he cabled to Dill. 'I hate babies and Iraqis, but will do my best for the little blighter.' Dill responded in kind: 'What a birthday present. Sincerely hope that you will be able to kill the little brute. Many happy returns of birthday but not of baby.'[8] Four days later, southern Iraq too came under Wavell's command. Of the various fronts on which he was fighting, Ethiopia was at last secured with Haile Selassie's triumphal entry into Addis Ababa on 5 May. Attacks on Italian positions continued for another ten days, but on 16 May the Duke of Aosta began negotiations for an armistice. Some resistance con-tinued throughout the summer, but Wavell's Italian East African campaign was effectively over.

Churchill, however, remained disgruntled by Wavell's behaviour over Iraq. Dill had spared Wavell the black thoughts in Churchill's mind, but was concerned for his friend's future. 'The Prime Minister wants to sack Wavell and put Auchinleck into the Middle East,' he informed Kennedy on 6 May.[9] In the event, with a vote of confidence debate taking place in the House of Commons, Churchill did not dismiss Wavell, but his com-mand in the Middle East remained a continuing subject of discussion. After a meeting of the Defence Committee on 10 May, Eden noted that Churchill had once more raised the issue of exchanging Auchinleck and Wavell. Although there was no unanimity, Eden admitted he felt Wavell's 'recent reactions' seemed to indicate that he was 'flagging'. 'In the end I weakly counselled delay and asked to wait for Crete result.'[10] Nerves in London were raw. Constant bombardment by the Luftwaffe was taking its toll. By the morning of 11 May, after the worst night of attack so far, an estimated 1,500 people were dead and more wounded. Harold Nicolson, author and MP, noted that the Houses of Parliament resembled 'a sort of Tintern Abbey'.[11]

Predictably, Wavell's suggestion that a political settlement in Iraq should be attempted was overruled, and the Chiefs of Staff accepted direct responsibility for sending the mobile cavalry brigade from Palestine to Iraq: 'Realities of the situation are that Rashid Ali has all along been with Axis powers.'[12] Wavell had either to acquiesce in their opinion, or proffer his resignation. He realized the force of Churchill's intent, and his subsequent cables were cooperative. Jumbo Wilson was charged with organizing the relieving column, 'Habforce', which was to free the pumping stations on the pipeline, already occupied by the Iraqis; it was then to march onwards to relieve the Habbaniya garrison. On 11 May Wavell flew to Lydda to confer with Wilson, travelling onwards by road to Jerusalem. As the commander of the 1st Cavalry Division Major-General John Clark recalled, Wavell's presence, and his clear and concise instructions, helped to relieve the inevitable tensions. Wavell's parting remarks expressed understated encouragement. 'It's a long-odds bet, but I think you will make it.'[13]

Wavell's main concern was Crete, where Freyberg recognized the poisoned chalice he had been handed, yet still bravely assured his men that they would meet the German attack 'on even terms'.[14] Defensive positions were being taken up at four locations – the port at Suda Bay, and around the three airfields at Heraklion, Retimo and Maleme – but Freyberg had already made it clear to both Wavell and the New Zealand Government that he believed the forces at his disposal, comprising approximately 20,000 men evacuated from Greece plus some poorly equipped Greek troops and the Cretan police force, were inadequate and that the whole question of holding Crete should be reviewed.

On the day Wavell travelled to Palestine to meet Wilson, he sent Dorman-Smith, his acting Director of Operations, to Crete. He took with him the latest Ultra information, outlining the anticipated German plan of attack. Earlier signals had reported a simultaneous combined air and sea attack; now, critically, Freyberg was told that countering the sea attack would be of secondary importance. As later indicated in an 'Appreciation' prepared by Freyberg's Brigadier General Staff Keith Stewart,[15] 'the entire plan is based on the capture of the aerodromes. If the aerodromes hold out, as they will, the whole plan will fail.'[16] If Ultra was right, redeployment was indicated, especially in the region of the Maleme airfield on the west of the island; however, on the grounds that there was not sufficient time, it did not take place. Two decades later Freyberg gave a more persuasive reason for this lack of response: had he redeployed his forces, it would have alerted the Germans that Britain had advance knowledge of the invasion plan, thereby compromising Ultra. However, at the time, and even with Ultra information to hand, Freyberg and his subordinates still considered a seaborne invasion possible: 'If they come as an airborne attack against our aerodromes, I feel sure we should be able to stop him if he attacks after the 16th,' Freyberg cabled Wavell after his meeting with Dorman-Smith. 'If, however, he makes a combined operation of it with a beach landing and with tanks, then we shall not be in a strong position.'[17] Preoccupied as Wavell was with Iraq and the Western Desert he neither ordered an immediate redeployment nor questioned Freyberg's actions.[18]

While 'Habforce' was making its 470-mile journey from Palestine to Iraq and Freyberg and his 'Creforce' awaited the German assault, Wavell turned his attention once more to the Western Desert. In the early hours of 15 May his first counter-offensive against Rommel – Operation 'Brevity' – was launched under Strafer Gott's command. Preceded by wireless silence, the attack initially achieved both surprise and success. But when Rommel sent troops forward, Gott ordered a withdrawal, leaving only a garrison at the newly captured Halfaya Pass. Two days later, the Germans retook it. Here was another failure to set against Wavell's name, and Churchill began to chafe again about retaining him as Commander-in-Chief in the Middle East. On 19 May he informed Dill once more that he had decided to replace Wavell with Auchinleck. As Dill later told Kennedy, since Churchill did not want Wavell back in London, staying in his club, he intended to send him to India where he could enjoy 'sitting under the pagoda tree'. Dill's advice was the same as before: 'Back him or sack him.'[19] In support of Wavell, Dill continued to maintain that he was the most outstanding commander of the war, one who enjoyed the confidence of his people and of his soldiers.

Tuesday 20 May was a perfect summer's day in Crete. After a heavy air bombardment, the Germans began their offensive, code-named Mercury. Even Freyberg admitted to being 'enthralled by the magnitude of the operation', as thousands of young men leapt in the 'crucifix' position from their aeroplanes. Led by General Kurt Student, ardent advocate and pioneer of the German paratroop division, the first drops were in the western sector of the island. Later in the day thousands more paratroopers landed in the centre and to the east. Although some were immediately shot down, others succeeded in circumventing the defences and engaging in heavy fighting. By midnight on 20 May Freyberg was cabling Wavell: 'Today has been a hard one. We have been hard-pressed. So far, I believe, we hold aerodromes at Retimo, Heraklion, and Maleme, and the two harbours.' But he went on to say that it would be wrong 'to paint optimistic picture . . . Scale of air attacks upon troops has been severe. Everybody here realizes vital issue and we will fight it out.'[20] Like the British, the Germans too were hard-pressed on the first night, but Freyberg did not manage to seize the advantage and mount an immediate counter-attack, which enabled the Germans to retain a vital foothold at Maleme airport. Freyberg was, however, still uncertain about German seaborne intentions, and how best to deploy his available resources. On the afternoon of 21 May he received a signal indicating that among the German operations planned for that day was an air landing of two mountain battalions and an 'attack [on] Canea'. In the next sentence the signal, which had the identifying Ultra initials 'OL', went on to say: 'Landing from echelon of small ships depending on situation at sea.' Freyberg's subsequent directive had important repercussions. 'Reliable information. Early seaborne attack in area Canea likely.' Without questioning further the probability of such an attack at a time when the Germans were still making all-out attempts to gain the airfield at Maleme, Freyberg ordered the 1st Battalion, The Royal Welch Fusiliers to remain at the seafront.[21]

As events in Crete took their inexorable course towards disaster, Wavell's position as Commander-in-Chief was at its most precarious yet. The catalyst was Syria. He had refused assistance to the Free French for an advance into Syria; when he heard that he had been overruled, he sent a curt cable to London urging the Government to trust his judgement, or relieve him of his command. Dill immediately sent Churchill a note to the effect that they had reached a point where they either had to permit Wavell to carry out the policy he believed to be 'sound', or relieve him of his command: 'My own feeling is that, at this juncture, we should trust Wavell. It is no time to make a change.'[22] When Churchill and Dill met at lunch on 21 May, Wavell's cable was the subject of discussion. Eden too was unhappy with the turn of events: 'Wavell has misunderstood our attitude over Syria. We realize he cannot spare troops from Crete or Western Desert, nor do we want him to from former in particular, but if the Free French are prepared to chance their arm in something like a Jameson raid, we are in favour of letting them have a shot, *faute de mieux*.'[23] Against both Dill's and Eden's advice, as well as that of David Margesson, the Secretary of State for War, Churchill responded to Wavell's telegram by calling his bluff, while firmly contradicting Wavell's assumption that pressure for the invasion into Syria had come from either the Free French leaders or Major-General Edward Spears, Head of the British Mission to the Free French.[24] It came, he said, 'entirely from the view taken here by those who have the supreme direction of war and policy in all theatres. Our view is that if the Germans can pick up Syria and Iraq with petty air forces, tourists and local revolts, we must not shrink from running equal small-scale military risks, and facing the possible aggravation of political dangers from failure.'

Churchill went on to take full responsibility for the decision; if Wavell were not able to put it into effect, arrangements would be made to meet 'any wish you may express to be relieved of your command'.[25] Dill took the precaution of warning Auchinleck to be ready to succeed Wavell as C-in-C, Middle East. He also wrote to Wavell with both his personal response and his professional opinion: 'What a time you are having. How I wish that I could be of more help to you . . . I feel the PM has only two alternatives – to trust or to replace. But even if he does not trust it would, I feel, be disastrous for you to go *at this moment* when you are handling so many difficult, if not critical situations.'[26] Wavell backed down, immediately giving orders to send the 7th Australian Division – less a brigade which remained in Tobruk – to Palestine in preparation for an advance into Syria. Only those closest to him knew how weary he was: 'the welcoming smile was a ghost of itself; the eye that so constantly gleamed with fun and mischief was bleak,' observed Dorman-Smith.[27]

Churchill might have his misgivings about Wavell's leadership, but he continued to send exhortations which Wavell in his turn answered from a Middle Eastern perspective, in his usual straightforward fashion. His cable dated 22 May set out in great detail his priorities, and his difficulties on all fronts. Ultimately, as his concluding paragraph made clear, his position in the Middle East depended entirely on air power and air bases: 'I know you realize all this and are making every effort to provide requirements and we are doing our best to secure Middle East. We have some difficult months ahead but will not lose heart.'[28] Churchill responded positively to this, thanking Wavell for his cable and commenting on each point. 'These are very hard times,' he noted, 'and we must all do our best to help each other.' Top of his list of requirements remained the Crete battle, which 'must be won': 'This will at least give you time to mobilize Tiger cubs and dominate situation Western Desert. While it lasts, it also protects Cyprus.' Churchill was also now minded to support Wavell vis-à-vis de Gaulle and the Free French: 'It is your views that weigh with us and not those of Free French. You had better have de Gaulle close to you. Let me know if I can help you with him. We cannot have Crete battle spoiled for the sake of Syria.'[29]

On 23 May Wavell flew to Basra to meet Auchinleck, to discuss reinforcements for Iraq and their respective strategies. He had acquiesced in military involvement but he was still anxious not to become over-committed, especially with his new responsibilities in Syria. As Wavell had already made clear to Dill, 'We must cut our coat according to cloth and simply have not the strength available at present for objectives India desire.'[30] It became clear to Wavell that Auchinleck was envisaging larger-scale operations which would mean occupying the oilfields of Mosul and Kirkuk. After their meeting he reported to Dill: 'It is obvious that we regard Iraq from somewhat different angles. My main task defence of Egypt and Palestine would be made more difficult but would not be greatly jeopardized by hostile control of Iraq. Whereas hostile control of Syria would affect me much more closely and dangerously. So long as my resources are inadequate, I am bound to be influenced by the closer and more threatening danger.' Wavell therefore suggested that, 'in view of her greater interest and greater stake in Iraq operations, India should resume control as soon as possible.'[31] Inevitably, perhaps, his return journey from Basra to Palestine was not without incident. 'One engine spouted oil all over us, and died,' recollected Coats. 'We hobbled across five hundred more miles of desert, sending appeals for help. Three German planes passed far to the north but seemed not to see us. On one engine and overloaded, we could only just overtop the mountains near Amman.' During the journey Wavell dozed and read Trollope. But he was obviously tired. 'As we thankfully clambered out of the plane, the Chief had a bad giddy spell; staggered and fell against me. He recovered in a minute, but he is exhausted, I fear, mentally as well as physically.'[32] Even so, within a day Wavell was in the air again, flying to Alexandria to discuss the deteriorating situation in Crete with Admiral Cunningham, whose ships were paying a heavy price for their part in the island's defence. At the same time he was briefing Dill about plans for his campaign into Syria, code-named 'Exporter', under Jumbo Wilson's command, and he was also being encouraged to attack again in Cyrenaica, in yet another operation, 'Bruiser'. Aware of his precarious relationship with Churchill, Wavell set his own responsibilities in perspective against those of the Prime Minister: 'We realize our burdens and responsibilities here, though heavy, are nothing to those you shoulder so gallantly.' In operation 'Tiger', more than two hundred tanks had arrived safely in North Africa by way of the Mediterranean, and he amused himself with a play on Churchill's own imagery: 'Weaning of Tiger cubs proceeding satisfactorily but even tigers have teething troubles.'[33]

Crete weighed most heavily on Wavell's mind. Queenie admitted that while her husband had been able to sleep during earlier battles, he was at this time so distraught that he 'walked the floor and was unable to rest'.[34] Churchill kept telling his Commanders-in-Chief in the Middle East to keep 'hurling in all aid you can',[35] but Wavell was obliged to report failure: 'Fear that situation in Crete most serious . . . There is no possibility of hurling in reinforcements . . . reinforcements have steadily become more difficult on account increasing enemy air force and may now be considered impossible . . . Such continuous and unopposed air attack must drive stoutest troops from positions sooner or later and makes administration practically impossible.' Repeating his earlier concerns about Germany's strength in the air, he said that Crete was no longer 'tenable'. Freyberg's only chance of survival was to withdraw across the mountains to Sphakia on the south coast, 'hiding by day and moving by night'.[36] On 27 May, as the British public rejoiced at news of the crippling of the German battleship *Bismarck* after the disastrous sinking of the *Hood*, Wavell authorized the evacuation. The Royal Navy could no longer operate in waters north of the island, so the evacuation of the western sector had to take place from the south.

The cost of these naval operations in Cretan waters was so high that when Wavell met Cunningham in Alexandria, he told him he and his colleagues had decided not to ask the Royal Navy to undertake any more rescue operations. Admiral Cunningham 'thanked us for our effort to relieve him of responsibility but said that the Navy had never yet failed the Army in such a situation, and was not going to do so now; he was going in again that night with everything he had which would float and could bring off troops.'[37] On the night of 28/29 May Freyberg sent back his personal staff and secret papers. He had also dictated a note for Wavell: 'We have had a pretty tough time. The troops were not beaten by ordinary conditions, but the great aerial concentration against us . . . The bombing is what has beaten us, the strafing having turned us out of position after position . . . We were handicapped by lack of transport, communications and lack of staff . . . I am sorry Crete could not be held. It was certainly not the fault of the troops.'[38] In the knowledge that Freyberg would not leave Crete without a direct order, Wavell signalled instructions for him to return to Egypt. On the night of 30/31 May Freyberg arrived in Alexandria and went directly to Cairo to see Wavell. 'It was a difficult meeting, and we were both overwrought. I presented a dishevelled appearance as I had not had my clothes off for several days, and had no clothes except what I stood up in.'[39]

For the returning soldiers Wavell managed to find the right words, as always: 'I thank you for the great courage and endurance with which you attempted the defence of the island of Crete. I am well aware of the difficulties under which you carried out your task and that it must have appeared to many of you that you had been asked to do the impossible and that you were insufficiently equipped and supported. As Commander-in-Chief I accept the responsibility for what was done. It was for strategical reasons necessary to hold the island of Crete if this could reasonably be done.'[40] Wavell also sent a signal to Cunningham praising the Royal Navy: 'I send to you and all under your command the deepest admiration and gratitude of the Army in the Middle East for the magnificent work of the Royal Navy in bringing back the troops from Crete. The skill and self-sacrifice with which the difficult and dangerous operation was carried out will never be forgotten and will form another strong link between our two services.'[41] Privately he was downcast by yet another disaster. 'I don't think I have ever seen our Archie quite so gloomy,' commented Lampson.[42] He was especially distressed by the heavy casualties The Black Watch suffered on the sea voyage back to North Africa. Crete never assumed the role originally anticipated by the Germans, however. Churchill described it as a Pyrrhic victory,[43] and a colonel of the German Air Force noted after the war that the occupation of the island 'achieved at such great sacrifice yielded no dividends on behalf of our offensive strategy, it merely improved the defensive position of the Axis in the Aegean.'[44] After the evacuation Churchill began the search for scapegoats. Already, in the aftermath of Greece, Longmore, who had been recalled to London in early May, had been replaced by his deputy, Tedder. Before Churchill had to explain to the House of Commons what had happened in Crete, Dill sent Wavell a list of questions about the conduct of operations. Wavell had realized that events in Crete were bound to require an explanation in London, and informed Dill that he had instituted a committee of inquiry to prepare a report on the battle. The Inter-Services Committee on Operations in Crete was chaired by Brigadier 'Guido' Salisbury-Jones, Coldstream Guards, who had assisted in training Greek troops on Crete, and for a short period Fergusson was also a member.[45] Its terms of reference were 'to ascertain the exact facts of the Operations' and 'to put up for consideration any lessons or guidance for the future'.[46]

Events in Iraq were proceeding slowly. By the end of May, British and Indian forces were within eight miles of Baghdad to the north-west and within three miles to the west. On 30 May Rashid Ali and his supporters fled to Persia; the following day an armistice was agreed, and Britain's right to station troops in Iraq was confirmed. While British forces continued to establish control over the country, a new pro-British Iraqi government was formed. In retrospect, Wavell realized that his attitude to Iraq had been wrong. 'I always disliked Iraq – the country, the people and the military commitment. From the military point of view I wanted it to remain quiet and give no trouble – at any rate while my forces were so small . . . it blew up at the worst possible time for me, when I had the Western Desert, Crete, East Africa and Syria on my hands and no troops. I probably didn't handle it too well, and was always a little defeatist about it. It came out all right in the end but it is not an episode of which I am particularly proud.'[47] On 18 June Iraq once more reverted to the India Command.

Wavell was also already considering his next campaign in the Western Desert, and he warned that his troops could suffer the same fate as those in Crete if German air superiority were not countered. Once it was clear that Crete had been lost, Churchill's attention also shifted. 'Everything must now be centred upon destroying the German forces in the Western Desert. Only by this deed will you gain the security on your Western flank which will enable you to keep the Germans out of Syria and yourself gain contact with Turkey.' It was vital, he said, before Germany recovered from its exertions and losses in Crete, to fight a decisive battle in Libya: 'In this way the loss of Crete will be more than repaired and the future of the whole campaign in the Middle East will be opened out.'[48] At the same time he was once more evaluating Wavell's performance, to the extent that even Dill was beginning to be 'in two minds' about him remaining as Commander-in-Chief in the Middle East. As related by Kennedy, when he met Dill on 30 May they acknowledged their debt to Wavell for his successes but came to the conclusion that 'Dill should advise that, if the Government could face the difficulty with the public, it would be best that Wavell should go: not merely because he had made mistakes, but because the Cabinet had lost faith in him.'[49]

Churchill had also been busy doing his housekeeping, and on 4 June had sent Wavell a long cable detailing his concerns. 'I have for some time been considering means by which I could lighten the burden of administration which falls on your shoulders while you have four different campaigns to conduct and so much quasi-political and diplomatic business.' He enumerated the tanks, guns, mechanical vehicles, and soldiers on ration strength sent to the Middle East: 'Yet you are evidently hard put to it to find a Brigade or even a battalion, and in continual telegraphs you complain of your shortage of transport which you declare limits all your operations.' He wanted to relieve Wavell of as much administration as possible, freeing him 'to give your fullest thought to policy and operations'. Comparing Wavell's situation to that of the C-in-C, Home Forces, General Alan Brooke, Churchill pointed out that Brooke was supported by the departments of the War Office and of the Ministry of Supply, and that a similar separation of functions should be established in the Middle East, although Wavell's authority as Commander-in-Chief would 'reign over the country'. Churchill then detailed what reinforcements he could send in the next four months and what field forces Wavell would be able to utilize for the autumn and winter campaigns, which might be 'severe'. His next point was the development and maintenance of the Army of the Nile operating in Cyrenaica and in Syria, which he believed would require organization and workshops on a far larger scale than Wavell had yet enjoyed. He proposed therefore setting up under Wavell's general authority an organization under 'an Officer of high rank' to be styled 'Intendant-General of the Army of the Middle East' whose duties would include the supervision and control of rearward administrative services. The man Churchill had selected as Intendant-General was VCIGS, General Sir Robert Haining, Wavell's successor in Palestine in 1938.

The final point in this long dispatch was the information that Averell Harriman, President Roosevelt's special adviser, would be arriving to assess potential American Lend-Lease supplies. 'He enjoys my complete confidence and is in the most intimate relations with the President and with Mr Harry Hopkins. No one can do more for you.' Churchill made it clear that it would be 'disastrous' if the supplies were not efficiently dealt with when they arrived, and commended Harriman to Wavell's 'most attentive consideration.'[50] The theme of Wavell's response was familiar: the 'Exporter' and 'Bruiser' forces were 'not anything like as large as desirable'; the Syrian operation was obviously 'in nature of gamble', and dependent on the response of 'the Vichys'. At a personal level, Wavell still did not find dealing with de Gaulle easy. Relations, he said, were not helped when the BBC announced 'that we have plans for Syria and that de Gaulle has arrived at Haifa. Much depends on secrecy and I was tying to keep Syria out of the news.'[51]

It was, however, no secret in the Prime Minister's inner circle that the Commander-in-Chief, Middle East was on the verge of dismissal. For reasons neither man understood, Wavell had never managed to play the role Churchill expected of a Commander-in-Chief. As his private secretary John Colville noted, the Prime Minister was saying 'some very harsh things' about Wavell, 'whose excessive caution and inclination to pessimism he finds very apathetic.'[52] Believing as he did that the Middle East had been 'so badly managed', Churchill suggested provocatively that if *he* could take over command there, 'he would gladly lay down his present office – yes, and even renounce cigars and alcohol.'[53]

Wavell too realized the effect of the setbacks he had suffered. 'I am feeling very far from being a successful commander after Cyrenaica, Greece and Crete,' he confided to Henry Jackson in early June.[54] Those close to him, like Dorman-Smith who had been 'in at the deaths' in May and June, were pained to see the whole structure of victory melt 'like a lump of sugar in hot tea.' Dorman-Smith later suggested that a possible explanation for Wavell's behaviour was 'a curious static loyalty to over-ruling authority, as if it was "fate"[;] perhaps his classical mind had something to do with this acceptance of fate.'[55] Nonetheless, with the disaster of Crete behind him

Wavell was once more thinking positively. 'If Syria and Battleaxe [as 'Bruiser' had been renamed] go well,' he cabled Dill on 6 June, 'there may be a partial lull in the Middle East till the autumn. If so I should like some weeks' rest and possibly you might like me home part of the time to report.'[56]

On 8 June the first advance into Syria took place. Whatever his private thoughts, Churchill was ready to advise, as always. 'I venture once again to emphasize that the objective is not the reaching of particular positions but the destruction by fighting of the armed force of the enemy wherever it may be found. As your force diminishes so should his. He has a far longer line of communication than you and must be in greater difficulties about supplies, especially of ammunition.'[57] As Wavell recorded, initially the advance made 'fair progress'. But when the Vichy forces realized how weak the British and Free French were, 'they soon took heart and their resistance stiffened.' Four days into the operations Wavell flew to Palestine to observe progress and the advance on Damascus. On 14 June, Vichy forces counter-attacked. 'The feeling between Vichy French and Free French was extremely bitter and the French professional soldiers were also undoubtedly fighting with a view to preserving their professional honour,' Wavell noted.[58] Churchill was watching keenly from London for any signs of flagging; rumours of a 'go slow' to avoid spilling French blood prompted a request that Wavell refute them.[59] Privately, Wavell admitted the strain. 'Well, we are still keeping our heads above water and tails and thumbs up, but it's a little difficult at times.'[60]

On 10 June Churchill had stood up in the House of Commons to defend British actions in Crete. But recriminations continued. After the evacuation, while the Inter-Services Committee continued to record its findings, Dill had asked Wavell to send home a senior officer who had experienced the fighting in Crete, to lecture about how best another German airborne attack might be countered. Brigadier Inglis had commanded the 4th New Zealand Brigade near Canea; unfortunately, at a meeting on 13 June he reported to Churchill how badly equipped the men had been, and how poor the defences. The next day Churchill minuted to the Chiefs of Staff this 'shocking' account of the state of the troops in Crete and of how slow Middle East HQ had been to act on the 'precise intelligence' – by which he meant Ultra – they had been given. Inglis's account had also fuelled Churchill's belief that the Middle East HQ had never shown that it had any 'real grip' on the operation, providing a further reason to replace Wavell.[61] But first there was the next offensive in the Western Desert.

At 4 a.m. on 15 June Operation 'Battleaxe' began. Unlike 'Compass', Wavell's latest offensive in Cyrenaica was no secret. The Germans called it *Sollumschlacht*, the Battle of Sollum. In a two-pronged movement British and Dominion forces attacked garrisons at Capuzzo and Halfaya and moved north to Bardia. By the evening Capuzzo had fallen; a second prong moved towards Bardia, whereupon there ensued the first tank-to-tank battle against the Deutsche Afrika Korps, with Rommel in personal command. The following day the Germans counter-attacked. By evening the XIII Corps had been obliged to withdraw, with the loss of 91 tanks as opposed to 12 German. Anxious about the progress of the offensive, on the morning of 17 June Wavell and Beresford-Peirse flew up to the front. But even this gesture backfired. As Tedder related: 'No one quite knew where the two Generals were, and it was only thanks to much good luck and a very heavy fighter escort that Wavell escaped. That evening, when he got back to Cairo, I told him politely that this had been an act of criminal lunacy. It was not merely a question of his personal value, but the effect that the loss of the General Officer Commanding would have from the point of view of prestige. We had lost enough Generals already.'[62]

The outcome of the visit was Wavell's realization that the offensive must be abandoned. As he himself had feared and Rommel had realized, the British were at a disadvantage because their heavy infantry tanks were so slow.[63] And the German anti-tank guns, as war correspondent Desmond Young noted, had armour-piercing ammunition which went through 'all our tanks like butter'.[64] In hindsight, Wavell also realized the troops had not been sufficiently organized or trained, a view with which Tedder concurred, adding for good measure that they were 'apparently unable to keep their own commanders informed, much less to keep the air forces informed.'[65] Wavell's cable to Churchill was dismal: 'Am very sorry for failure of "Battleaxe" . . . Fear this failure must add much to your anxieties.'[66] Soon afterwards Coats had to take some papers to Wavell in his office. He was sitting at his desk, 'playing with the many coloured pencils he always insisted on having, rolling them about and then gathering them up in one hand, then scattering them again.' He seemed unusually depressed. 'He looked up at me with his one sad eye and said, "Is this how it goes, Peter?" and quoted some lines of a speech in Hamlet: "If it be now, 'tis not to come;/ If it is not to come, it will be now;/ If it be not now, still it will come;/ The readiness is all."'[67]

Early in the morning of Sunday 22 June, yet another telegram arrived from the Prime Minister. The Chief of the General Staff Arthur Smith read it aloud, while Wavell was shaving: 'I have come to the conclusion that public interest will best be served by appointment of General Auchinleck to relieve you in command of armies of Middle East.' Having praised Wavell's conduct of the armies 'in success and adversity', Churchill suggested that 'a new eye and a new hand' were required.[68] Wavell showed no emotion but merely agreed that the job did indeed need 'a new eye and a new hand', and carried on shaving. Later that morning, Britons awoke to the news of the German invasion of the Soviet Union. Meanwhile, Wavell had taken his customary ride around the Gezira race course and then gone for a swim. In the changing-room were a number of young officers, who asked his opinion on the latest developments in Russia. With good humour he responded. John Connell, a staff captain who was present, saw the C-in-C surrounded by his friends: 'He looked like a man at the top of his form.'[69]

On the same day Churchill sent his telegrams to Wavell and Auchinleck, Dill drafted a long note to Churchill urging that Wavell should be allowed to come home for a rest, that Auchinleck should stay in India, and that Jumbo Wilson should take over temporarily in the Middle East; or that Wavell should come home and Alan Hartley, Commander-in-Chief, Northern Command in India, should take Auchinleck's place.[70] 'The alternative of allowing Wavell to replace Auchinleck in India, which I know you desire, has to my mind, many disadvantages. In the first place this idea arises largely, if not entirely, out of the kindness of your heart. But is it really a kindness to make Wavell C-in-C in India? In his place I should hate it. I should feel that my whole authority would be undermined by people in India, including Indians, regarding me as a failure. However you may write Wavell up, no one will think otherwise than that he has been relieved of his command in the Middle East because he has failed. Moreover, I do not think that Wavell would feel himself fully qualified to command in India.'[71] Yet however persuasively Dill argued, Churchill's mind was made up. From India, the Viceroy Lord Linlithgow's response was measured: 'I feel sure Wavell's shining achievements will secure to him a very warm welcome from the Indian Army and public opinion here. For myself I shall be proud to work with him.'[72]

Later that day Wavell responded to the Prime Minister's signal: 'I think you are wise to make change and get new ideas and action on the many problems in Middle East.' He thanked Churchill for his 'generous references', and requested a short period of leave in which to see his son and settle some business, acknowledging at the same time that 'public interest' might mean he had to leave immediately for India.[73] Churchill consulted with Linlithgow, then cabled to say the Viceroy thought it would be better for Wavell to 'get in the saddle' in India before coming home.[74] In his official history of the war, Churchill said Wavell received the decision to replace him in the Middle East 'with poise and dignity'.[75] To avoid farewells and explanations, especially to the Egyptians with whom he had formed a special rapport, Wavell expressed the hope that his departure could be announced after he had left Egypt, but Churchill did not think this possible. Wavell was informed that he and Auchinleck should arrange the date of the transfer of command between themselves, but that an announcement would be made on 1 July. Churchill's parting shot to Wavell was: 'Make sure operations do not suffer.'[76]

In the last days of Wavell's command in the Middle East he carried on with scheduled appointments. Damascus fell on 21 June; almost immediately after his dismissal he went to Palestine and Syria. In Jerusalem he stayed with the MacMichaels at Government House. As part of the evening's entertainment they played on the gramophone, while Araminta MacMichael sang, the popular – but 'lugubrious' – song by Edwin Ufford, 'Throw out the Lifeline': 'Throw out the lifeline across the dark wave, / There is a brother whom someone should save; / Somebody's brother! Oh, who then will dare / To throw out the lifeline, his period to share?' Wavell was back in Cairo on 24 June, and the following day set out for Addis Ababa to be the guest of a grateful Emperor. In recognition of his East African campaign Haile Selassie bestowed upon Wavell the Order of the Seal of Solomon, a rare honour normally awarded only to monarchs and heads of state. As they returned to Asmara, Wavell was once more beset by his flying gremlin: the pilot got lost, then they began to run out of petrol. An otherwise suitable emergency landing ground was occupied by peacefully grazing sheep, cattle and camels. After several unsuccessful attempts to scare the animals away, the pilot landed 'very skilfully' in their midst; as Wavell recalled, 'we finished up with a flock of sheep under one wing, some cattle under the other and a camel or two just in front of us.' A short time later an RAF plane picked them up. 'But it too had a misadventure, making a bad landing at Asmara and damaging the machine. None of the occupants was hurt.'[77] Wavell had not yet mentioned his impending departure to Coats. They reached Cairo to find that Auchinleck had already arrived; Wavell then told Coats, who felt that his 'world had collapsed'.[78]

The announcement in the papers of Wavell's appointment to India was accompanied by photographs of him posing with Auchinleck. As Churchill had already indicated, two additional appointments were also made: the Rt Hon. Oliver Lyttelton, DSO, MC, MP,[79] was appointed Minister of State and member of the War Cabinet resident in the Middle

East, and Bob Haining was confirmed as Intendant-General. Without bitterness Wavell observed that there were now three high-powered individuals to undertake the work he had done on his own for two years.[80] His Farewell Order showed none of the personal disappointment he may have been feeling. 'We have won some great successes, which will find a place in history, thanks to your skill, courage and hard work. We have had some failures and setbacks, when you have been outmatched in numbers and equipment, never in fighting qualities or endurance.'[81] Public reaction to his departure was mixed. The switch-over, remarked *The Times*, 'must undoubtedly come as a sharp surprise to public opinion. The people of this country have shown an enthusiasim for General Wavell's personality and have taken him to their hearts to an extent that is rare with soldiers, even in the midst of war.'[82] 'Whatever varnish was put on the transfer it could hardly disguise the fact that Britain's foremost soldier was being removed from the principal theatre of war to a quieter corner,' observed Liddell Hart in hindsight. But those behind the scenes were not surprised. They knew of the repeated disagreements between Churchill and Wavell, 'sharpened by a clash of temperaments'.[83] In Germany, Wavell's departure was greeted with surprise. 'The recall of Wavell is turning into a big sensation,' noted Hitler's propagandist Josef Goebbels. '[He is] Churchill's scapegoat for the lost Battle of Sollum.'[84]

Among Wavell's supporters, young and old, the feeling persisted that he had been badly treated. Dill immediately sent a message that he was going to miss him in command of the Middle East 'more than I can say'.[85] Dorman-Smith had a piece of paper in his pocket with the words *sic transit gloria mundi* on it: 'I must have felt his going very badly.'[86] Marshall-Cornwall later wrote that the Middle East had lost 'the guidance of the greatest strategist that the British Army had yet produced in the war.'[87] Alan Cunningham sent a message saying that all ranks in the East Africa Forces wished to express their 'great regret at passing from your inspiring and courageous leadership and to wish you Godspeed in the new and important task which lies before you.'[88] Sandy Reid Scott, a young lieutenant with the 11th Hussars who had lost his left eye in the Western Desert in December 1940 and had recently joined Wavell's staff as an ADC, commented that the change was a 'bombshell' for Wavell, who had done wonders juggling his troops 'and winning battles with two men and a boy'.[89] Another young officer, Tom Bird of the Rifle Brigade, whose brother, a contemporary of Archie John's at Winchester, had been killed in the Western Desert, was 'awfully sorry Wavell has gone. I had, and I think everyone had, terrific confidence in him, and in spite of setbacks still thought of him as a genius.'[90] 'What he did was to create the spirit of the Middle East, where every man was our friend and where every man did all that he could and more,' recollected Major Nial Charlton, who was on Wavell's General Staff at GHQ.[91] 'We said goodbye to a very great man, great in character and ability, a humble man who was absolutely straight,' Arthur Smith wrote to his family. 'No General in the history of the British army has had such a big job as he has had, and nobody at home can possibly understand the complications and difficulties with which he has had to contend.'[92] When Hermione Ranfurly went to say goodbye to the Wavells, she found Queenie and Nanny in their petticoats, packing. 'I felt as if my own family were leaving.'[93] Cairene society also viewed his departure with regret. But there was also a belief that Wavell was tired and needed a break, if not a change. In hindsight, Ismay believed he was 'a bit stale': the ideal would have been for him to take six months' leave, or six months' command elsewhere, and then come back – 'but one can't do that sort of thing in war'.[94]

Through it all, Wavell put on a brave face. 'In the conference room at GHQ,' noted the war correspondent Alexander Clifford, 'he reviewed his year of command. He went into no great details, but as he spoke I glimpsed how oblique, how ambiguous, how fantastically involved, had been the problems before him.'[95] If he was tired, he did not show it. 'Though his dark face was lined, he was as precise, as steady and as cheerful as I can ever remember.'[96] In his GHQ address Wavell recollected both his setbacks and his successes, pointing out that lack of equipment was always the key factor. 'But then I doubt if anyone will ever have enough of it.'[97]

On Monday 7 July Wavell departed, leaving Queenie and the girls behind: Joan had mumps. Coats also remained, to hand over to his successor and wind up 'unfinished Wavell business'. The Crete inquiry had just been completed and Wavell, in the belief that it was urgently required in London and since a courier was immediately available, initialled a copy and permitted its despatch, retaining another copy to read in India. Freya Stark was one of the crowd of supporters on the tarmac. 'He looked tired and sad, and kind, and the huge empty aerodrome, the sandy edges of the hills, the pale colour-wash – ochre and blue – of the early day, seemed all to lie attendant as a frame to a picture, round the group of uniforms and the weather-beaten faces, and the solitary figure who was handing over the defence of all this world and what it meant . . . the image was not inspired by any thought of lost causes, but by an atmosphere of loyalty and devotion that hung about the scene, and with it an acceptance of all that comes.'[98]

13

Conflict of the Hemispheres, 1941

The war from which Wavell had just been transferred now seems paro-
chial by comparison with the imminent conflict of the hemispheres.

Ronald Lewin[1]

I T TOOK WAVELL five days to fly from Egypt to India. Bernard Fergusson
and Reid Scott accompanied him, and according to Fergusson the new
Commander-in-Chief, India spent most of the first leg of the journey, to
Lydda, staring out of the window at the scenes of his exploits with Allenby
in 1917. Asked for something to read, Fergusson surrendered his copy of
James Elroy Flecker's play *Hassan*. Wavell looked at it, and before opening
it quoted in full the poem recited by Ishak, the Caliph of Baghdad's min-
strel, as he kneels awaiting the sword of the executioner Masrur: 'Thy
dawn, O Master of the world, thy dawn: / The hour the lilies open on the
lawn . . .'[2] He then read all the way to their next stop, at Habbaniya in Iraq;
there it was 'devilish' hot, and Wavell thought of going up to Deir-ez-Zor,
where skirmishing was continuing against the Iraqi rebels loyal to Rashid
Ali. Fearing he would be *de trop*, he contented himself with being driven
around the scene of recent fighting between the cantonment at Habbaniya
and the town of Fallujah.[3]

Moving on to Basra, which was even hotter than Habbaniya, Wavell
inspected the docks. He had hoped to make the journey from Sharja to
Karachi 'in a single hop', but they ran short of fuel in unfavourable head-
winds and had to stop for the night at Jiwani, on the Mekran coast of
Baluchistan. Wavell had the luxury of a hut, but his companions bedded
down on 'uncongenial' sand 'with a hot wind driving scratchy particles of
Mekran down our necks, and up our sleeves and trouser-legs.'[4] From
Karachi Wavell flew to Ambala, where thirty years earlier he had served
with his regiment. From there he went on by train, reaching Kakla, in the
foothills of the Himalayas, on 11 July; his destination, by way of the old
narrow-gauge mountain railway, was Simla, summer capital of the British

administration for more than a hundred years, set amid forests of deodar and pine trees on a ridge running seven or eight thousand feet above sea level, the air refreshingly cool compared with the heat of the plains. Every year the Government of India packed its bags – it took about a week – and moved to this pleasant hill station. Characteristically, Wavell's first order on his arrival was for a case of champagne to be sent to the agent stationed at Jiwani. Despite his long absence from India he remembered enough Urdu to speak to the servants, and 'the nearest thing to a smirk' Fergusson had seen appeared on his face when the bearer, 'obviously delighted, answered in a stream of words.'[5]

Compared with Cairo, the atmosphere in Simla seemed remote from the deprivations of war: 'I am His Excellency the C–in–C and Defence Minister and have two houses and as far as I can make out nearly 100 servants of all sorts, including a very good cook with several assistants, very bad for my figure. I don't feel my simple rather retiring nature can live up to it,' he wrote with fine self-mockery to Leonie Lemartine shortly after his arrival.[6] Wavell's residence in Simla was Snowdon, a rambling Edwardian house on several levels that bore the 'motley garb' of its many owners. The dining room, with a wonderful view overlooking the Himalayas, was baroque but generally, as Wavell noted, its present style exhibited more the 'autocratic hand of Kitchener'. Various 'improvements' had been made, one of which was to partition the rooms using torn-up Indian Army files as 'papier mâché' for the plasterwork.[7]

Wavell had the usual complement of ADCs and staff. His Chief of General Staff was Lieutenant-General Thomas Hutton, a gunner who like Wavell had worked in the War Office in the early 1920s, and had been serving as Deputy Chief of the General Staff under Auchinleck.[8] He also had the assistance of Ivor Jehu. At 31 he had been deemed 'too old' for the services, but as a war correspondent in the North-West Frontier in the 1930s, with experience of India's armed forces, he was put in charge of public relations.[9] In this position Jehu produced a series of books describing the exploits of Indian troops in the war; for the first book, dealing with operations in the Middle East during 1940–41, in which the 4th and 5th Indian Divisions had played such an important role, Wavell wrote the Foreword.[10] Over the next few years the two men became friends, and frequently golfed together. In the Middle East, Wavell had been most frequently in contact with Dill and then Brooke; in India he developed a lasting political relationship with Leo Amery, who had initially argued against the exchange with Auchinleck. But, as Amery later noted, once Linlithgow 'had enthusiastically accepted the swap, I obviously could not persist in opposing Wavell.'[11]

Inevitably Wavell had to get to know a new set of officers, men who might be familiar with his reputation but might not understand his frequent silences interspersed by the immutable 'I see'. At one of his first meetings with them, his new staff were surprised by the very few questions he asked, and the painful pauses that accompanied them. At length Wavell dismissed them, requesting the Master-General of the Ordnance to remain behind. According to Fergusson, who was present, he spelled out his immediate requirements: a set of all Indian Army regimental buttons 'for a girl friend of mine who collects them' – Araminta MacMichael.[12] Before leaving Cairo he had sent her his personal 'General's "escaping" button', which opened like a miniature pocket watch to reveal a compass. Thinking he would no longer be in a war zone, his accompanying note read 'I don't think I will be needing this now.'[13]

In Simla Wavell finally had time to read the Crete inquiry report. What he found was not to his liking, and 'he went through the roof'.[14] The report was heavily critical of the lack of defensive preparations on Crete, taking no account of the many other demands on the resources of the Middle East Command. Wavell immediately demanded that the report be withdrawn. As he informed the War Office, 'circumstances in the Middle East made it quite impossible to undertake a large programme of defence works on the island of Crete . . . GHQ had to decide how resources available should be distributed and had far more pressing and important commitments to meet, both for personnel and material, in the Western Desert, in Greece and on the northern frontiers of Palestine.' However, Wavell's and Freyberg's actions during the early stages of the German airborne assault on Crete damaged both men's reputations, and continued to haunt them professionally. Three years later Churchill was still complaining to his staff that Wavell had let them down 'atrociously' over Crete.[15]

When Wavell took command of the Indian Army it was twice the size of pre-war days, but, as with recruits in Britain, this did not mean all the enlisted men were ready for battle. Until 1940 soldiers depended on mules and camels for transport. There was no wireless, except at static HQs: all communication was by heliograph, lamp and flag, using Morse code and semaphore.[16] As for other equipment, what Wavell found on his arrival did not augur well. The most modern fighter planes were antiquated Audax machines; Wavell hoped Middle East Command might spare a few Gladiators, to enable pilots to train on more modern machines, and his first message from India was to Tedder: 'Have just seen India's most up-to-date fighter squadron armed with Audaxes. Does not this make your heart bleed?'[17] Tedder responded in kind: 'It does, but my heart's blood does not produce fighters. Do not think flight of our very part-worn Gladiators practicable from here to India. Am examining other possibility but prefer not to say more so as to avoid raising false hopes.'[18]

As Wavell was aware from the campaigns of 1940/1, the Indian Army had already sent a considerable number of men overseas. But they were needed at home, too, to police and guard the North-West Frontier, where the tribal areas bordering Afghanistan might provide a breeding ground for enemy agents, and to protect factories, depots, railways and ports. Indian soldiers had also to be encouraged to remain loyal to British interests, not influenced by the progressive political ideas of those Nationalists vociferously demanding India's independence. At the outbreak of war, the leaders of the Indian National Congress Party had made it clear that Britain's war against Germany was not their war, and had protested against the use of Indian soldiers beyond their own frontiers. Most articulate was Mohandas K. Gandhi, veteran Indian nationalist whose uncompromising campaign for the rights of Indians in South Africa at the turn of the century and later in India had gained him a revered and influential status as the 'Mahatma', or great soul.[19] In the autumn of 1940 he had called for 'civil disobedience' in response to Linlithgow's refusal to permit Indians freedom of speech to promote pacifist arguments against the war. By the time Wavell took command in India, more than 20,000 members of the Congress Party had been arrested.[20] Among the protesters was Subhas Chandra Bose, a Bengali politician and charismatic orator whose aggressive politics were too radical even for Gandhi and had led to his resignation as President of the Congress Party in 1939. Immediately after the declaration of war, his 'Forward Bloc' movement had embarked on further confrontational activities in Calcutta, leading to his arrest in July 1940; in early 1941 he escaped to Germany where he was put in charge of Hitler's 'Indian Legion', a group of Indian prisoners-of-war captured in the Western Desert who were opposed to British imperialism.[21] The attitude of the Muslim League, on the other hand, led by the Bombay lawyer Mohammed Ali Jinnah, was more cooperative.[22] Fearing domination by the Hindu population in any eventual devolution of power, however, in March 1940 Jinnah had taken the debate regarding India's future one step further with the historic 'Pakistan' resolution in Lahore, demanding the creation of a separate homeland for the Muslims in areas in the north-west and north-east of the subcontinent in which they were in the majority. At this stage, Wavell could hardly be expected to take much interest in the manoeuvrings between the various political parties; but the instablility arising from their anti-British actions was his concern.

Yet a more menacing external threat loomed. In India Wavell came into direct contact with events in Asia, where the United States and Japan were locked in a deadly game of brinkmanship. In 1931, in the wake of a power vacuum left between the warring Chinese Nationalists and Communists, the Japanese had invaded the north-eastern province of Manchuria, which they re-named Manchukuo.[23] This displeased the Americans, who were pursuing an 'open door' policy towards China and did not wish to be force-fully excluded from the region.[24] As fighting continued between the Japanese and the Chinese, the US goverment, without fully appreciating the Japanese national psyche or its military capabilities, turned to a com-bination of diplomacy and economic sanctions to force the Japanese to accept a dictated peace in China: in the summer of 1941 the US imposed an oil embargo on Japan.

Events elsewhere were working to Japan's advantage. As Wavell knew to his cost in the Middle East, one result of the fall of France in May 1940 was that its overseas possessions could no longer be regarded as 'friendly': in July the Vichy Government had been pressured by Japan to permit the development of air and naval bases in southern Indochina. At the stroke of a pen Japan was thus enabled to adopt forward positions two thousand miles from her frontiers, and only three hundred miles from British-held Malaya and the Dutch East Indies, rich in the raw materials the Japanese coveted. Thailand recognized Manchukuo early in August, Japan had troops in Indochina by the middle of the month, and in late August 1941 they bombed Kunming, the terminus of the road from Burma that followed an ancient track for 1,500 miles to Lashio, at the end of the railway from Rangoon. Churchill immediately cautioned Japan, whose menacing behaviour threatened Thailand, Singapore, the British link with Australia, and the Philippine Islands. But, like the warnings of the United States, those of the British Prime Minister went unheeded.

On Wednesday 13 August Wavell made his first broadcast as Commander-in-Chief in India, at the Simla Studio of All India Radio. He began by referring to the Middle East and to the role already played there by troops from India – both British and Indian: 'On behalf of the Middle East, I once more thank India for her efforts.' He hastened to correct any impression that Indian troops had been called upon to assume an unfair share of the fighting; in fact, proportionately the highest losses in the Middle East so far had been British. He also assured his listeners that the defence of Egypt, Palestine and Britain's whole position in the Middle East likewise constituted the defence of India.[25]

Inevitably Wavell kept in touch with his Cairo friends. His relationship with Freyberg had healed, and after his 13 August broadcast he wrote to tell Freyberg's wife Barbara he had just heard that her son Guy McLaren, Freyberg's stepson (feared dead in the Western Desert), was a prisoner and 'all right'. He also gave her a flavour of his life in India: 'I am pretty busy. I hob-nob with Rajahs one day and very political politicians the next, all quite interesting but not restful.'[26] When Prime Minister Peter Fraser considered replacing Freyberg as commander of the New Zealand forces, Wavell wrote in confidence to Dill: 'Freyberg produced one of the best trained, disciplined, fittest Divisions I have ever seen and he must be given fullest credit for their exploits in Greece and Crete . . . I should like him in India if New Zealand do no want him though I think they will be wrong to lose him.'[27]

Wavell's first priority in terms of external military commitments was Persia, bordering India in the east. Throughout the summer Reza Shah Pahlavi had been demonstrating pro-Axis sympathies, and there were a number of Germans in Teheran masquerading as 'tourists'. Churchill, anxious to safeguard Persia as a channel of supply to Russia and to protect the supply of oil, had proposed a joint campaign with the Russians. In late July Wavell had again requested a spell of leave in England, which Churchill had again refused, because of the impending action: 'You are responsible for the general conduct of the Persian campaign. A shock would be given to public opinion if you were not at the directing centre.'[28] On 17 August a joint Anglo-Russian ultimatum to remove the Axis agents in Persia was presented in Teheran. When it was rejected, columns of mainly Indian troops under the command of Lieutenant-General Quinan, GOC Iraq, moved into Persia to secure the oilfields.[29] As Wavell had predicted, Persian opposition was not serious and the Shah abdicated in favour of his son Muhammad Reza Pahlavi, who undertook to head a pro-Allied government. The legations of the Axis powers and their satellites were closed down. The Soviet Union and Britain guaranteed Persia's independence. On 30 August Churchill cabled Wavell: he was glad the Persian adventure had 'prospered', and there was now no reason why the C-in-C should not return home on leave.[30] The Prime Minister could afford a show of magnanimity: he had just returned from a secret meeting with Roosevelt at sea in Placentia Bay, Newfoundland at which the terms of a joint Anglo-American declaration of principles had been agreed. To be known as the 'Atlantic Charter', the document expressed a desire to see peace established 'after the final destruction of the Nazi tyranny'. As Churchill later admitted, 'the fact alone of the United States, still technically neutral, joining with a belligerent Power in making such a declaration was astonishing.'[31] Henceforward, the Prime Minister felt assured that Britain was no longer standing alone.

In early September Wavell returned to England. Somewhat peeved by Churchill's intimation that he was wanting to come home on holiday, he made it clear to him before his departure that his proposed visit 'was mainly to discuss future operations and India's further part in war, also to deal with certain personal business. I have no illusions about getting much leave or rest and proposed to return as soon as official and private business was settled. Private business can wait but I think personal discussion of certain problems of India's participation in the war would be valuable and is urgent.'[32] Sandy Reid Scott had not seen his family for three and a half years, so Wavell took his ADC with him, leaving Coats to look after his family, recently arrived from Cairo. On the way they stopped in Baghdad, to discuss the Persian offensive with Quinan, and at Cairo. 'Everyone delighted to see him,' Reid Scott noted in his diary. 'They all love him and are sorry he left.'[33] Fergusson was also back in Cairo, and had been preparing a draft of Wavell's final Middle East Despatch: 'This involved burrowing among mountains of signals, cables, appreciations, arguments, counter-arguments, which had accumulated over the seven or eight months before Wavell's final dismissal.' Together the two men worked on the draft until Wavell 'was satisfied that it was ready for the press.' According to Fergusson, during its preparation Arthur Smith had given him access to a file which contained 'every relevant scrap of signal or letter which had passed between [PM and C-in-C] . . . He was concerned that some day historians and others might be seeking to allocate praise or blame as between Churchill and Wavell.'[34] Wavell's onward journey to Malta, 'a veritable fortress bristling with guns and aircraft', was made in a large Sunderland flying-boat, causing Reid Scott to observe that the enemy must be 'cross-eyed as we are a cushy target in the moonlight and the exhaust shows for miles!'[35] After a stop at Gibraltar, early on the morning of 8 September Wavell landed at Plymouth, journeying on to London and the United Services Club in Pall Mall. When he arrived at the War Office he was greeted 'with open arms', according to Reid Scott.

It was Wavell's first visit to London for more than a year, and he had an audience of King George VI at Buckingham Palace in addition to his meetings with Churchill and the Chiefs of Staff. Discussions focused on aid to the Soviet Union through Persia – from the Persian Gulf to the Caspian Sea – and the defence of the Caucasus. He was also concerned to give substance to his argument that India was poorly equipped. Not only fighter planes but modern tanks and armoured cars were lacking, and there were only thirty anti-aircraft guns in the whole country; furthermore, despite a programme of training undertaken by Auchinleck, India was still desperately short of officers and technicians. Finally, Wavell was as anxious as his predecessors had been to state the case for Burma, semi-independent since 1937, to be placed under Indian rather than Malayan command. But the belief prevailed that Singapore was impregnable, and that Burma could best be administered from there. As Wavell later noted, this thinking was 'the cardinal mistake'.[36]

Wavell took time out from his busy round of meetings to invite Peter Coats's mother to lunch. He also met Joan Bright, a young woman with excellent secretarial skills whom Hastings Ismay (fulfilling a request from Churchill) had asked to organize a 'special information centre' in the Cabinet offices, so that visiting Commanders-in-Chief could be fully briefed on current developments. 'On the strength of what it was hoped would be a constant stream of distinguished visitors,' she later recalled, 'I was given a carpet, a long polished table, wall maps, an easy chair and some official secrets.'[37] When Wavell visited the office in September he seemed to Miss Bright as shyly unsure of what he was supposed to ask to see as she was uncertain what she should show him. 'He was perhaps rather surprised to find me – a young woman – instead of a uniformed officer sitting behind the desk.'[38] After he had looked at anti-aircraft defences and fighter strength Joan Bright took Wavell down to the Map Room, where the officers were 'thrilled' to meet him. On another visit Wavell invited Joan, to whom he had taken an 'immediate liking', to lunch at the United Services Club. His uneasy relationship with Churchill was still on his mind: walking through St James's Park, he asked her, 'Why does Winston dislike me?' As Joan recollected, it was a question to which she never found an answer; but it was obvious to her at the time that 'this quiet soldier, so lately a great victor in Africa and Egypt, was feeling out on a limb, shut off from the inner circle of affairs.'[39] Nevertheless, Wavell relaxed into some of his favourite pastimes. He dined with Brooke and Dill and numerous others. Archie John was in England, and shortly before Wavell returned to India he and his son went shooting with Arthur Wauchope on the Cranborne estate. Of the hundred brace of partridge they bagged between them, Wavell took three with him on his return journey as a present for the Governor of Gibraltar, the former CIGS Jack Gort.

On the eve of Wavell's departure from London his attention was drawn to the August edition of the *National Review* in which an article described

Churchill ruling the Cabinet as a 'complete autocrat, brooking no discussion, and no difference of view from the view he holds at the moment.' Wavell – 'a national hero' – was singled out as the object of Churchill's jealousy, this allegedly accounting for his transference away from 'the command he has so gloriously held in the Near East' to India. Wavell immediately sat down to write to the Prime Minister: 'I am very distressed if this sort of stuff is being written, with no vestige of truth in it. You, I know, and I, as I am sure you know, think of nothing but the national interest and the winning of this war and any talk of jealousy is absurd . . . You are carrying the heaviest burden of responsibility any man has ever shouldered, and I am very sorry if the Press add to your burdens in this way.' Churchill replied at once: 'I shall be ever grateful to you for all you have done to win the war, and I look forward with hope to your acting in a still wider field than the Nile valley . . . my admiration for your character, conduct and military capacity is constant.'[40] The tone of these two letters – cordial and to the point – suggested that a line might now be drawn under past differences. How Wavell dealt with what lay before him in South and South-East Asia would inevitably determine the warmth of their next encounter.

Wavell's return to India by air marked the first occasion on which a Commander-in-Chief had flown both ways – and his gremlin was in attendance: as they left Gibraltar the flying-boat was caught in a swell, and the sea came 'gushing into the cabin' through a hole in the hull. As the crew shouted 'abandon ship', a launch came to the rescue. Wavell had put his life-jacket on inside out but managed to save the official documents, while his personal effects in a bag were 'largely ruined'. He noted afterwards, in the first of many long letters to Joan Bright, that perhaps he had got his priorities wrong: 'The official papers were so dry that a soaking would have improved them.'[41] Another roll of soggy paper revealed a brassière: a present for Pamela from his sisters. After Malta and Cairo Wavell flew to Teheran, meaning to go on to Tiflis to meet General Koslov, commander of the Soviet Army in the Caucasus. But Koslov had been summoned to Moscow and bad weather prevented his return, so Wavell found himself having discussions with another general, 'a figurehead and no use for business'. With lively memories of his earlier encounters with Russians, he was critically appreciative of their strengths: 'I've seen a little of their army here, it looks good. I've always liked the Russians except to do business with when they are maddening – unpunctual, untruthful and unpractical.' Wavell's proposed visit to Tiflis had given Churchill an idea. Wavell, he told his old friend and confidant Max Beaverbrook, in Government since 1940 as Minister for Aircraft Production and currently on a mission in the Soviet Union, 'speaks Russian, and I contemplate his directing, or possibly, if the forces grow large enough, commanding, the right hand we shall give to the Russians in and about the Caspian basin.'[42] But the Caspian command never materialised. In Teheran Wavell did a little shopping, buying three 'not particularly good' carpets which were 'not particularly cheap' – for that very day the rate of exchange had apparently been altered.[43]

Wavell was back in Simla – 'pleasant and chilly' – at the beginning of October, so busy that he had no time to ride in the mornings and remained in his office until 7.45 p.m., which, as Reid Scott noted, 'horrifies GHQ.'[44] His main preoccupation was preparing for a three-day meeting of the newly formed National Defence Council, to be attended by Indian representatives from the provinces in British India and the Princely States. In his opening speech on 6 October Wavell reviewed the progress of the war, comparing the situation in which Britain found herself with that 150 years earlier when she was challenged by Napoleon. He also attempted to forecast the future, assessing that the Russians would stay in the war: 'Quite apart from the great fighting qualities of the Russians, I believe that they have a spiritual determination to see the war through, as they never had in the last war.' Despite Japan's belligerence in the Far East, Wavell spoke favourably of the Japanese people, suggesting that the 'vast majority . . . desire nothing better than to keep out of the struggle.'[45] This was perhaps unduly optimistic, for Japanese planes had already raided the Nationalist leader Chiang Kai-Shek's capital at Chungking, causing a number of casualties, and begun a blockade of the Chinese coast. Throughout September relations between the United States and Japan had become irretrievably strained, and on 9 October, an Anglo-US–Dutch agreement was signed against supplying oil to Japan. By the end of October the Chinese Foreign Minister was warning that the United States and Japan were on a collision course.

The growing inevitability of conflict in the Pacific did not prevent Wavell from settling into India. Numerous friends commented on his improved demeanour. Miles Lampson, meeting him in Cairo, said he had never known him 'so expansive and easy – there is no doubt that the physical strain here had got him down badly towards the end . . . India has set him on his feet again.[46] In mid October Wavell flew to Tiflis for his delayed meeting with Koslov. At a five-course dinner with ten different toasts, Wavell impressed the assembled company by emphasizing, in Russian, how closely his country and his hosts' were allied. During discussions the following day, Wavell again put forward the case for cooperation. 'The Chief,' noted Reid Scott, 'is quite excellent at getting stuff out of the stubborn and suspicious Russian general. When they start to get away from the subject by conveniently referring the whole thing to Moscow, he is good at getting them back to the point without treading on their toes.'[47] Even so, Koslov was not as forthcoming as Wavell had hoped. He later recalled that 'The Russians would tell us nothing of any of their plans for meeting any German attack through the Caucasus, were very willing to accept any assistance we could give them in the way of equipment and so forth, but not at all anxious to welcome British personnel of any kind.'[48] What was billed as 'an early supper' turned out to be 'a real Russian blind, and the company went to bed rather the worse for wear.'[49] By the time Wavell returned to India, the Government had packed its collective bags and returned to Delhi.

The city of Delhi to which Wavell returned as Commander-in-Chief had greatly altered since his time in India as a subaltern. At the Delhi Durbar of 1911, King George V had laid the foundation stone for a new 'Imperial' capital, to be called 'New Delhi', five miles from the old Mughal capital. Throughout the 1920s the architects Sir Edwin Lutyens and Sir Herbert Baker had created a new city whose buildings symbolized the splendour of the British Empire. The focal point was Viceregal Lodge, situated imperiously in beautiful gardens, flanked by Baker's government buildings at a lower elevation on either side; at the end of another imposing avenue was the Commander-in-Chief's house: 'rather large like a barracks – white with a good many pillars and a flag flying on top,' noted Tom Bird, one of Wavell's later ADCs. 'The garden is only fair, but the vegetable side of it very flourishing.' There were also numerous green parrots, doves, a mynah, squirrels, peacocks, green woodpeckers, and a porcupine.[50] There were excellent stables and a riding school, but no jumps, and no kennels for hound puppies.

Wavell had no sooner arrived in Delhi than he was off on his travels again for a look at his Eastern frontier, of which he had no prior knowledge. Burma and Malaya were outside his command, and the purpose of his visit was 'liaison'. Taking Jehu and Coats with him, he left Reid Scott behind to look after his three offices – those of ADC, Comptroller and GHQ – plus the 'whims' of Queenie and their three daughters. Reid Scott was also entrusted with searching the local bazaar for a horse-drawn tonga – which Wavell intended to use to help with petrol rationing.[51] After an overnight stop in Calcutta, where he had dinner with Sir John Herbert, a former Conservative MP and now Governor of Bengal,[52] Wavell flew on over the green swamps of Burma, reaching Rangoon at midday. The Governor of Burma was Sir Reginald Dorman-Smith, brother of Eric (who had remained in the Middle East with Auchinleck). During his visit Wavell was 'horrified' by what he observed to be 'the complete lack of organization, of military intelligence, and of planning generally to meet any Japanese attack'.[53]

The following day it was on to Singapore and Malaya, and yet again the flight had its problems. Half-way from Rangoon they flew into a 'howling monsoon'; visibility was nil and with petrol running low the plane had to turn back, eventually landing in pouring rain at Penang, south of the Kra Isthmus in Malaya. After viewing the newly constructed – and not very impressive – defences in the north-west of the Malay peninsula, Wavell spent two days in conference in Singapore, familiarizing himself with the command structure. The Commander-in-Chief, Far East, Air Chief Marshal Sir Robert Brooke-Popham, a distinguished RAF officer, had come off the retired list at the outbreak of war. The area of his command extended from Burma through Malaya, Singapore and British Borneo to Hong Kong.[54] Brooke-Popham commanded all land and air forces, but control of naval operations was under the authority of Vice-Admiral Sir Geoffrey Layton.[55] Civil authority belonged with the Governor of the Straits Settlements, Sir Shenton Thomas, who had been in his current position since 1934 and was, 'in Colonial office jargon, a "secretariat man".'[56] Major-General Arthur Percival – Chief of Staff under Major-General Dobbie in 1937/8 – had returned to Singapore as GOC, Malaya Command in May 1941.[57] Wavell had never met Percival before, but they both knew Dill, under whom Percival had served before the outbreak of war.

As Wavell realized from his time at the War Office in the 1920s, the security of Singapore – the 'Gibraltar of the Far East' – was believed to depend on the naval base constructed in the mangrove creeks of the Johore Strait. Five impressive 15-inch guns had been set up, three in the Johore Battery near Changi, two in another battery five miles west of the city; additional guns were located in batteries on islands at the eastern entrance to Johore Strait, giving Singapore the reputation of being protected 'by more guns than currants in a Christmas pudding'.[58] Nevertheless, as a report prepared by Percival and endorsed by the army commander, Major-General William Dobbie, had noted as early as 1937, the jungle to the north in Malaya was 'not impassable'.[59] Percival's warning that Japan might try to 'burgle Malaya by the back door' captured the interest of at least one national newspaper in Britain, but was not given the exposure it merited.[60] There was no naval battle fleet in port, and only 150 planes had been allocated for the defence of both Singapore and Malaya.

'The whole trip', remarked Coats of their tour to the Far East Command, 'has been a fantasia of crack-of-dawn starts, troop inspections in torrential downpours, dinners under punkas and rides in tanks through orchid-groves.'[61] On one occasion, Wavell was photographed wearing 'the most forlorn kind of waterproof cape and holding up an umbrella'; Coats, realizing that this did not reveal the Commander-in-Chief, India in the best light, noted that he must get the photograph suppressed.[62] At the end of Wavell's visit he expressed his dismay at Singapore's state of unprepared-ness; keen officers, he noted, were anxious to get away to an active thea-tre. At the same time his brief inspection led him to underestimate the ease with which the Japanese could progress down the jungle terrain of the peninsula: 'From the very little I saw and what I heard of the lay-out, I should think the Jap has a very poor chance of successfully attacking Malaya and I don't think, myself, that there is much prospect of his trying,' he wrote in a note to Auchinleck on 8 November.[63]

The possibility of Japanese movement through Indochina to attack the Burma Road, and thus threaten India, remained Wavell's major concern, and in Delhi he became even more convinced that Burma should be trans-ferred from the Far East to the India Command. A 'most secret' cable to Dill gave cogent reasons: the defence of Burma, he said, was vital to the defence of India, 'but NOT' to the defence of Malaya. An enemy in possession of Burma would be within bombing range of the principal munition works in India; in addition, it would be possible to develop land routes from Burma which would give access to India. In this connection, he took up the question of the construction of an all-weather road from Assam to Burma.[64] He also ordered that the 16th Indian Infantry Brigade should be sent immediately to bolster the forces in Burma.

Meanwhile, the Prime Minister was busy reshuffling his military commanders. It was no secret that ever since Greece, Churchill had lost confidence not only in Wavell but in Dill, whom he nicknamed 'Dilly Dally' and sometimes referred to as a 'ninny'. In November he decided to replace him as CIGS: promoted to Field Marshal, Dill was designated Governor of Bombay.[65] The new CIGS was General Sir Alan Brooke, whom Wavell had known since Aldershot. In a further reshuffle, Major-General Sir Henry Pownall, Vice-Chief of the Imperial General Staff, was sent to replace Brooke-Popham in Singapore.[66]

The drift towards war with Japan was gaining momentum. Speaking at a Lord Mayor's luncheon on 10 November, Churchill publicly announced that if the US became involved in such a war, the British declaration would follow 'within the hour'.[67] Wavell's 'Poppy Day' appeal on Armistice Day reminded his listeners of the sacrifices not only of the last war – twenty-three years before – but of those being made by men fighting in the present 'grim' struggle. He ended his speech with a comparatively little-known but appropriate verse of John McCrea's 'In Flanders Fields': 'Take up our quarrel with the foe: / To you from failing hands we throw / The torch; be yours to hold it high . . .' Later Wavell went with Linlithgow to see parachutists from the Nepalese Gurkha regiments, trained in India, do their first public jumps. To Queenie's horror, he said he would not mind doing one too.[68]

War clouds might be looming in the Pacific but Wavell, describing himself as 'a creature of routine', had adapted his Cairene way of life to Delhi. His early morning rides, beginning at 6.45 a.m. from literally outside his front door, returned along a lane where there were several jumps. He was accompanied by at least one ADC – normally Reid Scott, who unlike Coats shared his enthusiasm for riding; of Wavell's daughters it was Joanie, now nineteen, who most often came too. The day then fell into a set pattern: 'breakfast, office, luncheon (probably a party of some sort), more office, dinner (perhaps more guests) and so to bed.'[69] One such 'party' resulted from complaints about the conditions in which some of the Italian generals held as prisoners-of-war in India were kept: Wavell invited them to luncheon. He made a special effort, abandoning his notorious bored demeanour, as his guests enjoyed risotto, *vitello tonato* and gorgonzola with red wine. Afterwards Coats accompanied the generals on a sightseeing tour of the Red Fort in Old Delhi.[70] As Commander-in-Chief Wavell was also Minister for Defence, with a seat on the Viceroy's Executive Council – which, Wavell noted, Linlithgow handled 'admirably', although 'it does all take up time'. At the end of November, however, he was able to take time off from 'C-in-C ing' to travel in the Viceroy's train to shoot duck on the estate of the Nawab of Bahawalpur in the Punjab.

'I don't think the war is going badly,' he commented in a letter to Joan Bright written on his way to Bahawalpur. '1941 has on the whole been a better year than we had any right to expect with our backwardness of preparation.' Released from the pressures of the Middle East theatre, he had apparently recovered from the strains of his relationship with Churchill. 'I hope that whatever happens,' he continued, 'the Prime Minister's position will remain untouched; his courage and drive and leadership are indispensable. A very great man; if he had a better balanced judgement and chose men with his head rather than his heart, he would be almost superhuman, and how unpleasant people approaching the superhuman are!'[71] In early December Wavell was in Calcutta, staying again at Government House with the Herberts, and this time he met the Governor's wife, Lady Mary. According to Coats, she 'turned all her charm on the general, her face pinker than her ruby necklace and her black eyes rolling.' After dinner they played bridge; later they went to the popular 300 Club, and danced until four in the morning. The next day Wavell ate two helpings of bacon and eggs and told Coats that 'he had never felt better'. Herbert was apparently intrigued by this display of energy, remarking that he had always thought the Commander-in-Chief 'silent, stern and scholarly'.[72] It was Wavell's last comparatively carefree visit to Calcutta: the next time he and Lady Mary danced at the 300 Club, Britain was at war with Japan.

The first week of December 1941 began with a series of exchanges between the United States and Japan that seemed even more menacing than the war of words in which they had been engaged all summer. In his message to the Emperor of Japan President Roosevelt spoke of the 'sacred duty' their respective countries had to restore the traditional amity between them, but a point of no return had been reached. Late in the day on 6 December the Japanese replied, but the complete message, transmitted in parts, only arrived the following morning. By the time the critical part of the signal – stating that Japan was breaking off its relations with the United States – had been decoded, Japanese aircraft carriers were in position in the Pacific. At 07.55 local time on 7 December, a total of 423 planes made two separate attacks on the United States' fleet in Pearl Harbor. More threatening for British interests, Japanese troops landed in southern Thailand preparatory to a march southwards into Malaya. At the time of the attacks Wavell was asleep. Early morning in Hawaii was lunch time in Washington, early evening in London, and night-time in India. The news reached Wavell while he was on his early morning ride the following day.

The Japanese attack on Pearl Harbor brought the United States into the war and gave the British Empire in India an enemy on its doorstep. As Churchill had promised, the British declaration of war accompanied that of the United States;[73] the Netherlands, Free France and China followed suit. In Delhi, the reality of the situation was immediately brought home with the news that the Japanese had crossed into northern Malaya and attacked Hong Kong on 8 December. The sinking in an air-attack off the Malayan coast two days later of the *Prince of Wales*, flagship of the Eastern fleet, and the *Repulse* – sent by Churchill in the mistaken belief that their presence would deter Japanese aggression against the British Empire in the Far East – was even more devastating. Japanese troops had also landed in the Philippines. The Thai government was quick to grant the Japanese safe passage, followed by a ten-year treaty promising military, political and economic assistance. On 11 December, Japan, Germany and Italy signed a military pact for the prosecution of their war against the United States. The following day, belatedly, Wavell got what he had been requesting: 'You must now look East,' Churchill told him. 'Burma is placed under your command. You must resist the Japanese advance towards Burma and India and try to cut their communications down the Malay peninsula.' Wavell was also informed that 'at a convenient moment' Iraq and Persia would be transferred to the Middle East Command, and Churchill promised him a 'special hamper' of assistance: anti-aircraft and anti-tank guns; four fighter squadrons; and the 18th British Infantry Division, already in convoy around the Cape.[74] In the British press there was a brief reappearance of Wavell's name, when Churchill was credited with 'Olympian foresight' in having sent him to India before the onslaught.[75]

The attack on Pearl Harbor made an instant wartime ally of China, and both Britain and the United States sought to capitalize on whatever assistance the Chinese could provide. On Friday 19 December Wavell flew north from Delhi to meet 'Generalissimo' Chiang Kai-Shek at Chungking. En route he stopped at Calcutta, where he went racing and revisited the '300': 'With the Japs getting closer and Calcutta in a frenzy over the "certainty" of being bombed,' noted his ADC in his diary, 'it should have a stabilizing effect on them to see the Chief at the races and at a nightclub.' The following day Wavell travelled on to Rangoon, already aware of the deficiencies there. As Pownall, the new C-in-C, Far East commented: 'The arrangements for the defence of Burma seem sketchy, to put it mildly . . . I can see that Wavell is pretty sore at having been landed with such a deformed child.'[76] While he was there Wavell decided to replace the military commander in Burma, Lieutenant-General Kenneth McLeod,[77] who was nearly sixty and due to retire, with 'a commander with more experience of the organization and administration of troops on a large scale'.[78] Wavell chose his Chief of the General Staff, Hutton; not fully appreciating that operations in Burma were imminent, Wavell considered that his proven organizational ability as a staff officer would be sufficient to put the Burma command on a sounder footing.

On 22 December Wavell reached Chiang Kai-Shek's headquarters at Chungking, high in the hills above the Yangtze River. From their first meeting his impression of the Chinese leader was of a not 'particularly impressive figure . . . he speaks no English, but makes clucking noises like a friendly hen when greeting one.' His wife Madame Chiang, on the other hand, a woman of considerable infuence, spoke English perfectly.[79] Wavell's main objective was to obtain the services of the American Volunteer Group (AVG) for the defence of Rangoon; the two squadrons, commanded by Colonel Claire Chennault of the US Army Air Force, were under the control of the Chinese for the protection of the Burma Road.[80] Discussions lasted until midnight, and General Brett, commander of the US Army Air Corps, bore the brunt of the Chinese demands: as Wavell noted, 'the Chinese now obviously expected the Americans to be their Father Christmas for the rest of the war and to produce everything they wanted out of the bag.' His logical mind felt the discussions constantly veered away from the practical, as Chiang discussed 'global strategy in the widest sense'.[81]

Wavell also wanted to utilize some of the Lend-Lease material lying in the Rangoon docks, which was unlikely to reach China for at least six months. Chiang Kai-Shek was evasive, offering to send his 5th and 6th Armies (which amounted to two divisions)[82] to assist with the defence of Burma. Wavell accepted only one division of the 5th Army, which was already approaching the Burmese border, requesting that a second division (which was later utilized) be kept in reserve. He did not feel the military situation required acceptance of all the Chinese had to offer, conditional as it was upon a separate line of communication being made available for Chinese troops; they were also notorious for their 'locust' scouring of the land across which they passed. As he later noted: 'I had at the time every reason to suppose that I should have ample British, Indian or African troops available to defend Burma, which did not seem immediately threatened; obviously it was desirable that a country of the British Empire should be defended by Imperial troops rather than by foreign. The Chinese who had no administrative services of their own would have complicated the already difficult administrative problem in Burma.' Unfortunately his 'qualified acceptance' of Chinese aid was taken amiss by American public opinion, and he was accused of refusing Chinese help 'from imperialistic motives'.[83] It was evident the Chinese felt Japan would be quickly subdued by Britain and America. 'They seem to think the Chief had gone to Chungking to give them "a present",' noted Reid Scott, 'and were disappointed when he had nothing to give but rather to get.'[84]

Returning to Rangoon on Christmas Eve, Wavell had again to endure the vagaries of air travel. Initially there was no plane, and he had to wait for hours at Chungking; no sooner had a plane and crew appeared and they were airborne than an air raid warning forced them to turn back. Eventually the American pilot of a DC3 agreed to fly through the night to

Rangoon: he got lost, flew into Japanese-infested air space, then landed across the Gulf of Martaban from Rangoon at Moulmein, refuelled and headed off again. When they reached Rangoon there was an air raid in progress, so they spent half an hour in a slit trench, being 'blitzed' by fifty Japanese bombers. Wavell's trench was also occupied by an officer of Brett's staff: 'I cannot say that I was enjoying it, but the abject terror of my companion had the effect of heartening me.' While thus confined, he passed the time observing Japanese bombing techniques;[85] when the raid was over, he counted seventeen bombs which had fallen within fifty yards of the trench.[86] Such was Wavell's imperturbability, even though he had been 'within inches of death, of being blown to smithereens', that when he arrived at Government House, as Dorman-Smith noted, there was 'not a tremor in his hand' when he took his well-earned gimlet – a gin-and-lime cocktail. He might have just come in from a pleasant game of golf.'[87] At last he was able to celebrate what remained of Christmas Day, savouring Christmas pudding with brandy butter. On 26 December Wavell returned to Calcutta. Yet again there was no aircraft for him, so he had to pick up a Dutch plane. After all his exertions, Reid Scott thought his Chief would like a quiet evening, but he discovered that Wavell, 'to the amusement of all', had borrowed 50 rupees from the Viceroy's ADC and gone off 'round the town' with Lady Mary Herbert.

Wavell returned to Delhi, and a 'heap of work'. News from the Far East remained grim. On Christmas Day, after a valiant struggle, Hong Kong had surrendered to the Japanese. Churchill was already in the United States, accompanied not by his newly instated CIGS, Alan Brooke, but by Dill. As the Allied leaders conferred in Washington, Wavell felt free to go out for a day's pig-sticking with Joanie and Reid Scott. He returned to 'bombshell' news: he was to relinquish his position as Commander-in-Chief, India and assume that of Supreme Allied Commander of an entirely new command in the South-West Pacific, comprising four nations: ABDA.

14

Supreme Commander, 1942

The offer which I had to make to General Wavell was certainly one which only the highest sense of duty could induce him to accept. It was almost certain that he would have to bear a load of defeat in a scene of confusion.

Winston Churchill[1]

WHILE WAVELL WAS struggling back from China by way of Burma on Christmas Day, Churchill and Roosevelt were spending the holiday season together in Washington at a conference code-named 'Arcadia'. Prompted by the Japanese occupation of the Philippines and advances in Malaya, their objective was to review the deteriorating situation in South-East Asia. Roosevelt had suggested the creation of an entirely new position – 'Supreme Commander, South-West Pacific' – its holder to be in charge of all the Allied forces on land, at sea and in the air from Malaya, including Burma (once more removed from the India Command), through the Philippines and down to northern Australia. The acronym of this new command, ABDA, represented the American, British, Dutch and Australian troops under the Supreme Commander. The Americans suggested General Wavell for this appointment; Churchill was surprised: 'I was complimented by the choice of a British commander, but it seemed to me that the theatre in which he would act would soon be overrun and the forces which could be placed at his disposal would be destroyed by the Japanese onslaught.'[2] As Dill wrote to Alan Brooke from Washington, the British Government did not want one of their most respected commanders in place as the 'fall guy',[3] but it was indicative of the precedence the United States was beginning to take in the conduct of the war that Roosevelt prevailed. Churchill therefore found himself writing to inform Wavell that he was 'the only man who has the experience of handling so many different theatres at once, and you know we shall back you up and see you have fair play.'[4] Generalissimo Chiang Kai-Shek was to assume the position of Supreme Commander of all Allied forces in the China theatre to the north, comprising China, Thailand and Indochina; in return he had agreed to the appointment of an American deputy to head the Chinese 'Expeditionary Force' to Burma.

On paper it appeared that Wavell had been elevated to one of the most senior military positions in the war. But as his friend and confidant Liddell Hart later remarked, it was an empty honour which carried 'a hopeless prospect'. Wavell himself described it as 'a pretty tall order',[5] commenting that he felt like a man who wasn't expecting a baby and had been handed quadruplets.[6] His immediate circle of supporters saw his selection as a great compliment. 'They realize that things are in such confusion that the only thing to do is appoint the best man they have got,' Sandy Reid Scott noted in his diary.[7] As in the Middle East, Wavell's brief was formidable. He had to hold the line of islands from Malaya, Sumatra and Java to Northern Australia; he had to defend Burma and Australia as 'essential support positions', and re-establish communications with the Philippines; finally, he was to maintain general communications within the area under his command. And, as Churchill had already observed, 'we are no longer single, but married':[8] henceforth, deference to American views would be paramount. Instructions would come not only from London but from the Combined Chiefs of Staff in Washington, where Dill had been appointed head of the British Joint Services Mission. No doubt the unenviable task that lay ahead was in Wavell's mind when he broadcast on 1 January 1942. New Year's Day, he said, had had 'a red, stormy dawn'.[9]

On Monday 5 January Wavell left Delhi, seen off by Queenie and his daughters. Reid Scott again went with him, while Coats stayed with the family. Unperturbed by the dangers ahead, Queenie was already deliberating over what silver she should take with her when she joined her husband in his new posting.[10] In Singapore, Pownall, who had relinquished his position as C-in-C, Far East Command to become Wavell's Chief of Staff, was on the quay to meet his new superior. Together they spent the whole day at GHQ trying to formulate plans in what was obviously a fluid situation, when catastrophe was already looming in Malaya. From among those present, Wavell was disappointed to lose the services of Alfred Duff Cooper, former Secretary of State for War whom Churchill had appointed Resident Cabinet Minister and chairman of the War Council in Singapore in December 1941. But Churchill believed Wavell's arrival rendered Duff Cooper's office 'redundant' and instructed him to return home once he had conferred with Wavell and told him 'what you think and know'.[11] Cooper's prognosis for Singapore was not favourable: 'A breakdown on the civil side may well paralyse the fighting services. There exists a widespread and profound lack of confidence in the administration.' He went on to suggest that the simplest solution would be to declare a state of siege and appoint a military governor.[12] Wavell did not agree, maintaining that the Governor of the Straits Settlements, Sir Shenton Thomas, was a 'good figurehead' and should remain.[13]

Before Wavell travelled onwards to the Dutch East Indies, where his headquarters were to be based, he insisted on visiting the Malayan front, where the 3rd Indian Corps, consisting of the 9th and 11th Indian Divisions and commanded by Lieutenant-General Sir Lewis 'Piggy' Heath, veteran of the East African Battle of Keren, had been engaged in bitter fighting for a month in swamps and rain.[14] Depleted in numbers, the men were fatigued and short of equipment. The Japanese had air superiority except over Singapore Island itself, so Wavell travelled in the early hours of the morning, reaching Kuala Lumpur at dawn. He was immediately faced with the consequences of 'the Slim River disaster', in which Japanese tanks had succeeded in overrunning two brigades stationed north of Kuala Lumpur, thereby demoralizing the men still further.

From his brief preliminary survey Wavell had hoped the 11th Indian Division would be able to delay the Japanese advance through Malaya until the end of January. After touring the battle area, however, he concluded that he should order the 11th's withdrawal to the Muar River instead of waiting for a further Japanese offensive. The river, 100 miles south, in Johore Province, was the last natural obstacle before Singapore Island. While the withdrawal would allow the Japanese an unimpeded advance down the peninsula and access to the Malayan aerodromes, it would at least mean that an all-out stand could be made in Johore. To give the Indian troops some respite Wavell decided to bring up the 8th Australian Division, commanded by Major-General Gordon Bennett, currently in reserve in Johore.[15] Additional units, including the 9th Indian Division, were added to Bennett's command, designated 'Westforce'. Wavell's redeployment gave Bennett, with no experience of Indian units or of the Japanese, a very wide front to control, but Percival, the GOC, wrote respectfully that he did not see how 'any better plan could have been evolved in the circumstances.'[16] From Singapore Wavell cabled to the Chiefs of Staff outlining his proposal, noting how exhausted Heath's men were; they had been retreating continuously under most trying conditions, which did not bring out the 'best qualities of Indian troops.' They were 'utterly weary and completely bewildered by Japanese rapid encircling tactics, by enemy air bombing (though this had luckily been only intermittent) and by lack of our own air support.'[17]

After sending further telegrams explaining his strategy to the Chiefs of Staff and to General Sir Alan Hartley,[18] Acting Commander-in-Chief in Delhi, Wavell and Pownall finally set out for Batavia, capital of the Dutch East Indies, a conglomeration of islands east, south and west of Singapore and Malaya which in addition to Java, included Sumatra, Timor, Borneo and Celebes. His arrival was greeted by an array of admirals and generals and Wavell immediately went into conference with the Governor-General, Dr Van Mook. The senior positions in this multinational command were allocated to men from the four participating nations. As Deputy Supreme Commander Wavell agreed to the American General Brett with whom he had travelled to Chungking to meet Chiang Kai-Shek in December. Air Chief Marshal Sir Richard Peirse,[19] since 1940 Air Officer Commanding-in-Chief, Bomber Command, was appointed Air Commander, and the Dutch Lieutenant-General Hein ter Poorten was put in charge of ground forces. Even in peacetime, coordinating the forces of four different – and potentially rival – nationalities over such a vast area would have been a challenge. In wartime, with the Japanese assailing them from all sides, such a mission was assuredly doomed.

Wavell rose to the challenge, both professionally and domestically. It was, he said, 'an odd position for an indolent pleasure-loving military man of very moderate ability to have reached. I certainly never thought or desired to find myself responsible for part of the American Navy or Dutch air force.' Although he considered that both American and Dutch colleagues had been 'very kind' so far, 'these international four-in-hands are not easy for a rather amateur coachman to drive over very rough roads in stormy weather.' He also confessed to being 'old and bald (almost) but not yet as serious as I ought to be with my heavy responsibilities.'[20] For the first few days his new 'home' was the Hôtel des Indes in Batavia, a comfortable Indian bungalow-style hotel where he had a suite of bedrooms with bathroom, sitting room and a veranda. As Reid Scott recorded, the Dutch were 'quite charming' and had provided all requirements 'from aeroplanes for transport to torches for the blackout which is very strict.'[21] The ABDA headquarters were to be established at Lembang, just north of the Dutch military HQ at Bandung, with the navy stationed at the port of Sourabaya, at Java's eastern end, 400 miles from Wavell's HQ – a distance that compounded the already difficult problems of communication. As Pownall, his Chief of Staff, commented, never before had 'so many bricks' been expected 'from so little straw'.[22] From the outset Wavell had believed that Burma should have remained the responsibility of India, but as he later noted he was overruled 'on the grounds that Chiang Kai-Shek must feel himself connected with the new South-West Pacific Command. I think that this decision was a serious error from the military point of view. From my headquarters in Java, 2000 miles distant from Rangoon, and concerned as I was with an immense area and many international problems, it was impossible for me to give as close attention to the defence of Burma as was desirable; nor had I any reinforcements at my disposal to aid Burma.'[23]

Barely two days after arriving in Java, Wavell returned to Singapore to meet Gordon Bennett, whose 'Westforce' was moving up to the front line. After 'a quick run through' of the situation with Percival, Wavell set off for Segamet, eighty miles to the north, accompanied by Reid Scott and Percival's ADC, Ian Stonor. The whole show, as recounted by Reid Scott, was 'typically British': they started out with two new Ford cars and an escort of two military police despatch riders, but 'before 20 miles, all have fallen by the wayside.' One despatch rider skidded on the wet road and the second car broke down; the second despatch rider then broke down, 'so there was the most valuable General of the war heading towards the Japanese on a slippery road with a bad driver, through country infested with 5th column[ists], a constant possibility of running into a Jap patrol which had landed down the coast miles behind our lines, with the sole defence of Stonor's revolver for which I don't think he had any ammunition!'[24] It took them four hours to reach Bennett's headquarters at Segamet, and they returned to Singapore in a thunderstorm after nightfall. Wavell's reports to the Chiefs of Staff were gloomy: 'Battle for Singapore will be close-run thing and we shall need luck in getting convoys safe and up to time. Gordon Bennett and Australians in good heart and will handle enemy roughly I am sure.'[25]

But even as Wavell was formulating his plans, the Japanese were confounding them by moving more speedily and more aggressively than he could have anticipated; within a day of his arrival in Java, the Japanese declared war on the Dutch and landed troops on the eastern side of Borneo. A day later they occupied Celebes, a useful air base for further advances. When on 15 January Wavell formally assumed supreme command of ABDA, he made it clear that his scarce resources meant he would not be able to give General Douglas MacArthur, Commander-in-Chief of Allied Forces, South-West Pacific area, the support 'he appears to expect' in the Philippines.[26] With regard to Singapore and Malaya, so long as the Japanese did not make any further offensives against eastern Malaya, Wavell hoped that he could hold Johore in the south and possibly strike back. As with every situation he had so far faced, he was obliged to note: 'To meet above dangers over such wide area our resources by land sea and air are extremely limited.'[27] His reluctance to take responsibility for the Philippines was to make the Americans unnecessarily (and unjustifiably) wary of his intentions, suspicious that he wanted to avoid an especially difficult area. The Philippines, he was informed, were not excluded from the ABDA command.

Once Churchill returned from the United States, it was not long before Wavell was at the receiving end of a 'jet of telegrams . . . as from a firehose' regarding the defence of Singapore.[28] As Wavell had already informed him on 16 January, previous plans were all based on countering seaborne attacks.[29] When Churchill absorbed this he professed amazement, writing in his official history that he had had no idea the island fortress was so poorly defended: 'The possibility of Singapore having no landward defences no more entered into my mind than that of a battleship being launched without a bottom.'[30] It was also evident that, because of the belief that Singapore's defence was secured well to the north in the jungles of Malaya, even after the outbreak of war with Japan in December 1941 nothing had been done to construct defensive positions on the north of the island. For this Percival eventually took the blame, having told his Chief Engineer in late December, before the disasters in northern Malaya, that defences were bad for morale 'for both troops and civilians'.[31] Much was subsequently made of this statement, but the island had never been considered defensible from a close attack, as London was aware. When at a meeting of the Chiefs of Staff Churchill regretted the neglect of defences on the north shore, their view was that any last-ditch attempt would have to be made in Johore because, as John Kennedy recorded, 'The channel was narrow, mangrove swamps impeded the fire of the defences; and the aerodromes, water supply and other vital installations were within artillery range from the mainland.'[32]

To gain first-hand information of current preparations in Singapore, Wavell had sent a staff officer out from Java. On the basis of his report Wavell acknowledged that Percival was in a better position than himself 'to judge what troops are likely to be available at any given time', but had further instructions: 'You must think out problem of how to withdraw from mainland should withdrawal become necessary and how to prolong resistance on island.' In tune with Percival's concern for morale, he ordered that 'preparations must of course be kept *entirely secret*. Battle is to be fought out in Johore till reinforcements arrive and troops must not be allowed to look over shoulders.'[33] On the same day Wavell sent an even more pessimistic telegram to Churchill: 'I have ordered Percival to fight out the battle in Johore, but to work out plans to prolong resistance on island as long as possible should he lose Johore battle. I must warn you however that I doubt whether island can be held for long once Johore is lost.' He referred again to the heavy guns facing seawards, and – perhaps an indication that he had less than his usual grasp of the situation – informed Churchill that many of them could only fire seawards;[34] in fact, as he knew well enough from his initial visit, although such a prospect had not been envisaged when the guns were installed, most of them could fire landwards as well. Even more important, as Wavell recollected, was that 'the Air Force which might have saved Singapore by attack on the Japanese transports was not there at the right time, because it had to be elsewhere.'[35] Churchill was adamant that Singapore should not be lost without a fight. 'I was greatly distressed by your telegrams,' he responded, 'and I want to make it absolutely clear that I expect every inch of ground to be defended, ever scrap of material or defences to be blown to pieces to prevent capture by the enemy, and no question of surrender to be entertained until after protracted fighting among the ruins of Singapore City.'[36]

While Churchill was considering the vulnerability of Singapore, Wavell had been settling into his new headquarters in the Grand Hotel at Lembang. A heavily armed Dutch sergeant-major had been deputed to act as his bodyguard, with orders to die (if need be) in defence of the Supreme Commander, and insisted on sleeping on the floor, across the bedroom doorway. But Wavell did not linger long at his new headquarters: on 20 January, for the second time in a week, he was on his way to Singapore. The only car available when he arrived was a battered MG belonging to an RAF cadet. Wavell arrived at Percival's residence, Flagstaff House, as the day's first air raid was taking place. Yet again, their discussions focused on the defence of Singapore if the battle for Johore were lost. Wavell suggested it was likely the Japanese would attack on the north-west of the island, through the mangrove swamps; he therefore advised that the freshest troops – the newly arriving 18th British Division – should be positioned on the north-west, leaving the battle-hardened but weary Australians to defend the north-east. In Percival's despatch and his later writings he emphasized his own belief that the attack would come from the north-west, but during this meeting he pointed to the possibility of an attack coming from the north-east, down the Johore River towards Changi.[37] Leaving Percival to make his final dispositions, Wavell went back to Java, where he drafted a signal to the Chiefs of Staff in both London and Washington, indicating that a general withdrawal to the island of Singapore appeared to be only a matter of time. In an attempt to boost morale, Wavell also wrote a note for Percival: 'As in all other warfare, in thick or open country, in Asia or

Europe, in advance or retreat, in attack or defence, the leadership of the officer and the fighting spirit of the soldier – the determination to beat the other man whatever happens is the deciding factor. There are three principal factors in all fighting – good equipment, tactical skill and guts. But the greatest of these is *guts*.'[38]

Near escapes during air travel remained a recurring hazard. Wavell was to meet the Governor-General, Dr Van Mook, and since Batavia had two airports, the adjutant arranging the Supreme Commander's reception wanted to know which one would be used. Wavell's Dutch liaison officer Captain Reinhard Mackay could only recall the name of the older and smaller one. Asked on their arrival why that airport had been chosen, he avoided a direct answer – only to learn that the main airport had just suffered an unexpected bombardment. 'On our return voyage, General Wavell told me that even His Excellency the Governor-General had expressed his astonishment for our landing on the old airport and that he, Wavell, had failed to be able to explain. Then I told him the gospel truth; with the one eye he looked me all over for a while, but said nothing.'[39]

Books were as always a major solace in Wavell's life, and while browsing through a shop in Batavia he found a copy of the American edition of his Life of Allenby. 'He is in his element in a bookshop,' observed Reid Scott, 'and glances through detective stories and classics.'[40] Liddell Hart had sent him a copy of his book *The Strategy of Indirect Approach*, and Wavell wrote to thank him, touching again on familiar themes that now seemed particularly relevant: 'The more I see of war, the less I think that general principles of strategy count as compared with administrative problems and the gaining of Intelligence . . . But it is often outside the power of the general to act as he would have liked owing to lack of adequate resources, and I think that military history very seldom brings this out . . . for instance if Hannibal had had another twenty elephants, it might have altered his whole strategy against Italy. Heaven forbid that I should be mentioned in the same breath as Hannibal or any other commander of repute, but in operations for which I have been responsible I should, on more than one occasion, have acted differently if I had had another 200 or 300 lorries.'[41]

Elsewhere in Wavell's far-flung command, the situation was deteriorating: the Japanese, whose forces had been assembling along the Thai border since early January, had started their offensive against Burma. Like Singapore, the defence of this mountainous land required organisation and resources, both of which were lacking. As the GOC, Hutton, later admitted: 'There were very few metalled roads and transport was mainly by water or rail except in the case of the Burma Road to Mandalay, Lashio and Chungking. It was therefore quite unsuitable for forces dependant on mechanical transport.' Lack of intelligence also meant there was little indication of the invasion routes the Japanese were likely to take. Assuming their initial objective to be the Burma Road, it was thought that the attack would be directed either on Meiktila or, from Chiengmai, the railhead in Thailand, on Toungoo: 'Either of these would have cut the Burma Road and severed the communications from Rangoon to Mandalay with Chinese.'[42] On 15 January, however, the Japanese, taking advantage of obvious weakness in the south, had sent a battalion across the border between Thailand and Burma in the narrow stretch of land known as the Tenasserim coast facing the Andaman Islands. Within four days they had succeeded in capturing the town of Tavoy and its airfield, enabling them to fly in additional troops. The small garrison at Mergui withdrew, so that the Japanese, with comparative ease, had gained a foothold in southern Burma from where they could launch bombing raids northwards across the Gulf of Martaban against Rangoon as well as threatening Moulmein. In defence of this area was the hastily raised 17th Division, commanded by acting Major-General 'Jackie' Smyth who had earned a VC during the Great War and the MC fighting tribesmen on the North-West Frontier in 1920. He had only recently arrived in Burma, but had immediately sensed that whereas the Japanese 'were in top gear and overdrive, the British were in second gear, with no one coordinating or controlling the machine at all.'[43] As the Japanese moved up the river valleys, it became clear that the British would not be able to hold their advanced position.

Hutton urgently requested air forces and troops of Wavell. But the Supreme Commander had little comfort to give: 'We can spare nothing from here, India is obviously doing everything possible to help. You have done very well in air up to date and will continue to hit hard, I hope.'[44] Wavell's message to General MacArthur in the Philippines was the same: 'There is little I can do at present to help your magnificent defence except to organize supply of ammunition and food to you. This is in hand.'[45] In a show of good faith he offered to fly to the Philippines but MacArthur warned against attempting such a hazardous journey. Nevertheless, immediately after returning from Singapore Wavell felt compelled to go to Burma, flying through the night of 23/4 January, to confer with Hutton and Smyth. The Americans had put a heavy four-engined Flying Fortress at his disposal, but when they got to Batavia the pilot confessed that the runway was not long enough for him to take off with a full load of fuel, while with only a half-load they would not even be able to reach their first stop in Sumatra in the dark. Not surprisingly, Wavell was annoyed by the postponement; it was Reid Scott's sense that he thought 'the Americans should have known where they could take off.'[46] Wavell set off again, after a morning's work, for a small aerodrome in Bandung with a long runway for the Flying Fortress. It was 'very uncomfortable and the Chief spent the night on a lilo on a row of suitcases.' When they reached Burma, landing at Mingladon – 'in an air raid, at least we are the raid! They thought our Flying Fortress was a Jap!' – there was no one to meet them.[47] Hutton hurried to Rangoon, telling Smyth to hold Moulmein as long as possible and withdraw the disorganized troops, administrative units and stores across the Salween River.[48] After spending the day in Rangoon, with 'a good dinner and plenty to drink' hosted by Dorman-Smith at Government House, Wavell and his party returned to Java at midnight. Finding the atmosphere in Burma 'much calmer and more confident' than he had been led to expect, he concluded that evacuation would be premature, provided land and air reinforcements arrived and some naval force was available to prevent a landing near Rangoon from the Tenasserim coast. He also ordered a series of delaying tactics involving aggressive opposition to Japanese attempts to cross the Salween River.

Before leaving for Burma Wavell had received another interrogative cable from Churchill about his refusal of the entire complement of the Chinese 5th and 6th Armies at his December meeting with Chiang Kai-Shek in Chungking: 'I am still puzzled about your reasons for refusing Chinese help in the defence of Burma and the Burma Road,' the Prime Minister had cabled on 23 January. 'Burma seems in grave danger of being overrun. When we remember how long the Chinese have stood it alone and ill-armed against the Japanese and when we see what a very rough time we are having at Japanese hands I cannot understand why we do not welcome their aid.' He proceeded to enlighten Wavell regarding the American perspective, which had envisaged Wavell giving his 'left hand to China' in Burma while he focused on the other aspects of his command.[49] On his return from Burma Wavell responded, defending his position with a rare show of emotion: 'I did not refuse Chinese help.' It was the slowness of the Chinese that made it look as though he had only recently accepted two Chinese divisions: in fact, he had in December accepted – one immediately and one to be kept in reserve – the two divisions of the Chinese 5th Army. 'All I asked was that the Sixth Army should not be moved to Burmese frontier, as it would be difficult to feed and communications inside Burma could not deal with it. Generalissimo demanded a line of communications purely

Chinese and that Chinese troops should not be mixed with ours, a condition impossible to fulfil at that time.'[50] For once Churchill was satisfied with Wavell's explanation, and promised that he would 'not lose any chance' of explaining the situation to Roosevelt.[51]

Even as Wavell was giving his attention to Burma, the situation in Malaya was so grim that Churchill was beginning to think seriously about the reinforcements which were on their way. 'These', he later observed, 'could be doomed or diverted.' Though part of the 18th British Division had already landed, he still felt there was 'ample time to turn their prows northward to Rangoon.'[52] But when news of the possible diversion reached the Australian Prime Minister John Curtin, he sent Churchill a furious signal: 'On the faith of the proposed flow of reinforcements, we have acted and carried out our part of the bargain. We expect you not to frustrate the whole purpose by evacuation [of Singapore].'[53] Inevitably, the outcome of this exchange between the two Prime Ministers was critical for Wavell's command. Diverted to Burma, the 18th British Division would help its defence. But as Churchill noted in his official history, Curtin's reaction was not his only reason for deciding that they should carry on to Singapore: he had also become conscious of 'a hardening of opinion against the abandonment of this renowned key point in the Far East'.[54] By the end of January the 18th British Division, commanded by Major-General Beckwith-Smith, had fully disembarked in Singapore.

During Wavell's absence in Burma there were further exchanges between Churchill and Curtin. So concerned were the Australians for their own security following British reverses that Curtin wanted Churchill to back his demand for American naval and air assistance. Inevitably the person through whom that assistance would be channelled was Wavell, and on 24 January he was informed of a further extension to his command, to include 'not only the defence of Darwin but also . . . such portions of north-west coast of Australia as is necessary for successful defence of Darwin against enemy landings and for air operations from a base on the Australian coast in that area.'[55] Yet again Wavell took his new responsibilities in his stride, finding solace in his correspondents. He had set measures in train to improve the flow of mail to the Far East, and at the end of January reaped the benefit: a pile of letters arrived for him from India, including letters from his family in Delhi, and from Archie John in Scotland. Like his father, he felt it important to keep his friendships 'in constant repair' by writing hundreds of letters.[56] 'We are getting along quite happily,' Wavell replied to Archie John, 'in this very half-horse place up in the hills and have had no international disagreements yet.'[57]

Wavell's attempts to maintain the island chain were foundering. His report to the Combined Chiefs of Staff at the end of January again high-lighted the importance of getting enough of the promised Allied aircraft in time: only if Singapore could make 'a prolonged resistance' would the situation be saved.[58] But Japanese progress down the Malay peninsula was unrelenting, and Percival had to inform Wavell that withdrawal to Singapore Island would take place on the night of 30/1 January: 'I fully realize the wider repercussions of this step but in my opinion the risk which even now exists of the right and centre columns being cut off by swift enemy action down the west coast road does not justify any further delay.'[59] Wavell agreed, entreating Percival to fight for 'every foot of the island'.[60]

Before the withdrawal, Wavell flew overnight to Singapore, motored up to Heath's headquarters at Johore Bahru, and conferred with Gordon Bennett. It was agreed that martial law would be imposed once the army had withdrawn to the island, and that Percival would assume operational command. Those troops who could march were to cross the 1,000-yard causeway that night, before it was breached. By early morning on 1 February, the last remaining stragglers had crossed into Singapore. A piper of The Argyll and Sutherland Highlanders played the soulful 'Highland Laddie'; soon afterwards, an explosion left a seventy-foot gap in the cause-way. When Wavell received Percival's telegram stating that they had successfully withdrawn into Singapore 'Fortress', he laughed.[61]

In early February Burma was once more urgently demanding Wavell's attention, for despite his exhortations to fight forward, Moulmein had been evacuated on 31 January. He went to Burma again on 4 February, prompted by a message from the Military Attaché in Chungking that the Chinese were expecting both Rangoon and Singapore to be lost, and thought it prudent to conserve their strength and only fight the Japanese when threat-ened. Unfortunately, poor communications caused him to miss Chiang Kai-Shek, whom he had hoped to catch as he passed through Rangoon on Chiang's way to India. Reid Scott was with Wavell, who decided that since they were already half-way to India, his ADC should travel on to Delhi to tell Queenie, who was still thinking of joining him, and on whose behalf he and Reid Scott had been walking around the streets of Batavia in search of a home, 'what a one horse place it is, so that she does not come here and regret it afterwards.'[62] On his arrival Reid Scott was 'cross questioned' for an hour by Queenie and Pamela, at the end of which they decided they wanted to go to Java at once. 'Just the decision I hoped they would not make!'[63] The Chinese leader had reached Delhi; when Madame Chiang heard that Pamela was soon to marry her fiancé, Francis Humphrys, she made her a present of an embroidered red counterpane for the 'bridal bed'. Lady Wavell, noted Reid Scott, was slightly shocked.[64]

Wavell, meanwhile, remained in Burma. As he arrived on these flying visits he reminded the Governor, Dorman-Smith, of 'a Harley Street specialist, complete with black bag, coming to see a very sick patient.'[65] Referred to by Dorman-Smith's wife Doreen as 'Cyclops',[66] Wavell was 'a delightful guest and fortunately thoroughly enjoyed a really rough game of billiard fives – and could be rough!! I and my staff used to nurse our bruises for days afterwards.'[67] Dorman-Smith might admire Wavell's detachment and brilliant briefing, but he was also intrigued by what he described as the Commander-in-Chief's 'violent love affair' with a certain Miss Gibbs, also staying at Government House. 'We all understood as Miss Gibbs was a most attractive young person, as pretty as a picture and inclined at times to be a bit of a flirt. Our C-in-C fell heavily for her and tried his utmost to win his way into her heart with soft loving words – and bananas.' No further record exists of this encounter, and the 'affair', such as it was, seems most likely to have been no more than a romantic flirtation in the eye of the storm.[68]

Junior officers found Wavell more forbidding. During his early February visit, accompanied by Hutton, he went to visit Smyth in his forward position west of the Salween River. The impression Wavell made on this occasion was 'the reverse of welcoming'. 'After casting a glance of near-loathing at the lot of us, it seemed to me that he fixed me with his one good eye,' recalled James Lunt, a young officer with the 2nd Burma Brigade, part of the 17th Indian Division, 'and then barked out, "Take back all you have lost!" I did not dare open my mouth but I hope my expression showed that I would certainly do my best.'[69] Once more Wavell exhorted Smyth to 'fight forward' and regain the lost territory. But according to Smyth he offered no practical advice, instead telling the senior members of his staff that the Japanese were overrated and that their fighting ability was grossly exaggerated. 'It wasn't the sort of talk I had hoped for and it depressed them deeply as it made obvious that he was quite out of touch with realities.'[70] Even so, Wavell had not lost his eye for terrain. Observing the dry rice-paddies, he asked Smyth whether there was scope for using light tanks. With Smyth's affirmative, Wavell gave immediate instructions that the 7th Armoured Brigade and its light cruiser tanks, en route from the Middle East to Java, should be diverted to Rangoon. When the Indian Army and Allied forces were obliged to retreat, the tanks proved invaluable. As Lunt noted, the order to send the tanks was one 'for which everyone who served in Burma in 1942 had cause to be grateful to Wavell.'[71]

As British, Indian and Australian troops attempted belatedly to fortify the northern coastline of Singapore, the Japanese were working towards forcing their surrender. A severe Japanese artillery barrage against Singapore's north-eastern shoreline and reconnaissance reports of a Japanese invasion force anchored off the north-east of Singapore caused Percival to assign the north-east to the 18th British Division and the 11th Indian Division, now amalgamated with the depleted 9th. The mangrove swamps of the north-west were given to Gordon Bennett's 8th Australian Division, reinforced by the 44th Indian Brigade. These dispositions were the reverse of what Wavell had suggested at their 20 January meeting, but he was no longer on the spot to alter or advise, and signalled his agreement.[72] Across the water the Japanese, under the command of Lieutenant-General Tomoyuki Yamashita, were poised for their next victory. On the evening of 8 February approximately 4,000 Japanese troops crossed in plywood craft, concentrating their landings in the mangrove swamps in the north-west. Almost from the moment they landed, they gained the ascendancy. As Wavell later reported: 'Beach and searchlights had been installed but they were under the control of the local Infantry Commander and he had forbidden their exposure without a personal order. The order was never given.'[73] The Australians therefore lost the opportunity to attack the approaching Japanese, who succeeded in bringing over tanks and artillery. By dawn more than half the Japanese force of approximately 30,000 had landed, breaking ferociously through the Australian lines, capturing their first objective – Tengah airfield – and occupying the reservoirs which supplied water for the million-strong population of urban Singapore.[74]

On 10 February Wavell made his last visit to Singapore, arriving by Catalina flying-boat. They travelled low and slowly, without fighter-escort, and needed no instruments to find their destination: according to his liaison officer Reinhard Mackay, 'pitch dark clouds of smoke showed the right course.' After breakfast Wavell went with Percival first to see Gordon Bennett, to encourage him to strike back. But even as they met the futility of mounting a counter-offensive was manifest as their discussions were interrupted by a bombing attack during which 'the unedifying spectacle was seen of three general officers going to ground under tables or any other cover that was available.'[75] In hindsight, Wavell believed that Bennett 'seemed to have much more fight and vigour in him than most of the other Commanders . . . he was perfectly cool and unperturbed, but had obviously lost all hope of successful resistance.'[76] Percival, whose relations with Bennett had not been easy, observed that the Australian was less confident than he had been up-country: 'He had always been very certain that his Australians would never let the Japanese through and the penetration of his defences had upset him. As always, we were fighting this battle in the dark, and I do not think any of us realized at that time the strength of the enemy's attack.'[77]

Wavell returned to Flagstaff House, where he received a signal from Churchill which he first read, and then showed to Percival. Churchill had calculated that Percival had over '100,000 men', equivalent to five divisions. 'There must,' he insisted, 'be no thought of saving the troops or sparing the population. The battle must be fought to the bitter end at all costs.'[78] Before dinner Wavell wrote out his own version of Churchill's directive, which was equally blunt: 'It is certain that our troops on Singapore heavily outnumber any Japanese troops who have crossed the straits. We must destroy them. Our whole fighting reputation is at stake and the honour of the British Empire.' He went on to point out that the Americans had held out in the Baatan Peninsula in the Philippines against 'far heavier odds'. The Russians were turning back 'the picked strength' of the Germans. With an almost complete lack of modern equipment, the Chinese had resisted the Japanese for four and a half years: 'It will be disgraceful if we cannot hold our boasted Fortress of Singapore to inferior enemy forces. There must be no thought of sparing the troops or the civilian population, and no mercy must be shown in any shape or form. Commanders and Senior Officers must lead their troops, and if necessary, die with them.'[79] Both Churchill's and Wavell's messages were exemplary martial rhetoric. As the man on the spot, Percival replicated their orders: 'The spirit of aggression and determination to stick it out must be inculcated in all ranks . . . Every available man who is not doing essential work must be used to stop the invader.'[80] Privately Percival believed that the Supreme Commander was taking away with him on this last visit 'a false idea of the weight of attack which had been thrown against us, for the simple reason that, fighting blind as we were, none of us at that time had fully appreciated it ourselves.'[81]

Later that evening Wavell set out to return to Java. As related by Mackay, they were travelling with a number of bags laden with secret documents. As they arrived at the jetty – 'a wooden structure of quite some length but of little width, and without a railing' – the cars stopped. 'The five staff-officers of the two front cars alighted with their luggage to try and find the motor launch which was ordered to bring us back to the Catalina.' Wavell and Mackay were waiting in their car. 'Somewhat impatient', Wavell asked Mackay to find out the reason for the delay. 'Concerned about his one eye and being used to hold his arm firmly whenever darkness prevailed',

Mackay got out of the car, having first made 'a pressing demand' to the Supreme Commander 'to keep seated until my return. He nodded OK and I vanished in the pitch-dark, noticing that on my side of the car I had not quite two yards width to go.' Mackay had not advanced more than a few paces when he heard a loud cry. He and the other staff officers immediately realized what had happened: 'General Wavell had fallen off the jetty, and apparently right on the edge of beach and water, a fall of, say, four yards deep, but just on that spot a roll of barbed wire all along the beach had been mounted for defence purposes.' Mackay at once divined what lay behind Wavell's exit from the car: 'He had needed my absence to relieve himself before boarding the plane for a long flight, had opened the door, but had failed to notice that he had only about two feet of jetty to step on and no railing.'[82]

Wavell's fall onto broken concrete and barbed wire cut his back and broke two small bones. Unable to see a doctor, he was transported by motor-boat to the waiting Catalina in mid-harbour. To get him into the flying-boat, a machine gun mounted across the door had to be removed. At last he was taken aboard; his back was cleaned with iodine and he was given aspirins and a glass of neat whisky, whereupon he went to sleep. They could not take off, however, because the harbour was already crowded with small craft trying to escape under cover of darkness. The Catalina finally left at dawn. In Batavia Wavell was taken immediately to hospital, where it was hoped he would remain until he had fully recovered. But he was not so easily restrained: 'Doctors wanted to keep me flat in bed for a week or two, but I ordered myself out of hospital in 24 hours and they have had to admit that I have made a remarkable recovery.'[83]

By daylight on 11 February the Japanese controlled half Singapore Island. Wavell was obliged to report to Churchill that the battle for Singapore was not going well, and that the Japanese had succeeded in infiltrating in the west. 'I ordered Percival to stage counter-attack with all troops possible.' But, he said, the morale of some troops was not good: 'The chief troubles are lack of sufficient training in some of reinforcing troops and inferiority complex which bold and skilful Japanese tactics and their command of the air have caused.'[84] Wavell continued his encouragement to Percival to carry on the fight, while Percival was making it clear that, with dwindling water and food supplies, his commanders were 'too exhausted either to withstand strong attack or to launch counter-attack.' In such circumstances, Percival was requesting 'wider discretionary powers'.[85]

Wavell's signal of 14 February to Churchill foretold the end for Singapore: although he had ordered Percival to continue to inflict maximum

damage on the enemy, he feared 'resistance [is] not likely to be very prolonged.'[86] In consultation with Brooke, Churchill authorized Wavell to
instruct Percival as he thought best, when 'no further result' could be gained
in Singapore. On 15 February Wavell cabled Percival: 'So long as you are in
position to inflict losses and damage to enemy and your troops are physically
capable of doing so you must fight on . . . When you are fully satisfied that
this is no longer possible I give you discretion to cease resistance . . . Inform
me of intentions. Whatever happens I thank you and all your troops for your
gallant efforts of last few days.'[87] But the Japanese had already secured their
victory, as Percival's final brief cable to Wavell indicated: 'Owing to losses
from enemy action water petrol food and ammunition practically finished.
Unable therefore continue the fight any longer. All ranks have done their
best and grateful for your help.'[88] In the evening of 15 February – 'Black
Sunday' – Percival met the Japanese commander, General Yamashita, to sign
the surrender. The image that reached Wavell in Java was of 'three quarters
of a million panic-stricken Asiatics in a ravaged and blazing town, a pall of
black smoke visible for 40 miles and a ring of tired and dispirited troops.'[89]

Of the senior commanders, Gordon Bennett had succeeded in escaping
in a junk, leaving his second-in-command, Brigadier Callaghan, to surrender the Australian troops.[90] For the next three years, thousands of
Europeans, women and children as well as officers and soldiers, were kept
as prisoners-of-war. Amongst them were Percival, Beckwith-Smith (who
later died of diphtheria), Heath and Shenton Thomas. The Indian soldiers
were immediately taken separately to a small stadium near the Indian quarter on Singapore Island. Welcomed as brothers, they were addressed by
Colonel Mohan Singh, a radical Sikh nationalist and early defector who
announced the formation of an 'Indian National Army' which would fight
beside the Japanese to free Indians from Britain's imperial yoke. Those who
joined the INA went to a new 'Supreme Command' north of the city;
those who refused were incarcerated in large camps as prisoners-of-war. In
his official memoirs published in 1951 Churchill described the surrender at
Singapore as 'the worst disaster and largest capitulation in British history'.[91]

When apportioning blame for the fall of Singapore, Wavell believed
that 'the main causes of the disaster were the old British faults of under-
estimating the enemy, lack of preparation and over-confidence.'[92] His
report on the Malaya Campaign recognized that by November 1941 the
situation 'already contained many of the elements of disaster . . . The local
press, by consistently disparaging the quality of the enemy's air force, and
otherwise showing a poor opinion of his general efficiency, helped to build
up a dangerously complacent attitude, and in Malaya ease and complacency

flourish without outside assistance.' He also admitted that 'our estimate' of the Japanese Army and Air Force was 'disastrous in its consequences and incredible in its inaccuracy . . . From the very opening of hostilities it was obvious that there was something seriously wrong with our training, for not only was the method unsuited for meeting Japanese tactics, but individually our men were inferior as jungle fighters.' Wavell went on to say that the Australians had displayed a 'refreshingly offensive spirit' in North Johore, but after setbacks 'a rapid decline' had set in. The events on the night of 8/9 February, when they were subjected to a heavy bombardment, seemed 'to have destroyed almost completely their discipline and morale'. In fairness, Wavell also recorded that the bombardment, 'judged by the standard of any theatre of war, can only be described as very heavy; in addition, they had been under an only slightly less heavy pounding for at least 24 hours.' On the other hand, the 18th British Division were fresh and morale was excellent, but 'they were unacclimatized and ignorant of jungle ways.' They were, he said, 'rushed into action, soft and untrained, with the result that many a fine battalion was soon reduced to a collection of foot-sore, tired and depressed men.'[93]

Percival, whose name – rather than Wavell's – was to become synonymous with the surrender, also believed that 'in 1941 when the crisis came in the Far East, it was too late to put things right. Then we were engaged in a life and death struggle in the West, and war material which might have saved Singapore was sent to Russia and to the Middle East. The choice was made and Singapore had to suffer. In my opinion this decision, however painful and regrettable, was inevitable and right.'[94] Percival did not, however, take kindly to the criticism contained in Wavell's report regarding complacency, which shifted the blame from Wavell as Supreme Commander to his subordinates who had preceded his arrival. In defence of his actions as GOC, Malaya in 1940, Percival compared his experience in the region with Wavell's, who had never been in the Far East before. 'His opinions were based on two months' experience there and what other people told him.'[95]

Wavell's report on the evacuation from Singapore – submitted nearly a year later and embargoed for almost half a century – contained both criticism of 'deplorable' behaviour, and commendations. 'Some very fine work was done and much unselfish courage shown by some individuals . . . the conduct of others, officers and men, British and Australians, was, I regret to say, characterized by selfishness and regard for their own safety, which was most discreditable to British and Australian reputations, and must be attributed to the large-scale demoralization which set in at the end of the Malayan campaign.' He also acknowledged that 'for obvious reasons' his report was incomplete, but declared that he believed it gave 'an accurate general outline of events'.[96] Unfortunately for the future of British–Australian relations, while the report recognized that some British soldiers were 'no saints', the majority of Wavell's 'case-study' allegations of misconduct and petty theft, both in Singapore and after the evacuees reached Sumatra, were directed against the Australians. All praise went to the Dutch population who welcomed them, combining hospitality with efficiency in spite of many cases of 'barbaric ingratitude'.[97] When the report on the evacuation was made public in 1991 Wavell's criticisms opened old wounds, eliciting fierce rebuttals from Australian survivors.

For Wavell personally, the Singapore chapter of his ABDA command was closed: as Supreme Commander, he had to assume overall responsibility for another defeat. In the immediate aftermath his only course of action was to pick up the emotional pieces and focus on his next challenge: the Dutch East Indies and Burma.

After Singapore there was to be no let-up. On 16 February, Wavell sent Churchill a lengthy appraisal of the situation now facing him: 'Unless adequate naval and air reinforcements can be provided in time which seems improbable, Japanese invasion of Java seems likely to begin before end of February.' More importantly, Wavell was already inclining to the belief – like Churchill – that if it was a question of reinforcing Java or diverting troops to Burma or Australia, the latter two should take precedence.[98] The Australian Corps was on its way back from the Middle East: if it were not to return home, Wavell suggested, he believed it would be far more worthwhile for all or part of it to go to Burma. On the strength of this recommendation Churchill asked Prime Minister Curtin if the 7th Division – now nearing Ceylon – could be diverted to Rangoon. Then on 19 February a force of more than 150 Japanese bombers and torpedo bombers attacked Darwin in northern Australia. The Australian Government believed this attack might be the prelude to an invasion, so any chance of Curtin permitting the Australian Corps to go to Burma vanished. Bali had already fallen on 18 February; two days later, the Japanese landed on Timor, east of Java.

During the final stages of the Singapore catastrophe the situation in Burma was almost equally disastrous. As Wavell in faraway Java had always realized, it was extremely difficult for him to influence operations except when he was physically present. All telegrams had to be routed via Delhi, and could take a week in transit. Every report, instruction or order was out of date by the time it arrived. Following Wavell's January visit to Burma reinforcements were in place, and Hutton was continuing to put into effect Wavell's policy of delaying the Japanese advance as much as possible, 'having reserved to himself the decision to disobey this order if it should prove necessary to do so'.[99] But as in Malaya, the Japanese advance was unforgiving. On 16 February – the day after the surrender of Singapore – Japanese forces crossed the Bilin River north of Bilin. Bitter fighting ensued and yet again Smyth, who had been wanting to withdraw before his forces were completely destroyed, had to pull back to the last obstacle before Rangoon, the Sittang River. The reactions of Churchill in London, the Viceroy in India and Wavell in the Dutch East Indies – all far removed from the reality on the ground – were negative.

On 17 February, too late to influence events, Wavell had cabled Hutton: 'I do not know what consideration caused withdrawal behind Bilin River without further fighting. I have every confidence in judgement and fighting spirit of you and Smyth but bear in mind that continual withdrawal, as experience of Malaya showed, is most damaging to morale of troops especially Indian troops.' Time, he urged, could be gained as effectively by counter-offensive.[100] Privately he realized that things were not going well, and looked like becoming worse.[101] The Viceroy, Linlithgow, was even more damning in communicating with Churchill: 'Our troops in Burma are not fighting with proper spirit. I have not the least doubt that this is in great part due to lack of drive and inspiration from the top [i.e. Hutton].'[102] Churchill immediately sent the text of Linlithgow's telegram to Wavell, asking his opinion and suggesting that Hutton should be replaced by General Sir Harold Alexander, who had successfully commanded the 1st Division of the British Expeditionary Force at Dunkirk in 1940.[103] Although reluctant to make a change, Wavell's response was accommodating. He too believed that neither British, Australians nor Indians had shown 'real toughness of mind or body though Australians fought well in Johore', which he attributed to the 'softness' of the last twenty years. At the same time, he complimented Hutton: 'Leaders of real drive and inspiration are few . . . Hutton has plenty of determination behind quiet manner and will never get rattled but lacks power of personal inspiration . . . agree that Alexander's forceful personality might act as a stimulus to troops.'[104] Hutton subsequently maintained that the frank and often pessimistic telegrams he sent Wavell relating to Burma, which were decoded and sent to Churchill and Alan Brooke in London as well as Hartley and Linlithgow, contributed to his replacement.[105] And although Hutton lacked experience in operational command, to his credit he anticipated Rangoon's eventual fall and successfully moved vital stores up-country, near Mandalay: when the British and Indian soldiers were forced to retreat, the stores literally saved their lives. At this decisive stage in operations, Burma was removed from ABDA: with the loss of Singapore and Sumatra, the Combined Chiefs of Staff accepted that the country would 'inevitably become more closely linked to India which is her natural base'[106] and on 21 February Burma was returned, as Wavell had suggested from the outset, to the India Command.

The events of the past weeks had taken their toll on Wavell both physically and mentally. Rejoining him after a two-week absence, Reid Scott noted how tired and worried his 'Chief' appeared. His recovery from his fall had surprised the doctors, but he was still in pain, and Reid Scott felt remorse at not having been there for so long, 'not least of all to mix him a nice drink.'[107] Independently of Queenie, Wavell's middle daughter Felicity had come to his headquarters in Lembang to work in ciphers. Seeing the situation for herself, she agreed that it would have been 'madness' for her mother to leave Delhi.[108] Yet even at such a critical time, Wavell managed to inject humour into his correspondence with his friends back home: 'Six weeks ago I had two large houses, over 80 servants, about 8 horses, best cook in India, largest salary I am ever likely to earn and much pomp and ceremony. At present I am in one smallish room in an hotel, no horses, one char-man speaking no known language, very plain cooking and ? salary. Such changes', he wrote in response to Leonie Lemartine's Christmas letter, which had just reached him, 'keep one from getting mossy.'[109] Surprisingly, Wavell also confessed that he had little to do. 'That may sound strange in this crisis of the affairs of ABDA,' he wrote to Joan Bright on 20 February, 'but it is more or less true, at least I can think of nothing very useful to do . . . We have lost the battle here by a month or six weeks I think – the additional time that we should have gained at least in Malaya and Singapore and the time by which we should have built up in these islands an air force capable of holding and hitting back.' Although Wavell 'had a hunch' that the Japanese were stretched to the utmost in the air, he recognized that they were using their forces boldly, 'and have been too quick for us'.[110] He also foresaw that it would be only a matter of days before Java fell; it was therefore necessary to begin evacuation of the women, and that included his daughter. 'Felicity is very bolshie about going but Pa insists,' noted Reid Scott, who put her on a train to Batavia to pick up a boat to Ceylon. Lest Wavell should have to 'take to the hills and "sauve qui peut"', his ADC had prepared an 'escape kit' that included food, compasses, and whisky.[111]

As Japanese air raids on Java continued, Wavell sent Churchill a signal: 'I am afraid that the defence of ABDA area has broken down and that defence of Java cannot now last long. It always hinged on the air battle . . . I see little further usefulness for this HQ.' He took full responsibility, the persistent hallmark of his character: 'I have failed you and President here, where better men might perhaps have succeeded in altering time factor in our favour . . . I hate the idea of leaving these stout-hearted Dutchmen, and will remain here and fight it out with them as long as possible if you consider this would help at all.'[112] It was no more than Churchill had expected, however, and in response he praised Wavell's 'admirable conduct of ABDA operations in the teeth of adverse fortune and overwhelming odds.'[113] Wavell also signalled Curtin: 'It has been from the first a race against time and we have lost it by four or five weeks . . . Whether greater foresight and skill on my part could have gained the necessary time I am unable to say: I certainly offer no excuses.'[114]

On 23 February Wavell was ordered to close down ABDA headquarters and resume his position as Commander-in-Chief, India – bringing Burma once more under his command. Smyth's withdrawal across the Sittang River was turning into a disaster. As the 17th Division continued its retreat they realized that the Japanese had moved around their left flank, cutting off the leading brigade, already across the river, from the rest of the division. An overturned vehicle on the bridge blocked it for over two hours, leading to a six-mile tail-back. As the Japanese closed in Smyth gave the order to blow the bridge, not realizing two brigades were still on the wrong side. Such was the confusion that followed, it only later became apparent just how many men had been left behind. Of these, only a few managed to cross with their weapons on roughly made rafts; others attempted to swim, but with an incoming tide the current was strong, and they either drowned or were picked off by the Japanese. 'Friendly fire' by the RAF and the American Volunteer Group also caused casualties. From their respective headquarters it seemed to both Hutton and Wavell that the withdrawal could have been completed before the bridge was blown.[115] Smyth, as the divisional commander, held Wavell responsible for the disaster, because of his insistence that with inadequate troops the 17th Division should continue to try to fight forward. He also believed that the 'ill-judged and ill-informed directives' received by Hutton during these critical weeks were a result of Wavell's Singapore injury: 'I certainly was shocked at his appearance on his last visit to my headquarters in Burma . . . I realized afterwards how sick Wavell was at the time.'[116] As Wavell appreciated, the battle at the Sittang River bridgehead 'sealed the fate of Rangoon and Lower Burma'.[117]

On 25 February the ABDA command was formally dissolved and General ter Poorten took command in Java. The situation in Rangoon was so serious that Wavell wanted to fly to Burma directly from Java, but the weather in the region was so bad that his Acting C-in-C Hartley advised him to travel first to Delhi. Wavell set out in a Lincoln Zephyr, still with his faithful bodyguard, for an eight-hour drive – 300 miles – through the Javanese countryside to Jogjakarta on the south of the island, where there was a large enough strip for a Liberator to land. With two stops for petrol and two to admire – by moonlight – the great statues of Buddha and others of the ninth-century temple monument at Borabudur, they finally reached their destination at 10 p.m.

Before he left Java Wavell was able to do a good deed. Waiting in a nearby hotel, he noticed a civilian and his wife sitting with a group of servicemen. As one of the servicemen, Dudley Robinson, recalled, Wavell immediately sent over a chit offering the lady and her husband immediate safe passage off the island. The others, not so lucky, later became prisoners of war. 'But,' said Robinson, 'we thought how kind it was of Wavell to save the civilians from being captured.'[118] As Wavell left he presented a signed photograph and a signed copy of *Generals and Generalship* to his bodyguard, and a signed photograph to his driver. On the plane, he had 'a good and long night's rest'.[119] The following day, they arrived in Ceylon. Wavell was annoyed to learn that the Liberator was too big to land in Delhi, so he would have to go by way of Asanol near Calcutta, and change planes. 'The Chief is infuriated by going so far out of his way,' observed Reid Scott. 'Much damning of the RAF and draft telegrams starting "Asanol is obviously ridiculous" (none of which I sent).' Wavell arrived in Delhi on 27 February to be reunited with Queenie and Joan. Pamela had already left for Cairo to get married; Felicity was on her way from Java in a troopship.

Until Wavell formally resumed his position as Commander-in-Chief Hartley remained as Acting Commander-in-Chief, and with them both in Delhi there was 'much doubt at dinner, as to where people should sit – neither side are snobs and the Chief displays complete disinterest in that sort of thing.'[120] Immediately after dinner Wavell held a conference to discuss Burma. Dorman-Smith had already signalled to the Viceroy that 'unless some miracle happens' he would begin demolition of British installations in Rangoon on 1 March (the demolitions would include throwing 'a volley of billiard balls' at the portraits of past governors in Government House, to deny them to the Japanese as trophies).[121] Wavell, still believing evacuation to be premature, immediately cabled to suspend such action until he reached Burma. As Reid Scott marvelled, 'What with his fall and broken bones etc., coupled with so much travelling, the Chief ought to have three quiet days' rest but, as I expected, the outcome of the meeting is that the Chief should go straight to Burma leaving tomorrow: nothing will stop him if he wants to do something.'[122]

The failure of the ABDA command was a disappointment to Wavell. 'I feel I ought to have pulled it off but the dice were rather heavily loaded and the little yellow man threw them with considerable cunning,' he had confided to Joan Bright. 'I hate making excuses. I was given a job and have fallen down on it, whether it was "on" or not others can decide; I feel myself that it might have been but I think it wanted a bigger man than I have ever pretended to be. So that's that.'[123] To his friends in Britain it was not immediately clear whether or not Wavell had escaped. When Liddell Hart heard that he was safely back in Delhi he wrote expressing his relief: 'I had a mental picture of you sitting in captivity for weary years with nothing to read and re-read except *The Strategy of Indirect Approach!*'[124]

Those who had worked with Wavell also recognized that the odds had been against him. 'Of all the raw deals he has been given, the miracles he has been asked to produce without even a golden wand to wave, this ABDA Command has been the worst instance,' Pownall commented. 'I can think of no way in which he could have snatched victory; in just a few ways perhaps he could have held up for a little longer the Jap advances. But the eventual result was certain and the small delays he might have effected would not have made any appreciable difference to the final result.'[125] When it was all over, Churchill sent a telegram expressing his 'warmest admiration'.[126] With all around him collapsing, Wavell wondered why the Prime Minister had 'never parodied *Midsummer Night's Dream* in one of his addresses: "The course of true war never did run smooth", though the public always expect it to.'[127]

15

Adversity's General, 1942

It was Napoleon who said he preferred lucky Generals. He would have liked Alex but would have had little use for Wavell whose luck was abysmal.

Lieutenant-General Sir Thomas Hutton[1]

ARRIVING AT THE Burmese airfield at Magwe, Wavell at once held a meeting with Hutton, Dorman-Smith and Air Vice-Marshal Donald Stevenson.[2] Having lost Malaya and Singapore, he was extremely distressed at the prospect of evacuating Rangoon. Displaying rare anger, according to Hutton, Wavell 'stormed' at him 'in a most excited way'.[3] After lengthy discussions he reported back to the Chiefs of Staff that they would try to hold Rangoon, for which purpose he requested reinforcements: 'Even if Rangoon has to be evacuated all possible troops will be required in order to establish line across lower Irrawaddy valley to cover aerodromes in central Burma and to join up with Chinese in Shan States.'[4] Wavell then proceeded in a small plane to Rangoon. 'It was very hot. The threatened countryside slept underneath us in a golden haze of dust. Here and there, groups of refugees moved along the roads past banana groves,' recalled Coats.[5] Undaunted by the prevailing destruction, the following day they journeyed on, fifty miles north of Rangoon, and within a few hundred yards of the Japanese front line.

At Hutton's headquarters Wavell received a signal from Smyth suggesting that a withdrawal from Pegu should be made, whereupon he and Hutton immediately went to meet Smyth at his divisional headquarters. Though he conceded resources were limited, Wavell was keen for Smyth to hold on, believing that the 7th Armoured Brigade, which had disembarked at Rangoon, 'should impose caution on enemy'. Smyth was unwell, however, and was granted leave; he handed over to his second-in-command, General 'Punch' Cowan.[6] Wavell and his party (now including Smyth) then flew north from Mingladon to Lashio to meet Chiang Kai-

Shek. Wavell's mood was undoubtedly black: he and Smyth sat in silence at opposite ends of the plane, without a word. 'I realised what a shattering blow yet another defeat had been to him and I respected his silence,' Smyth noted, unaware that he was to be blamed for the Sittang disaster.[7] In Lashio, Wavell and Chiang Kai-Shek remained closeted with an interpreter. As Wavell later reported to Hutton, the Generalissimo expressed approval that they were continuing to hold Pegu and Rangoon. Wavell's message to Hutton, waiting for Alexander to arrive, was again to 'hang on hard'.[8]

Alexander's arrival had been delayed by bad weather, but on 2 March he finally reached India on his way to Burma to take over operational control from Hutton. As Wavell was returning from Burma the two men met briefly at the airfield at Calcutta. Smyth, still travelling with Wavell, was disappointed to be excluded from the discussions. 'I shall always think that it was quite inexcusable of him not to allow Alex at least to hear the opinion of the man who had been fighting the battle and knew ten times as much about the situation as did Wavell who had only descended from his faraway headquarters for a bird's eye view.'[9] Instead, Smyth was informed that Wavell would be travelling separately to Delhi, and that he would have to make his own way home. In his memoirs, Smyth writes of this bitterly: 'My baggage was removed . . . and piled on the tarmac. Wavell strode past me without any sign of recognition.'[10] When eventually Smyth got back to Delhi, he found himself immediately deprived of his Major-General's rank and retired from service on the Commander-in-Chief's orders. He went on to become a novelist and a Member of Parliament, but never quite forgave Wavell. It was an exceptional instance of Wavell letting his anger at the course of events colour his handling of personal relations.

From Delhi, Wavell immediately reported to Brooke his instruction to Alexander that Rangoon was not to be given up 'without battle as aggressive as our resources will permit'.[11] He would, he said, do everything possible to hold Burma, but ended his signal with a cautionary note on a recurrent theme: 'We are very thin on ground and in air and if troops and aircraft continue to be diverted elsewhere my difficulties are increased.'[12] On the day he composed this message, Japanese troops were entering one side of Rangoon while the British and Indian troops retreated from the other – miraculously, a Japanese commander had removed a road block once his own troops had passed, failing which Alexander and his army would have been trapped. Communications between Rangoon and Delhi were so confused that Wavell did not have Alexander's confirmation of the evacuation until 10 March.

True to form Wavell, well aware of the realities, had praise for Alexander: 'Well done. Responsibility for position in which you and troops were placed was wholly mine and I congratulate you all on determination with which you have extricated yourselves. Much regret casualties.'[13] Wavell later had the grace to admit in print that his decision to postpone the evacuation 'eventually placed General Alexander in a difficult position and led to his forces being nearly cut off.' On balance he believed that they had gained by the delay, because it had enabled them to land reinforcements. There were other mitigating circumstances: 'I was certainly guilty of an error of judgement in minimizing the danger to Burma, but it is doubtful whether, even if I had appreciated it thoroughly, I could have done much more to help Burma. India had been sucked dry of trained troops by the requirements of the Middle East, Iraq and Iran.' Referring again to reinforcements, he said that India was deficient in equipment for her own needs, and could not meet those of Burma as well. Most important was the fact that India had no modern air force with which to support the Burma Army.[14] Those who had suffered the consequences of Wavell's insistence on making a stand were more critical. 'I certainly felt then, and still feel, that if he [Wavell] had had his way the whole Army and a large number of civilians would have been captured in Rangoon by the Japanese,' noted Hutton (who, having been replaced by Alexander, was put in the embarrassing position of acting as his Chief of Staff before returning to Delhi in April). 'In fact by holding up the evacuation and ordering Alexander to counter-attack at Pegu he very nearly achieved that result.'[15] On the same day that Rangoon fell the Japanese, who had landed on Java at the beginning of March, took possession of the towns of Sourabaya and Lembang; on 12 March the Dutch, under General ter Poorten's command, formally surrendered.

In the Middle East, Britain had been the only major 'super' player; as with ABDA, Wavell's current command meant a continued sharing of strategy with the United States. In early March Major-General Joseph Stilwell, whom Wavell had met briefly in Calcutta on his return to Java at the end of February, had been appointed to command the Chinese 5th and 6th Armies, now concentrated around Mandalay and in the Shan States. His nickname – 'Vinegar (or sometimes, with heavy irony, 'Dextrose') Joe – characterized his acerbic temperament, and his relations with the British could be tense, because of his profound dislike of British 'colonialism'. Nevertheless, at a personal level Wavell liked him. But his feelings were not reciprocated. After his first meeting with Wavell, Stilwell described him as 'a tired, depressed man, pretty well beaten down.'[16]

In Wavell's effort to support Alexander's withdrawal in Burma, he summoned General Bill Slim, Commander of the 10th Indian Division, from the Middle East. After a reconnaissance mission to Maymo, to where Dorman-Smith had withdrawn after the fall of Rangoon, Slim went to see Wavell in Calcutta. He recalled the Commander-in-Chief standing in one of the visitors' sitting rooms in Government House 'in his usual firmly planted attitude . . . He held at that moment the most difficult command in the world – India and Burma. Yet it gave one confidence to look at him. I had seen him at the height of dazzling success, and he had stood and looked calmly and thoughtfully at me in the same way as he looked at me now.' The appointment Wavell requested him to undertake was not a staff job, as Slim had initially feared, but command of the 1st Burma Corps now being formed in Burma.[17] As usual, Wavell used words sparingly. 'Alexander has a most difficult task. You won't find yours easy.' A pause, and then: 'The sooner you get there the better.'[18]

On the world stage Wavell presided over a 'scene of confusion' perhaps worse than that Churchill had predicted for his ABDA command, but domestically the accustomed pattern of his life continued. Following his accident in Singapore he had started to ride again, the pain alleviated by Joanie's suggestion of using methylated spirits on his behind. The girls were now young women, as eager to assist in the war effort as to live life to the full. On 14 March Pamela married Lieutenant Arthur Francis Humphrys (of Charlton Park near Canterbury) at All Saints Cathedral in Cairo. None of her immediate family could be present. Smiling and confident, holding a single lily, Wavell's eldest daughter looked radiant. The service was short with one psalm ('God be merciful unto us') and one hymn ('The King of Love my Shepherd is'). The bride and groom departed to the singing of Mozart's *Alleluia*. Wavell was well pleased with his first son-in-law: he liked his daughter's 'young man', and hoped the marriage would be a success.[19] Privately he was trying to maintain his optimism about the outcome of the war: they were still passing through a 'dark time', but he believed they had come through worse. It was his fourth summer in the East and he felt rather weary and overworked, with hardly a day off since the war started.

On the bright side, the travel writer and Grenadier Guardsman Peter Fleming had arrived in India to join Wavell's staff. 'I still don't know what I am up to,' he wrote to his wife, the actress Celia Johnson, when he arrived.[20] 'The Chief, as we call him, is most charming and impressive but I don't ask, and he hasn't talked about my destiny. He is a v. good chap. I expect I shall hear in a day or two.' Fleming had met Wavell in the Middle East when he was engaged on stay-behind sabotage duties in Greece, and had already developed a rapport not only with Wavell but also with Queenie, whom he described as 'extremely nice: the shape of a cottage loaf but most sensible.'[21]

As the situation continued to deteriorate, at the end of March Wavell was back in Burma, taking Fleming with him on his first intelligence assignment. They landed at Mandalay, their destination Maymo. There were comforts – strawberries and wine – and noticeable deficiencies – soap and ice. Wavell travelled on to Alexander's headquarters on the Irrawaddy. Fleming, a newcomer to the jungle scene, experienced 'rather haphazard flights in a Blenheim; most uncomfortable, no parachutes, and the landing grounds either unlocatable or badly bombed.'[22] He then travelled onwards alone to Chungking; Wavell was sufficiently distressed by a rumour that his plane had been shot down for Fleming's reappearance at Maymo to elicit 'an almost emotional grunt', which 'touched me.'[23]

Returning to India, Wavell found the Viceroy preoccupied with the arrival of Sir Stafford Cripps. Recently appointed Lord Privy Seal and Leader of the House of Commons, he had been selected by Churchill to lead a mission to India with a two-fold objective.[24] Since Britain had agreed that India would achieve self-government once the war was over, it was necessary to prepare the ground for the drafting of a new constitution; more immediately, Churchill wanted Cripps to focus on how best the Indian political leaders could be encouraged to participate more actively in the war. As their representative spokesmen the Congress Party had nominated their President, Maulana Abul Kalam Azad, and Jawaharlal Nehru, who like his father Motilal had become an outspoken critic of British imperialism.[25] Among others with whom Cripps held meetings were Mohammed Ali Jinnah and the former premier of Madras, Chakravarti Rajagopalachari, who was more sympathetic than his compatriots to the impossibility of the British relinquishing all authority during the war. Cripps also met Gandhi, whose anti-war views extended to arguing that the British should leave India at once; the Japanese, he said, had no quarrel with the Indians and once the British had left, they would not attempt to invade. When Cripps revealed the British proposals – which effectively asked the Indians to postpone their demand for independence until after the war – Gandhi scathingly suggested that, if that was all Cripps had to offer, he should take the next plane home.[26]

Wavell was not directly involved in discussions regarding the future of India, but his role as Commander-in-Chief was relevant to the question of how much responsibility Indians should bear for the defence of their country. The document outlining Britain's proposals specified that until a new constitution could be framed, 'His Majesty's Government must inevitably bear the responsibility for and retain control and direction of the defence of India.'[27] The document went on to say that the task of organizing 'military, moral and material resources' should be the responsibility of the Government of India 'with the cooperation of the people of India', but the extent of that cooperation was unspecified. Not surprisingly, the Congress Party members rejected the proposals in a resolution one of the grounds of which was Britain's refusal to hand over the Defence portfolio to Indian hands.[28] Cripps, anxious to resolve what he believed to be the main issue preventing agreement – defence – suggested that Azad and Nehru should meet Wavell, who had just returned from Burma.

Cripps's proposal now, endorsed by the War Cabinet in London, was to create a new position on the Viceroy's Executive Council for a 'Defence Coordination Member'; Wavell, as Commander-in-Chief, would remain on the Council as 'War Member'. But despite the mission's best efforts – keenly watched by President Roosevelt through his representative, Colonel Louis Johnson – the discussions foundered.[29] The Indians were prepared to agree that the direction of strategy and control of operations should remain Wavell's responsibility, but were less pleased when they understood how 'hollow' their Defence Member's role would be. His functions seemed to amount to such minor tasks as overseeing amenities for the troops, canteens, stationery, schools, the entertainment of foreign missions, and demobilization after the war. Empty-handed, Cripps and his entourage returned to England on 12 April. Wavell was on the tarmac to see the delegation off.

This had been Wavell's first encounter with the tergiversations of Indian politicians. Fans of his, like Coats, believed that amid the heated discussions, Wavell was the only one who was 'calm, silent and wise'.[30] But, according to Brooke, who met Cripps soon after his return from India, Cripps (a fellow Wykehamist) was not impressed with Wavell because he was so silent.[31] Azad later gave the Indian viewpoint: 'the failure of the Cripps Mission led to widespread disappointment and anger in the country. Many Indians felt that the Churchill Cabinet had sent Sir Stafford only because of American and Chinese pressure, but in fact Mr Churchill had no intention of recognizing Indian freedom.'[32] This anger translated itself into a movement of civil disobedience that presented Wavell with more problems of internal security: Gandhi continued to preach non-violence but also exhorted his followers to non-cooperation, which more revolutionary elements interpreted as a licence to sabotage, communications installations being a favoured target.

Throughout Burma the British retreat continued. On 14 April demolition of the oilfields around Yenangyaung, north of Magwe, began, to deny them to the Japanese. As Mandalay was subjected to aerial bombardment, British and Indian troops withdrew up the Irrawaddy valley. Undaunted by the monsoon, which was making conditions for the retreating soldiers even more treacherous, Wavell was back in Burma in April. His objective was to reconnoitre Arakan, the 'wall of mountain and forest' bordering India, two hundred miles wide and stretching for six hundred miles from north to south.[33] Bernard Fergusson had recently been appointed from the Middle East to Wavell's Joint Planning Staff in New Delhi, and was with him during another 'Jonah' incident. Landing in a squall of rain on a brick airstrip, the aircraft skidded off the runway and ended on its nose. As its tail up-ended Wavell's travelling companions were thrown forward in a heap, with bits of luggage landing on him. When they attempted to get up, Wavell said, dead-pan: 'When you've all quite finished walking over your Commander-in-Chief . . .'[34] 'Chief' and former ADC soon found an opportunity to exercise their shared delight in poetry, versifying and playing about with words. When the Indian Parachute Brigade was raised, it included a British battalion with 30 'Jocks' from The Black Watch, and the two men amused themselves by composing a ballad, for which Wavell wrote this verse: 'Twould give the Indian ladies such a shock / To see how stoutly Scottish lads are built / So here's a word of warning to you, Jock: / Never go parachuting in the kilt.'[35]

Now that the Japanese were able to operate more or less with impunity in the Bay of Bengal, India's eastern coastline was vulnerable, as was the island of Ceylon. Colombo had already suffered a heavy air attack, resulting in the sinking of two cruisers, a destroyer and a light carrier, and the loss of thousands of tons of merchant shipping. Churchill's signal to Wavell expressed the 'grievous anxieties' he felt at their weakness: 'We are endeavouring to build up a fleet in the Indian Ocean sufficiently strong to cause the Japanese to make a larger detachment from their main fleet than they would wish . . . But if in the meantime Ceylon, particularly Colombo, is lost all this gathering of a naval force will be futile.' Satisfied that it was unlikely the Japanese would send four or five divisions 'roaming about' mainland India, Churchill also informed Wavell that he would not be able 'to provide air forces either to repel landings or to give an air umbrella for naval movements' along the eastern Indian coastline from Ceylon to Calcutta.[36] Wavell, aware of Churchill's insistence on carrying out intensive bombing raids in the heartland of Germany, had his own opinion about the availability of reinforcements: 'Unless a serious effort is made to supply our essential needs . . . I must warn you that we shall never regain control of the Indian Ocean and Bay of Bengal, and run the risk of losing

India. It certainly gives us furiously to think when, after trying with less than twenty light bombers to meet attack . . . we see that over 200 heavy bombers attacked one town in Germany.'[37]

In mid April Wavell journeyed to Bombay to spend three days at sea in HMS *Warspite* with Admiral Sir James Somerville, who had arrived as C-in-C of the Far Eastern fleet in February. Like Wavell, Somerville all too often found himself subjected to criticism from Churchill, who appeared to think that in requesting reinforcements he was 'asking for everything and giving the least possible.'[38] Also like Wavell, Somerville had enjoyed sitting in the comfortable armchair in Joan Bright's office, and had become one of her correspondents. The purpose of the *Warspite* meeting was to confer about the Japanese naval threat or, as Somerville put it, 'so that [Wavell] could see the fleet at work and also so that we could have a good heart to heart.' Like so many of Wavell's colleagues, Somerville, renowned for his larger-than-life presence, found him 'curious in some ways', noting his lack of small talk. 'At other times he talks on rather a high plane.'[39] Further discussions were held in Colombo, where Pownall had become GOC in Ceylon following the dissolution of ABDA. In Wavell's opinion, too much attention was being focused on Ceylon, denying him the resources he needed for the defence of India. He had already expressed his view to Churchill that Ceylon was mainly an air and naval problem: 'we should not lock up in island large number of troops which can be better employed elsewhere.'[40] The return flight from Colombo to Calcutta through a severe storm was the roughest of Wavell's life,[41] and he was relieved to be back home in time to celebrate Joanie's nineteenth birthday, for which Reid Scott had organized a party of sixty.

As the situation in Burma remained perilous Wavell continued to put on a brave public face, regardless of how he felt personally about the war: 'I am here, as the man on whom the main responsibility for the defence of India falls,' he stated in a broadcast speech on 21 April, 'not to give you false and easy assurances, not to tell you that danger does not exist; but to put that danger in a proper perspective and to tell you something of the measures that have been taken to meet that danger.' Wavell's delivery had none of the Churchillian ring, but he gave bold assurances of his confidence in ultimate victory, praising the quality of troops defending India. He ended by encouraging the people to resist 'defeatism'.[42] Privately, he was concerned about the future. 'I shall be relieved (and a little surprised) if we come through the next few months without serious loss,' he confided to Joan Bright at the end of April.[43] Though he had pronounced himself fully recovered from his back injury, he was still in pain, and after an X-ray the doctor recommended a massage every evening. Sometimes he watched films in the Residence's private cinema, finding diversion in the adventures of Walt Disney's Dumbo and Mickey Mouse.[44]

Bleak though his circumstances were, Wavell had in mind some original moves in Burma. His thoughts had been returning in particular to certain events of 1917. One evening in late April Fergusson and Peter Fleming were called into Wavell's study after dinner. 'He ran over once again the story of Colonel Richard Meinertzhagen dropping a haversack full of bogus information near Beersheba on 10 October 1917, which played a major part in deluding the Turks about Allenby's intentions.'[45] Wavell wanted to pull a similar trick on the Japanese with the idea of misleading them about both the precise route of Alexander's withdrawal and the military strength of India. The three men sat up until the early hours discussing the details. On 30 April, with Wavell's blessing, Fleming and Reid Scott set out for Burma to put the plan, code-named 'Error', into operation. 'The idea was that the Chief had just paid a hurried last-minute visit to the Burma front and had had a car accident, skidding when going too fast, then because the Japs were too close, had to evacuate the car in a hurry leaving most of his kit including his letter case full of faked information actually written by the Chief, i.e. "notes for Alexander" saying two armies were going to Burma and about a new secret weapon.'[46] To add authenticity to the package of deceptive documents, Wavell had included a much-loved photograph of Pamela. Peter Fleming had also concocted a letter supposedly written by Joan Bright, incorporating comments about fictitious plans and movements.[47]

Once Alexander had given his approval, the two men set off on the Mandalay road as far as the Irrawaddy. 'We arrived at dusk and found General Cowan straight away. He was delighted with the idea and knew a good place to stage it. We set it all up, made skid marks and pushed the car over.' As Fleming wrote in his official report: 'The results were not spectacular. The car flounced down the embankment without overturning, crossed a cart track, and plunged into a small nullah [valley], at the bottom of which it came to rest with its engine still ticking over self-righteously. We let the air out of one front tyre, punctured the other, and removed the ignition key.' In addition to Wavell's briefcase, they left a service dress jacket with the correct ribbons and the C-in-C's medal on the breast, and a case with a blanket marked 'Captain A. Reid Scott, 11th Hussars'. Wavell warned the War Office: 'Have just carried out stratagem in Burma which involved loss of my despatch case containing important documents some of which were genuine papers appropriately doctored. You will probably get official report stating documents lost. Might help if impression of anxiety over seriousness of loss of papers in Burma were fostered . . . Please ensure that absolute minimum persons know real truth of matter.'[48] It was difficult to determine the success of 'Error', but in 1944 Peter Fleming sent Wavell a note informing him that, according to the Chinese Director of Military Intelligence, it appeared that during the first Burma campaign the Japanese had captured important documents indicating that India's defensive potential was greater than they had supposed. As Fleming noted, 'I do not consider that this story constitutes proof that ERROR was successful, though it does suggest that it may have been successful. It is difficult to think of any other documents which the Japanese could have captured in Burma and which would have persuaded and even hinted to them that our forces in India were strong.'[49] Wavell responded light-heartedly to Fleming's note: 'When I am old and garrulous and blimping I shall probably tell a story of how I tricked the Japs and saved India from invasion!'[50] 'Error' was followed by numerous other schemes devised by Fleming and authorized by Wavell. It is in the nature of such stratagems that their effect is difficult if not impossible to assess, but like one of his Staff College 'heroes', Stonewall Jackson, Wavell certainly enjoyed making use of the potential 'to mystify and mislead' the enemy.

As early as February 1942, Wavell had also called for Wingate to organize irregular activities against the Japanese. He travelled to India on the same plane as Alexander, and thus arrived only shortly before the withdrawal began, but there was time enough 'for his active brain to grasp the essentials of fighting in Burma'. As in the Middle East, his proposal was for the formation of a 'Long Range Penetration Group' for action against Japanese communications. Wavell accepted his suggestions but warned him that he could not give him any 'picked troops'.[51] The idea was that Wingate's special brigade would form part of a large-scale operation against the Japanese in northern Burma which Wavell intended to mount after the monsoon in the autumn. In July, several thousand men – British, Indian and Burmese – assembled in the jungle region in the Central Provinces for four months of rigorous training in sweltering heat and the torrential rains of the monsoon. Raised as the 77th Indian Brigade, they took the name 'Chindits', after the Chinthe, the imaginary beast, half lion, half flying griffin, that traditionally guarded Burmese temples and which became their insignia.[52] Fergusson was given command of No. 5 column.

Throughout April and May, British and Chinese reverses in Burma continued. On 1 May Lashio fell; on the 4th the island of Akyab on the Arakan coast had to be evacuated. Chinese forces were defeated at Wanting on the

Burma Road, and at Bhamo on the Irrawaddy River. With complete control of the Burma Road, the Japanese could now enter China from Burma. Once Stilwell realized the extent of their rapid advance, and that there was no possibility of withdrawing into China, he saw that he must retreat with the remaining Chinese troops into India. To fray nerves still further and give credence to the widespread belief that Japan's next territorial goal was India, in mid May the Japanese bombed a small town in Eastern Assam, inflicting some damage and 'moderate casualties'. During Stilwell's withdrawal Wavell set out for Assam, travelling down the Manipur road along which the Burma Army would eventually make its way into India. American planes were already flying out refugees and the wounded. After a journey which involved Reid Scott driving along a road so narrow in places that 'one cannot afford to make a mistake without going over the edge', they arrived at the Imphal plain.

At one stop Wavell visited the 7th Queen's Own Hussars, bivouacked along the Imphal–Kohima road. Bereft of tanks, which they had had to jettison in the Chindwin River, the soldiers were waiting to return to India. Lieutenant Tim Llewellen Palmer described how Wavell, after thanking the men for all they had done during the retreat, asked him what they needed. Palmer's response – everything from ground-sheets to tanks – was met by the usual silence. Later that evening, a convoy of lorries arrived with Wavell's order: 'You are to have these.'[53] Having also visited an ammunition dump, an oil installation, a hospital and a rest camp, Wavell and his party arrived at the aerodrome to find it half under water. What ensued was a variation on Wavell's chequered encounters with flying. Reid Scott recorded the event in his diary: 'As our plane still has not turned up they offer us a Wellington. Having got on board we find the cooling system has broken down. At this moment the Macmillan plane arrives and while the poor chap is receiving a slight reprimand from the Chief (it was not his fault) we move the luggage. The refuelling arrangements are so primitive that I end up driving the petrol lorry myself and filling up the plane which takes ages as there are no tankers available. The Chief gets more and more irritable but a little gimlet out of a thermos soothes him. Temporarily.'[54]

Although the Japanese continued to advance in the Chindwin area, they too were exhausted, and unable to move beyond the Chindwin River. During the lull imposed by the monsoon Wavell observed in private correspondence that the Japanese were 'inactive', but was well aware that 'they may be boiling up something unpleasant and I have many uneasy weeks ahead.' He remained convinced that if he could get a long-range air striking force in India and attack Japanese aerodromes, bases and shipping, it would be 'the first nail in their coffin.' Looking to the future, he rephrased thoughts he had expressed at the beginning of the year: 'We shall win this war all right but shall we go back to our old ways again or can we regenerate ourselves?'[55] As to his own performance, he was as always self-deprecating: 'I will continue the work here as well as I can, but we want a fiery-headed crusader in this part of the world, and I'm certainly not that.'[56]

By the end of May, the surviving Allied forces had been brought safely to India. The withdrawal – the longest retreat in military history – was, as Slim later wrote, 'sheer misery'.[57] Afterwards, Wavell sent a message with his customary encouragement: 'Your main task during these months has been to occupy and delay large Japanese forces so as to give time for the defences of India to be reinforced and organized and this you have most successfully and gallantly accomplished.'[58] He also signalled Churchill: 'Alexander has performed fine feat in bringing back army.'[59] When Wavell came to write his official despatch, he pointed to a variety of circumstances which had caused the retreat, among them a faulty appreciation of Japanese fighting strength. 'More might have been done, in spite of all the deficiencies, to place the country on a war footing. Political considerations, the climate, under-estimation of the enemy, over-estimation of the natural strength of the frontiers, the complacency of many years of freedom from external threat, all combined to prevent the defence problem being taken sufficiently seriously.'[60]

Outwardly Wavell had been able to appear granite-like in his imperturbability, but those close to him were left in no doubt that the events of the past year had taken their toll. 'I'm not a great man, only a reasonably competent soldier, naturally somewhat lazy and now a little tired,' he wrote to Joan Bright at the beginning of June. 'But I'll keep on trying.'[61] Irritability over his inadequate resources was never far from the surface. Philip Mason, secretary to the Chiefs of Staff Committee, recalled Wavell coming into his office one hot evening in June: 'he stood, square and dogged, before the map of Burma, gazing at it, his hands behind him: "Think how stretched they must be!" he said. "This is the moment to hit the Japs if only we could! If I had one division in India fit to fight I'd go for them now!" But he had not.'[62] As for the safety of India's shores, confirmation of the decisive defeat of the Japanese fleet by the United States at Midway gave Wavell a much-needed breathing space. Henceforward the balance of sea power in the Pacific was tipped in the Americans' favour, and a Japanese naval attack on Ceylon was no longer a threat.

The July of 1942 was the hottest anyone in India could remember, and for once the Government of India had not undertaken the time-consuming process of moving to Simla. 'Delhi, that spreading leafy city of bungalows and palaces built of dirty white and tongue-coloured stone, settled down into torpor,' noted Coats.[63] It was Wavell's fourth summer in the East, and he was finding that the hot weather took it out of him. Air-conditioning was primitive, generally based on khus-khus tatties – screens of khus-khus grass 'which let the air through and were kept damp by coolies throwing water on them. They lowered the temperature by many degrees and at the same time gave off a rather good smell.'[64] Wavell was also frustrated by the way he had to spend his time: 'comparatively little war', but endless meetings of the Viceroy's Executive Council, focused on the politics of India and 'tiresome' matters of administration. After spending nearly a month in Delhi he went on a tour of southern India. In Bangalore he visited the Hindustan Aircraft Factory: production was slow, and he considerd they were making mainly obsolete aircraft.[65] At Poona he inspected a large number of troops from assorted regiments 'the way [noted Reid Scott] he says Allenby used to – dashing up with brakes screaming, making a brief tour, noticing every fault and disappearing after five minutes in a cloud of dust.'[66]

Wavell was also losing patience with the War Cabinet in London. 'They don't seem to realize the necessity to keep commanders informed of events and ideas that concern them as and when they happen.' As usual, he was complaining about lack of troops. He also 'nearly blew' up about a telegram forbidding him to repeat to Auchinleck his reports home, and vice versa. 'But I slept over and decided that they had quite enough to worry about at home at present without adding a rude and rather insubordinate C-in-C – however justified he thought himself.' Besides, he realized that he and Auchinleck had other means of keeping each other informed. He was also missing England. 'I wish I could see you in your little house,' he wrote to Joan Bright, 'and have a talk and eat eggs and bacon (or whatever you cook best) and drink beer, if there is still beer in England, and discuss the world as it is, and as it ought to be had men not Gods designed it.'[67]

At least there was serenity on the domestic front. Queenie was doing a lot of work with canteens and hospitals; Pam seemed 'very happy' in Cairo, though Francis was involved in 'the Western Desert battle'; Joan and Felicity were in 'quite good form', Joan working in Ciphers and Felicity, nicknamed 'Ferocity' by his ADCs because of her obviously strong will, in the Operations branch. She had just celebrated her twenty-first birthday, and during Wavell's visit to Ceylon in June he had bought her a beautiful sapphire. Nanny was in 'very good form and seems little affected by the heat. In fact we have all stood up to it fairly well so far, though I think my temper is several feet shorter.'[68] Wavell had also taken on a new ADC: the Hon. Simon Astley, 7th Queen's Own Hussars, younger son of Lord Hastings, had recently come out of the Burma jungle sick with malaria. In his moments of relaxation Wavell had embarked on an interesting enterprise which was to give him more pleasure than perhaps he ever imagined: the compilation of an anthology of all the poetry he knew by heart. It was 'an old-fashioned' collection which he believed would not interest anyone but himself.[69]

At the beginning of August 1942 Wavell was summoned to Cairo. His expectations were low: 'I doubt if I shall hear much to India's advantage, it looks as if everything I want will be wanted in Middle East and once again I shall have to battle with insufficient equipment, if I have to battle.'[70] More than a year since he relinquished command, he found that much had changed in Cairo. GHQ, which had started on such small foundations, was now a huge military base. The meeting had been convened by Churchill to discuss the Middle East Command. The Prime Minister's presence in Cairo was supposed to be a secret, but as Reid Scott, who had remained in Delhi, remarked, it was horrifying how many people even there knew. Nothing tangible had changed or occurred to make Wavell and Churchill more compatible, yet the next three weeks were probably the most harmonious period of their working relationship.

This time Auchinleck was the object of Churchill's displeasure. As with Wavell the previous year, Churchill had become irritated by Auchinleck's cautious responses and was seeking to replace him. His first choice was Strafer Gott, but Brooke cautioned that he was tired. Churchill then proposed that Brooke himself should take it on. The prospect of an operational job 'gave rise to the most desperate longings in my heart,' Brooke admitted, but he believed himself 'unsuited for the job, having never been trained in the desert.'[71] Churchill then reverted to Gott. He also wanted to split the command between the Near East and the Middle East, with Auchinleck taking over in the Middle East (Persia and Iraq) and Alexander, back from Burma, in the Near East, leaving Strafer Gott in charge of the 8th Army, successor to the embryo Western Desert Force of the 1940s, now opposing Rommel, who had finally secured Tobruk in June. But Auchinleck refused the Persia/Iraq command. No sooner had Gott been appointed than on 7 August the news came through that his slow transport plane had been shot down by the Germans twenty miles west of

Alexandria.[72] In place of Gott, General Bernard Montgomery, currently in Britain, was appointed to take command of the 8th Army while Alexander became Commander-in-Chief, Near East. Throughout these discussions, Wavell judged Churchill to be in his most Marlburian mood, seeing himself 'in the periwig and red coat of his great ancestor, directing Eugene (for which part Alexander is now cast) to begin the Battle of Blenheim' – of which the 238th anniversary happened to fall on 13 August.[73]

Wavell's visit to the Middle East was initially scheduled to last eight to ten days, but it soon became obvious that 'more was in the air than just Cairo' when he asked Reid Scott 'to send thick khaki etc. by quickest possible means'.[74] His destination was the Soviet Union. The purpose of Churchill's visit, accompanied by all his 'top brass', was to break the news to Stalin that the Allies were not strong enough to open 'a second front' in Europe that year. On Tuesday 11 August the delegation left Cairo for Teheran en route to Moscow. Unsurprisingly, perhaps, on the second part of the journey the Liberator in which Wavell, Brooke and Tedder were travelling developed engine trouble. They returned to Teheran for the night while another plane was found, a Russian one, a 'very good and comfortable machine of American make . . . Armchairs, a Persian carpet on the floor, radio-gramophone and all comforts.'[75] Setting out the following day, they flew at low altitude along the west coast of the Caspian Sea, where they expected to see Russian-built fortifications. As Tedder related, 'Wavell, Alan Brooke and I were seated one behind the other on the port side of the aircraft, and so got a perfect view,' but when he sought Brooke's and Wavell's opinion on what appeared to him to be non-existent fortifications, he found his timing was 'unfortunate' since both men were asleep.[76] When they reached Moscow, Churchill had already begun the difficult discussions with Stalin.[77] The previous evening the Soviet leader had apparently accepted Churchill's explanation; on the evening of Wavell's arrival he had reverted to his original demands.

The following day Brooke chaired a military meeting with the Chiefs of Staff at which they discussed again the Allies' inability to make a landing in the Cherbourg peninsula, as the Soviets wanted, to take the pressure off the Russians in the east. 'Throughout our discussion Wavell was most useful to me,' recalled Brooke. 'As he could understand Russian he wrote down a few notes and pushed them over to me even before the interpreter had time to get to work. I thus had a few additional seconds to frame my replies in.' The Russians were not pleased by the outcome of the discussions, but were eventually obliged to accept the Allied position. During the Moscow visit, Wavell told Joan Bright he found Churchill 'very pleasant, and we had a very friendly party. A very great man, but tiresome and unreasonable as a child at times.'[78] The gastronomical highlight was a three-hour-long, nineteen-course banquet in one of the State rooms in the Kremlin. When called upon to respond to the toast in his honour, Wavell did so in Russian, which, noted Brooke, 'met with great success'.[79] Churchill called Wavell's speech 'excellent'.[80]

The Prime Minister and his delegation left Moscow at dawn on 16 August. Once more Wavell and Brooke were travelling together in a Liberator, where they established themselves in the rear, 'lying on the floor, as there were no seats'. While Brooke read, Wavell was writing and the CIGS wondered whether he too should be making notes of the Moscow meeting. 'Suddenly he stopped and threw across to me the results of his labours.' It was a 'Ballade' for Churchill – and which, Wavell later noted with some amusement, pleased the Prime Minister. The 'Envoi' to the 'Ballade of the Second Front' succinctly summed up the outcome of their discussions: 'Prince of the Kremlin, / Here's a fond farewell / I've had to deal with many worse than you; / You took it, though you hated it like hell – / NO SECOND FRONT in 1942.'[81]

Back in Cairo, Brooke discussed the Iraq/Persia situation with Wavell. Since Auchinleck had refused the new Middle East Command, the plan was to hand Iraq and Persia to India – 'Archie Wavell to act as a foster parent and to prepare this Command for an independent existence at the earliest possible date.'[82] However, after further discussions, Churchill decided to make it into a separate command immediately and hand it over to Jumbo Wilson. In view of Churchill's desire to give Persia and Iraq 'a new independent nurse', Wavell considered himself fortunate to have been spared another 'unwanted' baby, although Churchill was still suggesting that the 'new infant would require to be nourished at India's nipple occasionally.'[83]

Before returning to Delhi, Wavell wrote to the Prime Minister with a request. It was, he said, the first time he had ever asked for anything: promotion to the rank of Field Marshal. 'I have commanded very considerable armies and held very responsible positions and had at least two very successful campaigns – in Cyrenaica in the winter of 1940–1 and in Italian East Africa in the first half of 1941 . . . I have also directed the operations that occupied Syria and reoccupied Iraq.' Pointing also to his setbacks, he suggested that 'how far they were due to my mismanagement I must leave to your judgement; but as I have since then been entrusted with very great, possibly even larger, responsibilities, I take it that my generalship has not been held to be radically at fault.' Stressing that he now had over a million soldiers under his command and that he was being asked to take on even greater responsibilities, he expressed a belief that he had 'fair claims' to the rank. Furthermore, and not least: 'It would considerably increase my influence and prestige with the Indian army and be taken as a compliment by them.' Had the opportunity presented itself, Wavell said, he would have spoken to Churchill in person, but he felt it would be less embarrassing if he put his request in writing 'in the first instance'.[84]

Churchill was in favour of granting Wavell's request, as was Alan Brooke; the Prime Minister therefore indicated to his new Secretary of State for War that he would like it to be announced in the New Year's Honours List. But Sir James Grigg[85] was shocked by Wavell's request and made his feelings plain to Churchill, stating, *inter alia*, that although Wavell had 'brains enough' he doubted his ability, and felt that if his name did go forward so should that of Gort, who was senior to Wavell. He also begged Churchill to postpone 'any question of making any special appointments to Field Marshal until the Army has some resounding success to its credit.'[86] For once Churchill was predisposed to stick up for Wavell, and Grigg reluctantly agreed to put Wavell's name before the King, while informing the Prime Minister that he did not think Wavell had 'any fire in his belly, or enough iron in his body'[87] – a view Churchill thought 'would astonish most people'.[88]

Unaware of any of this, soon after returning to Delhi Wavell made a broadcast marking the third anniversary of the outbreak of war. Once more he highlighted the role of Indian soldiers: 'The men who now protect India on all fronts from her foes, the men who fight as comrades side by side, whatever their caste and creed – these are the defenders of India in her hour of danger. Rajputs, Mahrattas and Madrassis; the great fighting races of the Punjab; Pathans from the Frontier; Jats and Garwalis and many others – men of the North, men of the centre, men of the South, from the whole countryside of India.' In conclusion, he exhorted his listeners to 'Lift up your hearts then, and trust in your fighting men.'[89]

A more personal worry was Reid Scott, whose horse had stumbled when he was riding with Joanie; it had fallen on his legs, and Reid Scott had suffered a broken ankle and dislocated shoulder. An injured ADC must inevitably inconvenience Wavell, but Reid Scott found his Chief was 'charming' about it, and expressed great concern over his leg and shoulder.[90]

Wavell was finding India 'tiresome'. The heaviest monsoon rains for years had flooded many places, damaging railways and disrupting communications to the Assam–Burma frontier. In addition, the Government of India was having to contend with the 'Quit India Movement' launched by the Congress Party following their disappointment with Cripps's proposals.

Gandhi and the main leaders of the Congress Working Committee had been detained in early August, but the movement still had a damaging effect. Supporters had torn up many miles of railway track, causing delays, so that troops under training for the Burma front had to be sent instead to deal with rioters or to guard the railways.[91] Malaria had taken its worst toll for a decade, and this at a time when they were short of hospitals and doctors. However, Wavell considered that the Indian people at large were carrying on as normal: 'We get all the recruits we want. There is no sign of any disloyalty in the Army.'[92]

Whatever Wavell's private feelings – and he admitted they were 'a little more anxious' than his official views – his public pronouncements remained upbeat. On 9 September he gave his customary address to the National Defence Council, choosing as his theme the weather and its effect on military operations.[93] 'I will begin by saying that these effects are, in my experience, apt to be exaggerated; and that a commander, provided he is prepared to face certain risks and casualties, can often operate in conditions which are considered impracticable according to accepted rules.' Taking as his examples Allenby's summer retention of a force in the Lower Jordan valley and his own operations in Abyssinia during the rains in May, Wavell admitted that the commander must nevertheless, 'always take them into very serious consideration.'[94]

Privately, the Wavells were concerned about a young man with whom Felicity was 'walking out', a 'parachutist' of whom they obviously disapproved. Wavell was aware of the lack of eligible young men, and appreciated that Felicity – at 21 – was at an 'impressionable' age. A further complication was the romance between Joanie and Simon Astley that had blossomed over the summer, when they earned the reputation for being the 'bright sparks' of Delhi. As Peter Coats recollected, it was difficult for the Wavells to approve Joanie's choice while disapproving of Felicity's, and for a while the 'four lovers moped'. Eventually, the parachutist 'faded' out.[95]

Throughout the summer Wavell had been trying to work out a new strategy for Burma. On 17 September he gave Major-General Edwin Morris, his Chief of the General Staff, a paper, 'Operation Fantastical', in which he asked for suggestions.[96] Believing the Japanese to be in greater trouble than was realized, Wavell was formulating a plan that would begin with a reoccupation of the island of Akyab to deny it to the Japanese as a refuelling base for their anticipated raids on Calcutta and Upper Arakan. 'The first thing I want is to create a spirit everywhere from GHQ downwards of determination to get as far into Burma this winter as possible.'[97] The Chiefs of Staff in London were less than enthusiastic. Brooke noted that capturing Akyab was an isolated operation; their main objective should be Rangoon, for which they did not yet have enough strength.[98] As Wavell plotted, his annoyance at not being able to achieve what he wanted was evident in his personal correspondence: 'I'm feeling a little frustrated,' he confided to Joan Bright at the end of September, because he had a 'hunch' that there was a big and successful battle to be fought 'if one had just a little more of everything and a little more time before the next monsoon.'[99]

But Churchill had at least granted Wavell's 'personal' request, and in early October came the news that his promotion to Field Marshal was to be announced in the next New Year's Honours List. Wavell's response seems rather out of character: he was not satisfied. In thanking Churchill, he expressed a hope that the announcement might be made forthwith: 'After all I feel it was in 1941 that I earned it not in 1942, and that it will look rather like an old age pension in the New Year List. Life is uncertain and my military career is beginning to draw to an end. I confess I should like to enjoy prestige as long as possible.' He then pointed to what perhaps lay behind his request in the first place. 'Also it might help in dealing with Americans and Chinese in forthcoming negotiations on Burma. Gingerbread is always gingerbread but may I have it with the gilt on please.' Churchill did not feel he could grant this request. Grigg, seeing what Wavell had written, thought he must be 'out of his mind.'[100] Archie John, who had recently arrived in India to join a battalion of The Black Watch in Bengal, was a little surprised that his father had requested the promotion, as was Coats: 'both Archie John and I slightly disapprove and feel that he is too young, and that it might spoil his market value; put him permanently on the shelf. Does he think he is about to retire into honourable obscurity? It would mean £3,000 a year for life, though, and I sometimes think he has money problems.'[101] Archie John's arrival in Delhi created a new dynamic in the family, and Coats, who considered himself the 'cuckoo' in the Wavell nest, regarded it with some apprehension. 'Fortunately, all was well. We had mutual friends in London and they had paved the way. After a day or two we were good friends and were to remain so always.'[102]

Wavell anticipated that the proposed attack on Akyab could be undertaken by sea with an independent brigade he hoped would be made available to him after completing operations taking place against Vichy forces in Madagascar. Meanwhile, Lieutenant-General Noel Irwin, Commander-in-Chief of the Eastern Army, had been instructed to mount the land advance from Chittagong into the Arakan.[103] The only force available, the

14th Indian Division commanded by Major-General Wilfrid Lloyd, though not yet fully trained, was given the task.[104] In early October Wavell was in Calcutta again, having stopped on the way to see Chinese troops training under American instructors at Ramgarh in central India. He then flew on to Burma, to Fort Hierty where, as recorded by Reid Scott, he found matters not to his satisfaction: 'The Chief had a scourge on the Medical arrangements in Eastern Army, having found at one hospital, where he was told that 90 per cent of the patients had malaria, that the drains were blocked and there was stagnant water.'[105] British resistance to increasing the number of Chinese troops at Ramgarh did nothing for Wavell's relationship with Stilwell. Initially Wavell had approved an increase, but Linlithgow had referred the question to London. To give substance to the British reluctance, Wavell highlighted the congested railroads, the demands the Chinese would make on valuable resources, and the fact that any additional presence would hinder his plans to expand the Indian Army – as Stilwell noted, 'if we get trucks, it will reduce his tonnage.' Stilwell was having difficulties persuading Chiang Kai-Shek to put his men in the field, and found Wavell's constraints exasperating. 'Well to hell with the old fool. We have just smoked them out. They don't want Chinese troops participating in the retaking of Burma. That's all. (It's OK for US troops to be in England though.) Discouraging encounter, after my labours to get the Chinese going.'[106] But as Stilwell realized, while it was not something Wavell could admit, there was a fear in London that if the Chinese assumed too great a role, they might seek to revive ancient claims on north Burma.

Politically India was quiet after the disturbances of the summer, and though his commitments were numerous, Wavell described some of his work during this period as 'dull'. Such was his mental energy that he was not content if he was not also writing. An article in the *Strand* magazine written by Liddell Hart in December 1941 that he had only just seen prompted him to write a response. 'Liddell Hart's writing is always a stimulant, often an irritant, to military thought.' With 'only a small fraction' of Liddell Hart's 'great knowledge of military history', he wrote of being inspired nevertheless to focus on generals who might be considered to have had military genius. 'Genius is a tiresome and misleading word to apply to the military art, if it suggests, as it does to many, one so gifted by nature as to obtain his successes by inspiration rather than through study.'[107] Some who might have been thought to have that quality, like T.E. Lawrence, he ruled out because their field of action and their exploits were on too small a scale;

the same was true of William Sherman and Stonewall Jackson, who had never been in supreme command nor had to bear the final strain of responsibility for the main armies of their government. Wavell's short list comprised Hannibal, Scipio, Alexander, Caesar and Belisarius from antiquity, Cromwell in the seventeenth century, Marlborough, Frederick, Napoleon, Wellington and Lee in the eighteenth and nineteenth centuries, and Möltke, Foch and Ludendorff in the twentieth. At the end of his analysis, Marlborough and Belisarius came top of his list as the most 'gifted and ablest' soldiers, followed by Wellington and Frederick, Lee and Napoleon. Wavell's article, captioned 'Military Genius', was published in *The Times* in October. Liddell Hart immediately penned a long Letter to the Editor, commending the article and indulging in his usual corrective tit-for-tat, dealing only with those points on which he and Wavell differed, rather than those where they saw eye to eye. 'Sir Archibald Wavell is a military writer and thinker with a touch of unconventionality, almost of whimsicality, who, even when he does not command universal agreement with his propositions, invariably compels thought and discussion.'[108] Another response came from the writer Robert Graves, author in 1938 of the first full account of the sixth-century campaigns of Belisarius to be published in English. Graves was anxious to point out the similarities between what Belisarius and Wavell had to face: Belisarius had operated from a distant base against an enemy who held Sicily as well as Africa and was strong at sea; later he had to free the Italians from their German masters, beginning with an invasion of Sicily. Graves's correspondence led Wavell to embark on what proved an unsuccessful attempt to have *Count Belisarius* republished.[109]

As a contrast to 'Military Genius', Wavell continued to work 'slowly' on his anthology, urged on by Peter Fleming. 'It has amused me for a little, but will not see print,' he noted in early November.[110] An additional diversion was that Joanie and Simon wanted to get married. Wavell had been 32 when he married Queenie, she 27, whereas Joanie and Simon's combined ages barely made 40, but still they expected him to take some action on their behalf.[111]

As 1942 drew to a close, Wavell's greatest disappointment was the offensive in Arakan. The 14th Division, advancing from Chittagong southwards through mangrove swamps and across tidal creeks, had to build the roads as they went: after one month they had barely covered a hundred miles. A typhoon that swept the Bay of Bengal in early November impeded their line of communications still further. Then came Wavell's bitter realisation that since the Madagascar operations were still incomplete he would have to forgo the idea of a seaborne assault and make do with ordering a land advance to the tip of the Mayu peninsula, from where the assault on Akyab might be launched. Wavell saw all the disadvantages of altering his original plan – not only was the terrain more difficult, but the troops had inadequate training in jungle warfare – but still hoped that a swiftly executed operation stood some chance of success. Stilwell was derisory, dismissing Wavell's limited objective as 'a joke'.[112]

Characteristically, with the progress of the war occupying his working hours, Wavell ended the year with thoughts on the aspect of his life which still afforded him the greatest mental relaxation: poetry. 'To my mind, writers and especially poets are the servants of the nation or, if they prefer it, of humanity', and should use their talents to help and inspire 'their less gifted comrades'. Poets – he continued in a long letter written to Joan Bright when he was 'rather torpid after lunch on Christmas day' – were 'the lineal descendants of the tribal ballad-makers who influenced by their songs the courage and beliefs of their tribes; of the minstrels who entertained and recorded in the earlier stages of civilization; and of the poets who in all ages have helped to inspire great deeds or have given pleasure and thought to their less gifted fellows.' As testimony to the inspiration he himself derived from poetry, he quoted two of his favourites. From Arthur O'Shaughnessy's ode 'The Music Makers' he chose 'One man, with a dream, at pleasure / Shall go forth and conquer a crown; / And two with a new song's measure / May trample an empire down.'[113] And from Flecker's *Hassan*: 'CALIPH: Ah, if there shall ever arise a nation whose people have forgotten poetry or whose poets have forgotten the people, though they send their ships round Taprobane and their armies across the hills of Hindustan, though their city be greater than Babylon of old, though they mine a league into earth or mount to the stars on wings, what of them? HASSAN: They will be a dark patch upon the world.'[114]

16

Field Marshal, 1943

> My new Field Marshal,
> When you have your baton,
> Your field-green breeches
> And your field-craft hat on,
> Your best field-glasses,
> Field boots,
> Field-grey hair,
> May I, a little field mouse,
> Come and stare?
>
> A.P. Wavell

WAVELL'S PROMOTION TO Field Marshal was announced in the New Year Honours List. Whatever his reservations about the timing, he was undoubtedly proud of the circumstance itself. Surpassing the achievements of his father and grandfather, he had joined the handful of men permitted to carry the symbolic baton.[1] Lady Linlithgow's private secretary, Ruby Hill, failed to notice the new badges signifying Wavell's promotion, and later apologized for not having congratulated him; if she had had his skill, she said, she would have written a poem. Wavell responded with what she, a 'little field mouse', might have composed.[2]

By the beginning of 1943 the best from Wavell's prodigious memory had been committed to paper, and his 'anthology' despatched to Peter Fleming's publisher, Jonathan Cape Ltd. Unfortunately Cape's editorial adviser Daniel George took a critical view of both Wavell's selection of poetry (a collection of 'familiar school recitations advancing in close formation') and his occasionally faulty memory; thoughtlessly, a copy of George's report was sent to Wavell. Fleming, understandably annoyed, enlisted the help of his friend and contemporary Rupert Hart-Davis, who was on the board of Jonathan Cape.[3] Hart-Davis rose to Wavell's defence, pointing out how tactless Cape's and George's response had been: 'Wavell,

like so many men of action, is extremely diffident about his literary lean-
ings, and clearly needs even more "jollying along" than most authors . . .
to describe his poetic treasures as "familiar school recitations advancing in
close formation" is tantamount to a sock on the jaw. You see, he looks on
the book as a lifelong treasure, which doesn't require much work on it. We
know there's a lot to be done, but really that's quite a minor point. The
important thing is, surely, that we have the complete bones of a tremen-
dously saleable book.'[4]

Wavell's leisure reading at this time was varied. He did not 'greatly like'
Lewis Namier's book *Conflicts*, in which he felt there was 'nothing new or
original or very striking',[5] but Carola Oman's *Britain Against Napoleon* he
considered 'well done'.[6] He managed to keep up his private correspondence, though when badly pressed for time he sometimes had to dictate
letters to his sisters – 'unsatisfactory', for it meant his 'PA', a Yorkshireman,
must know about all his private and family affairs. Joanie's wedding was set
for the end of January, but Felicity had contracted measles, a cause for concern lest the bride-to-be catch them too. But all was well, and on 27
January 1943 in the Church of the Redemption in New Delhi, Joan
Patricia Quirk Wavell – not yet twenty – was married to Captain the Hon.
Simon Astley, by the Bishop of Lahore. The well-known prayer of Sir
Jacob Astley – 'my new son-in-law's ancestor' – before the Battle of
Edgehill was quoted: 'O Lord, Thou knowest that I shall be very busy this
day: if I forget Thee, do not Thou forget me.' As Wavell observed, it was
quite a good prayer before battle, 'and perhaps before a honeymoon?' Joan
'was at the top of her form and thoroughly enjoyed it all. She's a cheerful
child, but with lots of common sense and character,' which, he commented, she would need to cope with 'her young man – quite a nice lad,
but inclined to be hot-tempered and intolerant!' Pamela was in Cairo but
Archie John was there, though suffering from malaria – 'a frightful
scourge', noted Wavell, affecting all the army.[7] Reid Scott was best man,
and Felicity, nor recovered, attended her sister.

Beyond his domestic circle, Wavell's attention was firmly fixed on the
operations in Arakan, where the 14th Division was continuing its uncertain advance down the Mayu peninsula. A high-level conference was
taking place at Casablanca at the same time, at which it was decided that a
much bigger offensive should be undertaken to recapture Rangoon. After
the conference Dill, accompanied by the US Army commander, General
Henry Arnold and General Bill Somervell, head of the American Service
of Supply, travelled to Delhi, as did Stilwell from Chungking. The plan
they evolved during meetings with Wavell at the beginning of February

was given the code-name 'Anakim'. As Wavell reported to the Chiefs of Staff, their main problems were physical and climatic. 'Only chance of success appears to be to extend enemy to utmost by concentric attacks with the object of engaging him simultaneously on every possible route of entry into Burma.' According to Wavell's report, he did not believe the major offensive could begin until November 1943, after the summer monsoon; in the meantime both British and Chinese forces 'should engage in minor offensive actions with the object of gaining positions for main offensive, and in road-making and administrative preparations.'[8]

In addition to his military concerns, Wavell was also keeping abreast of the Indian political situation. In the New Year Gandhi, under detention in Poona since the 1942 civil disobedience movement, had entered into correspondence with the Viceroy, Lord Linlithgow, to clear the Congress Party from blame for the violence which had erupted the previous summer. On 9 February he began a three-week fast, and there was anxiety lest he should die in prison. But when Linlithgow proposed releasing Gandhi for the duration of his fast, the Mahatma refused.[9] As a soldier, committed to maintaining law and order, Wavell was not predisposed to condone Gandhi's methods: 'I hope we shall have no more internal trouble though I don't know what trick that old humbug Gandhi will try after the failure of his fast.'[10]

On the Burma front Wavell, still anticipating that a combined operation with the Chinese would begin in early March, was looking forward to seeing the Chindits in action. But Chiang Kai-Shek had imposed a significant condition: he would only permit his troops to advance if the Allies had air superiority over Burma and command of the Bay of Bengal. When part of Britain's Eastern fleet was withdrawn to the Mediterranean to assist the landings in North Africa, Stilwell informed Wavell that the Chinese no longer intended to take part in the operation. In these changed circumstances Wavell flew to Imphal seeking reassurance that Wingate still considered it was worth sending in the Chindits 'with no strategical object'. 'I had to balance the inevitable losses – the larger since there would be no other operations to divide the enemy's forces – to be sustained without strategical profit, against the experience to be gained of Wingate's new method and organization. I had little doubt in my own mind of the proper course, but I had to satisfy myself also that Wingate had no doubts and that the enterprise had a good chance of success and would not be a senseless sacrifice.'[11]

The day before their departure, Wavell inspected the brigade. 'This is a great adventure. It is not going to be an easy one. I wish you all the very best of luck.' Finding nothing further to say, he brought up his hand in salute.[12]

As Wingate's biographer noted, 'stirring tales were told afterwards of how the Commander-in-Chief, overtaken by a noble impulse to pay tribute, saluted the troops before they could salute him. It is much more likely that he was prompted by his habitual shyness, and it is typical of the man that his embarrassed motion of the hand made an impression as deep as the most dramatic gesture imaginable.'[13] As more than three thousand men with their buffaloes and mules disappeared into the jungle towards the Indo-Burmese border, Wavell was in reflective mood. From Imphal he wrote to Jackson, his former divisional commander at Aldershot, reviewing the past nine months since the rain-soaked and demoralizing withdrawal: 'At the time, very many people, including quite a lot of Europeans, doubted our ability to hold India. I never had any serious doubts about that, though we were remarkably thin on the ground.' Wavell was now convinced that the danger of invasion had passed. They had also successfully defeated the attempts of the Congress Party 'to paralyse our war effort and we are definitely on the offensive rather than the defensive.'[14] Even so, he realized that the war might be 'a longish business yet, I am afraid. These Japs will give us some tough fighting, but we will fix them up all right in the end.'[15]

Hard as Wavell was working to reverse Allied setbacks in Burma, in London his ability to do so was being questioned. During Dill's South Asian tour, as he confided to Brooke, he had noticed in the Americans a certain distrust of Wavell as an 'unlucky General' who was 'too much in the hands of his experts'. The appointment of an American Deputy Commander-in-Chief was discussed. Ever Wavell's friend, Dill was prepared to defend him. In response to the assertion that there was not enough drive at the Army HQ, he commented: 'You know as well as I do that drive is not Archie's strong suit. It never was. I am sure he would appeal much more to Americans if he were obviously a "go-getter".'[16] Unaware that confidence in his command was once more on the wane, Wavell had returned from Imphal to Delhi, to another farewell. Sandy Reid Scott had been his ADC since June 1941 and on his departure from the Middle East Wavell had promised Reid Scott's commanding officer that he would return to his regiment as soon as his damaged eye was passed fit for desert work; he had now also recovered from the riding accident in late August, so the time had come. Wavell was sad to see him go: 'I have never met anyone old or young with a more attractive character,' he wrote to Reid Scott's father. 'He is one in a million. Everyone who has known him out here will regret his going. He has been a charming companion to me as well as a most efficient ADC.'[17] Reid Scott was equally complimentary about his Chief: 'I had worked for 18 months in the pocket of Archie Wavell, who will, I believe, be regarded by historians as the greatest statesman/soldier so far this century; from him I learnt a great deal about war and peace, politics and human nature, hard work and how to face disasters, and the real meaning of service to one's country.'[18] The fact that they both had only one eye had been recorded in verse. In response to a Canadian Army private who had observed that some people with one eye see better than many with two, Wavell had written: 'It's true I've one eye only, / My aide has but one, too. / So he looks east and I look west / When we want a wider view.'[19]

Wavell's new ADC was Tom Bird, who was already in New Delhi learning the ropes from Reid Scott, though having been in Archie John's house at Winchester, he was no stranger to the Wavell family. Being an ADC meant, among much else, being introduced to the family's games. Bird related an occasion when the Wavells and their guests – high-ranking Chinese generals – were dining with the Viceroy, and Archie John gave a party at home. As often happened, they played 'The Game', in which someone acted out an expression or phrase. To everyone's embarrassment, 'the Chief and Lady W. and the Chinese generals arrived back just as Joanie was acting out "Making a clean breast of it"!'[20] As Bird settled into his new position he learned, as his predecessors had, to understand Wavell's idiosyncrasies. When they were going out to an Old Wykehamist dinner, Bird tried to persuade Wavell to wear khaki battle-dress, 'which the rest of us have been told to wear, and not blue patrols'. Wavell asked if Bird thought he would be the only Field Marshal present. 'When I say yes, he says that in that case he thinks he can wear what he likes.'[21] There were also important lessons. 'Our baggage came from the aerodrome in a different car and took a long time arriving,' he noted when he went on his first trip as Wavell's ADC. 'Nobody had thought to tell me that one must never be separated from a small leather box which contains everything the Chief needs for the care of his eyes and his glass eye in particular.' Arriving at their destination, Wavell immediately asked for his leather box, and Bird was obliged to reveal that it had not yet arrived.[22] Like other ADCs before him, Bird considered he was working for 'one of the very few really very great men'.[23] He also observed how 'none of the Wavell family appeared to me to be in any way in awe of their father, and he obviously adored all his children, though he used to enjoy teasing Felicity. I have seen her upset the backgammon board into her father's lap and stamp out of the room when he was being particularly outrageous.'[24] Bird noticed too that, 'if anyone "talks horse" at all, they are always made to ride – any last-minute objections, like no riding clothes, "haven't ridden for ages", and so on are swept aside.'[25]

Throughout Wavell's time as Commander-in-Chief guests were constantly passing through his doors. Freya Stark arrived for a three-week stay in February, following her mother's death, and in early March the author and composer Beverley Nichols was in Delhi.[26] Having despatched his anthology, in what spare time he had Wavell had at last finished writing the second volume of Allenby's Life, as British High Commissioner in Egypt. He gave the manuscript to Freya Stark to read, which she considered a 'great privilege'.[27] Unlike other women, who felt a 'social failure' when sitting next to Wavell in silence, Freya had the talent to keep him amused, making life easier for his ADCs.[28] On top of Wavell's other concerns, he had to accommodate the presence in India of Auchinleck, who after refusing the Iraq/Persia command had returned to Delhi to write his despatch on his operations in the Middle East. As Bird noted, 'the situation is a bit awkward', and it was exacerbated by the fact that Auchinleck's wife Jessie had 'gone off' with Richard Peirse, who, after the dissolution of ABDA, had become Air Officer Commanding-in-Chief in Delhi.[29] Wavell handled the situation as best he could, sometimes asking Auchinleck's advice on matters relating to the Indian Army, but, with both past and present C-in-Cs, India in the same city, tongues were bound to wag. 'One rumour had it that the Auk was, yet again, to replace my Chief as C-in-C in India and that Wavell was to be sent as Governor-General to Canada,' noted Coats, 'an idea that appalled me.'[30]

By early March the Arakan operations were still not making the headway Wavell had envisaged, to the extent that even his friends were growing critical of his judgement. 'I was rather surprised to find Archie arguing on the lines that perhaps the Japs might have no air, no defences etc. It all seemed so much wishful thinking on which to plan a major operation,' wrote Somerville to their mutual correspondent, Joan Bright.[31] Later, on a visit to Durban, Somerville discussed Wavell's abilities with Smuts, who had 'a great opinion' of him as a soldier and leader; but he also believed Wavell was 'inclined to take a chance without weighing the odds.'[32] As he held to his belief that Arakan would bring some benefit, Wavell was also watching the progress of the Chindits. Such was the secrecy of the operation that next-of-kin had been told no more than that they would not hear from their husbands and sons for the next few months, though they should continue to write. Secrecy notwithstanding, Wavell took time to give Fergusson's parents 'some inkling of what was afoot'.[33]

At the beginning of the war Wavell had faced the Japanese with confidence; he now admitted that British and Indian troops had been demoralized by their fighting skill. 'The Japanese are setting us rather a fresh problem in tactics,' he wrote to Liddell Hart in mid March, 'by combining the fanaticism and mobility of the savage with modern weapons and training. He is refusing to surrender and fighting to the death with modern weapons very skilfully employed; and is showing an independence of lines of communication and an ability to live on the country which one does not expect from an organized modern army. We shall find the answer, but in the meantime our progress is slow, especially as both climate and topography are difficult.'[34] From Britain, Liddell Hart wrote back sympathetically: 'It seems to be your fate in this war to be always destined to tackle the most awkward problems, and under the most difficult conditions. What a succession you have had! The historians of the war are likely to appreciate it better than it is generally realized now.'[35] One problem in particular that troubled Wavell was the extent to which the Japanese treatment of prisoners should be made public; he wrote to ask Archie John what he felt were the views of the regimental soldier. 'By decision of the Foreign Office, we are at present debarred from publishing any information of such atrocities, their argument being, I think, that it will cause distress to people whose relatives are prisoners in the hands of the Japanese, or are fighting against them.' But Wavell thought it desirable that people should appreciate the sort of enemy they were facing 'and the reasons for hating him and dealing with him properly'. His own instinct was to publish, but he was not sure whether that would be the opinion of the 'modern soldier'. Archie John responded that he favoured publication because 'soldiers who know what their enemy is like are more likely to fight on in a hopeless spot rather than surrender.'[36]

Films continued to provide Wavell with occasional hours of relaxation, and when *In Which We Serve*, starring Celia Johnson, reached India, all the family sat together one evening with Peter Fleming to watch it. But when Joanie asked if her father would like to see the film of her marriage his reply was 'No thanks, I saw the wedding.'[37] Wavell was also filling a gap in his knowledge by reading books about the Mongol conquerors. His collection of poems was being edited in London, but unfortunately Cape had further annoyed him by asking £50 for Daniel George's editorial work. Wavell, however, was not inclined to pay 'some bloke' – George – for identifying the poems, something he felt he could quite well do himself.[38] Peter Fleming, equally outraged on his Chief's behalf, wrote to his wife how 'that ass' Jonathan Cape had written Wavell a letter 'which though sensible in some respects is not calculated to appeal to even the most bashful Field Marshal and would certainly antagonize a private individual like me.'[39]

Field Marshal he might now be, but Wavell had by no means abandoned his habit of exercising his sense of humour in doggerel verse. An Air Ministry wire detailing arrangements designed to smooth the passage of VIPs prompted the following:

> Oh it's nice to be a VIP
> And to travel with a zip
> When you take a little trip
> And be greeted with a 'Hip
> Hip hurrah, here he comes';

> While the common sort of CUB★
> (Like the Captain or the Sub)
> Just gets packed in any tub
> And goes to the smallest pub
> In the meanest kind of slums.

> But I think the CUB does more
> To win this ruddy war
> Than the VIP who's just a bore.[40]

Despite Wavell's best endeavours, his Arakan operations were a failure: in counter-attacking, the Japanese had adopted their familiar tactic of forming a hook behind Allied positions and forcing a withdrawal. On 17 March British and Indian troops were attacked just north of Rathedaung in Arakan and forced to fall back. On the Mayu peninsula four attempts to take Donbaik, south of Rathedaung, failed. Wavell was annoyed: 'Our tactics are completely without imagination or fire.'[41] Churchill was watching this dismal outcome. As he wrote in his official history, 'I felt that the whole question of the British High Command against Japan must come under review. New methods and new men were needed. I had long felt that it was a bad arrangement for the Commander-in-Chief India to command the operations in Burma in addition to his other far-reaching responsibilities.'[42]

The Chindit activities were also being circumscribed. Wingate's decision to cross the Irrawaddy River took them into more open terrain, and it was becoming difficult to drop supplies so far afield. On 24 March he was ordered to return to India; splitting up into small groups, the men began the weary journey home. At the beginning of April, as stragglers started to emerge from the jungle, there came a report 'with a wealth of confirmatory detail' that Fergusson had been killed. Wavell promptly ordered a temporary ban on the publication of any such information before facts had

---

★ 'Completely Unimportant Bloke'.

been confirmed. 'His wisdom saved my parents from unnecessary grief, and many other parents and wives as well.'[43] Militarily, the Chindits' exploits behind Japanese lines were not significant but, as Wavell (and Churchill) recognized, the boost to morale and the propaganda value – especially at this time of failure in Arakan – were not to be discounted.

When possible, Wavell continued to make his customary sorties to observe his command at first hand. In late March he went again to Imphal, leaving Queenie with the Herberts in Calcutta, inspecting canteens. For neither the first time nor the last, he took his life in his hands. 'We had an alarming time,' noted Tom Bird, 'when our pilot couldn't find the landing strip. We flew round and round for ages getting shorter and shorter of petrol. It was a great relief when we finally spotted it.'[44] For all the thousands of miles he had covered, Wavell still felt he was making little headway and as usual blamed himself for not teaching the soldiers better. 'But I really get very little time for honest soldiering, I seem to spend most of my time being War Minister,' he complained to Joan Bright, citing as an example the nearly three hours he had recently spent discussing the statutes of Delhi University, measures against speculators in cotton, and a Hindu marriage bill: 'Well, I ask you.'[45] To relieve the boredom of Executive Council meetings he usually took some military work to occupy his mind, and he retained his habit of doodling. But where once he had drawn hats, the only thing he felt competent to draw now was a black cat on a brick wall.[46]

It is scarcely surprising that Wavell felt restless and in need of a change. He contemplated a spring visit to General MacArthur, now based in Australia; he thought also of going to England in the early summer. Then came an immediate summons to London. Before leaving, he gave what proved to be his last address to the National Defence Council. Reviewing the war in its various theatres, he sought to clarify his position on Arakan. 'The Arakan operations were unfortunately described by some as an invasion of Burma. While it is true that we did cross the Burma frontier with small forces, it is quite impossible to invade Burma on any scale through Arakan, and we certainly had no intention whatever of doing so . . . My intention simply was to try to secure control of the northern strip of Arakan down to, and if possible including, Akyab. The only part of this strip that had any military value was Akyab Island, on which there are some good airfield sites.' Had he had the necessary shipping, he said, he would probably not have bothered about the Arakan coast at all. But the shortage of ships and assault craft made it necessary to secure control of the whole of the Mayu peninsula in order to launch an attack on Akyab.'[47] Queenie was in Assam when Wavell left India so abruptly on 19 April; he expected to be back by the middle of May at the latest.

Once in London Wavell was quick to renew his friendship with Channon, still living – in comparative luxury for war-torn Britain – at 5 Belgrave Square.[48] Although it was Good Friday and pouring with rain, when Wavell proposed a visit, Channon hurriedly arranged a cocktail party in honour of 'the greatest general of our day', noting afterwards that Wavell 'drank several cocktails, stayed for nearly three hours, and was charming.' Wavell also re-established contact with Joan Bright, who went with him over the Easter weekend to visit his sisters in Ringwood. 'It was a lovely drive,' noted Joan in her diary, and the sisters were 'charming', serving their guests a traditional English meal of breaded lamb cutlets and castle puddings. After church on Easter Sunday they had lunch with Bobbety and Elizabeth Cranborne, on whose estate the Wavell family had lived a lifetime ago.[49] Tea was taken with Cranborne's father the Marquess of Salisbury and his wife Mollie. Back in London, Wavell went to stay with Channon, who happily replicated Peter Coats's 'ADC-ish' role by arranging appointments for him.

Having apparently improved during their visit to Moscow the previous August, Wavell's relations with Churchill were again barely cordial. At their first meeting on Wednesday 28 April, and the following day with the War Cabinet, Churchill was extremely critical of the Arakan operations, 'though I pointed out to the War Cabinet their limited scope, that they would never have been undertaken at all if I had had shipping available for a direct assault on Akyab; and that I had at least kept the Japanese busy for a whole campaigning season without much encouragement from home and entirely on my own initiative; while the Chinese . . . had never moved at all.'[50] Churchill was also cool about Wavell's suggestion that a mission should go to Washington to discuss a new Far Eastern strategy. On a purely personal level, Churchill had not overcome the irritation induced by Wavell's taciturnity. 'I remember an embarrassing meeting,' recalled Lieutenant-General Ian Jacob, Military Assistant Secretary to the War Cabinet,[51] 'when he was asked to expound to those present including the Prime Minister his situation and plans, and was to all intents and purposes dumb.'[52] So adverse in its effect on his relationship with the Prime Minister was Wavell's failure to communicate that Joan Bright had asked him why he was always so tongue-tied. The response, from someone who loved to declaim poetry, was surprising: his shyness dated, he said, from his childhood, when his mother used to send for him from the nursery to be shown off to the assembled adults. Asked to say something, he found himself ter-rified of opening his mouth.[53]

Churchill did however see the merits of another Anglo-American Conference which would include a reassessment of the India Command. He christened the conference 'Trident', and it was scheduled to last a fort-night. For medical reasons the Prime Minister could not fly at the height required by a bomber, and sea-planes could not take the northern route until late May because of ice, so the journey to the United States was to be made by sea.

On Wednesday 5 May a delegation which included the Prime Minister, the Chiefs of Staff and the Indian Cs-in-C – Wavell, Somerville and Peirse – sailed from the Clyde aboard the passenger-liner *Queen Mary*, which had been converted into a troopship.[54] As Churchill noted, he had summoned the Commanders-in-Chief, India because he was sure that 'our American friends would be very anxious that we should do everything possible – and even impossible – in the way of immediate operations from India.'[55] Churchill was recovering from pneumonia, but throughout the journey he prepared papers and held discussions, mainly in his cabin. His remarks about Arakan in what he called his 'lengthy paper' on Indian and Far Eastern affairs made Wavell 'furious'. Brooke noted 'that Archie was indig-nant and I had to pacify him' – no easy task, for Wavell had taken Churchill's comments, which included such expressions as 'complete fail-ure' and 'deep disgrace', far more to heart than Brooke realized. He even told Brooke that he felt he must resign since the PM had lost confidence in him, and intended to write to Churchill to that effect. Brooke advised him against this: if he himself, he said, were 'to take offence when abused by Winston [since becoming CIGS] and given to understand that he had no confidence in me, I should have to resign at least once every day! But . . . I never felt that any such resignations were likely to have the least effect in reforming Winston's wicked ways!'[56] Later Wavell made his complaint to Churchill in person; Churchill immediately amended the offending sec-tion of the paper, thereby drawing even more attention to his remarks.[57] Wavell was also annoyed that Churchill should question the loyalty of the Indian Army: 'He accused me of creating a Frankenstein by putting modern weapons in the hands of sepoys, spoke of 1857, and was really almost childish about it.'[58] Those seated next to Wavell at dinner on this outward journey found his mood more taciturn than usual. 'It was awful!' recollected a young WRNS officer, Sheila MacLeod, who was working in the cipher unit. 'He sat for the entire meal without saying a word'.[59] The *Queen Mary* arrived in New York on 11 May in mist and rain that obscured the famous skyline, and the British party travelled on to Washington by special train.

At a private lunch with Roosevelt in Washington on 14 May, Churchill again criticized the direction of Arakan, and there was an unfortunate exchange over how air communications with China might be established through Burma and Assam. As Air Chief Marshal Sir William Elliot, Director of Plans at the Air Ministry, recalled the occasion, 'Wavell was quite at his worst, making the most heavy weather, in its most literal sense, about monsoons, floods and, finally, mosquitoes. This counsel of desperate despair was delivered in a dismal monologue with a dead-pan face. It was finally brought to a halt by the American General Bill Somervell, who, in withering tones, said, "And do you suppose we don't have mosquitoes in the Pacific?" '[60] Brooke too noted the general feeling of hopelessness with regard to Burma, and that Stilwell had vitiated relations between the British and Americans in South Asia.[61] In Stilwell's summary of the Washington conference he vented his long-felt frustration that all 'Bumble' Wavell ever saw were the difficulties: 'With Wavell in command, failure was inevitable; he had nothing to offer at any meeting except protestations that the thing was impossible, hopeless, impractical.'[62] In ignorance, no doubt, of such collective disapproval, Wavell spent some of his free time wandering through the Mellon Art Gallery, enjoying some 'wonderful' Rembrandts and other works. 'I fell rather in love with a little picture, by I think Bellini, called *The Feast of the Gods* in which the Gods and Goddesses had obviously done themselves well and were getting down to some slightly bibulous petting.'[63]

Once the 'Trident' conference was concluded, Churchill proposed to go to North Africa for further discussions on Anglo-American operations in the Mediterranean. Wavell was not included in the party, but ordered instead to fly back to London and wait there to discuss the set-up of the India Command on Churchill's return. 'I sensed that there was something working in the PM's mind which he was not prepared to discuss or mention to me at present. Alan Brooke swore that he did not know in the least what was in the PM's head.'[64] As Churchill journeyed onward, the question of Wavell's future did come up in conversation. According to Brooke, Churchill was trying to determine whether Wavell still had enough 'drive and energy' to carry on with his job, and was considering restricting the Commander-in-Chief, India to command of India alone. As an alternative, Brooke suggested that perhaps Wavell might be suitable as Governor-General of Australia. Churchill liked the idea enough to wire home about it, and mentioned it to the Australian Prime Minister, John Curtin.

While Wavell was still in Washington, but with his mind on his command in India, he composed an updated version of Kipling's 'Mandalay':

> By the old Moulmein pagoda, at the corner of my map,
> There's no Burma girl a-waiting, but a nasty little Jap;
> Yet the cipher wires are humming and the Chiefs of Staff they say:
> 'Get you back, you British soldier, get you back to Mandalay.'
>
>> Get you back to Mandalay,
>> Where mosquitoes swarm in May
>> And the Jap comes up through jungle
>> Like a tiger after prey.
>
> The anopheles* is buzzing, and his bite is swift, and keen,
> The rain pours down in torrents, and the jungle's thick and green,
> And the way back into Burma is a long and weary way
> For there ain't no busses running from Assam to Mandalay.
>
>> On the road to Mandalay,
>> Where the flying Zeros play
>> And the Jap comes up through jungle
>> Like a tiger after prey
>
> Ship some graders east of Suez and lots more trucks and jeeps,
> Let us have a few swift Spitfires and some transport planes for keeps,
> For at Washington we're learning what the weary Planner tells,
> That when Chiang-Kai Shek's a-calling, he'll never heed nought else.
>
>> But the ways to Mandalay
>> Where the Burma Road once lay,
>> Can't you hear Chungking a calling
>> For Rangoon and Mandalay.
>
> Well, we'll do our best to get there – and the Jap will do his worst –
> And whatever else may happen, we are bound to raise a thirst;
> But I wonder, how I wonder, whether Chiang-Kai Shek will play;
> Will his troops come up like thunder out of China cross the way?
>
>> On the road to Mandalay
>> Where the flying Zeros play
>> And the Jap comes up through jungle,
>> Like a tiger after prey.[65]

---

* Mosquitoes, carrying malaria parasite

IV
FROM SOLDIER TO STATESMAN

17

Designated Viceroy, 1943

> Lord help the next Viceroy whoever he is, he will be expected to do
> something drastic or dramatic.   A.P. Wavell[1]

A S THE HISTORIAN Ronald Lewin has so aptly related, finding a successor to Lord Linlithgow as Viceroy of India had much in common
with the caucus-race in *Alice in Wonderland*: 'There was no "One, two,
three and away!" but they began running when they liked, and left off
when they liked, so that it was not easy to know when the race was over.'[2]
Nor indeed who would win. Discussions had begun in the summer of
1942, when several names were canvassed. By the autumn the favourites
were Sir John Anderson, former Governor of Bengal and Lord President
of the Council in the British Government,[3] and Lord Cranborne,
Secretary of State for the Colonies. There was also talk of the return of
Lord Halifax, Viceroy from 1929 to 1931; Stafford Cripps's name had been
mentioned, as had that of the King's cousin Rear-Admiral Louis
Mountbatten.[4] After Cranborne turned the position down, Linlithgow was
asked to stay on for another six months, and discussions were not resumed
until 1943. By now the most obvious candidate and sometime favourite of
Churchill was Anthony Eden. Mountbatten's name was mentioned again,
as was Sir Miles Lampson's. As Commander-in-Chief in India, Wavell was
of course fully aware of the search, but he was not privy to the discussions
which began again in earnest in May. He did know that the short list now
included Oliver Lyttelton, because the only time he talked of the matter
directly with Churchill, on the outward journey to Washington, the Prime
Minister had indicated his feeling that Eden could not be spared, and his
inclination towards Lyttelton, currently Minister of Production and a
member of the War Cabinet.[5]

While waiting in London for Churchill's return, Wavell stayed with
Chips Channon, who had 'frenziedly rushed home to make arrangements'
when he knew the 'FM' was back in town. Over the next fortnight he

spent his time at the War Office and going to lunches and dinners, often organized by Channon, who combined Wavell's old friends and colleagues with other people he believed would interest and amuse him, like Mrs George Bambridge, Rudyard Kipling's daughter Elsie. Wavell dined frequently at the Naval and Military Club, Pratt's and Buck's Club, where Channon was a member, and at the Athenaeum. Rupert Hart-Davis, who had come to Wavell's defence earlier in the year over his poetry anthology, now in production, was able to advise on such niceties as how his name should be printed on the jacket. 'One day, while we were lunching at The Rag [the Army and Navy], I told Wavell we should have to decide what to put on the title-page – either A.P. Wavell (as in his Life of Allenby) or Field Marshal Sir Archibald Wavell, or some combination of the two. He thought in silence for a little while and then said very simply: "Everyone calls me Archie. Perhaps we ought to put that."' When Hart-Davis suggested it might look a little 'frivolous', they decided on 'A.P. Wavell', with his 'full dignities and initials' afterwards in brackets.[6]

Wavell also relaxed in the company of Leo Amery, Secretary of State for India and Burma. As a long-time political colleague of the Prime Minister he had sufficient experience of Churchill's personality to be able to sympathize with Wavell's frequent feelings of discomfort. Over dinner at the end of May, Wavell described to Amery how 'unfriendly' he considered Churchill had been, with 'no attempt to discuss the Arakan campaign'. Having talked over events in Washington, the two men turned to poetry. It amused Amery to note that Wavell knew nothing of George Meredith except 'Love in a Valley', 'so I introduced him to "The Thrush in February" and to "The Lark Ascending". I also inflicted my "Ulysses" and "Days of Fresh Air" on him before walking him back to Chips' house.'[7] Wavell was aware how long-winded Amery could be in his own political representations, but in the years to come he benefited from both his friendship and his hospitality. Amery likewise acknowledged that Wavell's 'personal attachments had a rare depth and sincerity and his loyalty to those who had earned his friendship was unshakeable'.[8]

Amery had also been informed by Churchill that he, Brooke and Ismay 'had come to the conclusion that Wavell had aged and was not up to the E. Asia command' and were thinking of appointing him Governor-General of Australia. But Amery believed it would be better to keep Wavell as Supreme Commander, and bring back Auchinleck as Commander-in-Chief in India.[9] Attlee feared the Americans might consider the appointment of Wavell as Governor-General in Australia an attempt to keep 'a military eye' on MacArthur.[10] Curtin, when consulted, was reluctant to upset MacArthur and in any case preferred a 'Royal' replacement for the previously agreed designate, the Duke of Kent, who had been killed in a plane crash in 1941.[11]

At the end of May Wavell took Channon – still proud of the company of 'his new great friend'[12] – to stay with George Spencer Churchill at Northwick Park.[13] Channon had learned to know when 'the great soldier' grew bored, as he did at Northwick ('his face goes grey, and he doesn't speak and there are long silences'). Wavell had also confided enough about the difficult time he had had on the American journey, with Churchill's criticism of the Burma campaign, for Channon to deduce that while he liked 'Society, with a capital S' and was enjoying his stay in Belgrave Square, Wavell was fearful for his future, appearing at times, as Amery too had detected, both lonely and unhappy. Nevertheless, he was benefiting from the break. In early June he was with his sisters in Ringwood, describing himself in correspondence as having 'a busman's holiday' looking at soldiers at various military and air force establishments, and feeling 'fit to face any PM'.[14]

When Churchill returned, discussions about the next Viceroy resumed; the Prime Minister had 'promised to settle [the matter] before Whitsun'.[15] On 9 June, having rejected all previous contenders, in conversation with Amery, Churchill revealed his chosen candidate: Wavell. 'I could not help saying that he was certainly better than some, which Winston remarked was a striking instance of understatement.' On reflection, as Amery wrote in his diary, he saw the advantages: 'Wavell has certainly got a broader outlook and wider reading than most soldiers. He has had to handle a good many political relationships in the Middle East and has the advantage of having been on the Executive Council in India and knowing the personalities . . . It is something to have a decision and if it is an experiment, it is at any rate better than appointing some rather colourless mediocrity.' With some foresight, Amery was already thinking that Wavell might prove more 'radical' than most politicians, 'witness Allenby in Egypt.'[16] Until Linlithgow's agreement to the appointment could be obtained, Amery was obliged to keep the information to himself.

Precisely when Churchill decided on Wavell as the next Viceroy is not clear. According to Brooke, it was during their stay in Washington that the thought first entered his mind. As Brooke later noted against his diary entry of 20 May regarding Churchill's desire to replace Wavell in command of operations in Burma, 'it was this same day when he began to consider Wavell as a possible candidate for the Indian Viceroyalty which he was having serious difficulties in filling.'[17] There is no clue in Churchill's official history.

Until the morning of 9 June, despite his concerns about losing Eden, he was still pressing him to take the position. Later in the day, 'rather than disrupt the War Cabinet', as Eden surmised, by insisting that either he or Lyttelton should go, Churchill selected Wavell.[18] Wavell, not unnaturally, had a different idea of his future. With absolutely no idea that his name was being considered as a future Viceroy, he had been contemplating changes in the India Command, and even growing enthusiastic about the idea of a new joint Anglo-American South-East Asia Command. 'Without vanity' he considered himself 'the obvious choice' for Supreme Commander – while realizing that, 'for some reason', Churchill would not want to appoint him.[19]

Channon enjoyed his guest, but admitted that keeping him occupied was a challenge. When Wavell appeared to have 'absolutely no plans' for the Whit Bank Holiday, Channon recorded in his diary that he 'secretly rang up the Amerys and persuaded them to invite him for the weekend' to Bailiff's Court, near Climping in Sussex.[20] Wavell's own recollection was a little different. Amery, he said, had several times invited him to the house but he had always refused, 'so I thought I would propose myself for a night and then motor on to my sisters' as well as speaking at Winchester on Whit Monday. He and Amery drove down together, and Amery discussed Indian politics. Wavell, thinking that whatever his future held he would not be dealing with Indian politics, took only a 'languid, even somnolent' interest in the discussion,[21] but from his remarks Amery concluded that he was 'shrewd' and 'not illiberal'. Amery was also thinking of the loss of Wavell to the military direction of the war. 'If there is to be a supreme C-in-C South-East Asia . . . I don't know who except Wavell can fill that bill. He does not strike me as tired and it would be making a better use of him.' So concerned was Amery that despite his age – nearly seventy – he thought of proposing himself to Churchill as an alternative Viceroy so that Wavell could remain in uniform. In the evening the talk became more general and Amery taught Wavell Chinese Chequers, 'at which he showed no great strategical aptitude.'[22]

The following morning Amery told Wavell the decision on the new Viceroy had reached the 'semi-final stage'. Wavell asked no further questions because Amery 'did not sound inclined for discussion'.[23] At lunchtime there was a surprise telephone call from Churchill's secretary, informing Wavell that the Prime Minister would like him to dine at Downing Street that Monday night. The early afternoon was spent sunbathing, and only as he was driving to his sisters' at Ringwood did Wavell think it 'conceivable' that Churchill might offer him the Viceroyalty. Rapidly dismissing the idea, he bent his mind to the speech he was to give at Winchester. After tea, he, Nancy and Molly went to see Cranborne. As he relates in his journal, when Bobbety greeted him with congratulations, his immediate response was: 'What on earth for?' In the face of Wavell's evident ignorance, Cranborne dropped the subject. 'I have since realized,' Wavell wrote, 'that probably everyone in the room, except myself and my sisters, knew that the choice for Viceroy had fallen on me.'[24]

Returning to London after speaking at Winchester the following day, accompanied by his sisters, Wavell at last realized the likely reason for Churchill's urgent invitation to dinner. In his journal he is candid about his feelings. He had 'no taste for the cares of Governorship'; at the same time, he realized that it might be difficult to refuse the Viceroyalty 'as a war appointment'. Wavell's meeting with Churchill was fixed for 8.30 p.m. at 10 Downing Street. As he was ushered into the basement where Churchill normally dined during the war, he saw that the table was set for two. Churchill, who was 'very pleasant', lost no time in telling Wavell he was being requested to give up the position of Commander-in-Chief and assume that of Viceroy. After dinner Ismay joined them, and Wavell was able to send Queenie a telegram informing her of his new appointment; it ended, 'What a fate for an unambitious soldier.'[25] Two days later Queenie's response came; Wavell then wrote Churchill a formal acceptance.[26]

The news of Wavell's appointment was greeted with incredulity by some, favourably by others. Halifax did not hide his dissent at the appointment of a soldier. 'How your father would have spat,' he wrote to Curzon's daughter Baba. 'I think between ourselves W. is a bad choice, tantamount to saying: "We don't care a d—n about the political side."'[27] Wavell wrote immediately to Eden: 'What a surprise, and what a shock! I wish you had been able to take it . . . Well, well. Yours apprehensively, Archie Wavell.'[28] When the official announcement was made, congratulations came at once from his supporters. 'Its difficulties and complexities are manifest,' wrote Liddell Hart, 'but it is certainly a great honour, not only for you, but for the Army, and an historical event.'[29] Wavell's younger admirers, like Tom Bird, saw only the honour: 'A man who can look back on so many successful campaigns, on so many commands successfully organized and administered, who can claim to have reached the topmost peak in a Military Career, and who is then invited to be Viceroy of India, as he reviews all this, must feel a fine sense of achievement, a feeling of having "got somewhere".'[30] The Indian reaction was positive. Some Indian newspapermen 'sniffed' at the press briefing, but when Amery told Sir A. Ramaswami Mudaliar, in London representing India at the War Cabinet and on the Pacific War Council, he seemed genuinely delighted, stating that Wavell's talks to them were 'the one thing that made the [National] Defence Council worthwhile'. Mudaliar also observed that Wavell's manner, 'though taciturn, was informal and easy with Indians.'[31]

Wavell himself had mixed feelings. 'What a surprise,' he responded to Jackson's letter of congratulation, 'and not altogether welcome.'[32] 'Not at all what I expected or desired but there it is, one must do what the authorities think will help most,' he wrote to Leonie Lemartine.[33] Until Queenie arrived he stayed on with Channon, who veered between enjoyment of such a distinguished guest, and finding him '*un peu sur le dos*'.[34] But as Viceroy-Designate Wavell was now the King's representative and his contacts with the London social scene were not only considered questionable by Buckingham Palace, but caused a certain amount of comment in Government circles. Channon was annoyed by the criticism. 'Such is the jealousy of this world. I have surrounded this poor lonely man with affection, have literally made his London life, and now people gossip.'[35] When Ismay raised the issue with Wavell using Joan Bright as an intermediary, he remained unperturbed, stating mildly that he enjoyed the company of Channon and his intellectual friends.[36]

On 20 June Archibald Wavell ceased to be Commander-in-Chief. The soldier who had entered the army 42 years earlier had become a civilian. 'He is out of uniform,' noted Channon on 22 June, 'and today he wore my blue suit, and looked well in it, almost skittish. I lent him everything, shirt, socks and studs.'[37] Wavell's Farewell Order of the Day to the Indian Armed Forces reviewed the past two years: 'Although these dangers have not been entirely removed, they have been held in check and Indian soil has been preserved from enemy invasion.' He ended by thanking the armed forces for the 'loyal service' they had given under his command.[38] This was Wavell's last military broadcast. On 5 July Auchinleck broadcast his Order of the Day assuming command of the armed forces; Wavell, he said, had applied his 'unrivalled knowledge, experience and ability to the reorganization of India's forces so as to fit them for the task.'[39]

As Viceroy-Designate Wavell immediately became involved in determining how best to fulfil the role of Viceroy in wartime. Throughout June and early July, dinners and luncheons in his honour filled his calendar. Coincidentally, his second volume of Allenby's Life, covering Allenby's time in Egypt as Commander-in-Chief and High Commissioner and detailing his progressive support for Arab nationalism, was shortly due for publication. Amery, shown proofs of three extracts which were to appear in the Daily Telegraph, was left wondering whether Churchill 'would have been so keen about Wavell as Viceroy if he had realized how thoroughly Wavell backs up Allenby's policy of sympathy with Egyptian nationalism. I should not be at all surprised if Wavell went a long way in trying to find a solution to the Indian problem.'[40] On 14 July Queenie arrived in London with Felicity, to stay in a suite of rooms reserved for Wavell and his family at the Dorchester Hotel. With no time to rest, Queenie's first engagement as Vicereine-Designate was a party at 10 Downing Street. A week later Simon and Joan – expecting their first child – arrived 'in quite good trim'. Wavell and Queenie also lunched with the King and Queen; Wavell recalled that there was no ceremony, and King George expressed a desire that Wavell should keep his telegrams shorter than those of the outgoing Viceroy.

In recognition of his appointment as Viceroy Wavell was created a viscount in the King's Birthday Honours List, taking the name Viscount Wavell of Cyrenaica and Winchester in the county of Southampton. His cousin Edward was overwhelmed by this further distinction: 'Upon hearing the announcement by the BBC in the 7 o'clock news this morning my first reaction was to say, "Lord, now lettest thou thy servant depart in peace." You have won an hereditary title for the Wavell family, the fulfilment of a hope that I have cherished for many years.'[41] On Wavell's behalf Edward had already been in touch with the College of Arms about a suitable coat of arms. The design eventually settled upon – costing £130 – was both ancient and modern: a scholar of Winchester and a soldier of The Black Watch supported on either side a shield displaying six merlettes and three fleur-de-lys for Normandy and France, neatly alluding to both the family's ancient de Vauville origins in the Cherbourg peninsula and Wavell's service at Ypres, with the family motto 'Pro Patria' beneath.[42] On a hot summer's day at the end of July, surrounded by his family and friends, Archibald Percival Wavell, aged 60, took his seat in the House of Lords. As described by Channon, 'Wavell was donning his ermine and velvet, and Lady Oxford – widow of former Prime Minister H.H. Asquith – rushed up to me in her dominating manner. "Will you introduce me to Wavell. He is the Empire's hero." And so I led her up to the Field Marshal, who was trying to get into his robes. He smiled and chatted with her for a minute, rather taken aback by her onslaught, and she was enchanted.'[43]

In early August Wavell and Queenie went to stay with his old friend Harry Dalmeny, sixth Earl of Rosebery, and his wife Eva at their magnificent home Dalmeny, on the outskirts of Edinburgh. The pre-eminent Shakespeare scholar John Dover Wilson, who lived near by, was invited to dinner: 'I dare to think that Wavell had especially asked to meet me, for the talk was mostly about Shakespeare.' Mostly, but not exclusively: the war featured too, especially Stalin's insistence on opening a second front. Wavell recited his poem 'No Second Front', which according to Dover Wilson – who initially thought it was by A.P. Herbert – left them all in 'fits of laughter'.[44] He gave Wavell a copy of his latest book, *The Fortunes of Falstaff*; Wavell enjoyed it 'thoroughly' and later returned the compliment by sending Dover Wilson his anthology and his Life of Allenby.[45]

By the time Wavell returned to London he had done some serious thinking about his new assignment, and decided that the deteriorating food situation in Bengal, where the failure of the 1942 winter rice crop was leading to famine, must be a priority. A 'Note' dated 20 August also outlined his somewhat revolutionary proposal for holding a meeting of leading Indian politicians, including those members of the Congress Party who were still in detention following their civil agitation in 1942. But as Amery wisely realized, his proposals 'would not have a ghost of a chance' at an ordinary Cabinet meeting, where there was still a general reluctance to contemplate Britain's departure from India, and he suggested instead a revival of the India Sub-Committee, with a few additional select members.

The last weeks of Wavell's time in England were so crammed with a 'hectic' round of lunches, dinners, interviews and discussions that he felt he would not get 'much peace' until he left. On 14 September he dined with Brooke, who briefed him on the Quebec Conference held in mid August at which Churchill and Roosevelt had agreed their future strategy for Europe and upon the creation of a new South-East Asia Command (SEAC). 'He was as delightful and charming as usual, but I do not think he spoke more than 100 words in the whole evening,' noted Brooke.[46] Of particular relevance to Wavell was the decision to appoint Mountbatten as Supreme Allied Commander. Mountbatten, whose ship HMS *Kelly* had gone down during the evacuation from Crete, had recently been a member of the Chiefs of Staff Committee. As Churchill had enthusiastically announced, he 'knows the whole of our war story from the centre.'[47] Mountbatten's youth (he was 43) and 'aristocratic playboy' reputation meant the appointment was controversial, but he was seen as an injection of fresh blood into a group of what were otherwise considered to be tired war leaders. As Eden's private secretary Oliver Harvey noted, the combination of Mountbatten and Wingate, who was preparing another Chindit operation, was 'at least a refreshing contrast to Wavell–Auchinleck.'[48]

Wavell remained preoccupied with his India policy, his draft of which had already undergone several revisions. When finally it was ready to be put up to the India Sub-Committee, which met for the first time on 17 September presided over by Attlee, it contained three principal clauses: a

Coalition Government of party leaders should be established at the Centre 'working under the existing Constitution and willing to support the war effort'; the method of establishing such a Government should be by inviting 'selected political leaders' to a conference; and the Viceroy should decide when such a move was desirable. All that was agreed at the first meeting was that Wavell should submit a revised draft. At the weekend he and Amery went to Kelvedon Hall, Channon's country home near Ongar, to work on his paper. They lunched on sandwiches and apples 'and oddments like baked beans' by the side of the swimming pool, and in the evening went through Wavell's paper 'and worked out some amendments which might improve it for his second draft.'[49]

Wavell managed to fit in other engagements. Two separate days were spent at Winchester, one to receive the Freedom of the City ('another long day'),[50] the other to be received 'ad portas' at his old school, which called for a speech in Latin in which he testified to his attachment to Winchester: '*Ille terrarum mihi praeter omnis Angulus ridet* [That spot smiles more for me than any other on earth].' One of the boys present, Geoffrey Howe, future Foreign Secretary, took note of Wavell's allusion to '*fulmina Hitleris* [thunderbolts of Hitler]', and used the expression to caption one of the nine snapshots he took that day.[51] Wavell was also sworn of the Privy Council, which entailed another visit to Buckingham Palace and lunch with the King and Queen. 'So ends a pretty strenuous week.'[52]

As the date for Wavell's departure to India drew closer, there was still no decision on the policy he was to adopt. His initial proposal for a conference of Indian leaders had been diluted into no more than a vague recommendation to try to break the political deadlock by approaching the political leaders, prior to which he must discuss the matter with the War Cabinet. He was frustrated by the lack of enthusiasm with regard to India, and revealed as much at a reception given by the East India Society. When Amery spoke with caution, saying that the sagacious elephant always tests the strength of a bridge before crossing it, Wavell riposted: 'This sagacious elephant has first to find a bridge!'[53] He was also battling for food for Bengal. But in this as with his political proposals, he found the Cabinet was not taking the situation as seriously as he believed they should; all was focused on events in Europe, where the tide was at last turning against Hitler: 'Apparently it is more important to save the Greeks and liberated countries from starvation than the Indians and there is reluctance either to provide shipping or to reduce stocks in this country.'[54]

These conflicting views collided at the Government Dinner in Wavell's honour hosted by Amery as Secretary of State for India on 6 October.

'When it came to speeches, Winston got up and after compliments to Wavell, made a pure die-hard speech, glorifying our past record in India, which of course I entirely agreed with, but without a word about the future except to say in effect that he believed his opposition to Indian self-government which was unchanged would be proved right.' When it was Wavell's turn, after complimenting Churchill as a remarkable war leader 'he sailed straight in with a passage of a mountaineering metaphor making it quite clear that the point we had reached, while a very fine climb indeed, was not the summit and that we must press on to the summit in spite of difficulties and risks.' As Amery noted, the speech was a direct challenge to Churchill's position, and it infuriated him. So diametrically opposed were the policies of Prime Minister and future Viceroy that it was decided it would be best if neither speech was published.[55] The following evening the Cabinet met to discuss Wavell's India proposals. Amery reported Wavell as arguing 'very well' and 'persuasively', yet the outcome was disappointing.[56]

Wavell's 'farewell' talk with Churchill took place on 8 October. As he recorded, Churchill 'produced a formula for a directive which was mostly meaningless, e.g. it exhorted me to get on with the war, to improve the lot of the Indian, to make peace between Moslem [sic] and Hindu, and indicated right at the end that political progress during the war was not barred.'[57] On reading the paper, Amery admitted that it was a 'curious document . . . most of it is pretty irrelevant but none of it harmful', but he thought there were 'sufficient passages' in it to give Wavell 'a free hand to do or recommend what he thinks right.' He realized Wavell was not pleased, and advised him to regard it as 'a gentle breeze to waft him on his way and accept it from Winston without cavil.'[58] Churchill was not prepared to go further: over his dead body, he said, would any approach to Gandhi take place. Wavell, though no politician, was astute enough to realize that Churchill was fearful lest any new initiative might split the Conservative Party, 'so is determined to block it while he is in power.' The two men parted 'on an outwardly friendly note', yet Wavell again observed that Churchill 'has always really disliked me and mistrusted me, and probably now regrets having appointed me.'[59]

Just before the Wavells left, Chips Channon hosted a party in their honour for more than a hundred people. 'For three hours', he noted, 'people poured in; young and old, gay and great, tight and sober; and soon the blue dining-room with its flickering candles was crowded . . . Freya Stark, dressed like an Eskimo in a white fur coat; Eve Curie, chic and military, in French uniform . . . Harold Nicolson in a corner with Lady Wavell . . . and ever so many more.'[60] It was the first – and only – time Queenie and Joan Bright met. Lady Wavell thanked Miss Bright for obtaining silver for Joanie when she married Simon Astley, but also showed her displeasure at Joan's familiar habit of writing to her husband as 'darling Archie'.[61] Even so, the letters continued. 'We've had some good talks and times since I've been home,' Wavell wrote on the morning of their departure. 'Thank you so much. Write and tell me your news and I will give you the lowdown on a Viceroy's life.'[62] On 11 October, nearly five months after leaving India as Commander-in-Chief, Wavell set off on the return journey. 'A distinguished galaxy' of friends and relations, policemen and cabinet ministers arrived at Airways House in Croydon to see the Viceroy-Designate and his family off[63] – except for Joanie, who remained in England to have her baby. It was unfortunate that after more than three months' preparation, Wavell left having concluded that 'the Cabinet is not honest in its expressed desire to make progress in India; and that very few of them have any foresight or political courage.'[64]

In India, the return of the former Commander-in-Chief as Viceroy was awaited with anticipation. 'The new Viceroy arrives in a few days' time,' wrote Captain John Irwin, ADC to the acting Governor of Bengal, Sir Thomas Rutherford (who had recently replaced Herbert, fatally ill with malignant cancer). 'Nobody knows quite what to make of Wavell. He has always been very reserved as a person but there's no doubt that he's more imaginative, less staid and "wooden" than Linlithgow. Indians are hoping that he will adopt a more courageous policy towards Congress and that he will do his best to find a solution to the present deadlock.'[65]

Wavell was already making his mark, insisting on a reduction in the pomp attending his arrival. 'A very serious discussion arose,' recalled a young Indian, Vidya Shankar, Deputy Secretary in the Home Department, 'over the ceremonial of his arrival prior to his assumption of office and subsequent ceremonial of assumption of office itself. The general approach of those who were in charge was to make him come to Delhi by a special train, whereas he preferred to come by air to the nearest place, thus reducing ceremonial to the simplicity of a drive to Delhi.'[66] The outgoing Viceroy greeted the incoming Viceroy at the top of the great flight of steps in front of the Viceregal residence, and the two men shook hands. As Wavell recollected, Linlithgow, tired after more than seven years in office, expressed relief: 'I do not think I have ever been so glad to see anyone.'[67] The night before Wavell's installation the Viceroys past and future exchanged views, as was customary. Linlithgow spoke frankly. 'He said we must be careful that we did not get into a position when we could not get out of India because of the chaos it would cause but were unable to control and administer it if we remained.'[68] Linlithgow and his family then departed, leaving Wavell in charge of India, still at war but yearning for independence from British rule.

Wavell was officially installed as Viceroy on 20 October in a majestic ceremony that passed off 'without a hitch.'[69] For her future role as Vicereine Queenie had been lent a magnificent tiara by Lord and Lady Denman, friends with whom more than thirty years earlier she had stayed in Australia.[70] As related by Peter Coats, 'H.E. wore his grey frock coat with an air . . . We, the staff, processed and bowed and deployed and bowed and processed once more, catching our spurs in the heavily embroidered carpet.'[71] Instead of divisions and brigades, Wavell now had under his authority approximately 300 million Indians in the eleven British provinces of India. Pending any alteration to the political system, as provided for by the 1935 Government of India Act, each province ran along quasi-constitutional lines with an Indian Premier responsible to a provincial legislature and a British Governor intended to act as much as possible as a figurehead. In cases where the Governor believed it necessary, Section 93 of the act entitled him to assume fuller powers. In 1939 more than half the premiers had resigned in protest when Linlithgow committed India to war without consulting the provincial ministries. Alternative ministries had been formed in some provinces, but when Wavell took over, five remained under the direct authority of their Governors under Section 93: Bombay, Madras, United Provinces, Bihar, and the Central Provinces. The remainder – Bengal, Punjab, Sind, Assam, Orissa, and the North-West Frontier Province – all had either anti-Congress or Muslim League ministries who were prepared to cooperate with the British. Of additional concern were the Indians who lived in the 562-plus 'princely states' ruled by the maharajas and nawabs holding one-third of India's land, with an estimated population of over 93 million.[72] As Viceroy, Wavell had to retain friendly relations with them at a time of political fluidity. While the rulers remained free to conduct affairs within their states as they wished, they owed paramount allegiance to the British Crown.

The British presence had remained proportionately, surprisingly, small: the Indian Civil Service had a complement of 1,200 men of whom 500 were British, 700 Indians. The Indian Political Service, previously known as the Foreign and Political Department of the Government of India, was responsible for the princely states; it had just 126 political officers, of whom 15 were Indian.[73] Wavell had a personal bodyguard, known as 'The Viceroy's Bodyguard'; his substantial staff were his 'employees', and he approved all appointments personally. He also relied upon his Indian Civil Service officers, of whom his Private Secretary, Evan Jenkins, had twenty years' experience in India;[74] when he later became Governor of the Punjab, his place was taken by George Abell, a member of the ICS since 1928.[75] Wavell had been a presence in Delhi since 1941, yet as Abell noted, 'apart from an occasional glimpse of a sphinx-like Commander-in-Chief' little was known of the new Viceroy.[76] Tom Bird returned to his regiment, but Peter Coats remained as his Comptroller and for a short time Pamela's husband Francis Humphrys was Wavell's Military Secretary.

The Wavells' home for the next few years was the magnificent sandstone and marble Viceregal Lodge. The Commander-in-Chief had a staff of more than a hundred; more than a thousand looked after the Viceroy. As Tom Bird noted, 'there was one man who did nothing except clean chickens.'[77] According to Joanie, it took another a year to change the blotting paper on the blotters throughout the residence.[78] A staff of a thousand notwithstanding, the formal aspects of a wartime viceroy's life were somewhat circumscribed as compared with pre-war years – Peter Coats, for example, had to use the available funds to entertain the maximum number of people – and Wavell was as ready to cut down on ceremonial on other occasions as he had been at his investiture. The State Rooms were but rarely used. Lunch was served in the garden, dinner in the 'small dining room'. When he had no engagements, Wavell would sit with his family after dinner and listen to the news on the radio or read the newspapers.[79]

Administratively, meetings of the Executive Council, held in a large room at Viceregal Lodge, were an even more important part of Wavell's routine than when he was Commander-in-Chief. Auchinleck now occupied that seat, with Wavell in the top chair where Linlithgow and so many distinguished predecessors had sat. Among the many men Wavell had inherited from Linlithgow's time was the Finance Member, Sir Jeremy Raisman, whom he found 'good and sound'.[80] Except for Raisman, the Home Member, and the Member for War Transport, the remaining ten were 'hand-picked' Indians.[82] Those who had believed that, as a former soldier, Wavell would leave administration to the bureaucrats found themselves mistaken. 'His bold and clear handwriting was in itself an ornament on the files which went up to him. His orders were short and crisp and were not liable to any misunderstanding,' noted Shankar. 'While he did not mince matters, there was no mistaking the fact that it was he who held the strings in his hands.'[83]

Pursuing the political initiative was of pressing urgency, but the first crisis with which Wavell had to deal as Viceroy was the famine in Bengal, which had already taken an estimated million lives. 'One cannot walk in the streets of Calcutta at any time of the day without coming across dead bodies, and the districts outside Calcutta are even worse.'[84] Within a week of his investiture Wavell and Queenie were flying to Bengal to see the situation for themselves. As Wavell noted to Amery, the number of destitutes who had poured into Calcutta to beg for food was 'loosely' put at 150,000. The sanitary conditions were 'shocking', and 'one has to walk warily and use an electric torch in the blackout.'[85] Wavell had meetings with Bengali ministers, impressing on them that 'they must get the destitutes out of Calcutta into camps, which should have been done long ago.'[86] Wavell was left wondering whether his visit had done any good, but it had a positive ripple effect, and even featured in the pages of Indian schoolboys' comics.[87] As noted by George Abell, it was not only an administrative success, 'it also gave him a very good start with Indian public opinion which wrote him down as active and sympathetic.'[88] Wavell immediately ordered a shake-up in the delivery of relief food supplies, and a young Indian officer on duty in Sind later remembered how swiftly his battalion was transferred to Bengal to assist with distribution.[89] In London, Amery was pleased to hear of this prompt action, advising Wavell that the Indian famine situation 'had stirred people here deeply.'[90]

Towards the end of November Wavell hosted a 'Governors' Conference' – the first, he recorded, since 1930 – for the governors of the eleven provinces, many of whom were or became personal friends. With famine an omnipresent threat, their discussions focused initially on food and statutory price control, broadening over the following days to include post-war work and general comments on the political situation. His governors, like Wavell, were beginning to realize the danger of trying to ignore India's political future until after the war: the Indian people were expecting change. No sooner was the conference over than Wavell went on tour to the Punjab and the North-West Frontier Province, where he had spent so much time as a subaltern.

Surprisingly – for their personalities were very different – in the early stages of Wavell's time as Viceroy he developed a good relationship with Mountbatten, who had arrived in India to take up his new position as Supreme Allied Commander before Wavell's departure from England. Wavell had not taken part in the recent 'Sextant' conference in Cairo but Mountbatten proved a useful informant, although he was 'more tired and depressed than I have seen him. He had had a difficult time at Cairo with PM and with Generalissimo and they had not got much settled. MB said there was little mention of India and her economics.' Mountbatten had for that reason chosen not to show Churchill the memorandum Wavell had prepared on India's capacity to assist the war effort; when he did mention India's political problems, apparently 'the PM blew up and damned not only him but me and all my works.'[91] Wavell enjoyed their exchange of views on the wartime situation. His mockery of his own failure to enjoy the 'sentimental-thriller' *Casablanca* illustrated the gulf between them, however: 'He is still youthful and I am afraid received the impression that I was a cheerless kill-joy not to like [such] films.'[92]

In early December Wavell and Queenie – now referred to by Wavell as 'Her Ex.' – heard that their first grandchild, a girl, had been born in England. Wavell at once put into verse some questions he wanted to ask her: 'What of your eyes, Diana Jane? / Are they deep-sea blue, like the deep blue main, / Or soft and grey, as an April rain, / Or pussy-green, with the cat's disdain?'[93] Joanie, who shared some of her father's talent, responded on behalf of her baby daughter: 'My eyes have stayed blue grandfather dear / They're set wide apart, they're deep and clear / They twinkle and wink I've already found / I shall use my eyes when men are around.'[94]

Wavell was to discover that the next few years were to be harder work than he ever could have imagined. After less than two months he concluded that the Viceroy's job was too big for one man, and would get him down. 'There is too much routine work, interviews etc., to give the Viceroy time for constructive thinking or the relaxation which is essential to a lazy man like myself,' he noted in his journal on 10 December. 'Today was an awful day: interviews, conferences, papers, visitors to all meals etc. literally from 10 a.m. to 10 p.m.; and my only relaxation was a ride 7.30–8.30 a.m.'[95] The same thoughts stayed with him over the next few days, but he had an inbuilt safety mechanism: 'However no one has as yet succeeded in working me beyond a certain limit. After that I do crossword puzzles or play golf.'[96] 'I really have three jobs,' he wrote to Freya Stark, 'each of them pretty well a full-time job – Prime Minister (and Foreign Minister) for a country about the size of Europe; representative Head of the State for constitutional functions (e.g., dealing with all mercy petitions from sentences of death), social performances etc: and Crown Representative for dealings with all the Indian States and their rulers. Also I am the equivalent of a Minister of State for dealings with the S.E. Asia command. It would be bad enough if things were smooth; but we have a food problem, and a coal crisis, and a political deadlock, and an inflationary threat – all in a very under-administered country.'[97] Yet, for all he felt that he had very little time for his private life, it was while he was Viceroy that Wavell began to write a journal which eventually ran to eleven volumes.[98]

Wavell might no longer travel to visit battle-fronts, but he made a point of getting to know the terrain under his authority. After staying with the Wavells, Somerville reported to Joan Bright that Archie was doing 'damn well', and described how, during his visit to north-west India, he rode through the villages dressed as a soldier and not a Viceroy.[99] Whenever possible Queenie went with him. She kept up what had become known as the 'Wavell Canteens' for the benefit of servicemen, working in them herself until the weight of convention forced her to stop. She was also Patroness-in-Chief of the Association for Moral and Social Hygiene, which was attempting to counter the prevalence of the brothels which had grown up near military bases and where venereal disease was rampant.[100]

In mid December the Viceregal party left for a ten-day tour of Orissa in the east, travelling onwards to Assam and Bengal. Wavell found it depressing: 'It was very strenuous and we had little or no let-up.' Sir John Herbert had succumbed to cancer on 11 December and a week later, in Calcutta, Wavell attended his memorial service. Lady Mary, whose 'entente' with Wavell had not passed unnoticed by his ADCs, went to Darjeeling to wait for a boat to take her back to Britain. Wavell had to give his first important public speech as Viceroy to the Chambers of Commerce in Calcutta. As usual he had not prepared it in advance, but, impromptu as it was, it examined the main issues affecting people's lives: food, coal, inflation, and post-war reconstruction. He refrained from talking about the political situation, however – not because it was not 'constantly in my mind; not because I have not the fullest sympathy with the aspirations of India towards Self-Government; not because I consider political progress impossible during the course of the war . . . but because I do not believe that I can make their solution any easier by talking about them just at present.'[101]

At the end of the year Bernard Fergusson arrived to stay with the Wavells in Delhi. Wavell's affection for his first ADC remained unchanged. Nearly a decade after their initial meeting, he described him to Freya Stark with some warmth: 'a good soldier, a good writer of prose and humorous verse, a lover of poetry, with a touch of mysticism (only a touch) and a strong stuffing of Presbyterianism.'[102] The two men discussed Fergusson's experiences with the Chindits, and especially Wingate, who, Fergusson thought, 'was, and is, extremely difficult – impossible at times.'[103] Wavell also enjoyed sharing with him an accolade he had received on his assumption of the Viceroyalty from an 'obsequious' Indian, who congratulated him for having now reached 'quite a respectable position'.[104] Looking back on 1943, Wavell characterized it as a 'hectic, and surprising, year.' The appointment as Viceroy had brought him prestige far beyond his expectations, yet he continued to brood about Churchill's criticism of the Arakan operations, which he believed the Prime Minister had misrepresented 'partly because he has never liked me'. As for the future, he was already beginning to realize that he should perhaps have secured more concrete guidelines from Churchill before accepting the Viceroyalty: 'I accepted the Viceroyalty in the spirit of a military appointment – one goes where one is told in time of war without making conditions or asking questions. I think I ought to have treated it in a political spirit and found out what the policy to India really was to be.'[105] Among those upon whom he felt he could depend, he was particularly heartened by Auchinleck's presence. 'It is a great comfort to have your help and advice. 1944 is going to be a difficult but interesting year.'[106]

18

Wartime Viceroy, 1944–5

Oh dear Chief, may you not be too drowned in politics and wickedness!

Freya Stark[1]

WAVELL WAS NOT looking forward to 1944 and its problems, the same that had preoccupied him since his assumption of the Viceroyalty three months earlier. Neither the situation in Burma nor that in India was likely to improve. To his disappointment, his suggestion that an Indian – Sir Ramaswami Mudaliar – be appointed Finance Member of the Executive Council in succession to Sir Jeremy Raisman, due to retire in April 1944, was 'torpedoed' by Churchill and Amery: instead, 'HMG' wished to appoint a Canadian.[2] Wavell also realized that without support from Whitehall he was limited in the actions he could take, and rather to his surprise he found that the lines between London and the Viceroy's office had all but fallen silent. A telegram from Churchill at the end of January was, he noted, his first communication from the Prime Minister since leaving England in October. During those early months Wavell had remained 'supremely anxious' about imports of food. As he wrote to Ismay, 'unless I can get a definite guarantee of a minimum of a million tons of grain imports in 1944, I do not think I can control the price or distribution of food throughout India, confidence which we are beginning to restore will disappear again, and all the progress we have made in these last months will be lost.' He proceeded to warn that a far worse and more widespread disaster than the previous year's could develop, with 'incalculable effects in loss of human life, on the whole political situation out here, and on our reputation at home and abroad. Please do impress on the Prime Minister that this is a really serious matter, and is the whole keystone of the present position in India.'[3] Ismay replied that the inability of HMG to give anything like adequate help was not due to lack of sympathy but lack of resources.[4]

On 17 February Wavell addressed the Central Legislature, sitting in Delhi for its Budget session.[5] As *The Times*'s correspondent in Delhi noted, the speech was being awaited in political circles 'with much interest but not, on the whole, with any great hopes that the Viceroy will be able to offer the new initiative which the Hindu nationalist and Moslem [sic] spokesmen have been demanding as a means of ending the political impasse.'[6] Adopting a familiar theme, Wavell began by observing that the post-war world for India would be one 'of the greatest opportunities and great dangers in which she has an outstanding role to play.' He described the subcontinent as a natural unit, and made his own feelings on India's future clear: 'What arrangements you decide to make for the two great communities and certain other important minorities as well as the Indian states, to live within that unit and make the best use of its wealth and opportunities is for Indians to decide.' Referring to Stafford Cripps's 'bold and generous' offer of 1942, he said that the offer of full self-government after the war under a new constitution was still open to those who had 'a genuine desire to further the prosecution of the war and the welfare of India.' Most importantly, in the knowledge that his speech would reach a wider audience beyond the Legislature, Wavell affirmed that at present there was no question of releasing those Indians whom the British held responsible for instigating the Quit India movement in August 1942 until he was convinced that their policy of non-cooperation and even obstruction had been withdrawn – 'not in sackcloth and ashes, that helps no one – but in recognition of a mistaken and unprofitable policy.' A coalition government by Indians for Indians was not an impossible ideal. They had, he said, 'come a long way together up the steep and difficult mountain at the summit of which was complete Indian self-government.' They were almost in sight of the top, but, as in the ascent of a mountain, 'the final cliffs were the steepest and most baffling of all.'[7] Wavell had been true to his principles, and spoken 'frankly' and 'bluntly as a soldier', but the reaction from both the Congress Party and the Muslim League was less than enthusiastic. Mohammed Ali Jinnah was 'understood to have taken the view that if, as Wavell had said, India's constitutional future was for Indians to decide,' then there was no need for the Viceroy to offer any opinion about India's future political disposition.[8]

Outside official fora Wavell went on holding discussions with those Indians who appeared eager to go at least some distance to understand what the British might be able to offer. While visiting Madras and the Central Provinces he met Shri Rajagopalachari, a less radical Congress politician who had openly expressed the view that the real obstacle to India's freedom was no longer the British, but the differences between the Congress Party and the Muslim League.[9] During their discussions Wavell outlined his idea for a Council of 'All the Talents', men recognized as representing the best elements in India who would work out India's problems under the present constitution, paying attention not to communal politics but to the 'interest of India as a whole'.[10] At the same time, while he might on occasion feel frustrated with the way Indians acted, he considered that in London there was less understanding, and consequently less scope for imaginative action. To cap it all, persistent demands for food were met with suggestions he considered impractical. As he recorded on 11 March, 'HMG's only reaction so far to my last telegram about food imports is a proposal that I should *export* 25,000 tons of rice per month to Ceylon in return for a similar quantity of wheat and flour several months later. I sent back a quick and stuffy one. I really think they are crazy at Whitehall, or else they never trouble to read one's telegrams.'[11] If Wavell considered India 'a very tiresome adolescent', he thought the India Office, the Home Department and others had not even got that far, but persisted in treating the subcontinent 'as a naughty child'.[12]

With Archie John still in the army and forty years' military service behind him, even as Viceroy Wavell remained thoroughly engaged in the military aspects of the war. He was pleased by an improvement in Allied fortunes in Arakan, congratulating Mountbatten in early March on his 'striking success': 'I have naturally been following with great interest the progress of the battle and have watched with admiration the steadfastness and skill with which commanders and troops have met a testing situation.' Mindful of the difficulties of fighting there, he wanted Mountbatten to inform the soldiers so recently under his command how he had 'admired and rejoiced in' their exploits.[13] He also watched with interest the continuing preparations for Wingate's second and much larger Chindit expedition, for which Archie John was currently undertaking training in jungle warfare with the 2nd Battalion, The Black Watch. Again the organization and drive were supplied by Wingate, who travelled tirelessly between his various forward positions. Unfortunately, the weather for the time of year was particularly bad: the monsoon was not yet due, but high winds and rainstorms with thunder and lightning were common. On the night of 24 March Wingate was due to return to his home base, but his plane never reached its destination. Not long after take-off, the aircraft plunged into the ground and burst into flames; all ten occupants, including two British war correspondents and the American crew of five, were killed instantly. For some days those close to Wingate hoped he might have survived, but on 28 March Wavell recorded in his journal that Wingate had been reported missing and 'that he had almost certainly been killed in an air crash between Imphal and Silchar.[14]

Wavell had known Wingate for less than ten years; during that time he had both promoted and taken a personal interest in his operations. 'I am glad', he wrote, 'that I was responsible for giving him his chance and encouraging him.' But he also admitted that he had never known him well enough as a man 'to like or dislike him'. Wingate, on the other hand, had not retained his early reverential opinion of Wavell. Fergusson was 'shocked at his callousness' when Wavell was relieved of his command as C-in-C in India: 'He said something like: "He wasn't up to the job anyway."'[15] When Wavell later wrote Wingate's obituary for the journal of the Royal Central Asian Society he did so in generous terms, at the same time pointing out Wingate's strong character: 'His forcible, challenging personality invoked antagonism, he often exasperated my staff by the vehement importunity with which his demands for priority of equipment and personnel were pressed.' The manner of his death, he said, was in keeping with his life – 'swift, meteoric, headlong'.[16] Wingate's place in command of the Chindits was taken by Brigadier Joe Lentaigne, awarded the DSO during the 1942 retreat from Burma. Wavell judged him to be 'more orthodox and less highly strung than Wingate', and he was selected in preference to Wingate's own choice for his eventual successor, Mike Calvert.[17]

Wavell's poetry anthology was published in March 1944. He had chosen to dedicate the book to Archie John, 'who shares my love for poetry but thinks his father's taste a little old-fashioned'. The title was *Other Men's Flowers*, a quotation – suggested by Coats – from the sixteenth-century French writer Montaigne: 'I have gathered a posie of other men's flowers and nothing but the thread that binds them is my own.' In inscribing a copy for Peter Coats, Wavell recognized his contribution in supplying 'the best thing in the volume, its title'.[18] He also acknowledged Peter Fleming's assistance: 'Since you were largely responsible for my publishing this, I send you a copy of the result.'[19] Other friends either bought or were given the book. Wavell sent Channon a copy for his birthday on 7 March. Freya Stark, who had read the manuscript, thought the selection 'very individual and clear-cut . . . all very sharply defined and gallant.'[20] When Wavell was requested by the writer Edward Thompson to forward two books to Nehru, incarcerated in Ahmednagar Fort, as an act of kindness, he included a copy of his anthology and a private letter 'in view of our respective positions'. Nehru thought the letter a good one, and that it 'indicated the decency of the man'.[21] Leonie Lemartine sent Wavell her copy to be signed, and he did so mindful of their long years of friendship: 'Leonie, sometime Lemartine, sometime Redwood, sometime Robinson, always a true friend, Moscow & St Petersburg 1911, London 1912–14, 1922–26 and so on.'[22]

In all, Wavell had included 255 poems under various headings. In addition to favourites from his schooldays and celebrated poems of the First World War poets, plus others about fighting of the sort one might expect to be firmly embedded in the military mind, there were poems about love and leisure. He held true to his earlier tastes – there was no Wordsworth, but plenty of Kipling and Browning. At the end of the book he had included his own 'Sonnet for the Madonna of the Cherries' as 'a wayside dandelion' in a special section on its own, which he called 'Outside the Gate'. He modestly confessed that he had not intended the poem, which had been inspired by a painting at Northwick Park, for publication but that 'the owner of the lady' – George Spencer Churchill – had requested its inclusion. Written in 1943 at a time when, before Wavell's appointment as Viceroy, he thought he would be returning to India as Commander-in-Chief, the poem is striking for its sensitivity.[23]

As Archie John realized, the poems which had remained in his father's memory opened a window to his soul and revealed facets of his personality 'to the public at large in the only way his nature allowed.'[24] George Abell was genuinely surprised by the anthology. 'It is an interesting book and throws much light on his character and gifts. Although the world knew him as an imperturbable, courageous figure, there was also in him the spirit of the Elizabethan buccaneer . . . the side of his genius which made him believe in new methods of warfare and encourage his long-range desert patrols and the Chindits was undoubtedly this impulsive questing spirit.' The book was 'evidence of his astonishing memory since in all the 400 pages there is no poem that he did not know by heart or at the least had known in full at some previous date.' From personal experience, Abell knew Wavell could recite 'a very large proportion when the book was published'. As Abell and others observed, the notes which accompanied many of the poems showed how 'youthful in spirit' Wavell was, and explained 'the affection that the young always had for him.'[25] Missing, however, was any strong indication of his spirituality. Although such hymns as 'Jerusalem' and Milton's 'Hymn on the Morning of Christ's Nativity' were included in the 'Music, Mystery and Magic' section, his selection suggests that while Wavell regularly went to church, he was not deeply religious. Ever critical of his own achievements, Wavell admitted the amusement he had derived from compiling his anthology 'in the short leisures of a very busy life', but felt that, with more time, he could have made 'a better job of it'. Much to his surprise the book, at ten shillings and six pence a copy, sold out almost immediately. Under the headline 'Field Marshal's choice' the *Times Literary Supplement* commended Wavell as 'the latest recruit to the ranks of the anthologists'.[26]

Wavell thought he was working harder now than ever he had as a soldier. 'When I am not on tour I have to spend 8 hours a day or more in the office and the tours are almost more strenuous than the office,' he complained to Joan Bright. 'I have to meet so many dull people and do so many 10–minute talks (it usually takes me 10 minutes to start talking at all to anyone new) and it is irksome to be always on the red carpet and my best behaviour (such as it is).' There was also the wearing business of persisting with his demands, as he felt he must; 'I am afraid I am making myself a thorough nuisance to HMG over food imports but I think I am saving them from serious errors and mean to go on.'[27] In the spring the province of Bengal at last got what Wavell termed a 'first-class nurse' – its new Governor, Richard Casey. Born in Australia, Casey had served at Gallipoli and won a DSO in 1918. Most recently he had been Minister of State Resident in the Middle East, and a member of the War Cabinet in Britain.[28] Like so many others, he considered Wavell 'one of the finest human beings I have known . . . a man of size . . . in character, personality and appearance he was most impressive. In spite of being solidly built, he was supple, with unusual muscular control.'[29] Wavell also faced a difficult situation in the Punjab, as Khizr Hayat Khan Tiwana, Premier since 1942, came into conflict with the Muslim League leader Jinnah. As a member of the Unionist Party, which represented the interests of both Muslims and Hindus in the Punjab and opposed the League's demand for a separate Pakistan, Hayat was resisting Jinnah's attempts to control the Punjab government. Jinnah took the line that since the Muslims in the Unionist Party were also members of the Muslim League, they were subject to his direction as President of the League; since they were also in the majority in the Punjab, this effectively gave Jinnah the control he sought. Wavell, however, adamantly refused to be drawn into automatically letting the will of the majority prevail at the expense of that of minorities. This became his stand not only when Hindus opposed Muslims, but when one group of Muslims opposed another. At this stage, he was also not prepared to admit that Jinnah represented solid Muslim opinion – 'but he can sway opinion and no one seems to have the character to oppose him.' He knew his views made him unpopular with Jinnah, but as usual remained unperturbed by personal criticism: 'I gather that Jinnah regards me as an enemy of the Muslim League and is determined to be as much of a nuisance as he can.'[30]

Among the names in the Visitor's Book at Viceregal Lodge was that of Cecil Beaton, acclaimed for his exhibitions of photographs, his paintings and his stage-designs. He was now on secondment to the Ministry of Information, and spent two weeks living 'in the vast domain', which he described as 'a city within a city'. Coming from war-torn wintry Britain, he was 'immensely impressed' by the 'sun, glitter and colour'. During his stay he became, as Coats described, 'almost an extra ADC . . . in a haze of well-deserved escapist luxury.'[31] He photographed Wavell and Queenie for *Life* magazine, and he drew cartoons, one of which, captioned 'Lady Wavell enjoys a picnic', showed the Wavell family on a traditional family outing. It was no secret that the Viceroy did not share the Vicereine's enthusiasm for picnics, which he famously described as like sitting on a nettle and eating a wasp.[32] Another visitor was the actress and writer Joyce Grenfell, in India on her first tour.[33] But amid the comings and goings there was always concern if one of those close to the Wavells went missing. In March Peter Fleming went on another intelligence mission, and did not return when expected. Once he was safely back in Delhi, Wavell sent for him. 'This was the cue for a typical Wavell–Fleming conversation':

w: Have a bad time?
F: No, sir, thank you, sir, not too bad. (*Pause.*)
w: Mph.
F: (*trying to make the grade*) Had a lot of luck, sir.
w: I see (*Pause.*)
F: (*telling all*) As a matter of fact it was rather interesting, sir.
w: Oh!
F: (*piling on the interest*) There's an awful lot of room in there, sir.
w: Room?
F: (*practically down to pidgin English*) Very big country, sir, very few Japanese.
w: I see. (*Pause.*)
F: I mean, you could hang about for a long time. With a small party, I mean. If you wanted to, of course.
w: Yes, I suppose you could. (*Pause.*)
w: Well . . .
F: Well, sir . . .
w: Thank you very much for coming to tell me all about it, Peter.
F: Not at all, sir. (*Exit.*)[34]

Despite the cares of high office, Wavell's humour was never far below the surface. When his private secretary Evan Jenkins temporarily ran out of work, he wrote a formal note to 'His Excellency' requesting the afternoon off. Wavell, at his most informal, responded, 'Hooray, hooray, when the cat's away the mice will play', and promptly went to play golf.[35] Wavell also found time to sit for his portrait by the artist Simon Elwes, a lieutenant-colonel in the 10th Hussars who was currently serving in the Public Relations department in India and engaged in painting 'military celebrities'.[36]

In early May, as the forest trees flamed into full bloom, heralding the coming of the hot weather, Wavell was on the move again after three days of National Defence Council meetings. He went first to Bombay to see what damage had been done to the docks following a recent fire, and then north to Sikkim, on the Nepalese border, close to the ancient Kingdom of Bhutan. Queenie had refused to accompany him on such a short visit, and Felicity went instead. For part of their journey they had 'to take to elephants' where floods had destroyed a bridge. The Resident with responsibility for both Sikkim and nearby Bhutan was Basil Gould, a contemporary from Summer Fields and Winchester and sometime 'Wykehamist contributor' to *The Summer Fields Magazine*.[37] As Wavell was amused to note, officially Gould was the 'despair' of Delhi – 'does none of the right bureaucratic things and has unorthodox views; but he is known affectionately as Uncle Basil by all the Maharaja's family, and has kept Sikkim and Bhutan good and happy all the war and is *persona grata* with the Tibetans.' The Viceroy therefore saw fit to extend Gould's tenure as Resident, rather than appoint 'a more orthodox official'.

During this visit, on 5 May, Wavell celebrated his sixty-first birthday. He had suffered numerous comparatively slight injuries since first breaking his collar-bone in South Africa more than forty years earlier, but remained in good health, though occasionally he awoke feeling 'rather rheumatic'. He was pleased to announce to Freya Stark that, like the Tibetan Lama in Kipling's *Kim*, he had acquired 'merit' on his birthday by walking round two monasteries before breakfast and turning a lot of prayer wheels. He went on to review his first six months as Viceroy, during which time he had visited all eleven provinces of British India and a few of the princely states: he believed that India as a whole was getting on 'fairly well', and that morale was much better than a year or two previously. But he was also well aware that 'A great part of India is always on the knife-edge of starvation.'[38] It was a time, too, for reflecting on his own achievements. 'I don't think I've been very successful but I've tried. I've certainly never worked harder,' he said in a long letter to Joan Bright; he now wrote to her more intermittently, but in the same uninhibited vein as if they were in touch every week. Returning to a familiar refrain, he complained that there wasn't time for hard thinking on all the problems confronting him, and that he was not 'extraordinary enough' to get the 'ponderous machine' of India out of its ruts, though he regarded himself as a slightly unorthodox Viceroy. The war was never far from his mind, and he felt it was now being fought mainly by 'tired, bored and rather disillusioned' people. 'If we are stale now, where are we going to get the fresh impetus of vitality and faith that the peace will require?' he wondered.[39]

While Wavell was away from Delhi a crisis occurred concerning the health of Gandhi, detained, like his political colleagues, since the 1942 civil disobedience movement. Gandhi, now 74, had fallen ill with malaria and it was feared that he might die in the Aga Khan Palace outside Poona, where he was confined. Wavell was unable through his absence to consult the members of his Executive Council, but somewhat reluctantly agreed to Gandhi's release. 'Personally, I could not see that we gained much credit by releasing him at the point of death; and if he was not at the point of death there was no need of such hurry.'[40] Far from dying, Gandhi rallied and returned to the political limelight, in due course writing to Wavell as 'Dear Friend' to request an interview. He also asked for permission to visit the detained members of the Congress Working Committee. Wavell, now back in Delhi, declined either to meet Gandhi or permit him to visit the detained Congress leaders, while suggesting that if, after his convalescence, Gandhi had 'a definite and constructive policy to propose for the further-ance of India's welfare', he would be glad to consider it.[41] Gandhi had altered his opinion on the value of a mass civil disobedience movement, but had publicly reaffirmed his commitment to the 'Quit India' movement; Wavell made it clear that, while he did not believe the Congress Party had any desire to help the Japanese, they must realize that the 'Quit India' res-olution would definitely hinder the war effort. Gandhi also remained firm in his demand for a national government that would assume complete con-trol of the administration.

In mid June, as the temperature rose steadily in Delhi, Wavell and Queenie managed to escape to Simla. It was a 'wearisome' drive, with twists and turns in the road that Queenie did not like, but the cooler air made the journey worthwhile. No sooner had they arrived, however, than a telegram reached them with the news that Archie John, now in Burma with the Chindits, had been seriously wounded. Inevitably this plunged the whole household 'in gloom, though', as Coats wrote, 'we have to go through the various functions . . . like some awful pre-ordained stage per-formance.'[42] The Wavells returned to Delhi the following day, flying on to Assam to await Archie John's evacuation, which was delayed 'partly owing to weather, mainly owing to his own refusal to be evacuated till all cases he considered more serious had gone.'[43] Archie John had had to have his hand and lower arm amputated but Wavell, while distressed, was also sanguine. As he wrote to Auchinleck, there was no chance of saving the hand: 'the boy is doing well and the doctors are pleased with him . . . It is very bad luck on him being crippled at his age by loss of a limb, but it might have been much worse.'[44] Later, during his convalescence, one of Archie John's visitors was Lieutenant-General Sir Adrian Carton de Wiart, who had lost both an eye and an arm at Ypres during the Great War.[45] It seemed, Wavell noted, that Carton de Wiart, currently serving as Special Military Representative with Chiang Kai-Shek, had passed through Delhi 'mainly, I believe, to tell my son how well he had managed without a hand. He is a charming person.'[46]

Amid these personal anxieties, the feeding of India remained a preoccupation. On 5 July Wavell had protested sternly to Amery about the delay in delivering wheat: 'If His Majesty's Government continues to disregard advice from here and refuses to face facts, I can see little hope of avoiding another disaster of which I have warned His Majesty's Government for many months now.'[47] Churchill had remained singularly silent, except for a telegram to Wavell asking 'peevishly' why Gandhi hadn't died yet.[48] There was also a new development on the Indian political scene, relating to a 'formula' suggested to Jinnah by the moderate Congress politician Rajagopalachari: if, Rajagopalachari said, Gandhi would be prepared to recommend it to the Congress Working Committee, and if Jinnah and the Muslim League would accept it, it might prove the beginnings of a way forward. According to the formula, contiguous districts in the North-West and North-East of India, where Muslims predominated, would be demarcated as constituting the Muslim League's objective 'Pakistan'. Before considering the plan, Jinnah wished first to consult his colleagues in the Muslim League; he also wanted to confer directly with Gandhi, rather than through Rajagopalachari as a go-between. But even at this early stage Wavell was sceptical that anything would be achieved. Gandhi's persistent requests to see the detained Congress Working Committee members made him believe that the Mahatma was not in fact working for a settlement, but 'to secure the release of the Working Committee as a prelude to further political agitation.'[49]

The Wavells went again to Simla to escape some of the midsummer heat, then Wavell returned south in August to continue with his constant round of meetings, burdened, he told Freya Stark, by paperwork which made him think of the opening lines of Kipling's poem: 'Files, files files / Oblige me by referring to the files.'[50] Seven strenuous months in India caused him to marvel at how Linlithgow had withstood the pressures for more than seven years. He was also becoming increasingly annoyed at the need constantly to refer to Whitehall: 'The PM wired me that the Cabinet was very perturbed that I had entered into negotiation with Gandhi, who should be dead – at least politically – according to the medical reports cabled home,' he noted in his journal on 4 August. Remembering the directive Churchill had given him on his departure as Viceroy the previous October, Wavell wired back that he was not negotiating with Gandhi, 'merely informing him that negotiation on his basis was impossible; that I had carried out the injunctions of his directive; and that the only provision of his directive which I had been unable to carry out was "to divert shipping to carry food grains", since HMG would give me neither shipping nor food grains.'[51] As far as larger issues were concerned, Wavell felt ignored: a significant conference on Palestine's future had been held, examining whether it should be partitioned. 'It will be noticed that, though India has over 90 million of Moslems, many of who feel very strongly about Palestine, HMG did not even think fit to inform me of this conference.'[52]

The various members of Wavell's family were busy with their own concerns. Queenie's life revolved around her voluntary duties. In Simla she organized a 'leave camp' in part of the Viceregal residence with Peter Coats's help, and it seemed to be 'a great success'. Pamela was expecting her first child – her parents' second grandchild – in October; Joan and little Diana, whom Wavell had not yet seen, were in England. Felicity was working with Peter Fleming. Visitors continued to arrive, one among them the popular playwright and composer Noël Coward, on his way to the Burma front to entertain the troops. Archie John was still recuperating from his injury, even managing to play a little golf, before having an artificial hand fitted in the expectation that he could return to his regiment 'and do some more fighting if the doctors will let him.'[53] When he went back to England on leave he made a point of touring the country to locate the families of those who had served under him, to give first-hand news of their 'distant sons'.[54] He also visited some of his parents' friends, including the Shakespeare expert John Dover Wilson, with whom Wavell had been corresponding since their meeting at Dalmeny the previous year. As Dover Wilson subsequently wrote to Wavell, he and his wife were 'delighted and cheered by your boy's visit, which left us feeling that life and living was more worth while, when such spirits as his existed to carry on the world.'[55]

Wavell also went 'back to the Army' that August, spending a 'strenuous' three days visiting Manipur and Assam, where the Naga tribesmen had borne the brunt of the Japanese two-pronged offensive against Kohima and Imphal. Tragically for the Naga, they were also fighting their countrymen: Subhas Chandra Bose had returned to the East from Europe in July 1943 to take over command of the Indian National Army, and its ranks, in the wake of his return, had swollen to an estimated 20,000. Although the INA was dependent on what the Japanese would spare them in the way of arms (generally captured British weapons), Bose's charisma still attracted recruits indoctrinated with the belief that by assisting the Japanese they were fighting a 'war of independence' against the British. To the British and Indians who had remained loyal, those who, for whatever reasons, broke the oath of allegiance sworn when they first joined the Indian Army were traitors: if captured, they received no mercy. Wavell flew first to Imphal, where he stayed with the Political Agent, Christopher Gimson, 'a bachelor of means'.[56] According to Wavell, Linlithgow had once claimed that during one of *his* visits a cat had dropped from the ceiling onto his bed during the night. When the story was related to Gimson, he replied casually that it was unlikely to have been a cat – 'quite probably a rat, though'.[57]

Wavell's main objective was to visit the soldiers, including those of the 6th Brigade and the 2nd Division, both of which he had once commanded. Formal occasions were far from his mind, so Edward Lydall, President of the Manipur State Durbar, had a difficult task breaking the news that the Maharaja wanted the Viceroy to conduct a coronation ceremony. Having met the Maharaja, Wavell drew Lydall aside to question him. Lydall explained that a crown found on the palace rubbish heap had given the Maharaja the idea; Wavell seemed to think he was 'trying to be funny'. The Maharaja was informed that he would have to crown himself. Like so many others before him, Lydall had his own experience of Wavell's forbidding reticence, when he met the Manipuri members of the Durbar: 'They were humble little men and they were scared out of their wits at the prospect of meeting a man who was not only the Viceroy but also a world-famous general. Wavell did nothing to put them at their ease. Indeed he was probably as little at ease as they were.' At each introduction, Wavell managed to utter no more than his customary 'I see'.

The ordeal was such that Lydall looked forward 'with dread' to dinner at the Political Agent's Residency – and he had heard a variation on the story about Gimson's cats: apparently a cat was quite liable to leap into the air during dinner and land on a guest's head 'with all its claws at the ready'. But he was pleasantly surprised. There were no such feline antics, and Wavell was far more talkative than he could have imagined. 'We sat entranced as the great soldier gave us his reminiscences of "Electric

Whiskers" and the rest. Occasionally we prompted him with a question. "Yes," he would say and launch out on some fresh aspect of desert warfare. Or "No . . . I think I must have been fighting some other battle somewhere else." It was a wonderful evening and it was fascinating to have glimpsed at last the very human person behind the frighteningly silent mask.'[58]

When Wavell returned to Delhi, he found that his continuing correspondence with Gandhi was proving even more troublesome than he had anticipated. The most recent letter related to consideration of a 'definite and constructive proposal' and forthcoming meeting with Jinnah, and Wavell wanted to respond – but, much to his annoyance, he was obliged first to send his letter to London for approval. Not surprisingly, when the draft was returned, he did not like the amendments. 'I got back a revised draft exactly the same in principle, but intransigent and discourteous in tone. It seems to me one of our great mistakes in this country is not to have realized the importance to the Indian mind of good manners and an appearance at least of consideration.'[59] Amery in London was doing his best. Wavell's plea to be allowed to write his own letter in his own language as long as it was consistent with Cabinet policy prompted him to note that 'he is of course perfectly right and Winston's insistence on Cabinet interference in these matters is intolerable.' But even Amery could not stick his neck out too far. Having at first prepared a telegram giving Wavell his 'personal authority' to act as he thought fit, on second thoughts he felt that 'so long as there is a chance of persuading the Cabinet to be sensible' it was his duty to try.[60] However, the constant scrutiny only resulted in making Wavell feel that Churchill and most of the Cabinet would prefer it if India were shelved until the war was over, but were not prepared to say so.

The issue of Wavell's response to Gandhi escalated into a minor row between Wavell and the Cabinet, where there was a fear that Wavell might even resign.[61] As Amery had the sense to realize, however, 'if there is to be a showdown it should come over food on which the case is obvious rather than over the precise wording of a letter to Gandhi.'[62] In the end Wavell followed Amery's advice 'not to go off the deep end by defying the Cabinet' and backed down on the grounds he had suggested – that it was not a suitable occasion for 'a head on collision'.[63] Privately, he remained irritated. 'I feel that many of our troubles in India, both administrative and political, are due to ignorance and prejudice among your colleagues,' he wrote to Amery. 'It is discouraging work to serve an obviously hostile Cabinet, who seem to have no confidence in my judgement on any matter.'[64] When, as expected, the Indians reacted adversely to his letter, terming it 'rude' and 'arrogant', Wavell was even more annoyed, asserting

Above: Cairo, August 1942. The Prime Minister liked to travel with his 'top brass': standing, Air Marshal Sir Arthur Tedder, Air Officer Commanding-in-Chief; General Sir Alan Brooke, Chief of the Imperial General Staff; Rear Admiral Sir Henry Harwood, Commander-in-Chief, Mediterranean; Rt Hon. Richard Casey, Minister of State Resident in the Middle East; seated, Field Marshal Rt Hon. Jan Christian Smuts, Prime Minister of South Africa; the Prime Minister, Rt Hon. Winston Churchill, General Sir Claude Auchinleck, Commander-in-Chief, Middle East, and General Sir Archibald Wavell, Commander-in-Chief, India

Right: Alan Brooke and Wavell in Teheran, 1942. Brooke told Wavell that if *he* were to take offence when abused by Churchill and given to understand that the PM had no confidence in him, he would have to resign at least once a day!

Commander-in-Chief's house, New Delhi. It was 'rather large like a barracks – with a good many pillars and a flag flying on top,' noted one of Wavell's ADCs

Wavell in Burma on reconnaissance

Wavell in Burma with Alexander and Slim. Wavell had sent Slim to help Alexander during the 1942 retreat from Burma. 'Alexander has a most difficult task,' he told Slim; 'You won't find yours easy'

Wavell at his lectern. In addition to official correspondence, he wrote thousands of letters by hand. As Viceroy, he also kept a journal

Wavell's youngest daughter Joan with her husband, The Hon. Simon Astley, 27 January 1943. 'Their combined ages barely reached forty years,' Wavell jokingly said

Nanny – Daisy Ribbands, who had lived with the Wavells since 1916: 'a great ally of the ADCs'

Wavell and Ivor Jehu, his Director of Public Relations, on the golf course, New Delhi. Throughout his life Wavell enjoyed golf. 'No one has succeeded in working me beyond a certain limit', he said as Viceroy; 'after that I do crosswords or play golf'

Wavell went to Imphal in 1944 to present medals and other accolades to British and Indian army troops who had defended it against the Japanese. Here he is decorating Jemader Singh Bahadur Gurung, 8th Gurkha Rifles, with the Indian Order of Merit (2nd class)

Wavell awarding the Victoria Cross to the widow of Sher Singh, 16 Punjab Regiment, 1944

CAN THEY MAKE UP THE JIGSAW?

Throughout the summer of 1946, the Viceroy Lord Wavell, Sir Stafford Cripps, Lord Pethick-Lawrence and A.V. Alexander worked on a plan to transfer power to Indian representatives in a united India. Newspaper commentators realised their difficulties

The Cabinet Mission: Cripps, Pethick-Lawrence and Alexander with their assistants seated behind. Wavell called them 'the three Magi': 'So far all the gifts . . . the frankincense of goodwill, the myrrh of honeyed words, the gold of promises – have produced little,' he wrot in April 1946

A morning ride from Viceregal Lodge; Wavell enjoyed his riding parties. Last-minute objections by guests – such as not having any riding clothes, or not having ridden 'for ages' – were swept aside

Lord Wavell greets his successor as Viceroy, Lord Mountbatten, March 1947. He described the appointment of Mountbatten as 'unexpected but clever'

Wavell as Colonel of the Regiment, 1948, with Lt. Col. Bernard Fergusson, (centre). When Wavell wore his kilt in Russia he created 'a veritable sensation'

Rededication of War Cloister, Winchester College, 14 November 1948. 'They fought, they endured, they died, in advance or retreat, in victory or disaster,' Wavell said in his speech

Wavell's grave, War Cloister, Winchester College. His widow preferred the Chantry Garth to a place near Allenby in Westminster Abbey

5 May 1883

WAVELL

24 May 1950

in his journal that the Cabinet had 'destroyed at one blow my reputation for fairness and good temper in my correspondence with Gandhi and has thus weakened my usefulness in any eventual dealings with Congress.'[65]

On 9 September the long-awaited meetings between Gandhi and Jinnah took place at Jinnah's home in Bombay. During their discussions, which lasted nearly three weeks, Gandhi offered Jinnah the 'Rajaji' formula of a divided Punjab and Bengal. Jinnah considered the area being offered both 'moth-eaten' and 'mutilated', and was unhappy with Gandhi's suggestion that the 'secession' of predominantly Muslim areas should take place after India was given its independence. Wavell, who already regarded both leaders as 'obstinate, intransigent, crafty old men',[66] was dismayed at the outcome. 'I did not expect statesmanship or a practical solution, but I did think the two would have got down to something, if only the best way to embarrass the [Government of India] . . . The two great mountains have met and not even a ridiculous mouse has emerged.'[67] As Wavell realized, the main point of disagreement was that Jinnah wanted Pakistan first and independence afterwards, 'while Gandhi wants independence first with some kind of self-determination for Muslims to be granted by a provisional Government which would be predominantly Hindu.'[68] Such a timetable would leave the minority Muslims vulnerable to the majority Hindus without the protective umbrella of British authority to safeguard their interests.

In the wake of the failure of the Jinnah–Gandhi talks, Wavell worked out another proposal. His suggestion was for the formation of a provisional Government, representing the main political parties, which would call a small conference of political leaders. It was his opinion that it would be better to show some movement forward before the end of the war, while Britain could at least retain some control of political aspirations. On this occasion it was Amery who raised objections, suggesting that since the two political parties, the Congress and the Muslim League, could not reach agreement, the National Defence Council might be used as a 'very suitable nucleus' because it already included representatives from the princes. Wavell disagreed, and did not mince words in letting Amery know he regarded the suggestion as 'quite impracticable'.[69] Wavell's mood during these deliberations was not improved by the fact that he had fallen ill with a 'slight chill and temperature', and for the first time in 'something like 10 years' – apart from his back injury – had been 'in bed for 2 or 3 days with a fever.'[70] His illness, diagnosed by the doctor as malaria, elicited the sympathy of at least one regular correspondent, Dover Wilson: to be under the weather 'must be very trying when you have so heavy a burden to carry as yours'.[71]

Every so often in the course of Wavell's official duties an unusual item came his way. One such was 'a very fine pair' of horns belonging to the *Ovis Poli*, the large sheep named after the late thirteenth-century Venetian travel-ler Marco Polo. As well as worrying about Indian politics and the war, in the autumn of 1944 Wavell was negotiating to send the horns to the Royal Central Asian Society in London (of which he had been a member since 1933). He was reliably informed by the Political Agent at Gilgit, Major E.H. Cobb, that the horns were of record size; they had been presented 'in token of their friendly relations' by Cobb's counterpart in Chinese Turkestan to mark the inauguration of the Indo-Sinkiang–China Postal Mail Service the previous spring. Cobb, also a member of the Royal Central Asian Society, had suggested the Society as a suitable recipient since its crest was the 'horns of Marco Polo's sheep'. When approached Wavell immediately agreed, organizing the transaction in correspondence with the Society's Chairman, General Sir John Shea, with whom he had served in Palestine.[72]

On 20 October Wavell celebrated his first anniversary as Viceroy, 'the hardest year's work I have done.' He felt able to congratulate himself on his handling of the food problem, but described the British Government's atti-tude as 'negligent, hostile and contemptuous.'[73] To mark the occasion he wrote a long letter to Churchill, pointing first to several instances of what had the appearance of a neglectful or unfriendly attitude to India: top of his list was the way he had 'literally to fight with all the words' he could command to secure food imports. He complained of the way soldiers' pay had been increased without prior consultation with the Government of India; this had already led to a bitter exchange between Viceroy and Prime Minister that autumn. He then proceeded to make a detailed report on the 'directive' Churchill had given him on his departure. His thesis was that it would be far better to make a fresh move towards Indian independence before the end of the Japanese war than afterwards, when food would still be short: 'Demobilization and the closing down of the war factories and overgrown clerical establishments will throw many people out of employ-ment. They will find a fertile field for agitation, unless we have previously diverted their energies into some more profitable channel, i.e. into dealing with the administrative problems of India and into trying to solve the con-stitutional problem.'[74]

In October Pamela presented the Wavells with their first grandson, 'a fine lusty infant', born in Viceregal Lodge and given the names Francis (after his father) Wavell Harold James. There were changes taking place in Wavell's staff. After two and a half years as his ADC, Simon Astley left to attend Staff College in England. Having initially thought him hot-headed and intolerant, Wavell had warmed to his son-in-law, later describing him as 'the quickest witted and most efficient ADC I have ever had . . . in many ways an attractive personality.'[75] At the end of November Wavell lost the services of Ivor Jehu, who retired as his Director of Public Relations and went back to writing for the *Times of India*. The two men remained in touch, as did their families. Jehu had married in early 1944 and Wavell stood godfather to his son, born in November, presenting him with a copy of *Other Men's Flowers*. Early in November there was news of the death through illness of Wavell's close friend Jack Dill; he was only 62. Serving in Washington during some of the most difficult days of the war, he had done much to defuse Anglo-American tensions. He was one of few foreigners to be granted the privilege of burial in America's National Cemetery at Arlington, Virginia. Of all Wavell's military contemporaries Dill was among his friends of longest standing – 45 years, since their arrival at Sandhurst in 1900 as awkward adolescents.

In December the Viceroy found himself 'speech-bound', trying to write several for a tour that was to take him to Bombay to visit the docks, recently repaired after an accidental fire earlier in the year, the Princely State of Hyderabad, and Calcutta. His visit to the Nizam of Hyderabad, largest of the princely states in central India, exposed him to 'a curious mixture of modern and medieval, of progress and of stagnation, under the despotic rule, except so far as British influence restrains him, of an odd personality.' Renowned for his innumerable pet dogs and his fortune – and his miserliness – the Nizam, Osman Ali Khan, had been undisputed ruler since a bitter contest for the succession between himself and his two brothers in 1911. There were three long days of official engagements, and 'her Ex' created 'a great impression'.[76] The next stop was Calcutta, to address the Calcutta Chamber of Commerce. Wavell then flew to Imphal. During this visit he knighted Slim, who, after countering the Japanese at Imphal and Kohima in the spring, had successfully taken the offensive back into Burma. The ceremony took place on a cleared field, with Slim kneeling on a velvet-covered stool. There had been rumours that King George might be coming to Assam to visit the troops, and would himself confer the honour, but the royal visit did not take place. Slim later said that there was no person apart from His Majesty by whom he would rather have been knighted than by Wavell as Viceroy.[77] Back in New Delhi, on Christmas Day there was a telegram from Amery saying that the War Cabinet would not make any move about India until Wavell went home and raised the issue in person: 'From his telegram it was obvious that they would much sooner I didn't hurry.'[78]

Among his successes for 1944 Wavell listed his achievement in getting a million tons of food for India's starving population. But on the political side he was forced to admit that he had made no progress, 'and I have undoubtedly disappointed the hopes of political India which were raised by Gandhi's release'. Although Wavell and Gandhi had still not met, he did not now regret having released him. He also believed that his insistence on supporting Khizr against Jinnah in the Punjab was correct. He felt a genuine affection for India, but his first year as Viceroy had made him extremely critical of Indian politicians – matched as usual by his own self-doubts. 'I have less opinion than ever of Indian capacity for leadership and statesmanship and commonsense; nor do I think that I have a strong enough personality to put through the almost superhuman task of persuading India to be a nation.' Nevertheless, he was determined to try. Still imbued with the patriotic values instilled a lifetime earlier, he also wanted to emphasize to Whitehall the benefits for Britain's 'prestige, security and prosperity' of securing 'a satisfactory but generous settlement of the Indian problem.'[79]

The new year opened 'quietly'. Wavell thought of going to London during the third week of January to state the case for some plan of action being put forward to break the political deadlock, but the response from London was not encouraging: a meeting between the 'Big Three' – Churchill, Roosevelt and Stalin – was scheduled at Yalta in the Crimea in February, and Wavell was informed that there was no possibility of his own meeting taking place before March. 'They obviously want to delay as long as possible the moment when they have to take a decision about India,' he noted in his journal on 7 January.[80] It did mean he could accept an invitation to go tiger-shooting in the Nepalese jungle in mid January. The pilots of the Viceroy's plane knew that when returning to Delhi they had to fly low over Viceregal Lodge to alert the cavalcade of cars to depart for the airport a short distance away. On this occasion Coats, sitting next to Wavell, saw that he was looking at the spreading gardens below. They were 'a carpet of bright colour, the fountains were playing in the sun, the mounted sentries were at their posts. Under its swelling dome, the Viceroy's House itself spread its four great wings. "Be it never so humble," H.E. said, "there's no place like home." '[81] Coats felt this typified Wavell's humour.

All attempts to secure political direction from London merely served to annoy Churchill, and Amery thought there was 'a real danger' that Churchill 'would drive Wavell into resignation.'[82] When the subject of India was discussed in Cabinet the week after Amery made this observation in his diary, he noted Churchill's hostile attitude to both Wavell and India, 'first of all treating Wavell as a contemptible self-seeking advertiser, and then talking about the handicap India is to defence.'[83] While Wavell waited to travel to London, he continued to seek whatever mileage could be gained from the various proposals emanating from the Indian political leaders. The leader of the Congress Party in the Legislative Assembly, Bhūlabhai Desai,[84] had suggested a 'national government' which would draw its members from the legislature. As far as Wavell could see, Desai's proposals were similar to ones he himself had already made. To find out whether they would be acceptable to the Muslim League, Wavell had proposed a meeting with Mohammed Ali Jinnah and Desai, to which the British Government had given its 'grudging' consent. Amery had suggested giving India 'Dominion status' under its present constitution and present Executive Council, but Wavell thought the idea 'unworkable' for both constitutional and psychological reasons. As he noted in his journal, Amery 'has a curious capacity for getting hold of the right stick but practically always the wrong end of it.'[85]

Freya Stark's friendship with the Wavell family had grown over the years, and in February she arrived in Delhi on a working visit to help Queenie with a committee which had been set up to find ways to involve Indian women in the war effort. Queenie had called upon Freya because the programme was 'beyond me and anyway I haven't the time.'[86] Freya had agreed to help, with the proviso that she could leave once Italy was liberated, to return to Asolo, near Trieste, her home before the war. No sooner had she reached Delhi than the Wavells left for a two-week tour to Mysore, Travancore and Cochin, accompanied by Archie John, just back in India after four months' recuperation in England. When they returned, Freya was able to see the customary ritual at first hand: 'Their Ex.s are back, and walking through rows of bows and curtseys looking like the fairy tale of the Children in the Wood, innocent and triumphant but strangers, with the creatures of an alien world all about them . . . it is hard to be easily chatty between two curtseys and with four ADCs listening.'[87] Freya remained with the Wavells for nearly five months, but it took her no time at all to conclude that 'their poor Ex.s are smothered in business and grandeur. What a heavy load! All the amusement is for the subordinates and all the weariness goes to the top.'[88]

In early March Wavell was still waiting to hear when he might return to England – 'I don't think the PM wants me at all and will procrastinate as long as possible'[89] – and in the meanwhile was kept busy with the day-to-day and the ceremonial, whether it was honouring Indian soldiers or their widows with the Victoria Cross, or an investiture with all its pomp and splendour. On such occasions he sat on the Viceregal throne with its velvet canopy embroidered with Britain's coat of arms, wearing a grey frock coat and looking, as Freya noted, 'so much what he is, good, and simple and direct'.[90] But his mood was not always placid, and when he heard that his visit to Britain was to be postponed until June because Attlee was going to San Francisco (to discuss the framing of a constitution for a United Nations Organization), he sent back an indignant protest. There had been, he said, no apology or explanation, 'just a contemptuous wave of the hand – "Tell India to wait till it's more convenient".'[91]

In London, Amery was – as so often – trying to state Wavell's case. When the India Committee finally recommended that Wavell should indeed come home, he had to pass the next hurdle: gaining the Prime Minister's approval. Fortunately Churchill did not ask to see the telegrams exchanged between Amery and Wavell, many of them so angry that 'he would have gone through the ceiling. As it is he spoke most bitterly and contemptuously of W. as never any real use as a soldier but who he had thought would at least carry on in India and not try and advertise himself by cringing to the Hindus etc. etc. I told him he was not fair, but didn't go on arguing as it was important to get his assent without more ado, and happily got it.'[92] Almost by return – after so much rejection – Wavell received a message indicating that a plane would be at Karachi on 21 March to fly him to England. Immediately Sir John – the Governor of Bombay – and Lady Colville, the 'Bombay Ducks', as Peter Coats called them – came to Delhi as Acting Viceroy and Vicereine. Wavell and Queenie left Delhi on 20 March, and with them went Pamela and her baby. After a short period as Wavell's Military Secretary her husband Francis was now in Greece, hoping for home leave. Simon, Joan and Diana were already in England while Simon was at Staff College.[93] Archie John had returned to his battalion. He had been passed 'A.1' fit, but the battalion was doing parachute training, and the parachute school 'maintained 2 hands were needed'; he therefore went instead to Peter Fleming's 'very ingenious department of Intelligence'.[94]

Chips Channon had obviously changed his mind about the Wavells since their previous visit. 'It is announced that the Wavells are arriving,' he noted in his diary on 21 March, 'but I have decided not to run them or run after them.' When they arrived in London two days later, he declined to go to meet them: 'The Viceroy can telephone to me when he feels so inclined.'[95] Even so, soon afterwards he went with Wavell and Queenie to see a *A Midsummer Night's Dream*. Staying again at the Dorchester, the Wavells found themselves in a city where, after the Allies' victories in Europe, there was at last a prospect of life returning to normal.

Eventually, on 26 March, Wavell was able to expound his views to the India Committee: 'I made a statement on situation in India and outlined my proposals. I was then cross-questioned, mainly on personalities and matters of detail and on the risks involved.' Wavell found the atmosphere of the committee, which included the 'obstructionists' Grigg, the Secretary of State for War, who had opposed Wavell's promotion to Field Marshal, and Simon, the Lord Chancellor, 'mainly friendly', but 'no one seemed to have any alternative proposals though they stressed the dangers and difficulties of making any move.'[96] Amery thought Wavell did well, 'making his points clearly and firmly but with great moderation and answering questions most effectively.'[97] A meeting with Churchill had been fixed for 29 March, their first since Wavell's departure for India as Viceroy-Designate in October 1943. His other commitments meant Churchill was anxious to state the case for India being 'kept on ice', while Wavell was adamant that India was 'very urgent and very important' and that the problems would be just as difficult after the war. As far as Wavell could make out, Churchill appeared to favour eventual partition of the subcontinent into Pakistan, Hindustan, Princestan, etc. 'He talked as if I was proposing to "Quit India", change the Constitution, and hand over India right away; and I had to interrupt him a number of times.' It was unlike earlier encounters between the two men in that Wavell found the Prime Minister – now 70 – 'friendly on the whole' but, he felt, 'depressed and lacking in fire.'[98] After five years of intense pressure, age was beginning to tell even on Churchill. Alan Brooke had weathered a relationship with the Prime Minister for two years; his diary reveals that for some months he had thought Churchill was losing his grip and meandering in his thoughts.[99]

Wavell attended meetings of the India Committee and the Cabinet, but over the next two weeks was obliged to record in his journal that no progress was being made in agreeing a new scheme that would move the issue of independence forward without compromising Britain's interests while war with Japan continued. 'I have no idea how long I shall be at home. I find things move very slowly here. I think a good many of the politicians are looking over their shoulders at the General Election prospects, which does not make getting decisions any easier.'[100] On 11 April Wavell flew to Germany to visit Montgomery's headquarters in a castle east of Osnabruck. 'Monty' had achieved high acclaim as Commander of the 8th Army which vanquished Rommel at El Alamein in North Africa, then gained further distinction as Commander-in-Chief of the Allied Armies in Northern France during the Normandy landings in 1944, and as Commander of the British Army of the Rhine. The two men spent about five hours together, during which, as Wavell commented, Montgomery 'talked pretty continuously'.[101] In London there was still 'nothing much doing', and the India Committee preserved 'a deep inertia and silence.'[102] As Wavell was returning from Germany on 12 April the dynamics of world leadership changed when Franklin Roosevelt, President of the United States since 1936, died suddenly at the age of 63, to be succeeded by his Vice-President, Harry S. Truman, son of a livestock trader and farmer from Missouri.[103] Wavell did not hear the news until the 13th. In an unprecedented gesture Churchill, 'overpowered by a sense of deep and irreparable loss', adjourned the House of Commons.[104]

Eventually, on 14 April, Amery informed Wavell that the India Committee had produced a scheme which he thought 'not too bad'. Wavell's suggestions were altered in two ways: it was proposed that the new members of the Executive Council should be selected from a group chosen by the provincial and central legislatures; and, to safeguard the Governor-General's (ie. Viceroy's) power to override the Executive Council in an emergency, that he be able to disregard the advice of his Council in specified fields. Wavell objected to the first of these suggestions on the grounds that consulting the provincial and central legislatures would result in a demand for the release of those members of the legislatures who were under detention, to enable them to participate, and this he thought premature; as to the second, it was Wavell's view that any attempt to increase the Governor-General's powers would cause an outcry from the Congress Party, whose objective was rather to diminish such powers. Further meetings followed that left Wavell feeling 'depressed and ruffled'.[105]

At one of these meetings four days later, Amery recorded that Attlee began by 'barking at Archie to the effect that he was in flat opposition to everything that the Committee favoured, after which we had a futile wrangle on the question whether Archie sufficiently recognized that what he was doing was an important constitutional departure.'[106] Much to Wavell's annoyance, he discovered that the India Committee was holding meetings without him, which made him feel like 'an Untouchable in the presence of Brahmins'. He realized they found him troublesome, and preferred 'to come to decisions without me', but thought this counterproductive, because 'they get annoyed if I raise objections to their work later on.'[107] At one stage John Simon, chairman in Attlee's absence, suggested that 'we had better drop any declaration and simply let Wavell go back to begin negotiating with Desai, Jinnah and Co.', but Amery pointed out that while they could have done so before Wavell's arrival, 'now something more definite was expected and in any case Wavell could not begin by an invitation to Indian leaders, whether broadcast or otherwise, without my being obliged to make an immediate statement in Parliament.'[108]

Private and social engagements offered a welcome contrast to political discussions. Wavell had agreed to sit for a bust by the sculptor Epstein, 'an odd, untidy, rather aggressive, self-opinionated little man whom I found attractive and intelligent.'[109] He dined at the fashionable West End restaurant Prunier's with the 'two reigning hostesses' of London, Lady Colefax and Lady Cunard, and he went to the theatre. He saw Laurence Olivier play *Richard III* – 'a marvellous piece of acting' – and John Gielgud as *Hamlet*, after which he dined with Gielgud and his leading lady Peggy Ashcroft, Rupert Hart-Davis's former wife, who was alternating Ophelia, Titania and the Duchess of Malfi in the Haymarket Repertory Season.[110]

Further discussions left Wavell still dejected by the end of April. 'I feel I have failed to make HMG realize the importance and urgency of the Indian problem or the real facts of the position. We have been talking for five weeks in a very disconnected way. The matter could have been settled in a week if they had really taken it seriously and wanted to. Now I think we have missed the bus in any case. The sudden complete collapse of the Germans, and the approaching reoccupation of the whole of Burma, will make Indian politicians much less accommodating than a few months ago. If I got my own way now, I feel it would be too late.'[111] But he realized it was inevitable that events in Europe should take priority. American forces had already reached Munich, and British troops had made their way from the toe of Italy to the Lido in Venice. The horrors of German war crimes had been revealed with the liberation of concentration camps at Belsen and Buchenwald. Mussolini had been executed by Italian patriots, his mutilated body hung up by the heels in the main square in Milan. On 30 April it was reported that Hitler had shot himself in his bunker in Berlin. The following day, 1 May, the German surrender in Italy became effective. In India, Coats was hearing rumours that Wavell might be sent to a defeated Germany as its 'Gauleiter': 'a beastly job and probably a knife in the back at the end of it.'[112] Yet despite the thrilling prospect of an end to the war, Amery noted, Churchill was as intransigent as ever when the Cabinet came to consider India. 'For half an hour or more Winston talked away, alternatively pouring contempt on the proposals as too trivial to have any effect anywhere and saying that the Indian problem could not be revolutionized in the last days of a dying Parliament. As usual he poured contempt on Wavell.'[113]

Wavell was still in London when VE – Victory in Europe – was cele-brated on 8 May. As people thronged the streets, Churchill's familiar voice crackled out over the radio. He was aware that there remained much to be done to reconstruct Europe, as well as a war in the Pacific to be concluded, and his speech was subdued. 'I told you hard things at the beginning of these last five years; you did not shrink, and I should be unworthy of your confidence and generosity if I did not still cry: Forward, unflinching, unswerving, indomitable, till the whole task is done and the whole world is safe and clean.'[114] On the afternoon of that momentous day Wavell went to the House of Lords to hear the announcement of the end of the European war, and later attended a service at Westminster Abbey. But despite the general euphoria and excitement he was still fretting, and eventually he 'blew off steam' to Amery about the way he was being kept hanging around. Amery counselled patience. There were, too, those who believed that despite the importance of what Wavell was trying to achieve, his visit to England was ill-timed. As Channon noted: 'He has been blundering and a bore to both Winston and the Cabinet. I am sorry for him.'[115]

Wavell, impervious to any such criticism, continued to be incensed by how badly he felt he was being treated.'One would think that with the Viceroy at home and available they would have asked his opinion on an important matter of great political significance which had been approved by the Governor-General in Council instead of contemptuously dismiss-ing it without even informing him . . . what a crew they are for a perilous voyage!'[116] Three days after this outburst in his journal, on Monday 14 May, Wavell had his first official contact with the India Committee for three weeks, a debate centred on safeguarding British business interests in India. Wavell responded to the various views for and against taking progressive steps by pointing out that only by force would it be possible to continue to treat India as a colony, a course which would in the long run be disas-trous: 'India's case merited and required sympathetic discussion.'[117] Privately he believed that while the Committee members maintained that the British Government wanted to give freedom to India, in reality they were opposing every suggestion for a step forward. At the end of the meet-ing it was agreed that Cripps's 1942 formula should be revived. Wavell could not refrain from pointing out that he had been in England for six and a half weeks, during three of which he had been 'completely ignored', and still there was no decision.[118]

For all Wavell's irritation, it was an inescapable fact that events in Britain and in Europe pushed India low on Churchill's list of priorities, which now included preparing for a General Election. Submitting his resignation to the King on 23 May, Churchill agreed to form a caretaker government pending elections in July. On 24 May Wavell sat down and wrote to Churchill, pointing out the length of time he had been at home, 'that I had had nothing from India Committee for 4 weeks or from himself for 7 weeks, and asking for a decision.' After discussions with Amery, he 'toned [his letter] down a bit'. Amery also had some good news: he had heard from Eden (who had been in the United States during most of Wavell's visit, first at Roosevelt's funeral and then at the San Francisco Conference) that Churchill planned to agree to a draft statement on India being made in Parliament, but that the timing was uncertain because of the impending dissolution. He might have agreed that a draft statement should be made, but Churchill was in no mood to hide his long-standing annoyance at Wavell's determination to come to England. Responding to the Viceroy's 'toned down' letter of complaint, he made it clear that they had not wanted him home, but that he had insisted on coming and 'that they had done their best for' him.[119]

On 30 May Wavell had an 'idle morning' while the Cabinet met to discuss his proposals for India. Churchill wanted to continue the talks at another Cabinet meeting in the early evening. When this went 'badly', yet another meeting was called for the following day, at which Wavell was to be invited to state his case, rather than having to rely on Amery to do so for him. That evening Wavell dined with Eden at the Athenaeum. Eden had always liked Wavell; he was sympathetic, and after 'a good talk' urged him to put his ideas to the Cabinet as convincingly as 'he had just put them to me.'[120] Churchill opened the meeting the next day 'with a long polemical statement'. Wavell then explained his belief that a meeting of Indian political leaders might offer a way forward. To his surprise, Churchill now declared himself prepared to agree to Wavell's proposals, with some amendments. Further discussions with the India Committee were scheduled for the afternoon; another Cabinet meeting would be held after dinner.

'The climax of my visit was an extraordinary one,' Wavell later noted. 'At the meeting of the Cabinet at 10.30 p.m. the PM made just as forcible an address in favour of my proposals as he had made in their damnation this morning.' He even approved Wavell's draft broadcast – with a couple of exceptions – 'and in fact exuded good will towards India and myself at every pore. He will change again but I suppose I can claim in the meantime some sort of personal triumph.' Wavell was under few illusions: Churchill had nothing to gain by making India an issue in the looming elections, and had decided 'to give way with good grace. What an extraordinary man he is!' At 11.30 p.m. – after six weeks, and just twelve hours before the Wavells' train was due to leave Victoria Station on the first stage of their return journey to India – Wavell got what he had come for: the go-ahead to hold a conference with India's political leaders in the hope of finding a way forward. 'It all ended in an atmosphere of good will and congratulations – only temporary, I fear.'[121] Amery was equally pleased: 'Everything ended on the happiest of happy notes and Wavell is still Viceroy and I Secretary of State, until at any rate the next row comes along.'[122] After midnight, standing in Horse Guards Avenue, Amery shook hands with Wavell. 'I told him that I believed we had, perhaps, pulled off a big thing, as big in its way as winning the war.' Later that day the Wavells set forth once more for India. In contrast to 1943, there were 'not many to see us off, thank heaven.' Lady Simon, the Lord Chancellor's wife, was there, however, 'and several times called down on me the blessing of St Patrick and all the saints.'[123]

19

Viceroy at Peace, 1945

We shall overcome our difficulties in the end. The future greatness of India is not in doubt . . . The failure of any political move narrows the field for future negotiations. A.P. Wavell[1]

B Y THE TIME the Wavells returned to India, the Pacific war was in its con-cluding stages: soon the world would be at peace once more. Wavell's immediate task was to put in motion his plans for a meeting of key members of the Congress Party and the Muslim League, as sanctioned in London. But when he presented his idea to the Executive Council in Delhi, it met 'with a very cold reception . . . what it really amounts to is that, as at home, nobody really wants to move at all.'[2] Indian public opinion welcomed Wavell's approach. 'I cannot help feeling that but for Lord Wavell's persistence, determination and genuine desire to give India its due, the current opinion held by Mr Churchill and the die-hards that India could be governed as it was before for another thirty years, could have held the field,' noted Vidya Shankar, Deputy Secretary in the Home Department.[3]

On 14 June Wavell broadcast his proposals. He explained that, with the exception of the Viceroy and the Commander-in-Chief, for the first time the Council would be made up entirely of Indians, who would hold the important portfolios of Home, Finance and Foreign Affairs previously held by British bureaucrats. The war against Japan was not yet over, and it was understood that the new Executive Council would continue to support offensive action. His Majesty's Government, said Wavell, had not lost sight of the need for agreement to be reached on a new constitution, and the purpose of the conference – to be held at Simla – was to make it easier to reach that agreement. Furthermore, those members of the Congress Working Committee detained since the 'Quit India' Movement in 1942 would be released. 'And so is launched a fresh attempt to help India to political freedom . . . whether it will crash on Indian intransigence, like the Cripps and other proposals, remains to be seen,' he noted in his journal.[4]

Shortly before leaving for Simla he wrote with characteristic generosity of spirit to Amery: 'I am annoyed that the proposals are being referred to as if mainly due to my initiative and the leading part you played is not being recognized out here. However your great sympathy for India will be known some day.'[5]

A week later Wavell arrived in Simla. Over the next fortnight, Peter Coats recalled that Viceregal Lodge, with its 'gilt chairs, silver throne . . . and tubs of hydrangeas', was full 'from dawn to dusk with the white-clad figures of Congress.'[6] The press were not invited, but an official statement on the conference's progress was issued each day. Even before the formal conference opened, Wavell had begun to appreciate the difficulties that lay ahead in dealing not just with the differences of opinion expressed by the Congress Party and the Muslim League, but with those of 'independent' figures who felt their interests were likely to be ignored by the major parties. Top of his concerns was the attitude of Khizr Hayat Khan Tiwana, Premier of the Unionist government in the Punjab, who informed Wavell that he was handing over power to the enemy, that his veto was 'dead as mutton', and prophesied chaos and disaster.[7] Wavell had his first encounter with Gandhi, who was not attending the conference but had travelled to Simla to be on hand for consultations. Millions of Indians might revere 'Gandhiji', but the Viceroy remained unconvinced of his sincerity. After their meeting – Wavell described it as 'mainly a discursive monologue' which included reminiscences of Gandhi's experiences in the Boer War – he conceded that Gandhi 'was friendly for the time being, but perfectly prepared to go back at any time on anything he had said.'[8] Archie John was less cynical: 'Whether he is a humbug or not in politics, there is no denying old man Gandhi's charm and it is clear that he is sincere in that the material comforts of this world matter not at all to him.'[9]

The conference opened on 25 June, after preliminary discussions. In all, twenty Indians from the provinces of British India were seated in the State Rooms of Viceregal Lodge with Wavell in the centre, the Congress Party to his left, the Muslim League to his right. Two secretaries were also present, Evan Jenkins and Rao Bahadur Vapal Pangunni Menon (known always as V.P.), an Indian civil servant born in Malabar in southern India who had assumed the position of Reforms Commissioner in 1942.[10] Among the key players were the President of the Congress Party, Maulana Azad, recently released from three years in prison; Mohammed Ali Jinnah, leader of the Muslim League, and his deputy Liaquat Ali Khan, a barrister from the United Provinces; Dr Khan Sahib, Premier of the North-West Frontier Province and Congress Party member; and Master Tara Singh, representing the Sikhs concentrated in the Punjab. Nehru too had been released from prison, but was not expected until the beginning of July. Only the Viceroy, the Commander-in-Chief and the Governor of the Punjab were permitted a car; for everyone else, travel was by rickshaw. As a matter of principle the Indian political leaders were reluctant to be transported by their fellow human beings, and when Nehru eventually arrived he insisted on riding a piebald pony.[11]

In summoning the Indian leaders to Simla, Wavell was providing them with an opportunity to discuss their political future freely for the first time since the war began. 'The statesmanship, wisdom and goodwill of all of us is here on trial,' he said in his opening remarks, 'not merely in the eyes of India but before the world.'[12] The significance of what he was trying to do was not lost on the Indian politicians. Those who had been jailed for three years were now being treated as future rulers. However, whereas agreement on the general principles under which a new, more representative Council would operate was straightforward, agreeing its composition – 'the real crux of the whole matter' – was far more difficult. As Wavell already realized, the sticking-point would be Jinnah's claim that the Muslim League had the right to nominate all Muslims on the Council, and Congress's belief that it also had the right to nominate a Muslim if it so wished (a view with which Wavell concurred). Wavell was especially concerned that the Punjab should be represented by a Punjabi Muslim, regardless of party affiliation. But Jinnah remained convinced that unless the Muslim League was permitted to nominate the quota of five Muslims, they would be outvoted. Wavell disagreed: 'I said that he was assuming that every vote would be taken on communal lines, and that if this was the spirit with which the Muslim League would enter the Council the whole purpose of it failed.' When Jinnah persisted in his claim that the League must nominate all Muslims, Wavell asked him 'bluntly whether he proposed to wreck the whole Conference on this issue.'[13]

As the man behind the initiative, Wavell's stock was rising. He was reported as having said that whatever their differing political opinions, the Indians were gentlemen. 'This remark of the Viceroy spread all over Simla and created a stir in both official and non-official circles,' noted Azad.[14] But within the framework of the conference, progress was uncertain. By 29 June Congress and the League had yet to agree on whose names they wished to submit; Wavell proposed that the two party leaders should each submit a list, from which he would choose an acceptable Council. Not for the first time he came to verbal blows with Jinnah, whom he described as being 'very difficult and argumentative, trying to corner me on some lawyer's point and refusing to give a straight answer.'[15] To give the leaders more time, Wavell adjourned the conference until 14 July. During the break, Jinnah again announced that he would not submit any names, because Wavell would not agree that the Muslim League represented all Muslims of the subcontinent. In consequence, even before the final meeting of the conference Wavell was recording its 'definite failure'. During these difficult weeks mealtime breaks with his family were a valued source of light relief: 'Every one of us, devoted to him, would try to make the short interval pass lightly, with talk of books or sport or even mild scandal – but never politics or war,' wrote Freya Stark, shortly to return to Europe after five months in the Wavell household.[16]

At the beginning of July Nehru reached Simla, his arrival coinciding with the first day on which Wavell felt free enough to go for a long walk. The sight of streets lined with police caused him a moment's irritation at what he considered unnecessarily heavy security, until he realized it was for Nehru. But the prospect of a breakthrough remained bleak: Jinnah was steadfast in his refusal to provide a list unless he could nominate all the Muslims; Wavell was not prepared to accept his right to do so; and he felt the Congress Party's list consisted of 'stooges' for the Party from the minority groups, including the 'scheduled castes' and the lowest in the Hindu caste system, the Untouchables. Under the circumstances Wavell felt compelled to make his own provisional selection, which included four members of the Muslim League and one Punjabi Muslim, and sent the list to London for Cabinet approval. Wavell had another meeting with Jinnah, who refused to change his stand, and with Gandhi, whose opinion he recorded: the British Government – sooner or later – would have to accept either the Hindu or the Muslim point of view, since the two were 'irreconcilable'.[17] 'So ends my attempt to introduce a fresh impetus and a fresh spirit into Indian politics,' he noted mournfully on 11 July.[18]

In Wavell's final address at Simla, he boldly took responsibility for the outcome of the conference. 'The main idea underlying [it] was mine. If it had succeeded, its success would have been attributed to me, and I cannot place the blame for its failure upon any of the parties.'[19] Such magnanimity in adversity earned him yet more respect; his concern was to avoid recriminations which might lead to a worsening of relations between the Muslim and Hindu communities. Writing privately to Amery, he laid the blame on Jinnah's 'intransigence about Muslim representation and Muslim safeguards,' but also conceded that a deeper cause was the keen distrust felt by Muslims – except for the pro-Nationalists – for the Congress Party and the Hindus. 'Their fear that Congress, by parading its national character and using Muslim dummies, will permeate the entire administration of any united India is real and cannot be dismissed as an obsession of Jinnah and his immediate entourage.'[20] Outwardly, as Archie John observed, he remained stoic. ' My father, as always, though he must have been very sad, concealed his disappointment and simply looked forward to the future without any looking back on might-have-beens.'[21] At least, Wavell noted, his pains had earned him two complimentary messages from the Cabinet – though as Amery noted regretfully, they 'mostly seem pleased' at its failure.[22]

Wavell was not the only person to experience disappointment that July of 1945. On the 25th the long-awaited British general election took place. Churchill had been busy meeting Stalin and Truman at Potsdam to discuss the future of Poland; as he later wrote, he had not burdened himself unduly with the elections 'while occupied with the grave business of the Conference'.[23] The following morning he and his fellow Conservatives awoke to the unexpected news of a landslide victory in favour of Clement Attlee's Labour Party. Wavell wrote immediately to Churchill, setting aside their past differences: 'My Dear Prime Minister (I must still call you so, as I still so think of you),

> I feel I must write you a few lines to try and express my feelings, now that you have laid down your long and glorious leadership of the country. I have served you for five years, to the best of my limited abilities, in various responsible posts with which you thought fit to entrust me. I think you have sometimes wondered whether I was more of a liability or an asset, but I hope that you have found me, with all my shortcomings, a loyal subordinate who always tried to carry out your plans. I would like you to know that at all times my admiration for your courage and for your vigorous direction of affairs has been unbounded.

He went on to thank Churchill for having trusted him with such responsibilities, and ended with a reminder that he had been promised a signed photograph, and that he would be proud to have one.[24] Whatever Churchill may have thought of such sympathy from the man he had so often rebuked, he replied graciously that he was 'much complimented' by Wavell's very kind letter, which he would 'preserve as a record of our eventful comradeship'.[25] Wavell also shared some of his feelings with Ismay – 'I shall feel rather lost without him as leader, after all these years I have worked for him' – and confided his disappointment over the conference.[26]

The Simla Conference was however more significant than perhaps even Wavell could have hoped. It raised the curtain on what was to become the biggest issue in future negotiations among the varying Indian factions. As Azad later noted, 'The Simla Conference marks a breakwater in Indian political history. This was the first time when negotiations failed, not on the basic political issue between India and Britain, but on the communal issue dividing different Indian groups.'[27] For the first time, the King's Representative had apparently been genuinely attempting to move forward. Azad was impressed 'by the frankness and sincerity of the Viceroy . . . I saw that his attitude was not that of a politician but of a soldier . . . It struck me that his approach was very different from that of Sir Stafford Cripps. Cripps had tried to present his proposals in as favourable a light as possible. He highlighted the strong points and tried to slur over the difficulties. Lord Wavell made no attempt at embellishment and he certainly was not trying to make an impression.'[28]

On 1 August Wavell and his eleven governors assembled for a two-day conference in Delhi. As well as the usual topics of food, coal, cloth, resettlement of soldiers, they reviewed the consequences of the Simla Conference. Discussion also revolved around the holding of elections in the autumn to the provincial and central assemblies, the first since 1937 – but Wavell was not satisfied. Elections, he said, were inevitable but without a definite policy might, 'after some months' dislocation of administration and communal agitation, leave us exactly where we were.'[29] Immediately after the conference he wrote to Attlee's new Secretary of State, Frederick Pethick-Lawrence,[30] who was 72 and who he feared might have 'fixed and old-fashioned ideas derived mainly from Congress contacts',[31] politely suggesting that he might like to visit India 'fairly soon' to acquaint himself with the current situation.[32] Meanwhile, the Viceroy had temporarily found a new golfing partner. Colonel Craig Smyser, a West Point graduate serving with the Engineer Corps, recalled Wavell as not a 'stylish golfer', but one who did 'remarkably well' considering his limited opportunities. He also, perhaps inevitably, became familiar with Wavell's poetic outbursts, remembering in particular one occasion when it took the Viceroy several strokes to get out of a bunker: 'On the last one, I heard him quote one of the stanzas of W.E. Henley's "Invictus", which goes: "Out of the night that covers me, / Black is the pit from pole to pole, / I thank whatever Gods may be, / For my unconquerable soul".'[33]

By late summer the war with Japan had entered its final and deadliest phase with the dropping of two atomic bombs on Hiroshima and Nagasaki on 6 and 8 August; an estimated 120,000 died in the two blasts.[34] Wavell was concerned about the advisability of using such a destructive weapon. 'I doubt whether man has yet the wisdom to use it wisely. It may end war or it may end civilization.'[35] The Japanese capitulated on 14 August 1945; one of Wavell's first 'horrors of peace' was to write a victory broadcast.[36] Characteristically, when three 'rather dreary pieces of scripture' were suggested for the Lesson he was to read at the Thanksgiving Service, he said he would prefer to read the triumphant Song of Deborah, the Jewish prophetess who helped lead an Israelite army against the Canaanites, as narrated in the Book of Judges. He was warned that it would not be in keeping with the 'spirit of the Service' but considered it entirely appropriate for a victory celebration, and duly read it: 'Praise ye the Lord for the avenging of Israel, when the people willingly offered themselves. Hear, O ye kings; give ear, O ye princes; I, even I, will sing unto the Lord.'[37] As well as keeping his journal, Wavell embarked on a review of his life from its beginnings. In what became known as his 'Recollections' he described his early life and schooldays, Sandhurst, the Boer War, his first years in India and so on. He had taken to working at a stand-up desk, commenting deadpan that in the land where heavy curry lunches were common, he would fall asleep in the afternoon at an ordinary desk.[38]

Instead of the Secretary of State visiting India, as Wavell had proposed, in late August he himself was back in London 'to make the acquaintance of the new Government and to get a line on their views about India.' In some ways Wavell was expecting Attlee and his colleagues to be easier to deal with than Churchill; in others, not. He was concerned, for example, that they might be 'much too sympathetic to the unpractical ideas of Indian politicians (and all Indian politicians are more or less unpractical), and thus more difficult, when it comes to keeping law and order.' On the Government's side, after the failure of Simla, Attlee wanted to see if Cripps's 1942 proposals could be revived, and whether a 'Constituent' body could be convened once the elections were over. But Wavell was sceptical about reviving the 1942 offer, believing the proposals much less likely 'to be accepted by the parties now than before.'[39]

On 29 August, after preliminary discussions with Attlee and Pethick-Lawrence, whom he found to be 'old, pleasant and amiable', Wavell went to Downing Street for a meeting of the newly named India and Burma Committee presided over by the Prime Minister. With Churchill no longer in the driving seat, the dynamics of the Indian problem had of course changed. Churchill was a self-confessed imperialist; Attlee, initially a Conservative but converted to Socialism by working in the East End of London, was set on decolonization. Wavell took Simla as his starting point. Its failure, he said, had narrowed the field and 'brought us up more firmly than ever against the communal issue.' It was his belief that Jinnah would be unlikely to enter into discussions 'without a previous guarantee of acceptance in principle of Pakistan.' And much as he had tried to accommodate the interests of non-Muslim League Muslims, it was now his view that 'Jinnah spoke for 99 per cent of the Muslim population of India in their apprehension of Hindu domination.' Whether or not this fear was well-founded, Wavell was convinced that it existed. Before further progress could be made he therefore believed it was essential to face up to 'the problem of Pakistan', which had never been objectively analysed. If Pakistan could be publicly shown to be 'a wholly impracticable proposition' it would, he thought, greatly reduce 'the vigour with which they would be prepared to go into action in support of it.'[40]

To demonstrate how difficult partition would be, in a separate 'Note' Wavell looked at what would happen in Punjab and Bengal: Muslims were in a majority, and Jinnah was suggesting the provinces should become part of Pakistan following a plebiscite held among the Muslim population only. For both provinces Wavell's conclusion was the same: it would not be fair to give a majority population of Muslims the right to determine the fate of a minority. He therefore concluded that there was no clear scheme of partition which the Government could announce 'as their notion of the ultimate safeguard for the Muslims. Nor can such a scheme be prepared immediately and without consultation with Indian opinion.'[41] In the meantime, the Cabinet decided to re-state Cripps's 1942 proposals with a view to the formation of a constitution-making body for a united India, unless the Indian leaders had agreed on another method before the end of the election period.[42]

The Wavells left England in the Viceregal train on 13 September. Felicity had come to England to act as her father's PA and 'stenographer' (which 'she did very well') and decided to stay on with Pamela, who was expecting her second child in March, having 'had enough of the East and of her parents for the time being.' But Joan and Diana returned to India with them, as did Wavell's sister Nancy. Simon Astley was now back in Delhi and so, said Wavell, 'we have quite a riding party again in the mornings'.[43] There were also goodbyes to be said in India. After nearly six years spent working for Wavell, Peter Coats had decided to go home. He had made up his mind before the Simla Conference, but found it hard to break the news, and did not tell Wavell until after the Viceroy had returned from London. After a game of golf and 'over a strong drink, I broached the topic. It took some doing. You know how sometimes he does not seem to understand things? Well, he just went blank on me and thought I meant leave. When I explained, he seemed upset and said "Well, that will be the breaking of a link. We've seen the war through together, Peter." '[44] Before Coats left the Wavells gave a farewell party for him 'and were kindness itself'. 'Late on the night before my dawn departure, I was alone in what had been my sitting-room. It was now dismantled; packing-cases and trunks stood about. There was a knock at the door, and it was the Viceroy, asking if he could come in. In all the two years we had lived under the same roof, I do not think he had ever just appeared like that. I gave him a drink, and he sat in silence on one of the boxes. For once I could not think of anything to say, and indeed there was nothing. After a few minutes he went away.'[45]

On 19 September Wavell announced the holding of elections. The British Government, he said, were determined to go ahead with bringing 'self-government' to India. 'It is now for Indians to show that they have wisdom, faith and courage to determine in what way they can best reconcile their differences.'[46] But his statement appeared vague, and disappointed Indian public opinion since there was no mention of independence. The issue of captured Indian National Army soldiers also came to a head when the first trial for 'waging war against the King' of three INA officers – symbolically, a Muslim, a Hindu and a Sikh – began in the Red Fort in Old Delhi on 5 November. In the post-war, pre-independence atmosphere, the general mood among Indian civilians – except for those who had suffered directly at the hands of the INA – was for leniency towards their compatriots.[47] 'Patriots not Traitors' read some of the billboards held high outside the Red Fort by sympathizers. The Congress Party opened a fund for their defence, and for a short period Nehru, who had not practised law for more than 25 years, sat among the defence lawyers. As a soldier, Wavell considered the actions of the INA treasonable; at the same time, he was able to understand the growing anti-British bias, as expressed to him in a letter from George Cunningham, Governor of the North-West Frontier Province: 'The thing is daily becoming more and more purely Indian versus British, and less and less ill-disposed Indians versus British cum well-disposed Indians.'[48] Wavell replied appreciatively: 'It is about as difficult a case as one could want.' However, he also believed that Indians should recognize 'that though we have gone to the limit of clemency, we have not entirely forgotten the 40,000 out of 60,000 of the Indian Army who were loyal to their allegiance and refused to give way to pressure and join the enemy.'[49] In his annual address to the Associated Chambers of Commerce, Wavell expressed himself publicly: 'Whatever your political views, if you cannot acclaim the man who prefers honour to his ease, who remains

341

steadfast in adversity to his pledged faith, then you have a poor notion of the character which is required to build up a nation.'[50]

Such was the pressure for leniency that both Wavell and Auchinleck had to re-think official policy. As Auchinleck wrote to the Viceroy at the end of November, 'It is impossible to apply our standards of ethics to this problem or to shape our policy as we would, had the INA been men of our own race.'[51] Henceforward Auchinleck, with Wavell's agreement, proposed to drop the charge of 'waging war against the King' and try only those accused of committing brutality and murder. When judgment was passed on the first three INA accused, Auchinleck reduced the sentence from transportation for life and cashiering and forfeiture of pay and allowances to cashiering and forfeiture of pay and allowances. In the years to come the 'myth' of the INA's 'patriotism' persisted. Subhas Chandra Bose, reported by the Japanese to have been killed in a plane crash soon after the surrender, became a hero of the Indian freedom movement. His older brother Sarat believed the crash had been 'staged'. At the time, Wavell recognized the potency of Bose's appeal. 'I wonder if the Japanese announcement of Subhas Chandra Bose's death in an air crash is true; I suspect it very much, it is just what would be given out if he meant to go underground . . . If it is true, it will be a great relief. His disposal would have presented a most difficult problem.'[52]

As 1945 drew to a close Wavell sent Pethick-Lawrence an appreciation of the political situation, outlining his objectives for 1946. According to his programme of action, he wanted to secure a 'reasonably efficient' Executive Council with representatives of the principal parties on a proportional basis, and to form a Constitution-making body which could produce a workable and acceptable Constitution to bring about provincial governments as far as possible on a coalition basis. Although elections were shortly to be held Wavell wanted to move as quickly as possible, which meant starting discussions to form the Executive Council in February, before all the results were known. Above all, Wavell remained concerned that, with the mood in the country still volatile, Congress could 'undoubtedly bring about a very serious revolt against British rule', which the British could still probably suppress but only 'after a considerable amount of bloodshed'. In other words, the British would be put in an 'untenable position' unless they found a solution. 'Our chief problem is to find some bridge between Hindu and Muslim.'[53]

On the same day in another long letter to Pethick-Lawrence Wavell fleshed out his thoughts on what should be done if there were a breakdown in negotiations and the British felt compelled to leave India without having reached a settlement, suggesting that all knowledge of any such plan should be restricted to a limited number of people. At this stage Wavell's 'break-down plan' consisted of 'exposing the dangers and disadvantages of the Pakistan scheme', and he felt a breakdown would be most likely to occur either because of 'excessive requirement by the Muslim League for repre-sentation and safeguards' or because of a demand by Congress 'for the abo-lition or weakening of the Governor-General's [Viceroy's] power of veto.' If the Muslims continued to insist on 'self-determination in genuinely Muslim areas', Wavell suggested it should be conceded; there could how-ever be no question of compelling the large non-Muslim population to remain in any future 'Pakistan' against their will. An additional considera-tion was the 'dangerous mood' which might be induced in the Sikhs, whose community would be divided. Furthermore, Wavell believed it would be 'embarrassing and not really honest' to concede the principle of 'Pakistan' without defining its area – but also that once the prospective new country had been demarcated, the Congress and the League would realize that their interests would be better served by remaining within the Federation.[54]

On New Year's Eve Wavell wrote a long and thoughtful letter to King George. 'There has been no real change of heart in Congress, but I think they have changed their tactics to the extent of trying to avoid any outbreak until after the elections, so that we may perhaps have a comparatively peace-ful month or two ahead.' He was pessimistic about the future: 'It is difficult to see how any agreement is to be secured between Congress and Muslim League on the composition of a new Executive Council or of a Constitution-making convention.' Failing agreement, he did not see how conflict could be avoided. 'I believe someone once described golf as "get-ting a small ball into a hole with instruments singularly ill-adapted for the purpose". The political leaders in India – Gandhi, Jinnah, Nehru and the others – are certainly singularly ill-adapted for delicate constitutional nego-tiation and will almost inevitably land one in the rough or some very deep bunkers.' His final thoughts were on the need to gain agreement in order to avoid an upheaval which might be more serious than the civil disobedience movement of 1942. 'I confess that I don't quite know how it is going to be done.'[55] Personally, Wavell felt overworked, as he told Freya Stark: 'The rou-tine seems heavier than ever and the political outlook gloomier, and the carpets redder and the boxes greener, and I have no time to read what I want to read or write what I want to write or meet those I want to meet.'[56]

Despite the very different peacetime climate in which 1946 began, as his letter to the King made clear, Wavell did not regard the New Year with much enthusiasm. He realized that everyone – both in India and in Britain – wanted to find a way to transfer power in India equitably, and with the least bloodshed possible. He also knew that the responsibility for finding that solution lay with him, and in his journal he wondered whether his 'brain power or personality' were equal to the task. As well as the political situation, Wavell had been pondering the future of the Indian Army, especially the Gurkha units who formed one-fifth of its forces. As both he and Auchinleck realized, it was unlikely the Nepalese soldiers would want to continue in an independent India as part of the Indian Army under Indian officers. An alternative would be for them to be employed directly by Britain 'as part of an Imperial strategic reserve, either in the Middle East or in the Far East, or elsewhere.'[57] As Wavell told Pethick-Lawrence, this was the option he favoured: 'I am sure you will recognize that this is a most delicate matter in which strict secrecy should be observed by all concerned.'[58] At a meeting with Jinnah on 5 January Wavell found him to be 'rather less difficult in manner than at Simla but just as uncompromising in substance.' On the same day he greeted a delegation of Members of Parliament from England, sent to India to reassure Indian politicians that Britain was genuinely intending to transfer power: 'quite a pleasant body with little knowledge of India but anxious to learn.'[59]

With the prospect of a hard year ahead, in early January Wavell and Queenie had a break from Delhi touring Bombay, with visits to Poona and Satara. As was usual on such a tour, the Viceroy had a variety of official and semi-official commitments, one of which was laying the cornerstone of the new stadium of the Maharashtra cricket club. Despite the mundane nature of the task he made what the Governor's ADC, Captain Michael Conville, called a 'very good' speech.[60] Sport, he said, was becoming 'so highly specialized, so competitive in spirit, and so international in outlook' that there was a danger of losing sight of its true aims, which were 'to encourage the many to take part in healthy recreation, whatever their standard of ability, rather than to exhibit the skill of a few chosen players.'[61] One thing Wavell found 'tiresome' was the custom of presenting the honoured guest with a garland: 'an Englishman feels a fool and looks a fool, when a very large garland of wet flowers is hung round his neck and a large tight bouquet of flowers pressed into his hand and a platoon of photographers crowd round to take photographs.' His main problem was deciding how soon he could decently remove the garland, which was 'usually dripping down one's neck and soaking one's collar . . . I have decided that as soon as the photographers have recorded the event, the garlander is quite satisfied and the garlandee can remove the garland.'[62]

In London, the India and Burma Committee was considering 'the Viceroy's Plan of Action' sent to Pethick-Lawrence at the end of 1945. On 10 January the Secretary of State circulated his own detailed comments on Wavell's proposals for re-forming the Executive Council, and his suggestion that a 'breakdown plan' should be in place in case negotiations failed. Overall, Pethick-Lawrence's response to Wavell's proposals was negative. He did not think it advisable, as Wavell had suggested, to advance the date for discussing the formation of the Executive Council; instead he believed that once the results of the elections were known in all provinces, it would be easier to determine exactly how much support there was for 'Pakistan' among Indians themselves. As to a 'breakdown plan', Pethick-Lawrence was prepared to acknowledge that the 'Viceroy is clearly right in saying that our plans must cater for the probability of a deadlock arising on the Pakistan issue or on the matter of the Viceroy's veto'; he was also prepared to concede that Wavell was justified in asking 'that we should have available a plan worked out in detail for a partition'; but at this stage in the negotiations neither he nor Attlee was prepared to move further in formalizing it. Furthermore, Pethick-Lawrence counselled delay in publicizing the proposed shape of a future Pakistan, on the grounds that such a delineation would tend to preclude 'any other solution of the Hindu–Moslem question'; in addition, it might adversely affect 'the prospect of the Indian [Princely] States coming into an all-India Constitution'.[63]

In Cabinet discussions with Attlee, a similar conclusion was reached. Jinnah was to be given no intimation as to the proposed frontiers of Pakistan before the Constitution-making body had had the opportunity of coming to an agreement among themselves, 'whether on an all-India or a Pakistan solution'. Moreover, like Wavell they believed the demand for 'Pakistan' might well break down because of practical difficulties, 'once Indian politicians could be brought to face up to them (which hitherto they had failed to do).' Ultimately, the Cabinet members believed, for both economic and defence reasons both Muslim and Hindu politicians 'might be brought together in some kind of federal solution.'[64]

Attlee's own preferred course of action remained a revival of Cripps's 1942 proposals, which envisaged the framing of a new constitution by the Indian political leaders themselves, for which purpose he intended to send another mission from London: on 24 January Wavell received a telegram informing him that a delegation of three ministers would arrive in Delhi in March. Past experience made him sceptical that a delegation which spent one or two weeks in India would achieve anything. 'From my own point of view, it relieves me of some of the immediate load of responsibility, I suppose; but it may increase it in the end, as I suspect that I may be left with all the loose and awkward ends to tie up and perhaps to implement a policy with which I do not agree.'[65] To prepare the ground for the delegation, Pethick-Lawrence finally asked Wavell for his recommendations 'as regards definition of genuinely Moslem areas if we are compelled to give a decision on this.'[66] While he was on tour in Bangalore Wavell responded: 'If compelled to indicate demarcation of genuinely Moslem areas' he recommended that in the west Sind, the North-West Frontier Province, Baluchistan and the Rawalpindi Multan and Lahore divisions of the Punjab should be included, 'less Amritsar and Gurdaspur districts'. In Bengal and Assam he made similar recommendations, excluding those areas which, although part of the province, did not have a majority of Muslims. As regards the Punjab, he was quite clear in specifying that the only Muslim-majority district that would not go to Pakistan was Gurdaspur, which for 'geographical reasons should go with Amritsar'; this, 'being sacred city of Sikhs must stay out of Pakistan.' He acknowledged that much of Lahore district was irrigated from the Upper Bari Doab canal with its headworks in Gurdaspur district, and that this was 'awkward but there is no solution that avoids all such difficulties.' The most important issue, as Wavell saw it, was to make provision for the Sikhs, whose homelands and sacred places were on both sides of any new frontier. 'This problem is one which no version of Pakistan can solve.'[67]

When Wavell learned the names of those making up the 'Cabinet Mission', he was unenthusiastic: Pethick-Lawrence, Cripps, and A.V. Alexander, the First Lord of the Admiralty, 'to act in association with the Viceroy'. 'I am afraid Cripps will be the operative element and I think he is sold to the Congress point of view, and I don't think he is quite straight in his methods . . . I cannot so far get from HMG any definite policy.'[68] Wavell was concerned to let the Government back home know prior to the arrival of the 'three Magi' that he did not propose to be treated as 'a lay figure', and wrote accordingly to Pethick-Lawrence, who assured him it was their 'firm intention' that the negotiations would be undertaken 'by you and ourselves acting together as a team'.[69] As far as Wavell could understand, they seemed to have no plans but were 'hoping to collect some out here by a long series of talks.'[70]

Still Wavell had to lobby for food: once more the spectre of famine loomed, and he was anxious to avert it. Indians remained disaffected because of the continuing INA trials; invariably their anger erupted in strikes and rioting in sympathy with the imprisoned soldiers. But Wavell and Auchinleck refused to halt those trials where the cases involved brutality.[71] Another grave concern was the mutiny of Indian sailors in Bombay which occurred in late February. As news of the disturbances spread, others joined in. By the end of the month the uprising had been quelled and the mutineers had surrendered, but the incident added more fuel to Wavell's argument that law and order were perilously close to breaking down.

The results of the elections held throughout British India marked a watershed. As the first test of political opinion since before the war, they demonstrated a dramatic change in the map of India. The Muslim League won all the Muslim seats in the Central Assembly, leaving the Congress Party with most of the rest. In the Provincial Assemblies a similar pattern was reflected, with the exception of the Muslim-majority North-West Frontier Province, where the Congress Party led by Dr Khan Sahib prevailed. In the Punjab the League won more than half the seats but a coalition of Sikhs, Hindus and the Unionist Party under Khizr Hayat's leadership excluded the League from control. The Muslim League's over-all success meant that henceforward, as Wavell was beginning to realize, Jinnah's claim to represent the Muslims of the subcontinent had to be taken seriously. Ever one to cherish the humorous side of an event where one was to be found, Wavell had noted that the 'one light touch' of the election campaign had been a petition from the Santals of Bihar objecting to the date which had been fixed: surely His Excellency knew that there was a great tribal holiday which meant they would be 'drunk for a week and unable to attend to any business'.[72]

Shortly before the Cabinet Mission's arrival, personal tragedy struck the Wavell family. On 21 March, while riding his motorcycle in Quetta, Simon Astley was killed. Wavell and Queenie flew at once to Quetta with Joanie for the funeral. It was, Wavell said, 'very hard on poor little Joan'.[73]

Three days later, the process by which the British Government was attempting to transfer power to a representative Indian Government entered its next phase with the arrival of the special 'Cabinet Mission' from Britain. Inevitably the press aroused interest and excitement with articles and editorials. One cartoon illustrated better than words the dilemma they faced. Entitled 'Can they make up the jigsaw?' it showed Wavell, Cripps, Pethick-Lawrence and Alexander staring at a number of jigsaw pieces on a table. On the wall was a map of India, with the title 'complete picture', showing Jinnah and Gandhi embracing, captioned 'Unified India fit to govern'.[74] Over the next three months, in the heat of a Delhi summer, with Wavell cast in the role of host, umpire and scapegoat, the 'three Magi' jointly worked on a plan to give independence to India.

20

Unity or Partition, 1946

> To establish in a stable form a united India under Indian rule is going
> to be an uncommonly difficult problem.   A.P. Wavell[1]

WAVELL'S NEXT FEW months as Viceroy of India were spent almost
entirely in trying to break the political deadlock between the
Congress Party and the Muslim League, while keeping the subcontinent
united. As his correspondence indicates, from the moment of assuming the
Viceroyalty he had no illusions about the difficulties. He had to endure not
only the prevarications of the Indian political leaders but the divergent
views and actions of the British politicians. Even as the 'three Magi' arrived
in India, Wavell thought that, 'pleasant and friendly' though they were, it
was questionable whether they had any definite plans in their heads.[2] The
Cabinet Mission's task was to try to agree with the Indian leaders 'a new
constitutional structure' for India, and to set up an 'Interim Government'
to carry on with the administration of the country; to this end the delegates
were instructed to 'discuss and explore all possible alternatives without proceeding upon any fixed or rigid pre-conceived plan.'[3] The objective was to
encourage the Indian leaders to make their own suggestions, rather than for
the British Government to dictate India's political future. Immediately after
the Mission's arrival Wavell wrote a 'Note' in which once more his fear of
impending disorder was plain: 'We are going into these negotiations with
an extremely difficult hand to play, owing to the necessity to avoid the mass
movement or revolution in India which it is in the power of the Congress
to start, and which we are not certain that we can control. It is obvious that
Congress will use the threat of such a movement to secure as much as possible of their demands, even unreasonable ones.'[4] Wavell was even contemplating the necessity of using the 'Big Stick' if no agreement could be
reached: sanctions of various kinds which would cut off India from
necessary supplies such as oil, kerosene and imports. For the time being,
however, the negotiating table was seen as the only way forward.

The members of the Mission began their work by having a series of consultations with Wavell, the governors of the provinces and the current members of the Executive Council. They then held discussions with the main Indian political figures; they also had to consider the future of the Princely States. Until recently the princes had chosen to wait and see what should arise from discussions with the major political parties, on the assumption that there was little to be gained by taking any decisions until the future of British India had been resolved. Wavell had already given an assurance that HMG had no intention of initiating any change in the relationship between the Princely States and the British Government without their consent; but it was inevitable that the Cabinet Mission, though the matter was not central to the main issue of giving independence to British India, would have to formalize exactly what the States' future relationship with the new Indian government would be.

At the outset Wavell found himself critical of the calibre of the three men sent to negotiate India's future: as Secretary of State for India Pethick-Lawrence was the most senior minister, but not 'a very good negotiator or questioner, he is inclined to be sloppy and long-winded and makes little speeches instead of asking questions.' Cripps, on the other hand, was 'an expert and incisive cross-examiner', but, mindful of his difficult encounters with Gandhi in 1942, appeared determined not to fall foul of the Congress leaders; this Wavell perceived as translating itself into an over-zealous desire to please them. Alexander did not speak much, and his knowledge of Indian affairs was 'scanty'.[5] Wavell was at the same time the éminence grise and, on occasion, the Cinderella kept away from the ball, and he was annoyed that Cripps held separate discussions with the Congress leaders to which he was not invited. As Vidya Shankar noted, 'different kinds of pulls were at work. This meant different sympathies and angles of vision which seem to have made it difficult for the Cabinet Mission to follow a clear strategy and a straight path despite Lord Wavell's well-meant efforts.'[6]

On 11 April the Mission issued a statement to the effect that, having heard the opinions of the most important political figures, they now proposed to enter the next stage: finding a solution. Four days later Azad gave the Congress position, which included a demand for complete independence, a united India, and a single federation comprising fully autonomous units. Congress hoped that Muslim fears of domination by the Hindu majority could be relieved without actually giving them an independent country. Jinnah meanwhile remained adamant that there was no scheme which could prevent the Hindus dominating the Muslims, and that the only solution was for complete sovereignty in the six provinces – Punjab, Sind, Baluchistan, NWFP, Bengal and Assam – in which Muslims were in the majority (not exactly the 'moth-eaten' Pakistan of predominantly Muslim areas in the north-west and north-east offered by Gandhi in 1944). By 18 April Wavell was recording in his journal that the inevitable outcome would be for him and the Cabinet Mission to suggest a solution, subject to the British Government's approval, which they would then have to put to the Congress Party and the Muslim League. 'So far all the gifts of these Magi – the frankincense of goodwill, the myrrh of honeyed words, the gold of promises – have produced little.'[7]

After these preliminary discussions the Cabinet Mission took a short holiday in Kashmir, leaving Wavell to enjoy 'the most peaceful weekend' he had had for a long time 'with the Delegation off and the Easter holiday on.'[8] Returning the next week the Mission put forward as a basis for negotiation a 'three-tier' proposal. At the top would be the union of India, composed of an equal number of representatives from the Hindu majority and Muslim majority provinces, together with representatives from the Princely States; in the middle, the sub-federations of 'Hindustan' and 'Pakistan' with separate legislatures; the bottom would be composed of provinces and States or groups of States which had agreed to join either Hindustan or Pakistan, which would deal with other issues relevant to their respective provinces.[9] It was suggested that the Congress Party and Muslim League should each nominate four representatives to go to Simla for a 'second Simla conference' to discuss the proposal. Azad's nominees were himself, Nehru (who he announced was to succeed him as Congress President in May), former Congress President Sardar Vallabhbhai Patel and Dr Khan Sahib's brother Abdul Ghaffar Khan, from the North-West Frontier Province. Jinnah chose Liaquat Ali Khan, plus Sardar Abdur Rab Khan Nishtar from the NWFP and Nawab Muhammad Ismail Khan from the United Provinces, both members of the Muslim League Working Committee. At the same time, Wavell was intending to proceed with negotiations for the formation of the Interim Government.[10]

At the beginning of May the Mission left the heat of New Delhi for Simla to begin its second phase. After preliminary discussions, deliberations began on 5 May – Wavell's sixty-third birthday, which left him wondering whether it was an auspicious day for such a critical meeting. As previously, Gandhi did not attend the meetings but was available for consultations. Yet again, the respective parties could only agree to differ. On the one hand, Congress wished to maintain a strong centre, precluded by the option for grouping; the Muslim League, while accepting a single union, had not given up its goal of achieving a separate Pakistan. Throughout the proceedings Wavell cast a disapproving eye on the negotiating style of both Pethick-Lawrence, whose 'benevolent generalities' made it impossible for the British to take a tougher stand, and Cripps, who evidently favoured Congress's position. Having entered into the negotiations with low expectations, Wavell was less disappointed when the second Simla Conference ended 'with much the same fate as the first', noting that it was a 'political show', and that his 'soldier's judgement and direct methods seem crude and clumsy to them.'[11]

The Cabinet Mission had at least formalized its position regarding the future of the Princely States. On 12 May a Memorandum on States' Treaties and Paramountcy was presented to the Nawab of Bhopal, Chancellor of the Chamber of Princes. It was already evident that once the British had left, the Chamber's members would no longer be in a position to enjoy the same relationship with the British Government as they had previously. As 'a logical sequence and in view of the desires expressed to them on behalf of the Indian States, His Majesty's Government will cease to exercise the powers of Paramountcy. This means that the rights of the States which flow from their relationship to the Crown will no longer exist and that all the rights surrendered by the States to the Paramount Power will return to the States.'[12] Until agreement could be reached on what new constitutional structure was to take the place of British India, no further arrangements could be made.

In New Delhi, in exceptional heat, the Mission set to work on further proposals. On 16 May a lengthy statement was published in the name of the 'Cabinet Mission to India and His Excellency the Viceroy' which analysed the negotiations so far. Included was an assessment of the 'Pakistan' claimed by the Muslim League, and of the smaller independent Pakistan confined to Muslim majority areas alone already rejected by the Muslim League as impracticable, and which the Cabinet Mission believed 'would be contrary to the wishes and interests of a very large proportion of the inhabitants of these Provinces.' In their opinion, the most practical and fairest solution was still the three-tier proposal with the country federated into three sections, A, B and C. Section A would comprise Madras, Bombay, United Provinces, Bihar, the Central Provinces and Orissa, Section B would include the Punjab, Sind, the North-West Frontier Province and Baluchistan, and Section C Bengal and Assam. Defence, Foreign Affairs and Communications would belong to the central government. Since most issues would be dealt with at the provincial level, Muslims would have almost complete autonomy in sections B and C in which they predominated. The constitution would be drafted by a Constituent Assembly which would be elected by members of the provincial legislatures. After ten years, by a majority vote of its legislature, any province could request its position within its respective section to be reconsidered.[13] After releasing the statement, Wavell and his political colleagues had to wait for a response from the Indian leaders.

As always, Wavell found mental relaxation in writing letters. His correspondence with Liddell Hart continued, but such was his eminence as Viceroy that the friendly exchanges had become more formal. He had also been obliged to decline to support Liddell Hart's application for the Chichele Chair in Military History, which had again become vacant at All Souls, having already promised support to another candidate. Nevertheless, the war was still a fruitful topic for a candid exchange of views. Liddell Hart had been interviewing surviving German generals and sent Wavell his notes; preoccupied as Wavell was with the Cabinet Mission, he read these with interest, and in replying maintained that he was not impressed with those Germans who blamed everything on Hitler: 'I feel that if we had lost, we should not have blamed it all on Winston.' He was especially interested in the Germans' early estimate that the campaigns in Greece and Crete had delayed their attack on Russia. 'It seems clear that the delay was at least a month, and that some of the armoured formations had not fully recuperated. There is no doubt, also, that Crete effectively stopped their using airborne formations again on any large scale. So that I think that Greece and Crete can claim to have paid a dividend, since the month's delay may well have saved Moscow; and to have shattered German faith in airborne formations must also have been well worth while.'[14]

Gandhi was the first person to raise objections to the 16 May Statement, which surprised the British politicians but, as far as Wavell was concerned, revealed him 'in his true colours'.[15] Gandhi complained primarily about the provision for 'grouping' which gave such obvious advantages to the Muslims in Sections B and C. Opposition was also voiced by the Sikhs of the Punjab, who feared being 'crushed' by the Muslims in Section B.[16] At this juncture Cripps was ill with colitis; both Wavell and Gandhi offered the services of their physicians, so the 'chief drafter' was able to choose between the natural therapies preferred by Gandhi and 'the canon of orthodox imperial medicine' advocated by the Viceregal doctor.[17] Cripps was absent until 3 June, during which time Wavell and the two remaining 'Magi' produced a document which Wavell called 'a small mouse after all these mountainous labours.' It did however contain an important passage indicating the Mission's belief that grouping of the provinces was an essential feature of the scheme 'which can only be modified by agreement between the two parties.'[18]

Wavell's personal life was still shadowed by Simon Astley's death, though Joanie had borne up 'wonderfully well'. Felicity was at home, working 'rather mysteriously' in a film writer's office; Pam and her two sons, Francis and Owen, were staying with Nancy and Molly at Ringwood. 'Her Ex' had remained in Simla, and Archie John was in Karachi running another education class, having taken with him all his father's copies of Shakespeare.[19] As always Wavell was reading widely, ordering directly from the London booksellers Truslove & Hanson.[20] He himself had had another slim volume published, by Macmillan, his 'broadcasts, orders and addresses in time of war' during the period he was Commander-in-Chief in the Middle East and in India. *Speaking Generally* was dedicated 'To my wife, who helped with these and with everything else'. At this time Wavell also gained the assistance of a man who became another firm friend – David Walker, who had served with Archie John in The Black Watch. Walker had been captured after the fall of France and spent nearly five years as a prisoner-of-war; after the war he worked as personal assistant to the Commandant of the Staff College at Camberley until in May 1946 he received a letter from Wavell, informing him of a vacancy on his staff for a Comptroller – as Walker described it, 'a glorified housekeeper, responsible for décor, meals, guests and an army of servants'.[21]

There was also a departure. Mountbatten had recently made a triumphal tour to Australia after completing the hand-over to civilian administrations in South-East Asia, and without having settled on a future career was on his way home to look for a new job.[22] In early June he wrote the last of what he called his 'bread and butter' letters to Wavell: 'I have come to look on Viceroy's House as a sort of second home, not only your hospitality in the house but for your friendship and unfailingly sound advice. I am sure you will realize how frightening it was for a substantive Captain RN to come out here as a Supreme Commander; but it was the example you set to everybody in India from the very beginning that helped to ease my task so greatly.' Well aware that Wavell was in the throes of strenuous – and still fruitless – negotiations with the Indian political leaders, he went on to congratulate him: 'In fact, if a satisfactory settlement is reached it will be regarded throughout India (and, I hope, England) as a personal and well deserved triumph for you.' With the mark of superiority even his junior position did not mask, he continued: 'I hope you will not think it presumptuous of me if I express great admiration for the way you have done your own job out here. I have fairly wide contacts from Ruling Princes down to VCOs and everyone is unanimous in the complete confidence they have personally in you.'[23] Throughout the course of their three-year working relationship Wavell had treated Mountbatten as a friend, and Mountbatten had always felt a great regard for Wavell.[24]

After two months 'without any decision', Wavell was feeling 'stale and over-worked'. He was not sleeping very well, and waking 'depressed and worried'. In his journal at the end of May he admitted that the strain of seven years' 'heavy responsibility' without rest was at last beginning to show. The enthusiasm with which he had embarked on his Viceroyalty more than two years previously had waned.[25] His gloom did not lift as June opened, and he found himself working out what he would do if the 16 May Statement was rejected. He was certainly expecting a negative response from the Muslim League, as no provision had been made in the Statement for a sovereign Pakistan. Yet his fears proved unfounded: on 3 June he met Jinnah, who appeared to be in 'good heart' and talked of submitting his names for the Interim Government. On 6 June the Muslim League accepted the scheme, and agreed to join the Constituent Assembly. Although the 16 May Statement as drafted did not meet the League's demands for Pakistan, it had certain advantages: not only would the groups in which Muslims predominated be virtually autonomous, but there was the possibility of secession after ten years. In the short term, Muslim interests would be protected; in the long term, a sovereign 'Pakistan' comprising the six provinces Jinnah had originally claimed might yet be achieved.[26] There was silence meanwhile from the Congress Party which, following the Muslim League's acceptance, was examining even more carefully the consequences of agreement.

The Cabinet Mission was anxious to complete its task and return home. As a means of forcing the issue, on 16 June Wavell announced his intention to move ahead by inviting fourteen individuals to serve as members of the Interim Government. He did not give the Muslim League parity, as Jinnah had requested, but he did select all the Muslim representatives from the Muslim League. Significantly, paragraph 8 of this 16 June Statement pledged that if one or other or both of the two parties proved unwilling to join in setting up the 'Coalition Government', 'it is the intention of the Viceroy to proceed with the formation of an Interim Government which will be as representative as possible of those willing to accept the statement of May 16th.'[27] However, the situation went 'all haywire again' when Gandhi insisted that Azad – as a Nationalist Muslim – should be included as one of the Congress Party representatives in the Interim Governmment.

In Wavell's opinion, putting forward Azad – a Muslim – as a Congress nominee was 'simply a manoeuvre to ensure Jinnah's refusal and thus put the onus of a breakdown on him.'[28]

Neither his heavy schedule nor the knife-edge on which the negotiations hung spared Wavell his Viceregal duty of entertaining visitors. Towards the end of June, Bernard Montgomery, the CIGS-Designate, had extended his tour to the Middle East at the request of his 'old friend, Archie Wavell' in order to come to India to discuss the future of the Indian Army in the wake of Britain's inevitable departure.[29] Since there was no agreed solution, their discussions were academic while Wavell recorded last-minute efforts to avert a breakdown in the negotiations. On 23 June he heard from Pethick-Lawrence (who had adopted the habit of going to Gandhi's prayer meetings, which Wavell regarded as 'a most unnecessary and undignified excursion') that the Congress Party would, after all, accept the 16 May Statement. On the 24th, more meetings took place. Wavell described them as being like a French farce, 'as some of the visitors had come unbeknownst to each other, and had to be interviewed in separate rooms.'[30] The outcome was the Congress Party's qualified acceptance of the 'long-term' objective of the 16 May Statement, the formation of a Constituent Assembly; but Congress was still not prepared to agree to an Interim Government, and still not in favour of the 'grouping' principle of dividing British India into Sections. Since the Muslim League had already agreed to the 16 May Statement, it seemed that at last – after years of fruitless negotiations – a breakthrough had been achieved. Wavell was unenthusiastic. In view of the Congress Party's reservations about grouping, he considered their agreement 'a dishonest acceptance, but . . . so cleverly worded that it had to be regarded as an acceptance.'[31] Whatever his private misgivings, however, on 26 June a joint statement by the Viceroy and the Cabinet Mission expressed happiness that 'constitution-making can now proceed with the consent of the two major parties and the [Princely] States.' Regret was expressed that it had not been possible to form the Interim Government, and the hope that after a short period of time a further attempt could be made. In the meantime a 'caretaker' government composed of Indian Civil Service (ICS) officers would be set up to administer the country. After three months in India, the Cabinet Mission could set a date for its departure: 29 June.

Congratulations were premature. The Congress Party had rejected the proposals for the Interim Government, but as far as the Muslim League was concerned paragraph 8 of the 16 June Statement pledged the Viceroy to go ahead even if one of the parties declined to join it. It now became clear – Congress and the League having both accepted the long-term objective of joining the Constituent Assembly – that the British politicians had elected to set aside this critical clause in anticipation of fresh negotiations with both parties for the formation of the Interim Government, pending which the Viceroy would, as they had announced, set up a caretaker government. Jinnah was outraged at what he termed a 'betrayal'; he asserted that the Mission were 'in honour bound to go ahead' on the basis of paragraph 8, and that by not doing so, they had revoked 'their plighted word'.[32] The Mission's actions appeared so contrary to their earlier statement that even the English-language press in India – normally favourable to the British Government – was critical. 'Politicians may do so, but it is not the business of statesmen to eat their words,' the *Statesman's* editorial opined. 'They should not risk bold, sweeping, unequivocal public undertakings unless they mean them, and can be relied upon to fulfil them. What was so emphatically considered needful and proper on June 16th cannot well, within ten days, have radically transformed its nature.'[33]

The *Statesman's* editor, Ian Stephens, whose sympathies lay with the Muslim League, was so surprised that he went to see Wavell. But his interview left him none the wiser, apart from a sense that the Viceroy was extremely tired. 'Talking with him there in his study, it was impossible to suppose him insincere and there was the further consideration that, besides daily collaboration with the Mission, he had throughout been carrying the full administrative load of the Viceroyalty.' Yet again Wavell had been outmanoeuvred by Cripps, who had drafted paragraph 8 with the express purpose, not of opening the door to a Muslim League Interim Government, but of encouraging the Congress Party to accept the 16 May Statement so that fresh negotiations could begin.[34] Once more the soldier's blunt honesty had come up against the politician's ability to finesse a difficult situation. Regardless of the rift which was now beginning to appear, on the evening of 27 June Wavell hosted a farewell dinner party for the delegation. Everyone was subdued except Alexander, who played the piano and sang until the early hours of the morning. After their departure, Wavell went to Simla for a rest 'and to think out the next move'.[35] Using his favourite 'family' analogy, he observed that the Mission had left him with 'one sickly child to be nursed through all its infantile complaints [the formation of the Constituent Assembly] and one still-born one to be revived [the Interim Government].'[36] Jinnah and the Muslim League remained deeply disappointed.[37]

Wavell subsequently wrote 'A Retrospect' summarizing the various phases of the Cabinet Mission's work. 'I am depressed at the future prospect. Congress have been encouraged and will set their claims higher than ever. The suspicion and dislike of Jinnah for the Congress have been enhanced; and to them is added, I fear, a mistrust of HMG, and perhaps of myself. Further negotiation will not be easy.'[38] As was his habit, Wavell found solace in versifying, inspired again by Lewis Carroll: ''Twas grilling [very hot]; and the Congreelites [animals rather like conger eels, very slippery, they can wriggle out of anything they don't like] / Did harge [haggle and argue] and shobble [shift and wobble] in the swope [a place open to sweepers]; / All Jinsy [supportive of Jinnah] were the Pakstanites [fierce noisy animals who live around mosques and can't bear Congreelites], / And the spruft [spruce and puffed up] Sikhs outstrope [went round shouting out that they weren't being fairly treated and would take direct action about it].'[39] Those of his staff, like Abell, who had witnessed the proceedings were full of admiration for the Viceroy, who 'made a considerable impression by his deep knowledge of the problem and by his wisdom . . . he was like a rock in his imperturbability. He was also recognized as being not only sympathetic to Nationalist aspirations but also an honest man who would not sacrifice justice to political expediency.'[40] Cripps, however, had not appreciated Wavell's manner; having returned to England, he determined that another Viceroy should step into his shoes.[41]

While he was in Simla, Wavell wrote to King George VI. Starting on a positive note (and perhaps concealing his private thoughts out of politeness) he said he thought no one could have worked 'more wholeheartedly and with greater patience and good temper' than the Mission. On the plus side, the Mission had convinced Indian public opinion that Britain really did intend to give India her independence. Furthermore, they had succeeded in getting both major parties to accept the compromise plan as expressed in the 16 May Statement; the failure over the Interim Government he claimed as 'more my fault' than theirs, while making no secret of his belief that Gandhi's insistence on including a Nationalist Muslim was what had thrown 'a spanner in the works' and caused that particular breakdown.[42]

Less than two weeks after the departure of the Cabinet Mission, even the fragile agreement which had been reached over the Constituent Assembly began to unravel. On 7 July, in his capacity as its new President, Nehru addressed the All-India Congress Committee. 'It is not a question of our accepting any Plan, long or short. It is only a question of our agreeing to go into the Constituent Assembly. That is all, and nothing more than that. We will remain in that Assembly so long as we think it is good for India, and we will come out when we think it is injuring our cause, and then offer our battle. We are not bound by a single thing, except that we have decided for the moment to go to the Constituent Assembly.' At a press conference three days later, on 10 July, he was asked to explain his position. Uttering similar sentiments, he predicted that the 'grouping' of provinces as provided for in the Mission's plan would probably not take place, since 'everybody outside the Muslim League was entirely opposed to grouping.'[43] Wavell was already trying to form an Interim Government to replace the Caretaker Council currently administering the country, but even before the impact of Nehru's statements hit home, Jinnah had refused to play a part. He was already sore following the paragraph 8 controversy, and his realization that the representation now offered was less favourable than previously rubbed salt into the wounds. He made his dissatisfaction plain to Attlee. 'It is not without deep regret that I have to say that the Cabinet Delegation and the Viceroy have, by handling the negotiations in the manner in which they did, impaired the honour of the British government and have shaken the confidence of Muslim India and shattered their hopes for an honourable and peaceful settlement.'[44]

The effect on the Muslim League of Nehru's press statements was disastrous. Jinnah immediately asserted that Nehru's remarks were 'a complete repudiation of the basic form upon which the long-term scheme rests', and on 29 July the League withdrew its acceptance of the long-term plan, announcing its intention to start a movement of 'direct action' to achieve Pakistan: 16 August was named as 'Direct Action Day'. 'What we have done today is the most historic act in our history,' Jinnah declared. 'Never [hitherto] have we in the League done anything except by constitutionalism. But now we are forced into this position. This day, we bid goodbye to constitutional methods.'[45] Even Azad later professed himself 'astonished' at what Nehru had said. 'It was not correct to say that Congress was free to modify the Plan as it pleased. These matters could not be changed unilaterally by Congress without the consent of other parties.'[46] The Indian civil servant Vidya Shankar agreed: 'Wavell is right in nursing a grievance against Pandit Nehru who, by his imprudent press statements and speeches, upset the whole apple-cart and played into the hands of Jinnah.'[47]

It seemed clear to Wavell that the problem originated in the Cabinet Mission's too-ready acceptance of the Congress Party's commitment to the plan; he believed both Cripps and Pethick-Lawrence had been 'dishonest' in instigating Congress to make this commitment public when it was clear that their acceptance was never wholehearted. He also blamed his own 'stupidity and weakness' in not realizing what was happening and standing up to it; finally, he criticized 'the irresponsibility of Nehru in making the statements he has since the Mission left.'[48] He was also annoyed with

Attlee, who had written him a long lettter at the end of July, congratulating him on the 'patience and skill' with which he had handled the Cabinet Mission negotiations but suggesting that he might want to consider appointing the 68-year-old former Chief Justice of India and President of the Federal Court, Sir Maurice Gwyer, as his political adviser. 'Politics has its own technique which can only be acquired by practice and not from text books . . . you as a soldier without political advisers must be somewhat in the same position as a Prime Minister would be without the advice of the Chiefs of Staff on military matters.'[49] Far from appreciating the Prime Minister's suggestion, Wavell was affronted. He resented the assumption that he was receiving 'nothing but official ICS advice' and that his political judgement was 'unsound, i.e. not sufficiently pro-Congress'. As usual, what he considered misplaced criticism was disregarded, and he confided to his journal that he thought his judgement better than 'HMG's and shall say so . . . If HMG don't like it their duty is to find another Viceroy, as I will not be a figure head.'[50]

In his lengthy response to Attlee, Wavell stated his position with his customary candour: 'I do not lay claim to any great measure of political wisdom but I do know something now of politics and politicians in India and the East . . . I feel that the suggestion has probably been made to you that I see no one except officials and take no advice except from them. I do not think that this impression is correct or fair to the officials. I see a good many unofficial persons of all types, as also do my advisers . . . I took up my present position as a war appointment, since the then Prime Minister judged, rightly or wrongly, that it was where I could best serve the war effort. I have no personal ambition, I have already reached a position far above my expectations or merits, and I have no desire except to serve the State to the best of my ability. But as long as I do so, I think I must be allowed to exercise my own judgement in the matter of the advice I give to HMG.'[51] This discursive defence surprised Attlee, and he replied briefly: 'In my suggestions I had no idea of indicating that you only saw officials or the officials were hidebound, but rather that inevitably from their position they are not very well acquainted with the technique of politics and democratic government.'[52] Wavell responded again at length, telling Attlee his letter was not adequate. 'From your silence on the matter, I assume that you wish me to remain in my present post. I will certainly continue to do my best, but I feel I must put before you certain matters on which I feel strongly. I think that it is essential that I should know your mind more fully as regards India; and also that I should have a definite policy from HMG.'[53] To this Attlee did not reply: he wrote three drafts, in which he assured Wavell that he wished him to remain in office, but none of the three was sent.[54] Wavell did not realize it at the time, but he was beginning to lose the Prime Minister's support. He did know he was extremely tired. 'I have a bad hour or two every morning now, when I wake early and think over the general state of India and the lack of a definite policy by HMG and the virtual certainty of serious trouble, and the way all constructive work I have been able to do in the last 2 and a half years seems likely to be wasted.' A ride and breakfast generally cheered him up, but he confessed to wanting a rest.[55]

On 10 August, in an attempt to repair some of the damage done by Nehru's July statements, the Congress Party came out with an acceptance 'in its entirety' of the Cabinet Mission plan, while continuing to express reservations about grouping. Once more Jinnah doubted the Party's sincerity, but the way was now open for Wavell to request Nehru, as his party's leader, to form the Interim Government. Privately, he was uncomfortable about this: 'I don't like it, but I think it is the only possible move.' Wavell had requested Nehru to offer the Muslim League some seats in the Interim Government, but Jinnah rejected the offer; instead, the Muslim League was concentrating its energies on its Direct Action Day. Originally Jinnah had planned to mark the day with nothing more than a statement regarding steps for Muslim 'self-preservation', but in Bengal, where the League Ministry headed by the Bengali Muslim League politician H.S. Suhrawardy had declared a public holiday, the situation turned ugly when looting, arson and rioting broke out.

Wavell flew immediately to Bengal, where the 'indescribable'[56] scenes of destruction and butchery – of Hindus by Muslims and Muslims by Hindus – were 'a sobering reminder that a much greater measure of toleration is essential if India is to survive the transition to freedom.'[57] Returning to Delhi, he asked Gandhi and Nehru to see him. He recorded the meeting in his diary as not being 'a great success', but it was more damaging than he realized. The tragic effects of communal violence in Calcutta had reinforced Wavell's determination to leave no stone unturned in his attempts to reconcile the Congress Party and the Muslim League. As he saw it, Congress's position on 'grouping' was the main obstacle to cooperation with the League. He had therefore prepared a formula for Nehru and Gandhi to sign on behalf of Congress which 'made a categorical statement that they would accept the position that the Provinces must remain in their Sections [A, B and C], as intended by the Mission, until after the first elections under the new Constitution.' But Nehru and Gandhi refused, deducing from the argumentative nature of the meeting that Wavell was operating under some strain. They also rejected the implied threat that Wavell would not be able to call the Constituent Assembly if they did not sign.

The following day Gandhi wrote to his 'Dear Friend' Wavell: 'Several times last evening you repeated that you were a "plain man and a soldier" and that you did not know the law. We are all plain men though we may not all be soldiers and even though some of us may know the law. It is our purpose, I take it, to devise methods to prevent a repetition of the recent terrible happening in Calcutta. The question before us is how best to do it.' After describing his tone as 'minatory' Gandhi went on, much to Wavell's annoyance, to advise that the Viceroy should be 'assisted, if necessary, by a legal mind enjoying your full confidence.'[58] Nehru also wrote to Wavell, affirming Congress's commitment to doing 'everything in our power to promote communal harmony.' But he told Wavell that his reference to the non-summoning of the Constituent Assembly, 'unless the course suggested by you was adopted by us, seemed to us extraordinary and this produced a feeling of resentment in my colleagues.' The summoning of the Constituent Assembly could not be held up 'because some people do not choose to join it and disturbances take place in the country.'[59]

Indirectly – and perhaps intentionally – the Congress leaders' criticism of the Viceroy was further undermining his position at home. Nevertheless, those who had seen Wavell at work and appreciated the realities on the ground continued to speak highly of him. The former Solicitor-General Sir Walter Monckton, who had been in India visiting the Princely State of Hyderabad, wrote to Churchill: 'I have heard a good deal of criticism of the Viceroy since I came back to England, most of it in general terms. It is only fair that I should say that none of the Princes with whom I have been in contact would wish to join in this criticism. They have found him before, during and after negotiations, to use the language of one of them, "a steadfast friend like the great soldier he is".'[60] On 2 September Wavell swore in a new 'Interim Government'. Despite his recent altercation with Nehru and Gandhi, the Congress Party representatives were in 'a sensible mood'. But Wavell remained committed to securing the entrance of the Muslim League, without which he believed 'there will be daily danger of really serious communal troubles which might amount almost to civil war.'[61] Henceforward Congress ministers, having set aside their policy of not accepting official hospitality from their rulers, enjoyed dining with the Viceroy and Vicereine.

Wavell had no illusions about the difficulties ahead, however, and since June had been working on his 'Breakdown Plan' and considering it in earnest with a small committee which included Auchinleck and Abell. On 7

September he sent his final draft to Pethick-Lawrence. For the first time a limit was to be set on Britain's presence: he suggested that the British withdrawal, undertaken in stages to the north-west and north-east of the country, with evacuation of all British citizens from Karachi and Calcutta, should be completed no later than the spring of 1948. Believing that Britain would be unable to retain effective control of India for more than 18 months, Wavell suggested that, come what might, even before any breakdown of law and order occurred, the withdrawal should begin no later than the end of March 1947. Alternatively, the British Government would have to resign itself to remaining in India for at least another 15 to 20 years. But Attlee, when Wavell's proposals reached his desk, considered them too extreme.

Finally, at the end of September, Jinnah began to signal that the Muslim League would, after all, enter the Interim Government. Wavell was pleased by this change of heart, and while he realized it would now be more difficult to convince the Congress members to share power,[62] he remained hopeful that if the Indian politicians could be kept together sitting around a table, 'they will learn to work together.'[63] On 26 October five nominees of the League took the seats in the Interim Government offered to them in July. Jinnah nominated his right-hand man Liaquat Ali Khan to lead the League in the government. Wavell, meanwhile, continued to demand a firmer course of action from London. 'If it is indeed the policy of HMG merely to carry on without any more definite programme than to hope for the best,' he wrote in a long letter to Pethick-Lawrence, 'they will inevitably place themselves, gradually or almost at once, completely in the power of the Congress, and even with a Coalition we cannot afford to postpone our withdrawal indefinitely.'[64] At the end of October Wavell wrote again to Attlee: 'The situation out here is tense and we may be faced with a crisis at any time. I am sure that we cannot safely continue to drift without a clear idea of how and when we are to leave India.'[65] Throughout the autumn, as the communal rioting that had begun with the 'Great Calcutta Killing' spread to East Bengal, it became Wavell's overriding concern – almost obsession – to create political harmony between the Muslim League and the Congress Party; unless this happened, he believed the whole of India could become a bloodbath.[66]

As Wavell had anticipated, with both the Congress Party and Muslim League in the Interim Government an argument had already broken out, over the distribution of portfolios. To maintain some element of fairness Wavell had insisted that Congress should offer the League one of the three 'senior' portfolios (Foreign Affairs, Defence or Home); Nehru had objected on the grounds that it would unsettle the country: Finance was the only portfolio Congress was prepared to surrender. Initially Wavell had favoured giving the Home portfolio to the Muslim League, Finance remaining with its current incumbent, Dr John Matthai, who, as a former professor of Indian economics at Madras University, had proved 'knowledgeable and sensible'.[67] But Nehru refused, and the Muslim League eventually took Finance and Commerce, plus Posts and Air, Health and Law. As Wavell also predicted, within a short time both parties formed themselves into 'blocs', gathering supporters from among the Indian civil servants. Of these, the most dedicated to the Congress cause appeared to be V.P. Menon, who although honest, Wavell observed, had for some time past been 'too much the mouthpiece of Sardar Patel', who held the important Home portfolio in the Interim Government.[68] Throughout the autumn political unrest continued. In late October Wavell gave up a day's shooting to stay in Delhi and issue a joint appeal for communal peace signed by the party leaders and himself, but since the Indian leaders could not agree on the text, he instead broadcast a personal appeal.[69] To cap it all, the princes were not happy. As the Nawab of Bhopal confided to Wavell's political adviser, Sir Conrad Corfield, former Resident of the Punjab States, 'The British seem to have abdicated all power and what is worse they have handed it over to their enemies and to the enemies of all their friends in this country.'[70]

Wavell was also assessing the impact of political developments in the rest of the country. In October Nehru had gone to the North-West Frontier, which Wavell described as a 'dangerous and foolhardy escapade'; in mid November the Viceroy therefore decided to visit the Frontier himself. The priorities of its people there differed from those of the politicians in Delhi.[71] At Landi Kotal he met a jirga (tribal assembly) of the Afridis whose lands straddled the Khyber Pass leading from Afghanistan: 'Their representation was to the effect that if we were going we should hand them back the Khyber Pass, that they had no intention of being ruled by Hindus and resented Nehru's visit and that anything in the way of a little extra cash would be very acceptable.' Wavell's response was that they should be 'good boys' and no one would interfere with their freedom, and that they would be able to state their case to any future Government of India. At Wana in Waziristan he presided over a jirga of the Ahmedzai Wazirs and then, journeying onwards to Miranshah, held discussions with Major Robin Hodson, the Assistant Political Agent. At the end of their meeting, 'the Viceroy turned to me and asked if I had anything to ask him'. Hodson wanted to know whether, in view of the unsettled situation, the Viceroy could authorize the use of air power and 'other measures' to contain any trouble. Wavell spread his hands over the table. 'I will do what I can, but my hands are tied by the Government at home.'[72] As always, the Viceroy was answerable to London.

On his return, Wavell found Nehru pressing for invitations to the Constituent Assembly to be issued: according to the original schedule, its work should have begun in early September. In an attempt to find a way out of the impasse, Wavell again met Jinnah and Nehru. Jinnah had reverted to his original theme of a sovereign 'Pakistan'. Agreement between Muslims and Hindus was impossible, he informed Wavell, and therefore there was no point in the League coming into the Constituent Assembly. 'He thought we should give them their own bit of country, let it be as small as we liked, but it must be their own, and they would live on one meal a day.'[73] This being Jinnah's attitude, Wavell realized there was little chance of persuading the Muslim League to change its stance; he also realized that he could not indefinitely postpone summoning the Constituent Assembly: the date was set for 9 December.

Attlee, meanwhile, had decided to shift the centre of political discussion from Delhi to London. On Sunday 24 November Pethick-Lawrence telegraphed suggesting that Wavell should return to England with two representatives from the Muslim League, two from the Congress Party and one Sikh, for further meetings before the Constituent Assembly convened. Nehru initially refused the invitation, believing acceptance to be tantamount to surrendering to the League's 'intransigence'; when prevailed upon by Attlee in person, he agreed. The next to voice concern was Baldev Singh, Defence Minister in the Interim Government, invited to represent the Sikhs. Then Jinnah changed his mind (prompting Wavell to comment, 'What an impossible set of people they are!').[74] But eventually the full complement of invited representatives was ready to leave for London, flying via Cairo and Malta. Including breakdowns, the journey took two days. Two hours after arriving in London at 9 a.m. Wavell was with Attlee, Pethick-Lawrence and Alexander. He had already prepared a note reviewing the 'short-term issue' and offering a 'long-term plan'.

In Wavell's 'short-term' review he made it clear that the Cabinet Mission Plan could have worked, but that neither the members of the Mission nor the British Government 'adhered to their original intentions with sufficient directness of purpose'. In the present uncertain situation, he now forcefully advocated consideration of a 'long-term' plan, and examined four possibilities. First, the British government could re-establish its authority and rule India for a further period, a course of action he realized had already been ruled out as impossible. Secondly, an attempt could be made to negotiate a fresh settlement that would involve 'some sort of Partition and would at once bring us into conflict with Congress'; again, Wavell rejected this as not being a 'practicable policy'. Thirdly, he suggested that they could 'surrender' to Congress as the majority party, while trying to secure for the minorities 'what fairness we can'; he rejected this course of action too, as not being 'an honourable or a wise policy'. Finally, having failed to bring about a settlement, Britain could announce her intention of withdrawing from India 'in our own method and in our own time', any attempt to interfere with the programme being regarded 'as an act of war'; this was in effect a re-statement of the 'Breakdown Plan'. However, before any of these options was considered, Wavell once more urged the Government to make 'the fullest use of the present discussions to try to restore the Mission plan'; if that was unsuccessful, he suggested the Government would have to opt for one of the courses of action he had outlined.[75] In his opinion, if agreement was not reached, option four, a gradual withdrawal, was the only possible way forward.

Over the next few days Wavell found himself caught up in a continual rush of conferences and engagements, among them a private audience of the King. Once more George VI complimented him on the clarity of his letters. He realized how hard had been Wavell's task: 'The Viceroy has done very well in trying to keep the 2 sides together and to have brought them here for conversations,' he noted in his diary. When the Indian leaders were entertained to lunch at Buckingham Palace, the King was left feeling that the leaders of the two main parties – Congress and the Muslim League – would never agree. 'We have gone too fast for them.'[76] During his discussions with Attlee Wavell began to believe that the Government was taking his suggestions regarding the Breakdown Plan seriously, and that he had 'got HMG down to face realities at last',[77] but agreement remained as elusive as ever. As so often before, Wavell found that poetry captured the mood better than prose, and added some Browning to the notes in his journal: 'Now, enough of your chicane of prudent pauses, / Sage provisos, sub-intents and saving-clauses!' As he recollected, the poem began 'Let them fight it out, friend! things have gone too far.'[78]

On 6 December – the last day of the conference – discussions were held at Downing Street regarding a draft statement. Summing up the Government's position at their last meeting, Attlee observed that the Indian leaders had been asked to London 'on this flying visit' with a view to resolving their differences over the Constituent Assembly. 'The British Government had done their part. They had secured acceptance in this country for a line of policy urged for many years by leading Indians. They were entitled now to ask for Indian cooperation. Since the Indian leaders were unable to reach agreement, the government therefore proposed to issue a statement.'[79] Wavell was never one to praise unnecessarily, but his journal was complimentary. Attlee, he noted, spoke 'quite well, concisely and clearly and on the right lines. (He begins to impress me as likely to be a notable PM.)'[80] The statement issued on 6 December was a combination of ideas expressed by Cripps, Alexander and Wavell, and in effect re-stated the Government's earlier position. Yet again it recognized that the sticking point was the interpretation of the 16 May Statement regarding grouping: 'The Cabinet Mission have throughout maintained the view that the decisions of the Sections should, in the absence of agreement to the contrary, be taken by simple majority vote of the representatives in the Sections. This view has been accepted by the Muslim League, but the Congress have put forward a different view. They have asserted that the true meaning of the Statement, read as a whole, is that the Provinces have a right to decide both as to grouping and as to their own constitutions.' To enable the Muslim League to reconsider its position, the Government urged the Congress Party to accept the view of the Cabinet Mission.[81]

In the wintry London climate tempers appeared to run less high. Nehru, while he made objections, did not reject the statement out of hand; both Jinnah and Liaquat Ali Khan seemed prepared to accept it, while asserting that referral of the disputed interpretation of the 16 May Statement to a Federal Court, as was suggested, would achieve nothing. Overall, however, the British Government's reaffirmation of its interpretation of the 16 May Statement appeared to vindicate the Muslim League's position, and to go some way towards standing up to the Congress Party, as Wavell had been urging.[82] Entirely familiar with the rhetoric favoured by both sides, he was realistic in his final analysis: 'So ends this phase of the long-drawn-out drama of negotiations with India. On the whole a better curtain than seemed likely at one time . . . the next Act will probably show all the Parties going right back to their original positions.'[83]

Immediately after the end of the 'Indian Conference' Nehru and Baldev Singh flew back to Delhi to attend the first meeting of the Constituent Assembly on 9 December, leaving Jinnah and Liaquat still out in the cold – literally – in London. Wavell too remained, hoping to move forward with discussions of his Breakdown Plan. For respite he saw old friends, including Leo Amery, who had slowed down considerably 'both physically and in terms of the current situation . . . His views on India are not up to date with the pace things have been going.'[84] He also lunched with the Australian war correspondent Alan Moorehead, who was writing a book on Montgomery and 'had represented me as opposing the expedition to Greece and Eden as having deceived me as to the possibilities of Turkey coming into the war. I told him neither was correct.'[85] As days passed into weeks, Wavell once more felt moved to protest at the way he was being left 'hanging about without any consideration for his convenience'. When at last he met the Prime Minister, Attlee agreed 'in principle' to the Breakdown Plan, 'if it was put in a different form', one that did not require parliamentary legislation.[86] But behind Wavell's back, Attlee was talking unfavourably about him. As King George VI noted, 'Attlee told me that Ld Wavell's plan for our leaving India savours too much of a military retreat & does not realize it is a political problem & not a military one. Wavell has done very good work up to now but Attlee doubts whether he has the finesse to negotiate the next steps when we must keep the 2 Indian parties friendly to us all the time.'[87] Unknown to Wavell, before Attlee met him for the last time, he had selected his successor.

After three weeks away, Wavell was anxious to get home to see 'Q. and the family'.[88] Deputing George Abell to state his case in future discussions of the Breakdown Plan, he left England on Sunday 22 December, arriving in New Delhi in time for dinner on Monday. The warmth of the Indian winter was enjoyable, but 'the comforts were nullified by cares of office and political worries.'[89] Regardless of what had transpired in London, he saw little hope for the future. Looking back on the last day of December over what had undoubtedly been one of his most difficult years, he noted that 'the Cabinet Mission was really our last chance to bring about a set-tlement in India, a temporary one which would have enabled us to leave India with peace and dignity.' Personally, Wavell considered it had been 'rather an unhappy year. While I have not had a day's real illness, I have never really been 100 per cent fit. The main trouble has been that I have been sleeping badly, waking up too early, to be assailed by doubts, fears and problems, official and private. It is a great strain on a small man to do a job which is too big for him, if he feels it too big. Health and vitality suffer. I am afraid that 1947 may be even more difficult, and more of a strain.'[90]

21

Dismissal, 1947

In all the history of British rule in India, there has never been a Viceroy with a harder task – made all the harder by the trend of circumstances – than fell to your lot.

Sir Alan Lascelles, Private Secretary to King George VI[1]

A S WAVELL HAD predicted, 1947 began with the same political impasse. The British Government's tougher stance regarding the Congress Party meant his first interview with Nehru on New Year's Day was 'not very satisfactory'. At one stage Nehru 'worked himself up into a denunciation of HMG and said that he would sooner India was divided into a hundred parts than that they should in any way abandon their principles and give in to the Muslim League.' Always concerned to maintain balance in any discussion, in response to Nehru's assertion that the British Government intended to give its unqualified support to the Muslim League Wavell told him 'the Muslim League took entirely the opposite view and thought that HMG had given unqualifed support to Congress.' Overall, he felt that Nehru's attitude was now one of 'sullen resentment' that the British Government had changed its position of 'unqualified support'.[2] In London meanwhile, in early January, the India and Burma Committee, chaired by Attlee, once more discussed Wavell's 'Breakdown Plan'.

However, as Wavell discovered to his regret, the interest in the plan apparently expressed by Attlee had evaporated. The Committee's Minutes recorded that, while they recognized the 'weight' of the arguments used by the Viceroy in support of gradual withdrawal, Attlee, Cripps, Pethick-Lawrence and Alexander had rejected the plan on the grounds that it could 'invite fractionalization of India into two or more parts.' The Committee also believed that the 'logical sequence to withdrawal from the four Southern Provinces would be withdrawal from further Provinces and this would lead straight in the direction of Pakistan.' In forming its opinions, the Committee noted that there was 'no reason why the Viceroy's plan should not be held in reserve for use in case of emergency, but they did not consider that the time had come to put it into force in the immediate future or to make any public announcement regarding it.'[3] Wavell considered the letter containing Attlee's formal rejection 'cold, ungracious and indefinite, the letter of a small man.'[4] With Mountbatten and Cripps, Attlee was already working out how to orchestrate Wavell's resignation rather than have to dismiss him. With this in mind, Attlee suggested that he return to England; Wavell refused the invitation on the grounds that he had no further policy to suggest. 'It is possible that the idea is to get me home and force my resignation,' he confided in his journal.[5]

In Delhi on 5 January the All India Congress Committee had passed a resolution accepting the 6 December Statement, but with reservations: no province should be subjected to any compulsion, and the rights of the Sikhs of the Punjab should not be jeopardized. Furthermore, if there were to be any compulsion, a province (or part thereof) had the right to take whatever action it deemed necessary. The Muslim League – which had not joined the Constituent Assembly – remained suspicious of Congress's true intentions, fearing that once the British had departed, Congress would assert the authority inherent in its majority status. Liaquat Ali Khan even suggested to Wavell that 'we [the British] ought to restore our authority and rule India for a further period of years, until the parties agreed.' When Wavell pointed out that the British Government could not break the pledge it had given to grant India self-government at an early date, Liaquat said it would be wrong to leave India to 'chaos but that if we were going to do it we should leave "fair chaos for both parties", and not remain to establish the Hindus in power.'[6] Subsequently, on 31 January, the Muslim League Working Committee passed a resolution affirming that it would not reconsider the withdrawal of its acceptance of the Cabinet Mission Plan. It further called upon the British Government to admit the failure of this Plan. Describing the Congress Working Committee's 5 January resolution as 'no more than a dishonest trick and a jugglery of words', it demanded the dissolution of the Constitutent Assembly. Two weeks later Congress reacted publicly: at a press conference, Sardar Patel declared that the British should either insist on the Muslim League's participation in constitution-making procedures or expel it from the Cabinet (as the Viceroy's Executive Council was now called).[7]

On 4 February Wavell was entertaining the Conservative MP Harold Macmillan, another Old Summerfieldian. Just after lunch a letter from Attlee arrived by special messenger. Writing on 31 January, Attlee began by referring to the 'wide divergence' which he believed existed between what Wavell was proposing for the interim period before India gained independence and what the British Government felt was the way forward. 'I am very conscious of the heavy burden which you have carried and of the great services which you have rendered during this difficult period. I know that you undertook this task from a high sense of duty.' Not wanting it to appear that Wavell was being summarily dismissed, Attlee put forward another reason for his replacement: 'You were, I understand, informed that your appointment was a war appointment and that while the usual term for a Viceroy is five years, this might not apply. I think that three years was mentioned.'

Attlee went on to point out that the Indian problem was entering a new phase, recalling that Wavell had once expressed his readiness to retire in the event of disagreement on policy – 'and this would seem to me to be the appropriate course to follow.' An announcement would be made as quickly as possible so that his successor could take over at the end of February or early in March. In conclusion, Attlee informed Wavell that he would like to submit his name 'for the dignity of an Earldom in recognition of the self-sacrificing and loyal service which you have displayed.'[8] Attlee also assured Wavell that he would not suffer financially if he were deprived of any leave. Wavell, not convinced by the 'wartime appointment' excuse, spent all next day with Queenie and Abell composing a reply. The final version was crisp and to the point:

> You are causing me to be removed because of what you term a wide divergence of policy. The divergence, as I see it, is between my wanting a definite policy for the interim period and HMG refusing to give me one . . . I do not of course question your decision to make a change. I have no desire except to serve the State to the best of my ability; obviously I cannot continue to do so if I have not the confidence of the Government in power. I think, however, that I am entitled to observe that so summary a dismissal of His Majesty's representative in India is hardly in keeping with the dignity of the appointment. It has been usual to give a retiring Viceroy six months' notice of his replacement . . . You can hardly have failed to appreciate the inconvenience and expense which you are causing to me and to the whole of my large personal staff by directing me to leave at such short notice; and I hope that I shall be given at least till the second week in March, to avoid the indignity, as well as the inconvenience of a scuttle.[9]

A week later, Attlee informed Wavell who his successor was to be: Viscount Mountbatten of Burma.[10] Wavell had only recently heard from Mountbatten the good news that Archie John had been belatedly awarded the MC for his service in Burma, and was agreeably surprised: 'An unexpected appointment but a clever one from their point of view; and Dickie's personality may perhaps accomplish what I have failed to do.'[11] In his hasty note of congratulations he told Mountbatten he was 'delighted', assured him the horses would be kept for him, and asked whether he wanted sad-dlery.[12] He signed himself 'Yours, Archie'. Mountbatten wrote back respectfully (and somewhat disingenously, in view of his discussions with Attlee regarding his removal): 'My dear Lord Wavell, I find it almost impos-sible to express my feelings on what has happened. I was most surprised when I was sent for by the Prime Minister, and told that your period of office had expired, and absolutely staggered when he told me that the Cabinet wanted me to succeed you . . . I took the liberty of telling the Prime Minister how much I admired all the decisions you had taken in such difficult circumstances, and what an extremely difficult man you were going to be to follow.'[13]

Wavell was not happy about having his replacement announced at the same time as a date was set for Britain's departure from India. He suggested to Attlee that the main announcement of a date for the transfer of power should be postponed: 'I said that I thought it was only fair on my succes-sor to let him have a week or two to study the situation before the final date was announced; and on me that I should not have the responsibility in my final weeks of office of carrying out a policy which I thought mis-judged and ill-timed.'[14] The next day telegrams arrived from Pethick-Lawrence, justifying the government's position, and accusing Wavell of inconsistency because in pushing for his Breakdown Plan he had urged that a firm date for the transfer of power be announced, and was now suggest-ing a postponement.[15]

As if Wavell had not enough to deal with in his last weeks as Viceroy, the marriage of his middle daughter Felicity to Peter Longmore, one of Arthur Longmore's sons, was fixed for Thursday 20 February. Wavell had already asked Attlee to put off the announcement of his dismissal – to have it announced just prior to the wedding would 'naturally be embarrassing' – and Attlee had agreed.[16] When the day came Wavell, resplendent in his Field Marshal's uniform, gave his daughter away. Among the fourteen hun-dred guests were close family and friends from England – Wavell's sister Molly, family friend Frances Hendry, George Spencer Churchill, Arthur Wauchope – as well as governors, maharajas, princes and nawabs. 'They all looked wonderful, driving away in their state carriages, followed by the Bodyguard in full dress,' remarked Jean, daughter of Leonard Grant, secretary of the United Services Club at Simla. There were 'glorious' wedding presents: 'heaps of gold and silver'.[17] The reception was held in the Mogul Gardens, already blooming in 'a riot of colour'.[18] As Wavell recorded, it all went 'smoothly,' thanks to Queenie's hard work and the efficiency of the staff.

Wavell's dismissal, though not yet made public, was an open secret. The previous November Wavell had visited the Wali of Swat, and one of the wedding guests was his son Aurangzeb, who had brought some beautiful carpets as a present. Finding his card attached to some carpets of lesser quality, and another man's to his fine ones, he protested. The other man was unperturbed: 'Why did you give such good carpets as a present when they are leaving?'[19] That same evening, Wavell had a series of short interviews with Nehru and Liaquat, who appeared to be 'genuinely sorry' that he was going.[20]

In England, on the day Felicity was married, Attlee stood up in the House of Commons to announce Wavell's replacement as a 'wartime' Viceroy. The House was crowded, and at first silent – until Churchill, as Leader of the Opposition, seized his opportunity to discomfit the Prime Minister: 'Will the Prime Minister lay before the House the reasons for the termination of the appointment of Viscount Wavell at this particular moment?' he demanded, to cheers from the Opposition benches. 'Will he indicate to us what differences or divergences or disagreements have arisen between the Viceroy and the British government?' Attlee's response was defensive: 'No. I have stated the announcement with regard to the termination of the Viceroyalty of Lord Wavell. I do not propose to add anything to it.' It was still midwinter, and Churchill, in his heavy overcoat, stood up again. 'Surely we are entitled to be treated in a reasonable manner. Is it not a fact that if Lord Wavell's Viceroyalty had ended with the war, it would have ended 18 months ago, and that if it had ended after three years it would have ended in June last? What then is the reason for this difference and disagreement which has led to the removal and dismissal of the Viceroy in full conduct of Government?' Again the Opposition cheered.

Attlee, no stranger to Churchill's taste for the theatrical, stood his ground: 'Mr Churchill knows very well that Lord Wavell was not appointed for a fixed term. As has been stated, it was thought that in the changed phase of the Indian problem it was the suitable time to make a change, and I do not propose to add anything to that statement.' Once more Churchill demanded an explanation, to further Opposition cheers: 'Surely the Prime Minister did not wake up one morning and say: "Oh, let us get another Viceroy." The Prime Minister must have some purpose or reason behind it, and we have a right to know what is that purpose or reason.' Despite his rising anger Attlee refused to be drawn into any further discussion, instead defending his prerogative, pointing out that Churchill as Prime Minister had made a number of military and civilian appointments and was not required to give reasons for them. Again Churchill invoked the drama of the occasion: 'Here we are dealing with an officer who has been serving Government in the most intimate relations and who is now dismissed . . . Surely this is a matter which, in all the history of either House of Parliament, has never been denied.'[21] After further provocative questions order was restored, and the House proceeded to the business of the day.

Churchill's staunch defence of Wavell was subsequently interpreted as a gracious gesture to the former Commander-in-Chief with whose career he himself had played musical chairs – 'The scarred veteran, in his magnanimity, did not forget how Wavell, "that brilliant chief, irregularly great", had done his best,' wrote Ronald Lewin in his book *The Chief*[22] – but Churchill was up to his old tricks, playing to the gallery, at which he was a past master. According to the liberal leader Clement Davies, Attlee's announcement came as no surprise to Churchill. When an important announcement was to be made in the House, it was customary procedure for the Prime Minister to forewarn the leaders of the other main parties. When, the evening before the announcement, Attlee informed Churchill and Davies of his intention to dismiss Wavell, Churchill had welcomed the decision, stating that Wavell was 'a bad general and a bad statesman'.[23] Even before that, however, Attlee had written to inform Churchill of the proposed change; replying, Churchill had expressed his desire to keep himself 'entirely free': until he knew the policy and directive and grounds for the change of personnel, he said, he could not 'form an opinion' nor give 'any undertaking of support'.[24] When the time came for Attlee's public announcement, he could not resist the opportunity to make political mileage of it in the House.

The impact of Wavell's dismissal was temporarily lost amid the columns of newsprint devoted to the Government's announcement of 'its definite intention to take the necessary steps to effect the transference of power to responsible Indian hands' on a date 'not later than June 1948'. Wavell, meanwhile, wrote as Viceroy to the King for the last time, outlining the four courses of action he had already put to Attlee. He noted his failure to elicit any definite policy from the Government: 'Their chief difficulty was reluctance to face Parliament with any proposal which would make it clear that we were withdrawing our control very shortly.' Wavell's personal view was that 'our own interests would probably best be served now by a definite decision to withdraw our control from India by a given date . . . we should also thus avoid being responsible for, and probably involved in, any widespread breakdown of law and order which may result from the communal situation or from labour troubles induced by revolutionary preaching or economic conditions.' At the same time he also recognized that it was probably in India's best interests that 'we should remain as long as we possibly can and still try and influence events in the direction of political sanity.'[25]

During King George's absence in South Africa, Wavell received a note of appreciation written on his behalf by his Private Secretary, Sir Alan Lascelles: 'For me to say how highly His Majesty values your services to the Crown in India, both as Commander-in-Chief and as Viceroy, seems to me, even though I write under orders, almost an impertinence; it would also be unnecessary, for I am sure you know it already. What you may not know, perhaps, is how fully the King has understood, all through these recent years, the immense difficulties with which you have had to cope. Nobody, not even the King, who is not actually in India can ever grasp to their full extent the problems with which a Viceroy is faced all day and every day and the peculiar complexity of the instruments with which he has to work.' Lascelles concluded his letter by conveying a further message from the King 'on the purely personal side', thanking Wavell for the 'extremely generous references' he had made to Mountbatten's appointment. 'The King feels that you have done a great deal towards giving him a good start, and is very grateful to you.'[26] As was his way, for the sake of the greater good Wavell had refrained from embarrassing the Government by publicly stating his feelings.

Polite Wavell may have been about Mountbatten, but he remained displeased about being given less than a month to manage his departure. Furthermore, it appeared that an attempt was being made to hurry him away without the customary formalities, and a curt but forceful correspondence ensued with the new Secretary of State for India, the Earl of Listowel, former Post-Master General, who had just taken over from Pethick-Lawrence.[27] Listowel's initial proposal was that Mountbatten should arrive in Karachi on the morning of Sunday 14 March, and suggested Wavell should meet him there that day to 'have a talk' with him. Mountbatten would then fly on to Delhi the following day, and the aircraft would return immediately to Karachi to take Wavell back to England. Mountbatten would be sworn in as soon as Wavell had left. This arrangement did not please Wavell at all, and he immediately telegraphed that he saw 'no reason' why the procedure followed when he succeeded Linlithgow should be changed: 'I arrived at Delhi one day, had a talk that afternoon and evening with Linlithgow, who left next morning.' He pointed out that what the Secretary of State suggested would be most inconvenient, both for himself and for the government of Sind. 'I am already being given unreasonably short time for my final arrangements and cannot consent to further curtailments by going to Karachi and waiting there.' Wavell informed Listowel that he would expect Mountbatten to arrive in Delhi while he was still there, and would himself leave the following day; he also indicated that 'a week later' than the proposed date would be easier for him, if it suited Mountbatten and the Government in England. He also had his personal staff to consider and was anxious to know which among them would be required to remain: 'Some of them have houses and all have personal effects such as horses to dispose of, if they are to leave.'[28] In this instance, Wavell won: he was informed that Mountbatten would arrive in Delhi, and a week later than originally indicated.

Inevitably 'in the throes of packings and windings up' Wavell found himself 'rather pressed', but with time to write in doggerel to Freya Stark: 'And in these glorious "average" days, / Shall all on equal terms cohabit? / The eagle with the babble wren; / The tiger with the sprightly rabbit?' There was a clear note of finality about his last days in India; one of his favourite horses, 'a hard puller' known as Puss, had to be put down, for instance. He marked the event in a poem entitled: 'Puss-in-Boots': 'Puss went to heaven, / That was only right. / Golden chestnut wings / Fashioned him for flight.'[29] As he also admitted to Freya, there was sadness in leaving India 'with the work unfinished, but shall certainly be glad of a rest, and shall certainly be spared very much anxiety and heart-burning.'[30]

Among colleagues who had known Wavell as both soldier and administrator there was genuine regret at his departure. 'I may perhaps be permitted to say,' wrote Sir Hugh Dow, Governor of Bihar, 'that I think this feeling of regret is shared by most of the members of the service to which I belong.'[31] In the days before he left Wavell continued to meet members of Congress and the Muslim League, discussing the future of the subcontinent, potential food shortages, and the INA. On 17 March Auchinleck (to whom Wavell had confided his feeling that he had been dismissed 'as if I were a cook') came to say goodbye.[32] He had wanted to hold a banquet in the departing Viceroy's honour, but Wavell had refused, preferring instead a 'quiet dinner'.[33] The two men had worked together on and off for fifteen years, ever since Auchinleck's arrival to view manoeuvres at Aldershot in the 1930s. Different as they were, their exchanges had always been marked by mutual respect. Most recently, Wavell had expressed gratitude for the army's role in the Punjab, where communal tensions had once more erupted into violence, leaving yet more dead.[34]

On the evening of 19 March Wavell presided over his final Cabinet meeting. The fate of the INA prisoners was again on the agenda. With a streak of schoolboy mischief, Wavell said he was sure the Cabinet would support demands for the release of the prisoners. When they agreed, he announced his intention of over-ruling them 'for the first and last time'. At the end of the meeting Wavell said a few brief words: 'I became Viceroy at a very difficult and critical time. I have tried to discharge my responsibility to the best of my ability . . . My appeal to you however would be that you should take no hasty decision. I am grateful to all of you for the cooperation I have received from you.'[35] Afterwards, as Azad noted, he collected up his papers and left quickly 'without giving any of us an opportunity to say anything.'[36] Before the Wavells left, Azad publicly acknowledged Wavell's contribution. 'I cannot help a feeling of regret that Lord Wavell, who was the instigator of a new chapter in the history of relations between India and England, is retiring from the scene.' He went on to describe how, after the failure of Cripps's 1942 mission, Churchill's government had decided to put the Indian question 'in cold storage' for the rest of the war: 'To Lord Wavell must belong the credit for opening the closed door.'[37]

For his successor Wavell had prepared a frank note on the Interim Government and the Cabinet. 'It is a very unreal Coalition. Though neither side shows any sign of wanting to leave the Government and though Cabinet meetings are carried on in a superficially friendly atmosphere, it is almost impossible to get members of the opposing groups to discuss things among themselves and they seldom meet except in my presence at Cabinet meetings. Meanwhile they go their opposite ways in the country.' Nevertheless, he concluded, the mere existence of the coalition was one of 'the reassuring features of the situation.'[38] The following day, one 'of farewells and packing', ended with Wavell's last dinner with the Cabinet.

In his final broadcast on All India Radio, after nearly six years in India as Commander-in-Chief and Viceroy, Wavell combined a nostalgic look back over his past service on the North-West Frontier with a wish for the future: 'Good bye and farewell – God be with you – and fare you well – as those words mean. They come from my heart, for I owe much to India.' He was, he said, leaving with 'a great affection' for Indian soldiers and the Indian people. 'During two world wars it was my fortune to see much of the prowess of the Indian soldiers and to profit by it.' He conceded that he might have made mistakes, but he had always tried to work for 'the welfare of India's inhabitants and for the advancement of India towards self-rule . . . You have hard, dangerous and difficult years ahead, but you will overcome them.' It was the last time the Indian people heard his voice.[39]

There was 'a good turn out' for Wavell's morning ride on his last day in India. He had lunch with some of Mountbatten's new staff, including Ismay and Sir Eric Mieville. Both Ismay and Mieville had worked for the former Viceroy Lord Willingdon in the 1930s, and therefore had experience of India. It was perhaps with slight resentment that Wavell concluded in his journal that they did not appear to have any 'very new or definite policy'.[40] Later, the new Viceroy-Designate and his Vicereine arrived. During Wavell's formal discussion with Mountbatten prior to handing over, Mountbatten asked what Wavell thought the next step should be, and how he could build on Attlee's 20 February Statement. The answer was self-evident: ultimately, everything would depend on the two main communities.[41] Mountbatten subsequently reported Wavell as saying: 'I am sorry for you. You have been given an impossible job. I have tried everything I know to solve the problem of handing over India to its people and I can see no light.'[42] Mountbatten revealed that Attlee had requested him to take over the Viceroyalty around the time of Wavell's return to India in December, news which led Wavell to conclude that 'Attlee's assurances of support at that time and subsequent letters were completely insincere.'[43] In fact the request to Mountbatten had been made on 18 December, two days before Wavell left England.[44]

Clement Attlee's later explanation of Wavell's dismissal included criticism of his Breakdown Plan. 'He produced a plan worked out by his ICS advisers for the evacuation of India with everybody moving from where they were by stages right up through the Ganges valley till eventually, apparently, they would be collected at Karachi and Bombay and sail away. Well, I thought that was what Winston would certainly quite properly describe as an ignoble and sordid scuttle and I wouldn't look at it. I came to the conclusion that Wavell [whom he had described as 'defeatist'] had shot his bolt and that I must find somebody else. I thought very hard on that and looked all round. And suddenly I had what I now think was an inspiration. I thought of Mountbatten.' According to Attlee, although Wavell had been 'a very good Viceroy in many ways', he was not suited to dealing with politicians, particularly Indian politicians. 'He was a soldier and a singularly silent soldier. A great man in many ways, but a curious silent bird, and I don't think silent people get on very well with Indians, who are very loquacious.'[45]

It was perhaps inevitable that Attlee's London-based perspective should not have recognized the esteem in which numerous Indians held Wavell, whose attempts to ensure fair play had been manifest both at Simla and in subsequent negotiations. Both sides may have been annoyed that he stolidly refused to favour their cause, but they admired him for it. The soldier-turned-statesman may have become impatient with their deliberations, but he had not wavered in attempting to find a solution. Eric Lumby, on the staff of the Cabinet Mission, observed that while the various Indian political parties had accused Wavell of siding with their opponents, once he left they had paid tribute to his sincerity in helping India gain independence. 'He had not succeeded in his aim: but it would be hard to over-estimate the value of his achievement in keeping open the path of negotiation so that the rival protagonists of unity and partition did not feel themselves compelled to resort to the desperate alternative of force.'[46] Lieutenant-General Attiqur Rahman considered Wavell to have been 'one of the first Britishers who appreciated the Pakistan stand . . . He may not have liked the abrasive personality of Mr Jinnah but there is no doubt that in his journal he has given a place to Muslim nationhood which became a reality.'[47] On the Congress side, Maulana Azad had recognized that Wavell's insistence on summoning the Simla Conference was the first clear indication that Britain really did intend to transfer power. Yet throughout the 1946 negotiations his position was undermined by the Congress leaders, who had the ear of the British Government; Nehru, as was later revealed, wrote to his friends in England that although Wavell was honest and sincere, he had 'lost all flexibility of his mind in his desire to appease Jinnah and the Muslim League.' Gandhi believed Wavell's state of mind had been 'unnerved owing to the Bengal tragedy' during the August riots.[48] Wavell was obviously tired in the latter stages of his Viceroyalty, and apparently unaware of the extent to which his plain-speaking had lost him support. Of all the dismissals he had suffered, this last hurt the most.[49]

After his talk with Mountbatten, Wavell spent his last evening in India discussing the Budget with Liaquat Ali Khan. Afterwards he and Queenie had dinner alone with the Mountbattens; later Ismay, Mieville and Abell joined them. They 'talked politics' for about an hour and a half. On Sunday 23 March Wavell made a ceremonial departure from a country on whose soil he had first set foot more than sixty years earlier, as a small boy, leaving Viceregal Lodge in a state carriage with the Bodyguard in their full regalia. In a break with precedent, the Mountbattens went to the airfield to see them off, a gesture Wavell described as 'friendly'. In Karachi he paid a short visit to the 2nd Battalion, The Black Watch, whose colonelcy he had recently assumed following Wauchope's retirement. They reached Habbaniya late at night and the following day they flew to Rome, where Peter and Felicity left them, to start their honeymoon. Wavell and Queenie spent the following morning in the Sistine Chapel, admiring the enduring work of Michelangelo. That evening they were in England.

22

The End

This the end
Foretold and dreamed –
'Colour and light and all warm lovely things.'
The last, Earth's last horizon eyes transcend,
Transcend the mirage.
Homeward, warrior poet, the evening brings.[1]

WHEN WAVELL LEFT India in the spring of 1947 he was nearly 64: the same age as Churchill when he became Prime Minister in 1940. Archibald Wavell, however, was going into retirement – or, as his admirers said, 'unsung into oblivion'.[2] He was to shoulder no greater responsibilities than those he had already borne. The step down must inevitably be painful, yet in his subsequent writings no note of bitterness accompanies his usual self-criticism. As in each new phase of his life, stoicism was the hallmark. For a while he stopped writing his journal; in August he began again, making entries at intermittent intervals, recapping on the past and constantly posing questions about his future. An indication of his feelings during the last years of his life is also to be found in the many letters he wrote to his regular correspondents, especially those with whom he had worked over the past years, who had invariably become close friends. He also continued to write about the family lineage to his cousin Edward, who had welcomed him home enthusiastically 'after so many years of absence'.[3] The lengthy handwritten letters to Joan Bright had ceased, however, and there is a sense that the relationship they had enjoyed through their correspondence ended with the war. He wrote to her just twice in 1946, once prompted by a newspaper announcement that she was leaving the War Cabinet Office: 'Your vitality and courage inspired many of us.'[4] In 1949 Joan married Colonel Philip Astley, a cousin of Wavell's deceased son-in-law Simon.[5]

★

The Wavells landed at Northolt airport, where Pethick-Lawrence and Alexander met them, Cripps having excused himself on the grounds of 'pressing business'. Wavell had a few 'innocuous' words for the Press and they went on to a suite at Claridges, reserved for them for ten days at Government expense. A few days later came an invitation to Downing Street where, as Wavell noted, he was questioned for about forty minutes 'in a rather routine and perfunctory fashion'. Towards the end of their meeting, Listowel, Secretary of State for India, asked whether Wavell had any advice on how to proceed. The response was understandably acerbic: 'I said that I had given them advice and that they had not liked it.' Even so – 'for what it was worth' – he recommended that they should make a final effort to bring all the parties together; if that failed, to avoid confusion the government should seriously consider arrangements for partition. Watch in hand, the Prime Minister bowed Wavell out 'without a single word of thanks or commendation',[6] excusing himself because of 'a luncheon arrangement'.[7]

In early April Wavell left for Scotland, going immediately to Dover Wilson's house at Balerno, south of Edinburgh. 'My memory of him sitting in my little library after lunch is almost too vivid. He was ever a silent man, and his first words, blurted out, were, "You know I've been sacked."' According to Dover Wilson, 'the depth and rawness of the wound were evident.' To a suggestion that he would now have more time to write, the former Viceroy almost shouted 'Not about India!'[8] Dover Wilson had hoped Wavell might become Master of Magdalene College, Cambridge, and with Wavell's agreement had put his name forward.[9] But though his distinction was evident, Wavell was already considerably beyond the optimum age, with no experience in the educational field. When an alternative was chosen, Wavell wrote amicably to Dover Wilson that he would have liked it, but had not been counting on it.[10]

Honours came thick and fast, however. The first was an honorary doctorate in law from the University of St Andrews, conferred on 9 April. George Cunningham, former Governor of the North-West Frontier Province, was being installed as Rector at the same time, and Dick O'Connor was also receiving an honorary degree. O'Connor recalled that, Wavell 'had to wear uniform for the ceremony and I found him cleaning his tunic buttons like any private soldier': comparatively recently, as Viceroy, 'he had hundreds of servants and orderlies, besides staff and ADCs at his beck and call.'[11] Bad weather did not prevent Wavell playing several rounds of golf at the Royal and Ancient at St Andrews, which had made him an honorary member on his return from India. 'We are anchorless at present,' he wrote to Freya Stark, 'no house, no particular ideas on where to live or what to do . . . The number of societies which want me to do unpaid honorary and probably tiresome work for them is large. So far I have succeeded in declining practically everything, also all invitations to write for the Press, to lecture, to make after dinner or luncheon speeches, to give away prizes at School commemoration days or to open bazaars, fetes, exhibitions. etc.'[12] He expressed similar sentiments to his former Comptroller David Walker, who was still in India, where the focus remained giving the subcontinent independence. It was already obvious that Mountbatten could not transfer power to a united India, and that a sovereign Pakistan was inevitable. But, warned Wavell with his usual foresight, 'it will not be easy to partition the baby'.[13] Without secretary or stenographer he felt 'overwhelmed' with correspondence, and sometimes used blue crayon to scribble his own responses on the letters he received, with apologies for his 'informal answer'.[14] During the summer the Wavell family's temporary 'home' was a flat in Mayfair. Bernard Fergusson arrived for 'bath and breakfast' after journeying overnight from Scotland. 'I rang the bell, and himself answered the door,' he recalled. 'When I emerged from the bathroom, shaven and clean, he called: "You'll find me along here."' The former Viceroy was in the kitchen frying eggs and making toast and coffee.[15] As Colonel of the Regiment, in early August Wavell visited the 1st Battalion, The Black Watch, which was stationed in Germany. As so often, his interest in history coloured his journal entry. Spending the night near the Minden Gap, he noted that it was here that, during the reign of Emperor Augustus in AD 9, the Roman general Varro's legions had met with disaster, which 'halted forever the spread of Roman civilization to Eastern Europe'.[16]

During the summer Wavell met Sir Ernest Oppenheimer, chairman of the South African De Beers diamond company. Wavell had no business experience, but his eminence resulted in an offer to join the board. 'I have become a dealer in diamonds,' he wrote to Freya Stark. 'I don't much fancy big business, but I must find some means to supplement the income, and there is some interest and even a little romance about diamonds . . . I think I shall pay a plutocratic visit to Kimberley this winter.'[17] Throughout this period Wavell felt that he and Queenie were wanderers, staying with friends or in clubs 'like egg-less Cuckoos'.[18] For over six months George Spencer Churchill's sister Agnes, Lady Cowdray, gave Wavell the use of a study in her house at Cowdray Park, near Midhurst in Sussex. He hated living in boxes but, as he noted on 15 August – India's Independence Day – 'I was trying to find something to do, since until this was more or less settled, it was not much use to look seriously for a house.'[19] By the autumn

Queenie was negotiating for a flat in a block at Kingston House South, Ennismore Gardens, near Hyde Park – 'not very attractive' but possible.[20] On 21 October Wavell carried the Sword of State at the Opening of Parliament in the company of two former colleagues-in-arms: Andrew Cunningham carried the Crown, and former Chief of the Air Staff Peter Portal the Cap of Maintenance.[21]

That same evening Wavell left for St Andrews, where he had agreed to lecture on 'The Triangle of Forces in Civil Leadership'. As he informed his audience, he would ordinarily have spoken about 'Military Leadership', but the last lecture in the series – delivered by Montgomery in 1945 – had been on that subject; he therefore chose to speak on aspects of civil leadership, ancient and modern. That he still felt unsettled is immediately evident in his speech, which he began with an apology for not having been able to research his lecture properly, not having his books at his disposal. He compared himself to the ancient philosophers who composed and delivered lectures while walking about, and managed to draw on his classical and historical knowledge to discuss the French and Russian revolutions, Pericles and Lincoln – 'two of the greatest democratic leaders of history' – Greece and Philip of Macedon, the Caesars of Rome. He ended on a note of optimism: 'I believe the essential qualities of Courage and Faith are still in us, and we deserve leaders of the same qualities, who will tell us the truth, the whole truth, and nothing but the truth, so that our national greatness and love of freedom may find as full expression in peace as in war.'[22] His address was later published as a pamphlet, and Liddell Hart wrote to congratulate him; it was, he said, 'one of the most penetrating things' Wavell had ever written. As usual, he included a note of his own detailed comments.[23]

The following day Wavell was installed as Chancellor of Aberdeen University. He had intended to speak on 'vitality and the spirit of adventure in men and nations', but an earlier address delivered by the Rector, Eric Linklater, 'sometime private in The Black Watch', caused him to change his mind. Linklater, he said, had covered the same subject 'with far more wisdom, grace and wit than are at my command'. Instead he chose 'Games and Athletics', and again began with an apology, in this case for his lack of qualifications to be Chancellor of a Scottish University: 'I did not receive the benefits of a University education and have had little opportunity to acquire knowledge of the organization of a University.' Furthermore, he was Scottish only by adoption in his Regiment. The theme of the speech, the historical development of games and athletics, followed the pattern of his life, from the early instruction he had received

as a boy at Summer Fields.[24] His hosts at Aberdeen, aware of Wavell's reputation for awkward silences, had initially viewed his first visit to the
University with some apprehension: 'We all laboured a bit heavily for a
quarter of an hour,' recalled Sir William Hamilton Fyfe, Principal and
Vice-Chancellor of the University. 'Then the talk turned to India, and for
the rest of the evening, without monopolizing the conversation, he kept
us keenly interested and amused, without ever exceeding the limits of
kindly comment and discretion.' Like others who knew Wavell personally,
Sir William found the silences far less disconcerting than he had expected,
and he recognized that 'perhaps supreme commanders, in the society of
their Staff, get into the habit of not talking when nobody has anything to
say. It's not a bad habit.'[25]

Wavell was back in London in November, when he and Queenie
attended the wedding of Princess Elizabeth and Philip Mountbatten at
Westminster Abbey. The King had ordered all the field marshals to carry
their ceremonial batons – the only time Wavell ever did. In the evening he
met Mountbatten, no longer Viceroy of India but now Governor-General,
and as 'voluble' as ever. Wavell detected that he had had a 'gruelling' time:
the outbreak of hostilities over the Princely State of Jammu and Kashmir,
still in dispute at Partition, meant that relations between Hindu and
Muslim were 'worse than ever before'. He was pleased, however, to hear
that his own 'stock stood high', and that all the political leaders respected
his integrity; Mountbatten also 'warned' him that 'Winston was no friend
of mine and had never been loyal to me.'[26] Later that night Wavell wrote
to Auchinleck, who had been instructed by Mountbatten to close down
Supreme Headquarters. 'I know how deeply you must be feeling the tragic
events in India and the disruption of the Indian Army and the apparent
destruction of your life's work.' He thought the Army might never again
be so effective a force, or have the same spirit. 'But the work that you and
all your officers did will live both in the past and future history of
India.'[27] Auchinleck did not reply for some months; when he did, he said
he had appreciated Wavell's 'very kind' letter 'more than I can say.'[28]

Wavell's despatch on Burma was shortly to be published. Lieutenant-
General Sir Leslie Hollis at the Ministry of Defence warned Churchill that
Wavell's criticism of the Chiefs of Staff and the Government for rejecting
his advice to place Burma under the India Command was likely to cause
some controversy. Having consulted Attlee and the Chiefs of Staff, Hollis
suggested that Churchill might add either a preface, giving the full political background to his decision to include Burma within the ABDA command, or explanatory footnotes; or they could refrain from comment,

'leaving it to the public to balance the political and military considerations'. On reflection, Churchill decided on the third course of action, noting: 'Naturally Lord Wavell does not fully relate what the political considerations were, but opportunity will arise to adjust that balance, and in the meantime I think it best to publish the Despatch as it stands.'[29]

At the end of November Wavell was awarded his fifth honorary degree in law, from London University.[30] As he recorded in his journal, he had missed the chance of achieving a long-cherished ambition. He had been tempted to ask for a D.Litt. instead, but had refrained from doing so; when he told the Vice-Chancellor over dinner that evening, the Vice-Chancellor said he wished they had thought of it. 'I had not liked to ask for it,' Wavell commented somewhat mournfully, giving a glimpse of the man who might have been an academic had fate and his father not directed him towards the army. 'But I might have had it and had it alongside Masefield.'[31]

By the end of the year the Wavells were at last ready to move into 23 Kingston House South. Wavell's sense of humour was equal to domestic upheaval: 'We are struggling to get into a flat,' he wrote to Walker, 'but so far all that has happened is that one van load of furniture has arrived and Her ex-Ex has a bad cold and is trying to decide what comes in the next van (I have suggested beds of which there are none at present but I don't think it is the right answer).'[32] In his journal he described 1947 as a thoroughly bad year: 'I think on the whole I am well out of India, though I hated the way they chucked me out and should have liked to see the thing through.' He still felt 'rootless and unhappy', and accepted invitations to functions 'of all kinds without really wanting to do any of them.'[33] What was more, he complained to Leonie Lemartine, with whom he was still in touch after 35 years, 'I seem to spend most of my time being my own ADC and Secretary – answering the telephone, looking out trains, dealing with correspondence, catching buses, shopping etc. which have all been done for me for the last 10 years or so, and I do it so badly.'[34] He was also distressed at the loss of his 'best friend' Arthur Wauchope, who had died in September, and admitted that he himself had not felt 'really well all year'.[35]

Nineteen-forty-eight looked brighter. At the end of January Wavell set off for South Africa, without Queenie. The journey was 'dull', and left him time for reflection. 'I don't like conversation in trains or planes or motors especially now that I'm rather deaf,' he confessed to Freya Stark, and went on to explain his lifelong preference for books over people: 'Why should one endure the tedious babble of some tiresome visitor, when at one's elbow is the wit and wisdom of all the ages and the best masters, clamouring for one's attention – or rather one's attention clamouring for them? . . . But I suppose that never to pull out one's social small-change and spend it in company is churlish and niggardly.'[36] Wavell spent five weeks in South Africa. Although he found that living with the 'VERY RICH' was 'a pleasant enough experience' and the Oppenheimers were 'charming and kind and interesting', he also felt out of place, 'like a sinner who has got a golden harp quite by mistake and doesn't know what to do with it.'[37] His programme was full, with mines and factories to visit and numerous meetings to attend. He also went to see Smuts in Cape Town, and found him – at 78 – 'as young in mind and body for his age as ever'. They discussed the state of Europe, and of South Africa, where the position of the 'Indian' and 'Native' populations was becoming explosive. 'How even the most liberal policy is going to secure the permanent domination of a mere handful, comparatively speaking, of white men in a country of predominantly black men, who are becoming conscious of their numerical advantage and of the happenings in Asia, no one can quite foresee.'[38]

Wavell returned to England in early March to find that it had taken Queenie all the time of his absence to obtain the necessary permits to redecorate their flat, so the painters had only just started. He busied himself with the pile of correspondence he found waiting for him, and got what the family called 'displaced books' (DBs) sorted into a library. In the House of Lords he had become the spokesman for British servicemen in India who had left the army to take up civilian jobs only to find that if they did not go on working in India after independence they faced premature retirement without a pension: on 7 April he moved a motion on behalf of approximately 700 men in subordinate positions in the provincial police forces, the secretariats of the Central Provinces, the forestry branch and on the railways. The officer classes had been fully compensated but the rank-and-file were left to 'shift for themselves', and this, he said, was not 'in accordance with British tradition'. As Commander-in-Chief and Viceroy, he had 'seen their work and can testify to the value of what they have done. The great and orderly expansion of the Indian Army would not have been possible without their effort. Secretarial work in an office is not exciting or dangerous during a war, but it is of vital importance.'

The Earl of Listowel, now Minister of State for Colonial Affairs, replied to the plea made 'by the noble and gallant Earl', defending the Government's position. It was unfortunate that their civilian status had deprived these men of certain rights they would have enjoyed if they had remained soldiers, but he reminded his listeners 'that it was at their own choice that they originally left the Army for Government service.' Wavell could not let this pass: 'A choice which was practically forced upon them. They had either to become civilians or to return as private soldiers to their units and give up lucrative employment.' The debate lasted for more than two hours. Wavell concluded his remarks by offering Listowel, in return for the sympathy he had offered the men, his own fullest sympathy for his 'having been put up to make such a weak and unconvincing case'. The Government, he said, had again written the matter off on a purely legal argument: 'If I press this matter no further today it is not because I feel satisfied, but because I hope that as a result of what has been said in your Lordships' House the Government will reconsider the question.'[39]

In the spring of 1948 Wavell received further literary exposure with the publication of *The Good Soldier*, a small book that included his Trinity College lectures on Generals and Generalship, his obituaries of Lawrence and Wingate, and several other studies. As usual, Liddell Hart was one of the first to write and congratulate him. Wavell seemed still to enjoy their discursive correspondence, which enabled him to sound out his own ideas. There is also a sense of the two men wanting to set the record straight: Greece, for instance, remained a recurring theme. Liddell Hart suggested that neither Churchill nor the War Cabinet had put pressure on Wavell to undertake the expedition, or to persist with it after Papagos changed his mind following the occupation of Bulgaria; Wavell defended his decision: 'It is true that no pressure was put on me to undertake the Greek Expedition or to persist in it after Papagos had changed his mind. Churchill did, after the latter event, have some qualms and did suggest the possibility of retraction. But all of us out there, Eden, Dill and myself, felt that it was not possible to do so.' Echoing his official opinion, he said he was 'quite sure that from the political and psychological point of view we were right to undertake it. And I believe that on the whole it may have had a favourable effect on the war.'[40] So determined was he to air his point of view that he and Eden had decided to write a book about the campaign, for which he had begun to write the Foreword.

Domestically, there were ups and downs. Cooks came and went, and so there was much experimental cooking. 'We did some quite good buttered eggs and fried bacon on telephoned instructions from Joan,' Wavell informed Freya Stark. In May Queenie went to Trieste, where Peter was serving in the RAF, to see Felicity's 'baby in, or rather out'. But Wavell was dissatisfied. 'England has had and is still having the most lovely spring in my memory and it has been heart-breaking to live in London,' he wrote to Freya, 'without room to swing even a kitten and with collars to wear and buses to queue for, and telephones to answer.' He also touched on world events. Thirty years ago he had walked through the Jaffa Gate in Jerusalem; he now considered Palestine 'a tragic business . . . the Jews must, I think, win in the end, they have money and brains and the cold ruthless selfishness that gets on in the world, and I can't see the Arabs hanging together or sticking it out, or countering the world propaganda of the Jews. For ourselves, it looks like meaning bad blood with Jews, Arabs and Americans. And we did mean so well. If ever a road to Hell was paved with good intentions, this one was.'[41]

On 1 June 1948 Wavell was installed as the 147th Constable of the Tower of London, an office held by eminent prelates of the Church, prominent politicians and distinguished soldiers from the time of William the Conqueror. Since the death of the Duke of Wellington the appointment, by 'Royal Letters Patent under the Great Seal', had always been filled by a soldier, on a five-year tenure since 1933. Once more, as when he was Viceroy, Wavell enjoyed the privilege of 'audience and direct communica-tion' with the King. 'The sun peered out from the grey sky at exactly the right moment: the uniforms shone, the beefeaters looked splendid,' noted Chips Channon, who later had tea with the Wavells, whom he found 'at their best and simplest – affectionate, muddled and charming.'[42]

Shortly afterwards Wavell made his annual visit to The Black Watch in Germany. On this occasion he had to preside over the merger of the 1st and 2nd Battalions, which he had tried unsuccessfully to prevent by asserting that there were enough regular volunteers to make up two battalions. 'It was a moving occasion,' recollected Fergusson, who had recently become the commanding officer, 'and one young soldier wept as he stood in the ranks.'[43] To lighten the mood, Wavell, Fergusson and Eric Linklater, who was also present, amused themselves by composing a 'Ballade of Bereavement' for Wavell's shaving-brush, left at the University of Aberdeen, whence he had just come: 'My chin, once glossy as a nectarine, / Now looks like holly on a Christmas card, / Or straggly hawthorns in a woodland scene / Such as is deftly drawn by Fragonard . . . I left my shaving-brush at Aberdeen.'[44] Wavell wanted to see where the 1st, 5th and 7th battalions had crossed the Rhine, the last obstacle to victory in Europe in 1945, so they took a picnic to Goch, Rees and Appeldorn, where Wavell's regimental comrades had fought and fallen.[45] This visit to the heart of Europe, with Berlin divided into Soviet and Allied Zones, also filled Wavell with foreboding: 'The world seems to be riding for a fall again and really will break its neck this time if it doesn't take care.' Yet as he had so often during the war, he remained optimistic. 'I still hope that somehow or other a way out will be found.'[46]

Wavell gradually adapted to the pace of his new life: 'I seem to be always extremely busy with something or other but don't get very much done. Like the Red Queen in Alice, I find it takes all the running one can do to keep in the same place.'[47] On 19 June Joanie, now 25, married again. In early July there was the family christening of Richard Martin Wavell, Felicity and Peter's baby. Nanny Ribbands was 'in good heart', and they had requested an Italian cook to come from Trieste. Francis and Pamela had been back in England since April, on six months' leave from India, where Francis was working with Burma Shell. Weekends and 'week-middles' were spent at the Longmores' home at Pipits Hill, Wentworth (for Air Marshals *vs* Generals golf), or at Hatfield staying with the Salisburys – Cranborne's father had died in 1947 and he was now the fifth marquess. The Wavells had acquired a dog, which they had called Rommel. Wavell also presided at the annual meetings of the Royal Society of Literature, the Royal Central Asian Society and the Sir Walter Scott Society, of the Army Historical Society, and of the Kipling Society (of which he had been a founder member in 1927). As Chancellor of Aberdeen University he conferred honorary degrees on Auchinleck and Arthur Smith.[48] However, when his Wykehamist friend Stephen Phillimore, now Vicar of St George's, Hanover Square, London, asked him to give a poetry reading to raise money for the church organ, he refused on the grounds that the church was not in his parish.[49]

Wavell might no longer be responsible for India, but he maintained an active interest in events there. Jinnah had died in September, and at the end of October Wavell dined in London with Liaquat Ali Khan, Pakistan's first Prime Minister. 'We spoke of Kashmir,' he noted, 'which he said was the only bar now to better relations with India; discussions with Nehru had led nowhere and Pakistan would never agree to Kashmir's accession to India.'[50] At Winchester in November a particularly memorable weekend saw the dedication of the War Memorial in War Cloister. He had been to Cowes on his own to sail in Sir Arthur Longmore's *Teal*, to Stratford-on-Avon to see productions of *Othello* and *Hamlet*. The latter, in Victorian dress, he thought 'not particularly good'; Anthony Quayle, former SOE operative who had parachuted into Albania, now the new director of the theatre, played the King in frock coat and mutton-chop whiskers. New books found their way onto his library shelves, such as Alan Paton's *Cry the Beloved Country* and the first volume of Churchill's *History of the Second World War* ('very good reading, but perhaps a little too self-righteous').[51] He 'savoured' Freya Stark's latest book, *Perseus in the Wind*: 'It is like a casket of jewels.'[52] The new cook from Trieste was regarded as 'favourable'.

Speaking engagements continued throughout the autumn. In mid October Wavell delivered the Presidential address to the Virgil Society, of which he had become President 'in an unguarded moment'.[53] The title of his address was 'Arms and the Man', and as usual he began by apologizing to his audience: as a soldier who had had no occasion and little opportunity for reading Virgil since passing into Sandhurst nearly fifty years before, he was in an impossible position. He then went on to deliver as learned a lecture as the audience could have expected – complete with Latin quotations (which he himself had used in time of distress, 'even fear') – supporting his thesis that Virgil, although opposed to war, had a shrewd apprehension of it; that Aeneas was quite 'an effective if rather pedestrian general' who has been misjudged; and, of course, that Virgil was a very great poet. Towards the end there was another apology: 'I have thrown out the best smoke-screen I could contrive to cover my retreat from an untenable position.' Above all, he said, Virgil had 'the grand gift of vision, a vision not of Arms and the Man but of something far higher and better – a golden era of peace on Earth and goodwill to all men.'[54]

Wavell had not lost his habit of self-criticism. 'I keep pretty well, but am getting old and fat and deaf and bald,' he told Leonie Lemartine. 'Moscow in 1911 seems a very long time ago.'[55] He was also frustrated by Archie John's career. After winding up the Army Education school in India, Archie John – now 31 and showing no signs of marrying[56] – had returned to Britain in November 1947 and was teaching at the Army School of Education in Cornwall. Wavell obviously thought that his son was wasting his talents and should have tried for the Staff College, but Archie John refused to do so, which Wavell found 'tiresome'.[57] The War Office he considered 'narrow-minded' because they had not allowed Archie John a year's leave of absence, to teach at Winchester and run their Cadet Corps.[58] Overall, he described 1948 as an 'aimless, purposeless, unprofitable year'.[59]

In 1949 Wavell embarked upon what promised to be a busy year of speeches and social functions. In early February he delivered a lecture on National and International History at the London School of Economics, in which he called the Old Testament 'the most striking example of nationalistic history', and as usual sent Liddell Hart a copy. The two men continued to discuss the threat presented by the Soviet Union to Western Europe. Possibly his own memories of Russia caused Wavell to take a more sympathetic view than most: 'I still believe that the present Russian attitude is defensive and is prompted mainly by fear of a German revival and another war on her western frontier,' he wrote to Liddell Hart in May. 'It is an understandable attitude in view of her losses in the last War and the way the Germans behaved. Naturally Russia would like to see Europe controlled by Communists . . . But I have never believed in a Russian desire for conquest or domination . . . This of course is not to minimize the danger . . . against which we have to be fully prepared.'[60]

Wavell had also begun an intermittent correspondence with Churchill through Pownall, who had retired at the end of the war. In April he sent Churchill a copy of his Presidential Address to the Virgil Society the previous autumn, in which he had mentioned Churchill's name.[61] Churchill graciously acknowledged it, and soon afterwards sent him provisional proofs of Volume III of his *History of the Second World War*, *The Grand Alliance*: it concerned, he said, 'all our most difficult affairs . . . Should you be inclined to look at it, I should be very glad to receive, in strict personal confidence, any comments you may care to make. Of course we may not find ourselves in agreement. Still, the more I ponder on those first fateful six months of 1941, the more I feel the sense of our comradeship and your great services.' He also enclosed an advance copy of Volume II, *Their Finest Hour*. Wavell told Churchill he would greatly look forward to reading it, 'both for the interest of the story and for the fine prose in which it is written'.[62] Having read the proofs he suggested no alterations concerning himself personally, commenting that Winston had 'on the whole' been 'very kind.' Churchill then sent him the chapter in Volume IV relating to the fall of Singapore. Wavell later wrote to Freya Stark that he found Churchill's account very much about 'Winston's war' but once more acknowledged that while it was rather 'one-sided history', Churchill had 'on the whole' been 'very kind'.[63] Norman Brook, who had been deputy secretary to the War Cabinet in 1942, subsequently noted that at this late stage Churchill had been rethinking his position on Wavell's capacities as a Commander 'very substantially – I believe – as a result of re-reading the telegrams and other material while he was at work on Volume III.' Despite their past differences, Wavell's post-war opinion of Churchill was positive: 'I have never loved, nor hated Winston. I have admired him intensely for his indomitable courage, his talents, his wit, his panache. I have disparaged him, almost despised him at times . . . But I have no doubt at all that admiration has always been predominant.'[64]

As in 1948, Wavell visited The Black Watch in Germany. The USSR had been blockading Berlin by road and rail since the previous summer, forcing Britain, France and the United States to organize a massive airlift: Wavell and Fergusson flew up to Berlin to see it. At the beginning of July Wavell once more spoke in the Lords on the pensions issue. Since he first raised the matter the Indian and Pakistani governments had agreed to grant the right of a proportionate pension to those retiring after 18 November 1948; Wavell welcomed this decision, but regretted that it had not been made retrospective to 15 August 1947.[65] He was supported by his friends, including Ismay and Salisbury. The Government eventually agreed to make some arrangement for those who had retired prior to the date stipulated by India and Pakistan, and indicated that recommendations from Wavell regarding those who might qualify would be considered. Wavell concluded the debate with the hope that the matter would be dealt with promptly, and a quotation from Shakespeare: to date those men could say that they had 'borne and borne and borne, and have been fobbed off, and fobbed off, and fobbed off from this day to that day, that it is a shame to be thought on. There is no honesty in such dealing.' He reserved the right to raise the matter again if they did not receive satisfaction.[66]

Archie John, meanwhile, was considering a political career, having been offered a seat to contest by the Liberals – but Wavell thought the Liberal Party had no future 'and I doubt whether he would find himself in congenial company with Welsh lawyers who seem to form the chief remnant of the Liberals.'[67] He himself was appointed Lord Lieutenant of the County of London; he did not want to accept, but 'it was intimated to me that I wasn't expected to refuse. I'm afraid it means more civil duties and parties.' Such were his commitments that Wavell told Freya Stark that at present, writing his autobiography was not possible.[68]

As had become his custom, Wavell spent part of the summer of 1949 in Scotland. David Walker was visiting from Canada, where he now lived, and they managed to play the Old Course at St Andrews, which they both preferred. Now that Wavell was freed from the cares of high office, Walker detected how his game had improved: 'The man who beat me at the Royal and Ancient was precisely the same person as, if more carefree than, the man I used to beat in Delhi.'[69] But his proneness to accidents continued to bedevil him. After three days' stalking in Ross-shire the previous September (and two stags) he sprained his ankle badly and so was able 'to stalk no more' that year.[70] Wavell told Walker he had been invited to visit The Black Watch of Canada, and asked whether he could 'spare a day or two' to help him on arrival. 'So diffidently asked,' Walker later recalled. 'If he had said Timbuktoo I would have been there to meet him.'[71] Wavell had also started work on a literary project he said he had 'rashly' undertaken – writing the section on 'Armies from 1900 to 1945' for a revised edition of the Cambridge Modern History. When he had reached 1939 he sent the 23 foolscap pages to Liddell Hart, with a view to finishing the section from

1939 to 45 after his return from Canada. Before he left, the Wavells held a 'Delhi party' that included many former aides and friends.[72]

Wavell set sail for Canada at the end of October. Queenie had refused to go with him because Joanie was expecting another baby, and she thought his programme 'too restless'.[73] As promised, David Walker spent a few days with him as 'unofficial aide-de-camp' and witnessed the 'tumultuous' welcome Wavell received at Montreal from The Black Watch of Canada, which had served in both wars. He had been asked to speak in Montreal, Toronto and Ottawa, and also in Washington, and he sent his draft speeches to Walker for comment. 'About only one, I think, I did help,' recalled Walker. In his speech to the Canadian Club in Montreal Wavell stressed the contribution the British had made to the world: clearly this would be 'meat and drink' to the English element, but Walker knew it might offend those of French descent. Acting upon his advice, Wavell adjusted his speech 'gratefully and gracefully, and also spoke a little French.'[74]

From Canada – 'an impressive country with a considerable future'[75] – Wavell went on to the United States. The evening before he started back to England he was due to address the American Academy of Poets, and David Walker had once more made himself available as unofficial ADC. With presentations, recitations, four eulogies and four main speakers, the dinner went on until well after midnight. Wavell – the fourth speaker – had chosen to speak on the soldier and poetry; quoting from memory from his anthology, he cited the concluding lines of Cameron Wilson's 'Magpies in Picardy': 'The beauty of the wild green earth / And the bravery of man.' These, he said, should be the chief themes of the poet, 'who should open our eyes to beauty and lead us to face the dangers and difficulties of this world with bravery'.[76] They were undeniably the chief themes of his own life.

The following day Wavell went shopping. Walker viewed the expedition 'with more trepidation' than the poets' dinner, 'never feeling much at ease among ladies' underclothes up for sale,' but Wavell 'the warrior, monocle in remaining eye, went about his task with seasoned aplomb.'[77] He left New York on 2 December and Walker accompanied him to the dock 'in a well-travelled New York taxicab, sharing the back seat with his well-travelled luggage.' As they neared their destination, a policeman stopped them and a long line of traffic built up behind them. The taxi driver deduced they must be waiting for 'some big shot', as Walker recalled. 'Eventually there passed across our bows a large and explosive motorcycle escort, a police car or two, and then a dignified Rolls-Royce . . . The Field Marshal smiled that wry grim smile of his and rumbled, "There goes

Monty." Neither rancour nor envy dwelt in him.'[78] Both Montgomery and Wavell were returning to England aboard the *Mauretania*.[79]

By the beginning of 1950 Wavell's morale had at last improved. Only the outdoors was missing: 'I wish we could live in the country but I have too much to do in London at present.'[80] There was his Cambridge entry on the Army to finish, and a waiting pile of correspondence (chorlettes, as he called them – chore letters). 'Next time I go away, instead of the formal "no correspondence will be forwarded" notice I shall try "all correspondence will be destroyed up to date of return",' he told Freya Stark.[81] During his absence Liddell Hart had produced four foolscap pages of comments on the already written section from 1900 to 1939. By early February Wavell had finished the first draft of the 1939–45 section on the Armies, but thought it 'too disjointed'.[82] Liddell Hart, however, described it as an 'excellent survey', and limited his comments to one and a half pages of single-spaced typed notes.[83]

There were also occasional visits to friends but these were not always happy. Jack Collins was dying of cancer, and his daughter Anne recalled how touched they were when Wavell made the effort to visit him in Winchester before his death in March 1950.[84] Wavell's own health was failing. At the end of March he told David Walker that he had been stricken by that 'foul plague', jaundice. In anticipation of another visit to The Black Watch in Germany in the spring, he also wrote to Fergusson, informing him of his illness. Freya Stark had recently returned from a trip to Cyrenaica, and Wavell was pleased to hear news of his wartime haunts. 'It brings back very many memories, of success and of failure and of days and nights in the desert.'[85] Wavell was also drafting a lecture for the British Academy, expanding his 1942 'Military Genius' article on Belisarius. And he also felt the need to finish the 'Recollections' he had been preparing for his family. They were marked 'private' – for family interest, and not to be published – but he had discussed his autobiography with Archie John and had even approached a publisher before he became ill. By the beginning of May he had succeeded in dictating his recollections up to the end of 1941.[86]

Wavell's condition was much more serious than he or his family realized. 'The doctors have now decided that this persistent jaundice of mine must be due to a gall stone,' he wrote to Fergusson on 1 May, 'and I am going into a nursing home this afternoon with a view to its removal. It is very tiresome.'[87] In fact he was suffering from a 'primary carcinoma of the hepatic duct'. The operation to excise the cancer – which took place on his sixty-seventh birthday – appeared to be successful, but he had a sudden haemorrhage. It was, as Queenie wrote to David Walker from the Beaumont Nursing Home in West London, a contest between 'his pluck, the skill of fine doctors and nurses, and death . . . This is perhaps the most gallant of all his battles and we can but pray that it will not prove the last.'[88] On the night of 23 May Archie John was sitting alone in the nursing home while his father slept. Seeking consolation, he took an anthology from the library shelves and found a poem he had never read before, then put the book down with a sad foreboding. The poem was Francis Bret Harte's 'Relieving Guard':

> Came the relief, 'What sentry, ho!
> How passed the night through thy long waking?'
> 'Cold, cheerless, dark – as may befit
> The hour before the dawn is breaking.'
>
> 'No sight? No sound?' 'No, nothing save
> The plover from the marshes calling
> And in yon western sky, about
> An hour ago, a star was falling.'
>
> 'A star? There's nothing strange in that.'
> 'No, nothing; but, above the thicket
> Somehow it seemed to me that God
> Somewhere had just relieved a piquet.'[89]

Wavell died on the morning of 24 May 1950.

It was a brilliantly hot day on Wednesday, 7 June 1950 as 'Judex' from Gounod's *Mors et Vita* was played in Westminster Abbey. Wavell's body had lain in state for two weeks in the Norman Chapel of St John in the Tower of London, where the Yeomen of the Guard kept vigil. On the morning of his funeral, as Lincoln bombers flew overhead and nineteen guns fired a salute, his body was transported along the River Thames to Westminster.[90] No pomp and circumstance was spared in what was the first State Funeral since the end of the war. Bernard Fergusson, commander of the 1st Battalion, The Black Watch, who had been ordered by the War Office to help with the funeral arrangements, was waiting on Westminster Bridge looking downriver.[91] 'A little flotilla of three launches was coming upstream in perfect symmetry, with their wake fanning out white behind them.' One Yeoman in full dress stood at the bow of the leading launch, the other at the stern. Arthur Smith was also on board, as was Archie John, now the 2nd Earl Wavell. Not since Nelson's funeral in 1805 had there been a 'state' river cortège. All river traffic was stopped, and the flags on the buildings were at half mast. People stood on rooftops, and workmen were stripped to the waist in the hot sun.

The launch stopped at Westminster and the coffin was carried up the steps. Fergusson, who confessed to admiring Wavell 'more than anyone else in the world', moved from observing the flotilla of launches to lead the officers.[92] 'Through the wide-open West door,' wrote John Connell for the *Evening News*, 'we could see the scarlet lines of the Yeomen Warders of the Tower. Round the tomb of the Unknown Warrior four tall candles burned steadily. Through the silence came the lonely and icy call of the pipes, faint and distant at first, as if heard down a mountain pass. Nearer came the cry, then the guard of honour halted, and from the gun-carriage slowly the coffin, swathed in the Union Jack, and topped by Lord Wavell's baton and plumed hat, was borne into the Abbey on the shoulders of the NCOs and men of The Black Watch.' As pall-bearers marched a glittering procession of great soldiers, sailors and airmen, all of whom, in Wavell's company, had borne high command in the Second World War: Alanbrooke, Montgomery, Mountbatten, Alan and Andrew Cunningham, Giffard, Platt, Smith, and many more.[93] Among those carrying Wavell's insignia were Dick O'Connor and an old friend from the North-West Frontier and the Great War, Amyas Borton. Mountbatten's presence as a pall-bearer had been opposed by 'his brother Lordships in the Admiralty, on the grounds that he was only a Vice-Admiral. He rightly retorted that for this occasion he was a former Viceroy, and characteristically got his way.'[94] Outside, a vast crowd had assembled in Parliament Square and Victoria Street.

Inside the Abbey there was silence. With representatives of the King and Queen stood Attlee, the Prime Minister, Anthony Eden, the Lord Chancellor, politicians, and members of the armed forces. Wavell's family was there with his sisters Nancy and Molly, Vere Bellairs who had introduced her cousin to his future wife so long ago, and Nanny Daisy Ribbands. An abbey-full of friends and well-wishers included people from all epochs of Wavell's life: Kenneth Buchanan, who had known him as a schoolboy; Neville Henderson, with whom Wavell had served in India (but not 'Long Man', who had died many years earlier in Linlithgow); Ivo Vesey, from his Staff College days (who lived to the age of 98); Henry Jackson and Jock Burnett-Stuart from his inter-war years. Conspicuous by his absence was Winston Churchill, who had sent Pownall to represent him. 'Some of us felt that he of all people might have come in person,' noted Fergusson,[95] but Churchill too, spending the summer in Chartwell writing his memoirs, was finding that 'old age was taking its toll'.[96]

Among the mourners was Yaqub Khan, formerly Wavell's adjutant in the Viceroy's Bodyguard, now a member of Pakistan's Foreign Service, who described how 'poignant and totally appropriate for the occasion' was the final reading from John Bunyan's *Pilgrim's Progress*: 'My sword I give to him that shall succeed me in my pilgrimage and my courage and skill to him that can get it. My marks and scars I carry with me, to be a witness for me that I have fought His battles who now will be my rewarder.'[97] After the prayers, the congregation sang Kipling's 'Recessional'. When the blessing had been given, the pipe-major, who had lost his eye at Tobruk, played 'Lochaber No More' and 'After the Battle'. The congregation then stood to attention for the bugler sounding the 'Last Post' and 'Reveille'. The effect in the Abbey, recalled Bernard Fergusson, was 'infinitely solemn', as the sound swelled and then died away. Soon after the service the funeral cortège left for Winchester, where Wavell was to be buried in preference to Westminster Abbey. At Staines the police, directed by the Assistant Commissioner of Police of the Metropolis, Major Philip Margetson, a former Scots Fusilier and old friend of Wavell's, 'had arranged for us all to have beer and tea and giant beef sandwiches,' recalled Fergusson. 'These were the more welcome since it was now nearly 2 p.m. and the Jocks had been on parade since some damnably early hour. I suddenly realized that, for the first time for a fortnight, nobody was actually watching over the Field Marshal: the hearse with his coffin lay quietly unattended in the yard. Just for a moment, I thought: "This won't do." Then it struck me that this was just how he would have liked it; and how much he would have enjoyed the banter of the Jocks and their reminiscences of the morning's events now that they were – for the moment – off parade and the tensions released.'[98] 'In the glorious still evening' Wavell was buried in the Chantry Garth at Winchester.[99] The scholar of Winchester had returned to his spiritual home.

23

Wavell's Legacy

Wavell with his integrity and his genius for soldiering, letters and friendship can neither be replaced nor forgotten.   Sir George Abell[1]

I N HIS JOURNAL Wavell wrote that he hoped some of the things he had done in his various responsibilities had 'been of some use to someone.'[2] It was a remarkably self-effacing comment from a man who had been Commander-in-Chief in the two most important theatres of the Second World War, and also Viceroy of India. But that was the character of the man. He neither craved fame nor clung to it. His disappointment at his dismissal as Viceroy had more to do with his dislike of leaving a job unfinished than with any distress at the loss of office. With his apparent lack of ambition, however, went an unwillingness to project himself favourably with his political colleagues; his failed relationship with Churchill is the most obvious example, that with Attlee a close second. Neither Cripps nor probably Pethick-Lawrence nor Stilwell applauded Wavell's manner. Even so, for all those who found him difficult there were legions who admired him, including such men as Brooke, Dill, Montgomery, O'Connor and Wilson.

Of the plethora of eulogistic obituaries that followed Wavell's death, Peter Fleming's in the *Spectator* aptly described his allure: 'An immense patient strength – perhaps that is the quality in Lord Wavell which seems, now that he is dead, the most important part of his character. With it went gentleness and wisdom and a remarkable humility. His one eye looked quizzically rather than sardonically upon the world, and he retained a certain innocence of spirit, the uprightness almost of a small boy who does not yet know that there are alternatives to uprightness.'[3] Dorman-Smith saw 'the perpetual youthfulness of Languedoc. He had none of the dreariness of the world of "oui".' At the same time, 'nobody really knew Archie. But I've seen him at various moments of crisis and of mirth, he was never grim . . . Without being sybaritic or sensuous he just enjoyed things as they

397

came along, gentle, and tough all in the same breath.' As to his poor relationship with Churchill, Dorman-Smith believed that Winston bored him:
'He therefore bored and perplexed Winston.'[4] Philip Mason thought the
affection he inspired had 'something more than respect, something more
like veneration. None of us, I think, could talk to him quite as an equal;
he was a being of a different and higher grade.'[5]

In judging Wavell's achievements after his death, Liddell Hart noted the
critical opinions of his generalship – 'that, as a soldier, his reputation was
unduly inflated by a few victories achieved over feeble Italian opponents,
and for which the credit should really go to the executive commanders
under him . . . he was over-cautious and lacking in decision . . . his con-
clusions were confused and too changeable . . . in various crises he was vac-
illating or evasive . . . while posing as a progressive soldier he was innately
conservative . . .'[6] Such extreme views have not stood the test of time, and
it is now appreciated how extremely complex and varied were the problems with which Wavell had to deal at a period when resources were inadequate and intelligence variable. No other wartime general faced similar
challenges – Greece, Crete, Singapore, Burma – or constraints with such
stoicism. Wavell never pretended he had all the answers, and was only too
willing to concede his mistakes. He was also always anxious that his commanders should share whatever praise he received. In the face of reversals
in the Western Desert and the evacuation of Greece and Crete, it was easy
to overlook the significance of Wavell's outstanding achievement in
destroying Italy's East African Empire, thereby safeguarding the Suez Canal
and Egypt, as well as the successful campaigns in Iraq and Syria. A further
measure of his generalship must be the loyalty he inspired despite his mis-
fortunes. Ismay always wished Wavell had never backed the Greek venture,
but years later still maintained that he would sooner have backed Wavell
than any other living soldier except perhaps Slim. 'He was a very very wise
old bird. His only grave error of judgement (Greece) was shared by 99 per
cent of the British High Command and was I believe in APW's case largely
the result of his ingrained loyalty to his political chiefs.'[7]

Among Wavell's critics in the political field Sir James Grigg was, inex-
plicably, perhaps the most antipathetic. Even before Wavell assumed the
Viceroyalty, Grigg believed, he had 'acquired a firm conviction that he was
ordained of Heaven to bring about a lasting settlement of the Indian problem and in spite of all we could say or do, this Messianic belief remained
with him.'[8] This view takes no account of the difficulty Wavell faced
simply in persuading Churchill that Indian policy should be discussed, both
during and after the war. Wavell's journal and his personal correspondence

reveal his own self-doubt, and his reluctant assumption of office; read in conjunction with the *Transfer of Power* documents, they also make clear his dogged determination to find a solution, and how circumscribed was his freedom of action. His relationship with Attlee as Prime Minister was less tempestuous than that with Churchill, but the two men had little in common and it was not in Wavell's nature to flatter Attlee any more than he had Churchill. In his confrontations with Churchill over India, he had at least had Amery's support; no such rapport ever developed with Pethick-Lawrence. Mountbatten had the advantage of having observed Wavell as he tried to reconcile the Muslim League and the Congress Party while at the same time reporting back to London; Mountbatten's insistence, before accepting the Viceroyalty, that he be granted plenipotentiary powers is evidence that he had learned from Wavell's experience.

As Viceroy, Wavell also demonstrated a capacity for realism not always shared by his political colleagues in England, who wished to keep the situation fluid. Rather than his 'vanity and ignorance' being the main cause in 'precipitating an avoidable abdication', as has been alleged, Wavell was constantly trying to warn the British Government of the dangers of letting India slide into chaos. His Breakdown Plan was not a plan to evacuate Europeans in an alarming emergency, but a political plan for a staged withdrawal of Britain's control, originally intended to shock the protagonists into agreement by indicating a date for Britain's eventual departure; by 1947 Wavell had come to believe that the British Government had exhausted all other available options. Nevertheless, throughout the course of the tortuous negotiations – from the time he opened the Simla Conference in 1945 until his dismissal in 1947 – Wavell's commitment to bringing the Congress Party and Muslim League together was both genuine and steadfast. Even Wavell's apparent tilt towards the Muslim League during the negotiations must be seen in the context of the evident sympathy shown by both Cripps and Pethick-Lawrence towards the Congress Party. As his daughter Lady Pamela said in 2000: 'My father wanted to be fair.'[9]

To see the Breakdown Plan as a 'scuttle' – Attlee's view of it – was also to overlook the fact that unless and until agreement was reached there was a real danger that the administration *would* break down, and with it law and order. Wavell had seen the warning signs even before the Calcutta killings in August 1946. Penderell Moon, who edited *The Viceroy's Journal*, believed it should have been adopted in the summer of 1946 as a means of putting pressure on the Congress Party. 'With the plan to fall back on, HMG and the Viceroy could have negotiated from strength instead of weakness.'[10] One reason for London's rejection of the Breakdown Plan – leading to

Wavell's dismissal – was the sense that a gradual withdrawal to the north-west and north-east of the subcontinent was tantamount to conceding Pakistan. Since partition formed part of the eventual solution, it may be conjectured that the Breakdown Plan – taking place over more than a year under Wavell's schedule – would have provided more time for tempers to subside; under Mountbatten, there were less than three months between the announcement of partition in June 1947 and the independence celebrations in August. Mountbatten argued that once the plan had been announced time was of the essence, but within Wavell's longer time-frame it is possible the violence that accompanied partition could have been considerably lessened, if not averted.

Wavell's supporters believe that had he remained as Viceroy and partition taken place, he would certainly have used the year of Britain's withdrawal to do what he could to enable the two new Dominions to establish themselves with less mistrust and hostility. Most importantly, they believe he would not have left unresolved the fate of Jammu and Kashmir, which has soured relations between India and Pakistan for more than fifty years. Undoubtedly Wavell would have striven for even-handedness between the parties, but whether or not he could have contained the explosive situation that developed over rival claims to the Princely State of Jammu and Kashmir which bordered both new countries is open to speculation. After partition Wavell expressed the view that with its Muslim ruler (who wanted to join Pakistan) and Hindu majority, the accession to India of the Princely State of Hyderabad in the heart of India could have been seen as fair exchange for conceding the majority Muslim state of Jammu and Kashmir to Pakistan.[11] While it is uncertain whether this would have been acceptable to an Indian government equally anxious to retain control of Jammu and Kashmir, a lengthier withdrawal would have given time for the adoption of a more reasoned approach to the state's political future.

Wavell's taciturnity is the characteristic which has attracted most comment. His family and close friends might claim that he was not as silent as legend would have it, but he was certainly far from loquacious in public, and it worked against him. Liddell Hart noted that he was 'exceptionally inarticulate, except on paper, for a man with such an active mind. It was rare for him to converse at all easily – and at times he seemed to be pulling out words as painfully as if he were pulling out his teeth.'[12] His letters, by contrast, were so interesting and fluent that Ivo Vesey believed that few apart from Winston Churchill were his equal in putting their thoughts on paper.[13] Even so, difficult though his 'professional silences' were, Philip

Mason recognized that in the right situation they could have a positive impact: 'the air of inattention, the secrecy, the silence, combined to make his subordinates regard him as primitive people regard a force of nature, something beyond their calculations, something liable at any moment to surprise them.'[14] Wavell frequently used these professional silences to considerable effect. He would wander around the room looking at books while plans were being discussed, then surprise those present by making it plain that he had missed nothing, indeed had already concocted a satisfactory plan. Conrad Corfield experienced Wavell's silences when he was interviewed for the position of political adviser, and emerged from the ordeal full of admiration: 'At the end of half an hour there had been more silence than talk, but he seemed satisfied and said, "Well, I'll be seeing you at dinner." I left with a feeling that here was a man I could serve with implicit confidence and trust . . . How did he communicate that feeling of confidence, and why did that confidence develop later into affection? I cannot explain. I learnt later what a potent weapon his silence was . . . It was his method: he didn't need to talk: he just waited and those who could not keep silent quickly gave themselves away. The others survived.'[15] John Benson noted that he 'seldom made conversation just for conversation's sake, and so at times might seem to be out of place to some people who did not know him. But if you could get onto a wave length with him he could be wonderful company. This did not happen often but it was all the more fun when it did.'[16] As even Queenie wrote, he could be 'so unexpectedly talkative as well as so disconcertingly silent'.[17] And as Dorman-Smith observed, 'Archie was never taciturn when he was happy or stimulated, he was always ready for a game or a joke.'[18]

Wavell's difficulties in communicating led him to form friendships with extrovert people – or as Queenie put it, he was apt to tolerate people 'if they amused him'.[19] Peter Coats and Chips Channon were ideal social companions. Wavell must have known of their more intimate relationship, but he liked them both and did not see it as an obstacle to friendship, or to retaining Coats on his staff. He recognized Coats's strengths, not the least of which was his ability to manage the household. Following Coats's death in 1990 the question of Wavell's own sexuality was raised, much to his family's distress. Patrick French wrote in 1997 that 'according to speculation in wartime Cairo, Wavell was himself homosexual – although most certainly an inactive one.' The allegation, based on correspondence with the editor of Channon's diaries, Robert Rhodes James, appears to be without foundation.[20] Nigel Hamilton's assertion that Wavell and Auchinleck were 'in all probability' homo-social is meaningless.[21]

At Wavell's death, Queenie and the family were bereft. 'After thirty-five years together in many lands the future without Archie seems pretty futile but my children are so good to me and I feel sure he is near us still,' she wrote to Henry Jackson.[22] Close friends likewise grieved: 'I feel as if life will just be a long straight seam now, without the lovely embroidery wrought upon it by Archie's friendship,' wrote Frances Hendry, who had known Wavell and his sisters from their youth. Nancy and Molly, whose 'strength and stay' he had been, were also lost.[23] Yet even Queenie had not always understood her husband completely, and aspects of his character remained hidden from her. 'Whether my Archie had an equable temperament I am not so sure,' she wrote to John Connell when discussing his proposed biography in 1961. 'I think it was more his immense self-control . . . He had such contempt for any display of nerves in men or women and even with children . . . that I think the appearance of equability arose from this . . . I am still wondering on many contradictions in a character so apparently simple but really very complicated.'[24]

Wavell left nearly £50,000 at his death, ensuring that Queenie was able to live in relative comfort, staying frequently at the International Sportsmen's Club in London and moving around the countryside to visit her daughters. But 1953 held one more sorrow to bear: the death of Archie John at 37 in an operation against the Mau-Mau in Kenya on Christmas Eve. Since he was unmarried, the title became extinct. When Lady Wavell died at the age of 100 in October 1987, her ashes were buried in the Chantry Cloister at Winchester, though no inscription marks her grave. As one of those present at her funeral said: 'She had been a "camp follower" all her life, where else was she to go?'[25] Of their three daughters, only Lady Pamela survived into the twenty-first century, dying at the age of 82 in March 2001; Lady Felicity died in 1994 and Lady Joan in 1999.

To date, no statue of Field Marshal the Earl Wavell graces a London square or street, there is no memorial, plinth or obelisk. There are no blue plaques on the houses in which he lived in London – in Cliveden Place, Hobart Place, Ennismore Gardens – to tell future generations that the only person to have been successively Commander-in-Chief, Middle East, Commander-in-Chief, India and Viceroy of India lived there. Yet there are reminders of Wavell's service to the nation scattered around the country. His birthplace in Colchester is indicated by a plaque on the house and the gate. In 1953 a plaque was unveiled in St Alban's Garrison Church, Aldershot to commemorate his command of the 2nd Division; there is also a window in the Memorial Chapel at Sandhurst. Wavell's coat of arms is mounted on the staircase at the Peers' entrance to the House of Lords; his ceremonial swords and medals take pride of place in a display cabinet at The Black Watch Regimental Museum in Perth, where the 'Wavell Gates' also stand. There is a Wavell block at Summer Fields, and a small collection of memorabilia is preserved at Winchester College, where there is also a memorial plaque in War Cloister.

Wavell's legacy is also to be found not only in the official military and political records but in the books and articles he committed to print. He published no autobiography, but his *Viceroy's Journal*, published posthumously in 1973, is central to an understanding of the last years of his life, revealing his frank, sometimes caustic thoughts to a wider public. Before his death Archie John had worked hard to compile and edit his father's papers, and had corresponded with as many as possible of those who had known his father, to record their views. These papers are a legacy that will enable future generations to further their understanding of Wavell's inner thoughts, as are Wavell's several volumes of 'Recollections', as yet unpublished, and the hundreds of letters he wrote. There is also the correspondence of earlier biographers with numerous friends and colleagues of Wavell, now also long gone.

From his youth until his comparatively early death, Wavell appears as a man with the capacity, behind a sometimes unfathomable exterior, for surprising compassion and warmth. What singles him out as an exceptional individual, both as soldier and statesman, is that he was always master of his destiny, regardless of the consequences. Each letter he wrote, every signal he sent, literally bore his signature. At all times he was prepared to stand by his actions. Above all, he retained his integrity.

That Wavell lived against the backdrop of two World Wars, when the world itself was on the threshold of change, gave him opportunities not shared by those coming before or after him. That he served in the Middle East, South and South-East Asia – covering such an immense area of the world – meant that he appeared to the public as 'our one general' who could be relied upon. That he then became Viceroy of India – albeit by default, since Churchill could not think whom else to appoint – enabled him to make a contribution in the realm of politics at an unprecedented time in South Asian history. A child of Empire, Wavell had the vision to see that times were changing, that the world map shared out between a few European countries was no longer relevant to the future.

The devotion his family felt for him rippled outwards to be shared by all ranks of men, from subaltern to fellow Field Marshal and by countless friends, their sons and daughters, even complete strangers. His tremendous love of literature which found expression in his anthology *Other Men's*

Flowers and for which his name is still so well known it could not have been compiled without deep feeling. Wherever he was, writing and recitation of poetry also gave him an emotional outlet. His sense of humour, most evident perhaps in his correspondence and compositions, was that of a man who enjoyed life. Despite achieving high office, he never lost sight of the foot soldier he had once been, marching on the South African veldt or in the foothills of the Himalayas. If Wavell's complete lack of showmanship inspired great loyalty, his modesty was regarded as 'a lesson to the nation'.[26] That, after so many challenges, he should have expressed fatigue is not surprising, and there is no doubt that although he carried his responsibilities unflinchingly, towards the end he certainly felt their weight.[27]

If an epitaph had been inscribed on Earl Wavell's simple gravestone in Winchester College's War Cloister, the words he learnt as a schoolboy and remembered always are perhaps the most apt:

> Who would true valour see,
> Let him come hither;
> One here will constant be,
> Come wind, come weather.[28]

Abbreviations

AJW	Archibald John Wavell
APW	Archibald Percival Wavell
AWM	Australian War Memorial (Canberra, Australia)
BLH	Basil Liddell Hart
BL	British Library (London)
BWRA	Black Watch Regimental Archives (Perth, Scotland)
CAC	Churchill Archives Centre (Churchill College, Cambridge)
EMW	Eugénie Marie Wavell (Queenie)
IWM	Imperial War Museum (London)
JMA	John Murray Archives, London
LHCMA	Liddell Hart Centre for Military Archives (King's College, London)
McMU	McMaster University (Hamilton, Ontario, Canada)
MUL	Manchester University Library
NA	National Archives (Kew, Surrey)
NAM	National Army Museum (London)
NB	University of New Brunswick (Canada)
NLA	National Library of Australia
NLS	National Library of Scotland (Edinburgh)
OIOC	Oriental & India Office Collection, British Library (London)
OU	Oxford University
RO'C	Richard O'Connor
RUSI	Royal United Services Institute (later Institute for Defence Studies) (London)
WSC	Winston Spencer Churchill

Wavell's decorations

PC	Privy Counsellor
GCB	Knight Grand Cross of the Order of the Bath
GCIE	Knight Grand Commander of the Order of the Indian Empire
GCSI	Knight Grand Commander of the Order of the Star of India
CMG	Companion of the Order of St Michael and St George
MC	Military Cross

Notes

IN MEMORIAM

1 Excerpt as quoted in Supplement to *The Wykehamist* No. 943, 1 Dec. 1948. Thompson, a Wykehamist, died fighting in Bulgaria. Information and further quotations are from the Supplement; additional information from private sources.
2 Arthur, Duke of Connaught (1850–1942) was Queen Victoria's third son. War Cloister was dedicated on 31 May 1924.
3 J. Osborne Harley, *Sunday Times*, 28 May 1950.

CHAPTER 1: A LATE VICTORIAN

1 As quoted in APW, *Allenby*, p. 11, and in APW's 'Notes & Ideas', 1939–46.
2 Archives de la Manche/Publications of the Jersey Society, private collection. The Chateau of Vauville – with the original castle keep – is now inhabited by Guillaume Pellerin: see 'To the manor born', Stuart Wavell, *Sunday Times*, 18 Nov. 2001.
3 APW, as quoted in *The Good Soldier*, p. 56.
4 R.J. Collins, *Lord Wavell*, p. 24.
5 APW, 'Recollections', John Connell fonds, McMU. The full text of Wavell's 'Recollections', incomplete at his death, remains with the family. For this, as for other works written by APW, copyright is with the Wavell Estate.
6 APW, 'Recollections', John Connell fonds, McMU.
7 APW related this incident to Sahibzada Yaqub Khan in 1945; Sahibzada Yaqub Khan to the author, 4 Feb. 2000.
8 APW, Farewell Broadcast, All India Radio, New Delhi, 21 March 1947, 559, *Transfer of Power*, IX, p. 1003, ed. Nicholas Mansergh.
9 In 1922 The Black Watch became the regiment's official name, as it is today.
10 APW, as quoted in *Other Men's Flowers*, p. 18; see also Kiernan, *Wavell*, p. 55.
11 Asked later in life why he was so tongue-tied at important meetings, Wavell himself attributed it to being made to speak in front of adults as a child: Joan Bright Astley to the author, May 2002.

12 Later Major-General Sir K.G. Buchanan, Kt, CB, CMG, DSO (1880–1973). As quoted in Kiernan, *Wavell* (1945), p. 48. Buchanan put the episode as occurring in 1889. But the Wavells were in India at the time and it must have been in 1893.

13 *Summer Fields Register, 1864–1960*, Introduction to the First Edition, Revd C.E. Williams, Oxford, 1929.

14 The boards are still in the same place, but as the wood darkened the red letters became semi-invisible, so they were overpainted in black in April 1902 (see *A Century of Summer Fields*, ed. Richard Usborne, Methuen & Co. Ltd, 1964, p. 49).

15 Nicholas Aldridge, OS 1948–54, Assistant Headmaster 1978–89, to the author.

16 A school chapel was built in 1897.

17 Nicholas Aldridge, *Time to Spare? A History of Summer Fields*, David Talboys publications, Oxford, 1989, pp. 4–5.

18 Sir Geoffrey Mander, OS 1892–95, as quoted in Usborne, *A Century of Summer Fields*, p. 22.

19 Aldridge, *Time to Spare?*, p. 30.

20 As quoted by 'A correspondent' in Usborne, *A Century of Summer Fields*, p. 26.

21 As quoted in Usborne, *A Century of Summer Fields*, p. 26.

22 Dr C. Eccles Williams to Colonel Wavell, December 1894, John Connell fonds, McMU.

23 Buchanan, as quoted in Kiernan, *Wavell*, p. 49.

24 As quoted in Usborne, *A Century of Summer Fields*, p. 26.

25 G.N.D. Grundy, *Recollections of A.P. Wavell at Summer Fields*, John Connell fonds, McMU (Box 9, F4); Norman Grundy's father, the Revd C.H. Grundy, was an assistant master of Summerfields until 1871.

26 APW to the Revd R.H. Lightfoot, 28 September 1943, as quoted in *The Summerfieldian*, 1993.

27 Buchanan, as quoted in Kiernan, *Wavell*, p. 49.

28 R.H. Dundas to AJW, 1952, as quoted in Connell, *Scholar and Soldier*, p. 30.

29 Dr Williams to Col. Wavell, Dec. 1894, John Connell fonds, McMU.

30 Ibid., December 1895.

31 Lillie Wavell's younger sister Florry had m. Augustus Longfield, of Longueville, Co. Cork, who had served with Major Wavell in The Norfolk Regiment.

32 Dr Williams to Col. Wavell, 1896, as quoted in Connell, *Scholar and Soldier*, p. 30. The scholarship board still displays his name.

33 A.L. Irvine, 'Sixty Years of School', John Connell fonds, McMU.

34 APW, 'Recollections', as quoted in Connell, *Scholar and Soldier*, p. 30.

35 APW to Dover Wilson, 14 May 1944, NLS. He added: 'This is probably entirely unfair to both poets, but it is just how they impress me.'

36 APW, *Other Men's Flowers*, 1944 (1948), p. 17.

37 APW to Dover Wilson, 21 Jan. 1945, NLS. The first plays he saw were *Julius Caesar* and *King John*.

38 APW to Freya Stark, 23 Dec. 1949, JMA.
39 APW, 'Recollections', as quoted in Connell, *Scholar and Soldier*, p. 33.
40 Elaine Strutt to the author, 30 May 2002.
41 Herbert Henry, 1st Earl of Oxford and Asquith (1852–1928); Prime Minister 1908–15.
42 Collins, *Lord Wavell*, p. 31.
43 As quoted in Connell, *Scholar and Soldier*, p. 33.
44 *The Summer Fields Magazine*, December 1897.
45 APW, 'Recollections', as quoted in Connell, *Scholar and Soldier*, p. 31.
46 John Connell fonds, McMU.
47 See Collins, *Lord Wavell*, p. 32.
48 APW, *Allenby*, p. 52.
49 Maj.-Gen. Andrew Wauchope, CMG, CB (1846–99).
50 Later Gen. Sir Arthur Wauchope GCB, GCMG, CB, CIE, DSO (1874–1946), a long-term friend of APW with whom he served in India and Germany. They regularly played golf together in Scotland. He never fully recovered from his Magersfontein injuries.
51 As quoted in Kiernan, *Wavell*, p. 50.
52 As quoted in the *Hampshire Chronicle*, speech by APW on being made a freeman of Winchester, 25 Sept. 1943; see Connell, *Scholar and Soldier*, p. 36.
53 John Connell fonds, McMU.
54 As quoted in Connell, *Scholar and Soldier*, p. 36.
55 *The Summer Fields Magazine*, Dec. 1900; the 'correspondent' was B.J. Gould.
56 As quoted in Kiernan, *Wavell*, p. 54.
57 Montague Rendall, CMG, MA, JP (1862–1950) to Gen. Wavell, John Connell fonds, McMU. He died shortly after Wavell, in October 1950.
58 APW, 'Recollections', as quoted in Connell, *Scholar and Soldier*, pp. 29, 30.

CHAPTER 2: LIFE IN THE ARMY, 1901–8

1 APW, 'Recollections', as quoted in Connell, *Scholar and Soldier*, p. 34.
2 In 1947 the Royal Military College and the Royal Military Academy, Woolwich, which had closed in 1939, were amalgamated as the Royal Military Academy, Sandhurst.
3 APW, 'Recollections', as quoted in Connell, *Scholar and Soldier*, p. 39.
4 Later Field Marshal Sir John Dill, GCB, CMG, DSO, DSM(US) (1881–1944).
5 APW, 'Recollections', John Connell fonds, McMU.
6 Letter of E.G. Wynard to Gen. Wavell, 9 Feb. 1901; see Connell, *Scholar and Soldier*, p. 39.
7 APW, Foreword, Bernard Fergusson, *The Black Watch and the King's Enemies*, p. 13.
8 APW, 'Government Houses', John Connell fonds, McMU.

9 Major Charles Raymond Barron Henderson, d. 1935; Major Neville George Boileau Henderson, DSO, d. 1957.

10 See Connell, *Scholar and Soldier*, p. 39.

11 APW to Nancy Wavell, Oct. 1901, John Connell fonds, McMU.

12 See APW, *The Good Soldier*, p. 48; 'McA' was killed at Loos.

13 Later Maj.-Gen. Sir Michael Rimington, KCB, CB, CVO (1858-1928).

14 Collins, *Lord Wavell*, p. 35.

15 APW to Nancy, 6 Jan. 1902, John Connell fonds, McMU.

16 APW, 'Diary', as quoted in Connell, *Scholar and Soldier*, p. 42.

17 APW in 1944, as quoted in Connell, *Scholar and Soldier*, p. 43.

18 APW to Nancy, 6 Jan. 1902, John Connell fonds, McMU.

19 Ibid., 24 April 1902.

20 Ibid., 7 March 1902.

21 Ibid., 1 April 1902.

22 Ibid., 27 March 1902.

23 Ibid., 1 April 1902.

24 Ibid., 10 April 1902.

25 APW, 'Diary', as quoted in Connell, *Scholar and Soldier*, p. 42.

26 Ibid., p. 43.

27 APW to Nancy, 3 July 1902, John Connell fonds, McMU.

28 In peacetime, under the regimental system then observed, one regular battalion was generally abroad while the other remained at home, so that the two rarely met.

29 APW to Nancy, 31 July 1902, John Connell fonds, McMU.

30 Ibid., 4 Sept. 1902.

31 APW, 'Recollections', as quoted in Connell, *Scholar and Soldier*, p. 45.

32 Col. the Hon. Malise Hore-Ruthven, CMG, DSO (1880-1969) to AJW, John Connell fonds, McMU.

33 As quoted in Connell, *Scholar and Soldier*, p. 52.

34 APW, 'Recollections', as quoted in Connell, *Scholar and Soldier*, p. 46; Col. the Hon. H.E. Maxwell, DSO (1857-1919).

35 Lt-Col. Neville George B. Henderson, John Connell fonds, McMU.

36 APW, 'Recollections', John Connell fonds, McMU.

37 Ibid.

38 APW to Nancy, 19 Sept. 1904, John Connell fonds, McMU.

39 Ibid., 21 May 1906.

40 Ibid., 30 Aug. 1904.

41 Ibid., 10 March 1905.

42 APW, 'Recollections', John Connell fonds, McMU.

43 Ibid., as quoted in Connell, *Scholar and Soldier*, p. 54. Later Air Vice Marshal Amyas (Biffy) Borton, CB, CMG, DSO, AFC (1886-1969).

44 Col. Archibald Bulloch, DSO, John Connell fonds, McMU.

45 APW, as quoted in Collins, *Lord Wavell*, p. 40.

46 APW, 'Recollections', John Connell fonds, McMU.

47 Hore-Ruthven to AJW, John Connell fonds, McMU.

48 APW, 'Recollections', John Connell fonds, McMU.

49 APW to Stephen Phillimore (undated, *circa* autumn 1905), private collection.

50 APW to Nancy, 21 May 1906, John Connell fonds, McMU. The knife reached him in August.

51 Ibid., 23 July 1906.

52 APW to Stephen Phillimore, 19 Nov. 1906, private collection.

53 APW to Nancy, 11 Oct. 1906, John Connell fonds, McMU.

54 APW, 'Recollections', as quoted in Connell, *Scholar and Soldier*, p. 54.

55 APW to Nancy, 6 March 1907, John Connell fonds, McMU.

56 See R.V. E. Hodson, *The Story and Gallantry of the North West Frontier*, Clio Publishing, 2002, p. 164.

57 See Kiernan, *Wavell*, p. 60.

58 APW, Farewell Broadcast, All India Radio, New Delhi, 21 March 1947, *559*, *Transfer of Power*, IX, pp. 1003–4. ed. Nicholas Mansergh.

CHAPTER 3: STAFF COLLEGE, RUSSIA AND THE WAR OFFICE

1 Sir William Robertson, as quoted in Kiernan, *Wavell*, p. 63.

2 APW, 'Recollections', as quoted in Connell, *Scholar and Soldier*, p. 59.

3 APW, 'Recollections', John Connell fonds, McMU; see A.R. Godwin Austen, *The Staff and Staff College*, p. 212–3 & p. 255.

4 Later General Sir Ivo Vesey, KCB, KBE, CMG, DSO (1876–1975), to John Connell, 26 Aug. 1961, John Connell fonds, McMU.

5 APW, 'Recollections', John Connell fonds, McMU.

6 Vesey to John Connell, 26 Aug. 1961, John Connell fonds, McMU.

7 Later Field Marshal Sir Henry Wilson, GCB, DSO. After the war he became an MP, and in 1920 was shot outside his house in London by Irish terrorists.

8 APW, 'Recollections', as quoted in Connell, *Scholar and Soldier*, pp. 62–3.

9 APW's maps were donated by the late Lord Ballantrae to LHCMA.

10 APW, 'Recollections', John Connell fonds, McMU. Lt-Col. Herman Gaston de Watteville (1875–1963) married Hope, Everard Calthrop's only sister.

11 Later Field Marshal Viscount Allenby, GCB, GCMG (1861–1936).

12 APW as quoted in Wavell, *Allenby*, p. 101.

13 APW as quoted in Connell, *Scholar and Soldier*, p. 64.

14 Later Field Marshal Sir William Robertson, GCB, GCMG, GCVO, KCVO, DSO (1860–1933).

15 As quoted in Connell, *Scholar and Soldier*, p. 65; see also Raugh, *Wavell in the Middle East*, p. 10; excerpts of APW's essay are reproduced in Victor Bonham-Carter, *The Strategy of Victory, 1914–18*, Holt, Rinehart & Winston, 1963, pp. 334–7.

NOTES TO PAGES 33-9

16 See Connell, *Scholar and Soldier*, note 5, p. 522; also John Connell fonds, McMU.

17 Vesey to John Connell, 26 Aug. 1961, John Connell fonds, McMU.

18 APW, 'Recollections', John Connell fonds, McMU.

19 As quoted in Kiernan, *Wavell*, p. 63. Col Robert Wallace (of that Ilk), CMG (1880–1970).

20 APW never understood who all the women were. After his death, AJW contacted Natalya (who had come to England and was then Mrs Duddington) and she explained the relationships in a letter dated 18 June 1953, John Connell fonds, McMU.

21 See notes 5 and 6, Connell, *Scholar and Soldier*, p. 523.

22 APW to Lillie Wavell, 5 March 1911, as quoted in Connell, *Scholar and Soldier*, p. 68.

23 Ibid.

24 APW, 'Recollections', as quoted in Connell, *Scholar and Soldier*, p. 68.

25 APW, 'Recollections', John Connell fonds, McMU.

26 APW to Lillie Wavell, 20 March 1911, John Connell fonds, McMU.

27 APW to Nancy, 13 April 1911, John Connell fonds, McMU.

28 APW to Gen. Wavell, 6 May 1911, John Connell fonds, McMU.

29 Later Maj.-Gen. C.G. Fuller, CB, CMG, DSO (1874–1960); Shahovsky also spelt Shahoffsky.

30 Capt. George Brooke Forbes Churchill was with the Royal Army Medical Corps.

31 APW, 'Recollections', John Connell fonds, McMU.

32 APW to Lillie Wavell, 3 June 1911, John Connell fonds, McMU.

33 APW, 'Recollections', John Connell fonds, McMU.

34 Natalya (later Mrs Duddington) to AJW, 18 June 1953, John Connell fonds, McMU.

35 See Connell, *Scholar and Soldier*, p. 72.

36 Ibid., footnote 10, p. 523.

37 Capt. Sir Mansfield Cumming, RN, KCMG, CB (1859–1923).

38 Gladys Robinson (née Sherwen, aka Leonie Lemartine) (1885–1965) to John Connell, John Connell fonds, McMU. Additional information from her daughter Peggy Box (b. 1910) to the author, 14 Jan. 2004. Leonie's first husband had died of pneumonia in 1911. She later became an actress.

39 APW, 'Recollections', as quoted in Connell, *Scholar and Soldier*, p. 74.

40 Ibid., John Connell fonds, McMU.

41 Ibid., as quoted in Connell, *Scholar and Soldier*, p. 77.

42 Ibid., p. 81; for the full account see pp. 78–81.

43 Later Maj.-Gen. Sir Ernest Swinton, KBE, CB, DSO, RE, MA (1868–1951).

44 Maj.-Gen. A. Elchaninov, *Tsar Nicholas II*, translated from the Russian by APW, Hugh Rees, London, 1913.

45 Collins, *Lord Wavell*, p. 59.

46 John Connell fonds, McMU.

47 APW, 'Recollections', John Connell fonds, McMU.

48 Connell, *Scholar and Soldier*, pp. 81–2. It is not clear who this lady was. She could not have been Leonie because she was only two years younger than APW.

49 APW to Nancy, 6 Nov. 1913, John Connell fonds, McMU.

50 Patricia (Peggy) Box (née Redwood) to the author, 14 Jan. 2004.

51 Veronica (Vere) Beatrice (d. 1957) m. 1909 Roger Mowbray Bellairs (later Rear-Admiral).

52 According to Gen. Sir Ivo Vesey, APW first met Queenie in Switzerland in 1911: Vesey to John Connell, 26 Aug. 1961, John Connell fonds, McMU.

53 Eugénie Wavell's notes on her family background, 1961, John Connell fonds, McMU.

54 Née Augusta Warburton; her husband was half-brother to John, 7th Duke of Marlborough; her son George and WSC's father were first half-cousins.

55 See Connell, *Scholar and Soldier*, p. 82.

56 Later Field Marshal Sir John French, 1st Earl of Ypres (1852–1925). A short, white-haired cavalryman, he had made 'one reputation in South Africa and another in ladies' bedrooms': Hew Strachan, *The First World War*, vol. 1, OUP, 2001, p. 202.

57 Later Gen. Sir Hubert Gough, GCB, GCMG, KCVO (1870–1963).

58 APW, as quoted in Connell, *Scholar and Soldier*, p. 85.

59 APW to Gen. Wavell, 23 March 1914, John Connell fonds, McMU.

60 Sir John French was succeeded by Gen. Sir Charles Douglas, GCB, KCB,CB (1850–1914).

61 APW to Gen. Wavell, 29 March 1914, John Connell fonds, McMU.

62 In 1890 Kaiser Wilhelm unwisely repudiated Bismark's 're-insurance' treaty with Russia.

63 Von Schlieffen continued to 'tinker' with his plan until his death in 1912: see John Keegan, *The First World War*, pp. 30–4.

64 Originally Haldane suggested 1 cavalry and 6 infantry divisions; this was later reduced to 1 cavalry and 4 infantry divisions.

CHAPTER 4: WAR IN 1914

1 Robert Browning (1812–1889), 'Childe Roland to the Dark Tower Came', as quoted in APW, *Other Men's Flowers*, p. 192.

2 Collins, *Lord Wavell*, p. 65.

3 Eric and Andro Linklater, *The Black Watch*. The 1st Battalion went across the Channel with the BEF; the 2nd Battalion arrived from India in October. Four Territorial battalions were immediately mobilised and additional battalions trained.

4 APW to Nancy, 12 Sept. 1914, John Connell fonds, McMU.

5 APW, 'Recollections', John Connell fonds, McMU.

6 Ibid.

7 Within a few weeks the BEF was reinforced by a 2nd cavalry division and two more infantry divisions. In 1914 the army's ration strength was 164,000, by 1918 it had risen to over five million.

8 APW, *Allenby*, p. 104.

9 Gen. Sir Horace Smith-Dorrien, GCB, GCMG, KCB, DSO, FRGS (1858–1930). His wife was honoured for her work in providing hospital bags for the contents of wounded mens' pockets.

10 APW to Nancy, 12 Sept. 1914, John Connell fonds, McMU.

11 Ibid.

12 APW, 'Recollections', as quoted in Connell, *Scholar and Soldier*, p. 93.

13 Leonie Lemartine to John Connell, 4 Nov. 1964, John Connell fonds, McMU.

14 APW to Nancy, 28 Sept 1914, John Connell fonds, McMU

15 Ibid.

16 APW, *Allenby*, p. 118.

17 Ibid., p. 119.

18 APW, 'Recollections', as quoted in Connell, *Scholar and Soldier*, p. 95.

19 APW, *Allenby*, p. 121.

20 APW, 'Recollections', as quoted in Connell, *Scholar and Soldier*, p. 100.

21 Buchanan, as recorded by Kiernan, *Wavell*, p. 68.

22 APW, 'Recollections', John Connell fonds, McMU.

23 This episode is related in Connell, *Scholar and Soldier*, p. 104.

24 APW to Nancy, 7 Jan. 1915, John Connell fonds, McMU.

25 Ibid.

26 Ibid., 20 Jan. 1915. Arguments over marriage and money were not unusual in wartime; if APW were to die, his wife (and perhaps child) would need to be assured of financial support.

27 Ibid., 26 March 1915.

28 Lt-Col. R.H. Pipon (b. 1882); in 1911–12 he had explored north from Burma to locate the source of the Irrawaddy river.

29 APW, 'Recollections', John Connell fonds, McMU.

30 APW to Nancy, 26 March 1915, John Connell fonds, McMU.

31 Ibid., 11 April 1915.

32 APW, 'Recollections', John Connell fonds, McMU.

33 As quoted in Connell, *Scholar and Soldier*, p. 108.

34 Gladys Robinson, aka Leonie Lemartine, to John Connell, 4 Nov. 1964, John Connell fonds, McMU.

35 APW to Nancy, 8 May 1915, John Connell fonds, McMU. The note-case arrived a month later.

36 Ibid., 28 May 1915.

37 APW, 'Recollections', John Connell fonds, McMU.

38 APW to Nancy, 3 June 1915, John Connell fonds, McMU.

39 APW, 'Recollections', John Connell fonds, McMU. This was in May 1915.

40 Ibid., as quoted in Connell, *Scholar and Soldier*, p. 109.

41 Eric Dorman-Smith was also present: 'In fact the battle was a shambles from the start . . . Our artillery was inadequate and communication with it did not work at all. The assaulting battalions had very heavy casualties initially and the reserve battalions came forward into the battle prematurely, partly because the German counter-assault fire on our forming-up trenches was so very heavy and accurate.' Dorman-Smith to John Connell, John Connell fonds, McMU.

42 APW, 'Recollections', as quoted in Connell, *Scholar and Soldier*, p. 110.

43 Ibid.

44 APW, 'Recollections', John Connell fonds, McMU.

45 Ibid., John Connell fonds, McMU.

46 Later Gen. Sir John Burnett-Stuart, GCB, KBE, CMG, DSO (1875–1958). APW as quoted in Connell, *Scholar and Soldier*, p. 112.

47 *The Times*, 28 Dec. 1915.

48 For a fuller account of the life of Arthur Wavell, see Kiernan, *Wavell*, pp. 33–47.

49 APW to Nancy, 9 March 1916, John Connell fonds, McMU.

50 APW, 'Recollections', John Connell fonds, McMU.

51 APW to Nancy, 16 Oct. 1916, John Connell fonds, McMU.

52 APW, 'Recollections', John Connell fonds, McMU.

53 APW, as quoted in Kiernan, *Wavell*, p. 83.

54 APW, 'Recollections', John Connell fonds, McMU.

55 Ibid.

56 Ibid.

57 Lt Gen. Sir Frederick Maude, KCB, CMG, DSO (1864–1917).

58 When published by the Bolsheviks in 1918, the terms of the Sykes–Picot agreement caused considerable controversy.

59 APW, as quoted in Connell, *Scholar and Soldier*, p. 117.

60 APW to Gen. Wavell, 21 April 1917, John Connell fonds, McMU.

61 Petrograd became Leningrad after Lenin's death in 1924; then reverted to St Petersburg in the early 1990s.

62 APW, 'Recollections', John Connell fonds, McMU.

63 A brevet was a way of advancing a rank, pending substantive promotion.

64 Ibid., as quoted in John Connell, *Scholar and Soldier*, p. 120.

CHAPTER 5: PALESTINE WITH ALLENBY, 1917

1 As quoted in APW, *The Palestine Campaigns*, p. 1.

2 APW, Ibid., p. 2.

3 Ibid., p. 88. In April, there were 'close on' 6,500 British casualties, as

compared with 2,000 Turkish losses; although these losses were significantly less than those on the Western Front, they served to impair morale.

4 Ibid., p. 96; see also APW, *Allenby*, p. 155.

5 In writing his book about the Palestine Campaigns, APW's eye for detail enabled him to correct the Official History, which had described Allenby as taking over at midnight on 28 June; as APW pointed out, this could not happen since midnight inevitably fell between two dates – thus 28/9 June.

6 APW, as quoted in Connell, *Scholar and Soldier*, p. 124.

7 APW, *The Palestine Campaigns*, p. 73. See Judges xvi, 3.

8 Ibid., p. 102.

9 Ibid., p. 95.

10 APW, *Allenby*, pp. 164–5.

11 Later Maj.-Gen. Guy Dawnay, CB, CMG, DSO, MVO (1878–1952).

12 APW, *Allenby*, p. 169. Later Field Marshal 1st Baron Chetwode, GCB, OM, GCSI, KCMG, DSO (1869–1950). Later Colonel Richard Meinertzhagen, CBE, DSO (1878–1967).

13 As recorded by Maj.-Gen. S.S. Butler, CB, CMG, DSO, 'Memoirs', PP/MCR/107, IWM.

14 APW, *The Palestine Campaigns*, p. 117.

15 Ibid., p. 124.

16 APW, *Allenby*, p. 173.

17 'Balfour Declaration', as quoted in Lord Melchett, *Thy Neighbour*, p. 124.

18 APW, *Allenby*, p. 199, fn.

19 APW, 'Recollections', as quoted in Connell, *Scholar and Soldier*, p. 129.

20 APW, *Allenby*, p. 179. The 'one' is obviously APW.

21 APW, as quoted in Connell, *Scholar and Soldier*, p. 130.

22 APW, *Allenby*, p. 182.

23 As quoted in David Thomson, *Europe since Napoleon*, Pelican, 1973, p. 629.

24 APW, *The Palestine Campaigns*, p. 142.

25 APW to Nancy, 17 Nov. 1917, John Connell fonds, McMU.

26 APW, *Allenby*, p. 193.

27 Later Gen. Sir John Stuart Mackenzie Shea, GCB, KCMG, DSO (1869–1966).

28 T.E. Lawrence, *Seven Pillars of Wisdom*, Jonathan Cape, 1946, p. 453 & p. 462.

29 APW, *The Good Soldier*, p. 57.

30 APW, *Allenby*, p. 199.

31 APW, 'Recollections', as quoted in Connell, *Scholar and Soldier*, p. 133.

32 Leon Wolff, *In Flanders Fields*, Longmans, 1959, p. 264.

33 Joint note of the Military Representatives Supreme War Council, as quoted in Anglesey, *History of the British Cavalry*, 5, Leo Cooper, 1994, p. 214.

34 John Connell fonds, McMU.

35 Later Maj.-Gen. Rt Hon. Sir Frederick Sykes, GCSI, GCIE, GBE, KCB, CMG, KJStJ (d. 1954).

36 APW, 'Recollections', as quoted in Connell, *Scholar and Soldier*, p. 135.

37 The predecessor was Maj.-Gen. Arthur Bartholomew, CB, CMG, CBE, DSO (1879–1945). APW, 'Recollections' as quoted in Connell, *Scholar and Soldier*, pp. 135–6.

38 Chetwode, as quoted in Connell, *Scholar and Soldier*, p. 136.

39 Rt Hon. Jan Christian Smuts, PC, OM, CH, FRS, Field Marshal. (1870–1950). In WWI, he had worked to quell pro-German separatist groups in South Africa, and for Anglo-Boer co-operation; Prime Minister 1919–24 and 1933–48.

40 APW, *Allenby*, p. 128.

41 As quoted by APW in *Allenby*, p. 215 and Anglesey, *History of the British Cavalry*, 5, p. 230.

42 APW, 'Recollections', as quoted in Connell, *Scholar and Soldier*, p. 138.

43 Anglesey, *History of the British Cavalry*, 5, p. 233.

44 APW, *Allenby*, p. 225.

45 Anglesey, *History of the British Cavalry*, 5, p. 256.

46 APW, 'Recollections', as quoted in Connell, *Scholar and Soldier*, p. 142.

47 Collins, *Lord Wavell*, p. 97.

48 APW, *Allenby*, p. 231.

49 Ibid., p. 232.

50 APW, *Allenby*, p. 235. APW's account is full of comparisons and anecdotes from ancient history.

51 Ibid., p. 237.

52 Ibid., pp. 145–6. Unfortunately the subsequent fate of the horses was less happy; after the fall of Damascus all 20,000 were 'cast' as unfit for military service and sold in Egypt: see Jilly Cooper, *Animals in War*, pp. 47–8.

53 APW, 'Recollections', John Connell fonds, McMU.

54 Leon Wolff, *In Flanders Fields*, p. 272.

55 APW, *The Palestine Campaigns*, p. 242.

CHAPTER 6: PEACETIME

1 APW, *Allenby*, p. 256.

2 AJW, Introduction to *Other Men's Flowers*, Memorial Edition, 1952, p. 10.

3 Norman Davies, *Europe*, OUP, 1996, Appendix III, p. 1328.

4 John McCrae (1872–1918); born in Ontario of Scottish parents; served as an artillery officer in the Boer War. 'In Flanders Fields' was published in *Punch*, vol. cxlix, 8 Dec. 1915.

5 Rudyard Kipling, 'My Boy Jack', as quoted in *Other Men's Flowers*, p. 425.

6 Lt-Col. Reginald Norton Knatchbull (1872–1917).

7 APW, *Other Men's Flowers*, p. 372, 1948 edn.

8 APW to Nancy, 17 Nov. 1917 from GHQ Egypt, John Connell fonds, McMU.

9 J.R. Macdonald to Bernard Fergusson, 12 Jan. 1962, John Connell fonds, McMU.

10 APW, *Allenby*, p. 257.

11 Ibid., p. 258.

12 APW, 'Recollections', as quoted in Connell, *Scholar and Soldier*, p. 147.

13 APW, from *T.E. Lawrence, by His Friends*, ed A.W. Lawrence, as quoted in APW, *The Good Soldier*, p. 57. Feisal Ibn-Hussein (1885–1933).

14 APW, 'Recollections', John Connell fonds, McMU.

15 APW to Stephen Phillimore, 21 April 1920, private collection.

16 Collins, *Lord Wavell*, p. 111. 'Commanding Officer's orders', relating to offences against military law and their punishment, could be dull. As a brevet lieutenant-colonel, APW still only had the substantive rank of major.

17 APW, 'Government Houses', John Connell fonds, McMU.

18 APW, 'Recollections', John Connell fonds, McMU.

19 John Connell fonds, McMU.

20 APW, 'Recollections', John Connell fonds, McMU.

21 Lt-Gen. Sir George Macdonogh, GBE, KCB, KCMG, CB (1865–1942).

22 APW, 'Recollections', as quoted in Connell, *Scholar and Soldier*, p. 149.

23 See Brian Bond, 'The Army between the Two World Wars 1918–1939', in *The Oxford History of the British Army*.

24 Gen. Sir Ivo Vesey to John Connell, 26 Aug. 1961, John Connell fonds, McMU.

25 Collins, *Lord Wavell*, p. 117.

26 'The Imperfect Guest', 'Wavell poems', private collection. 'The Perfect Guest', Anon. reads: 'She answered by return of post / The invitation of her host. / She caught the train she said she would / And changed at stations where she should.' *Desk Drawer Anthology*, ed. Alice Roosevelt Longworth & Theodore Roosevelt, Doubleday, Doran & Co., New York, 1937, p. 367.

27 APW, 'Recollections', as quoted in Connell, *Scholar and Soldier*, p. 151.

28 APW, 'The End of the Lausanne Conference' (from 'Nathaniel in Wonderland'), 'Wavell poems', private collection.

29 Burnett-Stuart to AJW, ibid.

30 APW, 'Recollections', John Connell fonds, McMU.

31 Earl of Cavan, KP, GCB, GCMG, GCVO, CBE, KCB, CB, MVO (1865–1946); Admiral of the Fleet 1st Earl Beatty, OM, PC, GCVO, KCB, KCVO, DSO, MVO (1871–1936); Marshal of the RAF, 1st Viscount Trenchard, GCB, OM, GCVO, DSO (1873–1956).

32 APW, 'Recollections', as quoted in Connell, *Scholar and Soldier*, p. 152.

33 'Not by argument but by the superior dining-out power and long-standing prestige of the Admiralty': BLH notes, 31 Aug. 1964, John Connell fonds, McMU.

34 APW, 'Recollections', as quoted in Connell, *Scholar and Soldier*, p. 153.

35 Later Sir Basil Liddell Hart, Hon. D.Litt (1895–1970).

36 BLH to APW, 14 Jan. 1926, as quoted in Connell, *Scholar and Soldier*, p. 153.

37 APW to BLH, 18 Jan. 1926, LH 1/733, LHCMA.

38 See Kiernan, *Wavell*, p. 103.

39 Later Maj.-Gen. John F.C. Fuller, CB, CBE, DSO (1878–1966).

40 APW to BLH, 29 April 1948, LH 1/733, LHCMA. Published in the RUSI *Journal* under the title 'The Army and the Prophets' (vol. LXXV, Nov. 1930, pp. 665–80). It is likely that APW had submitted it for the *Army Quarterly's* 1926 Bertrand Stewart Prize Essay, the theme of which was 'Problems of Imperial Defence Today'.

41 'Wavell' by BLH, *The Times*, 8 May 1950, LH 10/1950/7a, LHCMA.

42 In 1971 it became the Royal United Services Institute for Defence Studies.

43 Mary Medlycott (née Eden; 1916–2002), to the author, Oct. 2001; a distant cousin of Anthony Eden; Archie John was godfather to her third daughter.

44 APW, *The Good Soldier*, p. 59.

45 John Connell fonds, McMU.

CHAPTER 7: MANOEUVRES

1 'Man is the main instrument of battle: let us then study man in battle because he is the one who makes it real.' Charles Ardart du Picq (1821–1870). Inscribed above a hall door at Versailles, noted by APW when he was there on a course in Dec. 1934. APW to BLH, 5 Jan. 1935. LH 1/733, LHCMA.

2 APW, 'Recollections', as quoted in Connell, *Scholar and Soldier*, p. 154.

3 APW, 'Government Houses', John Connell fonds, McMU; *House & Garden* 1950.

4 Ibid.

5 APW, 'Recollections', John Connell fonds, McMU.

6 Later Maj.-Gen. R.J. Collins, CB, CMG, DSO (1880–1950).

7 Gen. Burnett-Stuart to AJW, as quoted in Connell, *Scholar and Soldier*, p. 155.

8 APW to BLH, 27 June 1927, LH 1/733, LHCMA.

9 APW to BLH, 15 July 1927, LH 1/733, LHCMA.

10 BLH to APW, 24 Dec. 1927, John Connell fonds, McMU.

11 APW, 'Recollections', John Connell fonds, McMU.

12 BLH, *Memoirs*, I, p. 135.

13 APW, speech at Staff College, as quoted in Connell, *Scholar and Soldier*, p. 157.

14 APW, 'Recollections', as quoted in Connell, *Scholar and Soldier*, p. 158.

15 Collins, *Lord Wavell*, p. 132.

16 Ann Grantham (née Collins), to the author, 28 Sept. 1999. She was later in India when APW was Viceroy. Her first husband was Robin Ridgeway, private secretary to Auchinleck and a master at Winchester.

17 APW, *The Good Soldier*, p. 59.

18 APW, 'Recollections', as quoted in Connell, *Scholar and Soldier*, p. 158.

19 Collins, *Lord Wavell*, p. 136.

20 APW, 'Recollections', as quoted in Connell, *Scholar and Soldier*, p. 158.

21 Later Gen. Sir Henry Jackson, KCB, CMG, DSO (1879–1972).

22 Eric Dorman-Smith (1895–1969); he later changed his name to O'Gowan Dorman. His brother was Sir Reginald Dorman-Smith, Gov. of Burma 1941–2.

23 APW, 'Recollections', as quoted in Connell, *Scholar and Soldier*, p. 165.

24 BLH, Notes, 31 Aug. 1964, John Connell fonds, McMU.

25 APW, 'Recollections', as quoted in Connell, *Scholar and Soldier*, p. 160.

26 Eric Dorman-Smith to John Connell, 1 July 1961, John Connell fonds, McMU.

27 BLH said that to call the experimental infantry brigades 'mechanised' was a euphemism since most of their transport was merely motorized. In 1933 the 6th was 'de-mechanized' and only the 7th retained: BLH notes, 31 Aug. 1964, John Connell fonds, McMU.

28 Buchanan, as quoted in Kiernan, *Wavell*, p. 103.

29 APW to BLH, 8 Nov 1930, LH1/733, LHCMA.

30 Ibid., 31 May 1932.

31 Eric Dorman-Smith to John Connell, 29 Nov. 1961, 15 Dec. 1961, John Connell fonds, McMU.

32 John Connell fonds, McMU.

33 Elaine Strutt, daughter of Estelle Dorman-Smith, to the author, 30 May 2002; she and EMW designed the doll.

34 APW, *The Good Soldier*, pp. 121–9.

35 Eric Dorman-Smith to John Connell, 9 Sept. 1961, John Connell fonds, McMU.

36 APW, 'Recollections', as quoted in Connell, *Scholar and Soldier*, p. 168.

37 Eric Dorman-Smith to John Connell, 15 Dec. 1961, John Connell fonds, McMU.

38 APW, 'Recollections', as quoted in Connell, *Scholar and Soldier*, p. 169. APW was not the first person to advocate use of liaison officers. In 1920 BLH had been urging what he called 'liaison forward': BLH, Notes, 31 Aug. 1964, John Connell fonds, McMU.

39 APW, Lecture at the RUSI, 15 Feb. 1933, as quoted in *The Good Soldier*, 'Training for War', p. 120.

40 BLH, *Memoirs*, I, p. 252; private information.

41 APW, 'Recollections', as quoted in Connell, *Scholar and Soldier*, p. 170.

42 APW, 'Government Houses', John Connell fonds, McMU.

43 Gen. Sir Ivo Vesey to John Connell, 26 Aug. 1961, John Connell fonds, McMU.

44 APW to BLH, 1 Jan. 1934, LH 1/733, LHCMA.

45 Collins, *Lord Wavell*, p. 149.

46 Later Air Marshal Sir Lawrence Fleming Pendred, KBE, CB, DFC, DL (1899–1986); Pendred to John Connell, John Connell fonds, McMU.

47 APW, 'Recollections', John Connell fonds, McMU.

48 APW to BLH, 29 Nov. 1934, LH 1/733, LHCMA.

49 Later Gen. Sir James Marshall-Cornwall, KCB, CBE, DSO, MC, FRGS

(1887–1985); later Lt-Gen. Sir Bernard Freyberg, VC, GCMG, KCB, KBE, DSO, LLD, DCL (1889–1963).

50 James Marshall-Cornwall, *A Memoir: Wars and Rumours of Wars*, p. 95.

51 Gen. Sir James Marshall-Cornwall to Paul Freyberg, 5 July 1977, as quoted in *Bernard Freyberg*, pp. 178–9.

52 Joint Report on the *Cycle d'Information des Généraux et des Colonels* by Maj.-Gens Wavell, Freyberg and Marshall-Cornwall, as quoted in Connell, *Scholar and Soldier*, p. 172.

53 APW, *The Times*, 19 April 1945, as quoted in *The Good Soldier*, p. 94.

54 APW to BLH, 5 Jan. 1935, LH 1/733, LHCMA.

55 BLH to APW, 7 Jan. 1935, LH 1/733, LHCMA. Correspondence continued Jan.–Feb.

56 Later Lord Ballantrae, GCMG, GCVO, DSO, OBE (1911–80).

57 As quoted in Bernard Fergusson, *Portrait of a Soldier*, p. 16.

58 APW to Edward Wavell, 2 and 14 March 1935, private collection; Edward Wavell (1880–195?), private detective (6th or 7th cousin of APW).

59 APW as quoted in Connell, *Scholar and Soldier*, p. 173.

60 Mary Medlycott, to the author, Oct. 2001; see also Gen. Sir Ivo Vesey to John Connell, 26 Aug. 1961, John Connell fonds, McMU

61 John Connell fonds, McMU. EMW's mother died in 1937. 'No one spoke ill of her,' said APW, who was obviously fond of his mother-in-law.

62 Later Field Marshal Lord Wilson of Libya and of Stowlangtoft, GCB, GBE, DSO (1881–1964).

63 Later Maj.-Gen. Sir Victor Fortune, KBE, CB, DSO (1883–1949).

64 Later Lt-Gen. Sir Arthur Smith, KCB, KBE, DSO, MC (1890–1977).

65 APW, 'Government Houses', John Connell fonds, McMU.

66 Fergusson, *Portrait of a Soldier*, p. 19.

67 APW to Nancy, 28 May 1935, as quoted in Connell, *Scholar and Soldier*, p. 175.

68 APW, as quoted in *The Good Soldier*, p. 58.

69 APW to BLH, 22 Feb. 1936, LH 1/733, LHCMA.

70 Later Field Marshal Sir Claude Auchinleck, GCB, GCIE, CSI, DSO, OBE (1884–1981); he refused a peerage.

71 APW to BLH, 5 July 1935 (from Somborne, Farnborough, Hants), LH 1/733, LHCMA.

72 Fergusson, *Portrait of a Soldier*, p. 39.

73 Gen. Sir Ivo Vesey to John Connell, 26 Aug. 1961, John Connell fonds, McMU.

74 Mrs Michael Ingram to the author, 1999.

75 Fergusson, *Portrait of a Soldier*, p. 39; Fergusson ceased to be APW's ADC in March 1937.

76 Ibid., p. 21.

77 Ibid., pp. 34–5.

78 APW, 'The Higher Commander', lecture 4 Dec. 1935, RUSI *Journal*, vol. LXXXI, Feb.–Nov. 1936.

79 Fergusson, *Portrait of a Soldier*, p. 37.

80 Later Field Marshal John Gort, 1st Viscount (UK), VC, GCB, KCB, CB, CBE, DSO, MVO, MC (1886–1946).

81 Later Field Marshal Alan Brooke, 1st Viscount Alanbrooke GCB, CB, OM, DSO (1883–1963).

82 Later Lt-Gen. Sir Brian Horrocks, KCB, DSO, MC (1895–1985); Horrocks's recollection, as quoted in Philip Warner, *Horrocks*, p. 48, also in John Connell fonds, McMU.

83 APW to BLH, 4 Feb. 1937, LH 1/733, LHCMA.

84 APW to Dill, 23 July 1936, WO 32/4157, NA. Other members of the delegation were Lt-Gen. Sir Giffard Le Quesne Martel, Major E.C. Hayes and Wing Cdr H.E.P. Wigglesworth and two private 'soldier-servants'. Manoeuvres were also attended by French and Czechoslovak delegations.

85 Maj. Hayes to APW, Martel and Wigglesworth, 31 Aug. 1936, WO 32/4157, NA.

86 APW, report on visit to manoeuvres in White Russian Military District, WO 32/4157, NA.

87 Memorandum by Col. E.O. Skaife, Military Attaché, Moscow, 11 Nov. 1936, WO 32/4157, NA.

88 *Daily Telegraph* 14 Sept. 1936.

89 APW, report on visits to establishments in Soviet Union after manoeuvres, WO 32/4157, NA. Marshal Kliment Voroshilov (1881–1969).

90 The average age of generals and lieutenant-generals in employment was 60, compared with 57 in 1914. Rt Hon. Leslie Hore-Belisha, PC, MP (1893–1957).

91 'Some Noteworthy Officers', LH 11/HB 1937/29, LHCMA.

92 Later Gen. Sir Charles Deedes, CMG, OBE (1879–1969); in South Africa and at the Staff College at the same time as APW.

93 Deedes to APW, 1 July 1937, as quoted in Connell, *Scholar and Soldier*, p. 184.

94 APW to Nancy, 4 July 1937, John Connell fonds, McMU.

95 APW to BLH, 31 July 1937 LH 1/733, LHCMA.

CHAPTER 8: PRELUDE TO WAR

1 Keitel, *Deutsche Wehr*, as quoted in Raugh, *Wavell in the Middle East*, p. 37. Keitel was Hitler's Oberkommando der Wehrmacht.

2 APW, to Edward Wavell, 31 July 1937, private collection.

3 Collins, *Lord Wavell*, p. 168.

4 APW, as quoted in Collins, *Lord Wavell*, p. 168.

5 APW to BLH, 31 July 1937, LH 1/733, LHCMA; his appointment began 19 Aug. 1937.

6 APW, 'Government Houses', John Connell fonds.

7 Brig. G.S. Brunskill, CBE, MC (1891–1982); Memoirs, PP/MCR/136, IWM.

8 Clarke as quoted in Mure, *Master of Deception*, p. 57; later Brig. Dudley Clarke, CB, CBE (1899–1974)

9 EMW to John Connell, John Connell fonds, McMU and as quoted in Connell, *Scholar and Soldier*, p. 189.

10 APW as quoted by Leo Amery, Diary, 2 July 1943, AMEL 7/37 CAC.

11 See Collins, *Wavell*, p. 174; see also John Connell fonds, McMU.

12 BLH, note, 28 July 1938, LH 1/733, LHCMA.

13 Talk with Hore-Belisha, 1 Oct. 1937, LH 11/HB 1937/47, LHCMA.

14 Talk with Hore-Belisha, 15 Oct. 1937, LH 11/HB 1937/56, LHCMA; see also BLH to John Connell, 22 June 1962, John Connell fonds, McMU.

15 Lunch with Hore-Belisha, 19 Oct. 1937, LH 11/HB 1937/58, LHCMA.

16 As related in Connell, *Scholar and Soldier*, p. 194; see also Fergusson's account, *Portrait of a Soldier,* pp. 45–6.

17 Fergusson, *The Trumpet in the Hall*, p. 44.

18 Later Air Chief Marshal Sir Roderic Hill, KCB, MC, AFC, MA (1894–1954).

19 APW, 'Recollections', as quoted in Connell, *Scholar and Soldier*, p. 195.

20 General Sir Reginald Wingate, GCB, GCVO, GBE, KCMG, DSO (1861–1953). Later Maj.-Gen. O.C. Wingate, DSO (1903–44).

21 As quoted in *The Good Soldier*, p. 62; see also APW's Foreword to *Wingate's Raiders* by Charles Rolo (1944).

22 Brunskill, Memoirs, PP/MCR/136, IWM.

23 APW to Leonie Lemartine, 8 Jan. 1938, private collection.

24 APW, as listed in Connell, *Scholar and Soldier*, p. 197. He also noted: 'C-in-C Home Defence; decide policy if continental war; grouping of infantry units; Mobile Division; abolish promotion exams; confidential reports to include fitness for war; close touch with science; more brevets'.

25 APW, 'Recollections', John Connell fonds, McMU.

26 BLH to APW, 2 March 1938, LH 1/733, LHCMA.

27 APW to BLH, 9 March 1938, LH 1/733, LHCMA.

28 Gen. Sir Arthur Wauchope, as quoted in Fergusson, *The Trumpet in the Hall*, p. 33.

29 APW to Nancy, 10 March 1938, John Connell fonds, McMU; Sir Harold MacMichael, GCMG, DSO (1882–1969).

30 APW, 'Recollections', as quoted in Connell, *Scholar and Soldier*, p. 197.

31 Ibid., John Connell fonds, McMU.

32 APW, 'Government Houses', John Connell fonds, McMU.

33 APW to Nancy, 23 April 1939, John Connell fonds, McMU.

34 APW to Leonie Lemartine, 24 Dec. 1938, private collection.

35 Later Field Marshal Bernard Law Montgomery, 1st Viscount Montgomery of Alamein, KCB, GCB, DSO (1887–1976).

36 *The Memoirs of Field Marshal the Viscount Montgomery of Alamein*, p. 46.

37 APW to Sir Ernest Swinton, 22 May 1938, LH 1/733, LHCMA. BLH was the obvious successor, but Swinton did not like him and therefore determined to prevent him from having the Chichele Chair by offering it to APW.

38 BLH to John Connell, 22 June 1962, John Connell fonds, McMU. APW's later successes in the Second World War indicate that BLH's negative view was not borne out. But his opinion must also be seen in the context of his criticism of the slow promotion system, of which he considered APW a victim.

39 William Henry Dudley Boyle, later 12th Earl of Cork and Orrery, GCB, KCB, CB (1873–1967).

40 APW, 'Recollections', as quoted in Connell, *Scholar and Soldier*, p. 200.

41 APW to BLH, 16 Aug. 1938, LH 1/733, LHCMA.

42 APW to Leonie Lemartine, 22 Oct. 1938, private collection.

43 APW, 'Recollections', as quoted in Connell, *Scholar and Soldier*, p. 202.

44 Ibid.

45 APW to Edward Wavell, 6 Jan. 1939, 'Chronological list of References to the name of Vauville, Wauville, Wayvill, Wavell, 1050 to 1940', private collection.

46 APW to Leonie Lemartine, 3 Jan. 1939, private collection.

47 APW to BLH, 13 Jan. 1939, LH 1/733, LHCMA.

48 APW, as quoted in *The Good Soldier*, p. 29.

49 Michael Fox to AJW, as quoted in Connell, *Scholar and Soldier*, p. 201.

50 APW, 'Recollections', as quoted in Connell, *Scholar and Soldier*, p. 206.

CHAPTER 9: MIDDLE EAST COMMAND, 1939

1 APW as quoted in Moorehead, *The Desert War*, first page.

2 APW to Leonie Lemartine, 5 Aug. 1939, private collection. APW was given the rank of local General specific to his new command; promoted 1 Oct. 1940.

3 Alan Moorehead, *The Desert War*, p. 3.

4 Later Lord Killearn, PC, GCMG, CB, MVO (1880–1964); his second wife Jacqueline's father was Aldo Castellani, physician to the Royal houses of Savoy and of Aosta; he and Lady Lampson were known as 'Samson and Delilah'. See also Peter Coats, *Of Generals and Gardens*, p. 75.

5 Tedder, *With Prejudice*, p. 43.

6 Lampson, as quoted in Raugh, *Wavell in the Middle East*, p. 49.

7 Lt-Col. Sir Stewart Symes, GBE, KCMG, DSO (1882–1962).

8 Later Admiral of the Fleet Viscount Cunningham of Hyndhope, KT, GCB, OM, DSO, LL.D (1883–1963); see S.W.C. Pack, *Cunningham, The Commander*.

9 Air Chief Marshal Sir William Mitchell, KCB, CB, CBE, DSO, MC, AFC (1888–1944).

10 General Sir Robert Cassels, GCB, GCSI, DSO, IA (1876–1959).

11 When Egypt became independent, Britain's special interest in the Suez Canal was recognized and she was granted permission to retain a garrison there for 20 years.

12 APW, Notes for BGS [Brigadier, General Staff], Middle East Command, as quoted in Raugh, *Wavell in the Middle East*, p. 42.

13 APW, as quoted in Connell, *Scholar and Soldier*, p. 213. see also note 1, p. 527.

14 Arthur Smith, 'Reminiscences for his grandchildren', private collection.

15 Fergusson, *Portrait of a Soldier*, p. 47; later Lt-Col. John Benson (d. 2001).

16 Later General Sir Richard O'Connor, GCB, DSO, MC (1889–1991).

17 Later Maj.-Gen. W.J. Cawthorn CB, CIE, CBE (1896–1970).

18 Maj.-Gen. W.J. Cawthorn to Sir Walter Crocker, 12 July 1965, 'Diaries of Sir Walter Crocker', MS 5019, NLA.

19 Raugh, *Wavell in the Middle East*, p. 40; Collins, *Lord Wavell*, p. 195. Cawthorn's tasks also came under the 'Minister of State' organization which WSC instituted soon after APW's dismissal in 1941.

20 APW to Gort, 3 Aug. 1939, demi-official letter, NA.

21 APW to Leonie Lemartine, 5 Aug. 1939, private collection.

22 Joseph Raanan, 'Unpublished Memoirs', private collection.

23 APW to Gort, 10 Aug. 1939, demi-official letter, NA. During his command in the Middle East, Wavell never had an aircraft of his own; he had therefore to travel by troop carrier, bomber or whatever other plane was available, and put up with the consequent delays and discomfort, in slow and unsuitable machines: Connell, *Scholar and Soldier*, p. 213.

24 Corelli Barnett, *The Desert Generals*, p. 24.

25 Alan Moorehead, *African Trilogy*, Hamish Hamilton, 1944, p. 22.

26 Sir Douglas Dodds-Parker (b.1909) to the author, 8 March 2002.

27 Later General Sir William Platt, GBE, KCB, DSO (1885–1975).

28 Figures from BLH, 10/1950/28a, LHCMA.

29 APW to Gen. Sir Henry Jackson, 21 Aug. 1939, Wavell Album, BWRA 0335; APW wrote to Jackson as 'Jacko'.

30 APW to Gort, 'Notes on Strategical Situation in the Middle East', 24 Aug. 1939; Raugh, *Wavell in the Middle East*, p. 45.

31 Beck had also been responsible for negotiating the non-aggression pact with Hitler in Jan. 1934.

32 APW to Gort, 2 Sept. 1939, as quoted in Connell, *Scholar and Soldier*, p. 215.

33 Later Field Marshal Lord Ironside, GCB, CMG, DSO (1880–1959).

34 Ironside to APW, 11 Sept. 1939, as quoted in Connell, *Scholar and Soldier*, p. 216.

35 APW to Mrs Mary Peckitt (Molly), 24 Oct. 1939, Misc U9 Spec, IWM. It is not clear who this lady is: quite possibly the widow of Reginald Peckitt, CBE, Chief Mechanical Engineer, Egyptian State Railways, who d. 1937.

36 General Maxime Weygand (1867–1965); arrested by Gestapo in 1941 for opposing German policies in French Africa, imprisoned in Germany until 1945. The sentence of 'infamy' passed upon him as a member of the Vichy Govt. was quashed.

37 APW, as quoted in Collins, *Lord Wavell*, p. 211.

38 Collins, *Lord Wavell*, p. 203.

39 Gort to APW, 11 Sept. 1939, as quoted in Connell, *Scholar and Soldier*, p. 216.

40 APW, 'Recollections', as quoted in Connell, *Scholar and Soldier*, p. 217. See 'Notes on Conference held at Ankara on 20–10–39 between Marshal Fevzi Cakmak, Gen. Weygand and Gen. Wavell', WO 201/1044, NA.

41 Freya Stark, *East is West*, p. 4; Freya Stark. DBE (1893–1993); see Caroline Moorehead, *Freya Stark*; and for a critical examination of her reputation, Molly Izzard, *Freya Stark*, Hodder & Stoughton, 1993.

42 APW, 'Note on Visit to Turkey, 18–22 Oct. 1939', WO 201/1044, NA.

43 Later Maj.-Gen. Sir Percy Hobart, KBE, CB, DSO, MC (1885–1957). See Kenneth Macksey, 'Hobart', in *Churchill's Generals*, ed. John Keegan, p. 245.

44 Jumbo Wilson as quoted in Macksey, 'Hobart', in *Churchill's Generals*, ed. Keegan, p. 246.

45 After the German *blitzkrieg* Hobart was restored to the active list on WSC's insistence to raise the 11th Armoured Division in 1941–2 and the 79th (specialized) Armoured Division in 1942, which he commanded until 1945. In 1948 BLH questioned APW on the removal of Hobart and APW defended his decision as quoted: APW to BLH, 13 May 1948, LH 1/733, LHCMA.

46 See Dudley Clarke, *Seven Assignments*, p. 28.

47 APW, 'Government Houses', John Connell fonds, McMU.

48 Auchinleck to John Connell, 12 Sept. 1961, John Connell fonds, McMU.

49 Araminta, Lady Aldington, to the author, February 2002.

50 Dudley Clarke, *Seven Assignments*, p. 29.

51 Later Admiral Sir Dudley Pound, GCB, OM, GCVO, KCB, CB (1877–1943); later Marshal of the RAF Lord Newall, GCB, OM, GCMG, CBE (1886–1963).

52 APW, 'Recollections', as quoted in Connell, *Scholar and Soldier*, p. 219.

53 APW to Leonie Lemartine, 25 Jan. 1940, private collection.

54 Later General Lord Ismay, GCB, CH, DSO (1887–1965).

55 APW to Jackson, 22 Jan. 1940, Wavell Album, BWRA 0335.

56 The fortifications, later disarmed by the Italians, proved useful to Rommel and a nuisance to Montgomery.

57 APW, 'Recollections', as quoted in Connell, *Scholar and Soldier*, p. 220.

58 APW to Nancy (undated), Connell, *Scholar and Soldier*, n. 6, page 527.

59 APW to Jackson, 22 Jan. 1940, Wavell Album, BWRA 0335.

60 APW to Leonie Lemartine, 25 Jan. 1940, private collection.

61 APW, appreciation, 26 Jan. 1940, Connell, *Scholar and Soldier*, p. 221.

62 *The Eden Memoirs: The Reckoning*, pp. 85–6.

63 Freyberg had been invalided out in 1937 but remained on the Army List; he had been educated in New Zealand, and on the outbreak of war offered his services to the NZ Government. He commanded 2 New Zealand Division and 2 New Zealand Expeditionary Force.

64 Later Field Marshal Sir Thomas Blamey, GBE, KCB, CMG, DSO (1884–1951).

65 Paul Freyberg, *Bernard Freyberg*, p. 203.

66 Captain Peter Coats (1910–90); ADC and Private Secretary to APW 1940–6.

67 Peter Coats, *Of Generals and Gardens*, pp. 49, 50, 52.

68 Ibid., p. 55.

69 Ibid., p. 57.

70 APW to Ironside, 3 April 1940, as quoted in Connell, *Scholar and Soldier*, pp. 223–4.

71 In 1952 Farouk finally had a son, to whom he relinquished the throne that year.

72 Coats, *Of Generals and Gardens*, p. 59.

73 APW to Ironside, 15 April 1940, as quoted in Connell, *Scholar and Soldier*, p. 226.

74 To spread the work-load of the chiefs of staff, Chamberlain had decided to create a new office of 'vice-chief'. APW to Dill, 28 April 1940, WO 106/5045, NA.

75 Coats, *Of Generals and Gardens*, p. 59. Coats's chronology is erratic: his note is dated '4 April' but the Wavells' wedding anniversary was 22 April.

76 Ibid., pp. 58–9.

77 Later Brigadier Eric James Shearer, CB, CBE, MC (1892–1980).

78 Later 1st Earl Halifax, KG, PC, OM, GCSI, GCIE (1881–1959).

79 Rt Hon. Leopold Amery, PC, CH, MP (1873–1955).

80 WSC, as quoted in *Their Finest Hour*, p. 24.

81 Lord Ismay, *Memoirs*, p. 158. Ismay was also Chief of Staff Officer to WSC and a member of the Chiefs of Staff Committee.

82 Lt-Col. John Benson to Harold Raugh (undated), private collection.

83 See Raugh, *Wavell in the Middle East*, p. 60.

84 APW to Dill, 22 May 1940, as quoted in Connell, *Scholar and Soldier*, p. 229.

85 The document was not circulated, but APW did send it to Dill. When it came to the attention of WSC, he used it as a reason to label APW 'defeatist', John Connell fonds, McMU.

86 Dill to APW, 27 May 1940, as quoted in Connell, *Scholar and Soldier*, p. 231.

87 APW to Dill, Ibid., p. 233.

88 WSC to Anthony Eden, 6 June 1940, as quoted in WSC, *Their Finest Hour*, p. 145.

89 Later Air Chief Marshal Sir Arthur Longmore, GCB, DSO (1885–1970).

90 See Connell, *Scholar and Soldier*, p. 234.

91 Later Lt-Gen. Sir Noel Beresford-Peirse, KBE, CB, DSO (1887–1953); later Maj.-Gen. Sir Michael O'Moore Creagh, KBE, MC (1892–1970).

92 See Maj.-Gen. I.S.O. Playfair, *The Mediterranean and Middle East*, vol. 1, p. 94; Wavell had approx. 86,000 men.

93 APW, 'Recollections', John Connell fonds, McMU.

94 Later Sir Michael Wright, GCMG (1901–76), British Embassy, Cairo, 1940–3; Sir Terence Shone, KCMG (1894–1965), British Minister, Cairo, 1940; Ernest Francis Withers Besly, CMG (1891–1965), legal adviser to British Embassy in Cairo since 1937.

95 APW, 'Recollections', John Connell fonds, McMU.

CHAPTER 10: HOLDING AFRICA, 1940

1 BLH, 'Wavell', 8 May 1950, LH 10/1950/7a, LHCMA.

2 APW, 'Recollections', as quoted in Connell, *Scholar and Soldier*, p. 237.

3 APW as quoted in Julian Amery, *Approach March,* p. 206.

4 APW, Order of the Day, 17 June 1940, as quoted in APW, *Speaking Generally*, p.11. Four years later when Alan Cunningham met Wavell at the Staff College, he reminded APW of his confidence in the ability of the British Empire to survive, to which Wavell replied: 'Yes, but I can't think why now!' Collins, *Lord Wavell*, p. 244.

5 WSC to APW, 1 July 1940, CHAR 20/14, CAC.

6 APW, 'Recollections', as quoted in Connell, *Scholar and Soldier*, p. 241.

7 Dill to APW, 26 June 1940, as quoted in Connell, *Scholar and Soldier*, p. 239.

8 Later Acting Lt-Gen. W.H.E. 'Strafer' Gott, CB, CBE, DSO, MC (1897–1942).

9 Later Brig. R.A. Bagnold, OBE, FRS (1896–1990).

10 See Saul Kelly, *The Hunt for Zerzura*, pp. 133–77.

11 Bagnold, *Sand, Wind and War*, p. 128, as quoted in Kelly, *The Hunt for Zerzura*, p. 143. The LRDG was also supported by the Special Operations Executive (SOE) in London.

12 APW to Maj. R.A. Bagnold, 1 Oct. 1940. See C.25, CAC.

13 Haile Selassie (1891–1975), grand-nephew of Emperor Menelik II.

14 Later Brig. D.A. Sandford, CBE, DSO (1882–1972).

15 Remotely controlled by SOE in London but answerable to APW and Platt, commander of British forces in the Sudan; see M.R.D Foot, *SOE: The Special Operations Executive*, p. 175. Douglas Dodds-Parker was the SOE 'anchor man' in Khartoum.

16 APW, 'Recollections', as quoted in Connell, *Scholar and Soldier*, p. 246.

17 Ibid., p. 248.

18 See Christopher Sykes, *Orde Wingate*, p. 232.

19 APW as quoted in Connell, *Scholar and Soldier*, p. 249.

20 APW, 30 July 1940, cable, WO 169/11, NA.

21 Eden, *Memoirs*, p. 129.

22 Hastings Ismay, who had served in Somaliland 1914–20, believed the 'proper course' would have been to evacuate the capital and withdraw to the Somaliland plateau, where with the Somaliland Camel Corps and British troops could have interrupted Italian lines of communication to Ethiopia: see Ismay, *Memoirs*, pp. 193–4. APW does not appear to have considered this as an option.

23 Shearer, private memoir, as quoted in Lewin, *The Chief*, p. 36.

24 Eden, *Memoirs*, p. 130.

25 Ismay, *Memoirs*, p. 192.

26 Shearer, private memoir, as quoted in, Lewin, *The Chief*, p. 37.

27 APW, 'Recollections', as quoted in Connell, *Scholar and Soldier*, p. 256.

28 Shearer, private memoir, as quoted in Lewin, *The Chief*, p. 23; Chequers in Buckinghamshire is the official Prime Ministerial country residence.

29 Eden, *Memoirs*, p. 130.

30 John Colville, as quoted in *Action This Day: Working with Churchill*, ed. Wheeler-Bennett, p. 61; later Sir John Colville, CB, CVO (1915–87).

31 Ismay to John Connell, 21 Aug. 1961, John Connell fonds, McMU.

32 Diary, 13 Aug. 1940, Eden, *Memoirs*, p. 131

33 WSC to Eden, 13 Aug. 1940, CHAR 20/2 A42 43, CAC; see also Eden, *Memoirs*, p. 131 and Colville, *Downing Street Diaries*, Hodder & Stoughton, 1985, p. 222.

34 Eden to WSC, as quoted Eden, *Memoirs*, p. 132. See also Douglas Wimberley to Ronald Lewin, 12 June 1981, who said that there was no other regular army officer in the whole of the British Army who could have tackled the problems APW had to face, as well as he did, except Alanbrooke: RLEW 7/21, CAC.

35 WSC, as quoted in Eden, *Memoirs*, p. 133.

36 Eden, *Memoirs*, p. 133.

37 WSC, *The Grand Alliance*, p. 242. See also WSC, CHUR 217/A-C & CHUR 4/167, CAC.

38 Diary, 15 Aug. 1940, Eden *Memoirs*, p. 133.

39 WSC, *Their Finest Hour*, p. 376.

40 APW, broadcast, 21 Aug. 1940, as quoted in APW, *Speaking Generally*, p. 15.

41 APW as quoted in Lewin, *The Chief*, pp. 43, 45. With the invasion of Britain still a possibility, 'all felt his lash, to the nation's benefit. If he sought – excessively, indeed – to whip on the Commander-in-Chief in Cairo, some plea in mitigation must be allowed': p. 46. See also WSC, *Their Finest Hour*, pp. 379–82.

42 Dill, as quoted in Lewin, *The Chief*, p. 25, also quoted in Raugh, *Wavell in the Middle East*, p. 83. See also Fergusson, *Portrait of a Soldier*, p. 52: 'It was this unlucky phrase which had annoyed the Prime Minister, and started the rot in his relations with Wavell.'

43 APW to DCGS, 'Note on Genesis and Working Out of "Compass" Plan', Appendix A, 11 Sept. 1940, Auchinleck papers, *121* MUL, also quoted in

Connell, *Scholar and Soldier*, p. 273. WSC had also thought of a plan to inflict 'strangulatory hernia' on the Italians by advancing into Libya.

44 Hitler and Mussolini met three times at the Brenner Pass, in March and Oct. 1940 and in June 1941; it was a convenient distance from both Berlin and Rome.

45 Eden to APW, 8 Oct. 1940, as quoted in Connell, *Scholar and Soldier*, p. 276.

46 Freyberg, *Bernard Freyberg*, p. 234.

47 Ibid.

48 APW, 'Recollections', as quoted in Connell, *Scholar and Soldier*, p. 277, and APW to Wilson, 20 Oct. 1940, 'Note on Genesis of Compass', Appendix C, Auchinleck papers, *121*, MUL.

49 Eden, *Memoirs*, p. 154.

50 Ibid., p. 163.

51 See Christopher Sykes, *Orde Wingate*, p. 244 for a fuller account; also Eden, *Memoirs*, p. 164.

52 APW, Foreword, Charles Rolo, *Wingate's Raiders*, p. 6; Wingate and Sandford later quarrelled.

53 APW, 'Recollections', as quoted in Connell, *Scholar and Soldier*, p. 277.

54 APW despatch, 'Operations in the Western Desert from 7th Dec. 1940 to 7th Feb. 1941', WO 106/2133, NA.

55 In 1936 the small Mark I tanks were called 'Matildas'; subsequently the name became the formal title for the heavy Mark II tanks used in N. Africa.

56 Straker, *Memoirs* [unpublished] p. 80.

57 APW to Wilson, 2 Nov. 1940, 'Note on Genesis of Compass', Appendix D, Auchinleck papers, *121*, MUL.

58 Ismay, *Memoirs*, p. 195.

59 See S.W.C. Pack, *Sea Power in the Mediterranean*, p. 183.

60 WSC to APW, 14 Nov. 1940, CHAR 20/14, CAC. Neville Chamberlain had retired from the House of Commons and leadership of the Conservative Party in Sept. 1940. He had unfailingly supported WSC, notwithstanding WSC's responsibility for the Norwegian fiasco.

61 WSC to APW, 22 Nov. 1940, CHAR 20/14, CAC.

62 WSC to Dill and Eden, 22 Nov. 1940, as quoted in Connell, *Scholar and Soldier*, p. 283.

63 APW, 'Note on Genesis of Compass', 15 Dec. 1941, Auchinleck papers, *121* MUL.

64 WSC to APW, 26 Nov. 1940, as quoted in Connell, *Scholar and Soldier*, p. 286.

65 Dill to APW, 29 Nov. 1940, Ibid., p. 282.

66 APW to Wilson, 28 Nov. 1940, 'Note on Genesis of Compass', Appendix F, Auchinleck papers, 121, MUL, as quoted in Connell, *Scholar and Soldier*, p. 286.

67 Later Gen. Sir Alan Cunningham, GCMG, KCB, DSO, MC (1887–1983).

68 Later Lt-Gen. Sir Iven Mackay, KBE, CMG, DSO, VD Hon. LL.D (1882–1966).

69 APW to Dill, 6 Dec. 1940, as quoted in Connell, *Scholar and Soldier*, p. 288.

70 WSC to Dill, 7 Dec. 1940, Ibid., p. 289.

71 APW, 'Recollections', Ibid., p. 289.

72 Coats, *Of Generals and Gardens*, p. 73.

73 Alexander Clifford, *Three Against Rommel*, p. 36.

74 APW, as quoted in Moorehead, *African Trilogy*, p. 65.

75 As told to Hermione Ranfurly, *To War with Whitaker*, p. 78. Fellers was unaware when, soon afterwards, the cipher he used in reporting news picked up from the British was broken by both the Germans and the Italians. His telegrams to Washington thus became an important source of information for Rommel after his arrival in North Africa. It was not until 1942 that the British, through Ultra, realized what had happened, and Fellers was removed.

76 APW, Special Order of the Day, Dec. 1940, as quoted in APW, *Speaking Generally*, p. 18.

77 WSC to APW, 13 Dec. 1940, CHAR 20/14, CAC.

78 APW to Collingwood, 10 Dec. 1942, RLEW 4/6, CAC. It is not clear who this is – perhaps Lt-Gen. Sir George Collingwood, KBE, CB, DSO, who served in the Middle East and Burma.

79 APW to Dill, 17 Dec. 1940, WO 106/5127, NA.

80 WSC to Ismay, 11 Dec. 1940. CHAR 30/102, CAC. There is no record of what WSC thought of the books. They were returned to the library in March 1941.

81 BLH, *The Listener*, 9 Jan. 1941, LH 10/1941/1C, LHCMA.

82 See John Baynes, *The Forgotten Victor*, p. 99. APW used the same argument in his despatch, 'Operations in the Western Desert from 7th Dec. 1940 to 7th Feb. 1941', WO 106/2133 NA.

83 See Raugh, *Wavell in the Middle East*, p. 101 and Baynes, *The Forgotten Victor*, pp. 100–1 for a discussion of the pros and cons. Fergusson called it 'one of the neatest and most skilful bluffs of the whole war', since it was such an unexpected action to take, as quoted in Fergusson's unpublished review of BLH's *History of the Second World War*, private collection.

84 WSC to APW, 16 Dec. 1940, CHAR 20/14, CAC.

85 WSC to APW, 18 Dec. 1940, CHAR 20/14, CAC.

86 APW to WSC, 19 Dec. 1940, as quoted in WSC, *Their Finest Hour*, p. 543.

87 *To War with Whitaker*, Ranfurly, 11 Dec. 1940, pp. 73–4.

88 Unique among the wives, Hermione had trained as a secretary in London – her qualifications were invaluable.

89 Ranfurly, *To War with Whitaker*, p. 75. APW's letter is dated 24 Dec. 1940; she did not receive it until 4 Jan. 1941.

90 Maj. J.F. MacKinnon to John Connell, 30 March 1964, John Connell fonds, McMU.

91 RO'C, 'Report on Operations in Libya', O'Connor collection, NAM.

92 APW to Dill, 17 Dec. 1940, WO 106/2136, NA.

93 Freyberg, *Bernard Freyberg*, pp. 236, 237.

94 APW to Dill, 17 Dec. 1940, WO 106/5127, NA.

CHAPTER 11: ALL FRONTS, 1941

1 J.C. Smuts quoted this poem to Peter Coats prior to the Greek campaign; as quoted in Coats, *Of Generals and Gardens*, p. 89.

2 APW, New Year's Day, 1941, *Speaking Generally*, pp. 17–18.

3 Coats, *Of Generals and Gardens*, p. 75. Robert Rhodes James, editor of Channon's extensive diaries, reveals that Channon was bisexual and that his relationship with Peter Coats effectively ended his marriage to Honor Guinness: *'Chips': The Diaries of Sir Henry Channon*, Preface to the 2nd edn, 1993.

4 Channon, *Diaries*, 2 Jan. 1941, p. 280.

5 See Channon, *Diaries*, 4 Jan. 1941, p. 281. Channon left for Greece on 8 January, en route for Belgrade.

6 WSC to APW, 7 Jan. 1941, as quoted in Connell, *Scholar and Soldier*, p. 306.

7 APW to WSC, 8 Jan. 1941, ibid.

8 Not until Feb. 1941 did Middle East Command receive 'Ultra' intelligence, as a digest; only from mid March was all relevant material directly transmitted, but even then it was frequently paraphrased. The use/non-use of Ultra intelligence had important consequences for Wavell's actions and Churchill's criticism of him: see F.W. Winterbotham *Ultra Secret*; Ronald Lewin, *Ultra Goes to War*; Paul Freyberg, *Bernard Freyberg*; Corelli Barnett, *The Desert Generals*.

9 APW to Dill, 9 Jan. 1941, as quoted in Connell, *Scholar and Soldier*, pp. 309–10.

10 WSC to APW, 10 Jan. 1941, *The Grand Alliance*, pp. 16–17. Here, WSC qualifies his order by stating that 'our intentions at this time did not amount to the offer to Greece of an army, but only to special and technical units.'

11 Araminta, Lady Aldington to the author, Feb 2002.

12 General John (Ioannes) Metaxas (1871–1941).

13 Coats, *Of Generals and Gardens*, p. 79.

14 John Shearer to Peter Coats; see *Of Generals and Gardens*, p. 80.

15 Freya Stark to Lucy (Mrs John) Beach, 19 Jan. 1941, *Letters*, vol. 4, p. 113.

16 APW to Dill, 24 Jan. 1941, as quoted in Connell, *Scholar and Soldier*, p. 318.

17 APW to Jackson, 27 Jan. 1941, Wavell Album, BWRA 0335.

18 Channon, *Diaries*, p. 284.

19 John William Burgon (1813–88); quoted in Coats, *Of Generals and Gardens*, p. 81.

20 Fergusson, *Portrait of a Soldier,* p. 49

21 Ibid., p. 50.

22 WSC, Personal Minute, 31 Jan. 1941, PREM 3/209, NA.

23 Eric Dorman-Smith, as quoted in Connell, *Scholar and Soldier,* p. 321.

24 RO'C, as quoted in Raugh, *Wavell in the Middle East,* p. 118, Connell, *Scholar and Soldier,* p. 326, and John Connell fonds, McMU.

25 Statistics vary: WSC says they had advanced 500 miles, overwhelmed more than nine divisions, taken 130,000 prisoners, 400 tanks, 1,290 guns. Of Wavell's force of 35,000, 500 men were lost, 1,373 were wounded and 55 missing.

26 Speech titled 'Give us the tools and we will finish the job', as quoted in *Never Give In! The Best of Winston Churchill's Speeches,* ed Winston S. Churchill (WSC's grandson), Pimlico, 2003, p. 261.

27 Channon, *Diaries,* 9 Feb. 1941, p. 291.

28 There is no evidence that the detailed secret and personal letter written by Leo Amery to Dill pointing out the advantages of a rapid advance to Tripoli was given the consideration it perhaps deserved: see Connell, *Scholar and Soldier,* pp. 321–3, and Dorman-Smith to John Connell, 9 Sept. 1961, John Connell fonds, McMU.

29 War Cabinet Defence Committee (Operations) 10 Feb. 1941, DO (41) CAB 69/2, NA, as quoted in Raugh, *Wavell in the Middle East,* p. 119.

30 APW, as quoted in Corelli Barnett, *The Desert Generals* (1983 edn), p. 63.

31 Cable No. 51265, 12 Feb. 1941, Principal War Telegrams, NA, as quoted in Raugh, *Wavell in the Middle East,* p. 138.

32 Corelli Barnett, *Engage the Enemy More Closely,* pp. 328–9: 'The Premier actually opted for the Greek adventure in the face of apparent odds far more adverse than in reality.' See also F.H. Hinsley, *British Intelligence in the Second World War,* p. 359.

33 APW to Eric Dorman-Smith, as quoted in Connell, *Scholar and Soldier,* p. 330.

34 Cable No. 51265, 12 Feb. 1941, as quoted in Raugh, p. 138.

35 WSC, as quoted in Connell, *Scholar and Soldier,* p. 333.

36 APW to WSC, Secret Cipher, 12 Feb. 1941, WO 106/2144, NA.

37 APW, John Connell fonds, McMU.

38 Later Maj.-Gen. Sir John Kennedy, GCMG, KCVO, KBE, CB, MC (1893–1970).

39 Dill as quoted in Kennedy, *Business of War,* p. 75 (in error, Raugh gives the reference as Fergusson).

40 Ibid., p. 76.

41 Later Gen. William J. Donovan; a Republican Wall Street lawyer of Catholic/Irish descent. In June 1941 he was appointed Coordinator of the newly established Office of Coordination of Strategic Information (or Services – hence OSS), the American equivalent of SOE.

42 See Raugh, *Wavell in the Middle East,* p. 141; see also Joseph P. Lash, *Roosevelt*

and Churchill 1939–41, p. 305, where Donovan maintains that the decision to send British troops to Greece was made not by the Cabinet or Churchill but by Wavell.

43 Kiernan, *Wavell*, p. 178.

44 Ibid., p. 171.

45 APW, 'Major-General Orde Wingate', *The Good Soldier*, p. 63.

46 Special Order of the Day, GHQ, Cairo, 14 Feb. 1941, as quoted in *Speaking Generally*, p. 23. See also APW despatch, 'Operations in the Western Desert from 7th Dec. 1940 to 7th Feb. 1941', WO 106/2133.

47 *Illustrated London News*, Feb. 1941.

48 *The Times*, 17 Feb. 1941. The lectures were subsequently printed in booklet form and translated into several languages, including German. After Rommel's death, his family sent Rommel's annotated copy to the Wavell family.

49 *The Times*, 21 Feb. 1941.

50 Anthony Eden, 'Story of Greece', Avon papers, University of Birmingham, as quoted in Raugh, *Wavell in the Middle East*, p. 141.

51 Later Field Marshal Sir Thomas Blamey, GBE, KCB, CMG, DSO (1884–1951).

52 APW, 'Despatch of British Forces to the Balkans', 17 Feb. 1941, WO 169/918, NA.

53 APW, 'War is an Option of Difficulties', 19 Feb. 1941, WO 169/924, App X, 30, NA.

54 Marshall-Cornwall, *Wars and Rumours of Wars*, p. 185.

55 See Raugh, *Wavell in the Middle East*, p. 148: 'there seems to be little doubt that Donovan's persistent pro-intervention posture, as a representative of the United States, influenced significantly Wavell's decision to send a force to Greece.' The source for this information is Col. Vivian Dykes, CBE, MBE (1898–1943), who was Donovan's British Army escort officer. His diary is in the Donovan Papers, USA Military History Institute.

56 Eden, *Memoirs*, p. 195.

57 Sir John Dill, 21 Feb. 1941, PREM 3/206/3, NA.

58 See Raugh, *Wavell in the Middle East*, p. 150.

59 WSC to Eden, 21 Feb. 1941, PREM 3/206/3, NA.

60 Eden, Cable No. 358, 21 Feb. 1941, as quoted in Raugh, *Wavell in the Middle East*, p. 151.

61 Sir Michael Palairet, KCMG (1882–1956).

62 Later Lord Caccia, GCMG, GCVO (1905–90).

63 Caccia to Raugh, 1990, as quoted in Raugh, *Wavell in the Middle East*, p. 152.

64 Koryzis, as quoted in Connell, *Scholar and Soldier*, p. 339.

65 On 23 Feb. 1941 British forces at El Agheila were attacked by heavy tanks and motorcycle combinations 'believed to be German': War Diary, WO 169/924, NA.

66 War Cabinet, COS Cttee, 24 Feb. 1941, CAB 66/15, NA as quoted in Raugh, *Wavell in the Middle East*, p. 154.

67 WSC, 24 Feb. 1941, as quoted in Gilbert, *Churchill*, 6, p. 1013.

68 WSC to APW, 1 March 1941, as quoted in Raugh, *Wavell in the Middle East*, p. 178. On 16 March British Somaliland was reclaimed.

69 WSC, 6 March 1941, ibid., p. 157.

70 APW, 6 March 1941, ibid.

71 Cunningham, *A Sailor's Odyssey*, p. 315.

72 J.C. Smuts, as quoted in Raugh, *Wavell in the Middle East*, p. 158.

73 APW to WSC, 13 March 1941, CHAR 2/423, CAC.

74 Randolph Churchill, MBE (1911–68).

75 WSC to APW, 28 Jan. 1941, CHAR 1/362/1, CAC.

76 Randolph Churchill to WSC, 14 March 1941, CHAR 1/362, CAC.

77 APW to WSC, 29 Mar. 1941, CHAR 2/423, CAC.

78 Auchinleck to APW, 13 March 1941, Auchinleck papers, 130, MUL.

79 Lt-Gen. (later Sir) Philip Neame, VC, KBE, CB, DSO (1888–1978).

80 Later Lt-Gen. Sir Leslie Morshead, KCB, KBG, CMG, DSO (1889–1959).

81 APW to RO'C, 27 June 1945, RLEW 4/6, CAC. Neame's son states that his father had already warned APW: 'For Wavell to claim that he was unaware of the dangerously poor mechanical state of the armoured troops until a few days before the attack (as he did in his Despatch) is clearly untrue'. Neame to Lewin, RLEW 4/6, CAC.

82 APW to RO'C, 27 June 1945, RLEW 4/6, CAC.

83 Coats, *Of Generals and Gardens*, p. 91.

84 Erwin Rommel (1891–1944). Suspected of complicity in the July 1944 plot against Hitler, he took poison rather than face a people's court.

85 The Ambassador's wife, Lady Lampson.

86 APW, 'The Jug (with apologies to Lewis Carroll)', CHAR 1/362, in letter from Randolph to WSC, 6 April 1941. See also Coats, *Of Generals and Gardens*, p. 88 and Lewis Carroll, *Through the Looking Glass*, ch. 6, Humpty Dumpty: 'I sent a message to the fish: / I told them "This is what I wish".' During the Mad Hatter's Tea Party in *Alice in Wonderland* the dormouse keeps falling asleep while he relates his story.

87 Anti-Comintern pact signed by Germany and Japan on 25 Nov. 1936, by Italy on 6 Nov. 1937. In Jan. 1939 Hungary signed, followed by Spain, and in 1941 other satellite countries also joined.

88 Beevor, *Crete*, p. 32: in fact, far more divisions than were necessary.

89 APW, 'Operations in the Middle East from 7th Feb. 1941 to 15th July 1941', supplement to *London Gazette*, 3 July 1946, p. 3427.

90 WSC, *The Grand Alliance*, p. 178. Maj.-Gen. M.D. Gambier-Parry, MC (1891–1976); he took over from Maj-Gen. Tilly, who had died shortly after arriving in Egypt.

91 APW, 'Recollections', as quoted in Connell, *Scholar and Soldier*, p. 375.

92 APW to WSC, 27 Mar. 1941, *The Grand Alliance*, p. 179. Lewin, *The Chief*, p. 119, wrongly dates this as 23 Mar. 1941, as does Carver, *Dilemmas of the Western Desert*, Batsford, 1986, p. 21.

93 See Carver, *Harding of Petherton*, p. 67; later Field Marshal Lord Harding of Petherton, GCB, CBE, DSO, MC (1896–1989).

94 RO'C as quoted in Connell, *Scholar and Soldier*, p. 392.

95 Notes from an interview with RO'C by Ronald Lewin: RLEW 4/1, CAC. APW's decision to retain both RO'C and Neame at Barce was contrary to the accepted principle of retaining unity of command; see Raugh, *Wavell in the Middle East*, p. 195.

96 RO'C to APW, 27 June 1945, RLEW 4/6, CAC.

97 Harding to Raugh, 21 Sept. 1987, as quoted in Raugh, *Wavell in the Middle East*, p. 195.

98 Sir Kinahan Cornwallis, GCMG, CBE, DSO (1883–1959).

99 Major General F.W. von Mellenthin, *Panzer Battles*, p. 39.

100 WSC, *The Grand Alliance*, p. 309.

101 Later Maj.-Gen. Sir Francis de Guingand, KBE, CB, DSO (1900–79); de Guingand, *Operation Victory*, Hodder & Stoughton, 1947, p. 75. After the war, various reports emerged regarding the reason for their capture. In *The Chief*, Lewin blamed Neame for insisting on going in a particular direction when he was in fact lost. Neame's son hotly contested this account. RO'C exonerated APW and did not criticize Neame, but pointedly told APW that Neame had never apologized for making him a prisoner: see RLEW 4/6, CAC.

102 APW to Collingwood, 10 Dec. 1942, RLEW 4/6, CAC.

103 See Collins, *Lord Wavell*, p. 368.

104 At the time, not everyone endorsed APW's decision to hold Tobruk. John Kennedy, Dir. of Mil. Ops, recorded: 'I was astonished by this decision of Wavell's. The force in Tobruk would not be strong enough to break out once it was surrounded or to harass the German communications': *Business of War*, p. 91. WSC said it should be held 'to the death': WSC to APW, 7 April 1941, WO 106/2144, NA. Tobruk fell to Rommel in June 1942.

105 This story is related in detail in Collins, *Lord Wavell*, p. 369–71 as told to him by Major the Earl Amherst. See also Carver, *Harding of Petherton*, p. 69.

106 See David Fraser, *Knight's Cross*, p. 294.

107 WSC, *The Grand Alliance*, p. 190.

108 Collins, *Lord Wavell*, p. 372.

109 *Goebbels Diaries*, 16 April 1941.

110 Dill to WSC, 19 April 1941, PREM 3/52/1, NA, as quoted in Raugh, *Wavell in the Middle East*, p. 200.

111 Tedder, *With Prejudice*, p. 74. Later Marshal of the Royal Air Force, 1st Baron Tedder, GCB (1890–1967).

112 Coats, *Of Gardens and Generals*, p. 98.

113 Hetherington, *Blamey*, p. 105.

114 APW to WSC, 22 April 1941, 'Most Secret and Personal', PREM 3/206/3, NA.

115 APW to WSC, 25 April 1941, *The Grand Alliance*, p. 192. WSC's use of the name 'Tiger' predates British knowledge of the German 'Tiger' tanks.

116 WSC to APW, 28 April 1941, Ibid.

117 Dorman-Smith to John Connell, 29 Sept. 1962, John Connell fonds, McMU.

118 See Raugh, *Wavell in the Middle East*, p. 202–4.

119 WSC, Personal Telegram, 28 April 1941, PREM 3/109, NA.

120 Freyberg, as quoted in Paul Freyberg, *Bernard Freyberg*, p. 266.

121 See Paul Freyberg, *Bernard Freyberg*, pp. 268–9; see also Callum Macdonald, *The Lost Battle*, p. 160–1.

122 APW to RO'C, 27 June 1945, RLEW 4/6, CAC.

123 APW, 'Operations in the Middle East', as quoted in Woollcombe, *Campaigns*, p. 108.

124 APW, 'The British Expedition to Greece, 1941', in *Army Quarterly* vol. LIX (Jan. 1950); see also Lewin, *The Chief*, pp. 106–7, who believes that APW did not avail himself of the opportunities he had to inform WSC of the military risks. Maj.-Gen. Sir Francis de Guingand was extremely critical; see *Generals at War*, Hodder & Stoughton, 1964, p. 46: 'I have never been able to find any evidence to suggest that it was a reasonable military risk.'

125 Air Chief Marshal Sir Arthur Longmore to John Connell (undated, *circa* 1964), John Connell fonds, McMU.

126 Lt-Col. John Benson to Harold Raugh, 2 March 1989, private collection.

127 APW, Notes after seeing proofs of WSC, *The Grand Alliance*, John Connell fonds, McMU.

128 RO'C, private memoirs on Western Desert Campaign 1940–1, sent from POW camp in Italy, RLEW, 4/1, CAC.

129 Kennedy, *Business of War*, pp. 138–9.

130 Eric Dorman-Smith to John Connell, 9 Sept. 1961, John Connell fonds, McMU.

131 RO'C to John Connell, 22 Sept. 1964 (?), John Connell fonds, McMU.

132 Amery to Dill (undated but before 8 Feb. 1941), as quoted by Eric Dorman-Smith to John Connell, 12 Sept. 1961, John Connell fonds, McMU.

133 Rommel, *The Rommel Papers*, ed. BLH, p. 95.

134 Philip Neame, Jr to Ronald Lewin, RLEW 4/6, CAC.

135 APW, 'The British Expedition to Greece', *Army Quarterly* vol. LIX (Jan., 1950).

136 Air Chief Marshal Sir Arthur Longmore to John Connell (undated but *circa* 1964), John Connell fonds, McMU. See also Arthur Longmore, *From Sea to Slay*, Geoffrey Bles, 1946, p. 284.

137 WSC to APW, 1 May 1941, Cable No. 64484, Principal War Telegrams and Memoranda, 1940–3: Middle East, PREM 3/206/3, NA.

138 J.C. Smuts as quoted in Collins, *Lord Wavell*, Foreword, p. 10.

CHAPTER 12: CHURCHILL'S AXE, 1941

1 Alan Moorehead, *African Trilogy*, p. 176.
2 APW as quoted in Ranfurly, *To War with Whitaker*, 2 May 1941, p. 90; Hermione says 1917, but it was 1916 when EMW made the journey.
3 Ibid.
4 WSC as quoted in Raugh, *Wavell in the Middle East*, p. 207.
5 Air Marshal Sir J.H. D'Albiac, KCVO, KBE, CB, DSO (1894–1963), 'Report on Operations in the Baghdad Area 2nd May to 31st May 1941', private collection. The women and children were evacuated without casualties.
6 Ranfurly, *To War with Whitaker*, 3 May 1941, p. 91.
7 APW, as quoted in a private communication to John Connell, John Connell fonds, McMU.
8 As quoted in Kennedy, *Business of War*, p. 117; see also Connell, *Scholar and Soldier*, pp. 438–9 and Coats, *Of Generals and Gardens*, p. 103. Kennedy gives the date of 6 May.
9 Kennedy, *Business of War*, p. 116.
10 Eden, Diary, 10 May 1941, *Memoirs*, pp. 250–1.
11 Hon. Sir Harold Nicolson, CMG (1886–1968) MP (Nat. Lab.) 1935–45, author and critic. See *Diaries and Letters 1930–62*, 1966–8.
12 Chiefs of Staff, 6 May 1941, Auchinleck papers, *184*, MUL.
13 Later Lt-Gen. J.G.W Clark, CB, MC (1892–1948); as quoted in Collins, *Lord Wavell*, p. 397.
14 Freyberg's Order of the Day: see Callum Macdonald, *The Lost Battle*, p. 146.
15 Later Maj.-Gen. Sir Keith Stewart, CB, CBE, DSO (1896–1972).
16 'Most Secret Appreciation – German plan for attack on Crete', as quoted in Freyberg, *Bernard Freyberg*, p. 283. According to Paul Freyberg, this copy is probably the only one to survive; all others would have been destroyed.
17 Freyberg to APW, as quoted by Antony Beevor, 'Clash of views on battle of Crete', letter to *The Times*, 9 May 1991. See also Macdonald, *The Lost Battle*, p. 161.
18 See Freyberg, *Bernard Freyberg*, pp. 280–9. In *Ultra Goes to War* Lewin does not examine whether or not APW and Freyberg could have acted on Ultra intelligence without alternative sourcing. Instead he criticizes both men for getting 'the message but not the meaning': see pp. 158–60; see also Antony Beevor, *Crete*, p. 82 for his assessment that Freyberg was 'fixated' on a seaborne invasion. The British were already aware of the presence of German paratroopers in Greece because Hitler had ordered an attack on the bridge at Corinth: a redeployment to reinforce the Maleme airfield would not have been unexpected. But since the very existence of Ultra intelligence remained Classified Information until 1974, APW took his explanations to the grave.

19 Kennedy, *Business of War*, p. 120.

20 Freyberg to APW, 20 May 1941, as quoted in WSC, *Grand Alliance*, p. 254.

21 OL (Orange Leonard) 15/389: see Antony Beevor, *Crete*, pp. 156–8.

22 Dill as quoted in Kennedy, *Business of War*, p. 120.

23 Eden, Diary, 21 May 1941, AP 20/1/21 Avon papers, Univ. of Birmingham, as quoted in Raugh, *Wavell in the Middle East*, p. 219.

24 Maj.-Gen. Sir Edward Spears, KBE, MC (1886–1974).

25 WSC to APW, 21 May 1941, as quoted in WSC, *Grand Alliance*, p. 290. Kennedy believed APW should have refused to fight in Syria because it meant jeopardizing Operation Battleaxe in the Western Desert: *Business of War*, p. 122.

26 Dill to APW, as quoted in Connell, *Scholar and Soldier*, pp. 462–3.

27 Eric Dorman-Smith, John Connell fonds, McMU.

28 APW to WSC, 22 May 1941, CHAR 20/39/11–14 , CAC.

29 WSC to APW, 23 May 1941, CHAR 20/39/15, CAC.

30 APW to Dill, Most Secret Cipher, 12 May 1941, Auchinleck papers, *204*, MUL.

31 APW to Dill, Most Secret Cipher, 25 May 1941, Auchinleck papers, *230*, MUL.

32 Coats, *Of Generals and Gardens*, p. 108.

33 APW to WSC, 25 May 1941, CHAR 20/39/29, CAC.

34 EMW to Bernard Freyberg, while he was staying at C-in-C's house 31 May/1 June 1941, as quoted in Freyberg, *Bernard Freyberg*, p. 313.

35 WSC to Commanders-in-Chief, Middle East [via APW], 27 May 1941, CHAR 20/39/31, CAC.

36 APW to WSC, 27 May 1941, CHAR 20/39/33, CAC.

37 APW, 'Recollections', John Connell fonds, McMU.

38 Freyberg to APW, as quoted in Freyberg, *Bernard Freyberg*, pp. 311–12.

39 Freyberg as quoted in ibid., p. 313.

40 APW, personal, to Commanders of Formations which served in Crete, and Officers Commanding Units which served in Crete, GHQ, Middle East, June 1941, as quoted in APW, *Speaking Generally*, p. 24.

41 APW to Cunningham, 22 June 1941, as quoted in Cunningham, *A Sailor's Odyssey*, p. 64.

42 Lampson, Diary, as quoted in Beevor, *Crete*, p. 228.

43 WSC, *Grand Alliance*, p. 268.

44 Former Col. W. Gaul, 'Operation Merkur', US Navy restricted, John Wheeler-Bennett papers, Series B, St Antony's, Oxford.

45 Later Maj.-Gen. Arthur Guy Salisbury-Jones, CMG, CBE, MC (1896–1985). The members of the cttee were Cdr C. Wauchope, RN, Lt-Col. G.E.R. Bastin, and Wing-Cdr E.C. Hudleston, RAF.

46 APW to Under-Sec. of State, War Office, 19 Aug. 1941, WO 106/3126, NA.

47 APW, 'Recollections', as quoted in Connell, *Scholar and Soldier*, p. 429; Box 4, John Connell fonds, McMU.

48 WSC to APW, 28 May 1941, CHAR 20/39/36, CAC.

49 Kennedy, *Business of War*, p. 129.

50 WSC to APW, 4 June 1941, CHAR 20/39/73–75 , CAC. Gen. Sir Robert Haining, KCB, DSO (1882–1959).

51 APW to WSC, 5 June 1941, CHAR 20/39/81–83, CAC.

52 John Colville, 3 June 1941, *Fringes of Power*, p. 394.

53 Ibid., 25 May 1941, p. 391.

54 APW to Jackson, 5 June 1941, Wavell Album, BWRA 0335.

55 Eric Dorman-Smith to John Connell, 11 Sept. 1962, John Connell fonds, McMU.

56 APW to Dill, 6 June 1941, as quoted in John Connell letter to Ismay, 6 Sept. 1961, John Connell fonds, McMU.

57 WSC to APW, 9 June 1941, CHAR 20/39/104, CAC.

58 APW, 'Recollections', John Connell fonds, McMU.

59 WSC to APW 16 June 1941, CHAR 20/39/128, CAC. The third phase took place from 23 June–12 July, by which time APW had been replaced as C-in-C, Middle East.

60 APW to Leonie Lemartine, 11 June 1941, private collection.

61 Raugh, *Wavell in the Middle East*, p. 229.

62 Tedder, *With Prejudice*, p. 125.

63 *The Rommel Papers*, ed. BLH, p. 146.

64 Desmond Young, *Rommel*, p. 96.

65 Tedder, *With Prejudice*, p. 127.

66 APW to WSC, 21 June 1941, CHAR 20/40/34, CAC.

67 Coats, *Of Generals and Gardens*, p. 113. Coats's (or APW's) recollection of *Hamlet* is a little faulty. The correct quotation is, 'If it *be* not to come . . . yet it will come' (Act V, sc.iii).

68 WSC to APW 21 June 1941, CHAR 20/40/32, CAC.

69 John Connell to Ismay, 6 Sept. 1961, Ismay 4/9/38a, LHCMA.

70 Later Gen. Sir Alan Hartley, GCIE, KCSI, CB, DSO (1882–1954).

71 Dill to WSC, 21 June 1941, Box 4, John Connell fonds, McMU.

72 Linlithgow to WSC, 21 June 1941, CHAR 20/40/29, CAC.

73 APW to WSC, 22 June 1941, CAB 66/17/143, NA.

74 WSC to APW, 26 June 1941, CHAR 20/40/54–5, CAC.

75 WSC, *Grand Alliance*, p. 310.

76 WSC to APW, 1 July 1941, CHAR 20/40/90, CAC.

77 APW, 'Recollections', John Connell fonds, McMU.

78 Coats, *Of Generals and Gardens*, p. 117.

79 Later 1st Viscount Chandos, KG, PC, DSO, MC (1893–1972).

80 APW, 'Recollections', John Connell fonds, McMU.

81 Farewell Order, July 1941, as quoted in APW, *Speaking Generally*, p. 25.

82 *The Times*, 2 July 1941, LH 1/733, LHCMA.

83 BLH, 'Wavell', 8 May 1950, LH 10/1950/7a, LHCMA.

84 *The Goebbels Diaries*, 3 July 1941.

85 Dill to APW, 21 June 1941, as quoted in Connell, *Scholar and Soldier*, p 505.

86 Eric Dorman-Smith to John Connell, 29 Nov. 1961, John Connell fonds, McMU.

87 Marshall-Cornwall, *Wars and Rumours of Wars*, p. 189.

88 Gen. Sir Alan Cunningham to APW, 5 July 1941, Alan Cunningham papers, NAM.

89 Sandy Reid Scott, Diary, 4 July 1941, private collection; Capt. Alexander Reid Scott, MC (1918–60).

90 Bird, Letters Home, 5 July 1941, private collection. Tom Bird (b. 1918) later went to India as Wavell's ADC, 1943.

91 Col. Nial Charlton, TD (1910–82) to John Connell, 28 Jan. 1961, John Connell fonds, McMU.

92 General Arthur Smith, Family letter, 7 July 1941, private collection.

93 Ranfurly, *To War with Whitaker*, p. 99.

94 Ismay to Connell, 13 Sept. 1961, Ismay 4/9/39, LHCMA.

95 Alexander Clifford, *Three Against Rommel*, p. 106.

96 *News Chronicle*, 5 July 1941, LH 1/733, LHCMA.

97 APW, ibid.

98 Freya Stark, *East is West*, p. 130.

CHAPTER 13: CONFLICT OF THE HEMISPHERES, 1941

1 Lewin, *The Chief*, p. 147.

2 James Elroy Flecker (1884–1915), *Hassan*, Heinemann, 1922, p. 76.

3 Fergusson, *Portrait of a Soldier*, p. 62.

4 The pilot was Squadron-Leader Burberry, and the party also included 'a rather lugubrious' group-captain from Air HQ, India: Fergusson, *Portrait of a Soldier*, pp. 60, 62.

5 Ibid., p. 64.

6 APW to Leonie Lemartine, 27 July 1941, private collection.

7 Coats, *Of Generals and Gardens*, p. 120 and APW, 'Government Houses', *House and Gardens*, 1950.

8 Later Lt-Gen. Sir Thomas Hutton, KCIE, CB, MC (1890–1981).

9 Ivor Jehu, CIE (1908–1960). In Nov. 1944 he returned to writing for *The Times of India*.

10 This was *The Tiger Strikes*, Government of India, 1942.

11 Amery, 23 June 1941, *The Empire at Bay*, p. 695. He believed Auchinleck was 'the one person who inspired confidence from all classes of Indians.'

12 Fergusson, *Portrait of a Soldier*, p. 66. Fergusson spent only 6 weeks in India before returning to his battalion in the Middle East; he returned to Wavell's staff as a Joint Planner in April 1942.

13 Araminta, Lady Aldington to the author, Dec. 2004. The button was made by Asprey's, who had turned their factories to the production of necessary items as part of the war effort: Angus Robb, in charge of heritage at Asprey's, to the author, Jan. 2005.

14 Fergusson to Sir Alister McIntosh, 16 Sept. 1977, as quoted in Freyberg, *Bernard Freyberg*, p. 316.

15 APW to Under Sec. of State, War Office, 19 Aug. 1941, p. 1. WO 106/3126, NA. The report was withdrawn, mainly because of its leading references to Ultra intelligence. A second, 'anodyne' report was prepared under Brigadier Erskine. The Salisbury-Jones report was finally released in 1972 (available in the National Archives). See also Freyberg, pp. 316–18. Fergusson says APW read the report on the plane in early July, but on 19 Aug. APW says that he had only read it 'a few days ago'. I have accepted his more contemporary account. Dalton, 3 Aug. 1944, *The Political Diaries of Hugh Dalton, 1940–45*, as quoted in Freyberg, p. 281; later Lord Dalton, PC, MA (1887–1962).

16 Henry Hall, *Memoirs* [unpublished]. During the war the Indian army expanded to 1,800,000.

17 APW, as quoted in Fergusson, *Portrait of a Soldier*, p. 63.

18 Tedder, *With Prejudice*, p. 138.

19 Mohandas Karamchand Gandhi (1869–1948).

20 B.R. Tomlinson, *The Indian National Congress Party and the Raj*, Macmillan, 1976, p. 151.

21 Subhas Chandra Bose, educated at Cambridge (1895–1945); Gandhi admired his steadfast stand against the British; see Azad, *India Wins Freedom*, p. 40.

22 Mohammed Ali Jinnah (1875–1948).

23 After defeat by Mao Tse-Tung's Communist army in 1949/50 Chiang Kai-Shek fled to Formosa (Taiwan).

24 See Fred Alexander, *The Simon-Stimson Myth*, Univ. of Western Australia, 1954 for a discussion of the effect which the Japanese incursion into Manchuria had on Anglo-American relations.

25 APW's first broadcast, 13 Aug. 1941, private collection.

26 APW to Barbara Freyberg, 13 Aug. 1941, private collection.

27 APW to Dill, 21 Aug., 27 Aug. 1941, Auchinleck papers, *298 and 301*, MUL.

28 WSC to APW, 26 July 1941, CHAR 20/42A/15–16, CAC.

29 Later Gen. Sir Edward Quinan, KCB, KCIE, DSO, OBE (1885–1960).

30 WSC to APW, 30 Aug. 1941, CHAR 20/41/38, CAC.

31 WSC, *Grand Alliance*, p. 394.

32 APW to WSC, 27 Aug. 1941, CHAR 20/42A/21, CAC.

33 Reid Scott, *Diary* [unpublished], 3 Sept. 1941.

34 Fergusson, *Trumpet in the Hall*, pp. 122–3. Fergusson says that so far as he knew only two copies of Arthur Smith's special file were kept, one for 'the record' and the other for APW. See APW, 'Operations in the Middle East from 7th Feb. to 15th July 1941', Supplement to *London Gazette*, 3 July 1946.

35 Reid Scott, Diary, 5 Sept. 1941, private collection.
36 APW, 'Operations in Burma', Dec. 1941–May 1942, RLEW 4/2, CAC.
37 Joan Bright Astley, *The Inner Circle*, p. 66. Joan Bright (Mrs Philip Astley, OBE; b. 1910). Joan Bright's work developed into the compilation of extensive Special Information Centre files (now in the National Archives) and as Administrator of the 'Big Three' Conferences until the end of the war.
38 Joan Bright Astley to the author, Sept. 2003.
39 Astley, *The Inner Circle*, p. 71; see also APW to Joan Bright, 30 Sept. 1941, IWM.
40 APW to WSC, 20 (?) Sept. 1941; WSC to APW 19 Sept. 1941, CHAR 30/102, CAC.
41 APW to Joan Bright, 30 Sept. 1941, IWM. Their correspondence continued until 1946.
42 WSC to Beaverbrook, 21 Sept. 1941, as quoted in WSC, *Grand Alliance*, p. 431; William Maxwell Aitken, lst Baron Beaverbrook, PC (1879–1964).
43 APW to Joan Bright, 30 Sept. 1941, IWM.
44 Reid Scott, Diary, Oct. 1941.
45 Address and statements to the National Defence Council, as quoted in APW, *Speaking Generally*, pp. 84–100. In his address on 3 Dec. 1941 he outlined Japan's 'menacing attitude'.
46 Sir Miles Lampson, later Lord Killearn (cr. 1943), *Diaries*, as quoted in Coats, *Of Generals and Gardens*, p. 120.
47 Reid Scott, Diary, 15/16 Oct. 1941, private collection.
48 APW, 'Recollections', as quoted in Connell, *Supreme Commander*, p. 35.
49 Reid Scott, Diary, 15/16 Oct. 1941, private collection.
50 Tom Bird, Letters Home, 7 April 1943.
51 Reid Scott, Diary, 25 Oct. 1941.
52 Lt-Col. Sir John Herbert, GCIE, DL, JP (1880–1943).
53 APW as quoted in Connell, *Supreme Commander*, p. 41.
54 Air Chief Marshal Sir Robert Brooke-Popham, GCVO, KCB, CMG, DSO, AFC, KStJ (1878–1953).
55 Later Admiral Sir Geoffrey Layton, GBE, KCB, KCMG, DSO (1884–1964).
56 Sir (Thomas) Shenton Thomas, GCMG, OBE, KStJ (1879–1962).
57 Later Lt-Gen. Arthur Percival, CB, DSO, OBE, MC (1887–1966).
58 From an Australian newspaper, as quoted in Costello, *Pacific War*, p. 107. With the exception of one of the 15-inch guns in the Johore battery, these guns had an arc of fire of 360 degrees. They were silenced by aerial bombing and lack of ammunition. To talk of the guns 'facing the wrong way round' is 'nonsense': John Terraine, *Daily Telegraph* 1 Feb. 1982. However, it was never expected that the guns would have to fire landwards. See also Ch. 14 pp. 235–6 and n. 34.
59 Costello, *The Pacific War*, p. 107.
60 Kinvig, *Scapegoat*, pp. 107–8.
61 Coats, *Of Generals and Gardens*, p. 132.

62 Ibid., p. 133.

63 APW to Auchinleck, as quoted in Connell, *Supreme Commander*, p. 41.

64 APW to Dill, 11 Nov. 1941, IOR L/WS/1/846, OIOC, BL; see also Lewin, RLEW 4/2 CAC.

65 Dill had just remarried after the death of his first wife in Dec. 1940; WSC later changed his mind and appointed him Head of the Joint Staff Mission in Washington (a role he ably filled during some of the most contentious discussions between the US and the UK over the conduct of the war).

66 Later Lt-Gen. Sir Henry Pownall, KCB, KBE, DSO, MC (1887–1961).

67 WSC, Lord Mayor's luncheon, 10 Nov. 1941, private collection.

68 Reid Scott, Diary, 11 Nov 1941, private collection.

69 APW to Joan Bright, 30 Nov. 1941, IWM.

70 Coats, *Of Generals and Gardens*, p. 139.

71 APW to Joan Bright, 29/30 Nov. 1941, IWM.

72 Coats, *Of Generals and Gardens*, p. 140. Lady Mary was the daughter of the Earl of Ilchester; her brother, the Hon. John Fox-Strangways, was a POW in Italy.

73 WSC's formal announcement in the House of Commons came at 3 p.m. on 8 Dec. 1941 – two hours before Roosevelt's, in fact.

74 WSC to APW 12 Dec. 1942, as quoted in *The Grand Alliance*, p. 564.

75 Woollcombe, *The Campaigns of Wavell*, p. 158.

76 Pownall, *Diaries*, 20 Dec. 1941.

77 Lt-Gen. Sir Kenneth McLeod, KCIE, CB, DSO, DL (1885–1958).

78 APW, Supplement to the *London Gazette*, 11 March 1948, p. 1669.

79 Chiang Kai-Shek's 3rd wife, Soong Mei-Ling, and her two sisters, married to men who alternately held the office of prime minister, foreign minister and finance minister, were part of an influential clique opposed to the Communist faction led by Mao Tse-Tung.

80 Later Maj.-Gen. Claire Chennault (1890–1958). In 1937 he had resigned from the US army and become aviation adviser to China in its war against Japan. Organized volunteer American aviators into a corps known as 'Flying Tigers'; recalled to the US army in 1942, given command of China Air Task Force.

81 APW, 'Recollections', as quoted in Connell, *Supreme Commander*, p. 62.

82 *The Stilwell Papers*, p. 44.

83 APW, 'Operations in Burma, Dec. 1941–May 1942', RLEW 4/2, CAC. APW also pointed out that the Chinese troops moved so slowly that they would not have helped the situation, but admitted that it would have saved such criticism if he had 'wholeheartedly' accepted the offer.

84 Reid Scott, Diary, 24 Dec. 1941.

85 *The Times*, 1 Jan. 1942.

86 APW, 'Recollections', as quoted in Connell, *Supreme Commander*, p. 66.

87 Dorman-Smith, 22 Dec. 1941 Unpublished memoirs, Dorman-Smith Collection, MSS EUR E215/32b OIOC, BL.

CHAPTER 14: SUPREME COMMANDER, 1942

1 WSC, *The Grand Alliance*, p. 600.
2 Ibid., p. 597.
3 Alanbrooke, *War Diaries*, p. 216.
4 WSC to Lord Privy Seal to transmit to APW, 29 Dec. 1941, as quoted in *The Grand Alliance*, p. 600.
5 Coats, *Of Generals and Gardens*, p.146.
6 Reid Scott, Diary, 2/3 Jan. 1942; APW to Joan Bright, 4 Jan. 1942, IWM.
7 Reid Scott, Diary, 30 Dec. 1941.
8 WSC to Lord Privy Seal, 3 Jan. 1942, as quoted in *The Grand Alliance*, p. 607.
9 Broadcast by APW, 1 Jan. 1942, private collection.
10 Connell, *Supreme Commander*, p. 76.
11 WSC, *The Grand Alliance*, p. 544; WSC to Duff Cooper, 6 Jan. 1942, as quoted in Connell, *Supreme Commander*, p. 79. Rt Hon. Sir (Alfred) Duff Cooper, later 1st Viscount Norwich, PC, GCMG, DSO (1890–1954).
12 Duff Cooper to WSC and Secretary of State for Colonies, Lord Moyne, as quoted in Lewin, *The Chief*, p. 164.
13 APW to Brooke, 1 June 1942, Report on the Malaya campaign, WO 106/2564A.
14 Lt-Gen. Sir Lewis Heath, KBE, CB, CIE, DSO, MC (1885–1954).
15 Later Lt-Gen. Henry Gordon Bennett, CB, CMG, DSO, VD (1887–1962).
16 Percival, *The War in Malaya*, p.210. Later he wrote more critically that Wavell's plan was 'not his plan': see *Sixty Years On*, ed. Farrell and Hunter. See also Kinvig, *Scapegoat*, p. 127 on Percival's misgivings about Bennett. Percival also had strained relations with Heath.
17 APW to Chiefs of Staff, 8 Jan. 1942, as quoted in Connell, *Supreme Commander*, p. 85.
18 Gen. Sir Alan Hartley, GCIE, KCSI, CB, DSO (1882–1954).
19 Air Chief Marshal Sir Richard Peirse, KCB, DSO, AFC (1892–1970).
20 APW to Mary Peckitt, 1 Feb. 1942, IWM.
21 Reid Scott, Diary, 10 Jan. 1942, private collection.
22 Pownall, 13 Jan. 1942, *Diaries*, p. 76.
23 APW, 'Operations in Burma', RLEW 4/2, CAC.
24 Reid Scott, Diary, 13 Jan. 1942, private collection.
25 APW to Chiefs of Staff, 14 Jan. 1942, as quoted in Connell, *Supreme Commander*, p. 95. As Lt-Gen. Yamashita's diary later revealed, at the Battle of Muar, 'the most savage of the campaign', the Australian infantry battalions delayed the Japanese advance for five days: MSS1450, AWM.
26 Later General of the Army Douglas MacArthur, Hon. GCB (1880–1964).
27 APW to Combined Chiefs of Staff, 15 Jan. 1942, as quoted in Connell, *Supreme Commander*, p. 99.
28 Kennedy, *Business of War*, p. 196.

29 APW to WSC, 16 Jan. 1942, as quoted in WSC, *The Hinge of Fate*, p. 42.

30 WSC, *The Hinge of Fate*, p. 43.

31 Percival, as quoted in Kinvig, *Scapegoat*, p. 197.

32 Kennedy, *Business of War*, p. 196.

33 APW to Percival, 19 Jan. 1942, as quoted in Kirby, *War Against Japan*, p. 316.

34 APW to WSC, 19 Jan. 1942, as quoted in *The Hinge of Fate*, pp. 47–8. In a footnote Churchill also notes that Wavell's comment regarding the guns only firing seawards was inaccurate.

35 APW, 'Recollections', as quoted in Connell, *Supreme Commander*, p. 106.

36 WSC to APW, 20 Jan. 1942, as quoted in *The Hinge of Fate*, pp. 46–7; see also WSC to APW, 19 Jan. 1942, CHAR 20/68B/124, CAC.

37 Kirby, *War Against Japan*, pp. 318–19 and Woollcombe, *Campaigns of Wavell*, p. 188. In *The War in Malaya*, p. 261, Percival wrote that everything pointed to the attack developing from the west, but in a letter to Maj.-Gen. Stanley Kirby he says that this assertion was incorrect and based on hindsight. See also Louis Allen, *Singapore*, pp. 162–3, and Kinvig, *Scapegoat*, p. 198: 'The issue is not nearly as clear-cut as this "Wavell was right, Percival was wrong" interpretation would suggest.'

38 APW, Note to Percival, as quoted in Connell, *Supreme Commander*, p. 114.

39 Capt. R.A Baron Mackay, Memoirs, 'A Dutchman at ABDA and British Headquarters', 99/19/1, IWM.

40 Reid Scott, Diary, 15 Jan. 1942, private collection.

41 APW to BLH, 23 Jan. 1942, LH 1/733, LHCMA. *The Strategy of Indirect Approach* was first published in 1929 and revised in 1946. It is not clear why BLH sent it to APW just at this time.

42 Hutton, Personal Record, Rangoon 1940–1, RLEW 4/5, CAC.

43 Later Brig. Rt Hon. Sir John Smyth, VC, MC, PC (1893–1983).

44 APW to Gen. Hutton and Air Vice Marshal Stevenson, 21 Jan. 1942, as quoted in Connell, *Supreme Commander*, p. 115.

45 APW to Gen MacArthur, 21 Jan. 1942, ibid., p. 118.

46 Reid Scott, Diary, 23 Jan. 1942, private collection.

47 Ibid., 24 Jan. 1942.

48 Hutton later took issue with Connell's statement, *Supreme Commander*, p. 121: 'Hutton told Smyth to get the main body of his Division back to the Sittang River as quickly as he could and to hold Moulmein with one Brigade in order to deny it to the enemy as long as possible', stating that: 'It surely should have been obvious that had I issued any such orders I should quite rightly have been relieved of my command as soon as Wavell arrived later the same day!' Hutton to Editor, *Times Literary Supplement*, 2 Oct. 1969, RLEW 4/5, CAC.

49 WSC to APW, 23 Jan. 1942, *The Hinge of Fate*, p. 119–20.

50 APW to WSC, 26 Jan. 1942, ibid., p. 120.

51 WSC to APW, 28 Jan. 1942, ibid.

52 WSC, *The Hinge of Fate*, p. 49.

53 Curtin to WSC, 23 Jan. 1942, ibid., p. 51.

54 WSC, ibid., pp. 51–2. APW was later criticized for not diverting the 18th British to Burma, but it is clear the decision was WSC's.

55 Combined Chiefs of Staff to APW, 24 Jan. 1942, as quoted in Connell, *Supreme Commander*, p. 124. A further proposal for the whole of Australia to come under ABDA did not materialize.

56 Bruce M. Cooper, 'Archie Wavell – Portrait of a Soldier', BBC Broadcast, 19 March 1967, David Walker papers, NB.

57 APW to AJW as quoted in Connell, *Supreme Commander*, p. 126.

58 APW, despatch on SW Operations, as quoted in Woollcombe, *Campaigns*, p. 181.

59 Percival to APW, 28 Jan. 1942, as quoted in Connell, *Supreme Commander*, p. 127.

60 APW to Percival as quoted in ibid., p. 128.

61 Reid Scott, Diary, 3 Feb. 1942, private collection.

62 Ibid., 5/6 Feb 1942.

63 Ibid., 7 Feb 1942.

64 Ibid., 10/11 Feb 1942.

65 Dorman-Smith Unpublished Memoirs, Dorman-Smith collection, MSS EUR E215/32b, OIOC, BL.

66 Lady Dorman-Smith, Diary, March 1942, Dorman-Smith collection, MSS EUR E215, OIOC, BL.

67 Dorman-Smith to John Connell, 17 Nov. 1964, John Connell fonds, McMU.

68 Miss Gibbs was perhaps the sister of Air Vice Marshal Sir Gerald Gibbs, CIE, CBE, MC, Senior Air Staff Officer, HQ, 3rd Tactical Air Force, South-East Asia, 1943–4: see Dorman-Smith, Unpublished Memoirs, Dorman-Smith collection, MSS EUR E215/32b, OIOC, BL.

69 James Lunt, *A Hell of a Licking*, p. 123.

70 Smyth, *Milestones*, p. 176.

71 Lunt, *A Hell of a Licking*, p. 154.

72 See *Sixty Years On*, ed. Farrell and Hunter: 'The C in C's opinion, like Percival's own, was no more than a preliminary judgement which neither commander was able to back with strong intelligence': p. 257. Brig. James Percival to the author: 'Whether the Japanese had attacked from the NW or the NE the result would not have been much different', May 2005.

73 APW, Report on Malaya Campaign, WO 106/2574A, NA.

74 Water (15 million gallons a day) also came from south Johore, which was already in Japanese hands.

75 Percival, *The War in Malaya*, p. 275.

76 APW to Lt-Gen. Sir Iven Mackay, 10 Oct. 1944, Papers of Lt-Gen. Sir Iven Mackay, 3DRL 6433 – Item 11, AWM, Canberra.

77 Percival, *The War in Malaya*, p. 275.

78 WSC to APW, 10 Feb. 1942, as quoted in *The Hinge of Fate*, p. 87. APW corrected WSC, saying that Percival did not have quite the number of troops WSC estimated, but that he had 'quite enough to deal with enemy who have landed if the troops can be made to act with sufficient vigour and determination': APW to WSC, 11 Feb. 1942, p. 88. The figure traditionally given is 85,000. Lt-Col Denis Russell-Roberts, 5/11 Sikh Regiment, called this 'the world's most misleading figure' and suggested that 22,000 fighting infantry was more realistic: letter to the *Daily Telegraph*, 2 Feb. 1982.

79 APW, 'Last Order', WO 106/2593, NA.

80 Percival as quoted in *Scapegoat*, p. 210.

81 Percival, *The War in Malaya*, p. 278.

82 Mackay, Memoirs, 99/19/1, IWM.

83 APW to Leonie Lemartine, 18 Feb. 1942, private collection. According to *The Stilwell Papers*, APW had also been wounded in Java, but it was kept a secret from the press. 'Lady Hartley let it out': p. 66.

84 APW to WSC, as quoted in *The Hinge of Fate*, p. 88.

85 Percival to APW, 13 Feb. 1942, as quoted in ibid., p. 91.

86 APW to WSC, 14 Feb. 1942, as quoted in ibid., pp. 91–2.

87 APW to Percival 15 Feb. 1942, as quoted in ibid., p. 94 and Percival, *The War in Malaya*, p. 292. Percival writes that this telegram was 'the only thing to cheer our gloom'.

88 Percival to APW, 15 Feb. 1942, as quoted in Connell, *Supreme Commander*, p. 168.

89 APW, Report on Malaya campaign, WO 106/2574A, NA.

90 See M.R.D. Foot and J.M. Langley, *MI9*, p. 278. The expression 'to do a Gordon Bennett' – i.e., to run away' – is still current.

91 WSC, *The Hinge of Fate*, p. 81. The hyperbole masks the fact that once the *Prince of Wales* and *Repulse* had been sunk, Singapore had lost its use as a port for a Far Eastern fleet. Bereft of fighter aircraft, Singapore was doomed once the inadequate defences in northern Malaya had been breached. See also Louis Allen, *Singapore*, p. 1.

92 APW to Lt-Gen. Sir Iven Mackay, 10 Oct. 1944, Mackay papers, 3DRL 6433– Item 11, AWM.

93 APW, Report on Malaya Campaign, WO 106/2574A, NA.

94 Percival, *The War in Malaya*, p. 306.

95 Percival, as quoted in Louis Allen, *Singapore*, p. 201.

96 APW to Brooke, 20 Jan. 1943, 'Report on Evacuation from Singapore across Sumatra Feb–March 1942', WO 141/100, NA.

97 'Report on Evacuation', WO 141/100 NA. See also Hank Nelson, Fall of Singapore controversy, MSS 1450, AWM.

98 APW to WSC, 16 Feb. 1942, as quoted in Connell, *Supreme Commander*, p. 172.

99 Hutton to Editor, *Times Literary Supplement*, 2 Oct. 1969, RLEW 4/5, CAC.

100 APW to Hutton, 17 Feb. 1942, as quoted in Connell, *Supreme Commander*, p. 181.

101 APW to Joan Bright, 17 Feb. 1942, IWM.

102 Linlithgow to WSC, as quoted in *Supreme Commander*, p. 181.

103 Later Field Marshal Harold Alexander, 1st Viscount Alexander of Tunis, KG, GCB, GCMG, CSI, DSO, MC (1891–1969).

104 APW to WSC and Brooke, 18 Feb. 1942, as quoted in *Supreme Commander*, p. 182.

105 Hutton, Personal Record, Rangoon 1940–41, RLEW 4/5, CAC.

106 Combined Chiefs of Staff to APW, 18 Feb. 1942, as quoted in *Supreme Commander*, p. 182.

107 Reid Scott, Diary, 17 Feb. 1942, private collection.

108 Ibid.

109 APW to Leonie Lemartine, 18 Feb. 1942, private collection.

110 APW to Joan Bright, 20 Feb. 1942, IWM.

111 Reid Scott, Diary, 21 Feb. 1942, private collection.

112 APW to WSC, 21 Feb. 1942, *The Hinge of Fate*, p. 127–8.

113 WSC to APW, 22 Feb. 1942, ibid., p. 128.

114 APW to Rt Hon. Mr Curtin, PM of Australia, 21 Feb. 1942, RLEW 4/12, CAC.

115 See Connell, *Supreme Commander*, p. 186.

116 Smyth, *Milestones*, p. 183.

117 APW, 'Recollections', as quoted in *Supreme Commander*, p. 189.

118 Dudley Robinson to the author, 9 Feb. 2005. He was with '153 Maintenance unit', servicing Brewster Buffalo monoplanes in Kuala Lumpur. Evacuated from Malaya to Java, he later became a POW in Sourabaya, Bandung and Changi.

119 Reid Scott, Diary, 25 Feb. 1942, private collection.

120 Ibid., 26 Feb. 1942.

121 Dorman-Smith to Linlithgow, 27 Feb. 1942, as quoted in Connell, *Supreme Commander*, p. 202. See also Dorman-Smith, unpublished Memoirs, Dorman-Smith Collection, MSS EUR E215/32, for policy of 'immobilizing' everything which might give pleasure to a 'Nip' officer.

122 Reid Scott, Diary, 27 Feb. 1942, private collection.

123 APW to Joan Bright, 20 Feb. 1942, IWM.

124 BLH to APW, 3 March 1942, LH 1/733, LHCMA.

125 Pownall, *Diaries*, p. 94.

126 WSC to APW, 5 March 1942, CHAR 20/71A/52, CAC.

127 APW to Joan Bright, 20 Feb. 1942, IWM.

CHAPTER 15: ADVERSITY'S GENERAL, 1942

1 Lt. Gen. Sir Thomas Hutton, Personal Record, Rangoon 1941–42, RLEW 4/5, CAC. 'Alex' is Alexander.
2 Air Vice-Marshal Donald Stevenson, CB, CBE, DSO, MC (1895–1964).
3 Hutton, Personal Record, Rangoon 1941–42, RLEW 4/5, CAC.
4 APW to Chiefs of Staff, 1 March 1942, as quoted in Connell, *Supreme Commander*, p. 203.
5 Coats, *Of Generals and Gardens*, pp. 152–3.
6 APW to Brooke, 1 March 1942, as quoted in Connell, *Supreme Commander*, p. 204. Maj.-Gen. David Cowan, CB, CBE, DSO, MC (1896–1983).
7 Smyth, *Milestones*, p. 201.
8 APW to Hutton, 3 March 1942, as quoted in Connell, *Supreme Commander*, p. 204.
9 Smyth, *Milestones*, p. 202.
10 After this incident, Smyth says he never spoke to APW again. In 1943 APW sought to have Smyth's rank of Maj.-Gen. restored; regulations prevented it, but he was made an honorary Brigadier. After entering politics in 1945, Smyth said the rank of Major-General would have been an embarrassment. His sad memories of Burma were compounded by the death of his eldest son at Kohima in 1944, aged 22. See *Milestones*, pp. 203–7.
11 APW, as quoted in Connell, *Supreme Commander*, p. 205.
12 APW to Chiefs of Staff, 7 March 1942, as quoted in Connell, *Supreme Commander*, pp. 215–16.
13 APW to Alexander, 11 March 1942 as quoted in Connell, *Supreme Commander*, p. 209.
14 APW, 'Operations in Burma', December 1941–May 1942, Despatch by Field Marshal Lord Wavell, RLEW 4/2, CAC, later published in *The London Gazette*, 11 March 1948, p. 1672, NAM. The Burma Army comprised mainly Indian units with some local Burmese units, e.g. Burma Rifles.
15 Hutton, Personal Record, Rangoon 1941–2, RLEW 4/5, CAC. See also Philip Mason, *Matter of Honour*, pp. 190–1.
16 Joseph P. Stilwell (1883–1946) *The Stilwell Papers*, 1 March 1942, letter to Mrs Stilwell p. 68.
17 See Robert Lyman, *Slim: Master of War*, p. 267 for discussion of why Slim thought he was going to be asked to be CGS to Alexander.
18 As reported by Slim in *Defeat into Victory*, p. 31. See also *Churchill's Generals*, ed. John Keegan, 'Slim' by Duncan Anderson, for a discussion of the Alexander/Slim relationship, p. 310.
19 APW to Joan Bright, 26 March 1942, IWM. The marriage was a success and lasted more than 57 years, until Francis's death in 1999; Lady Pamela died in 2001.

20 Celia Johnson (1908–82), m. Peter Fleming (1907–71) in 1935. She later starred with Trevor Howard in *Brief Encounter*.

21 Peter Fleming to Celia Johnson, 18 March 1942, private collection.

22 Ibid., 28 March 1942.

23 Duff Hart-Davis, *Peter Fleming*, p. 264.

24 Rt Hon. Sir Stafford Cripps, PC, FRS, KC, JP, MP (1889–1952).

25 Maulana Abul Kalam Azad (1888–1958); Jawaharlal Nehru (1889–1964).

26 Gandhi, as related to his biographer Louis Fisher. Contrary to popular belief, Gandhi did not call Cripps's offer 'a post-dated cheque on a failing bank'. In Sitaramayya's official *History of the Congress*, *Roy's Weekly* (Delhi) first used the expression 'a post-dated cheque on a crashing bank': S.M. Burke and Salim Al-Din Quraishi, *The British Raj in India*, OUP, 2000, p. 370.

27 Declaration, para (e), as quoted in Eric Estorick, *Stafford Cripps*, p. 307 and Burke and Quraishi, *The British Raj in India*, p. 365.

28 Congress resolution, 2 April 1942, as quoted in Burke and Quraishi, *The British Raj in India*, p. 370.

29 It is beyond the scope of this biography to analyse Johnson's precise role. For more detail, see Peter Clarke, *The Cripps Version*, p. 315.

30 Coats, *Of Generals and Gardens*, p. 158.

31 Alanbrooke, *War Diaries*, 24 April 1942, p. 252.

32 Azad, *India Wins Freedom*, p. 70.

33 Mason, *A Shaft of Sunlight*, p. 167.

34 Fergusson, *Portrait of a Soldier*, p. 74.

35 Ibid.

36 WSC to APW, 18 Apr. 1942, *The Hinge of Fate*, p. 163–4.

37 APW to Chiefs of Staff, 12 Apr. 1942, ibid., p. 165.

38 WSC to Alexander and Pound minute M 186/2, 15 May 1942, Adm. 199/1935, as quoted in Roskill, *Churchill and the Admirals*, p. 205.

39 Somerville to Joan Bright, 26 April 1942, IWM.

40 APW to WSC, 5 March 1942, CHAR 20/71A/66, CAC.

41 Reid Scott, Diary, 23 April 1942, private collection.

42 Broadcast by C-in-C from Delhi, Tuesday 21 April 1942, private collection.

43 APW to Joan Bright, 29 April 1942, IWM.

44 Reid Scott, Diary, 17 April 1942, private collection.

45 Fergusson, *Portrait of a Soldier*, p. 75.

46 Reid Scott, Diary, 30 April 1942, private collection.

47 Duff Hart-Davis, *Peter Fleming*, pp. 266–9.

48 Wavell Notes from files made available to Ronald Lewin by General Sir David Fraser, 3 Feb. 1979, RLEW 4/12, CAC; Connell, *Supreme Commander*, p. 213.

49 Peter Fleming, 1944, private collection.

50 APW to Fleming, 30 Aug. 1944, private collection.

51 APW's Foreword to Charles Rolo, *Wingate's Raiders*. See also Connell, *Supreme Commander*, p. 203; Alexander, *Memoirs*, p. 91 and Sykes, *Orde Wingate*, p. 359.

52 Wingate misunderstood 'Chinthe' as 'Chindit', which was adopted before the error was realized.

53 Lt Tim Llewellen Palmer, as quoted in Connell, *Supreme Commander*, p. 226; Cdr of 'A' squadron, 7th Hussars, Acting Capt. from May 1941.

54 Reid Scott, Diary, 10 May 1942, private collection.

55 APW to Joan Bright, 20/22 May 1942, IWM.

56 Ibid.

57 Slim, *Defeat into Victory*, p. 116.

58 APW, Message, *Speaking Generally*, May 1942, p. 61.

59 APW to WSC, Most Immediate, 22 May 1942, Winterton collection, 02/54/1, IWM.

60 APW, Operation Despatches, WO 106/2666, NA.

61 APW to Joan Bright, 1 June 1942, IWM.

62 Philip Mason, *A Matter of Honour*, p. 494; Philip Mason, CIE, OBE (1906–99).

63 Coats, *Of Generals and Gardens*, p. 172.

64 Ibid., p. 164.

65 Reid Scott, Diary, 17 July 1942, private collection.

66 Ibid., 19 July 1942.

67 APW to Joan Bright, 23 July 1942, IWM.

68 APW to Padre Joseph McKew, 9 July 1942, John Connell fonds, McMU; McKew had been Chaplain at Aldershot, 1934–7.

69 APW to Joan Bright, 2 Aug. 1942, IWM. See Coats, *Of Generals and Gardens*, pp. 167–8 for his account.

70 APW to Joan Bright, 2 Aug. 1942, IWM.

71 Alanbrooke, *War Diaries*, 3 Aug. 1942, p. 290.

72 A German plane, driven out of high altitude in combat, came across the slow transport plane in which Gott was travelling and shot it down in flames: see Alanbrooke, *War Diaries*, 7 Aug. 1942, p. 295.

73 APW to Joan Bright, 9 Aug. 1942, IWM.

74 Reid Scott, Diary, 2/3 Aug 1942, private collection.

75 As quoted by Rt Hon. Sir Alexander Cadogan, PC, GCMG, KCB (1884–1968); Cadogan, *Diaries*, p. 470.

76 Tedder, *With Prejudice*, p. 329.

77 Vyacheslav Molotov (1890–1986) was also present.

78 APW to Joan Bright, 21 Aug. 1942, IWM.

79 Alanbrooke, *War Diaries*, 14 Aug. 1942, p. 301.

80 WSC, *The Hinge of Fate*, p. 444.

81 'Ballade of the Second Front', 16 Aug. 1942, Wavell Poems, private collection. APW also sent this poem in his letter to Joan Bright, 21 Aug. 1942; see also Alanbrooke, *War Diaries*, 16 Aug. 1942, p. 307, and Cadogan, *Diaries*, 15 Aug. 1942, p. 474.

82 Alanbrooke, *War Diaries*, 18 Aug. 1942, p. 308.

83 APW to Joan Bright, 21 Aug. 1942, IWM.

84 APW to WSC, 20 Aug. 1942, WO 259/66, NA. APW had always been senior to Gort until Hore-Belisha appointed Gort CIGS (in preference to APW).

85 Rt Hon. Sir (Percy) James Grigg, PC, KCB, KCSI (1890–1964), appointed Secretary of State for War, Feb. 1942.

86 Grigg to WSC, 1 Sept. 1942, WO 259/66, NA.

87 Ibid., 15 Sept. 1942.

88 WSC to Grigg, 16 Sept. 1942, WO 259/66, NA.

89 APW, Broadcast, 3 Sept. 1942, *Speaking Generally*, p. 62. APW later said that he got a rocket from WSC for this broadcast because the PM wanted to issue orders that no C-in-C should broadcast without his sanction, and found he had no control over C-in-C India: APW to Joan Bright, 23 Dec. 1942, IWM.

90 Reid Scott, Diary, 2–3 Aug. 1942, private collection.

91 Burke and Quraishi, *The British Raj in India*, p. 388.

92 APW to Gen. Sir Henry Jackson, 19 Nov. 1942, Wavell Album, BWRA 0335.

93 See Coats, *Of Gardens and Generals*, p. 164, although he says that his suggestion was for a speech given by APW in the summer.

94 APW address to the National Defence Council, 9 Sept. 1942, *Speaking Generally*, pp. 129–30.

95 Private information to the author; see Coats, *Of Generals and Gardens*, p. 182.

96 Later General Sir Edwin Morris, KCB, OBE, MC (1889–1970), Chief of the General Staff, India 1942–4.

97 APW to Morris, 17 Sept. 1942, as quoted in Connell, *Supreme Commander*, p. 239.

98 Alanbrooke, *War Diaries*, 30 Sept. 1942, p. 325.

99 APW to Joan Bright, 28 Sept. 1942, IWM.

100 APW to WSC, WO 259/66, NA.

101 Coats, *Of Generals and Gardens*, p. 183. According to Coats, AJW not APW told him about the request.

102 Ibid., p. 182.

103 Lt-Gen. Noel Irwin, CB, DSO, MC (1892–1972).

104 Maj.-Gen. Wilfrid Lewis Lloyd, CBE, DSO, MC (1896–1944).

105 Reid Scott, Diary, 23 Sept 1942, private collection.

106 *The Stilwell Papers*, 17 Oct. 1942, p. 162.

107 *The Times*, 23 and 24 Oct. 1942, LH 1/733, LHCMA.

108 BLH, *The Times*, 3 Nov. 1942.

109 Robert Graves (1895–1985); *Count Belisarius* (1938) was awarded the Stock Prize in 1938; see LH 1/733, LHCMA.

110 APW to Joan Bright, 3 Nov 1942, IWM. In his memoirs Peter Coats says the anthology was his idea. 'When soon after our arrival in India, I suggested that he should compile an anthology, he rather scouted the suggestion, saying something about being too busy fighting the war to bother about anthologies. But that was not the end of it' (pp. 168–9). Ronald Lewin, *The Chief*,

says that Wavell was inspired to compile the anthology by AJW and Peter Fleming (p. 243).

111 APW to Joan Bright, 15 Nov. 1942, IWM.

112 *The Stilwell Papers*, p. 168.

113 APW to Joan Bright, Christmas Day 1942, IWM. The verse is correctly quoted in *Other Men's Flowers*, p. 61 as 'three with a new song's measure, Can'.

114 Flecker, *Hassan*, p. 86. Taprobane was the ancient name for Sri Lanka (Ceylon).

CHAPTER 16: FIELD MARSHAL, 1943

1 A Field Marshal is presented by his Sovereign with a magnificent baton covered in red velvet and surmounted by a gold figure of St George slaying the dragon, as a symbol of his authority, so rarely used even ceremonially that no one was sure how it should be carried: *Journal of the Society for Army Historical Research*, Vol. 38, 1960, p. 84. APW was presented his baton on 14 May 1943, in England.

2 'Ode to a Field Marshal', written by APW in response to Miss Ruby Hill's apology. Wavell Poems, private collection. Also quoted in Connell, *Supreme Commander*, p. 265.

3 Rupert Hart-Davis (1907–99).

4 Rupert Hart-Davis to Jonathan Cape, 22 April 1943, Jonathan Cape papers, as quoted in Ziegler, *Rupert Hart-Davis*. By 1979 *Other Men's Flowers* had sold 119,898 copies plus 8,000 for the Book Society: see Lewin, *The Chief*, p. 245.

5 Lewis Namier, FRA, MA (1888–1960), Professor of Modern History, Manchester since 1931. A Russian by birth, Namier was a naturalized British citizen.

6 Carola Oman (Lady Lenanton, 1897–1978).

7 APW to Joan Bright, 28 Jan. 1943, IWM.

8 APW to Chiefs of Staff, 10 Feb. 1943. A further meeting was held in Calcutta on 9 Feb. 1943 when Chinese Generals Ho and T.V. Soong were present. As quoted in Connell, *Supreme Commander*, p. 266.

9 See Judith M. Brown, *Gandhi*, pp. 341–2, for a detailed discussion of his fast.

10 APW to Stephen Phillimore, 7 Feb. 1943, private collection.

11 APW, as quoted in Christopher Sykes, *Orde Wingate*, p. 385.

12 APW, as quoted in Connell, *Supreme Commander*, p. 258.

13 Sykes, *Orde Wingate*, p. 386.

14 APW to Gen. Sir Henry Jackson, 7 Feb. 1943, Wavell Album, BWRA 0335.

15 APW to Leonie Lemartine, 3 Feb. 1943, private collection.

16 Dill to Brooke, 12 Feb. 1942, Wavell Notes from files made available by Gen. Sir David Fraser to Ronald Lewin, 3 Feb. 1979, RLEW 4/12, CAC.

17 APW to Col. Reid Scott, 20 Feb. 1943, private collection.

18 Reid Scott, Diary, April 1947, private collection.

19 APW to Private Florin, *Daily Telegraph* 28 Dec. 1942, LH 1/733, LHCMA. In fact, both men had lost their left eye. Verses repeated to the author by Mrs Jean Wright, sister of Sandy Reid Scott.

20 Tom Bird, Diary, 12 Feb. 1943, private collection. At this stage Peter Coats was Private Secretary, Simon Astley ADC and Tom Bird ADC/Comptroller.

21 Ibid., Feb. 1943.

22 Ibid., 14 March 1943.

23 Bird, Letters Home, 17 Feb. 1943, private collection.

24 Tom Bird, 'Recollections', p. 80, private collection.

25 Bird, Letters Home, 16 March 1943, private collection.

26 John Beverley Nichols (1898–1983); known for his unorthodox views.

27 Freya Stark to Nigel Clive, 13 Feb. 1943, *Letters*, IV, p. 270.

28 Mrs T.A. Bird to the author, 1999.

29 Tom Bird, Diary, 22 March 1943; Peirse later married Jessie Auchinleck.

30 Coats, *Of Generals and Gardens*, p. 186.

31 Somerville to Joan Bright, 7 March 1943, IWM.

32 Ibid., 4 April 1943.

33 Fergusson, *Portrait of a Soldier*, p. 77.

34 APW to BLH, 14 March 1943, LHCMA.

35 BLH to APW, 16 April 1943, LHCMA.

36 APW to AJW, 24 March 1943 and AJW to APW, private collection.

37 Tom Bird, Diary, 5 March 1943, private collection.

38 APW to Joan Bright, 24 March 1943, IWM.

39 Peter Fleming to Celia Johnson, 18 March 1943, private collection.

40 APW, 23 March 1943, Wavell Poems, private collection, also quoted in Coats, p. 180 ('Oh it's fun . . .') and sent to Joan Bright, 8 April 1943, IWM.

41 APW to Joan Bright, 14 March 1943, IWM.

42 WSC, *Closing the Ring*, p. 70.

43 Fergusson, *Portrait of a Soldier*, p. 77.

44 Tom Bird, 'Recollections', private collection.

45 APW to Joan Bright, 8 April 1943, IWM.

46 Ibid., 24 March 1943.

47 APW, Address to the National Defence Council, 14 April 1943, *Speaking Generally*, pp. 159–60.

48 Channon, *Diaries*, 23 April 1943, p. 355. Coats says he tried to keep his two lives apart, and makes it appear that it was some time before APW set foot in Belgrave Square: see *Of Generals and Gardens*, p. 196. Channon's account seems more reliable, since Wavell reached England on 22 April and Good Friday was the following day.

49 Viscount Cranborne, later 5th Marquess of Salisbury, KG, PC (1893–1972).

50 APW, *The Viceroy's Journal*, pp. 1–2.

51 Later Lt-Gen. Sir (Edward) Ian Jacob, GBE, CB, DL, JP (1899–1993).

52 Ian Jacob, Notes, 1976, private collection.

53 Joan Bright Astley to the author, London, 27 May 2002.
54 The party consisted of WSC, Averill Harriman, Beaverbrook, Leathers (Minister of Transport), Charles Wilson, Cherwell, APW, Peirse, Somerville, 3 Chiefs of Staff, all Joint Planners etc.: see Alanbrooke, *War Diaries*, 5 May 1943, p. 398.
55 WSC, *The Hinge of Fate*, p. 701.
56 Alanbrooke, *War Diaries*, 8/9 May 1943, pp. 400–1.
57 In his official history WSC quotes only paras 5–15 of this 'lengthy paper'; see *The Hinge of Fate*, pp. 702–5.
58 APW, *The Viceroy's Journal*, p. 4.
59 Hon. Mrs Robert Phillimore (née Sheila MacLeod) to the author, Feb. 2005.
60 Air Chief Marshal Sir William Elliot, KBE, CB, DFC (1896–1971) to General Sir Henry Jackson, 11 Dec. 1961, Wavell Album, BWRA 0335.
61 Alanbrooke, *War Diaries*, 14 May 1943, p. 403.
62 *The Stilwell Papers*, p. 198.
63 APW to Tom Bird, April 1945, private collection.
64 APW, *The Viceroy's Journal*, p. 4.
65 'Mandalay', APW 21 May 1943, written in Washington, enclosed in a letter to Joan Bright, 6 June 1943, IWM. Also in Wavell Poems, private collection. Kipling's original reads: 'By the old Moulmein Pagoda, lookin' eastward to the sea, / There's a Burma girl a-settin', and I know she thinks o' me; / For the wind is in the palm-trees, an' the temple-bells they say: / "Come you back, you British soldier; come you back to Mandalay!"'

CHAPTER 17: DESIGNATED VICEROY, 1943

1 APW to Joan Bright, 3 Nov. 1942, IWM.
2 Lewis Carroll, *Alice in Wonderland*, as quoted in Lewin, *The Chief*, p. 215.
3 Rt Hon. Sir John Anderson, PC, GCB, OM, GCSI, GCIE, FRS, MP (Nat), later 1st Viscount Waverly (1882–1958).
4 Spectator's Diary, *Spectator*, 25 Sept. 1941; Julian Amery to Lord Mountbatten, 5 Feb. 1968, Listowel collection, MSS EUR C357/B, OIOC, BL; later 1st Earl Mountbatten of Burma, KG, PC, GCSI, GCIE, GCVO, KCB, DSO (1900–79).
5 Leo Amery's 1943 diary is extremely interesting on the 'selection process': see AMEL7/37 CAC.
6 Rupert Hart-Davis, 25 April 1962, John Connell fonds, McMU.
7 Amery, Diary, 28 May 1943, AMEL7/37, CAC.
8 Amery, *The Times*, 28 May 1950.
9 Amery, Diary, 30 May 1943, AMEL7/37, CAC.
10 Ibid., 31 May 1943.
11 David Day, *The Politics of War*, p. 502.

12 Channon, 31 May 1943, *Diaries*, p. 363.

13 George Spencer Churchill's mother Lady Edward, EMW's godmother, had been killed in a car crash in September 1941.

14 APW to Joan Bright, 6 June, 1943, IWM.

15 Amery, Diary, 5 June 1943, AMEL7/37, CAC.

16 Ibid., 9 June 1943, AMEL7/37, CAC.

17 Brooke, as quoted in *The Turn of the Tide*, ed. Arthur Bryant, p. 624.

18 See Cadogan, 9 June 1943, *Diaries*, p. 536, and Eden, *Memoirs*, p. 385.

19 APW, *Viceroy's Journal*, p. 5.

20 Channon, 12 June 1943, *Diaries*, p. 365. See also *Viceroy's Journal*, p. 6. Channon's version seems a little odd: surely Wavell must already have arranged to speak at Winchester. The edited *Viceroy's Journal* omits all reference to the time APW spent at Belgrave Square. In his diary Amery says Wavell had 'invited himself': 11 June 1943, AMEL7/37, CAC.

21 APW, *Viceroy's Journal*, p. 6.

22 Amery, Diary, 13 June 1943, AMEL7/37, CAC.

23 APW, *Viceroy's Journal*, p. 6.

24 Ibid., p. 7.

25 Bird, 'Recollections', p. 79, private collection.

26 In his diaries Channon suggests that Wavell was dumbfounded 'as he had never taken my hints and jokes on the subject seriously.' He indicates that the offer came as no surprise to him personally. See *Diaries*, p. 366 and also Coats, *Of Generals and Gardens*, p. 185. That APW asked his wife's approval also raised a few eyebrows at the War Office: private information to the author.

27 Lord Halifax to Lady Alexandra Curzon, as quoted in Anne De Courcy, *The Viceroy's Daughters*, Phoenix, 2000, p. 405.

28 APW to Eden, 17 June 1943, as quoted in Eden, *Memoirs*, p. 385.

29 BLH to APW, 25 June 1943, LH 1/733, LHCMA.

30 Bird, Letters Home, 21 June 1943, private collection.

31 Amery, Diary, 18 June 1943, AMEL7/37, CAC. Diwan Bahadur Sir Arcot Ramaswami Mudaliar, KCSI (1887–1976).

32 APW to Gen. Sir Henry Jackson, 26 June 1943, Wavell Album, BWRA 0335.

33 APW to Leonie Lemartine, 29 June 1943, private collection.

34 Channon, 21 June 1943, *Diaries*, p. 367.

35 Channon, 23 June 1943, *Diaries*, p. 368. Because of their friendship and Channon's political and social network, there were allegations (unsubstantiated) that Channon had 'rigged' the Viceroyalty in favour of APW (Channon, 25 June 1943, *Diaries*, p. 369).

36 Joan Bright Astley to the author, London, 27 May 2001.

37 Channon, 22 June 1943, *Diaries*, p. 367.

38 APW, Farewell Order of the Day, Press Note, 28 June 1943, private collection.

39 General Sir Claude Auchinleck, Order of the Day, 5 July 1943, private collection.

40 Amery, Diary, 28 June 1943, AMEL7/37, CAC.

41 Edward Wavell to APW, 1 July 1943, private collection.

42 Edward Wavell to APW, 23 July 1943, private collection; see also L.G. Pine, *The House of Wavell.*

43 Channon, 28 July 1943, *Diaries,* p. 373.

44 Dover Wilson, *Milestones on the Dover Road,* p. 251; John Dover Wilson, CH, Litt D FBA, MA, (1881–1969).

45 APW to Dover Wilson, *Milestones on the Dover Road,* p. 251.

46 Alanbrooke, *War Diaries,* 14 Sept. 1943, p. 452.

47 WSC, as quoted in Ziegler, *Mountbatten,* p. 222.

48 Sir Oliver Harvey, GCMG, CB, later 1st Baron Harvey of Tasburgh (1893–1968), as quoted in Ziegler, *Mountbatten,* p. 222.

49 Amery, Diary, 19 Sept. 1943, AMEL7/37, CAC.

50 See Pine, *The House of Wavell.*

51 Lord Howe to the author, 16 Jul. 04.

52 APW, *Viceroy's Journal,* 25 Sept. 1943, p. 19.

53 Ibid., 21 Sept. 1943, p. 18.

54 Ibid., 24 Sept. 1943, p. 19.

55 The speeches were later published in *164, Transfer of Power,* IV, pp. 377–8.

56 Amery, 7 Oct. 1943, *Empire at Bay,* p. 946.

57 APW, *Viceroy's Journal;* see Directive, Enclosure to *172, Transfer of Power,* IV, p. 387.

58 Amery, 8 Oct. 1943, *Empire at Bay,* p. 947.

59 APW, 8 Oct. 1943, *Viceroy's Journal,* p. 23.

60 Channon, 7 Oct 1943, *Diaries,* p. 377.

61 Joan Bright Astley to the author, Sept. 2003.

62 APW to Joan Bright, 11 Oct. 1943, IWM.

63 Channon, 11 Oct. 1943, *Diaries,* p. 377.

64 APW, 8 Oct. 1943, *Viceroy's Journal,* p. 23.

65 Capt. J.C. Irwin to his mother, Govt House, Calcutta, 13 Oct. 1943, private collection.

66 V. Shankar (1909–81); Unpublished Memoirs, private collection.

67 Linlithgow as quoted by APW to Amery, 25 Oct. 1943, *187, Transfer of Power,* IV, p. 407.

68 APW, 19 Oct. 1943, *Viceroy's Journal,* p. 33.

69 APW to Amery, 25 Oct. 1943, *187, Transfer of Power,* IV, p. 407.

70 Rona Smith, the Denman's granddaughter, to the author, 2003. The tiara was subsequently returned to the family but later stolen, and has never been traced.

71 Coats, *Of Generals and Gardens,* p. 213.

72 E.W.R. Lumby, *The Transfer of Power in India 1945–7,* Hyperion Press, 1981, pp. 202, 267.

73 See *Viceroy's Journal,* p. 31, and information from Major Henry Hall.

74 Later Sir Evan Jenkins, GCIE, KCSI (1896–1985).

75 Later Sir George Abell, KCIE, OBE, Hon. LL.D (1904–89).

76 George Abell to Dr Minto Robertson, 8 Aug. 1950, private collection.

77 Bird, Recollections, private collection. Tom Bird declined APW's offer to stay on as ADC, but before leaving wrote a short report on the running of the Viceroy's house.

78 Joan (Wavell) Astley to Araminta MacMichael (Bowman, later Araminta, Lady Aldington) to the author, Dec. 2004.

79 Josephine Ross, *Beaton in Vogue*, p. 68, reference American *Vogue*, June 1944.

80 Sir Jeremy Raisman, GCIE, KCSI (1892–1978).

82 From 1921 to 1939 the Executive Council was normally composed of eight members, five British, including the Viceroy, and three Indian. Since 1941 the Council had been enlarged to include more Indians; when APW became Viceroy the total number was fourteen, of whom ten were Indians.

83 V. Shankar, Unpublished Memoirs, private collection.

84 Capt. J.C. Irwin to his mother, 3 Nov. 1943, private collection.

85 APW to Amery, 1 Nov. 1943, *199*, *Transfer of Power*, IV, p. 430.

86 APW, 29 Oct. 1943, *Viceroy's Journal*, p. 35.

87 Partha Sarathi Gupta to the author, New Delhi, Dec. 1998. He was nine years old in 1943.

88 George Abell to Dr Minto Robertson, 8 Aug. 1950, private collection.

89 Maj. Monty Palit to the author, 1999.

90 Amery to APW, 3 Nov. 1943, *205*, *Transfer of Power*, IV, p. 446.

91 APW, 1 Dec. 1943, *Viceroy's Journal*, p. 40.

92 Ibid., 7 Dec. 1943.

93 APW, 'Questions for Diana Jane', Wavell poems, private collection.

94 'Answers to My Grandfather', by Joan Wavell Astley, Wavell Poems, private collection.

95 APW, 10 Dec. 1943, *Viceroy's Journal*, p. 40.

96 APW to Joan Bright, 12 Dec. 1943, IWM.

97 APW to Freya Stark, 29 Dec. 1943, JMA.

98 Edited by Penderell Moon and published as *The Viceroy's Journal* in 1973.

99 Somerville to Joan Bright, 5 Dec. 1943, IWM.

100 See Bayly and Harper, *Forgotten Armies*, p. 300.

101 APW, 22 Dec. 1943, *Viceroy's Journal*, p. 42.

102 APW to Freya Stark, 29 Dec. 1943, JMA.

103 Fergusson as quoted in *Viceroy's Journal*, p. 44.

104 Bernard Fergusson to Ronald Lewin, RLEW 4/13, CAC. Lewin's notes state this was when APW was appointed Field Marshal, but further correspondence indicates that it was when APW became Viceroy; George Fergusson to the author, Jan. 2005.

105 APW, summary of 1943, *Viceroy's Journal*, pp. 44–5.

106 APW to Auchinleck, 24 Dec. 1943, Auchinleck papers, *1047*, MUL.

CHAPTER 18: WARTIME VICEROY, 1944–5

1 Freya Stark to APW, 14 Jan. 1945, *Letters*, V, p. 130.
2 Raisman stayed on for another year and was replaced in April 1945 by Sir Archibald Rowlands, GCB, MBE (1892–1953).
3 APW to Lord Ismay, 8 Feb. 1944, Ismay 4/9/16a, LHCMA.
4 Ismay to APW, 7 March 1944, Ismay 4/9/17, LHCMA.
5 The Legislature consisted of two chambers, the Legislative Assembly and the Council of State.
6 *The Times*, 17 Feb. 1944.
7 APW speech to the Legislature, 17 Feb. 1944, as quoted in *The Times*, 18 Feb. 1944.
8 Leader comment, *The Times*, 18 Feb. 1944.
9 See Azad, *India Wins Freedom*, p. 68.
10 APW, 3 March 1944, *Viceroy's Journal*, p. 57.
11 APW, 11 March 1944, *Viceroy's Journal*, p. 59.
12 Ibid., 19 March 1944, p. 61.
13 APW to Mountbatten, 4 March 1944, Mountbatten Collection, OIOC, BL.
14 APW, 28 March 1944, *Viceroy's Journal*, p. 63.
15 Fergusson, *The Trumpet in the Hall*, p. 177.
16 APW, 'Major-General Orde Wingate', *The Good Soldier*, p. 66.
17 APW, 8 May 1944, *Viceroy's Journal*, p. 71; later Major-General Walter David Alexander Lentaigne, CB, CBE, DSO (1899–1955).
18 Lewin said the title was Peter Fleming's idea. This was contested by Peter Coats, who sent Lewin a photocopy of APW's inscription in his copy of the book: RLEW4/14, CAC.
19 APW to Peter Fleming, private collection.
20 Freya Stark to Sir Sydney Cockerell, 1 April 1944, *Letters*, V, p. 78.
21 M.J. Akbar, *Nehru*, p. 361. Edward Thompson (1886–1946); Fellow of Oriel College, Oxford and prolific writer.
22 APW, private collection.
23 See APW, *Other Men's Flowers*, p. 439.
24 AJW, John Connell fonds, McMU.
25 George Abell to Dr Minto Robertson, 8 Aug. 1950, private collection.
26 *Times Literary Supplement*, 18 March 1944. See APW, Preface to *Other Men's Flowers*.
27 APW to Joan Bright, 26 March 1944, IWM.
28 Rt Hon. Richard Casey, PC, CH, DSO, MC (1890–1976).
29 Casey, 'Personal Experiences', as quoted by Dorman-Smith, 4 Aug. 1962, John Connell fonds, McMU.
30 APW, 29 March 1944, *Viceroy's Journal*, p. 63.
31 Coats, *Of Generals and Gardens*, p. 218.
32 Cecil Beaton (1904–80).

33 Joyce Grenfell CBE, actress and writer (1910–79).

34 Peter Fleming to Celia Johnson, 21 March 1944, private collection.

35 APW, 16 April 1944, *Viceroy's Journal*, p. 65.

36 Simon Elwes, DL, JP, Kt of Malta (1902–75).

37 Sir Basil Gould, CMG, CIE (1883–1956).

38 APW to Freya Stark, 3/5 May 1944, JMA.

39 APW to Joan Bright, 5/8 May 1944, IWM.

40 APW, 8 May 1944, *Viceroy's Journal*, p. 70. Accounts vary as to Gandhi's age, but he was born on 2 Oct 1869: see Judith M. Brown, *Gandhi*, p. 15.

41 See *539*, *Transfer of Power*, IV, Gandhi to APW, 17 June 1944, p. 1032; *544*, APW to Gandhi, 22 June 1944, pp. 1039–40.

42 Coats, *Of Generals and Gardens*, p. 228.

43 APW, 19 June 1944, *Viceroy's Journal*, pp. 74–5.

44 APW to Auchinleck, 22 June 1944, Auchinleck papers, *1058*, MUL.

45 Coats, *Of Generals and Gardens*, p. 217. Lt-Gen. Sir Adrian Carton de Wiart, VC, KBE, CB, CMG, DSO (1880–1963).

46 APW, 26 June 1944, *Viceroy's Journal*, p. 77.

47 APW to Sec. of State, 'Wavell Notes' from files made available by Gen. Sir David Fraser, 3 Feb. 1979 to Ronald Lewin, RLEW 4/12, CAC.

48 APW, 5 July 1944, *Viceroy's Journal*, p. 78.

49 Ibid., 19 July 1944, p. 80.

50 APW to Freya Stark, 3 Aug. 1944, JMA. The actual quotation is 'Files – The Files – Office Files! / Oblige me by referring to the Files. / Every question man can raise, / Every phrase of every phase / Of that question is on record in the Files': Rudyard Kipling, 'The Files' (1903).

51 APW, 4 Aug. 1944, *Viceroy's Journal*, p. 82.

52 Ibid., 22 July 1944 p. 80.

53 APW to Leonie Lemartine, 24 Sept. 1944, private collection.

54 Fergusson, 'Obituary, Major the Earl Wavell, MC', *The Red Hackle*, January 1954.

55 Dover Wilson to APW, 5 Nov. 1944, NLS.

56 Lydall to John Connell, 15 Dec. 1964, John Connell fonds, McMU; Christopher Gimson, CIE, BA, ICS (1886–1975).

57 APW, 9 Aug. 1944, *Viceroy's Journal*, p. 83.

58 Lydall to John Connell, 15 Dec. 1964, John Connell fonds, McMU.

59 APW, 9 Aug. 1944, *Viceroy's Journal*, p. 84.

60 Amery, 12 Aug. 1944, *Empire at Bay*, p. 994.

61 Alanbrooke, *War Diaries*, 15 Aug. 1944, p. 581.

62 Amery, 12 Aug. 1944, *Empire at Bay*, p. 994.

63 Ibid., 14 Aug. 1944, p. 995.

64 APW to Amery, as quoted in *Viceroy's Journal*, p. 86.

65 APW, 22 Aug. 1944, *Viceroy's Journal*, p. 87.

66 APW to Freya Stark, 3 Aug. 1944, JMA.

67 APW, 20 Sept. 1944, *Viceroy's Journal*, p. 91.

68 APW to Amery, 3 Oct. 1944, *37, Transfer of Power*, V, p. 75.

69 Ibid., 22 Oct. 1944, *61*, p. 123.

70 APW, 11 Oct. 1944, *Viceroy's Journal*, p. 92; APW to Amery, 10 Oct. 1944, *52, Transfer of Power*, V, p. 104.

71 Dover Wilson to APW, 5 Nov. 1944, NLS.

72 APW to Gen. Sir John Shea, GCB, KCMG, DSO, 16 Sept. 1944, and further correspondence, private collection. The horns remain on the Society's premises to this day.

73 APW, 20 Oct. 1944, *Viceroy's Journal*, p. 93.

74 APW to WSC, 24 Oct. 1943, as quoted in *Viceroy's Journal*, pp. 94-9.

75 APW, 29 Oct. 1944, *Viceroy's Journal*, p. 100.

76 APW, 16 Dec. 1944, *Viceroy's Journal*, p. 105.

77 Viscount Slim to the author, April 2005.

78 APW, 25 Dec. 1944, *Viceroy's Journal*, p. 107.

79 Ibid., 31 Dec. 1944, p. 108.

80 Ibid., 7 Jan. 1945, p. 109.

81 Coats, *Of Generals and Gardens*, p. 236.

82 Amery, 19 Jan. 1945, *Empire at Bay*, p. 1026.

83 Ibid., 25 Jan. 1945, p. 1027.

84 Bhulabhai Jivanji Desai (1877-1946).

85 APW, 20 Jan. 1945, *Viceroy's Journal*, p. 111.

86 EMW, as quoted in Freya Stark, *Dust in the Lion's Paw*, p. 229.

87 Freya Stark to Hon. Mrs Hore-Ruthven, 20 Feb. 1945, *Letters*, V, p. 146.

88 Freya Stark to Gerald de Gaury, 19 Feb. 1945, *Letters*, V, p. 145.

89 APW, 10 March 1945, *Viceroy's Journal*, p. 115.

90 Freya Stark to John Grey Murray, 13 March 1945, *Letters*, V, p. 154.

91 APW, 15 March 1945, *Viceroy's Journal*, p. 117.

92 Amery, 16 March 1945, *Empire at Bay*, p. 1032.

93 Bird, 10 April 1945, Letters from the Wavell family, private collection.

94 AJW to Walter Oakeshott, 22 Aug. 1945, John Connell fonds, McMU.

95 Channon, 21 March 1945, *Diaries*, p. 400.

96 APW, 26 March 1945, *Viceroy's Journal*, p. 119; John, 1st Viscount Simon, PC, GCSI, GCVO (1873-1954); according to Eden, he called APW 'a foolish, woolly-headed old man': Eden, *Memoirs*, p. 540.

97 Amery, 26 March 1945, *Empire at Bay*, p. 1033.

98 APW, 29 March 1945, *Viceroy's Journal*, p. 120.

99 Alanbrooke, *War Diaries*, 8 Sept. 1944, p. 589 and 19 Jan. 1945, p. 647.

100 APW to Tom Bird, 10 April 1945, private collection.

101 APW, 11 April 1945, *Viceroy's Journal*, p. 124.

102 Ibid., 12 April 1945, p. 124.

103 Harry S. Truman (1884-1972), 33rd President of the USA, 1945-1952.

104 WSC, *Triumph and Tragedy*, p. 412.

105 APW, 18 April 1945, *Viceroy's Journal*, p. 126.
106 Amery, 18 April 1945, *Empire at Bay*, p. 1037.
107 APW, 23–5 April 1945, *Viceroy's Journal*, p. 126.
108 Amery, 23 April 1945, *Empire at Bay*, p. 1037.
109 APW, 6 April 1945, *Viceroy's Journal*, p. 123. The bust was displayed for the Festival of Remembrance, 'Other Men's Flowers – Fifty Years On', 16–18 June 1995 at Winchester College.
110 Coats, *Of Generals and Gardens*, p. 249.
111 APW, 29 April 1945, *Viceroy's Journal*, p. 127.
112 Coats, *Of Gardens and Generals*, p. 247; a '*Gauleiter*' was the governor of a district in Nazi Germany.
113 Amery, 30 April 1945, *Empire at Bay*, p. 1039.
114 WSC, as quoted in *Triumph and Tragedy*, p. 479.
115 Channon, 6 May 1945, *Diaries*, p. 405.
116 APW, 11 May 1945, *Viceroy's Journal*, p. 129.
117 APW, War Cabinet, India Committee, *449, Transfer of Power*, V, pp. 1029–37.
118 APW, 14 May 1945, *Viceroy's Journal*, p. 130.
119 APW, 28 May 1945, *Viceroy's Journal*, p. 133.
120 Eden, 30 May 1945, *Memoirs*, p. 540.
121 APW, 1 June, 1945, *Viceroy's Journal*, p. 136.
122 Amery, 31 May 1945, *Empire at Bay*, p. 1045. On 2 Dec 1947 he added a note: 'The immediate wrecker [of the Simla Conference] was Jinnah, but the real wrecker perhaps the long delay before Archie was allowed to try, and so Winston.'
123 APW, 2 June 1945, *Viceroy's Journal*, p. 136. Kathleen, Viscountess Simon, DBE (1871–1955), was a champion of 'freedom' causes.

CHAPTER 19: VICEROY AT PEACE, 1945

1 APW, Annexure to Confidential Note, No. 8, 14 July 1945, Wavell collection, MSS EUR D977/5, OIOC, BL, and APW to Amery, 15 July 1945, ibid.
2 APW, *Viceroy's Journal*, 6 June 1945, p. 139.
3 V. Shankar, Unpublished Memoirs, private collection.
4 APW, 14 June 1943, *Viceroy's Journal*, p. 142.
5 APW to Amery, 17 June 1945, Wavell collection, MSS EUR D977/4, OIOC, BL.
6 Coats, *Of Generals and Gardens*, p. 251.
7 APW, 23 June 1945, *Viceroy's Journal*, p. 144.
8 Ibid., 24 June 1945, p. 146. See also Wavell collection, MSS EUR D977/5, OIOC, BL.

9 AJW to Walter Oakeshott, 22 Aug 1945, John Connell fonds, McMU.

10 That Menon (1889–1966) worked in the Viceroy's office during the critical negotiations of 1946 and 1947 has led to allegations that, with a pro-Congress bias, he did not act with the complete impartiality expected of a civil servant. 'It was an association which had much more to do with the shaping of India's future than has hitherto been realized': Leonard Mosley, *The Last Days of the British Raj*, Weidenfeld & Nicolson, 1961, p. 89, MSS Eur A221, OIOC, BL.

11 John Raisman to the author, Feb. 2005.

12 APW, 25 June 1945, Wavell collection, MSS EUR D 977/5, OIOC, BL.

13 APW, 27 June 1945, *Viceroy's Journal*, p. 149.

14 Azad, *India Wins Freedom*, p. 114.

15 APW, 29 June 1945, *Viceroy's Journal*, p. 150.

16 Freya Stark, *Dust in the Lion's Paw*, p. 247.

17 Gandhi to APW, 11 July 1945, Wavell collection, MSS EUR D977/5, OIOC, BL.

18 APW, 11 July 1945, *Viceroy's Journal*, p. 154.

19 APW, Annexure to Confidential Note No. 8, 14 July 1945, Wavell collection, MSS Eur D977/5, OIOC BL.

20 Note on the Conference to Amery, 15 July 1945, Wavell collection, MSS EUR D977/5, OIOC, BL.

21 AJW to Walter Oakeshott, 22 Aug. 1945, John Connell fonds, McMU.

22 Amery, *Empire at Bay*, 12 July 1945, p. 1048.

23 WSC, *Triumph and Tragedy*, p. 583.

24 APW to WSC, 28 July 1945, CHAR 2/560/77, CAC.

25 WSC to APW, 5 Aug. 1945, CHAR 2/560/75, CAC.

26 APW to Ismay, 31 July 1945, Ismay 4/9/19, LHCMA.

27 Azad, *India Wins Freedom*, p. 117.

28 Ibid., p. 113.

29 APW, 2 Aug. 1945, *Viceroy's Journal*, p. 160.

30 1st Baron Pethick-Lawrence, PC (1871–1961).

31 APW, 3 Aug. 1945, *Viceroy's Journal*, p. 161.

32 APW to Pethick-Lawrence, 5 Aug. 1945, 4, *Transfer of Power* VI, p. 27.

33 Colonel Craig Smyser to John Connell, 26 Aug. 1963, John Connell fonds, McMU; W.E. Henley, 'Invictus', *Other Men's Flowers*, p. 86.

34 A uranium fission bomb was dropped on Hiroshima, a plutonium bomb on Nagasaki.

35 APW, 7 Aug. 1945, *Viceroy's Journal*, p. 162.

36 Ibid., 11 Aug. 1945, p. 162.

37 Ibid., 19 Aug. 1945, p. 163; Judges v, 2–31.

38 Colonel Craig Smyser to John Connell, 29 Nov. 1963, John Connell fonds, McMU. Lt-Col. F. Burnaby-Atkins, ADC also confirmed to the author that APW worked at a stand-up desk.

39 APW, 22 Aug. 1945, *Viceroy's Journal*, p. 164.

40 India and Burma Committee, 2nd Meeting, 29 Aug. 1945, *78*, *Transfer of Power*, VI, p. 174.

41 APW, 'Note by the Viceroy on Pakistan', 31 Aug. 1945, *82*, *Transfer of Power*, VI, p. 190.

42 APW to Sir John Colville, 29 Aug. 1945, *79*, *Transfer of Power*, VI, p. 180.

43 APW to Freya Stark, 26 Sept. 1945, JMA.

44 Coats, *Of Generals and Gardens*, p. 250.

45 Ibid., p. 261.

46 APW, Broadcast 19 Sept. 1945, *116*, *Transfer of Power*, VI, p. 282.

47 Their names were Shah Nawaz Khan, P.K. Sahgal and G.S. Dhillon. Not all Indians were sympathetic. Nirad Chaudhuri was incensed at 'the surrender' to the 'allies of Axis': *Thy Hand, Great Anarch!*, p. 781.

48 Cunningham to APW, 27 Nov. 1945, Cunningham collection, MSS EUR D 670/7, OIOC, BL.

49 APW to Cunningham, 30 Nov. 1945, ibid. See Kulkarmi and Murty, *First Indian National Army Trial*. They were tried 'irrespective of caste or creed'.

50 APW, 10 Dec. 1945, Royal Exchange, Calcutta, as quoted in *The Times*, 11 Dec. 1945.

51 Auchinleck to APW, 26 Nov. 1945, Auchinleck papers, *1119*, MUL.

52 APW, 24 Aug. 1945, *Viceroy's Journal*, p. 164. So persistent was the belief that Bose might still be alive that in 1956 the Indian government sent a mission to Japan to conduct an inquiry into his death, during which 67 witnesses were interviewed; see Louis Allen, *The End of the War in Asia*, p. 144.

53 APW to Pethick-Lawrence, 27 Dec. 1945, *315*, *Transfer of Power*, VI, pp. 686–8. See also *Viceroy's Journal*, pp. 196–200.

54 APW to Pethick-Lawrence, 27 Dec. 1945, *316*, *Transfer of Power* pp. 700–1.

55 APW to HM King George VI, 31 Dec. 1945, *Transfer of Power*, *322*, VI, pp. 714–15.

56 APW to Freya Stark, 23 Dec. 1945, JMA.

57 Auchinleck to APW, 6 Nov. 1945, Auchinleck papers, *1110*, MUL.

58 APW to Pethick-Lawrence, 1 Jan. 1946, *325*, *Transfer of Power*, VI, p. 723.

59 APW, 5 Jan 1946, *Viceroy's Journal*, p. 202.

60 Captain Michael Conville (1924–2004) to the author, May 2002.

61 HE The Viceroy's Speech, Poona, 10 Jan. 1946, private collection.

62 APW, 15 Jan. 1946, *Viceroy's Journal*, p. 204.

63 Pethick-Lawrence, 'Memorandum', 10 Jan. 1946, *347*, *Transfer of Power*, VI, pp. 757–62.

64 India and Burma Committee, 14 Jan. 1946, *355*, *Transfer of Power*, VI, p. 787.

65 APW, 24 Jan. 1946, *Viceroy's Journal*, p. 206.

66 Pethick-Lawrence to APW, 29 Jan. 1946, *387*, *Transfer of Power*, VI, p. 860.

67 APW to Pethick-Lawrence, 7 Feb. 1946, *Transfer of Power*, VI, *406*, p. 912. Mountbatten has frequently been criticized for awarding most of Gurdaspur

district to India at partition, thereby improving India's land access to Jammu and Kashmir. But it was Wavell's suggestion, in the interests of the Sikhs.

68 APW, 12 Feb. 1946, *Viceroy's Journal*, p. 211.

69 APW/Pethick-Lawrence correspondence 17/21 Feb. 1946, as quoted in *Viceroy's Journal*, pp. 213–14; see also Pethick-Lawrence collection, MSS EUR D540/1, OIOC, BL.

70 APW, 27 Feb. 1946, *Viceroy's Journal*, p. 218.

71 APW to Auchinleck, 20 Feb. 1946, Auchinleck papers, *1139*, MUL.

72 APW, 16 Feb. 1946, *Viceroy's Journal*, p. 211.

73 APW to Mountbatten, 27 March 1946, Mountbatten collection, MSS EUR F200, OIOC, BL.

74 *The Bulletin and Scots Pictorial*, 20 March 1946, Pethick-Lawrence collection, MSS Eur D540/2, OIOC, BL.

CHAPTER 20: UNITY OR PARTITION, 1946

1 APW to Sir Alfred Zimmern, 17 Jan. 1945, MS Zimmern 49, Folio 2, Bodleian Library, OU.

2 APW, 24 March 1946, *Viceroy's Journal*, p. 229.

3 Brief from British Cabinet, as quoted in Burke and Quraishi, *The British Raj in India*, p. 426.

4 APW, Note for the Cabinet Delegation, 29 March 1946, *Viceroy's Journal*, p. 232.

5 APW, 2 April 1946, ibid., p. 234.

6 V. Shankar, Unpublished Memoirs, p. 191, private collection.

7 APW, 18 April 1946, *Viceroy's Journal*, p. 248.

8 Ibid., 21 April 1946, p. 249.

9 See Ayesha Jalal, *The Sole Spokesman*, p. 189.

10 APW, 27 April 1946, *Viceroy's Journal*, p. 253. Sardar Vallabhbhai Patel (1875–1950).

11 Ibid., 12 May 1946, p. 267.

12 Memorandum on States' Treaties and Paramountcy presented by the Cabinet Mission to His Highness the Chancellor of the Chamber of Princes, 12 May 1946, as quoted in Lumby, *Transfer of Power*, pp. 220–1.

13 Statement by the Cabinet Mission and His Excellency The Viceroy, 16 May 1946, as quoted in *Viceroy's Journal*, Appendix II, p. 479. See also *303, Transfer of Power*, VII, pp. 582–91. A detailed analysis of Pakistan was also made in London, which concluded that a united India would better suit Britain's strategic interests. See L/WS/1/1029, OIOC, BL.

14 APW to BLH, 17 May 1946, LH 1/733, LHCMA. See Sir John Wheeler-Bennett papers, Series B, St Antony's College, Oxford. The belief that Operation Barbarossa was delayed because of the Balkan campaign was questioned by Martin Van Creveld, *Hitler's Strategy 1940–1941 – The Balkan Clue*,

Cambridge University Press, 1973, who argues that slow distribution of mechanical transport to units earmarked for Russia accounted for the delay. See p. 173–6 & p. 182.

15 APW, 20 May 1946, *Viceroy's Journal*, p. 274.

16 See Moon, *Divide and Quit*, p. 50.

17 Peter Clarke, *The Cripps Version*, p. 436.

18 APW, 22 May 1946, *Viceroy's Journal*, p. 275.

19 APW to Freya Stark, 27 May 1946, JMA; APW to Dover Wilson, 25 Sept. 1945, NLS.

20 APW to S.R. Fuller, Truslove & Hanson, misc. corresp. 1946, MSS EUR B337, OIOC, BL; among books ordered by APW were *The Drawings of Leonardo da Vinci*, Napoleon's *Memoirs*, a biography of Augustus John (who had drawn APW) and C.S. Forester's *Lord Hornblower*.

21 David Harry Walker, *The Wavell Rock*, David Walker collection, NB.

22 Ziegler, *Mountbatten*, p. 344.

23 Mountbatten to APW, 1 June 1946, Mountbatten collection, MSS EUR F200, OIOC, BL.

24 Countess Mountbatten to the author, 29 May 2002. There was a family connection: in Oct. 1946 she had m. 7th Lord Brabourne; APW's aunt Elizabeth was m. to Colonel Norton Knatchbull, a cousin of 5th Lord Brabourne.

25 APW, 31 May 1946, *Viceroy's Journal*, p. 282.

26 Moon, *Divide and Quit*, p. 51.

27 APW, 16 June 1946, as quoted in Moon, *Divide and Quit*, p. 53.

28 APW, 20 June 1946, *Viceroy's Journal*, p. 298.

29 Montgomery, *Memoirs*, p. 425; see also APW, 20 June 1946, *Viceroy's Journal*, p. 298.

30 APW, 24 June 1946, *Viceroy's Journal*, p. 301.

31 Ibid., 25 June 1946, p. 305.

32 Jinnah, as quoted in Stephens, *Pakistan*, p. 99.

33 Ibid., p. 98.

34 Peter Clarke, *The Cripps Version*, p. 454.

35 APW, 30 June 1946, *Viceroy's Journal*, p. 309.

36 APW to Joan Bright, 27 June 1946, IWM.

37 See Stephens, *Pakistan*, p. 99.

38 APW, 1 July 1946, *Viceroy's Journal*, pp. 312–15.

39 See *Viceroy's Journal*, p. 316.

40 George Abell to Dr Minto Robertson, 8 Aug. 1950, private collection. 'The ultimate agreement between the parties secured by Lord Mountbatten owes more than has been recognised to the patience and fairness of Lord Wavell during this time.'

41 Peter Clarke, *The Cripps Version*, p. 455. Cripps even thought he himself might like the position.

42 APW to HM King George VI, 8 July 1946, reproduced in the *Viceroy's Journal*,

Appendix VIII (with slight omission) by gracious permission of HM The Queen, pp. 493–6.

43 See Peter Clarke, *The Cripps Version*, p. 461 and Stephens, *Pakistan*, p. 102. Statement of 10 July 1946 as quoted in *The Indian Annual Register* (1946), vol. II, pp. 145–7, as quoted in *Speeches and Documents on the Indian Constitution, 1925–47*, vol. II, pp. 612–15. Anita Inder Singh, *The Origins of Partition*, p. 176 suggests that Nehru said nothing that differed from earlier statements against grouping.

44 Jinnah to Attlee, 23 July 1946, *68*, *Transfer of Power*, VIII, p. 106.

45 Jinnah as quoted in Stephens, *Pakistan*, p. 103.

46 Azad, *India wins Freedom*, p. 166. These remarks made in hindsight are contained in the new edition, published 30 years after Azad's death and long after Nehru's.

47 V. Shankar, Unpublished Memoirs, private collection.

48 APW, 29 July 1946, *Viceroy's Journal*, p. 324.

49 Attlee to APW, 22 July 1946, *64*, *Transfer of Power*, VIII, pp. 99–101.

50 APW, 29 July 1946, *Viceroy's Journal*, p. 324.

51 APW to Attlee, 1 Aug. 1946, *102*, *Transfer of Power*, VIII, pp. 167–8.

52 Attlee to APW, 20 Aug. 1946, *184*, *Transfer of Power*, VIII, p. 271.

53 APW to Attlee, 28 Aug. 1942, *212*, *Transfer of Power*, VIII, p. 328.

54 Drafts by Mr Attlee, Annex (i) (ii) (iii), *212*, *Transfer of Power*, VIII, p. 331.

55 APW, 6 Aug. 1946, *Viceroy's Journal*, p. 329.

56 Stephens, *Pakistan*, p. 105.

57 APW, broadcast, 24 Aug. 1946.

58 Gandhi, 28 Aug. 1946, *207*, *Transfer of Power*, VIII, p. 322, and *Viceroy's Journal*, p. 342.

59 Nehru to APW, 28 Aug. 1946, *211*, *Transfer of Power*, VIII, p. 327.

60 Sir Walter (later Lord) Monckton to WSC, 4 Sept. 1946, Dep Monckton 1, Bodleian Library, OU.

61 APW to Sir Hugh Dow, Gov. of Bihar, 6 Sept. 1946, Dow Collection, MSS EUR E373/9, OIOC, BL.

62 APW to Freya Stark, 23 Sept. 1946, JMA.

63 APW to Sir Hugh Dow, 16 Oct. 1946, Dow Collection, MSS Eur E373/9, OIOC, BL.

64 APW to Pethick-Lawrence, 23 Oct. 1946, *501*, *Transfer of Power* VIII, pp. 794–9.

65 APW to Attlee, 30 Oct. 1946, *531* *Transfer of Power* VIII, p. 839.

66 Moon, *Divide and Quit*, p. 59.

67 APW to Nehru, 24 Oct. 1946, *503*, *Transfer of Power*, VIII, p. 800; APW to P-L, 30 Oct. 1946, *534*, ibid., p. 840.

68 APW, 28 Nov. 1946, *Viceroy's Journal*, p. 384.

69 APW to Pethick-Lawrence, 30 Oct. 1946, *534*, *Transfer of Power*, VIII, p. 840.

70 Nawab of Bhopal to Corfield, 23 Nov. 1946, *83*, *Transfer of Power*, IX, p. 156.

71 APW to Pethick-Lawrence, 30 Oct. 1946, *534*, *Transfer of Power*, VIII, p. 840.

72 Major Robin Hodson, MBE, Notes of the Viceroy's visit, 15/16 Nov. 1946,

to the author. Nehru blamed IPS officers who were sympathetic to the Muslim League: see Enc. to *520*, *Transfer of Power*, VIII, pp. 816–19.

73 APW, 19 Nov. 1946, *Viceroy's Journal*, p. 378.

74 Ibid., 29 Nov. 1946, p. 385.

75 Ibid. 2 Dec. 1946, pp. 387–8.

76 HM The King's Diary, 3 Dec. 1946, as quoted in Wheeler-Bennett, *King George VI*, p. 706.

77 APW, 5 Dec. 1946, *Viceroy's Journal*, p. 392.

78 Robert Browning, 'Before'. Ibid., p. 391.

79 Indian Conference in London, 6 Dec. 1946, Appendix to *166*, *Transfer of Power*, IX, p. 297; see also *163–169*, ibid., pp. 288–99.

80 APW, 6 Dec. 1946, *Viceroy's Journal*, p. 394.

81 Indian Conference in London, 6 Dec. 1946, Appendix to *166*, *Transfer of Power*, IX, p. 297.

82 See Indian Conference in London, 6 Dec. 1946, *163*, ibid., p. 289.

83 APW, 6 Dec. 1946, *Viceroy's Journal*, p. 394.

84 Ibid., 16 Dec. 1946, p. 395.

85 Ibid., 18 Dec. 1946, p. 396; Moorehead, *Montgomery* (1948). Conflicting reports about Greece, had decided Eden and APW to collaborate on a book to which APW would contribute the military chapters and Eden the political. APW only got as far as writing the preface before his death in 1950: see Eden, *Memoirs*, p. 203 and Appendix D.

86 APW, 20 Dec. 1946, *Viceroy's Journal*, p. 397.

87 HM The King's Diary, 17 Dec. 1946, as quoted in Wheeler-Bennett, *King George VI*, p. 710.

88 APW, 20 Dec. 1946, *Viceroy's Journal*, p. 398.

89 APW to Joan Bright, 28 Dec. 1946, IWM.

90 APW, 31 Dec. 1946, *Viceroy's Journal*, p. 403.

CHAPTER 21: DISMISSAL, 1947

1 As quoted in Wheeler-Bennett, *King George VI*, p. 712.

2 APW, 1 Jan. 1947, *Viceroy's Journal*, p. 404, see also 1 Jan. 1947, *239*, Transfer of Power, IX, p. 438.

3 'Future Policy in India', India and Burma Cttee, 10 Jan. 1947, *257*, *Transfer of Power*, IX, p. 475.

4 APW, 12 Jan. 1947, *Viceroy's Journal* p. 410.

5 Ibid.

6 Ibid., 7 Jan. 1947, p. 407.

7 See Stephens, *Pakistan*, p. 118.

8 Attlee to APW, 31 Jan. 1947, *Viceroy's Journal*, App. IX, p. 497, also *331*, *Transfer of Power*, IX, pp. 582–3.

9 APW to Attlee, 5 Feb. 1947, *Viceroy's Journal*, App. IX, p. 498; also *351*, *Transfer of Power*, IX, p. 624.

10 Attlee to APW, 12 Feb. 1947, *381*, ibid., p. 679.

11 APW, 13 Feb. 1947, *Viceroy's Journal*, p. 419; also APW to Pethick-Lawrence, 17 Feb. 1947, *410, 411*, *Transfer of Power*, IX, p.733.

12 APW to Mountbatten, 14 Feb. 1947, *392*, *Transfer of Power*, IX, p.703.

13 Mountbatten to APW, 18 Feb. 1947, *417*, ibid., p. 744.

14 APW, 17 Feb. 1947, *Viceroy's Journal*, p. 421.

15 Pethick-Lawrence to APW, 18 Feb. 1947, *423*, *Transfer of Power*, p. 753, 19 Feb. 1947, *429*, ibid., p. 762.

16 APW to Attlee, 14 Feb. 1947, *391*, ibid., p. 703.

17 Jean Grant, diary, Thursday 20 Feb. 1947, private collection.

18 *The Times*, 21 Feb. 1947.

19 Miangul Hasan Aurangzeb to the author, Islamabad, April 2002.

20 APW, 20 Feb. 1947, *Viceroy's Journal*, p. 422.

21 Parliamentary proceedings, 20 Feb. 1947, as quoted in *The Statesman*, 22 Feb. 1947: 'Mr Churchill causes a storm in Commons'; also *The Times*, 21 Feb. 1947.

22 Lewin, *The Chief*, p. 241.

23 As related by Rt Hon. Clement Davies, PC, KC, MP, leader of the Liberal Party since 1945, to Godfrey Carter (a friend of Davies' son), then to Lewin, 19 Dec. 1980, RLEW4/14, CAC.

24 WSC to Attlee, 18 Feb. 1947, *424*, *Transfer of Power* IX, p. 754.

25 APW to the King, 24 Feb. 1947, as quoted in Wheeler-Bennett, *King George VI*, p. 709.

26 Sir A. Lascelles to APW, 30 March 1947, as quoted in Wheeler-Bennett, *King George VI*, pp. 712–13.

27 William Hare, 5th Earl of Listowel, PC (1906–97).

28 APW to Listowel, Mountbatten collection MSS EUR F200/176, OIOC, BL.

29 Wavell Poems, private collection.

30 APW to Freya Stark, 13 March 1947, JMA.

31 Sir Hugh Dow to APW, 3 March 1947, Dow collection, MSS EUR E372/9, OIOC, BL.

32 APW to Auchinleck as recorded by Shahid Hamid, 8 Feb. 1942, *Disastrous Twilight*, p. 133.

33 Shahid Hamid, 15 March 1942, ibid., p. 142.

34 APW to Auchinleck, 22 March 1947, Auchinleck collection, *1219*, MUL.

35 APW, as quoted in Azad, *India Wins Freedom*, p. 193. Azad also quotes APW as saying that he had resigned – not strictly true since he was dismissed.

36 Azad, *India Wins Freedom*, p. 194.

37 Ibid., p. 192.

38 APW, unsigned and undated note, *561*, *Transfer of Power*, IX, p. 1009.

39 APW, Farewell Broadcast, All India Radio, New Delhi, 21 March 1947, *559*, ibid., pp. 1003–4.

40 APW, 22 March 1947, *Viceroy's Journal*, p. 432. Sir Eric Mieville, GCIE, KCVO, CSI, CMG (1896–1971).

41 Minutes of meeting between Mountbatten and APW, 22 March 1947, *562*, *Transfer of Power*, IX, p. 1011.

42 Mountbatten to H.V. Hodson as quoted in Close, *Attlee, Wavell and Mountbatten*, p. 9.

43 APW, 22 March 1947, *Viceroy's Journal* p. 432.

44 Philip Ziegler, *Mountbatten*, p. 356.

45 Attlee, as quoted in *A Prime Minister Remembers*, p. 209. In Jan. 1946 Pethick-Lawrence had passed on to Attlee a message from former Vicereine Lady Willingdon suggesting Mountbatten: Pethick-Lawrence to Attlee, 30 Jan. 1946, *391*, *Transfer of Power*, VI, p. 87.

46 E.W.R. Lumby, *Transfer of Power in India*, p. 144.

47 Lt-Gen. Attiqur Rahman, Frontier Force Regiment, to Ronald Lewin, 20 July 1981, 4/12, RLEW7/21, CAC.

48 See Leonard Mosley, *The Last Days of the British Raj*, 1961; MSS EUR A221, OIOC, BL, pp. 46–7.

49 AJW to Private Wood, 1 March (undated, but 1947), 82/37/1, IWM.

CHAPTER 22: THE END

1 Excerpt from 'An Ordinary Soldier', in the *Sunday Times*, 28 May 1950. AJW found this among the most moving tributes to his father: AJW to Eric Linklater (undated), NLS.

2 Shahid Hamid, 17 March 1947, *Disastrous Twilight*, p. 147.

3 Edward Wavell to APW, 1947, private collection.

4 APW to Joan Bright, 27 June 1946, IWM.

5 Col. Philip Astley, CBE, MC (1896–1958). Joan Bright met Philip Astley not through the Wavells but through his sister, married to a colleague in the War Cabinet Office.

6 *Viceroy's Journal*, p. 434.

7 Information given to John Dover Wilson by AJW, as quoted in *Milestones on the Dover Road*, p. 259.

8 John Dover Wilson, Ibid., p. 160.

9 John Dover Wilson, Ibid., p. 160.

10 APW to Dover Wilson, 24 May 1947, NLS.

11 General Sir Richard O'Connor, 'A Pentagonal Portrait', *Aberdeen University Review*, Vol. XXXIII, No. 103, Autumn, 1950, p. 387.

12 APW to Freya Stark, 17 April 1947, JMA.

13 David Walker papers, NB.

14 APW to Edward Wavell, 4 June 1945, private collection.

15 Fergusson, *Portrait of a Soldier*, pp. 82–3.

16 APW, 15 Aug. 1947, *Viceroy's Journal*, p. 436.

17 APW to Freya Stark, 4 Sept. 1947, JMA.

18 APW to Freya Stark, 8 June 1947, JMA.

19 APW, 15 Aug. 1947, *Viceroy's Journal*, p. 436.

20 APW, 14 Oct. 1947, Ibid., p. 436.

21 Marshal of the Royal Air Force Charles Frederick Algernon Portal, 1st Viscount Hungerford, KG, GCB, OM, DSO, MC (1893–1971).

22 'The Triangle of Forces in Civil Leadership' by Field Marshal the Right Honourable Earl Wavell, PC, GCB, GCSI, GCIE, CMG, MC, LL.D., Walker Trust Lectures on Leadership No. IX, Geoffrey Cumberledge, OUP, 1948.

23 BLH to APW, 31 March 1948, LH 1/733, LHCMA.

24 'Games and Athletics', by Field Marshal the Rt Hon. Earl Wavell, PC, GCB, GCSI, GCIE, CMG, MC, LL.D, reprinted from *The Aberdeen University Review*, Vol. XXXIII, No. 98.

25 Sir William Hamilton Fyfe, MA, LL.D, FRSC, Hon, FEIS, JP (1878–1965). 'A Pentagonal Portrait', *Aberdeen University Review*, Vol. XXXIII, No. 103, Autumn, 1950, p. 387.

26 APW, 20 Nov. 1947, *Viceroy's Journal*, p. 437. Mountbatten remained in India as Governor-General until 1948.

27 APW to Auchinleck, 20 Nov. 1947, Auchinleck papers, *1287*, MUL, as quoted in Connell, *Auchinleck*, p. 934.

28 Auchinleck to APW, 4 May 1948, Auchinleck papers, *1312*, MUL.

29 WSC, CHAR20/251, CAC. Later General Sir Leslie Hollis, KCB, KBE (1897–1963).

30 APW had also been awarded an LL.D. by Cambridge, and a doctorate in Civil Law (DCL) from Oxford.

31 APW, 1 Dec. 1947, *Viceroy's Journal*, p. 438. Masefield's D.Litt. was awarded by Oxford in 1922.

32 APW to David Walker, 13 Dec. 1947, David Walker papers, NB.

33 APW, 31 Dec. 1947, *Viceroy's Journal*, p. 438.

34 APW to Leonie Lemartine, 22 Dec. 1947.

35 APW, 31 Dec. 1947, *Viceroy's Journal*, p. 439.

36 APW to Freya Stark, 15 Feb. 1948, JMA.

37 Ibid.

38 APW, 15 Feb. 1948, *Viceroy's Journal*, p. 440.

39 Parliamentary Debates (Hansard), House of Lords, Official Report Vol. 154 No. 57, 7 Apr. 1948, Ismay 3/9/20, LHCMA.

40 APW to BLH, 13 May 1948, LH 1/733, LHCMA.

41 APW to Freya Stark, 17 May 1948, JMA.

42 Channon, 1 June 1948, *Diaries*, p. 426.

43 Bernard Fergusson, *The Black Watch and the King's Enemies*, p. 374.

44 'A Ballade of Bereavement', quoted in Fergusson, *Portrait of a Soldier*, p. 87; Wavell Poems, private collection.

45 Fergusson, *Portrait of a Soldier*, p. 84.

46 APW to Gen. Sir Henry Jackson, 22 July 1948, BWRA 0335.

47 APW to Leonie Lemartine, 12 May 1948, private collection.

48 Wavell Family Courier – VI, July 1948, David Walker papers, NB.

49 APW to Stephen Phillimore, private collection.

50 APW, 31 Oct. 1948, *Viceroy's Journal*, p. 443. See also APW to Michael Close, 13 Dec. 1949, MSS Eur Photo Eur 393, OIOC, BL.

51 Family News VI, Nov. 1948, David Walker papers; APW to Freya Stark, 9 Sept. 1948, JMA; APW tells Freya that if he ever wrote his autobiography the title would be 'Call it a Life' – and suggests that 'Stark Naked or Stark Staring' would hardly do for hers.

52 APW to Freya Stark, 23 Dec. 1948, JMA.

53 Ibid., 9 Sept. 1948, JMA.

54 Pamphlet *Arms and the Man*, by Field Marshal Earl Wavell, the Presidential address to the Virgil Society, 13 Oct. 1948, LH 1/733, LHCMA.

55 APW to Leonie Lemartine, 20 Dec. 1948, private collection.

56 Ibid., 12 May 1948, private collection.

57 APW to Freya Stark, 23 Dec. 1948, JMA.

58 David Walker papers, NB.

59 APW, Summary of 1948, *Viceroy's Journal*, p. 444.

60 APW to BLH, 11 May 1949, LH 1/733, LHCMA.

61 APW to WSC, 6 April 1949, CHUR 4/21, CAC.

62 WSC to APW 6 May 1949; APW to WSC, 10 May 1949, CHUR 4/21, CAC.

63 APW to Freya Stark, 24 Oct. 1949, JMA.

64 Sir Norman Brook KCB to Gilbert Laithwaite, KCMG, KCIE, CSI, 9 Aug. 1950, CAB 21/5854, NA. APW to Grigg, 10 March 1950, John Connell fonds, McMU.

65 Parliamentary Debates (Hansard) 6 July 1949: Ismay 3/9/17a, LHCMA.

66 Correspondence continued throughout August, as those who considered themselves able to qualify made their representations to APW. Those affected included about 30 policemen, 30 or 40 European railway officials, and two men from the Security Printing Press. After his death, Ismay continued to speak on their behalf. The quotation from Shakespeare is Mistress Quickly, King Henry IV, Part 2, Act II, Scene I.

67 APW to Freya Stark, 31 July 1949, JMA.

68 Ibid., 24 Oct. 1949, JMA.

69 Walker, *Lean, Wind, Lean*, p. 265.

70 APW to Eric Linklater, 29 Sept. 1949, NLS.

71 Walker, *Lean, Wind, Lean*, p. 287.

72 APW to Freya Stark, 24 Oct. 1949, JMA.

73 Ibid.; Joan gave birth to another girl, Anthea Leila.

74 Walker, *Lean, Wind, Lean*, p. 290. APW's speech was published in *The Ottawa Citizen*, 17 Nov. 1949.

75 APW to Leonie Lemartine, 27 Dec. 1949, private collection.

76 As quoted in Walker, p. 291; see also Bernard Fergusson, *Portrait of a Soldier*, p. 79. Cameron Wilson was killed in the Great War.

77 Walker, *Lean, Wind, Lean*, p. 291.

78 Ibid., pp. 189, 294.

79 Walker, *The Wavell Rock*; also narrated *in Lean, Wind, Lean*, p. 294.

80 APW to Gen. Sir Henry Jackson, 7 Feb. 1950, BWRA 0335.

81 APW to Freya Stark, 23 Dec. 1949, JMA; 'I am beginning to think it would be a useful refreshment of the mind and body to go to bed for some weeks and do nothing but read.'

82 APW to BLH, 3 Feb. 1950, LH 1/733, LHCMA.

83 BLH to APW, 11 Feb. 1950, LH 1/733, LHCMA.

84 Anne Grantham to the author, 28 Sept. 1999.

85 APW to Freya Stark, 18 April 1950, JMA.

86 The 'Viceroy's Journal' begins in 1943, leaving a gap of a year and a half in APW's own recollections of his life. There are nine volumes of 'Recollections'. By his bedside after he died were found pencil notes of the chapter headings of the autobiography he never wrote.

87 APW to Fergusson, 1 May 1950, LH 1/733, LHCMA.

88 EMW to David Walker, May 1950, David Walker papers, NB.

89 Poem by Francis Bret Harte (1839–1902), sent by AJW to Eric Linklater (undated letter), NLS.

90 The idea for Wavell's body to be taken from the Tower by river was EMW's, troops being unobtainable to line any other route: AJW to David Walker, 5 July 1950, David Walker papers, NB. Channon said that he 'sadly suggested' to Attlee's PPS that Wavell should have a state funeral: Channon, *Diaries*, p. 444. Alanbrooke succeeded Wavell as Constable.

91 Lord Ballantrae (Bernard Fergusson), 'An affectionate memory of the Field Marshal whose funeral was 30 years ago today', in *The Times*, 6 June 1980.

92 Ibid.

93 John Connell, 'Farewell to Wavell, Poet and Soldier', *Evening News*, John Connell fonds, McMU. When Brooke was elevated to the peerage in 1945, he took the name of Alanbrooke.

94 Fergusson, *The Trumpet in the Hall*, p. 250.

95 Fergusson, *Portrait of a Soldier*, p. 92. 'I have never found it in my heart to forgive him for not being present,' Fergusson wrote in *The Times* 30 years later; he died a few months after writing the article.

96 Gilbert, Martin, *Churchill, A Life*, p. 891. Churchill died in 1965 at the age of 90.

97 John Bunyan, *The Pilgrim's Progress*, Order of Service, Wednesday 7 June 1950. Sahibzada Yaqub Khan to the author, London, 2000.

98 Lord Ballantrae, *The Times*, 6 June 1980.

99 Lady Wavell preferred the Chantry Garth to a place near Allenby in Westminster Abbey: Fergusson, *The Trumpet in the Hall*, p. 249.

CHAPTER 23: WAVELL'S LEGACY

1 Sir George Abell to Dr J. Minto Robertson, 8 Aug. 1950, private collection.
2 APW, 31 Dec. 1947, *Viceroy's Journal*, p. 439.
3 Peter Fleming, *Spectator*, 26 May 1950.
4 Dorman-Smith to John Connell, 29 Jan. 1962, John Connell fonds, McMU.
5 Philip Mason, *A Shaft of Sunlight*, p. 183.
6 BLH 'Wavell', 8 May 1950, LH 10/1950/7a (published after APW's death in *Evening Standard, Yorkshire Post, Auckland Star*), LHCMA.
7 Ismay to Fergusson, 25 Aug. 1960, RLEW4/10, CAC.
8 Grigg, *Prejudice and Judgement*, Jonathan Cape, 1948, p. 328. The allegation quoted is cited in BLH, 'Wavell'.
9 Lady Pamela Humphrys to the author, October 2000. See Penderell Moon to George Abell, 6 Jan. (undated, but probably 1973), private collection.
10 Penderell Moon to George Abell, 3 Dec. (undated, but probably 1972), private collection.
11 APW to Michael Close, 13 Dec. 1949, MSS EurPhoto 393, OIOC BL.
12 BLH, 'Wavell', LH 10/1950/7a.
13 Gen. Sir Ivo Vesey to John Connell, 26 Aug. 1961, John Connell fonds, McMU.
14 Mason, *A Shaft of Sunlight*, p. 184.
15 Corfield recollections, private collection; later Sir Conrad Corfield, KCIE, CSI, MC (1893–1980).
16 Lt-Col. John Benson to Philip Warner, 15 March 1985, private collection.
17 EMW to Eric Linklater, 6 Feb. 1953, NLS.
18 Dorman-Smith to John Connell, 29 Jan. 1962, McMU.
19 EMW as quoted by John Connell to Ismay, 4/9/1936, LHCMA.
20 Patrick French, *Liberty or Death*, p. 175. Robert Rhodes James, editor of Chips Channon's diaries, to Patrick French, July 1996. Rhodes James later denied having made this comment: private information.
21 Nigel Hamilton, *The Full Monty*, Allen Lane, 2001; p. 559.
22 EMW to Gen. Sir Henry Jackson, 20 July 1950, BWRA.
23 Frances Hendry to Willa Walker, 8 July 1950, David Walker papers.
24 EMW to John Connell, 13 Oct. 1961, John Connell fonds, McMU.
25 Private information.
26 Sir George Abell to Dr J. Minto Robertson, 8 Aug. 1950, private collection.
27 See Pownall, *Diaries*, p. 95.
28 John Bunyan, 'To Be a Pilgrim', as quoted in APW, *Other Men's Flowers*, p. 85.

Acknowledgements

I T WOULD NOT have been possible to write the life of Earl Wavell without the assistance of numerous individuals to whom I owe a great debt of gratitude. I should like to express my thanks first to the late Lady Pamela Humphrys, Wavell's eldest daughter, whom I met before her death in 2001; to her son, Owen Humphrys; to the late Lady Joan's daughter, Mrs Robert Kellie; and to Andrew Longmore, the late Lady Felicity's son. Throughout my research, Wavell's private papers remained closed; however, I am grateful to the Wavell Estate for permission to quote extracts from Wavell's unpublished letters and poems in other manuscript collections, as well as from his many publications.

I should also like to give special thanks to Araminta, Lady Aldington and Joan Bright Astley, OBE who supported me in my endeavour with unfettered enthusiasm; to Michael Belkine, for permission to quote from John Connell's correspondence and publications; to Tom Bird for permission to quote from his diary and letters; to Kate Grimond, who made excerpts from her father's letters to her mother, from which I have quoted; to Maybe Jehu, who lent me her father's private papers for an extended period of time; to William T. Reid, who trawled through the archives in Australia on my behalf; to the family of the late David Walker, who undertook invaluable research for me at New Brunswick University, Canada; to Mrs Jean Wright, the sister of Captain Alexander Reid Scott, who laboriously copied out long passages of her brother's wonderfully descriptive diaries, from which I have quoted. I am also grateful to many others whose publications, private correspondence and memoirs I have consulted and from which I have quoted, as listed in the notes and bibliography.

The Rt Hon. Leopold Amery's diaries are cited by permission of his grandson Leo Amery; quotations of Field Marshal Sir Claude Auchinleck are reproduced by courtesy of the University Librarian and Director, the John Rylands University Library, the University of Manchester; Sir Winston Churchill's correspondence and writings are reproduced with permission of Curtis Brown Ltd, London on behalf of the Estate of Sir

Winston Churchill; Lord Ismay's correspondence is cited by permission of the Hon. Mrs Susand Evetts; General Sir Henry Jackson's correspondence is cited by permission of the Trustees of The Black Watch Regimental Museum; an extract from Rudyard Kipling's poem 'My Boy Jack' is cited by permission of the National Trust for Places of Historic Interest or Natural Beauty; Captain Sir Basil Liddell Hart's correspondence is cited by permission of the Trustees of the Liddell Hart Centre for Military Archives; Captain Baron R.A. Mackay's memoirs are cited by permission of Mrs S.G. Croiset van Uchelen-Mackay; Viscount Monckton's correspondence is cited by permission of Balliol College, Oxford; Earl Mountbatten's correspondence is cited by permission of The Countess Mountbatten of Burma; Admiral Somerville's correspondence is cited by permission of the Somerville family; Brigadier G.S. Brunskill's collection is held in the Department of Documents at the Imperial War Museum: every effort has been made to contact the copyright holder, so far without success. Crown copyright material is reproduced with the permission of the Controller of Her Majesty's Stationery Office.

I am grateful to all those who read either all or part of my manuscript and made invaluable comments: Corelli Barnett, CBE; Professor Brian Bond, FRHistS; General Sir David Fraser, GCB, OBE, DL; David Page; Brigadier James Percival; General Sir Robin Ross, KCB, OBE and Viscount Slim, OBE.

My thanks also to Nicholas Aldridge, who generously shared his experiences of Summer Fields; Patrick Maclure at the Wykehamist Society, Winchester, who answered my many and frequent questions; Dr P.J. Thwaites, Curator, who showed me around Sandhurst; Tom Smyth, Archivist, The Black Watch Regimental Archives; Alan Packwood and his colleagues at the Churchill Archives Centre; Roderick Suddaby and his colleagues at the Imperial War Museum; Michael Ball at the National Army Museum; Dr Iain Brown at the National Library of Scotland; Catherine Stewart and her colleagues at McMaster University; John Montgomery, Librarian at the RUSI; and the staffs at the Oriental and India Office Collection, the British Library, the Liddell Hart Centre for Military Archives, King's College, London, the London Library, Manchester University Library, the National Archives, the Teen Murti Library, New Delhi, and the University of Reading. Then there are all those listed in the bibliography to whom I have spoken, many of whom have kindly let me borrow books on a long loan. My thanks also to M.J. Gohel and the Asia–Pacific Foundation, which gave me a travel bursary to undertake research abroad. Unless otherwise stated, all views expressed in this biography are my own.

A number of friends have supported me emotionally and practically, offering both hospitality and advice, as well as introducing me to further contacts for my research: Sir Nicholas Barrington, KCMG, CVO; Charlotte Breese; Sir Keith and Lady Bright; Amanda Buchan; Brian Cloughley; Michael Crawley; Jonathan and Belinda Davie; Howard and Christobel Flight; Rowan and Davina Freeland; Hugo and Annabel Gamble; Dr Helen Likierman and Julian Hale; Christopher and Dana Kinder; Mark and Lucy Le Fanu; Roderick and Jenny Ingham Clark; Major Robin Maclean; Ann Mytton; John and Anne Raisman; Michael and Sue Rose; Dr Rashmi Shankar; Lord and Lady Tugendhat; the late Frances Tulloch; Richard Warner; Elizabeth Willis; Brigadier Bill Woodburn and Nigel Wright. My thanks to them as well as to my fellow biographer Colin Clifford, who understood only too well the challenges of trying to fit a life into a circumscribed number of pages.

My final thanks go to my agent Sara Menguc, my commissioning editor Caroline Knox, my editor Roland Philipps and the staff at John Murray, especially Rowan Yapp, Caroline Westmore and my copy-editor Liz Robinson; and to my family: my husband Stephen Willis and our children Alexandra, Anthony and Olivia, to whom Wavell's name became as familiar as that of any twenty-first-century icon; my father-in-law, Dr John Willis; and my sister Elizabeth. My acknowledgements would not be complete without mentioning my mother, whose encouragement was unwavering until her death in 2004, and my father, Vice Admiral B.B. Schofield, CB, CBE, who, like Wavell, was a late Victorian. As a serving naval officer in both world wars he inspired my interest in military history, and it was upon his library shelves that I first discovered Wavell's *Other Men's Flowers*.

Sources and Select Bibliography

1. Correspondence and interviews
(* since deceased)

J.N. Abell*; Abraham Akavia; Lady Araminta Aldington; Nicholas Aldridge; Mrs Philip Astley, OBE (Joan Bright); Corelli Barnett, CBE; Dr Christopher Bayly; Antony Beevor; Yusuf Beg; Michael Belkine; Roger Berthoud; T.A. Bird, DSO, MC; Prof. Brian Bond, FRHistS; Patricia Box; Field Marshal Lord Bramall, KG, GCB, OBE, MC; Prof. Christopher Brooke; Dr Iain Brown; Prof. Judith Brown; Lt-Col. F.R. Burnaby-Atkins; Charles Burrell; Dame Frances Campbell-Preston; Field Marshal Lord Carver, GCB, CB CBE, DSO and Bar, MC*; Mohammed Iqbal Chawla; Michael Close*; Maj. Stephen Connelly (Rtd); Michael Conville*; Mrs Walter Courage; James D'Albiac; Prof. John Dancy, MA; Lord Deedes, KBE, MC, PC; Lord Denman, CBE, MC, TD; Prof. David Dilks, FRHistS, FRSL; Sir Douglas Dodds-Parker, MA, FRCS; Mrs Gerald Draper; Robert Ellgood; Celia Elmhirst; George Fergusson; Margaret Fergusson; Gen. Sir David Fraser, GCB, OBE, DL; Ms Annabel Freyberg; Lady Freyberg; Jim Glendinning; Carol Ann Goodall; the Duke of Grafton, KG; Ann Grantham*; Lord Grantley; Kate Grimond; Penelope Greenwood; Partha Sarathi Gupta; Maj. Henry P. Hall, CMG, MBE*; Robert Harling; Dr Tim Harper; Lord Healey, CH, MBE, PC; Maj. Robin Hodson, MBE; Maj.-Gen. David Horsfield, OBE, FIEE; Prof. Sir Michael Howard, CBE, MC; Lord Howe, CH, Kt, PC, QC; Owen Humphrys; Lady Pamela Humphrys*; Mrs Michael Ingram; J. Gabriel Irwin; Maybe Jehu; Sir John Keegan, OBE, FRSL, FRHistS; Mrs Robert Kellie; the Rt Hon. The Lord Kelvedon; Sahibzada Yaqub Khan; Clifford King; Capt. John King; Andro Linklater; Magnus Linklater; Nicolas Maclean, CMG; Patrick Maclure; Maxine Magan; William Magan; Col. Patrick Massey, MC*; Chris Masters; Mary Medlycott*; Revd Aubrey Moodie; The Countess Mountbatten of Burma, CBE, CD, JP, DL; John Murray; Christina Noble; David Page; Maj. Monty Palit; Brig. James Percival; Anne Raisman; John Raisman, CBE; Lt-Col. Harold E. Raugh, Jr, PhD; Sir Peter Redwood; W.A. Reid; Dudley Robinson; Lt-Gen. David Rose, DSO, MC; Gen. Sir Robin Ross, KCB, OBE; Sir Ian Scott, KCMG, KCVO, CIE*; Dorothea Shepherd; John Shipman; Nicholas Shreeve; Patwant Singh; Viscount Slim, OBE; Rona Smith*; Alexandra Hockenhull Soskin; Thomas W. Straker; Elaine Strutt; Maj.-Gen. Sir John

Swinton, KCVO, OBE; Nora Taee; Sir Wilfred Thesiger, KBE, DSO, MA★; Dr P.J. Thwaites, MA, MSc, DMS, AMA, MIMgt; Dr Robert Travers; David Twiston-Davies; Walter Ulrich; Sir Robert Wade-Gery, KCMG, KCVO; Lady Wade-Gery; Willa Walker; Philip Warner★; Stuart Wavell; Pamela Weldon; Lt-Gen. Sir James Wilson, KBE, MC, DL★; Lady Wilson; Richard Woodman; Jean Wright; Philip Ziegler, CVO.

2. *Manuscript Collections*

Abell, Sir George, KCIE, OBE, private collection

Amery, Rt Hon. Leopold, PC, DH, Amery papers; Churchill Archives Centre

Astley, Joan Bright, OBE, Imperial War Museum; private collection

Auchinleck, Field Marshal Sir Claude, GCB, GCIE, CSI, DSO, OBE, John Rylands University Library, the University of Manchester

Bagnold, R.H., OBE, FRS, Churchill Archives Centre

Beamont, Christopher, British Library

Benson, Lt-Col J.E., private collection

Bird, T.A., DSO, MC, private collection

Brunskill, Brig. G.S., CBE, MC, Imperial War Museum

Burrell, Hon. Judith (née Denman), private collection

Butler, Maj.-Gen. S.S., CB, CMG, DSO, Imperial War Museum

Cawthorn, Maj.-Gen. W.J., CB, CIE, CBE, National Archives of Australia

Christie, W.H.J., British Library

Churchill, Sir Winston, PC, OM, CH, FRS, Churchill Archives Centre

Close, Michael, British Library

Connell, John, William Ready Division of Archives & Research Collection, McMaster University Library, Hamilton, Ontario, Canada

Crocker, Sir Walter, CBE, National Archives of Australia

Cunningham, Gen. Sir Alan, GCMG, KCB, MC, National Army Museum

Cunningham, Sir George, GCIE, KCSI, OBE, British Library

D'Albiac, Air Marshal Sir John, KBE, CB, DSO, private collection

Dorman-Smith, Col. Rt Hon. Sir Reginald, GBE, British Library

Dover Wilson, John, CH, LittD, FBA, MA, National Library of Scotland

Dow, Sir Hugh, GCIE, KCSI, KStJ, British Library

Fleming, Peter, OBE, University of Reading and private collection

Freyberg, Bernard, VC, private collection

Forrester, Charles, K-i-H, AHWC, FRIC, British Library

Fuller, S.R., British Library

Grant, Jean, private collection

Hall, Maj. Henry P., CMG, MBE, private collection

Hockenhull, A.J.W., OBE, private collection

Hodson, Henry, private collection

Hodson, Maj. Robin, MBE, private collection

Hutton, Lt-Gen. Sir Thomas, KCIE, CB, MC, Lewin collection, Churchill Archives Centre

Irwin, Captain J.C., private collection

Ismay, General Lord, KG, PC, GCB, CH, DSO, DL, Liddell Hart Centre for Military Archives

Jackson, Gen. Sir Henry, KCB, CMG, DSO, Black Watch Regimental Museum and Archives, Perth

Jacob, Hon. Maj.-Gen. Sir Ian, KBE, CB, private collection

Jehu, Brig. Ivor, CIE, private collection

Jenkins, Sir Evan, GCIE, KCSI, National Archives

Lemartine, Leonie (otherwise Gladys Robinson), private collection

Lewin, Ronald, Churchill Archives Centre

Liddell Hart, Captain Sir Basil, Liddell Hart Centre for Military Archives, King's College

Linklater, Eric, CBE, TD, National Library of Scotland

Listowel, Earl, PC, British Library and private collection

Mackay, Lt-Gen. Sir Iven, KCE, CMG, DSO, VD, Hon LL.D, Australian War Memorial, Canberra

Mackay, Captain Baron R.A., Imperial War Museum

Mason, Philip, CIE, OBE, private collection

Melville, Lt-Col. A.D., TD, MA, JP, Imperial War Museum

Monckton, 1st Viscount, KCMG, KCVO, KC, MC, Bodleian Library, Oxford University

Mountbatten of Burma, Earl, KG, PC, GCB, OM, GCSI, GCIE, GCVO, DSO, British Library

Nelson, Hank, Australian War Memorial, Canberra

O'Connor, Gen. Sir Richard, GCB, DSO, MC, Liddell Hart Centre for Military Archives, King's College

Pethick-Lawrence, Baron, PC, MA, British Library

Phillimore, Ven. Hon. Stephen, MC, private collection

Reid Scott, Capt. Alexander, private collection

Robinson, Gladys, see Lemartine

Shankar, V., private collection

Stark, Freya, DBE, John Murray Archive

Straker, Thomas W., private collection

Walker, David, Harriet Irving Library, University of New Brunswick, Canada

Wavell, Earl, PC, GCB, GCSI, GCIE, CMG, MC, Australian War Memorial, British Library, Imperial War Museum, Liddell Hart Centre for Military Archives, National Archives, Royal Society for Asian Affairs, and private collections

Wavell, Edward, private collection

Winterton, Maj.-Gen. Sir John, CB, CBE, Imperial War Museum

Zimmern, Sir Alfred, Bodleian Library, Oxford University

3. Published Sources
(The place of publication is London unless otherwise stated.)

Akbar, M.J., *Nehru: The Making of India*, Viking, New York, 1988

Alanbrooke, Field Marshal Lord, *War Diaries, 1939–1945*, ed. Alex Danchev and Daniel Todman, Weidenfeld & Nicolson, 2001

Allen, Louis, *The End of the War in Asia*, Hart-Davis MacGibbon, 1976

——*Singapore 1941–42*, Frank Cass, 1993

Alexander Memoirs, The, ed. John North, Cassell, 1962

Amery, Julian, *Approach March*, Hutchinson, 1973

Amery, L.S., *The Empire at Bay: The Leo Amery Diaries*, ed. John Barnes and Davis Nicholson, Hutchinson, 1988

Attlee, Clement, *A Prime Minister Remembers*, Heinemann, 1961

Arthur, Sir George, *From Wellington to Wavell*, Hutchinson, n.d.

Astley, Joan Bright, *The Inner Circle: A View of War at the Top*, Little Brown & Co., Boston, 1971

Azad, Maulana Abul Kalam, *India Wins Freedom*, Orient Longman, India, 1988

Barnett, Corelli, *The Desert Generals*, William Kimber and Co. Ltd, 1960, 1983 (new ed.)

——*The Sword Bearers*, Eyre & Spottiswoode, 1963

——*Engage the Enemy More Closely*, Hodder & Stoughton, 1991

Baynes, John, *The Forgotten Victor*, Brassey's, 1991

Bayly, Christopher and Harper, Tim, *Forgotten Armies*, Allen Lane, 2004

Bell, Sir Gawain, *Shadows on the Sand*, C. Hurst & Co., 1983

Beevor, Antony, *Crete*, John Murray, 1991

Beevor, J.G., *SOE, Recollections and Reflections 1940–45*, The Bodley Head, 1981

Birkenhead, the Earl of, *Halifax: The Life of Lord Halifax*, Hamish Hamilton, 1965

Bond, Brian, 'The Army between the Two World Wars 1918–1939', *see* Chandler, David

Bramall, E.N.W. and Jackson, W.G.F., *The Chiefs*, Brassey's, 1992

'Brown, Judith M., *Gandhi, Prisoner of Hope*, Yale University Press, 1989

——*Nehru*, Longman, 1999

Bryant, Arthur, *Turn of the Tide 1939–1943*, Collins, 1957

Cadogan A., *Diaries 1938–45*, ed. David Dilks, Cassell, 1971

Carver, Michael, *Harding of Petherton*, Weidenfeld and Nicolson, 1978

Chandler, David G., ed. *The Oxford History of the British Army*, OUP, 1994

Chaudhuri, Nirad C., *Thy Hand, Great Anarch!*, Hogarth Press, 1990

'Chips': *The Diaries of Sir Henry Channon*, ed. Robert Rhodes James, Weidenfeld and Nicolson, 1993

Churchill, W.S. *The Second World War*, vols I–VI, Cassell, 1948–54

Ciano, Galeazzo, *Diary 1939–43*, ed. Malcolm Muggeridge, Heinemann, 1947

Clarke, Dudley, *Seven Assignments*, Jonathan Cape, 1948

Clarke, Peter, *The Cripps Version*, Allen Lane, 2002

Clifford, Alexander, *Three Against Rommel*, George G. Harrap & Co. Ltd, 1943

Close, Michael, *Attlee, Wavell and Mountbatten and the Transfer of Power*, National Book Foundation, Islamabad, 1997

Coats, Peter, *Of Generals and Gardens*, Weidenfeld & Nicolson, 1976

Collins, R.J., *Lord Wavell*, Hodder & Stoughton, 1948

Colville, John, *The Fringes of Power*, Hodder & Stoughton, 1985

Connell, John, *Auchinleck*, Collins, 1959

——*Wavell, Scholar and Soldier* (to June 1941), Collins, 1964

——*Wavell, Supreme Commander, 1941–43*, ed. Michael Roberts, Collins, 1969

Cooper, Artemis, *Cairo in the War 1939–45*, Hamilton, 1989

Cooper, Duff, *Old Men Forget*, Rupert Hart-Davis, 1953

Cooper, Jilly, *Animals in War*, Heinemann, 1983

Corfield, Sir Conrad, *The Princely India I Knew*, Hoe & Co., Madras, 1975

Costello, John, *The Pacific War, 1941–1945*, Atlantic Communications Inc., 1981

Cunningham, Admiral of the Fleet Viscount, *A Sailor's Odyssey: The Autobiography of Admiral of the Fleet Viscount Cunningham of Hyndhope, KT, GCB, OM, DSO*, Hutchinson, 1951

Curie, Eve, *Journey Among Warriors*, Heinemann, 1943

Danchev *see* Alanbrooke

Day, David, *The Politics of War*, Harper Collins, Sydney, 2003

Dilks *see* Cadogan *and* Tedder

Dover Wilson, John, *Milestones on the Dover Road*, Faber & Faber, 1969

Eden, Rt Hon. Anthony, Earl of Avon, *Memoirs: The Reckoning*, Cassell, 1965

Estorick, Eric, *Stafford Cripps*, Heinemann, 1949

Farrell, Brian and Hunter, Sandy, *Sixty Years On: The Fall of Singapore Revisited*, Eastern Universities Press, 2002

Fergusson, Bernard, *Beyond the Chindwin*, Collins, 1945

——*The Black Watch and the King's Enemies*, Collins, 1950

——*Wavell: Portrait of a Soldier*, Collins, 1961

——*The Trumpet in the Hall, 1930–1958*, Collins, 1970

Foot, M.R.D. and Langley, J.M., *MI9*, Bodley Head, 1979

——*SOE, The Special Operations Executive 1940–46*, BBC, 1984

Fraser, David, *Alanbrooke*, Collins, 1982

——*Knight's Cross*, Harper Collins, 1993

French, Patrick, *Liberty or Death*, Harper Collins, 1997

Freyberg, Paul, *Bernard Freyberg, VC: Soldier of Two Nations*, Hodder & Stoughton, 1991

Fry, Michael G., *Lloyd George and Foreign Policy*, McGill/Queen's University Press, 1977

Gilbert, Martin, *Finest Hour: Winston S. Churchill, 1939–41*, Heinemann, 1983

——*Churchill: A Life*, Heinemann, 1991

Glendevon, John, *The Viceroy at Bay: Lord Linlithgow in India 1936–43*, Collins, 1971

Godwin-Austen, A.R., *The Staff and Staff College*, Constable, 1927

Goebbels Diaries 1939–41, The, tr. Fred Taylor, Hamish Hamilton, 1982

Hamid, Shahid, *Disastrous Twilight*, Leo Cooper, 1986

Harper, Tim *see* Bayly

Harris, Kenneth, *Attlee*, Weidenfeld & Nicolson, 1982

Hart-Davis, Duff, *Peter Fleming*, Jonathan Cape, 1974

Hastings, Robin, *An Undergraduate's War*, Bellhouse Publishing, 1997

Hetherington, John, *Blamey*, F.W. Cheshire, Melbourne, 1954

Hinsley, F.H., *British Intelligence in the Second World War*, vol. 1, HMSO, 1979

Howard, Michael, *Strategic Deception in the Second World War*, Pimlico, 1990

——*The First World War*, OUP, 2002

Hunter *see* Farrell

Ismay, *The Memoirs of General the Lord Ismay*, Heinemann, 1960

Jackson, W.G.F. *see* Bramall

Jalal, Ayesha, *The Sole Spokesman*, Cambridge University Press, New Delhi, 1994

James, Lawrence, *Raj: The Making and Unmaking of British India*, Little Brown & Co., 1997

Jenkins, Roy, *Churchill*, Macmillan, 2001

Kazimi, Muhammad Reza, *Liaquat Ali Khan and the Freedom Movement*, University of Karachi, 1997

Keegan, John, *Churchill's Generals* ed., Weidenfeld & Nicolson, 1991

——*The First World War*, Hutchinson, 1998

Kelly, Saul, *The Hunt for Zerzura*, John Murray, 2002

Kennedy, Major-General Sir John, *The Business of War*, Hutchinson, 1957

Kiernan, R.H., *Wavell*, George G. Harrap & Co. Ltd, 1945

Kinvig, Clifford, *Scapegoat: General Percival of Singapore*, Brassey's, 1996

Kirby, S. Woodburn, *The War Against Japan*, vol. 1, HMSO, 1957

Kulkarmi, V.S. and Murty, K.S.N., eds, *First Indian National Army Trial*, Law Academy, Delhi, 1946

Langley, J.M. *see* Foot

Lash, Joseph P., *Roosevelt and Churchill 1939–1941*, Andre Deutsch, 1977

Lawrence, A.W., ed., *T.E. Lawrence by His Friends*, Jonathan Cape, 1937

Leach, Hugh with S.M. Farrington, *Strolling about on the Roof of the World*, Routledge Curzon, 2003

Lewin, Ronald, *Ultra Goes to War*, Hutchinson & Co. Ltd, 1978

——*The Chief*, Hutchinson & Co. Ltd, 1980

Liddell Hart, Capt B.H., ed., *The Rommel Papers*, tr. Paul Findlay, Collins, 1953

——*Memoirs, Vols. 1 & 2*, Cassell, 1965

——*History of World War 1*, Cassell, 1970

——*History of World War 2*, Putnam, New York, 1971

Linklater, Eric and Andro, *The Black Watch: The History of the Royal Highland Regiment*, Barrie & Jenkins, Penguin Press, 2002

Lunt, James, *A Hell of a Licking: The Retreat from Burma 1941–2*, Collins, 1986

Lyman, Robert, *Slim, Master of War*, Constable, 2004

Macdonald, Callum, *The Lost Battle: Crete 1941*, Macmillan, 1993

Mansergh, Nicholas and Moon, Penderell, eds, *Transfer of Power 1942–47*, Vols IV–XI, HMSO, 1976

Marshall-Cornwall, James, *A Memoir: Wars and Rumours of Wars*, Leo Cooper, 1984

Mason, Philip, *A Shaft of Sunlight*, Andre Deutsch, 1978

——*A Matter of Honour*, Papermac, 1978

Melchett, Lord, *Thy Neighbour*, Frederick Muller, 1936

Mitchell, Norval, *Sir George Cunningham*, Blackwood, Edinburgh & London, 1968

Montgomery, Bernard, *The Memoirs of Field Marshal Montgomery*, Collins, 1958

Moon, Penderell, *Divide and Quit*, OUP, 1999; *see also* Wavell

——*Transfer of Power*, see Mansergh

Moorehead, Alan, *The Desert War: The North African Campaign, 1940–43*, Hamish Hamilton, 1965

Moorehead, Caroline, *Freya Stark*, Viking, 1985

Muggeridge, Malcolm *see* Ciano

Moran, Lord, *Winston Churchill: The Struggle for Survival*, Constable, 1966

Mure, David, *Master of Deception*, William Kimber, 1980

Murty *see* Kulkarmi

Nehru, Jawaharlal, *Selected Works, Second Series Vols 1 and 2*, Jawaharlal Nehru Memorial Fund, 1984

Owen, Frank, *Tempestuous Journey: Lloyd George*, Hutchinson, 1954

Pack, S.W.C., *Sea Power in the Mediterranean*, Arthur Baker Ltd, 1971

——*Cunningham the Commander*, Brassey's, 1974

Percival, Lt-Gen. Arthur, *The War in Malaya*, Eyre & Spottiswoode, 1949

Pine, L.G., *The House of Wavell*, private publication, 1948

Playfair, I.S.O, *The Mediterranean and Middle East*, HMSO 1954–1988

Pownall, Lt-Gen. Sir Henry, *Diaries*, ed. Brian Bond, Leo Cooper, 1974

Ranfurly, Countess, *To War with Whitaker*, Mandarin, 1995

Raugh, Lt-Colonel Harold, *Wavell in the Middle East, 1939–41*, Brassey's, 1993

Rolo, Charles J., *Wingate's Raiders* (Foreword by Field Marshal Viscount Wavell), George G. Harrap & Co. Ltd, 1944

Rose, David, *Off the Record*, Spellmount Ltd, 1998

Roskill, Stephen, *Churchill and the Admirals*, Collins, 1977

Ross, Josephine, *Beaton in Vogue*, Thames & Hudson, 1986

Rowan-Robinson, Maj-Gen. H., *Wavell in the Middle East*, Hutchinson & Co. Ltd, 1942

Seervai, H.M. *Partition of India: Legend and Reality*, OUP, 2005

Singh, Anita Inder, *The Origins of Partition, 1936–47*, OUP, 1987

Slim, Field Marshal Sir William, *Defeat into Victory*, Reprint Society, 1957

Smith, Colin, *Singapore Burning*, Viking, 2004

Smuts, J.C., *Jan Christian Smuts, By His Son*, Cassell & Co. Ltd, 1952

Smyth, Sir John, *Milestones*, Sidgwick & Jackson, 1979

Stark, Freya, *Letters*, vols IV, V, VI, ed. Lucy Moorehead, Michael Russell, 1977

——*Dust in the Lion's Paw*, John Murray, 1961

——*East is West*, John Murray, 1945, Arrow edition, 1991

Stephens, Ian, *Pakistan*, Ernest Benn Ltd, 1967

Stilwell, Joseph, *The Stilwell Papers*, Macdonald, 1949

Sykes, Christopher, *Two Studies in Virtue*, Collins, 1953

——*Orde Wingate*, Collins, 1959

Tedder, *With Prejudice: The War Memoirs of Marshal of the Royal Air Force Lord Tedder, GCB*, ed. David Dilks, Cassell, 1966

Transfer of Power, see Mansergh

Tuchman, Barbara W., *Sand against the Wind: Stilwell and the American Experience in China, 1911–45*, Macmillan, 1971

Von Mellenthin, Major-General F.W., *Panzer Battles*, tr. H. Betzler, ed. L.C.F. Turner, Ballantine Books, 1956, 1971

Walker, David, *Lean, Wind, Lean: A Few Times Remembered*, Collins, 1984

Warner, Philip, *Auchinleck*, Buchan & Enright, 1981

——*Horrocks*, Sphere Books, 1985

Wavell, A.P. (*later* Field Marshal Earl Wavell), *The Palestine Campaigns*, ed. Maj-Gen. Sir Charles Calwell, Constable, 1928, 2nd edn 1929

——*Allenby: Soldier and Statesman*, Harrap, 1946 (originally publ. in 2 vols: *Allenby: A Study in Greatness*, 1940, and *Allenby in Egypt*, 1944)

——*Other Men's Flowers*, Jonathan Cape, 1944, Memorial Edition 1952

——*Speaking Generally*, Macmillan, 1946

——*Notes & Ideas*, private publication, 1947

——*The Good Soldier*, Macmillan, 1948

——*The Viceroy's Journal*, ed. Penderell Moon, OUP, 1973

Wheeler-Bennett, John, *King George VI*, Macmillan, 1958

——ed. *Action This Day: Working with Churchill*, Macmillan, 1969

Whitehouse, Arthur, *Epics and Legends of the First World War*, Frederick Muller Ltd, 1964

Wingate, Reginald, *Lord Ismay: A Biography*, Hutchinson, 1970

Winterbotham, F.W., *The Ultra Secret*, Dell Publishing Co., 1974

Wolpert, Stanley, *Jinnah of Pakistan*, OUP, 2000

Woollcombe, Robert, *The Campaigns of Wavell, 1939–43*, Cassell & Co. Ltd, 1959

Young, Desmond, *Rommel*, Collins, 1950

Ziegler, Philip, *Mountbatten*, Collins, 1985

——*Rupert Hart-Davis, Man of Letters*, Chatto & Windus, 2004

Zubair, Zeba, *From Mutiny to Mountbatten: A biographical sketch of and writings by Altaf Husain*, Kegan Paul, 1996

Journals and Magazines

Army Quarterly, 1950
Illustrated London News, February 1941
House & Garden, 1950
Journal of the Society for Army Historical Research, Vol. 38, 1960
The Journal of the Royal United Services Institute, November 1930
The Journal of the Royal United Services Institute, Feb–Nov 1936
The London Gazette, July 1946, March 1948
The Red Hackle, July 1950
The Times, selected issues
The Trusty Servant, selected issues
The Spectator, May 1950
The Summer Fields Magazine, selected issues
The Wykehamist, selected issues

Index

Index

Field Marshal Earl Wavell is referred to as APW.
Titles and ranks quoted are generally the highest achieved.
For ease of reference, entries under British, Dominion and Empire Land Forces are in alphabetical and numerical order rather than in strict order of military precedence.
British warships are entered under Royal Navy.

ABDA Command (South-West Pacific; American, British, Dutch Australian) 229–31, 233–5, 250, 251, 252, 253
Abdullah (Regent of Iraq) 133, 183–4
Abdullah, King (of Transjordan; *later* Jordan) 84
Abell, Sir George 303, 304, 312, 357, 367, 370, 397
Aberdeen University 382–3, 388
Afrika Corps, Deutsche *see* Rommel, General Erwin
Akyab Island 263, 271–2, 275, 284
Alanbrooke, Field Marshal Alan Brooke, 1st Viscount 110, 120, 224, 267, 269, 293, 327, 395
Albania 166
Aldershot 98–102
Aldridge, Nicholas 10–11
Alexander, Rt. Hon. A.V. 346, 380
Alexander, Field Marshal Harold, 1st Viscount 249, 255–6, 265, 267, 349, 364
Alexandra, Tsarina (of Russia) 61
Aliakmon Line (Greek defensive position) 178, 181, 186

Alington, Revd Hugh 10
All India Radio 216–17, 376
All Souls College (Oxford) 121, 352
Allenby, Field Marshal Edmund, 1st Viscount 32, 66–8, 70–2, 74–80, 84–5, 86, 110; APW's life of 113, 118, 161, 122, 281, 296
Aly, Prince Mohammed (of Egypt) 140
American Volunteer Group (AVG) 228, 251
Amery, Leopold ('Leo') 141, 145; relationship with APW 214, 292–7, 299–300, 320, 323–5, 326, 329, 332, 366, 399
Amherst, Major the Earl 185
Anderson, Sir John (*later* Viscount Waverly) 291
Andrews, Lewis 115
Anglo-Egyptian Treaty (1936) 128
Anglo-Iraq Treaty (1930) 133
Anglo-Polish Treaty (1939) 131
Aosta, Duke of 130, 196
Arakan offensive 260, 272, 274–5, 281, 283, 284, 307

Arbatskaya, Lydia 36–7
Arcadia Conference (1941–2; Washington) 230
Army Quarterly 92
Arnold, General Henry 277–8
Ashcroft, Peggy 329
Asquith, Herbert Henry, 1st Earl 13, 41, 42–3, 297
Asquith, Raymond 13, 82
Assam 264, 302, 306, 346, 350, 351
Astley, Diana Jane (APW's grand-daughter) 305, 388
Astley, Sir Jacob 277
Astley, Joan (APW's daughter) *see* Wavell, Joan Patricia Quirk
Astley, Joan Bright (friend of APW) *see* Bright, Joan
Astley, Colonel Philip 379
Astley, Captain the Hon. Simon 267, 271, 274, 322–3, 347
Atlantic Charter (1941) 217–18
Attlee, Clement: joins National Coalition government (1940) 141; opposes APW's appointment as Gov. Gen. of Australia 292; Indian Independence negotiations 298–9, 328, 339, 345, 364, 365–6, 367, 368–9; wins General Election (1945) 337; dismisses APW as Viceroy 369–70, 377; and decision attacked by Churchill 372–3; appoints Mountbatten as Viceroy 370–1, 377; at APW's funeral 395
Auchinleck, Field Marshal Sir Claude 108, 152, 388; relationship with APW 135, 307, 375, 383, 401; as C-in-C India 179, 184, 296, 342; replaces APW in Middle East Command 196, 198, 200, 208, 209; criticised by Churchill 267
Auchinleck, Lady Jessie 281
Aurangzeb (son of Wali of Swat) 372
Australia 216, 230, 248, 292

Azad, Maulana Abul Kalam 258, 259, 334, 335, 338, 349, 350, 354, 355, 378

Bacon, Francis: 'Great Place' 196
Baghdad Times 134
Bagnold, Brigadier R.A. 146–7
Bahawalpur, Nawab of 225
Baker, Sir Herbert 222, 301, 306
Baldwin, Stanley 91, 111
Balfour, Arthur James 67, 68–9
Balfour Declaration (1917) 67, 68–9, 71, 114
Baluchistan 350, 351
Bambridge, Mrs George 292
Bardia 163–4, 192, 207
Bartholomew, General Sir William 83, 121
Basra 183, 184, 195, 200, 212
Beaton, Cecil 314
Beatty, Admiral of the Fleet David, 1st Earl 92
Beaverbrook, Max 220–1
Beck, Josef 131
Beckwith-Smith, General M.B. 240, 246
Beda Fomm, Battle of (1941) 170
Belisarius 274, 393
Bellairs, Veronica (*née* Wavell; APW's cousin; 'Vere') 40, 395
Bengal: famine 299, 302, 303–4; Independence negotiations 321, 340, 346, 350, 351; rioting 360
Benghazi 182, 183, 185, 193
Bennett, Lieutenant-General Henry Gordon 232, 234, 241, 243, 246
Benson, Lieutenant-Colonel John 129, 142, 191, 401
Beresford-Peirse, Lieutenant-General Sir Noel 144, 160–1, 174, 207
Bergonzoli, General 170, 319–20
Bernard, Canon 40
Bernard, Caroline 40
Besly, Ernest Francis 144

Bhopal, Nawab of *see* Khan, Hamidullah
Bihar 302, 351
Bilin river 249
Bird, Tom 210–11, 222, 280, 284, 295, 303
Bismarck (German battleship) 202
Black Watch, The *see* British and Commonwealth Land Forces: Royal Highland Regiment
Blamey, Field Marshal Sir Thomas 138, 187
Boer War 14, 31, 67 *see also* South Africa
Bolkhovitinov, General 62, 63
Bols, Major-General Sir Louis 84, 85, 86
Bombay 302, 347, 351
Borneo 234
Borton, Air Vice-Marshal Amyas 25, 52, 59, 66, 79, 83, 89–90, 395
Bose, Subhas Chandra 215, 242, 319, 342
Boyle, Admiral of the Fleet William 122
Breslau (German battleship) 45
Brest-Litovsk, Treaty of (1918) 72
Brett, General 228, 233
Bright, Joan (*later* Astley): friendship and correspondence with APW 219, 220, 225, 250, 253, 266, 268–9, 272, 275, 284, 301, 313, 315, 379
British, Dominion and Empire Land Forces
  ARMIES: 1st Army 140; 8th Army 267, 268, 327; Burma Army, 256, 264
  CORPS: 1st Burma 257; 3rd Indian 232; XIII (*formerly* Western Desert Force) 179, 183, 207
  DIVISIONS: 1st Cavalry 197; 1st Infantry 111, 249; 1st South
African 169; 2nd Armoured 179, 182; 2nd Infantry 106, 107, 108, 319; 3rd Infantry 95; 4th Indian 130, 144, 156, 159, 160, 162, 173, 179, 213; 5th Indian 173, 213; 6th Australian 156, 159, 162, 164, 166, 174–5, 184; 7th Armoured (*formerly* Mobile) 144, 149, 156, 170, 179; 7th Armoured Support Group 146; 7th Australian 174–5, 184, 185, 200, 248; 7th Infantry (*later* 6th) 129, 132, 144; 8th Australian 232, 243; 9th Australian 180; 9th Indian 232, 243; 10th Indian 184, 195, 256; 11th Indian 232, 243; 14th Indian 273, 274–5, 277; 17th Indian 242; 17th Infantry 238, 251; 18th Infantry 227, 236, 240, 243, 247; 64th Highland 59; New Zealand 138, 155, 174, 179; West African Frontier Force 151
  BRIGADES: 1st Armoured 175, 179; 2nd Burma 242; 4th Guards 107, 108; 4th New Zealand 156, 206; 5th Infantry 107, 108, 110; 6th Infantry 98–100, 107, 108, 319; 7th Armoured 242, 254; 7th Infantry 96; 11th Indian 130; 44th Indian 243; 77th Indian ('Chindits') 263; Australian Light Horse 78; Indian Parachute 260; South African 149, 150
  REGIMENTS AND FORMATIONS: 1st Lincolnshire 53, 54; 1st Northumberland Fusiliers 53; 1st Royal Scots Fusiliers 53; 2nd Cameron Highlanders 163; 4th Royal Fusiliers 53, 55; 7th Queen's Own Hussars 264, 267; 7th Royal Tank 156;

British, Dominion and Empire Land Forces (*cont.*)

REGIMENTS AND FORMATIONS (*cont.*):

Argyll and Sutherland Highlanders 241; Gordon Highlanders 26; Gurkha Rifles 344; King's African Rifles 28; Middlesex Yeomanry 138; Nottingham Sherwood Rangers Yeomanry 163; Queen's Regiment 31; Royal Engineers 35; Royal Highland Regiment (Black Watch) 8–9, 14, 18–19, 20, 21, 23, 26, 114, 116; *1st Battalion* 381, 387, 394; *2nd Battalion* 149, 310, 378; *5th Battalion* 387; *7th Battalion* 387; Royal Norfolk Regiment 7, 8, 55; Royal Welch Fusiliers 199; Seaforth Highlanders 21

British Expeditionary Force (BEF): First World War 44, 49–52, 99; Second World War 131, 142, 143

Brook, Norman 390

Brooke-Popham, Air Chief Marshal Sir Robert 223, 224

Browning, Robert 12, 49, 312, 365

Brunskill, Brigadier George 114

Buchanan, Major-General Sir K.G. 9, 11, 12, 53, 100, 395

Bulfin, General 85

Bulgaria 157–8, 166, 171, 176, 178, 181, 184

Bulloch, Colonel Archibald 25, 88

Bunyan, John: *Pilgrim's Progress* 396

Burgon, John 169

Burma: APW urges Burma be under India Command 219, 222, 224, 227, 230, 250; Burma Road 224, 228, 238, 264; Japanese advance on 237, 248–9; Allied withdrawal completed 264–5

Burnett-Stuart, General Sir John 59, 90–1, 95, 96, 103, 109, 116, 395

Butler, R.A. 165

Caccia, Harold 176

Cairo Conference (1943; Sextant) 304

Cakmak, Marshal Fevzi 133, 134

Calcutta 304, 360, 362

Callaghan, Brigadier 246

Callwell, Major-General Sir Charles 93

Calthrop, Everard 31, 38, 59, 83

Calvert, Mike 311

Campaigns and their Lessons (ed. Callwell) 93

Cape Matapan, Battle of (1941) 182

Capuzzo 207

Casey, Richard 313

Cassels, General Sir Robert 128, 179

Cavan, Frederick, Earl of 91–2, 96

Cawthorn, Major-General Walter 129–30

Central Powers (First World War: Germany, Austria–Hungary, Turkey, Bulgaria) 64

Central Provinces 302, 351

Ceylon 260, 261, 265

Chamberlain, Neville 111, 119–20, 122, 131–2, 137, 141, 142, 157

Channon, Henry ('Chips') III 165–6, 169; friendship with APW 166, 171, 285, 291–2, 293, 294, 300, 326, 401

Chardigny, Colonel 62–3

Charlton, Colonel Nial 211

Chennault, Major-General Claire 228

Cherat Times (newspaper) 27

Chetwode, General Sir Philip 68, 69, 74, 75, 77

Chiang, Madame (wife of Chiang Kai-Shek) 227–8, 242

Chiang Kai-Shek 221, 227, 228, 230–1, 239, 254, 273, 278

China 216, 221, 228, 230–1, 263–4, 273, 278; armies 228, 239, 256

'Chindits' (Long Range Penetration Group; Burma) 263, 278–9, 281, 283–4, 298; *see also* Wingate, Captain O.C. (Orde)

Chindwin river 264

Cholmley, George 82

Chungking 227–8, 238

Church of the Redemption (New Delhi) 277

Churchill, Augusta, Lady Edward Spencer (Countess Wavell's godmother) 41, 54, 56, 106

Churchill, Captain George (Medical Corps) 35, 37

Churchill, George Spencer 123, 293, 312, 371, 381

Churchill, Randolph 179, 181

Churchill, Winston 41–2, 91, 120, 123, 132, 141, 146; relationship with APW (Middle East Command) 143, 146, 148, 150–3, 157–9, 161, 162–3, 166–7, 172, 177, 182, 188–9, 195; replaces APW with Auchinleck 196, 199–200, 205, 208–9; relationship with APW (India and ABDA) 230–1, 239–40, 251, 253, 260–1, 267, 285–7, 307; fall of Singapore 243–6; relationship with APW (as Viceroy of India) 293–5, 300, 325, 326; attacks Attlee over APW's dismissal 372–3; reconsiders opinion of APW 390; *History of the Second World War* vol. I 388; vols. II, III and IV 390

Clark, Geoffrey 82

Clark, Lieutenant-General J.G.W. 197

Clarke, Brigadier Dudley 114, 136

Clifford, Alexander 160, 211

Coats, Captain Peter 138–9, 141, 165–6, 167, 168, 201, 207, 209, 224, 272, 311, 340–1, 401

Cobb, Major E.H. 322

Colefax, Lady 329

Collins, Ann *later* Grantham 97, 393

Collins, Major-General R.J. 8, 49, 96, 97, 103, 393

Colville, John 151, 205

Colville, Sir John and Lady 326

Congress Party, Indian National 215, 258, 259, 279, 316, 335, 341; Congress Working Committee 271, 316, 317, 333

Congreve, General Sir Walter 86

Connaught, Duke of 2, 17

Connell, Captain John 208, 395, 402

Conville, Captain Michael 344

Cooper, Sir (Alfred) Duff (*later* Lord Norwich) 231–2

Corfield, Sir Conrad 363, 401

Cornwallis, Sir Kinahan 183, 195

Cowan, Major-General David ('Punch') 254, 262

Coward, Noël 318

Cowdray, Agnes, Lady 381

Cranborne, Lord Robert ('Bobbety') 285, 295; *later* 5th Marquess of Salisbury 391

Creagh, Major-General Michael O'Moore 144, 161, 174

Crete 142, 156, 172, 187, 189, 190; defence and evacuation of 197–9, 201–3, 206, 214, 352; Creforce 198; *see also* Greece

Cripps, Sir Stafford: Indian Independence proposals 258–9, 309, 330, 338, 339, 340, 345; negotiations 291, 346, 349, 351, 356, 357, 368

Cumming, Captain Sir Mansfield RN 37

Cunard, Lady 329

Cunningham, Admiral of the Fleet Andrew, Viscount 128, 131, 143, 164, 174, 182, 201, 202, 382, 395

Cunningham, General Sir Alan 159, 169, 173, 178, 186, 210, 395

Cunningham, Sir George 341, 380
Curie, Eve 300
Curtin, John (PM of Australia) 240,
 248, 251, 287, 292–3
Curzon, Lord 22–3, 24, 27
Cyrenaica 167, 171, 175, 182, 201,
 207, 269

Daily Telegraph 296
Damascus 73, 75, 78, 209
Darwin (Australia) 240, 248
Davies, Clement 373
Dawnay, Major-General Guy 67
Deedes, General Sir Charles 112
Delhi 222, 225
Denman, Lady 302
Denman, Lord 41, 302
Desai, Bhulabhai 325
Dill, Field Marshal Sir John: meets
 APW at Sandhurst 17; as Director
 of Military Intelligence 104, 110;
 as GOC Palestine and Transjordan
 111, 113, 115; as Vice-Chief of
 Imperial General Staff (VCIGS)
 140; as CIGS 143, 146, 150–1,
 158, 164, 172, 175, 178, 186–7,
 196, 198, 199, 279; promoted to
 Field Marshal 224; in Washington
 229, 230, 231; death 323
Dobbie, Major-General William 223
Donovan, General William J. 172,
 175
Dorman-Smith, Doreen (wife of Sir
 Reginald) 242
Dorman-Smith, Captain Eric (*later*
 O'Gowan-Dorman) 99, 188, 197,
 252; comments on APW 100, 170,
 200, 205, 397–8, 401
Dorman-Smith, Estelle (wife of
 Captain Eric) 101
Dorman-Smith, Sir Reginald 222–3,
 229, 242
Dow, Sir Hugh 375

Dundas, Robert 12
Dutch East Indies 216, 232, 233

East Africa: APW's offensive campaigns
 (1941) 159, 162, 166, 168, 169,
 170, 173, 178, 182, 186, 269
École des Maréchaux (French military
 academy) 104–5
Eden, Anthony (*later* 1st Earl of
 Avon): appeasement resignation
 119; friendship with APW 137–8;
 as Secretary of State for War 141,
 145; comments on APW and
 Churchill 150, 151–2; visits APW
 in Middle East 154–5; and
 Churchill's reaction to 'Compass'
 plan 157; as Foreign Secretary 167,
 174, 175, 181; as candidate for
 Viceroy 291, 294; at APW's
 funeral 395
Eden, (*later* Medlycott) Mary 94
Edward VII, King 18
Edward VIII, King 111
Egypt 188–9, 190, 209
El Agheila 170, 182
Elchaninov, Major-General Andrei
 Georgievich 39
Eliot, T.S. 106
Elizabeth, Princess (*later* Queen
 Elizabeth II) 1, 383
Elliot, Air Chief Marshal Sir William
 287
Elwes, Simon 315
Encyclopaedia Britannica 92, 96
Entente Cordiale (Anglo-French
 agreement; 1904) 43–4
Epstein, Jacob 329
Ertel, Madam (APW's Russian
 landlady) 33–4, 35–6
Ertel, Natalya 34, 36
Ethiopia *see* Selassie, Emperor Haile
 (of Ethiopia)
Evening News 395

Farhan, Sheikh 115
Farouk, King (of Egypt) 140
Feisal I, King (of Iraq) 84, 85, 133,
    183–4
Feisal II, King (of Iraq) 133
Fearon, Dr W.A. 13, 15
Feast of the Gods, The (painting;
    Bellini) 287
Fellers, Bonner 160
Fergusson, Bernard (Lord Ballantrae):
    APW appoints as ADC 106;
    comment on APW 108–10, 129,
    213, 214, 262, 381; as intelligence
    officer in Jerusalem 116; journeys
    with APW 169–70, 212; involved
    in Crete inquiry 203; drafts APW's
    final Middle East dispatch 218;
    joins planning staff in Delhi 260,
    262, 263, 306, 381, 387, 393,
    394–6; joins Chindits 263, 306;
    APW's affection for 306; in
    command of Black Watch 387;
    APW's funeral 394–6
Fergusson, General Sir Charles 106
Flecker, James Elroy: *Hassan* 212, 275
Fleming, Peter 257–8, 262–3, 274,
    276, 282, 311, 314, 397
Foch, Marshal 132
Fortune, Major-General Sir Victor 107
'Forward Bloc' (Indian political
    movement) 215
Fox, Michael 124
France: First World War 43–4, 50,
    63–4, 73; Second World War 132,
    136, 142, 145–6, 199, 206
Franz Ferdinand, Archduke 44
Franz Josef, Emperor 44
Fraser, Peter (PM of New Zealand)
    217
French, Field Marshal Sir John, 1st
    Earl of Ypres 41, 42, 50, 59
French, Patrick 401
Freyberg, Barbara 217

Freyberg, Lieutenant-General Sir
    Bernard: early meeting with APW
    104; problem of divided loyalties
    138, 154–5; considered for Middle
    East Command 152; Greece and
    'Lustre' force 174, 179; defence
    and evacuation of Crete 190, 197,
    198, 199, 202, 212, 214; APW's
    support for 217
Fuller, Major-General C.G. 35, 36–7
Fuller, Major-General John F.C.
    ('Boney') 93
Fyfe, Sir William Hamilton 383

Gambier-Parry, Major-General M.D.
    182, 184–5, 194
Gandhi, Mohandas K. ('Mahatma'):
    civil disobedience movement 215,
    259, 271, 316; demands British
    withdrawal from India 258, 316;
    imprisonment 278, 316; failure of
    talks with Jinnah 320–1; role at
    Simla Conferences 334, 350;
    APW's opinion of 334;
    Independence negotiations 350,
    352, 354, 360–1; comment on
    APW 378
de Gaulle, Charles 146, 184, 200, 205
Gaza, third Battle of (1917) 66–70
Geddes, Rt Hon. Sir Eric 89
George II, King (of the Hellenes)
    167, 187
George V, King 45, 59, 100, 222
George VI, King 1, 218, 343, 365,
    367, 374
George, Daniel 276–7, 282
German Army: 5th Light Panzer
    Division 180; 15th Panzer Division
    195
Germany (First World War): outbreak
    of war 43–5; Western Front
    49–60, 75; use of gas 56, 57;
    armistice 79

Germany (Second World War):
  occupies Ruhr 111; and annexes
  Austria 120; Munich Agreement
  122, 124; Nazi–Soviet Pact (1939)
  131; occupies Poland 131;
  Tripartite Pact with Italy and Japan
  (1940) 154; Rommel's offensives in
  North Africa 182–3, 184, 191,
  192, 267; see also Crete; Greece
Ghazi I, King (of Iraq) 133
Ghurkha 344
Gibbs (primary school; Kensington)
  90
Gibbs, Miss 242
Gielgud, John 329
Giffard, General Sir George 124, 395
Gimson, Christopher 319
Gladstone, William 113
Godwin-Austen, Major-General 152,
  153
Goebbels, Josef 186, 210
Goeben (German battleship) 45
Goering, Herman 149
Gordon, General Charles 139
Gort, Field Marshal John, 1st Viscount
  110, 116, 121, 123, 124, 131, 133,
  142, 219
Gott, Acting Lieutenant-General
  W.H.E. ('Strafer') 146, 195, 198,
  267–8
Gough, General Sir Hubert 42, 43
Gould, Sir Basil 315
Gouraud, General 105
Government of India Act (1935) 302
Grant, Jean 371
Grant, Leonard 371
Graves, Robert: Count Belisarius 274
Greece: defence and evacuation 156,
  157–8, 166, 167–8, 171, 174–8,
  179–80, 182, 184, 186, 187, 189,
  190–1, 193, 352; see also Crete
Grenfell, Joyce 314
Grigg, Sir James 270, 272, 327, 398

Grundy, Norman 11
de Guingand, Major-General Sir
  Francis 185
Gwyer, Sir Maurice 359

Habbaniya 195, 197, 212
Haig, Field Marshal Douglas, 1st Earl
  59, 66, 72–3
Haining, Intendant-General General
  Sir Robert 205, 210
Haldane, Richard 31, 44
Halder, General Franz 189
Halfaya 198, 207
Halifax, Lord 141, 291, 295
Hamilton, Nigel 401
Haram-el-Sharif ('noble sanctuary')
  71, 115
Harding, Field Marshal John, Baron
  183
Harriman, Averell 205
Harrismith (Transvaal) 20, 21
Hart-Davis, Rupert 276–7, 292, 329
Harte, Francis Bret: 'Relieving Guard'
  394
Hartley, General Sir Alan 208, 233,
  252
Harvey, Sir Oliver (later Baron) 298
Hastings, Lord 267
Heath, Lieutenant-General Sir Lewis
  232, 246
Henderson, Major Charles ('Long
  Man') 18, 24, 25, 27, 83, 395
Henderson, Lieutenant-Colonel
  Neville ('Piccanin') 18, 23, 83, 395
Hendry, Frances 371, 402
Henley, W.E.: 'Invictus' 338
Herbert, A.P. 298
Herbert, Lieutenant-Colonel Sir John
  222, 301
Herbert, Lady Mary 226, 229, 306
Herman-Hodge, Hon. George 82
Hill, Air Chief Marshal Sir Roderic
  117

Hill, Ruby 276
Hitler, Adolf 111, 122, 329
Hobart, Major-General Sir Percy
134–5, 144
Hodson, Major Robin 363
Hollis, Lieutenant-General Sir Leslie
383–4
Holy Trinity Church (Knightsbridge)
56
Hong Kong (1941): Japanese attack on
226, 229
Hopkins, Harry 205
Hore-Belisha, Leslie 111–12, 116, 136
Hore-Ruthven, Colonel the Hon.
Malise 23, 26
Horrocks, Lieutenant-General Sir
Brian 110
Hôtel des Indes (APW's HQ in
Batavia) 233, 236
Howe, Geoffrey (*later* Lord) 299
Humphrys, Lieutenant Arthur Francis
242, 266, 303, 322, 326, 388
Humphrys, Francis (APW's grandson)
322, 353
Humphrys, Owen (APW's grandson)
353
Humphrys, Pamela *see* Wavell,
Eugénie Pamela
Hungary 184
el Husseini, Haj Amin 114–15, 183
Hutton, Lieutenant-General Sir
Thomas 213, 227, 237–9, 249, 251,
254, 255, 256
Hyderabad, Nizam of (Osman Ali
Khan) 323, 400

Illustrated London News 174
Imphal 264, 278, 279, 284, 323
In Which We Serve (film) 282
India: APW posted to 22–9; APW
takes command of Indian Army
(1941) 208, 213–14; anti-British
politics 215–16; 'New Delhi' 222;
ABDA Command created 229–31;
APW resumes C-in-C India role
(1942) 251; civil disobedience
campaign 259, 270–1, 278; APW
appointed Viceroy 291–7, 301–3;
food shortages 298, 299, 303–4,
308, 310, 317, 324, 346; Simla
Conferences 334–8, 350–1;
Mountbatten appointed Viceroy
370–1, 377
Indian independence: 1941
negotiations 258–9; 1943
negotiations 258–9, 298–300,
302–4; 1944–5 negotiations 308–9,
310, 313, 316–18, 320–2, 324–31;
1945 negotiations 333–47; 1946
negotiations 348–52, 354–67; 1947
negotiations 368–9, 372–4, 376–8;
summary 398–400
'Indian Legion' (anti-British troops)
215
Indian National Army (INA) 246,
319, 341, 342, 346, 376
Indochina 216, 224, 231
Inglis, Brigadier L.M. 206
Iraq 183–4, 190, 195–7, 200–1, 203;
Habforce 197, 198
Ironside, Field Marshal William
Edmund, Baron 131, 132, 139,
140, 143
Irrawaddy valley and river 254, 258,
260, 262, 264, 283–4
Irvine, A.L. 12
Irwin, Captain J.C. 301
Irwin, Lieutenant-General Noel 272
Ismay, General Hastings, Baron: as
Secretary for Committee of
Imperial Defence 136, 141;
Churchill and APW 150, 151, 161;
comment on APW 211, 398;
organises Cabinet Office
information centre 219; food
shortages in India 308; joins

Ismay, General Hastings, Baron (*cont.*)
Viceroy's (Mountbatten) staff 377,
391
Issus, Battle of (33 BC) 79
Italy (Second World War): invades
Abyssinia 111; size of Middle East
forces 130; prelude to and
declaration of war 137, 139–40,
142, 144–5; attack on British
Somaliland 149, 152; capture of
Sidi Barrani 154; invades Greece
156; *see also* East Africa; Operation
Compass (Parts I and II)
Ivanovitch, Reuben 34

Jackson, General Sir Henry 98–9,
106, 131, 205, 279, 395, 402
Jackson, Stonewall 32, 263, 274
Jacob, Lieutenant-General Sir
(Edward) Ian 285
Jaffa, fall of 70
James, Robert Rhodes 401
Japan 111, 154; invades Manchuria
216; bombs Kunming 216;
blockades Chinese coast 221;
attacks Pearl Harbor 226; and
Hong Kong 226, 229; treatment of
prisoners 282; Hiroshima and
Nagasaki 338; *see also* Burma;
Singapore, fall of
Java 231, 234, 248, 256
Jehu, Ivor 213, 222, 323
Jenkins, Sir Evan 303, 314–15, 334
Jerusalem, capture of 66, 70–1, 74
Jinnah, Mohammed Ali: demands
Muslim homeland 215; comment on
APW 309, 313; attempts to control
Punjab government 313; failure of
talks with Gandhi 317, 320–1; Simla
Conferences 334–8; Independence
negotiations 340, 345, 354, 356, 358,
362, 364, 366, 378; Direct Action
Day riots 360; death 388

Joffre, General Joseph 50
John Constable & Co. (publisher) 93,
97
Johnson, Celia 257, 282
Johnson, Colonel Louis 259
Johore 235–6, 249
Jonathan Cape Ltd (publisher) 276–7,
282
Journal (Royal Central Asian Society)
311

Kailani, Rashid Ali el 183, 195, 197,
203, 212
Keitel, Field Marshal Wilhelm 113
Kennedy, Major-General Sir John
172, 188–9, 191, 196, 198, 204, 235
Kent, George, Duke of 293
Kerensky, Alexander 63
Khan, Sir Hamidullah (Nawab of
Bhopal) 170, 179, 351, 363
Khan, Liaquat Ali 334, 350, 362, 366,
369, 378, 388
Khan, Nawab Muhammad Ismail 350
Khan Sahib, Dr 334, 347, 350
Khan, Sahibzada Yaqub 396
King David Hotel (Jerusalem) 113
Kipling, Elsie *see* Bambridge
Kipling, John 81
Kipling, Rudyard: 'My Boy Jack' 81;
'The Road to Mandalay' 288;
'Recessional' 396
Kitchener, Lord 20, 23, 45, 60, 155
Knatchbull, Elizabeth Florence
Norton (*née* Wavell; APW's aunt;
'Betsy') 82, 90,
Knatchbull, Lieutenant-Colonel
Reginald Norton (APW's cousin)
82, 90
Knox, Frank 172
Knox, General Harry 102
Kohima 264, 323
Koryzis, Alexander 168, 171, 176,
187

Koslov, General 220, 221–2
Kosovo, Battle of (1389) 44

Lampson, Jacqueline 169
Lampson, Sir Miles (*later* Lord
    Killearn) 128, 144, 203, 221, 291
Lascelles, Sir Alan 368, 374
Lashio 238
Lausanne Conference (1922) 91
Lausanne, Treaty of (1923) 82
Lavarack, Major-General John 185
Lawrence, Colonel T.E. (of Arabia;
    also John Hume Ross; *also* Shaw)
    71, 77, 78, 84, 85, 94, 97, 107–8,
    273
Layton, Admiral Sir Geoffrey 223
Le Cateau 50
League of Nations 111
Lees Knowles, APW's lectures 123–4,
    386
Lemartine, Leonie (*also* Gladys
    Redwood; *later* Robinson): APW's
    friendship with 37, 40, 51, 56–7,
    213, 250, 296, 311–12, 384, 389
Lentaigne, Major-General Walter 311
Lewin, Ronald 212, 291; *The Chief*
    373
Libya 157–8, 204
Liddell Hart, Sir Basil: friendship and
    correspondence with APW 92–3,
    96–7, 99–100, 105–6, 108, 231,
    273, 274, 282, 295, 389–90; advises
    Hore-Belisha 112, 116; comment
    on APW 121, 210; quoted 145;
    comment on *Allenby* 161; APW
    unable to support for All Souls
    Chair 352; judgement on APW
    121, 398, 400; *The Ghost of
    Napoleon* 104; *The Strategy of
    Indirect Approach* 237, 253
Life (magazine) 314
Lightfoot, Robert 12
Linklater, Eric 382, 387

Linlithgow, Lord 208, 214, 215, 249,
    278, 301–2, 319
Listowel, Earl of 374, 375, 380, 385–6
Lloyd, George 145
Lloyd, Major-General Wilfrid 273
Lloyd George, David 65–6, 73, 75, 82
Long Range Desert Group (LRDG;
    earlier Long Range Patrol) 147
Longfield, Jack (APW's cousin) 12,
    55, 59, 82
Longfield, Katherine (APW's cousin)
    14
Longmore, Air Chief Marshal Sir
    Arthur 143, 164, 167, 174, 178,
    186, 191, 193, 371, 388
Longmore, Felicity *see* Wavell, Felicity
    Ann
Longmore, Peter 371–2, 388
Longmore, Richard Martin Wavell
    (APW's grandson) 388
Ludendorff, General Erich von 79, 274
Lumby, Eric 378
Lunt, James 242
Lutyens, Sir Edward 222
Luze Simonds, John de 82
Lydall, Edward 319–20
Lyttelton, Rt Hon. Oliver (*later* Lord
    Chandos) 209–10, 291, 294

'M.M.' (handwriting expert) 39
'McA' (APW's batman) 19
MacArthur, General of the Army
    Douglas 234–5, 238, 284
McCrea, John: 'In Flanders Fields' 81,
    225
MacDonald, Ramsay 91
Macdonogh, Lieutenant-General Sir
    George 88
Mackay, Lieutenant-General Sir Iven
    159, 164, 174
Mackay, Captain Reinhard 237, 243,
    244–5
MacKinnon, Major J.F. 163

Maclaren, Archibald 9, 10
Maclaren, Gertrude Isabella 9–10, 11
Mclaren, Guy 217
Maclaren, Wallace 10
McLeod, Lieutenant-General Sir Kenneth 227
MacLeod, Sheila (*later* Phillimore) 286
MacMichael, Araminta (*later* Lady Aldington) 135, 167, 209, 214
MacMichael, Sir Harold 119, 128, 209
Macmillan, Harold 369
Madras 302, 351
Magersfontein, Battle of (1899) 14–15, 25
Malaya 216, 222, 223, 224, 226, 231
Mandalay 238, 250, 258, 260
Manoeuvres Act (1911) 108
Margesson, David 199
Margetson, Major Philip 396
Marne, Battle of the (1914) 50, 51
Marshal-Cornwall, General Sir James 104, 105, 169, 175, 210
Mason, Philip 265, 398, 400–1
Matthai, Dr John 363
Maude, Lieutenant-General Sir Frederick 62
Maxwell, the Hon. Henry Edward 23, 26
Megiddo, Battle of (1918) 77–9
Meinertzhagen, Major Richard (*later* Colonel) 68, 262
Menon, Rao Bahadur Vapal Pangunni ('V.P.') 334, 363
Menzies, Robert 171, 172
Meredith, George: 'Love in a Valley' 292; 'The Thrush in February' 292; 'The Lark Ascending' 292
Metaxas, General John (Ioannes) 167, 168, 176
Mieville, Sir Eric 377, 378

Milne, General Sir George 96
Minto, Lord 27
Mitchell, Air Chief Marshal Sir William 128, 131
Mittelhauser, General Eugène 146
Monckton, Sir Walter 361
Mons, Battle of (1914) 50
Montgomery, Field Marshal Bernard Law, 1st Viscount 120, 122, 268, 327–8, 355, 392–3, 395
Mook, Dr Van 233, 237
Moon, Penderell 399
Moorehead, Alan 130, 194, 366–7
Morris, General Sir Edwin 271
Morshead, Major-General Sir Leslie 180
Moulmein 241
Mountbatten, Admiral of the Fleet Louis, 1st Earl: first considered for Viceroy role 291; appointed Supreme Allied Commander (SEAC) 298; relationship with APW 304–5, 310, 353–4, 383; as Viceroy of India 369, 370–1, 374, 375, 377, 378, 381, 383, 399; APW's funeral 395
Mountbatten, Philip (*later* Prince Philip) 383
Mudaliar, Sir A. Ramaswami 295–6, 308
Murray, General Sir Archibald 65–6
Muslim League 215, 309, 313, 325, 335, 347
Mussolini, Benito 111, 120, 131, 329

Nablus 77
Naga (tribesmen) 318–19
Namier, Lewis: *Conflicts* 277
Napoleon, Emperor 254, 274
National Defence Council (India) 221, 315, 321
National Review 219–20

Neame, Lieutenant-General Sir Philip 179, 182–3, 184–5, 188, 194

Nehru, Jawaharlal: criticises imperialism 258; APW sends poetry anthology to 311; Simla Conferences 335, 350; as defence lawyer for INA 341; address to All-India Congress Committee 357–8; damaging meeting with APW and Gandhi 360–1; Constituent Assembly arguments 362–3, 364; comment on APW 378

Nehru, Motilal 258

Nepal 344

Newall, Marshal of the RAF Cyril, Baron 136

Nicholas II, Tsar 39, 45, 61, 63

Nicholas Nicholaivitch, Grand Duke 61, 63

Nichols, Beverley 281

Nicolson, Harold 196, 300

Nishtar, Sardar Abdur Rab Khan 350

Noguès, General August 136

North-West Frontier Province 302, 304, 341, 346, 347, 350, 351

Oakeshott, Walter 1, 103

O'Brien, Octavius (Countess Wavell's grandfather) 41

O'Connor, General Sir Richard 129, 132, 144, 146, 155, 157–64, 170, 174, 184–5, 191, 380, 395

Olivier, Laurence 329

Oman, Carola (Lady Lenanton): Britain against Napoleon 277

Operation Anakim 277–8

Operation Battleaxe (earlier Operation Bruiser) 201, 205–7

Operation Brevity 195, 198

Operation Bruiser (later Operation Battleaxe) 201, 205–7

Operation Canvas 169

Operation Compass 155, 156–7, 158–61, 162, 164, 166, 167, 168–9, 170, 171, 173–4

Operation Demon 189

Operation Emily 159

Operation Error (deception plan) 262–3

Operation Exporter 201, 205

Operation Fantastical 271

Operation Lustre (later 'W' force) 174–5, 179, 180, 182, 184, 186

Operation Mercury (German) 198

Operation Sunflower (German) 180

Operation Tiger 188, 201

Oppenheimer, Sir Ernest 381

Orissa 302, 306, 351

Osborne Harley, J. 3

O'Shaughnessy, Arthur: The Music Makers 275

Oxford, Lady 297

Paget, General Sir Arthur 41

Pahlavi, Muhammad Reza 217

Pahlavi, Reza Shah 217

Pakistan: creation of 313, 321, 340, 343, 345, 346, 350, 364, 381, 388; see also Indian Independence

Palairet, Sir Michael 176

Palestine 114; APW's views on 115, 387

Palmer, Lieutenant Tim Llewellen 264

Papagos, General Alexander 167–8, 177, 178, 181, 187, 191, 386

Patel, Sardar Vallabhbhai 350, 363, 369

Paton, Alan: Cry the Beloved Country 388

Paul, Prince (of Yugoslavia) 165, 169, 180, 181

Paulus, General Friedrich von 189, 194

Pearl Harbor (1941) 226

Peel, Lord 114

Peirse, Air Chief Marshal Sir Richard 233, 281, 286

Pendred, Air Marshal Sir Lawrence 104

Percival, Lieutenant-General Arthur 223, 232, 235, 243–8

Percival, Eliza Bull *see* Wavell, Eliza Bull

Persia 217

Pétain, Marshal Henri 145–6

Peter, King (of Yugoslavia) 169, 182

Pethick-Lawrence, Lord Frederick 338, 342, 344, 345, 346, 349, 351, 355, 364, 368, 371, 399

Peto, Clement 82

Philippine Islands 216, 227, 230, 231, 235

Phillimore, Stephen 26, 86, 388

Picot, Georges 62–3

Picq, Ardant du 95

Pipon, Robert 55

Platt, General Sir William 130, 159, 166, 168, 169, 173, 178, 186, 395

Poland: Polish Brigade 184

ter Poorten, Lieutenant-General Hein 233, 252

Portal, Marshal of the RAF Charles, 1st Viscount 382

Pound, Admiral Sir Dudley 136, 151

Pound, Ezra 106

Powell, Richard 82

Pownall, Lieutenant-General Sir Henry 224, 227, 231, 253, 261, 390, 395

Princip, Gavrilo 44

Punch (magazine) 29

Punjab 302, 313, 321, 334, 335, 340, 347, 350, 351

Quayle, Anthony 388

Quebec Conference (1943; Quadrant) 298

Queen Mary 286

Quinan, General Sir Edward 217, 218

Quirk, Eugénie (*née* O'Brien; Countess Wavell's mother) 41

Quirk, Eugénie Marie (Countess Wavell) *see* Wavell, Eugénie Marie, Countess

Quirk, Colonel John Owen (Countess Wavell's father) 41, 97

'Quit India' movement 259, 270–1, 278, 298, 309, 316, 333

Rahman, Lieutenant-General Attiqur 378

Raisman, Sir Jeremy 303, 308

Rajagopalachari, Chakravarti 258

Rajagopalachari, Shri 309–10, 317

Ranfurly, Dan, 6th Earl of 184, 194

Ranfurly, Hermione, Countess of 163, 196, 211

Rangoon 216, 222, 228, 229, 238, 252, 254, 255, 277–8

Rawalpindi General Hospital (nr Boulogne) 58

Red Hackle, The (regimental magazine) 87

Redwood, Gladys *see* Lemartine, Leonie

Redwood, Peggy (*later* Box) 40

Reid Scott, Captain Sandy 210, 221–2, 231, 252–3, 262–3, 264, 270, 273, 279–80

Rendall, Montague 16

Ribbands, Daisy (Wavell family nanny) 60, 85, 135, 141, 211, 267, 388, 395

Rimington, Major-General Sir Michael 19–20

Roberts, Field Marshal Frederick Sleigh 26, 66

Robertson, Field Marshal Sir William 30, 33, 60, 66, 67, 71, 72–4

Robinson, Dudley 252

Robinson, Esmond 40, 51

Robinson, Gladys *see* Lemartine, Leonie
Romania 166, 172, 178, 184, 189
Rommel, Field Marshal Erwin 180, 182, 183, 186, 189, 191, 194–5, 198, 207, 267
Roosevelt, President Franklin D. 172, 205, 226, 259, 287, 328
Rosebery, Eva, Countess of 297
Rosebery, Harry Dalmeny, 6th Earl of 297
Ross, John Hume *see* Lawrence, T.E.
Royal Air Force (RAF) 92, 96, 166; No. 4 Squadron 101
Royal Australian Navy: HMAS *Hobart* 153
Royal Flying Corps (RFC) 52, 96
Royal Highland Regiment *see* British and Commonwealth Land Forces: Royal Highland Regiment
Royal Naval Air Division (RNAD) 96
Royal Navy 202–3; HMS *Hampshire* 60; HMS *Warspite* 131, 261; HMS *Hood* 202; HMS *Prince of Wales* 226; HMS *Repulse* 226; HMS *Kelly* 298
Royal United Services Institute (RUSI) 102, 109, 123; *Journal* 93
Russia: APW's visits to 33–7, 38–9, 60–4, 110–11; APW negotiates in Caucasus 220–2; APW visits with Churchill 268–9
Rutherford, Sir Thomas 301

St Andrews, University of 380, 382
St Mary and St Bartholomew Church (Cranbourne) 94
Salisbury, 4th Marquess of 285; 5th Marquess of 391
Salisbury-Jones, Major-General A.G. 203
Salween river 239

Sandford, Brigadier D.A. 147, 156, 173
Sandhurst, Royal Military Academy 16–18, 124
Sandy Lane Golf Club 89
Schlieffen, Marshal Alfred von 43, 44, 50
School of Musketry (Hythe) 18–19
Scott, George 62
Seeckt, General Hans von 93
Seely, Colonel J.E.B. 41, 42
Selassie, Emperor Haile (of Ethiopia) 111, 147–8, 155–6, 159, 168, 173, 196, 209
Shakespeare, plays: 13, 207, 253, 329, 391
Shankar, Vidya 301, 333, 349, 358
Shea, General Sir John 70, 322
Shearer, Brigadier Eric James ('John') 141, 145, 149–50, 151, 160
Shepheards Hotel (Cairo) 85
Shone, Sir Terence 144
Sidi Barrani *see* Operation Compass (Parts I and II)
Simla 213, 221
Simla Conferences (Indian Independence) 334–8; 350–1
Simon, Lady 332
Simon, John, 1st Viscount 327, 328
Sind 302, 350, 351
Singapore: fall of 92, 216, 219, 223, 224, 231–2, 234–6, 241, 243–8
Singh, Baldev 364, 366
Singh, Colonel Mohan 246
Singh, Maharaja Pratap 24
Singh, Master Tara 334–5
Sittang river 249, 251, 255
Slim, Field Marshal William, 1st Viscount 256–7, 265, 323
Smith, Lieutenant-General Sir Arthur 107, 129, 187, 207–8, 211, 218, 388, 394, 395
Smith, Auriol (*later* Ingram) 109

Smith, Brigadier-General Douglas 52

Smith, Geoffrey 82

Smith-Dorrien, General Sir Horace 50

Smuts, Rt. Hon. Field Marshal Jan Christian 75, 139, 178–9, 193, 280, 385

Smyser, Colonel Craig 338

Smyth, Brigadier Rt Hon. Sir John 238, 239, 242, 249, 251, 254–5

Sollum, Battle of (1941) 207, 210

Somervell, General Bill 277–8, 287

Somerville, Admiral Sir James 261, 280, 286, 306

Somme, Battle of (1916) 60

Sophie, Duchess of Hohenberg 44

South Africa: APW's father in 15; APW in 19–22; 384–5; 150

Soviet Union see Russia

Spears, Major-General Sir Edward 199

Special Night Squads (SNS; Palestine) 18

Spectator (journal) 397

Staff College (Camberley) 28, 30–3, 102

Stalin, Josef 268, 298

Stark, Freya: friendship and correspondence with APW 168, 211, 305, 308, 311, 315, 325, 336, 343, 375, 380–1, 384–5, 386–7, 390; *Perseus in the Wind* 388; *The Valley of the Assassins* 134, 306

Statesman (newspaper) 356

Stepan (APW's Russian batman) 62

Stephens, Ian 356

Stevenson, Air Vice-Marshal Donald 254

Stewart, Major-General Sir Keith 197

Stilwell, Major-General Joseph 256, 264, 273, 275, 277–8, 287

Stoner, Ian 234

Strand (magazine) 273

Student, General Kurt 198

Suhrawardy, H.S. 360

Sumatra 231, 250

Summer Fields (APW's prep school) 9–10, 82, 90, 97, 383, 403

Summer Fields Magazine, The 14, 16, 315

Supreme War Council (Versailles) 72–4, 75

Swinton, General Sir Ernest 39, 121

Sykes, Major-General Rt Hon. Sir Frederick 73–4

Sykes, Sir Mark 62–3

Symes, Lieutenant-Colonel Sir Stewart 128, 155

Syria 199–201, 205, 206

Taranto, Battle of (1940) 157

Tavoy airfield 238

Tedder, Air Marshal Sir Arthur 187, 207, 214, 268

Tenasserim 238, 242

Thailand 216, 226–7, 231

Thomas, Sir Shenton 223, 232, 246

Thompson, Edward 311

Thompson, Frank 1

Times Literary Supplement 92, 313

Times of India 323

Times, The 59, 92, 174, 210, 274, 308–9

Titterton, W.R. 174

Tiwana, Khizr Hyat Khan 313, 324, 334, 347

Tobruk: APW's capture of 167, 168–9; Rommel's attacks on 184, 185, 186, 188, 192, 194, 195, 267

Tower of London 387, 394

Trenchard, Marshal of the RAF Hugh, 1st Viscount 92

Trident Conference (1943; Washington) 286–7

Trinity College (Cambridge): APW's lectures 123–4, 174, 386

Tripartite Pact (Germany, Italy and Japan; 1940) 154, 178; Bulgaria joins 178

Triple Alliance (Germany, Austria–Hungary and Italy; 1882) 43–4

Triple Entente (Britain, France and Russia; 1907) 44

Tripoli 172, 182, 191–2, 193

Truman, President Harry S. 328

Truslove & Hanson (booksellers) 353

Tuckey, Major 156

Turkey: First World War 65–80; Second World War 133–4, 157, 167, 168, 170, 171, 174–6, 178, 180, 191

Twain, Mark 106

'Ultra' intelligence reports 166, 171–2, 188, 189–90, 197, 199, 206

Unionist Party (Punjab) 313

United Provinces 302, 351

United Services Club 218, 219

United States of America: 'open door' policy towards China 216; imposes oil embargo on Japan 216, 221; Japanese attack on Pearl Harbor 226; APW accused of imperialism 228; Stillwell appointed to Chinese army (Burma) 231; APW visits 287; APW's appt as Supreme Cdr 230

US Army Air Corps 228

US Army Air Force 228

Vaughan-Thompson, Reginald 82

Verdun, Battle of (1916) 59, 60

Vereeniging, Treaty of (1902) 21

Versailles, Treaty of (1919) 84, 87; APW visits 72–4, 104–5

Vesey, Geraldine 103

Vesey, General Sir Ivo 31, 33, 89, 103, 109, 395, 400

Virgil Society 389, 390

Voluntary Auxiliary Division (VAD) 135

Voroshilov, Marshal 111

'W' force see Operation Lustre

Walker, David 353, 381, 391, 393, 394

Wallace, Col. Robert 33, 83

Watteville, Lt.Col Herman de 32, 93

Wauchope, Major-General Andrew 14, 25

Wauchope, General Sir Arthur 14–15, 25, 30, 104, 114, 119, 384

Wavell of Cyrenaica and Winchester, Field Marshal Sir Archibald Percival, 1st Earl (1883–1950)

PERSONAL LIFE: birth 7; antecedents 7–8; early childhood 8–9; love of poetry and doggerel 9, 12–13, 31, 71, 90, 91, 169, 181, 267, 269, 275, 283, 288, 298, 311–12, 365, 375, 387; academic ability 9, 11–13, 15, 32, 33; appearance and character 9, 11, 12, 16, 18–19, 23, 39–40, 53, 56, 78, 88, 89, 110, 171, 194, 205, 229, 285–6, 397–8, 400–1, 402; schooldays 9–16; sporting ability 12, 13–14, 23–4, 32; interests 13, 19, 20–1, 25; health 21–2, 201, 244–5, 250, 257, 261–2, 265, 315, 321, 367, 391, 393–4; linguistic skills 25, 27, 30, 34, 36, 37, 39, 75; financial difficulties 25–7, 28, 55, 56; marriage to Eugénie Quirk ('Queenie') 41, 51, 54, 55–7; birth of son (Archibald John) 60; and daughter (Eugénie Pamela) 79, 83; loss of friends and relatives (First World War) 82; and second daughter (Felicity Ann) 87; has skiing accident

Wavell of Cyrenaica and Winchester,
Field Marshal Sir Archibald
Percival, 1st Earl (1883–1950) (*cont.*)
  PERSONAL LIFE (*cont.*):
    87, 123; birth of third daughter
    (Joan Patricia Quirk) 90; death
    of mother 94; happy family life
    97–8, 266–7; death of father
    106–7; flying skills 117; declines
    Oxford professorship 121;
    receives knighthood 123; and
    Order of the Bath 174; created
    Viscount 297; Earl 370; birth
    of grandchild (Diana Jane) 305;
    religious views 312; wounding
    of Archie John (son) 122,
    316–17, 318; birth of grandson
    (Francis) 322; death of John Dill
    323; death of Simon Astley (son-
    in-law) 347; honours 380, 382,
    384, 387, 391; travels to South
    Africa 384–5; speaks in Lords
    on army pensions issue 385–6,
    390–1; frustration over Archie
    John's career 389; visits Berlin
    390; and Canada 392–3; and US
    392–3; final illness 393–4; and
    death 394; funeral 394–6;
    unsubstantiated allegation of
    homosexuality 401; memorials
    402–3; *see also* Bright, Joan;
    Lemartine, Leonie; Stark,
    Freya
  MILITARY CAREER: enters
    Sandhurst 16–18; gazetted to
    Black Watch 18–19; Boer War
    experiences 19–22; posting to
    India 22–9; and Staff College
    (Camberley) 28, 30–3; studies
    and travels in Russia 33–7,
    38–9; appointed to War Office
    37–9, 49–50; 'Curragh mutiny'
    crisis 41–3; sees action in
    France (First World War) 51–9;
    wounded 58–9, 82; awarded
    military cross 59; appointed to
    General Staff (France) 59, 60;
    liaison duty with Russian Army
    60–4; as liaison officer to
    Allenby (Palestine Campaigns)
    64–72; meetings with T.E.
    Lawrence 71, 94, 97, 107–8;
    attends Supreme War Council
    (Versailles) 72–4; appointed
    brigadier-general 74, 83;
    returns to Palestine Campaigns
    74–80; great influence of
    Allenby 79–80; posted to Egypt
    83–6; rejoins Black Watch in
    Germany 86–8; duties at War
    Office 88–92; Singapore
    defence debate 92; work with
    experimental 'mechanised force'
    (Salisbury Plain) 95–7;
    commands 6th Infantry Brigade
    98–101; interest in military
    training and mechanisation
    99–102, 108; appointed aide to
    George V 100; promoted
    major-general 102; undertakes
    Middle East reconnaissance
    (1934) 103–4; expounds on war
    theory 105, 108, 109, 123–4;
    commands 2nd Infantry
    Division 106, 107, 108; leads
    delegation to Russia 110–11;
    takes command in Palestine
    (1937/8) 112–19; first meeting
    with Wingate 117–18;
    appointed to Southern
    Command (1938) 119–24;
    promoted to lieutenant-general
    119; appointed GOC-in-Chief,
    Middle East (1939) 124; general
    127; responsibilities 127–8;
    writes 'The Worst Possible

Case' (Egypt withdrawal
scenario) 142, 188 189;
relationship with Churchill
(Middle East Command) 142,
143, 148, 150–3, 157, 161,
162–3, 166, 172, 177, 182,
188–9, 195, 196; forms Long
Range Desert Patrol 147;
foments Ethiopian rebellion
147–8, 155–6, 159, 168, 173;
evacuation from British
Somaliland 149, 152, 153;
triumph of Operation Compass
155, 156–7, 158, 161, 162, 164,
166, 167, 168, 170, 173; defence
and evacuation of Greece 156,
157–8, 166, 167–8, 170, 171,
174–8, 179–80, 182, 184, 186,
187, 189, 190–1, 193, 398;
successful campaign in East
Africa 159, 162, 166, 168, 169,
170, 173, 178, 180, 182, 186,
196, 209; failure of Operation
Brevity (Western Desert) 195,
198; success of Operation
Habforce offensive (Iraq) 195,
196, 197, 203; replaced by
Auchinleck in Middle East
(1941) 196, 199–200, 205,
208–11; defence and evacuation
of Crete 197–8, 199, 201–3,
206, 212; Operation Exporter
(Syria) 199–201, 205, 206;
failure of Operation Battleaxe
(earlier Operation Bruiser;
Cyrenaica) 201, 206, 207;
replaces Auchinleck in India
208–9, 213–14; receives rare
honour from Haile Selassie 209;
anger at Crete inquiry report
214; concerns over equipment
levels 214–15, 217; and anti-
British politics (India) 215–16;
and growing threat from Japan
216, 224; secures Persian oil
fields 217; visit to London
218–19; urges Burma be under
India Command 219, 222, 224,
227, 230, 250; Churchill and
National Review article 219–20;
negotiates with Caucasus
Russian authorities 220–2;
horrified by Far East
Command's lack of preparation
222–3; and Singapore's defences
223, 224, 231–2; relationship
with Churchill (India and Far
East Command) 225, 251, 253,
260–1, 267, 268–9, 285, 286,
287, 307; surrender of Hong
Kong 226, 229; Chiang Kai-
Shek and defence of Burma
227–8, 239–40, 254; takes
ABDA Command 229–31,
233–5, 250, 251, 252, 253; fall of
Singapore 216, 219, 223, 224,
231–2, 234–6, 241, 243–8;
responsibility for defence of
Darwin 240; disaster of Sittang
river withdrawal 249, 251,
254–5; resumes C-in-C India
role (1942) 251; evacuation of
Rangoon 255–6; appoints Slim
to 1st Burma Corps 256–7;
problems with 'Quit India' and
civil disobedience 259, 270–1,
278; 'failure' of Arakan offensive
260, 263, 271–5, 277, 281, 283,
284–5, 286, 287, 307; Operation
Error (deception plan) 262–3;
Burma withdrawal completed
264–5; with Churchill in Russia
268–9; spared Iraq and Persia
responsibility 269; seeks
promotion to Field Marshal
269–70, 272, 276; appointed

Wavell of Cyrenaica and Winchester,
Field Marshal Sir Archibald
Percival, 1st Earl (1883–1950) (cont.)
MILITARY CAREER (cont.):
Viceroy of India (1943) 291–7,
301–3; relationship with
Churchill (as Viceroy) 293–5,
300, 325, 326; concern over
food shortages 298, 299, 303–4,
308, 310, 317, 324, 346; Indian
independence (1943
negotiations) 298–300, 302–4;
Indian independence (1944–5
negotiations) 308–9, 310, 313,
316–18, 320–2, 324–31; Indian
independence (1945
negotiations) 333–47; Indian
independence (1946
negotiations) 348–52, 354–67;
relationship with Mountbatten
353–4; relationship with Attlee
359–60; Indian independence
(1947 negotiations) 368–9,
372–4, 376–8; dismissed by
Attlee (1947) 369–71, 374, 375,
377–8; last evening in India 378
WRITINGS AND LECTURES: articles
92–3, 274, 393; 'War and the
Prophets' 93; The Palestine
Campaigns (1928) 96–7, 161;
Field Service Regulations (vol. I;
rewrite) 103; Allenby (1940)
110, 113, 118–19, 122, 161;
lectures 123–4, 174, 382, 386,
389, 390, 393; Generals and
Generalship (1941) 174, 252;
Other Men's Flowers (poetry
anthology; 1944) 267, 274,
276–7, 282, 292, 311–13, 323,
403–4; 'Military Genius' (for
The Times) 274, 393; Allenby in
Egypt (1943) 281, 296; begins
journal 305, 379; 'Sonnet for

the Madonna of the Cherries'
(Other Men's Flowers) 312;
'Recollections' (unpublished)
339, 393, 403; Speaking Generally
(1946) 353; The Good Soldier
(1947) 386; unfinished book on
Second World War Greek
campaign 386; 'Armies from
1900 to 1945' (for Cambridge
Modern History) 391–2, 393;
The Viceroy's Journal (post-
humous; 1973) 399, 403; see
also Liddell Hart, Sir Basil
FAMILY HOMES: 10 The Avenue
(Colchester; APW's birthplace)
7; Englefield Green (Berks) 14,
17; Cranborne Lodge
(Cranbourne Estate, Dorset) 22,
26, 31, 54, 72, 93–4; 53a Pall
Mall (London) 38; 10 Cliveden
Place (London) 83; Villa Heller
(APW's home in Egypt) 85; 5
Hobart Place (London) 89, 94;
Little Somborne (Ringwood;
final home of APW's father) 94;
Little Somborne House
(Stockbridge; childhood home of
APW's father) 94; Brigmerston
Farm House (Brigmerston) 95,
97, 98; Blackdown House
(Aldershot) 98, 102; Churchill
House (Aldershot) 107;
Government House (Salisbury)
119; 23 Kingston House South
(Ennismore Gdns, London) 382,
384
Wavell, General Archibald Graham
(APW's father) 31, 93–4, 97;
military career 7, 8–9, 14–15, 17,
22; relationship with APW 28–9,
40, 42, 54–5; death 106
Wavell, Archibald John (APW's son;
'Archie John'): birth 60; childhood

and schooldays 62, 83, 85, 90, 94,
97–8, 103; meets Bernard
Fergusson 106; studies at
Sandhurst 108; posted to Palestine
114, 119, 122; interest in politics
122–3, 391; prolific letter writing
240, joins Black Watch 272;
surprise at APW's request for
promotion 272; APW consults on
POW treatment 282; *Other Men's
Flowers* dedicated to 311–12;
wounded 122, 316–17, 318, 326;
comment on Gandhi 334; awarded
MC 370; teaches at Army School
of Education 389; death of APW
394; and own death in Kenya 402
Wavell, Arthur (APW's cousin) 12,
17, 40, 41, 59, 82
Wavell, Arthur (APW's uncle) 8
Wavell, General Arthur Goodall
(APW's grandfather) 7, 90, 94
Wavell, Edward (distant cousin of
APW) 106, 113, 123, 297, 379
Wavell, Eliza Bull (*née* Percival; APW's
mother; 'Lillie') 7–8, 94, 106
Wavell, Eugénie Marie, Countess (*née*
Quirk; APW's wife; 'Queenie'):
background 41; marriage to APW
51, 54, 55–7; relationship with
APW's female friends 57, 301, 325;
APW wounded in action 58–9;
birth of son (Archibald John) 60;
foreign travels with APW 61–3,
85–6, 104, 113, 135–6, 211, 231,
241–2, 252, 266; birth of daughter
(Eugénie Pamela) 79, 83; birth of
second daughter (Felicity Ann) 87;
and third daughter (Joan Patricia
Quirk) 90; death of Eliza Wavell
(APW's mother) 94; relationship
with APW 109; appearance 138,
257; in England as Vicereine-
Designate 297, 300–1;

grandchildren 305, 322, 388;
voluntary work in India 306, 318,
325; death 402
Wavell, Eugénie Pamela (*later*
Humphrys; APW's daughter;
'Pam') 83, 106–7, 135, 138;
marriage to Francis Humphrys
241–2, 257, 266, 388; birth of son
(Francis) 322; death 402
Wavell, Felicity Ann (*later* Longmore;
APW's daughter; 'Fizzie') 87, 114,
123, 135, 141, 250, 266, 271, 277,
280; marriage to Peter Longmore
371–2; christening of son (Richard)
388; death 402
Wavell, Florence Anne Paxton (APW's
sister; 'Nancy') 7, 31, 32, 85, 94,
395; correspondence with APW
13–14, 19, 20, 21, 25, 28, 40, 50–1,
54–5, 57, 70, 83
Wavell, Joan Patricia Quirk (*later*
Astley; APW's daughter; 'Joanie';)
90, 123, 135, 141, 225, 261, 266;
marriage to Simon Astley 271,
274, 277, 301; death of husband
347; remarriage 388; own death
402
Wavell, Lillian Mary (APW's sister;
'Molly') 7, 20, 31, 51, 85, 94, 295,
371, 395
Wavell, Colonel Llewellyn (APW's
uncle and godfather) 8, 18
Wavell, Raymond (APW's cousin) 40,
82
Wavell, William (APW's uncle) 8
Weizmann, Dr Chaim 71
Western Desert Force (*later* XIII
Corps) 144, 146, 154, 156, 161,
267
Westforce (Singapore) 232, 234
Weygand, General Maxime 132, 133,
136, 142, 146
Weyvill, Sir John 124

de Wiart, Lieutenant-General Sir
    Adrian Carton 317
Wilhelm II, Kaiser (of Germany) 45,
    74, 79
Willcocks, General Sir James 28
Williams, Revd Charles Eccles 10,
    11–12
Willingdon, Lord 377
Wilson, Cameron: 'Magpies of
    Picardy' 392
Wilson, Field Marshal Sir Henry 31,
    37, 42, 49, 72–4
Wilson, Field Marshal Henry
    Maitland ('Jumbo'), Baron 107,
    129, 134, 147, 152, 157, 158, 161,
    174, 184, 197, 201, 269
Wilson, Hester 135
Wilson, John Dover 297–8, 318, 321,
    380; The Fortunes of Falstaff 298
Winchester College 1–3, 12–16, 82,
    97–8, 103, 295, 299, 396, 403

Wingate, Major-General O.C. (Orde)
    117–18, 148, 156, 306, 310–11;
    'Gideon' force 173; 'Chindits'
    263, 298, 310
Wingate, General Sir Reginald 117
Wolfe, General James 175
Wordsworth 12
Worthington-Evans, Sir Laming 97
Wright, Sir Michael 144
Wykehamists see Winchester College

Yalta Conference (1945; Argonaut)
    324
Yamashita, Lieutenant-General
    Tomoyuki 243, 246
Young, Desmond 207
Ypres, Battles of 52, 56, 57–8, 59, 82
Yugoslavia 165–9, 174–6, 178, 180,
    181, 184, 186, 191

Zionism 115, 117, 118, 148